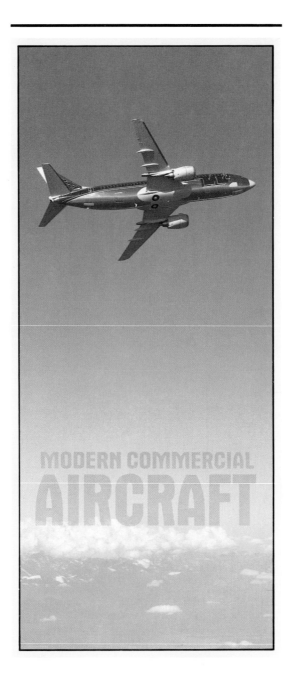

MODERN COMMERCIAL
AIRCRAFT

MODERN COMMERCIAL AIRCRAFT

William Green • Gordon Swanborough • John Mowinski

PORTLAND HOUSE
New York

This 1987 edition published by
Portland House,
distributed by Crown Publishers, Inc.
225 Park Avenue South
New York
New York 10003

ISBN   0-517-63369-8

hgfedcba

CREDITS

Editor:
Philip de Ste. Croix

Designers:
Nick Buzzard
Carol Warren, Kathy Gummer

**Color profiles, cutaways, and
three-view drawings:**
© Pilot Press Ltd

Diagram artwork:
Mike Badrocke © Salamander Books Ltd

Filmset:
Rapidset Ltd, England

Color and monochrome reproduction:
York House Graphics Ltd, England

Printed in Italy

MAIN AUTHORS

William Green entered aviation journalism early in World War II with the *Air Training Corps Gazette* (now *Air Pictorial*) and has gained an international reputation for his many works of aviation reference, covering both aeronautical history and the current aviation scene. Following RAF service, he was European correspondent for US, Canadian and South African aeronautical journals and British correspondent for several European publications. He was technical director of the RAF *Flying Review*, then editorial director when it became *Flying Review International.* In 1971 he and Gordon Swanborough jointly created the monthly *Air International,* now one of Europe's foremost aviation journals, and they have also produced a number of books under joint authorship, including *The Illustrated Encyclopedia of the World's Commercial Aircraft, An Illustrated Anatomy of the World's Fighters,* and *Flying Colours.*

Gordon Swanborough has spent his working life as an aviation journalist and author, with the exception of a year-long appointment in 1964 as a Sales Publicity Officer with the British Aircraft Corporation. From 1943 until 1963 he was a member of the editorial staff of the weekly magazine *The Aeroplane,* specializing for much of that time in air transport affairs. In 1965 he became editor of *Flying Review International,* and in 1971 joined forces with William Green to create *Air International.* As a team, these two authors are also responsible for the production of the thrice-yearly *Air Enthusiast,* devoted exclusively to aviation history, the annual RAF *Yearbook* and a series of authoritative works on both current aircraft and various aspects of aeronautical history.

John Mowinski has become an established contributor to a number of well-known aviation journals, newspapers and books (among them *An Illustrated Guide to the World's Civil Airliners*), writing on subjects ranging from aircraft manufacturers and operators to the development and application of high-technology materials in the aerospace field. He has been employed on a wide range of military, airliner, and corporate aircraft programs. He currently works for British Aerospace, Inc., in the United States, and lives in Reston, Virginia, with his wife Kirsti.

CONTRIBUTORS

Roy Braybrook is a freelance aviation writer and consultant. An engineering graduate, he was formerly a senior project engineer with Hawker Aircraft, then head of sales support activities at Hawker Siddeley Aviation at Kingston, and technical marketing advisor to the Kingston-Brough Division of British Aerospace.

Ken Fulton, currently working with Fokker Aircraft on promotion of the Fokker 50 and 100, has maintained a specialist interest in aero-engines for most of his working life. After an editorial appointment on the staff of *The Aeroplane*, he more recently held public relations appointments in industry, and regularly contributes articles and news columns to aviation publications on both sides of the Atlantic.

Bill Gunston, a former RAF pilot and flying instructor, has spent most of his working life accumulating a wealth of information on aerospace technology and history. Formerly Technical Editor of *Flight International*, he is an assistant compiler of *Jane's All The World's Aircraft*, and author of numerous books on aerospace and defence topics.

Don Parry spent 33 years as a flight engineer with the RAF, BOAC and British Airways. Now a full time freelance writer, he specialises in aerospace, defence and electronics subjects.

Brian Walters is now a freelance writer, following early experience as an airline sales representative and then engagements with aviation and defence journals. A practising pilot, he maintains a wide-ranging interest in all aviation subjects and often writes also on technological subjects in other fields.

CONTENTS

AIRCRAFT TECHNOLOGY

Since the advent of the jet airliner in the fifties, the shape of the civil transport aeroplane has changed little. Most of the world's air travellers fly in aeroplanes that fall into one of a few well-established and proven configurations. Indeed, some types of aircraft, emanating from factories that may be half a world apart, look so similar that they are hard to differentiate. It would be wrong to assume, however, that technology has been standing still for the past three decades. The purpose of the six chapters making up this first section is to show just what advances are being made in the field of airliner design, construction and operation.

Under an airliner's skin — which is now likely to incorporate panels or surfaces in one of the new 'composite' materials — much has changed. Computers have taken over and enhanced control of the aircraft, helping it to fly more safely and more comfortably, whatever the weather. On the flight deck, two men now do the work of four, more easily and more accurately. Passengers enjoy better facilities in larger cabins but pay — in real money terms — less per mile or per kilometre than ever before, thanks to the subtle design changes brought in by aerodynamicists to improve operational economy.

As described in the appropriate chapters, more exciting developments are to come. The shape of aeroplanes *is* changing, as wings gain 'winglets' and fuselages grow 'noseplanes'. And as the changes take place, even more radical developments can be foreseen in the field of propulsion, where 'propfan' has become the buzzword of the late 'eighties. A marriage of propeller and jet engine technologies, the propfan engines under development as this book was prepared hold the promise for the next big step forward in air transportation, ensuring that it remains one of the most dynamic industries of the 20th century.

ANATOMY OF A FLIGHT

For the individuals who make up the crew of Flight 123 the day starts just like any other: relaxed breakfast; take the dog for a walk; deliver children to school or just quietly read the mail. Packing is done quickly and with little concern; it is all part of a long established pattern.

Depending upon how far away from the airport each ones lives, their departure times are scattered, and cars, buses or trains finally deliver three flight deck crew members and 14 cabin crew members to the airport.

The aeroplane that is to take them – or, more specifically that they are to take – to New York is already airborne as they make their departures, inbound from Zurich at the end of a flight from Australia. It lands at about the time that the first crew member leaves home to begin a 75-minute journey. The incoming crew has handed over details of any mechanical problems or defects, and the engineering staff begins to ready the aircraft for its next flight.

In the airline's operations centre the flight planning staff has already interrogated the computer for flight plan details and these are being printed out to offer the most fuel-efficient operation, within the constraints of the available North Atlantic track systems. Approximate passenger figures are being assessed, to confirm the amount of freight that can also be accommodated in the large underfloor holds, which are a distinctive feature of the Boeing 747 that is operating the service.

Catering staff supervise the loading of the catering trays, food and beverages into metal containers that are then packed into easy-loading trucks, ready to be taken out to the aeroplane.

Although the complete crew will be operating as a well-trained team in a closely-knit environment for the next few hours, they see little of each other on arrival at the airport. Members of the cabin crew meet for a briefing under the supervision of the chief steward, and are apprised of the number of passengers and any special requirements. These can

The Route

Above: Many passengers scanning their London to New York route map in the in-flight magazine must wonder why it seems to follow a curved path north over Canada. In fact, when viewed on the globe, the path can be seen to be a straight line between the two points. It is part of the 'great circle' route.

Below: London's principal airport, Heathrow, is one of the busiest in Europe, providing a gateway for millions of travellers every year. Three passenger terminals are grouped in the central area, which is surrounded by runways. To increase capacity, a fourth terminal had to be located beyond the runways.

vary from care for an invalid or handicapped passenger, through various forms of dietary requirements (six vegetarian and four kosher meals have been requested on this flight) to VIPs or the occasional show-biz personality, with the accompanying complications of press and public interest.

The three flight deck crew (captain, co-pilot and flight engineer) meet at the flight planning office. Often they are complete strangers to each other, and it is a remarkable testimony to standardization and training procedures that within an hour of their first meeting, these total strangers can take a massive 800,000lb (362,880kg) aeroplane into the air with complete confidence in each other's abilities.

The flight plan is offered for the crew's inspection and a close look is taken at the meteorological reports. Today the weather looks good, with no problems greater than a little clear air turbulence (CAT) about half way across. The whole of the New York area is forecast to be fine and warm. There is, nevertheless, one slight complication for the crew's attention. Last night, an aircraft flying to London from Miami suffered an engine failure and diverted to New York, where a spare engine was situated. Now, it is necessary to get a replacement spare to New York and today's flight from London has been chosen as the carrier.

SPARE ENGINE

Few, if any, passengers will be aware that on this occasion the aeroplane in which they are flying appears to be a five-engined machine. The spare engine is fitted with streamlining fairings, and bolted under the wing root, where it adds slightly, and asymmetrically, to overall drag. For the flight crew, this means that the calculations for aircraft performance have to be revised and the cruising speed must be reduced. This implies a slightly longer flight than normal, but otherwise there is little evidence, either on the flight deck or in the cabin, of the additional load.

Above: While the captain and his crew are responsible for conducting the aircraft from take-off to landing, a great deal of the necessary planning goes on on the ground. Airlines with fleets running into dozens or even hundreds of aircraft must maintain flight planning and operations centres such as this one to arrange the daily schedules for each aircraft.

As the time for take-off approaches the complete load figure has been decided by the control centre and this allows the final fuel figure to be calculated and approved by the captain. Already a provisional figure has been sent to the refuelling team which has started loading the many tons of fuel that will be needed to fly the aeroplane the 2,600 naut mls (4,830km) or so across the Atlantic and to provide the reserves that may be called upon should some unforeseen circumstance extend the flight's destination.

At this point, the flight engineer heads out to the aircraft to begin his pre-flight checks. The two pilots attend to the remaining paperwork and the captain familiarizes himself with a quick read of a confidential file. This contains details of security procedures or related subjects, underlining the constant concern and care now taken by airlines to minimize the problems of international terrorism.

On arrival at the aircraft, the flight engineer ensures that the final fuel figure is acknowledged and he is briefed by the ground engineering supervisor about the state of the aircraft. Any defects or problems are invariably known as 'snags', and these are considered at this point; there is an established practice of allowing certain defects, which in no way affect flight safety, to be carried over, under the name of acceptable deferred defects (ADDs). Typically, these include parts of a galley, lighting or a broken seat arm which cannot be replaced in the time available before scheduled departure. Occasionally, a more complex ADD may be in the book and this has to be checked to ensure that the deficiency does not entail an operational limitation, which would then have to be allowed for.

The flight engineer now begins the short safety check, which is a method of ensuring that the aircraft is in a suitable condition to receive electrical and pneumatic power without the accidental operation of a system. He also checks out the three inertial navigation systems (INS) and inserts the coordinates of the present position (in this case the airport ramp), details of which are supplied in a manual. This is an important aspect of the preparation, for the INS equipment needs some time to run up and align in a process that cannot be commenced until the units receive the initial input from the flight engineer or pilot.

The two pilots having now arrived on board, the co-pilot settles down to begin his own series of checks. All the pre-flight checks are divided between the co-pilot and flight engineer, while the captain ensures that all of the required paperwork is in order, and then proceeds to load the three INS units with the waypoints as depicted on the flight plan: these are the pre-computed points along the aircraft's planned course that the INS will use to fly the aircraft accurately from London to New York.

The flight engineer leaves the flight deck to carry out an external check and takes a special note of the

Above: At first glance, this looks like a five-engined Boeing 747—notice the extra nacelle under the wing root. Actually, this fifth engine is non-operational, the 747 being one of several types of jetliner that can carry an extra engine in this way to return it to home base for repair or to take a new engine 'down the line'.

Below: The captain (left) and first officer prepare for take-off in a Boeing 767, going through a carefully prepared and well-rehearsed sequence of pre-flight checks. Modern cockpit technology allows the largest of jetliners to be flown by a two-pilot crew, instead of the three or four specialists once required.

fifth pod, now firmly bolted under the wing. Refuelling is almost complete, but it has been noticed that one of the tyres has a deep cut near the crown. It is quickly agreed that this has to be changed before take-off. The flight engineer makes a mental note to warn the co-pilot to leave the brakes alone until the job is finished – otherwise, brake plates are likely to be falling out of place and a real delay would ensue.

Returning to the flight deck, the flight engineer begins his own instrument panel check and assures the captain that all pre-flight preparations are going well and to schedule.

During this time, members of the cabin crew are 'dressing' the aeroplane – putting out the magazines, supervising the loading of the food and amenities, and ensuring that all the equipment is working properly. This quickly reveals a problem: a hot cup in one of the rear galleys is not working. The chief steward heads to the flight deck to pass on the complaint. Along the way he is told by a stewardess that one of the lavatories does not flush. Passing these snags to the flight engineer, the chief steward makes the point that with a full passenger load there is a need for a full set of serviceable lavatories.

Perhaps the only bad thing about the Boeing 747 is the sheer size of the aeroplane. Crew members can lose a lot of weight running up and down stairs trying to find other staff. It can also take a lot of time, and in the 60 minutes of pre-flight preparation, time is at a premium. Fortunately, all airlines have a useful radio link with their respective control and maintenance departments, and this is usually known as company frequency. This is now used by the flight engineer to call for a replacement hot cup and attention for the lavatory.

Meanwhile, the first passengers appear on board, and the cabin crew swings into its well-rehearsed routine of polite firmness and distant familiarity, which are the hallmarks of their trade.

Suddenly, in a flurry of activity, three airline ground staff appear on the flight deck – refueller, engineering supervisor and a young lady with the completed loadsheet. The signing of these documents represents the handing over of the aeroplane to the captain's control, and it is time to go. Pre-start checks proceed, with all three crew members taking

part and with a particular emphasis on the INS. Some Boeing 747s are now fitted with flight management systems (FMS) and these have automated much of the flight planning and cruise control procedures – another important step along the road to complete automation of the flight.

READY TO GO

The co-pilot now obtains start-up clearance from the control tower together with the initial airways clearance, which will allow the aeroplane to go on its way. This is known as the standard instrument departure (SID) pattern and it is carefully reviewed by all three crew members.

Start-up and taxi out are quickly done, as the cabin crew provide the cabin briefing on emergency procedures – a task that on some aircraft is now performed by means of a video presentation. Another ritual that often interests passengers is the call from the flight deck for all doors to 'automatic'. This is an operation which arms the door escape slide mechanisms. In the event of an incident re-

Above: Airline catering, using meals prepared prior to take-off, is now an advanced science.

Right: Most travellers today spend as much time in the airports of departure and arrival as on the flight. This is Heathrow's Terminal 4.

quiring rapid evacuation of the cabin, simply opening the door will drive it out under the force of compressed gas and initiate inflation of the escape slide. It can be appreciated that it is also important to return this system to 'manual' after landing to prevent embarrassment!

As the Model 747 taxies out to the runway holding point, other checks are being made, including setting of the wing flaps and ensuring that everything is ready for take-off. The height of the Model 747's flight deck above the ground means that judgement

increased and the flight engineer carefully adjusts the levers under the captain's hand to ensure that the maximum power settings for the prevailing conditions are not exceeded. As the aeroplane accelerates down the runway the co-pilot calls out the airspeed indications: V_1 the 'decision' speed, after which it is safer to continue take-off in the event of engine failure: V_R the 'rotation' speed at which the nosewheel is lifted to get the aircraft into its take-off attitude; and V_2 the lowest speed at which the aircraft can safely be lifted off the runway. Another flight is on its way.

As the climb progresses and the flaps are retracted, the automatic pilot is selected and the crew settles down to a six- or seven-hour stint of careful monitoring and closely co-ordinated procedures. As England's West Country slides past underneath, the co-pilot calls the oceanic air-traffic control (ATC) centre at Shannon to receive details of the clearance across the Atlantic. This should match the agreed track presented at London. There are times when this has not happened, because of congestion of the transatlantic airways, in which case there is a short period of intense flight deck activity as the new set of co-ordinates is accepted and placed into the computers.

Today, all is well and the operation settles down at the requested flight level, which is the current optimum for the weight of the aircraft. As fuel is burnt *en route*, the weight goes down and the aircraft will be climbed, in a series of steps, to ensure the most efficient use of fuel.

The workload on the flight deck is reduced at this point and if necessary one crew member at a time can take a few minutes rest away from the flight deck, or eat a crew meal. The two remaining crew members can still reach all the necessary controls to deal with any emergency that may arise. As the flight progresses and careful navigation checks are made, a reading of the figures for fuel consumed indicates that all is proceeding well, with even a suggestion that, by the time the aeroplane reaches New York, there will have been a slight saving in fuel over the original calculated figure. Perhaps it is a particularly clean aeroplane today, the fifth engine notwithstanding.

of ground speed is not always easy, and here the INS is useful in displaying an indication of ground speed to the pilot in the cockpit.

Among his pre-flight calculations, the co-pilot has worked out a set of speeds to suit the prevailing conditions. These take account of variables such as aircraft weight, meteorological conditions (temperature, wind speed and direction, etc), length of runway and airfield height. With the help of an individual graph for each runway and airfield, a set of figures can be derived. Known as V_R, V_1 and V_2,

these signify critical aspects of the flight envelope during the take-off run, and are set on the airspeed indicator by means of small plastic cursors or 'bugs' for rapid visual identification.

Final take-off clearance is received from the airport control tower, and the aeroplane is carefully lined up at the end of the active runway. A last look around, and the captain pushes the thrust levers forward a small amount. The flight engineer carefully checks the response of the engines, notes all parameters and calls 'Engines stabilized'. Power is then

Left: The control tower is an important and easily-recognised part of every airport, although the control of aircraft along their designated routes is exercised chiefly from darkened radar rooms in control centres. The visual control room—this one is at Aberdeen—is concerned only with the aircraft's final approach, its take-off, and ground movements.

Above: Controllers at work in the London Air Traffic Control Centre, which looks after the aircraft flying on the designated airways over most of England. This particular group is concerned with one of the Terminal Control Areas (TMAs), responsible for traffic around London's four major airports of Heathrow, Gatwick, Stansted and Luton.

Right: This diagram shows the airways in the airspace over the UK, up to 24,500ft (7,467m). They are divided between two Flight Information Regions, London and Scottish, and the aircraft flying in them are controlled from one of three centres (London, Manchester and Scottish) at any given time during their flight. As will be seen, the airways actually link Terminal Control Areas (TMAs) that block off all of the airspace around busy intersections and airports, the latter each having its own control zone extending from ground level to about 25,000ft (7,620m). The airways are normally 10mls (16km) wide and aircraft fly along them at carefully controlled intervals, different altitudes in 1,000ft (300m) steps being used for aircraft that are flying in opposite directions.

Airways in UK Airspace

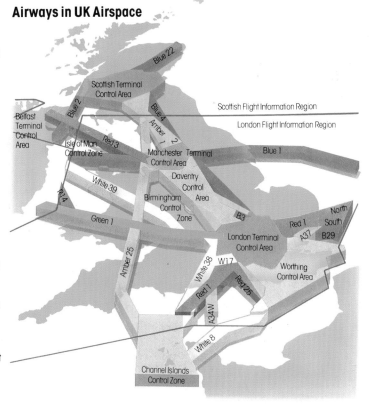

As the flight continues, other vapour trails can be seen, all of them pointing roughly in the same direction, which is comforting! As each waypoint is reached, the co-pilot calls the applicable control centre to report the position and, if appropriate, requests a change in height. The INS can carry up to nine waypoints at a time and about half way across the ocean the system has to be replenished with a new set of data to take the aeroplane on to New York. As was the case in London, this procedure is carefully checked by each crew member. Radio contact over the ocean is by voice HF (high-frequency radio), although a VHF set is kept tuned to the emergency frequency and at least one crew member maintains a listening watch. This is always a requirement of ocean flying, but it is no less important to listen out for a message over sparsely populated land masses.

Back in the cabin, the passengers have by now been adequately fed, served with duty-free requirements and are now being given little choice but to watch the in-flight entertainment, or listen to one of the alternative audio entertainment channels. To ensure that the film can be adequately viewed, it is usually necessary to pull down the cabin blinds; consequently, most passengers miss the awesome sight of the pack ice usually to be seen off Labrador.

As the North American land mass appears over the horizon, the crew begins to consider preparations for arrival at New York. *En-route* meteorological broadcasts have confirmed the good weather expectations, and the only concern now is the possibility of long air traffic delays. As Boston slips by, contact is established, on the company frequency, with New York and assurance is given that delays are minimal and a gate number is provided, this latter telling the crew where the aircraft will be parked on arrival.

Crew checks concerned with the arrival procedures are completed and a new set of performance figures compiled by the flight engineer, including details of the amount of diversion fuel available if for some reason it is not possible to land as planned at New York.

Clearance for descent is passed by the ATC and power is reduced as the Model 747 starts to nose down, some 30 minutes before the estimated time of arrival (ETA). The passengers barely notice any change in attitude, although a loud hiss of air as the engine bleed valves function often gives a clue to what is happening.

Most of the world's major airports offer a facility known as the automatic terminal information service (ATIS). This is a frequently updated recorded message giving details of local weather conditions, runway in use and any unusual conditions. ATIS takes some of the verbal work-load off the air traffic controllers, although the Americans tend to have a habit of recording the details at very high speed, which can be irritating to tired crew members attempting to copy the information in long hand.

Today's message is mercifully brief, and the crew settles down to a period of concentration. Check lists are read in order and a sharp look-out is maintained at all times, for this is a very busy area for aerial activity. At regular intervals the ATC calls with a brief 'Traffic 12 o'clock – height unknown' mess-

age and scanning usually reveals a small light aeroplane well below the Model 747.

ARRIVAL

As the airport comes into view, it can be seen that our flight is but one of many arrivals, expertly threaded by ATC into a long line of aircraft curving across the sea. Chatter on the radio is now virtually constant as aircraft are sequenced into the final landing pattern. As the arrivals runway grows larger, other aircraft are to be seen taking-off from the parallel runway, creating a scene of carefully organized three-dimensional chess.

Final landing checks completed, the wheels are lowered and flaps and throttles adjusted. Although the weather is good, all on-board equipment, including the instrument landing system (ILS), is used to ensure adequate monitoring and to prevent the

Below: Flying may still be a thrill for a few, but it is boring for many, and in-flight entertainment has become commonplace, with films, video displays and piped music offered on long flights.

Right: The safe conduct of a flight from A to B calls for the integration of many aids, some inside the aircraft and others outside. In the last few moments of a flight, visual cues from runway lights are vital.

Left: There are times when aircraft seek to arrive at busy airports more quickly than the airport can receive them, even if two parallel runways are used simultaneously. When this situation arises, the aircraft are instructed by the approach controller to circle around a designated reporting point, usually by flying a 'racetrack' pattern. As each additional aircraft reaches this waiting point, it is given a new height, thus forming a 'stack'.

aircraft lining up with the wrong runway. The intensity of the whole operation is emphasized by the rapidity with which aircraft land and clear the runway as ATC gives clearance to the following aircraft.

Everything is now looking good: the radio altimeter is ticking off the feet in precise steps, all the needles are pointing in the right direction and all systems are prepared for landing. There is just one more aeroplane ahead, and as this touches down a large cloud of blue smoke marks the contact of rubber on concrete. It rolls along the runway, visibly slowing and aiming for the first high-speed turn off, but suddenly it appears to brake and slow down, coming to a stop just as it turns off, with the tail protruding over the active runway.

Instinctively, the crew of Flight 123 makes a mental preparation for an overshoot and as ATC calls 'go around, airplane blown tyre on runway' the oper-

ation is carried out precisely, smoothly and in accordance with well rehearsed drills. Go-around power is applied and the nose raised, 'Flaps 20' (a 20-deg setting) are selected, and as the co-pilot notes and calls out 'Positive rate of climb' the gear is selected up.

The crew finds this development more irritating than inconvenient; it will add another 20 minutes or so to the flight time and use up the fuel that had been saved by careful procedures on the way across. ATC is equal to the situation and by a series of rapid instructions brings the Model 747 back into a slot that enables the crew once again to establish the aeroplane on the ILS and this time accomplish a successful landing.

As the runway is cleared the aircraft's auxiliary power unit (APU) is started, to provide power after engines are shut down, and the final set of checks is started to prepare the aeroplane for parking. The members of the cabin crew quickly pass around the cabin to hand out the various coats and belongings that have been stored in the wardrobes – pausing also to place all doors in 'manual' in response to a call from the flight deck on the PA system.

As the parking bay is approached, the crew carefully lines up the aeroplane with a set of lights, to ensure accurate placing, and carefully edges the aircraft into position. As the brakes are applied by the captain, the flight engineer switches all of the services over to the APU and shuts down the engines. The remainder of the check list is read out and the paperwork is completed. Any defects which have become apparent are written up and the total time since starting engines is carefully noted in the log. The flight deck is then tidied up and the crew leaves for the pre-arranged hotel.

Tomorrow, the the whole process starts all over again – in reverse!

Above: The world-wide spread of air transportation has at times outpaced the provision of ground facilities, but modern aircraft—this is a Saab SF-340—are designed and equipped to be able to fly safely into and out of small and simply-equipped airfields.

Below: Journey's end: passengers on an Air Portugal flight disembark at Lisbon. Duty hours for the pilots are carefully controlled, but would allow a return flight to be made, for example, between London and Lisbon. On some very long flights, relief crews have to be carried.

Right: Only a few of today's air travellers find flying frightening but many display their anxiety while awaiting the arrival of baggage in the destination airport! Few frequent air travellers have avoided the misery of a lost bag at some time but the airline record overall is good.

THE FLIGHT DECK

To the untutored eye, the first sight of the flight deck of a large transport aircraft often suggests a rather confused mass of dials, indicators, switches, controls, warning lights and associated displays. There appears to be little order in their presentation, their positioning a result of someone's whim, and the controls apparently fitted in convenient spaces.

The truth is that the layout is based upon many years of careful development and the application of sound ergonomic principles in design, presentation, layout and operational requirements. This is necessary because any aircraft's cockpit or flight deck is a collection point for a vast amount of information. Detectors, sensors and receivers mounted throughout the airframe collate a great deal of data which are continually displayed for the benefit of the crew. To assist the process of assimilation, the information tends to be presented in 'blocks', each of which is concerned with a specific area or system.

Taking the flight deck of a currently operated Boeing 747 as an example, the view is best described from the position of the captain's seat – which is always the left-hand position of the two forward-facing seats. Until quite recently, most large aircraft have been operated by three-men flight crew, but there is now a clear trend towards two-pilot operation of aircraft even as large as the Boeing 747.

Immediately in front of the captain is a set of instruments which are duplicated on the co-pilot's side. These make up the modern version of what used to be called the blind flying panel. The basic philosophy remains the same, as this group of instruments gives the pilot the vital cues of heading, speed and attitude. The modern instruments use electronic techniques for additional refinements and selections, which allow different types of information to be 'called up' as required. The only instrument that seems to have escaped the electronic revolution is the vertical speed indicator (VSI), which provides an indication of the rate of climb or descent. An additional source of height information is available from a radio altimeter, which comes into its own in the final landing approach and during automatic landings.

Other indicators on this panel include automatic flight warnings, instrument warnings and computer selectors, emphasizing the considerable degree of automation inherent in modern aircraft.

The co-pilot's panel is virtually identical, with the addition of a large flying control position indicator, an air temperature gauge and hydraulic brake pressure indicator.

These two panels are separated by a large central panel containing the main engine parameter gauges. These indicate engine speeds, temperatures and fuel flows. A stand-by artificial horizon is mounted in this area, enabling the third crew member (flight engineer) to monitor all three attitude indicators. If either of the pilots' instruments becomes suspect, the faulty instrument can be quickly identified by reference to the stand-by.

This area also includes a central warning panel, covering all the primary systems. Any incipient defect will illuminate one of these lights to attract the crew's attention. Flap indicators show the position of leading- and trailing-edge flaps, by a combination of twin needles and lights. The distinctive hallmark of many Boeing transports is the large handle for the landing gear selection, with the adjacent warning lights to monitor correct operation.

The Model 747 has a number of on-board computers, with the addition of a separate small computer which is fed with basic information to offer a read-out of engine power values for all aspects of the flight envelope. This read-out display is also mounted on the central panel, where it can be monitored easily, particularly during the climb, to ensure that maximum values are not accidently exceeded.

Immediately above, mounted on the windscreen coaming, is the automatic pilot selection and control panel. The aircraft is usually fitted with a triple autopilot installation to enable fully automatic operations under very restricted visibility, right down to landing. All commands to the autopilots can be made through this panel, as well as the selection of associated navigation facilities. It is noteworthy that there is even a special mode for automatic flight in turbulence. To each side of this panel are radio navigation selectors to enable the correct frequency to be set up for navaids or the instrument landing system (ILS).

ENGINE CONTROLS

Between the two pilot's seats is the central console. Most prominent here is the set of four throttles, or thrust levers, which control the power output of the engines and enable reverse thrust to be selected on landing. Other control levers include the flap selector and the speed brake selector. Boeing has always been concerned about the need to ensure that both leading-edge and trailing-edge flaps are correctly sequenced in operation. To achieve this desirable situation, the flap selector lever operates a programmed controller during its movement to ensure that the flaps are always properly sequenced when being extended and retracted.

Also prominent in this area are the three inertial navigation system (INS) control and display units. The Model 747 was the first commercial aircraft to feature this system as a fully integrated element in

Above: Even when allowance is made for a telephoto lens, this Saab SF-340 has been brought in unusually close, providing a glimpse of the pilots' place of work from the outside. The aircraft captain always sits on the left side.

Below: The flight deck of a British Aerospace 146 shows early eighties state-of-the-art, the best that could be achieved with 'clock' type instruments. The next stage was to introduce electronic displays—but compare this with the Boeing 747 (right).

the design. Earlier aircraft, like the Boeing 707 and Douglas DC-8, had been fitted with INS but these were add-on solutions which did not represent the best ergonomic answer.

Other navigation and communication system frequency selectors are also in the area in close proximity to all three crew members for ease of operation from any of the seats. This emphasizes the basic design philosophy and layout of all equipment, which enables complete integration of the crew members and ensures adequate monitoring of all flight deck functions.

Immediately to the rear of the pilot's seats and mounted on the right hand (starboard) side of the aeroplane, in three-crew layouts, is the flight engineer's position. This enables control to be exercised over aircraft systems such as the auxiliary power unit, electrics, hydraulics, fuel management, pneumatics, air conditioning and pressurization.

Overhead, another wide panel carries additional selectors including the engine start units and the all important fire handles. In the event of an engine fire, a warning bell sounds and the relevant handle illuminates with an ominous red glow.

Also fitted to the roof structure are a number of circuit breaker (fuse) panels which protect the many electrical circuits. Other flight deck systems include oxygen, inter-communication and emergency equipment, the last comprising lifejackets and escape ropes to enable the crew to descend to the ground via a roof-mounted hatch.

This necessarily brief review of the layout of the flight deck is sufficient to indicate the considerable amount and disposition of instrumentation. For many years, the instruments have been based upon

Boeing 747-200 Flight Deck

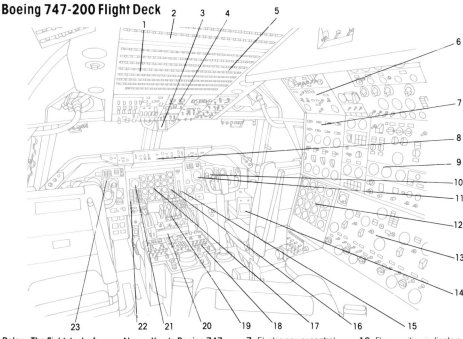

Below: The flight deck of the Boeing 747-200 (a four-engined aircraft like the BAe 146 illustrated on the left) reflects the standards of the seventies, and is laid out for three-crew operation. New 747s are now being developed for two-crew operation.

Above: Key to Boeing 747-200 flight deck (below)

1 Essential services bus bar
2 Circuit breakers
3 Standby compass
4 Systems controls
5 Radio bus bar
6 APU and auxiliary power control panel
7 Electric power control panel
8 Autopilot mode selector
9 Cabin air control panel
10 Attitude director
11 Machmeter
12 Engine instruments
13 Fuel system panel
14 Weather radar scope
15 Landing gear selector
16 Flap position indicators
17 Engine instruments
18 Radar and communications
19 Throttles
20 Autopilot controls
21 Standby attitude director
22 Master warning panel
23 Captain's main flight instruments

Left: If they are to be operated safely alongside large aircraft and in an international airline environment, even small commuterliners must have fully-equipped flight decks. The BAe Jetstream 31 shows how it can be done.

Right: Moving up the size scale a little, from 19 seats to 30 seats, the Embraer Brasilia shows a layout strikingly similar to that of the Jetstream. Note, however, the modest use of electronic displays for primary flight information for the two pilots.

Below: The ATR 42, a product of Franco-Italian co-operation, represents another step up in size from the types illustrated left and right. The greater width of the fuselage and flight deck is obvious, but the instrument layout is similar.

electro-mechanical technology, tending to take up a great deal of panel space and often proving to be less reliable than desired.

Ergonomically, such a layout tends to be self-defeating, because at any one time the crew is interested in only about 10 per cent of the total displayed information. The remaining 90 per cent is not only unwanted but can be distracting, even confusing, as it can create ambiguity in the monitoring of the wanted data. To ensure maximum operational efficiency, it has therefore become necessary – pending the arrival of the much more advanced flight decks now becoming available – to devise a series of drills and procedures to deal with all aspects of the operation and emergencies. These are then committed partially to memory and backed up by comprehensive check lists, which are read out by one crew member and monitored by another.

In general, transport aircraft are operated within carefully controlled parameters reflecting ambient conditions and relative to height, weight and air traffic control restrictions. These parameters are broken down into tables and graphs which are used by the crew to establish the correct flight profile for the prevailing conditions, all of which comes under the general heading of 'cruise control' procedures.

It can be appreciated that the crew is constantly in receipt of a considerable amount of information which can be processed for use in managing the progress of the flight. This is, of course, pure computational work and ideally suited to modern electronic computers. Computers are also free of the 'human' problems of workload, stress, emotion and fatigue, all of which can lead to the making of errors in calculations.

Perhaps the major watershed in air transport philosophy occurred during the oil crisis of the early 1970s. Until that time, the price of fuel had been of relatively little consequence among all the other factors in the equation of direct operating costs. The massive increase in oil price, over a very short period, led to drastic rethinking about all aspects of commercial operations. This sparked off a strong move towards greater efficiency and cost awareness on the part of the airlines.

Coincidentally, the electronics revolution was also under way and digital techniques combined with miniaturization were offering new types of equipment which were light, compact, highly capable, extremely reliable, demanding of minimal power and relatively cheap to produce.

This computational potential offered the chance for a re-evaluation of the whole operation, and a programme of rationalization was undertaken to assess flight deck workload and composition, the intention being to develop a greater degree of automation and, as a consequence, to reduce manning levels, in an attempt to reduce costs and improve efficiency wherever possible.

Such thinking revived many of the older controversies about flight deck manning. Crew complement had become a very vexed question during the 1950s and early 1960s, leading to considerable industrial unrest as first, navigators, and then radio operators were displaced.

As the early piston engine transports grew into the mechanically complex multi-engined airliners of the 1940s, their operation required a number of highly specialized crew members on the flight deck. Apart from the basic job of flying the aeroplane, a long-range communications specialist was needed, and the continuous task of navigation also demanded a specialist crew member. Certain airlines made polar operations a normal part of their schedule, though it is less well known that such operations required the services of two navigators on the flight deck in order to handle the high work load occasioned by the vagaries of natural magnetic phenomena at high latitudes.

In addition, the increasingly complex airframe systems and piston engines called for a flight engineer, with the result that by the end of World War II a new generation of airliners had appeared requiring five- and at times six-man crews. The pace of war had also accelerated the development of electronically-based systems, and it had already become

apparent that long-range voice communications could be conducted on automatically-tuned radio sets. This set the scene for the demise of the specialist radio operator as the pilots took over in-flight communications.

GLASS COCKPITS

As electronics became ever more dominant, the advent of the INS saw the demise of classical navigation and the flight crew complement stabilized, on the larger aircraft, as two pilots and a flight engineer. Now it would seem that the industry is reducing this number to just two pilots as computers take over more of the flight deck management role and the development of the so-called 'glass' cockpit.

This innovation has occurred as a consequence of the ability to translate many of the flight monitoring, cruise control, navigation and communications management tasks into computer software, which can then be stored and used to provide information on a 'call up' basis. Modern computers can store a vast amount of information, and can even 'prioritize' certain aspects. By use of suitable electronic display screens, this information can be presented to the pilot as and when it is required, all other extraneous data being with-held. The system can also be configured to display additional data such as weather radar pictures, check lists and airfield landing diagrams. In the event of a problem developing in a system, the pilot is warned of the situation and the

applicable drill is also displayed automatically. In this manner, the flight deck clutter is dramatically reduced, ambiguity is avoided and greater efficiency in information handling is achieved.

As with any new developments, the transition has not been as rapid as was once predicted. This type of equipment is not cheap, and its maintenance costs are still largely to be evaluated. Some criticism has been based upon the fact that continuous displays of information on the old electro-mechanical instruments often gave an early warning of developing problems: thus a trend could be recognized by an experienced crew member – always a useful pointer in engine condition monitoring. The computer only acts when an incipient incident reaches a predetermined threshold, which may take the crew by surprise and leave less time for corrective action and for options to be considered.

Despite these factors, the new types of flight deck are becoming increasingly common, both as initial fit or as a retrofit. The Boeing 747 has undergone radical review and a long-range version, the Model 747-400, is now emerging with a fully computerized 'glass' flightdeck and a two-man crew.

Significantly, though, one airline has decided to retain the older type of instrumentation, even in its new aircraft, and this decision may well have been swayed by the realities of local labour costs. It does serve as a good example of the current ambivalence in the industry.

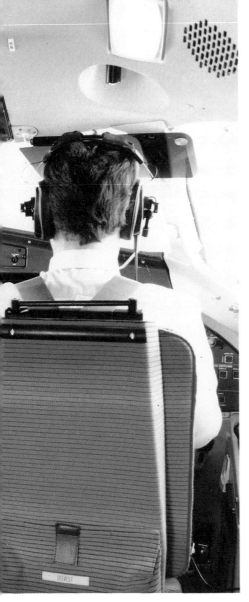

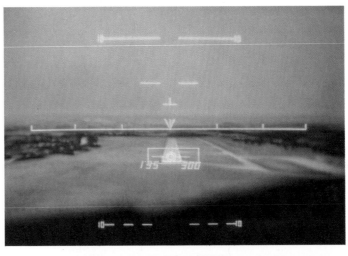

Left: Borrowing from military technology, some manufacturers have offered such features as a head-up display in their current airliners, such as this McDonnell Douglas MD-80. See how the pilot is given vital flight information while still looking straight ahead.

Below: The two-pilot flight deck of the Boeing 767 shows the clean, uncluttered look obtained with new instrumentation, including so-called 'glass' electronic displays.

Air transport has developed over some six decades and has learned some hard lessons along the way. There is an innate conservatism that is not always in sympathy with every aspect of technical innovation. This is especially true when it is achieved by a large increase in the initial cost of ownership. At one time this was acceptable, in the face of rapidly escalating fuel costs. Today, in the mid-1980s, fuel costs have fallen again from 40 per cent or more of direct operating costs (DOCs) to just 20 per cent. This cyclical instability is no new experience in aviation, but it does suggest that in the foreseeable future the emphasis is more likely to be upon a reduction in new aircraft purchase costs, rather than the drive to reduce fuel consumption through new engine technology or improved operating efficiency derived from flight deck innovation. Put more simply, the question is how long the higher first cost of a fully 'glass' cockpit takes to be repaid through reduced DOC.

Perhaps the most controversial of all of these 'reduction' campaigns has been in the drive to offer long-range, trans-oceanic operations by twin-engined airliners. This is an emotive subject best summed up by an old aviator who admitted that the only reason he flies the Atlantic on a four-engined airliner is because there is not a six-engined one!

Safety is always an emotive and difficult subject. The many thousands of safe flights are quickly forgotten in the face of a single, inevitably highly-publicized, disaster. Aviation strikes a primeval nerve in the soul that seems to obscure the larger picture of events. The question of long-range oceanic twins will continue to cause discussion, although an increasing number of these operations are now taking place.

A320 DESIGN

To ensure maximum integrity within the limitations of the design, a number of additional back-up systems are applied and much reliance is placed upon the extremely high reliability of the modern jet engine. The one certainty, in the long term, is the increasing importance of the avionic equipment which will continue to expand in capability and offer very real advances in flight safety. The best example of this overall approach is to be found, at the time of writing, is the Airbus A320, which offers the single most importance advance yet in flight deck design and procedures.

The full set of electronic flight instrumentation creates a clean uncluttered look, which in this case is enhanced even more by the absence of the large, traditional flying control column. Instead, there is a neat, unobtrusive sidestick controller mounted on a small ledge, adjacent to each pilot's seat, on the left- and right-hand sides of the cockpit. This layout is

A320 Avionics

Right: Certainly the most advanced airliner flying in 1987 is the Airbus A320. This schematic diagram shows the main elements incorporated in the A320's flight management and guidance systems (FMGS) and fly-by-wire (FBW) system. The avionics fit is being developed by SFENA with Sperry and Bodenseewerk.

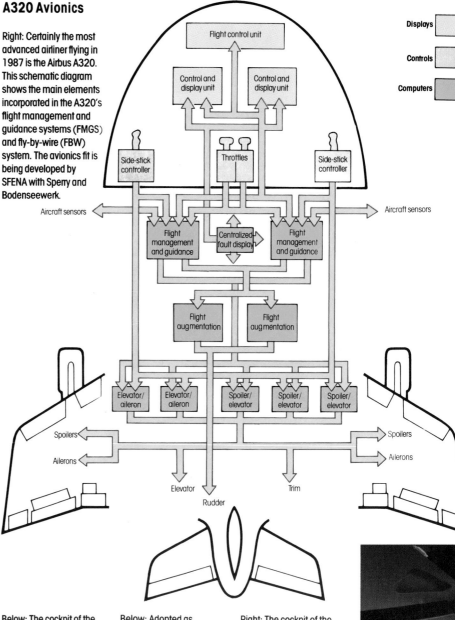

Displays

Controls

Computers

Below: The cockpit of the Airbus A310 shows a number of advanced features and was one of the first for an aircraft as large as this to adopt the Forward Facing Crew Cockpit (FFCC) arrangement, dispensing with the services of the flight engineer and his side-mounted controls.

Below: Adopted as standard in the A320 are side-stick controllers, an idea borrowed from military practice, to take the place of the usual central control column. This diagram shows how pilot inputs to the SSC are used—via flight computers—to command control surface movements.

Right: The cockpit of the A320—shown here in a full-scale mock-up—presents a singularly uncluttered look, thanks to the use of side-stick controllers and almost all 'glass' displays, using six identical colour cathode ray tubes. Each pilot has two CRTs for flight displays.

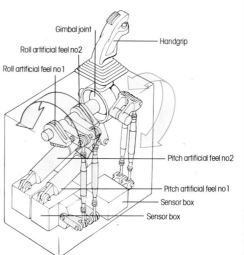

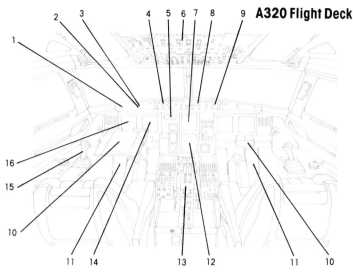

A320 Flight Deck

Above: Key to Airbus A320 flight deck (below); note that the pilot's primary flight displays and controls are duplicated on the co-pilot's side.

1 Autoland control
2 Master warning 'amber'
3 Master warning 'red'
4 EFIS controls, captain
5 Standby ASI, altimeter and attitude indicator 'clock' instruments
6 Systems control panels, fuel flow management
7 Engine and warning displays, part of electronic centralised aircraft monitoring (ECAM) system

8 Flight control unit, to dial in required heading, speed, altitude and vertical speed
9 EFIS controls, first officer
10 Slide-out table, shown stowed and in use (port)
11 Rudder pedals
12 Systems display, part of ECAM
13 Throttles
14 Navigation display CRT, one for each pilot
15 Side-stick controller, one each side 'handed' for captain and first officer
16 Primary flight display CRT, one for each pilot

the most obvious external evidence of the revolutionary fly-by-wire system that offers precise, controlled and safe computer control of all flight conditions. The choice of this type of system also offers significant weight savings and reduction in mechanical parts. Instead, the main flying control surfaces are all signalled electrically under computer control. As the data banks have been supplied with all the speeds, attitudes and permissable manoeuvres of the flight envelope, the aircraft will never overspeed, overstress or stall.

The design of the A320 and its systems provide a significant pointer to the future. Most aeroplanes are built to withstand greater strains than should be expected. This is to allow for the human element, which may impose too high a loading on the airframe through careless handling, or by accident. This need to 'over-engineer' the airframe inevitably increases its structural weight and thus reduces aerodynamic efficiency.

Above: Entering service in 1987, the Fokker 50 shows how a relatively elderly design (the F27 Friendship) can be modernised. Using state-of-the-art instruments and equipment, Fokker has been able to give the Fokker 50 a thoroughly modern flight deck, with a much less 'cluttered' appearance than that of the F27.

The advent of fly-by-wire and computer-controlled flight envelopes offers the designer the opportunity to build an aeroplane that is stressed more efficiently, is lighter, and therefore more efficient – hence less expensive – to operate.

inevitably, developments along these lines lead to arguments about the role of the pilot in future transport aeroplanes. Certainly it is within the scope of aeronautical engineering to build a totally automated aeroplane, but such a development is just as obviously socially unacceptable, at least within the new few decades. Space flight may be the forerunner in this application. Instead, the pilot is becoming a systems manager, supervising a highly automated process, but always ready to intervene if any aspect appears to become divergent.

Unfortunately, the human is not a very efficient monitor over a long period and in a repetitive environment. Already there have been reports of incidents caused through an element of inattention, said to have been engendered by the atmosphere of the new flight decks.

There is nothing new in this, for crew alertness has long been a problem in aviation. In the past, the problem was alleviated by a constant and often extremely variable workload and the presence of large crews. Now, it appears that an era of small (two-man) crews, long flights and considerable automation is to be the pattern. Yet, although the technical abilities of the aircraft are undoubtedly greater than ever before, the human still remains the fallible, weak link in the control loop.

No doubt industrial psychologists are already agonizing over such things, but in a more practical way it may be that the computers will have the final answer. It is not outside the bounds of possibility for the human crew member to be kept under surveillance as well. Regular 'attention getter' actions may be instituted by the computer systems, to ensure a high level of pilot awareness. Typically, these could include exercises which have to be carried out at regular intervals, requiring an element of tactile, aural and physical co-ordination.

It seems that the aeroplane is approaching a point of extremely safe and efficient operation. Perhaps the real doubt about the future must be over the ability of the world-wide infrastructure – air traffic control, airfield facilities and en-route communications – to attain a similarly high standard. But that is another story.

THE CABIN AND ACCOMMODATION

When an airliner taxies to the passenger terminal at the end of a flight and the captain shuts down the engines, the aeroplane is rapidly surrounded by many different kinds of vehicle. So many, in fact, that it seems a wonder that they can all find room to perform their functions without getting in each other's way. That they can go about their tasks with unimpeded access to the aeroplane is a measure of the care which has been taken in the design of the airliner. Baggage and cargo trucks, water replenishment and lavatory trolleys, power and air-conditioning units, a special food truck with an elevating platform – these and other vehicles are driven onto the airport apron to ensure that the airliner is quickly made ready for the next leg of its journey.

Most passengers are unaware of the almost military precision necessary to speed the turnaround of an airliner after its arrival, but the key to the success of the operation has been established long before – in the drawing offices of the aircraft manufacturer. It is there that the shape and detail of the aircraft are determined, the final result always representing a compromise. For the designer must try to satisfy demands made by many individuals, including those who want to make sure that the airliner will be profitable, while others are more concerned with comfort, or safety, or the ease with which the cabin crew can get on with their job.

Somewhere during the evolution of the design, these compromises have to be made. To achieve the maximum profit, the designer is asked to get as many seats into the cabin as possible – but the result may be so uncomfortable that passengers will prefer to travel on a different type of airliner. Or perhaps

757 Ground Servicing

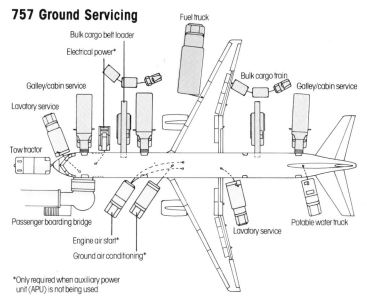

Fuel truck
Bulk cargo belt loader
Electrical power*
Bulk cargo train
Galley/cabin service
Galley/cabin service
Lavatory service
Tow tractor
Passenger boarding bridge
Engine air start*
Ground air conditioning*
Lavatory service
Potable water truck

*Only required when auxiliary power unit (APU) is not being used

Left: When an airliner comes to rest on the airport apron, usually alongside an 'air bridge' as shown here, a swarm of vehicles arrives to undertake a variety of tasks related to the off-loading of passengers, baggage and waste, and preparation for the next flight.

Below: Providing seating on two decks is one way to increase passenger capacity without going for very long tubular cabins, but to date only the Boeing 747 has made use of this arrangement. This picture shows the top deck of the 747-400.

Below: As airliners have grown steadily larger and passenger capacities have increased, wider cabins have been introduced, to allow twin-aisle arrangements that offer a welcome alternative to the 'long, thin tube' look of large single-aisle aircraft. The spacious cabin of the Boeing 767, here, includes enlarged-capacity overhead baggage bins.

Right: The galley of the modern airliner—this one is in the Boeing 767—must be capable of holding ready-prepared meals and beverages for hundreds of passengers, and keeping them hot and appetizing for service any time up to several hours after take-off.

Below: The galley requirements on commuter aircraft, such as the de Havilland Canada Dash 8, illustrated here, are much smaller than those on larger aircraft, not just because there are fewer passengers, but because only light snacks and hot drinks are needed on short flights.

the aeroplane will not be powerful enough to lift all the passengers and cargo that could be crammed into the available space on board.

The question of safety must always be paramount: are there, for example, enough emergency exits to ensure the swift evacuation of the cabin, if necessary? Maybe the demands of safety regulations are met, but if the seats are too tightly packed, there may not be enough room for the passengers and cabin crew to use the aisles at the same time.

The answer to every problem must always be a compromise, although advances in technology are constantly making such compromises easier. Indeed, flexibility is the trend nowadays: simple adjustments can be made to enable the configuration of the cabin to be changed quickly to account for different demands. Modules can now be produced to enable airlines to effect changes of this kind in what amounts to a matter of hours.

COMFORT AND SAFETY

Whilst conscious of the need for safety, most passengers have comfort and convenience uppermost in their minds as they climb aboard an airliner to begin their journey. However, someone, somewhere, has already made the compromises which have largely decided the issue. If the journey is to be a short one, perhaps of an hour's duration or less, it is probable that the airline will have decided that it need not install reclining seats in that particular cabin. If this is a holiday charter airliner about to embark on a slightly longer journey, it may have been judged that the passengers will not mind a little discomfort for the very low air fare which is part of the holiday 'package'.

A scheduled-service flight lasting about two hours, on the other hand, must offer a higher standard of comfort, with more space between the seats and more legroom. A really long journey, to the far side of the world, is tiring for even the most experienced passenger, so this demands that the airline provide the maximum level of comfort commensurate with profitability – compromise again.

More space for galleys is necessary for the really long-distance airliners, because passengers expect – and need – hot meals and plenty of refreshments. For the shorter 'commuter' journey, a cup of coffee and a packet of biscuits are all that most carriers offer – and few passengers expect more. So the level of comfort is largely determined by the length of the journey, and by the fare paid by the passenger. From the earliest days of commercial aviation, passengers have found themselves in some kind of tube because that is the best compromise that designers have been able to find. The long thin tube of Concorde is shaped that way so that it can achieve speeds in excess of Mach 2; the giant Boeing 747 flies subsonically, however, so the designer has been able to produce a three-deck airliner (with passengers on two of these decks and cargo at the bottom).

Many demands are made upon aircraft manufacturers to produce profitable airliners, so a generous underfloor baggage and cargo area is now essential. This enables airlines to boost their revenues by carrying freight in passenger aircraft, as well as the passengers' own baggage. Indeed, the Boeing 747 cabin can accommodate more cargo in its belly than the all-cargo version of the earlier Boeing 707 could carry in the main cabin. Uniquely, Boeing's Jumbo can also carry as many as 69 passengers in an upper cabin located above the main passenger deck behind the cockpit, thus making the maximum use of the generous space available.

The pressures on aircraft designers to get more out of their airliners certainly do not diminish. New lightweight materials, combined with design ingenuity, ensure that more passengers and cargo can be carried in a given size of aircraft, without having to sacrifice comfort levels. Indeed, the advanced technology now being applied will ensure that standards of comfort will increase – sometimes in 'invisible' areas such as cabin air conditioning, or by ironing out bumps which can make a flight uncomfortable. Airliners of tomorrow, such as the Airbus A320, will have gust-alleviation systems in which a computer, far out of sight of the cabin, will automatically respond to turbulence faster than the pilot could manage, activating control surfaces to smooth the passage of the aircraft. Computers are also being used at the design stage to determine the best position for the air-conditioning outlets to provide a draught-free circulation within the cabin. Both Airbus and Boeing have employed computer techniques in this way to determine the most comfortable flow of air. Boeing has also used computer modelling to discover the best method of removing cigarette smoke, devising a special ducting system just below the stowage bins on its new short-haul airliner for the 1990s. One day, this particular problem may go away altogether: some airlines now make their flights 'no smoking' completely, and virtually all have separate areas in the cabin for smokers and non-smokers.

Another invisible aid to passenger comfort in the cabin is the pressurization system. The early airliners did not have this facility, and therefore had to fly in the often turbulent weather at relatively low altitudes. By designing a strong pressure cabin, aircraft manufacturers ensure that airliners can fly 'above the weather' while protecting passengers from the discomforts of high-altitude flying.

Aspects of passenger comfort cover a multitude of subjects in a modern airliner, and the most basic element of all is perhaps the seat. Here, again, compromise is essential because seat manufacturers must provide designs which are as light as possible whilst being hard-wearing and comfortable, as well as conforming to safety standards in rigidity, etc. The earliest seats in pre-World War II airlines were simple wicker chairs that were not even securely fixed to the cabin floor, but seat design has now become a highly technical matter, with a reclining mechanism and carefully placed cushions combining to give maximum support to all parts of the body.

The size of the seat varies according to the class of travel (and therefore according to the fare paid). Real luxury is to be found in the exclusive atmosphere of the first class cabin where there is usually a gap (or 'pitch') of 38in (96.5cm) or more between seat rows, whereas a pitch of 30in (76cm) or so is all that economy-class passengers may expect. The more recently introduced business or coach class is, as one might expect, somewhere in between, with a typical 34in (86cm) separation between seat rows. Sleeperette seats on some airlines enable first-class passengers to get a good night's sleep, although this is not a new development, real beds (or rather bunks) having been provided in the early days of piston-engined airliners.

Convenient baggage bins (enclosed luggage racks above head level in the cabin) are an aspect of passenger comfort, too. The ability to stow hand baggage out of the way makes for an uncluttered floor and therefore more legroom, as well as greater safety. Considerable thought goes into the design of stowage bins and manufacturers vie with each other to provide just a little more space than the competition. A few airlines even boast of their ability to provide sufficient space for skis in their overhead baggage stowage facilities. Soviet airlines offer a different solution to the hand baggage problem: the Il-86, for example, offers a 'below decks' baggage

A320 Cabin Layouts

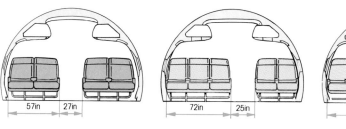

12 super first (36in pitch) + 138 economy (32in pitch)

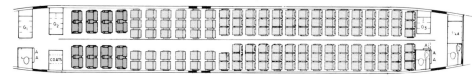

16 super first (36in pitch) + 30 business (36in pitch) + 89 economy (32in pitch)

164 economy (32in pitch)

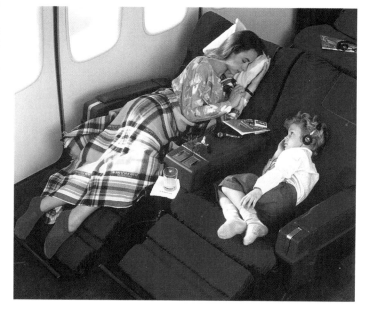

Above: Several different passenger seating layouts are available in modern airliners, the choice depending on the routes over which the aircraft is to operate. Up to three classes are available, shown here in the A320: super first class (red), business (blue) and economy (green).

Left: For really long journeys, and for those passengers who can afford first-class fares, some airlines provide seats that are comfortable and large enough to sleep in. Those shown here are 'sleeperettes' installed in a Boeing 747 of Air France.

area through which boarding passengers pass on their way to the main cabin. Thus, if a passenger has a bulky item that will not be needed on the journey, it can be placed on a shelf to be picked up again on arrival. Soviet designers have another unusual requirement to satisfy – that of providing wardrobe space for the winter coats of 150-300 passengers (depending on aircraft type). In some cases, this means rearranging cabin layouts between summer and winter, with the loss of up to six passenger seats in the latter case.

Air journeys can be boring – indeed most are, because there is little to be seen from 30,000ft (9,145m) or so, and even the majestic clouds lose their attraction after a while. So airlines have devised various ways of reducing the tedium and making the journey more comfortable. Food is one of the most obvious methods of keeping passengers from getting bored (especially on long journeys), the term being used to embrace liquid refreshment.

In the pioneer days of air transport, when airliners lumbered their way at low altitudes and slow speeds, passengers could expect little more than a sandwich prepared by the steward in a tiny kitchen. The main meals were taken on the ground in an hotel because the leisurely pace required frequent stops for servicing, a rest for the crew and an overnight stay for passengers and crew alike on longer journeys. Today, more and more airliners offer the opportunity for non-stop flights, even over very long distances. Just as transatlantic non-stop flights have long been taken for granted, so today services from London to Singapore, Johannesburg or San Francisco have quickly become routine. On these very long flights, it is necessary to serve every passenger with at least one main meal and perhaps several snacks, all of which have to be loaded on to the airliner before the journey begins. Cabin crews have to work hard to ensure that these are properly prepared before they are served, usually from a trolley

Comparative Cabin Dimensions

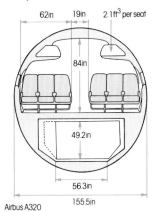

Airbus A320

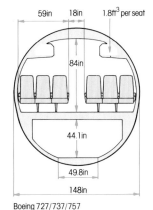

Boeing 727/737/757

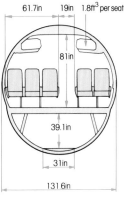

McDonnell Douglas MD-80

Above: Aircraft interior cabin designers go to great lengths to avoid giving passengers the impression of being overcrowded, but there is an ever-present pressure to maximise the payload within the 'envelope' of the given cabin diameter. These diagrams show a comparison between the Airbus A320 (left), the Boeing 727/737/757 and the MD-80 (right).

Left: Although the A320 has a fairly high density layout in the economy-class section, this mock-up shows that the cabin designers have been able to achieve quite a light and spacious appearance.

Below: The first-class section of the A320 offers a striking contrast to the economy cabin (shown left) and features wider aisles and seats.

wheeled up and down the aisle from the galley. With the exception of first-class meals on some airliners, all food is prepared long before it is served, in an airport kitchen, each ingredient having been measured according to an airline manual so that all the portions are as near equal as possible.

The meals sometimes include lobster, caviar or some delicacy designed to convey an atmosphere of luxury – but the aim of providing an appetising hot course can fail because the meal has been reheated just a little too long. It is, nevertheless, a considerable achievement for any airline to provide hundreds of meals (often with a choice), several times during a long flight.

Modern technology has come a long way since the early airborne kitchens were introduced. Some wide-body airliners such as the DC-10 and Tristar have underfloor galleys reached by a lift, so that a few crew members can prepare meals 'downstairs', while others serve them in the cabin from trolleys. Just as the latest technology is applied to the design of cabin seating and air conditioning, galleys also are being constantly developed with the objective of providing the lightest possible facility in the smallest possible space. Flexibility is the watchword in cabin design these days, so modular galleys are often produced to enable airlines to switch them around and take them off certain airliners, if for some reason they need to put in more seats for a particular journey or season.

IN-FLIGHT ENTERTAINMENT

Another method of relieving the tedium of long flights is to provide entertainment, in the form of films or taped music. This is not so new, either, for airborne musical entertainment was first provided on an aluminium piano in the great Zeppelin airships of the 1930s, and 16-mm film projectors were to be found on some airliners of the period too. On the giant Jumbos of today, however, there are many passengers who cannot see out of the windows, so film entertainment has come to be considered essential, although some airlines do provide cabin space for those who prefer to work or read.

Most airliner film systems make use of screens and projectors which retract into the ceiling, but there is an increasing tendency towards the use of television-type screens fixed at various points in the cabin. Entertainment programmes for such systems increasingly include advertisements (just like home TV!), helping to pay for the equipment, and it is probable that the medium will eventually be used to provide safety bulletins, in place of the demonstrations traditionally given by the cabin crews. Already, some airlines use the cabin channels to advertise duty-free goods on board, and their own future flights. Others (notably Virgin Atlantic) have sought to encourage live entertainment by offering free transatlantic flights to 'buskers' and pop groups of an acceptable standard who give performances en route. A more extreme form of cabin entertainment was tried by a German operator some years ago, with topless stewardesses on some special charter flights!

Toilets, lavatories, powder rooms: call them what one will, the facilities are an essential aspect of comfort in an airliner cabin, and are an aspect which is not neglected in terms of modern technology. For example, the latest version of the Boeing 747 (the Model 747-400) will feature a vacuum waste disposal system and a modular design which will enable the location to be varied according to the demands of individual airlines. The maximum use is made of the smallest possible space; mirrors and diffused lighting creating a comfortable atmosphere, while careful design ensures that practical needs (such as a nappy changing table) can be met.

Even the most experienced traveller cannot be unmindful of the hazards that may one day be encountered on an air journey. Yet despite the occasional tragic accident, safety standards continue to rise, year by year. The constraints placed upon the airliner design team put safety aspects at the top of their scale of priorities, and no one would have it otherwise. However, it must be acknowledged that compromises have to be made in this aspect of cabin design, too. For example, some experts insist that it is safer for passengers to be placed in rearward-facing seats than the more customary forward-facing layout, yet it is only some military operators who have adopted such a configuration in their transport aircraft. It is reasoned that in the event of a crash-landing, the sudden deceleration would force passengers into rearward-facing seats instead of out of them. However, airlines in general argue that passengers would not welcome such a seat layout, which would be considered unnatural, so designers have tended to concentrate on making seats safer in other ways. Seat manufacturers have produced new models in carbon-fibre laminates which are very light but also very strong. The authorities also lay down strict regulations regarding the strength of the method of anchoring seats to the floor.

Much thought and research has also gone into the development of safer cushions and seat coverings. Materials which had previously been thought to be safe have actually proved to be dangerous in a fire because otherwise harmless gases given off by different components in a cabin have sometimes combined to produce a lethal mix. Good old-fashioned wool is gaining in popularity as one of the safest materials, and its natural flame resistance can be enhanced by special treatment with an additive

such as Zirpro; this has been tested by the authorities in seven major aircraft-producing countries and found to be safer than some man-made materials (which tend to melt easily).

Nowadays, the certification authorities demand that cabin seats must include 'fireblockers' which will inhibit the spread of burning materials. The polyurethane foam cushions used on most seats are highly flammable, but if they are covered with such fireblocker materials, ignition can be delayed for vital seconds, or prevented altogether. In a trial carried out in the USA, it was estimated that the survival time in a cabin fitted with fireblocking covers was increased by 40 seconds. Some companies have developed flame retardants for man-made materials

such as polyester and nylon; Flamebar for example, has produced a solution which imparts self-extinguishing properties and eliminates flaming droplets, themselves often the source of secondary fires within the cabin of an aircraft.

Considerable research into the matter of cabin materials has been carried out in government establishments in various parts of the world, and gradually the right combinations have been found. Both Boeing and Airbus have played a pioneering role in the establishment of smoke and toxicity standards for cabin materials. Indeed, Airbus has tested over 20,000 samples of materials and has established its own specifications, which have been adopted as an aircraft industry standard. In fact,

Right: Two British Aerospace 146 aircraft supplied to the Queen's Flight are equipped to a very high standard, with comfortable seating and tables. They show what is possible when space is available and fares do not have to be charged!

Below: Even quite small aircraft—in this case a Beechcraft Super King Air 300—can be fitted with comfortable seating to become mini-airliners, and sometimes are used in this rôle, as well as for corporate travel.

Airbus will not use some plastic materials in the cabin for although lightweight and strong, these give off smoke and gas at low ignition temperatures.

Many accidents which have claimed lives in the past have been deemed 'survivable' by present-day standards but for the emission of smoke and gases which have either prevented passengers from finding escape exits, or have hindered their movement because of their toxicity. To speed the evacuation of a cabin in the event of fire, floor-mounted emergency lighting is now being fitted to airliners. This will help passengers to find the exits in dense cabin smoke conditions, and they are battery powered to ensure their independence from the aircraft's power supply which may be severed in an accident.

Left: The CAA Fire Service Training School is a recognised leader in the field. As well as fire crews from British airports, it trains students from as far afield as Saudi Arabia and Hong Kong on its courses at the school's Tees-side facility, in County Durham.

Below: New technology is appearing in the cabin, as elsewhere in the modern airliner. This panel with its keypad and coloured lights allows cabin staff to control and monitor many of the cabin facilities from one spot. It is a feature of the Airbus A320.

Fires in aircraft lavatories have sometimes been the source of a subsequent disaster and a recent development involving an alloy with a low melting point has helped the design of an automatic fire-fighting system. This is set off when a certain temperature has been reached: the alloy melts and so triggers a piston which releases Halon gas into the overheated area.

It is rare for a pressurization failure to occur in an airliner, but all modern aircraft are fitted with an emergency oxygen system in which masks drop out above the heads of passengers so that they can be quickly donned. As a further safety measure in the event of a sudden decompression at altitude, airliners are fitted with vents in the cabin to ensure that an explosive pressure does not build up. These and other measures have been developed in the light of earlier experience, and are examples of the way that designers quickly apply the latest safety techniques to modern airliners.

Inflatable escape chutes are another feature of airliner emergency equipment: they are designed to help passengers evacuate the cabin speedily in the event of an incident. In addition to carrying individual life jackets under each seat, airliners operating over major stretches of water are also equipped with large inflatable liferafts. Thus, in the unlikely event of an airliner ditching at sea, there are a number of emergency aids quickly available.

FUTURE DEVELOPMENTS

Many new developments will ensure that the airliner of tomorrow will be both safer and more comfortable even than those operating in the mid-1980s. For example, it can often be difficult for disabled passengers to get on board, so Airbus has devised a special wheelchair which makes access to the cabin much easier. In fact, on the A320, a lavatory with a folding wall facilitates the entry of wheelchair or stretcher-borne passengers. When British Airways refurbished its Model 747 fleet, it included lavatories specifically designed for use by disabled passengers.

Airbus has also developed a control panel which will make life easier for cabin crews in the future. In the A320 a series of lights and buttons on a panel provides cabin attendants with a visual indication of the status of such items as cabin lighting and water tank levels.

Bendix has introduced something called the Integrated Data Management System, which includes a Cabin Management Terminal. This enables cabin crews to maintain a direct electronic link with the ground, not by voice communication but by means of a keyboard. Items such as on-board sales reports, inventories, meal reports and crew time reports can be completed and transmitted before landing. In addition, special passenger requests, connecting flight information and reservations can be handled without involving the flight deck crew. The Data Management System includes a Duty-Free Terminal which can record sales, calculate currency exchanges and print customs documents. Other electronic gadgets of direct benefit to passengers include on-board telephones, which enable businessmen to call their contacts before arrival or to check with their offices to ensure that all is well.

Despite the trend towards ever bigger aircraft (Boeing is talking of 600- or even 800-seat airliners), modern technology will be increasingly employed to ensure that safety standards as well as comfort levels, are constantly improved. The cabin of an airliner may look like a simple tube, but for the aircraft designer it is very much more complex. Passengers, however, remain largely unaware of such complexity – unless they glance at all those support vehicles which crowd around before take-off.

DESIGN AND MANUFACTURE

The art of successful commercial aircraft design can be defined as sizing the product correctly to meet current and future market demands, and using modern technologies in such areas as power plants, aerodynamics, structural materials, aircraft systems and manufacturing techniques in order to achieve a worthwhile reduction (e.g. 10 per cent) in direct operating costs (DOCs).

The overwhelming importance of economics in this field of design may simplify the decision-making process in comparison with that of combat aircraft, but the designer of airliners is nonetheless faced with some extremely difficult matters of judgement. For example, in selecting the power plant, one of the crucial factors is how the price of fuel is going to vary during the selling-life of the aircraft. In the mid-1970s, it was being forecast that fuel prices would continue to rise as oil reserves threatened to dry up during the 1990s, and that even by the mid-1980s fuel would account for 44 per cent of DOC. In the event, fuel prices have stabilized (as a result partly of the fact that new oil reserves continue to be found), and associated costs now typically represent only 25 per cent of DOC.

The stabilizing of fuel prices has had various ramifications for the airliner designer. Perhaps most importantly, since the choice of engines is the most fundamental decision in any aircraft design, it makes it considerably less easy to justify the adoption of a totally new power plant concept (such as the unducted propfan) aimed specifically at a major reduction in fuel consumption. In addition, the de-emphasizing of fuel costs causes the designer to pay greater attention to other aspects of DOC, notably maintenance costs. Aside from the mechanical engineering aspects, maintenance costs will benefit from a new generation of highly reliable avionics, automatic health-monitoring systems, and databus systems that replace huge bundles of cables and connectors.

The basic shape of the airliner is the result of many different considerations, starting with the need to accommodate the predetermined number of passengers and quantity of cargo in a fuselage that will combine a largely constant cross-section for ease of manufacture with a cabin interior that appeals to the travelling public. The payload/range performance of the finished product dictates its take-off weight (for a given level of technology), which in turn determines the wing area required to achieve the desired approach speed and landing performance. For a given wing area, the span is selected to produce a reasonable compromise between lift-induced drag and structure weight.

ASPECT RATIO

Between the mid-1970s and mid-1980s, the high price of fuel encouraged the use of relatively high aspect ratios (i.e. a large wingspan in relation to mean chord) despite the higher wing weights produced, but this trend may now be reversed. Wing sweep and thickness/chord ratio are selected in combination, in order to achieve the chosen cruise speed or maximum operating Mach number for a reasonable structure weight. In the case of long-range aircraft, there is naturally a strong demand for the highest feasible cruising speed, because of the significant potential savings in block time. There is thus a move to increase the speed of aircraft such as the Boeing 747SP from Mach=0.85 to 0.90, although this does represent a considerable challenge.

Once the wing area has been chosen (and hence initial wing loading), take-off performance demands generally establish the thrust/weight ratio required, although the designer will check that this also provides the cruising altitude planned. Knowing the total thrust required, the designer can then

Right: The price of fuel has a significant influence on airliner design and, more particularly, on the choice of engine for a new design. This graph shows just how dramatic was the rise in fuel prices from the mid seventies onwards.

Below: The modern airliner embraces many engineering disciplines, not all of which are immediately obvious to the passenger. This picture gives some idea of the amount of electric cable used in a Fokker 100.

Fuel Prices

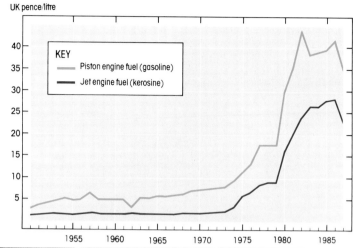

UK pence/litre

KEY
— Piston engine fuel (gasoline)
— Jet engine fuel (kerosine)

Left: Designing for best performance and economy needs to be tempered with other requirements. Rear-mounted engines on the MD-80, for example, have many advantages but are seen here to be difficult to reach for routine maintenance.

Below: In their constant search for superior performance and operating economy, aircraft designers have tried every conceivable configuration. The Boeing 727's three-engined layout proved a classic.

select engines and consider how they should be mounted on the airframe. The greater the number of engines, the more capable the aircraft should be to survive a single engine failure, and thus the safer the passenger. Twin-engined airliners are nevertheless increasingly being operated over long overwater sectors and there is pressure to relax regulations specifying the period (usually 60 or 90 minutes) in which aircraft should be able to reach an airfield in the event of one engine failing. However, it seems likely that a significant number of passengers will insist on at least three engines for long trans-oceanic flights, no matter how safe the twin-engined types can be made to appear statistically.

Three engines are generally better than two in emergency situations, such as the ability to ferry the aircraft (empty) back to the operator's maintenance base with one engine inoperative. On the other hand, it is difficult to achieve a really satisfactory installation for the centreline engine. If it is located inside the rear fuselage, access may be difficult, and there may be development problems in providing satisfactory airflow to the engine at the end of a long S-shaped intake. If the engine is located in the vertical tail, then it clearly requires special equipment for maintenance personnel to reach it. Nonetheless, a three-engined airliner is possibly less expensive than the equivalent aircraft designed on the basis of using four smaller but more easily accommodated engines.

Before leaving the subject of three- and two-engined airliners, it should be added that because of the need to allow for an engine failure during take-off, a twin is comparatively overpowered. With both engines operating, it thus achieves a very high climb angle at take-off, and may thus produce a much smaller noise 'footprint' around the airport than a three- or four-engined aircraft.

In selecting a location for engines, economics favour hanging them on the wing, since wing weight is primarily associated with providing bending strength to withstand lift loads, and since the weight of the engines subtracts from the lift-induced bend-

Left: While aerodynamic and structural developments have been plentiful in recent years, airliner production techniques have advanced less rapidly. This view of the de Havilland Dash 8 final assembly line shows little to have changed for several decades.

Right: The aspect ratio that a designer chooses for the wing of any new airliner is based on a number of considerations. This diagram shows a variety of aspect ratios on aircraft of various configuration. The Lockheed Electra (1), with a straight wing and turbo-props, had an ar of 7.5, closely matched by the 8.0 of the Fokker F28 Fellowship (3). In a class of its own, the delta-winged Concorde (5) has an ar of about 2. One of the highest aspect ratios of any is sported by the Shorts 360 (2), at 12.4; the Airbus A320 (4), at about 9.4, is typical of today.

Comparative Aspect Ratio

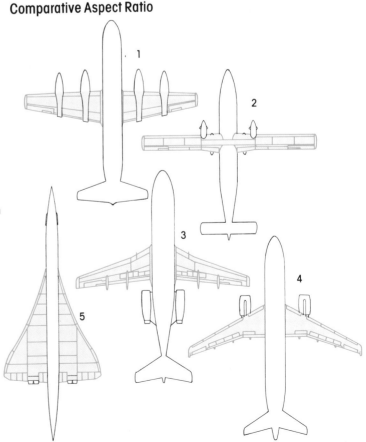

ing moments. The loads produced by the engines can furthermore be fed directly into the wing spars, whereas a rear fuselage mounting demands considerable strengthening in that area to diffuse thrust, weight and inertia loads into the structure. However, wing-mounted engines may well restrict the percentage of trailing edge available for flaps, or require much more complex flaps for the same lift coefficient to be achieved. It may also be noted that, when this type of arrangement originated with the Boeing 707, the (turbojet) engines were proportionally quite small and had little effect on the aircraft's stalling characteristics. Conversely, the turbofan engines of the twin-engined Boeing 757 are much larger in relation to the wing, so stalling characteristics had to be checked very carefully.

It may be argued that a rear-fuselage engine mounting minimizes not only cabin noise but also the yawing moment produced by engine failure and thus reduces the size of the vertical tail, although this is not to say that airliners with wing-mounted engines cannot deal even with outboard engine failures. One very real drawback associated with rear-mounted engines is that the designer is virtually obliged to use a high-set horizontal tail. Such a tailplane usually provides a long tail-arm, and it operates in clean air above the wing wake, but at high angles of attack it may be blanketed by the wing and possibly the engine nacelles. There is then a tendency to pitch up into a deep stall condition, from which recovery may be impossible. As a result, it may be necessary to add a stick-shaker or even a stick-pusher in the aircraft's control system to en-

sure that such conditions are not encountered in the course of airline operations. Conversely, a low tail makes the aircraft increasingly stable as AOA (angle-of-attack, a measure of the aircraft's nose-up attitude in relation to the airflow) increases, but in normal flight operates in the wing wake, which may produce some buffeting and non-linearity of response.

Since the first jet-powered airliner (the de Havilland Comet) entered service in 1952, a wide variety of configurations has been used. Some concepts, such as the 'buried' engines in the wing roots of the Comet, have been ruled out (in that case because of difficulties in access and in re-engining) while other ideas have become the norm, especially at the upper end of the weight range. Long-range aircraft have proportionally small payloads, hence there are the largest possible gains to be had from weight-

Above: The high-wing layout chosen for the BAe 146 was relatively unusual for its size but results in engine intakes well clear of the ground for easy access.

Left: The Boeing 737's low wing puts the engines very close to the ground and when larger engines were adopted for the 737-300, the intakes had to be flattened.

saving and aerodynamic refinement. In this context, the Boeing 747's arrangement, with four engines mounted under the wing, reigns supreme, and it is difficult to visualize anyone today proposing a rear-engined configuration such as that of the Vickers VC-10 or Ilyushin Il-62.

By the same token, it is virtually certain that any large passenger-carrying airliner will have a low-set wing, since the wing carry-through structure then passes neatly through the underfloor freight area, with no interruption of the interior of the cabin. In smaller airliners with proportionally less of the fuselage cross-section devoted to freight, there are arguments in favour of a high wing, although this necessitates a bulge over the top line of the fuselage if the wing carry-through is not to restrict headroom in the cabin. In the case of the BAe 146, it is argued that having a continuous upper surface to the wing

Engine Location

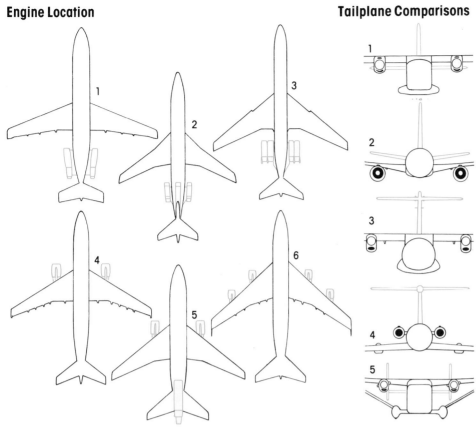

Above: Two, three or four engines, rear-mounted or on the wing—all layouts have been successfully used. These layouts are shown here as applied to the BAC One Eleven (1), Boeing 727 (2), Ilyushin Il-62 (3), Airbus A300 (4), McDonnell Douglas DC-10 (5), and Boeing 747 (6).

Below: Just how different designs for the same job can be is shown by the British Aerospace 146 (1) and the Fokker 100 (2), which are 100-seat airliners for short/medium ranges. Four engines and a high wing or two engines and a low wing do the same job for different customers.

Tailplane Comparisons

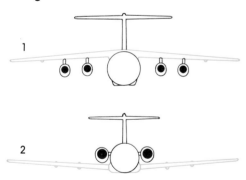

Below: Providing for the carriage of freight is an important part of the civil transport designer's job today, as freight becomes more significant proportionally in total air traffic. Many of the standard airliners can be fitted with freight doors, like this British Aerospace 146.

Above: Tailplane position and configuration vary as much as wing and engine locations, and are related to the overall aircraft design. These diagrams show, top to bottom, the tail units of the Dornier 228 (1), Boeing 767 (2), ATR 42 (3), Tupolev Tu-134 (4) and Shorts 330 (5).

originally designed to operate from well-swept paved surfaces, hence it was perfectly acceptable to mount its engines below a low wing, although this does restrict the use of flaps. It is also noteworthy that in the case of the Model 737-300 with large CFM56 turbofans, the lower rim of the intake had to be flattened to increase separation from the ground.

One of the arguments used against high-wing aircraft is that this arrangement frequently leads to a long, stalky (engine nacelle-mounted) landing gear, which is not suited to rough surfaces. On the other hand, a high wing normally means a low floor line and easier access from the ground, which may be a significant factor at small airports. BAe argues that the low wing of the BAe 748 places most of the aircraft systems at a very convenient height for ground servicing, since they are located in the belly of the aircraft, within easy reach of a man standing on the ground. In the case of the ATP derivative, it is also argued that the low wing makes possible compatibility with modern airport Jetways and Airbridges. The ATP is also a good illustration of the fact that a low-set wing lifts the fuselage higher off the ground and thus makes it easier to stretch the cabin, whereas an aircraft that sits low on the ground may be restricted in fuselage length by rotation considerations at take-off.

DESIGNING FOR FREIGHT

The carriage of freight is becoming an increasingly important factor in airliner design, due both to the growth in cargo traffic and to the need for operational flexibility. Boeing's first design in the evolutionary process that led to the highly successful Model 747 was actually a double-decked project, since this gave the highest number of passengers for a given cross-section. However, in the early 1960s, when jet fuel cost around 10 cents per US gallon, there was a widespread perception that Concorde and subsequent SSTs would win most of the long-haul passenger business. Boeing accordingly revised the Model 747 design to give it the best possible potential for cargo-carrying.

Wing Position

generates four per cent more lift with eight per cent less drag at high AOA than in the case of the equivalent low wing. It is also argued by BAe that the high wing keeps the intakes well clear of the ground (and thus avoids debris ingestion) while permitting the use of relatively deep pylons that take the engine efflux will below the wing, allowing the use of a flap over almost 80 per cent of the trailing edge. It may be noted in this respect that the aircraft's tabbed Fowler flap was intended to give a lift coefficient of 3.38, and that a figure of 3.45 has been achieved.

The ability to operate from unpaved runways in undeveloped regions of the world was an important consideration in the design of the BAe 146, hence the high intakes and also the short fuselage-mounted landing gear, which is more like that normally fitted to a military tactical transport. A more conventional aircraft such as the Boeing 737 was

Cargo considerations led Boeing to abandon the double-deck arrangement in favour of a single deck that was wide enough to take up to 10 seats abreast (US tourist class) or two freight containers 8ft by 8ft (2.44m by 2.44m) side-by-side. In establishing how the containers were to be loaded, the company looked at swing-noses and at visor-noses with the flight deck either below the cabin floor or above it. In the end it was decided to locate the cockpit above the main cabin, though this necessitated a long fairing behind the flight deck in order to achieve an acceptable drag at the design cruise speed. The associated space was initially used as a lounge for first-class passengers, and later as a cabin for up to 32 extra passengers. In the case of the stretched upper deck Model 747-300 this second cabin has been extended by 280in (7.1m) to take up to 69 economy-class passengers. An incidental advantage of the stretched upper deck is that the increased fineness of the aerodynamic bulge improves optimum cruise speed from Mach=0.84 (for the standard airframe) to Mach=0.86.

Before leaving this discussion of basic airliner configuration considerations, it may be useful to mention the two principal changes that could occur before the end of the century. Firstly, although (in this writer's view) wing-mounted engines may well continue to find general favour in the context of turboprops and jet-propelled airliners, the introduction of unducted propfans could necessitate a return to rear fuselage mountings in order to achieve acceptable cabin safety. The individual blades of the propfan may have so much kinetic energy that failure considerations will lead to regulations demanding that they are mounted aft of the pressure cabin. On the other hand, at least one manufacturer (Rolls-Royce) is considering the use of internal ties that would retain the blade after failure of its primary structure, and this may permit the use of wing-mounted unducted propfans.

Secondly, it is possible that some airliners will be designed using a canard configuration, so that all the horizontal surfaces develop positive lift, and also to improve airfield performance. A conventional aft tail normally carries a download, whereas a foreplane carries an upload to trim. On the other hand, it currently appears that in the case of a naturally stable aircraft the maximum lift coefficient achievable is restricted by foreplane stall, and that the CG range of a canard configuration may well be less than for an aft-tail arrangement. In the circumstances the widespread adoption of canard layouts seems unlikely.

ADVANCED TECHNOLOGIES

A wide range of improvements is being introduced in order to improve the economics of current-generation airliners. One of the most important advances relates to the computer-aided design of wings that (for a given sweep angle) achieve unprecedented combinations of thickness/chord ratio and lift/drag ratio at high subsonic Mach number. Traditional aerofoils had triangular lift distributions with a peak suction far forward, associated with very high local velocities and a strong shock wave well forward on the section. Modern aerofoils produce a comparatively flat-top suction over most of the upper surface, with a weak shock well aft, and the undersurface is shaped to give positive lift toward the trailing edge. The whole chord is thus working effectively, and much higher efficiencies are produced. In addition, it is normal to take the maximum thickness forward at the wing root in order to give the wing the highest effective sweep back angle.

The comparatively thick sections made possible by this 'supercritical' approach to wing design benefit structure weight and allow increased aspect ratios to be used. Other possible aerodynamic refinements include the variable-camber (or 'mission-adaptive') wing, which changes its shape to match the flight regime. However, considerable work remains to be done on this concept. More extensive trials have been conducted with winglets, which reduce induced drag without the bending moments produced by normal wingtip extensions. Winglets reduce the rotational flow around the wingtips and may generate a small forward thrust component.

A more radical form of drag reduction is the use of laminar flow control (LFC), which is conventionally achieved by sucking away the boundary air from the upper wing surface through a multiplicity of small holes. McDonnell Douglas is promoting the development of 'hybrid LFC', in which suction is used over only a small part of the wing chord, aft of which a large area of natural laminar flow is achieved by means of a favourable pressure gradient. Fuel gains of around 15 per cent are predicted.

Trim drag can be reduced in various ways, including the use of inverse camber on the inboard sections of a swept wing. The CG should be as far aft as possible, which is encouraging the use of the tailplane as a trim tank, although fuel pumping for CG adjustment was introduced with the Concorde. In time, airliners may follow combat aircraft in adopting naturally unstable configurations (i.e. with the CG even farther aft), and relying on artificial stability and fly-by-wire (FBW) controls.

The use of FBW controls will have other advantages, in saving weight and in making possible the use of gust alleviation systems, which may reduce structure weight. At present, the tendency in new airliners is to use FBW with mechanical reversionary systems, but it seems likely that in future these rods, cranks, pulleys and cables will be eliminated in the interest of weight-saving. Other moves to reduce system weight include the use of fibre-optics in place of conventional cables, and new actuator concepts such as Boeing's projected electrostatic actuator (EHA), which would eliminate long runs of hydraulic piping.

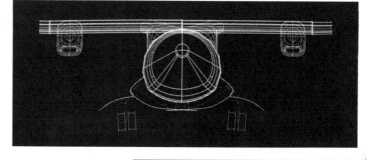

Right: Large drawing offices where draughtsmen prepare blueprints from which each individual item of an airliner is manufactured are becoming things of the past. The norm now or in the near future is to use CAD (computer-aided design) techniques, as for this ATR 42.

Below: Wind tunnels are valuabable tools during the early stages of airliner design, helping to establish the basic configuration. On test here is a detailed model of the MD-91X.

Right: Airbus Industrie has been pushing forward the frontiers of safe commercial flying with such innovations as fly-by-wire systems and side-stick controllers, giving new levels of control.

Above: Computers play a vital part in modern airliner technology, at all stages from design to operation. At the manufacturing stage, as shown here on a Boeing 757 wing panel, computers aid precision machining.

Airframe materials are changing to reflect the emphasis on weight-saving. Composite materials are being used increasingly, even in primary structure. Recent tests include a vertical tail for a DC-10 and five tailplanes for Boeing 737s, with weight savings in the order of 20 per cent. Carbon wheelbrakes provide major savings. Aluminium-lithium alloys offer a weight reduction of eight per cent relative to current aluminium alloys.

Costs are also being reduced through improved manufacturing techniques. Computer-aided manufacturing (CAM) is making possible increased automation, although this is unlikely to approach the levels achieved in car factories. Boeing presentations indicate a growing use of thermoplastic materials, allowing complex parts such as wing ribs to be formed as a single piece (rather than 20 or more pieces and up to 500 fasteners), with a cost saving of 30-40 per cent. New techniques such as superplastic forming and diffusion bonding promise to combine savings in both weight and cost. The airliner of the future may well change little in appearance, but the materials from which it is constructed and the manner in which its components are manufactured will certainly be different from those of today's aircraft.

ENGINE TECHNOLOGY

The airline engine of today has evolved along a long and difficult path, with many technical challenges on the way, since the pioneer commercial turbines of the early 1950s. Most of the engines in that period, (the de Havilland Ghost turbojet in the D.H. Comet, the Rolls-Royce Avon turbojet in the later Comets and the Sud-Aviation Caravelle, and the Pratt & Whitney JT3C turbojet in the Boeing 707 and Douglas DC-8) were adapted from military combat powerplants. The first real commercial power units, based on first-hand experience with turbine engines in airline operation and designed from the outset for passenger-carrying service, were the Rolls-Royce Tyne turboprop and Spey turbofan designed in the mid- to late 1950s.

From that time onwards, an increasing variety of fully-fledged commercial turbines began to emerge, with the big Pratt & Whitney JT9D turbofan developed in the late 1960s for the Boeing 747 representing perhaps the most dramatic single step forward. General Electric, which made a belated but highly successful entry into the airline market, did not entirely break with early practice, its CF6 series of big turbofans being initially derived from the TF39 turbofan powering the Lockheed C-5A, though this was in any case a purpose-built transport engine, not a combat engine.

What made these later-generation commercial engines so different from their predecessors were the differing performance and operating criteria applied to their design, compared with those for military engines. The airline operator wants low fuel

Right: Suited to propulsion at speeds of around M0.6, the turboprop consists of a gas turbine driving a propeller via a gearbox. The large, relatively slow-moving prop slipstream provides the majority of the engine thrust.

Right: Simplest of the turbine powerplants, the turbojet expels its low mass flow exhaust gases rearwards at high speed to produce thrust. It is most suited to economic propulsion at supersonic speeds – as for the Concorde SST.

Right: Offering attractive fuel economy at M0.85, the turbofan uses its fan to accelerate additional air around the outside of the engine (the bypass flow) to produce a larger, slower-moving exhaust mass for efficient high subsonic propulsion.

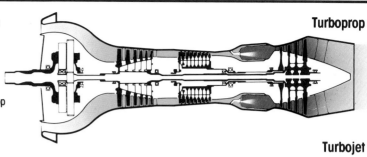

Turboprop

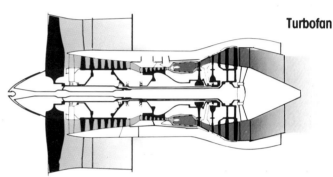

Turbojet

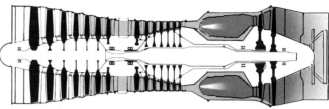

Turbofan

burn; high reliability, durability and maintainability; low noise and exhaust emissions; and competitive pricing. By contrast, the military combat engine tends to emphasize specific performance – that is, pounds (or kg) thrust per pound (kg) of engine weight and per square unit of frontal area, and pounds (kg) thrust per pound (kg) of air mass flow through the engine. Less stress is placed on specific fuel consumption (SFC) than is the case for an airline engine, and the various commercial criteria play a part, but less importantly.

The final outcome of this growing divergence between civil and military engines is that interchange in their roles has become limited to special cases only. Today, over 30 years since military engines powered many of the early turbine airliners, the cross-fertilization has changed direction: the P&W JT9D and PW2037, the GE CF6-50 – GE/Snecma CFM56 and the Rolls-Royce RB.211 – all developed in the first instance for commercial use, how each has at least one military transport application.

COMMERCIAL ENGINE TYPES

Since the introduction of the Vickers Viscount in the mid-1950s, powered by the Rolls-Royce Dart turboprop, airliner propulsion has undergone a radical

Above: One of the world's outstanding commercial turbine engines, the Rolls-Royce Dart civil turboprop was in production from 1953 (when the Dart RDa3-powered Viscount entered service with BEA) through to 1986, by which time over 7,000 units had been built. More than 110 million hours have been flown in service. One of the latest versions was the 2,330 ehp Dart Mk 552, shown here installed in a Fokker F27 Friendship.

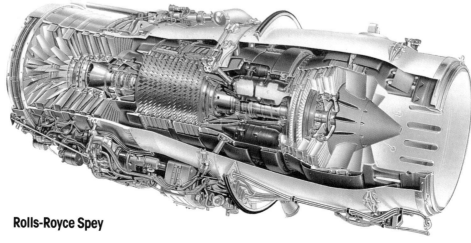

Rolls-Royce Spey

Left: The first turbine aero engine to be designed from the outset for airline use was the Rolls-Royce Spey turbofan which first ran in December 1960. Applications include the BAe Trident and One-Eleven, Fokker F28 Fellowship, Gulfstream II and III and Rombac 1-11. A higher rated, re-fanned derivative, the Rolls-Royce Tay, powers the Fokker 100 and Gulfstream IV. The Tay more than trebles the Spey's bypass ratio.

series of changes of engine type. The turboprop was early relegated to mainly short-haul operations as the greater speed and glamour of the turbojet, and then the turbofan, displaced what came to be regarded as old-fashioned propeller propulsion. Fuel prices were considerably lower in the 1960s, so neither the better fuel economy of the turboprop nor its less noisy operation were enough to sustain it in the front line of airline propulsion. Conversely, it was the poor fuel economy of the turbojet, combined with its excessive exhaust noise, which resulted in its fairly rapid replacement by the quieter and more fuel efficient turbofan.

Today, the turbojet has been effectively eliminated from the commercial transport scene. At present, the major responsibility for airline propulsion rests with the turbofan. Now emerging as an entirely new form of propulsion, however, is the propfan, planned for entry into service in the early 1990s. The reason for the expected breakthrough of the propfan into what might otherwise appear to be a stable and well-established market for the turbofan, can be found in the differing propulsion characteristics of the competing engine types.

Aside from the component and thermal efficiencies of the core engine (the main gas generating compressor, combustor and turbine), which are broadly comparable between one manufacturer and another, it is the basic configuration and propulsive efficiency of the overall powerplant system that influence an engine's position in the propulsion spectrum. A major parameter of configuration is bypass ratio (BPR), representing the ratio between the external mass of air accelerated by the system and the air passing through the engine proper.

The highest BPR of all is in fact the piston engine/ propeller combination, where the ratio can be as high as 200:1. Next in order is the turboprop, at between 70 and 100:1. In these two engine systems, the primary characteristic is their moderate acceleration of a relatively large mass of air through the propeller disc. In terms of propulsion efficiency, propeller engine combinations are suited to aircraft cruise speeds up to the equivalent of Mach=0.75. Above this flight condition, the propeller begins to experience compressibility problems (its helical tip speed is considerably higher than the aircraft's forward speed), and its efficiency in accelerating air rearwards becomes increasingly impaired. Although advanced technology propellers have raised the limiting Mach number somewhat, this basic limitation to propeller propulsion remains.

The turbojet, where all the propulsive air passes through the engine core, is at the other end of the BPR scale, and has a ratio of zero. This means that regardless of the thermal efficiency of the core section, the fact that the turbojet accelerates a relatively small mass flow to a very high exhaust speed, the propulsive efficiency is low except at very high air-

Comparative Noise Footprints

5,000

0

5,000

20

(000ft)

10

0

737-300

10

727-200

20

Above: The diagram shows the benefit of a quieter, higher bypass ratio turbofan in the Boeing 737-300 compared with the earlier 727-200.

Below: The Pratt & Whitney JT9D pioneered the introduction of high bypass ratio turbofans offering high thrust, enhanced fuel economy and quieter operation. The P&W engine, shown here in its JT9D-7R4 version, entered airline service powering the Boeing 747 in January 1970. Competing turbofans are the General Electric CF6 series and the Rolls-Royce RB211 family.

Rolls-Royce Olympus

Right: The world's only turbine engine in supersonic passenger-carrying service is the Rolls-Royce Olympus 593 turbojet with reheat developed by Snecma. As powerplant for the Anglo-French Concorde SST, the Olympus 593 produces an impressive 38,000lb (17,235kg) of thrust on take-off. Although a turbojet (the only one in civil use) the engine provides a competitive fuel economy at supersonic flight speeds.

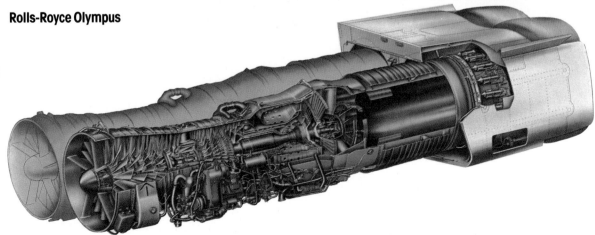

craft speeds. Hence the deliberate use of turbojets in the Concorde, and their virtual disappearance from subsonic areas of airline propulsion.

The turbofan was introduced specifically as a means of overcoming this fundamental limitation in the turbojet. While progressive improvements in component efficiency, and higher compressor pressure ratios and turbine entry temperatures, tended to raise thermal efficiency more or less regardless of engine type, the turbofan concentrated on improving the propulsive efficiency by raising the BPR. As the fuel economy of an aero engine is the product of its thermal and propulsive efficiencies, this tactic offered potentially large benefits in the high subsonic speed regime.

The earliest airline turbofans, the Rolls-Royce Conway and Pratt & Whitney JT3D, had low BPRs in the range of 0.3:1 to 1.4:1. The benefits they offered over the Avon and JT3C turbojets were thus discernible but not dramatic. Even the next generation of purpose-built turbofans, the R-R Spey and P&W JT8D, still had BPRs of less than 1:1, although these engines have subsequently been refanned and, as the Tay and JT8D-200, have BPRs of about 2:1. The really big step forward was pioneered in 1960 by the P&W JT9D, which had a ratio of 5:1. This had a profound effect on fuel burn, corresponding to a 25 per cent reduction in SFC compared with other engines of the period. The GE CF6 and R-R RB.211 series of turbofans followed in the wake of the JT9D.

More recent generations of turbofans with BPRs of around 5:1 and 6:1 (the all-new Pratt & Whitney PW2000 and PW4000, the International Aero Engines V2500 and the largely-new CFM International CFM56) have offered further improvements in SFC. The reduction in cruise fuel consumption made available by the V2500 and later CFM56 models – both strongly contesting for orders to power the Airbus Industrie A320 – is around 20 to 25 per cent compared with current in-service turbofans.

In the early 1980s, when the price of crude oil reached about $25 per barrel, an airline's fuel bill represented as much as 30 per cent of the aircraft total operating costs. General Electric, which was seeking to contest Pratt & Whitney's dominance of the short/medium-haul market with the JT8D turbofan, decided that the propfan concept represented a viable means for achieving much higher BPRs and hence significantly lower fuel consumptions. In 1984, developed was started of the GE unducted fan (UDF) engine with a BPR of 35:1. Using thin, highly swept propfan blades designed to delay the onset of compressibility effects, the UDF is optimized for propulsion at a cruise Mach number of around 0.85, making it competitive with current turbofan equipment.

Below: The Rolls-Royce RB211 turbofan has a unique three-spool layout which enhances fuel efficiency and throttle response. Shown here is the most powerful version, the 58,000lb (26,305kg) thrust RB211-524D4D.

Right: The Pratt & Whitney JT8D is the world's most successful commercial turbofan to date, with over 12,000 units built and production continuing of the re-fanned JT8D-200 series for the McDonnell Douglas MD-80 family.

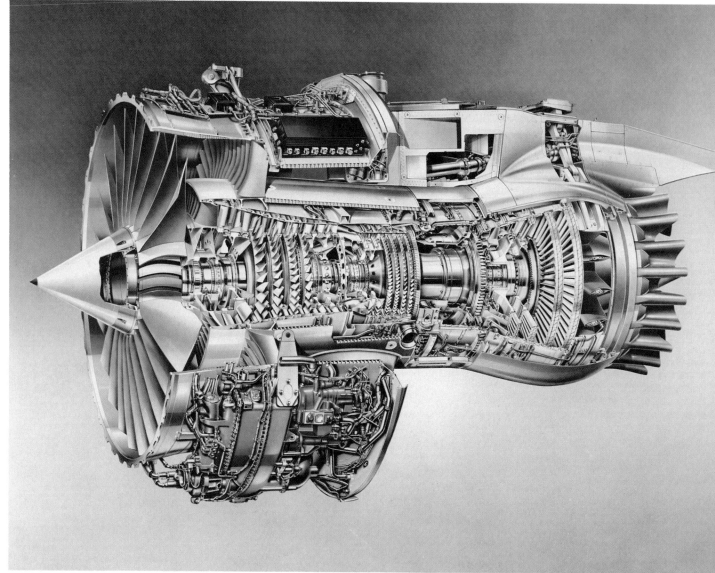

Comparative Engine Thrusts

Right: The contrasting configurations and sizes of turboprop, turbojet and turbofan engines – with three sizes of turbofan shown with differing magnitudes of bypass ratio (bpr). Top-to-bottom: 2,272ehp (equivalent to 8,620lb thrust for the ATP) Pratt & Whitney Canada PW124 turboprop of 70 to 100:1 bpr; Rolls-Royce/Snecma Olympus 593 reheated turbojet of zero bpr; Rolls-Royce RB211-524D4D turbofan of 4.4:1 bpr; Pratt & Whitney JT8D-219 turbofan of 1.77:1 bpr; and Avco Lycoming Textron ALF 502R-7 turbofan of 5.7:1 bpr. The length of the rectangle behind each engine is proportional to the unit's thrust output. The height of the rectangle indicates the relative diameter of the engine's slipstream or exhaust. The colour represents the temperature of the slipstream, ranging from a cool blue for the turboprop, through mauve for the turbofans, to a hot red for the turbojet.

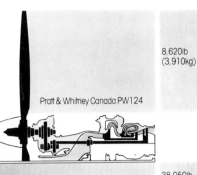

Pratt & Whitney Canada PW124

8,620lb
(3,910kg)

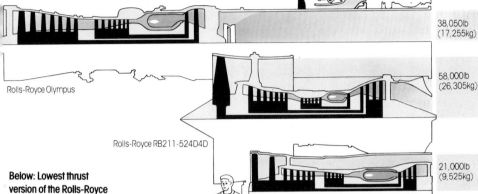

Rolls-Royce Olympus

38,050lb
(17,255kg)

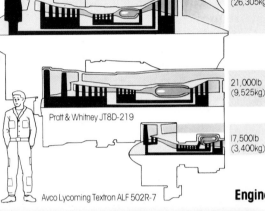

Rolls-Royce RB211-524D4D

58,000lb
(26,305kg)

Pratt & Whitney JT8D-219

21,000lb
(9,525kg)

Avco Lycoming Textron ALF 502R-7

17,500lb
(3,400kg)

Below: Lowest thrust version of the Rolls-Royce RB211 family of turbofans is the 40,100lb (18,185kg) 535E4 which has a smaller, lower airflow fan and other modifications. The 535E4 and earlier 535C power the Boeing 757-200 airliner.

Below: Comparison of cruise performances (height/speed/sfc) of (1) Olympus 593 in Concorde; (2) JT8D-219 in McDonnell Douglas MD-80; (3) RB211-524D4D in Boeing 747; (4) ALF 502R-7 in BAe 146; and (5) PW124 in BAe ATP.

Engine Cruise Performances

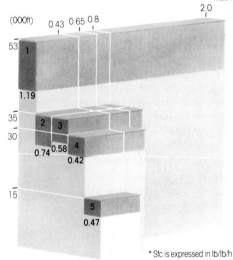

Mach
2.0

(000ft)   0.43 0.65 0.8

53   1
     1.19

35   2   3
30   0.74 0.58   4
            0.42

15   5
                  0.47

* Sfc is expressed in lb/lb/h

General Electric's promotion of the propfan engine (the UDF is to power Boeing's new 7J7 150-seat transport) has led to other engine manufacturers initiating their own projects. In contrast with turbofan engines, however, where the various manufacturers' products have tended to become increasingly like each other, the propfan had already inspired a variety of different configurations. Estimated reductions in SFC compared with current airline engines are an impressive 25 to 35 per cent.

THE TURBOFAN

Turbofans power the great majority of airline transports in service today, and range from the 6,700lb (3,040kg) thrust Avco Lycoming Textron ALF502 in the British Aerospace 146 commuterjet to the 59,000lb (26,760kg) thrust General Electric CF6-80C2 in the Boeing 747 and 767, and the Airbus Industrie A300 and A310 wide-body transports. The typical configuration is two-shaft, with a single-stage fan plus turbine on the low-pressure rotor, and the core section comprising an axial compressor

Propfan

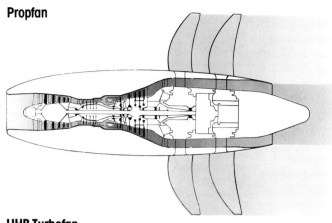

UHB Turbofan

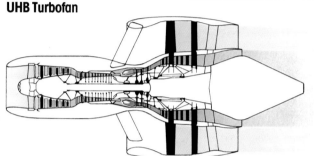

(and combustor) plus turbine on the high-pressure rotor. An exception to this layout is the RB.211, which has three shafts, the compressor and HP turbine being split into intermediate- and high-pressure rotors.

Other features of turbofans include the use of thrust reversers, normally of cascade type, acting on the fan slipstream which provides the major part of the engine's thrust; modular construction to avoid having to remove the entire engine in the event of a defect in one component; engine health or condition monitoring facilities on the combustor and main rotative assemblies to enable incipient failures to be detected; and increasingly more sophisticated engine control systems leading ultimately to fully automatic digital engine controls (FADECs).

THE PROPFAN

The state-of-the-art with propfans is still at an early stage: General Electric started ground testing of its 25,000lb (11,340kg) thrust proof-of-concept UDF in 1985, and flight testing started on a Boeing 727 in August 1986. This engine, the 9,000-16,000lb (4,080-7,260kg) thrust Allison/Pratt & Whitney Model 578-DX propfan, and certain of Rolls-Royce's design studies are all of similar concept in that they each feature aft-located open (or unducted) contra-rotating fans. Internally, the units differ quite markedly. GE's UDF incorporates no reduction gearing between the LP turbine and propfan, and the turbine itself is unusual in having intermeshed contrarotating rotors.

The Allison 578-DX is the most conventional of the three types in its layout, using the core engine to energize a power turbine driving a gearbox which drives the fan. The power turbine gases, after exhausting to atmosphere, flow over the fan blade roots. This latter feature is avoided in R-R's more recent designs by ducting the turbine gases internally, over wide-chord turbine-shaped hubs carrying the fan blades.

The foregoing propfan layouts all use 'pusher' fans, which ensure that the engine intake inducts 'clean' air. However, the vulnerability of open fans to foreign object damage (FOD) means that virtually all the installations proposed for these engines utilize rear-mounted nacelles with the fans behind the aft pressure bulkhead. As an alternative arrange-

Above: Full-scale mock-up of the projected Rolls-Royce ContraFan ultra high bypass turbofan of 50,000 to 65,000lb (22,675-29,480kg) thrust, intended for long-range transports.

Below: Full-scale mock-up of the 10,000shp PW-Allison Engines 578-DX propfan engine with contra-rotating Hamilton Standard Prop-Fan at rear. Centre are the exhaust ports.

Top: Propfan — representative of small/medium size propfans, with two-spool gas generator and rear-located gearbox driving a contra-rotating open fan in pusher mode.

Above: UHB Turbofan — representative of ultra high bypass, high thrust turbofans with forward mounted gas generator and 'gearless' contra-rotating ducted fan.

ment, the Allison Model 501-M78 driving a single-rotation propfan (scheduled to be flight tested in 1987) and some R-R studies make use of 'tractor' fans which can be wing-mounted.

A contrasting group of propfan designs is aimed at alleviating the noise, vibration and safety problems of the open fan, and makes use of single-rotation ducted fans, in most instances driven via a gearbox. These units correspond to ultra-high bypass turbofans (typically in the region of 15:1 to 25:1 BPR) and the duct provides both for containment of 'thrown' fan blades and a more efficient high-speed cruising performance. However, the lower BPRs mean that the reduction in SFC is less than with the UDF concept.

Pratt & Whitney and Motoren- und Turbinen-Union (MTU) are collaborating in researching this configuration. Rolls-Royce's corresponding concept features a mid- to aft-mounted counter-rotating ducted fan and, in some 'gearless' designs, incorporates GE's form of intermeshed counter-rotating fan turbine.

Overall, the trend is emerging that open-fans may be limited to use on short/medium-haul transports, while ducted fans will be more suited to long-range Jumbo-type transports where wing-mounted engines are expected to be favoured. This implies that open fans are likely to be in the medium-thrust bracket, and ducted fans in the high-thrust bracket. Almost certainly, the first propfan to enter passen-

Rolls-Royce Dart Mk 552

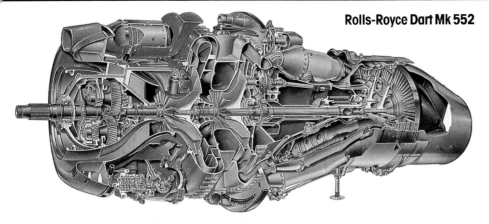

Above: This layout is representative of small/medium power turboprops, with (l to r) gearbox, compressor, combustor and turbine.

Right: Pratt & Whitney PW 124 turboprop with BAe/Hamilton Standard six-bladed propeller on BAe Viscount flying test bed.

Below: Rolls-Royce Tay turbofan mounted on R-R's engine noise test facility at Hucknall, Notts. The 12,420 to 15,100lb (5,635-6,850kg) thrust Tay powers the Fokker 100 and Gulfstream GIV, and enables both aircraft to meet all existing and projected international noise regulations.

ger-carrying operations will be General Electric's pioneering UDF powering Boeing's 7J7 150-seat transport, planned for entry into service in 1992.

THE TURBOPROP

To date, the most widely used configuration of turboprop has been the single-shaft layout as typified by the 2,000-3,000shp (1,500-2,240kw) R-R Dart and 4,000-5,000shp (2,985-3,730kw) Allison Model 501/T56. The former uses a centrifugal compressor and integral gearbox, and the latter an axial compressor and strut-mounted gearbox. At the low/medium end of the power scale, suited to commuter and short-haul operations, two-shaft and three-shaft free turbine layouts have more recently come into service. At the high power end, the 5,000-8,000shp (3,730-5,970kw) R-R Tyne has been unique in its use of a twin-spool compressor arrangement, also with integral gearbox.

For the future, there is the possibility that the Pratt & Whitney PW3005 and/or General Electric GE27 5,000shp (3,730kw) turboshafts developed under US military funding as Modern Technology Demonstrator Engines, could be modified as commercial turboprop engines.

FUTURE DEVELOPMENTS

NASA, in reviewing (during 1986) future aeropropulsion opportunities, graded these as first, evolutionary; second, novel heat engine developments; and third, revolutionary concepts requiring radical changes in the structure of the aerospace industry. The stage applicable to today's commercial engines is 'evolutionary', and here NASA saw large rather than small gains in performance still to be won. The three main avenues of progress that can be exploited are via advanced aerodynamics, innovative design and new materials.

Advances in aerodynamics can be seen in the steady increase in compressor pressure ratios, with 40:1 being proposed with a similar number of stages as existing 30:1 ratio engines. Aerodynamics also form part of what Rolls-Royce calls aero-thermal technology, in particular concerning turbine blade cooling. This has already enabled R-R to achieve turbine entry temperatures on the RB.211-524D4D of 2,510°F (1,377°C). The company's high-temperature demonstrator unit has run at close to 2,870°F (1,577°C), and temperatures of 3,140°F (1,727°C) are being proposed for demonstration by Rolls-Royce in the late 1980s.

Innovative design is well exemplified in GE's development of the UDF, and the diversity of competitive designs which it has inspired. And if the open fan has enabled BPRs of 35:1 to be achieved with impressive effect on propulsive efficiency, then on the materials' front, what NASA calls the 'non-metallic' engine will have comparable impact on such aspects as mechanical and structural design and thermal efficiency.

Composite materials purpose-conceived for individual components are being proposed, in which the material and the component are designed together as a single integrated function. Weight, strength, mechanical and thermal integrity, and most other design parameters will be measurably enhanced, together with improved cost effectiveness. For hot-end components, in particular turbine blades, the introduction of high-temperature ceramic materials is moving ever closer. Success with ceramics will enable impressive increases in turbine temperature, leading to further advances in thermal efficiency and power being achievable for a given size of engine.

Not without reason has the commercial aero engine been described as being at the cutting edge of advanced technology and industrial competition.

FUTURE DEVELOPMENTS

Commercial aircraft come in different shapes and sizes, for contrasting purposes. It is clearly impossible to predict the future of giant passenger jets, heavy freighters, local-service turboprops and STOL utility machines for the so-called 'bush' market all in the same breath – to say nothing of helicopters and perhaps airships! This chapter, which looks as far ahead as one dare attempt, a little way into the 21st century, is concerned chiefly with the mass passenger market. Like most aircraft, big passenger carriers can be studied under four main subheadings: aerodynamics, structure, propulsion and systems.

Fifty years ago, the DC-3 era established the cantilever monoplane wing as the undisputed lifting surface for most airliners, and virtually all such wings have flaps to increase lift on take-off and increase lift and drag on landing. With the coming of jets in the 1950s, wings became generally thinner: at least the ratio of thickness (measured from top to bottom) to chord (distance from leading edge to trailing edge) became significantly reduced, typically from around 17 per cent to barely half this value. To some degree this was accomplished by sweeping the wings back at an angle of about 35°. The trend seemed to be towards thinner wings and more sweepback, but – except for the special case of the Concorde SST – the reverse has happened.

AERODYNAMICS
Today's advanced jetliners have wings with greater thickness/chord ratio, typically around 12 per cent, and sweepback reduced to between 15 deg and 28 deg. On the other hand, aspect ratio (the slenderness in plan shape, defined as the square of the

span divided by wing area) has never ceased to increase, from around 6 (6.96 for the Boeing 747) to 7.77 for the Boeing 757, 7.9 for the Boeing 767, 8.8 for the Airbus A310 and 9.39 for the A320. All this has been made possible by so-called 'supercritical' wing profiles, which enable wings to be relatively deeper at Mach numbers around 0.8-0.85 without any extra drag. In turn this reduces structure weight, leaves more room for fuel and has other advantages. Greater aspect ratio has a direct effect upon efficiency in cruising flight, so that range is increased for any given amount of fuel. There is no reason to doubt that, with improved materials, aspect ratios will reach 12 by 2000. Combined with improved engine cycle efficiency this will improve the 'miles per gallon' figure by 25-35 per cent.

This has already revolutionized the sector distances that can be flown economically by any given size of aeroplane. After World War II, a long-range airliner was one that could fly sectors longer than 1,000 statute miles (1,610km). To fly the North Atlantic was virtually impossible, without flight refuelling. It could just be attempted, with totally uneconomic payload, by colossal aircraft such as the Bristol Brabazon. Today, heavy passenger and cargo loads can be flown over the North Atlantic by quite modest twin-engined machines. A sector of 1,000 statute miles (1,610km) is short range; medium-haul is around 3,000 statute miles

Below: Constant efforts by designers and engineers in recent years have resulted in a number of small but significant innovations. One such that seems to have universal applications is the winglet or, on this Airbus 310, wing-tip fence, which increases aspect ratio.

Above: The Airbus A320, shown here making its first flight on 22 February 1987, looks conventional enough at first sight. It can justly claim to be the most advanced airliner of the eighties, however, thanks to many advanced features in its aerodynamic design, manufacture, structural ideas and systems.

Mission Adaptive Wing

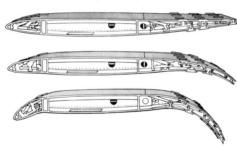

Left: Thanks to the pliability of new non-metallic materials that can be used for structural members of an airframe, Boeing has been able to develop this Mission Adaptive Wing, which can change its profile in flight without the usual drawbacks of gaps being opened up when slats or flaps are operated.

Above: The Boeing Mission Adaptive Wing is being test-flown by NASA on a modified F-111A, showing how military hardware can aid civil innovations.

Left: Laminar flow control, as mentioned in this chapter, is a promising area for development. NASA has been using this JetStar to test wing sections with LFC.

(4,830km); and the long-haulers do upwards of 6,000 statute miles (9,665km) – a distance that was far beyond even the future plans of anyone designing aircraft 40 years ago.

It has often been stressed that the one thing aircraft have to offer is speed, and it has sometimes been assumed that it is natural to offer as high a speed as possible. Until about 1960 this was true. Piston-engined airliner designers sought more speed by every means possible but lost out to the turboprop, which in turn was almost swept away by the jet. Jet designers sometimes failed badly when trying to get more speed, the classic case being the Convair CV-990 Coronado. Today, not only has the propeller come back to the world's airports, but the jet has all the speed it needs and is being developed entirely along such fresh directions as greater reliability, reduced fuel burn, less noise, improved digital avionics and, above all, reduced costs.

From the aerodynamic point of view this means an all-round reduction in drag. Many former excrescences, such as wing fences, vortillons (underside fences on the MD-80) and vortex generators are being eliminated, while the winglet (or as Airbus calls it, the wingtip fence) is definitely on the way in. But a much more fundamental goal is the attainment of laminar (non-turbulent) flow. The thin sheath of air surrounding today's airliners is almost always highly turbulent, and it gives rise to considerable drag. If this so-called boundary layer can be made laminar, drag can be reduced by more than half. Almost 40 years ago, engineers were working on ways of designing a laminar airliner, typically by sucking the boundary layer inside the aircraft through porous or finely perforated skins. This proved difficult to accomplish, and the slightest surface irregularity (such as a fly squashed against the leading edge on take-off) caused severe turbulence.

Though not evident externally, future transports are certainly going to have cleverer wings than those flying today. The A330 and A340 are heralding a new era in which aerofoil section, or profile, will be varied throughout each flight under computer control to achieve the highest lift/drag ratio at all times. These new European aircraft simply use the trailing-edge flaps for this purpose, but the ideal solution is a fully variable profile, with no hinges or discontinuities, rivalling the variation in profile of a bird's wing. The Boeing Military Airplane Co. has fitted a crude form of such a wing, called a Mission Adaptive Wing (MAW) to an F-111, and it could be that by about 2010 the designers of airliners will be thinking in terms of refined MAWs as a matter of course.

Today the battle for laminar aircraft is on again, and it looks as if it may be won well before 2000. Indeed, by the use of radically new wing profiles, with little or no sweepback, it is theoretically possible to achieve 'natural' laminar flow, without expenditure of energy on sucking and blowing. By the time this book appears someone may have decided to flight-test a full-scale piece of wing to see if such benefits can be realized in practice. Meanwhile, drag of ordinary jetliners can be reduced by cutting a thin slit along the wing upper surface just ahead of the shockwave, cutting a second slit just behind the shockwave, and then joining the two slits under the wing surface: differences in pressure cause air to flow into one slit and out of the other, weakening the shock and stabilizing its position, the big advantage being that the weak shock no longer causes such massive separation from the wing of the boundary layer downstream. This could reduce drag by 2-3 per cent by about 1998, and the same year might see almost as great a reduction in drag from limited natural laminar flow on engine pods and parts of the fuselage.

STRUCTURES

Turning to structures, it is a general rule that civil aircraft tend to introduce new technologies anything from three to 15 years later than do advanced combat aircraft, and on this basis the structure of the year-2000 airliner is likely to be made chiefly of advanced composites. The latter can be thought of either as plastic materials reinforced by very strong fibres or, alternatively, as millions of fibres stuck together with glue, the latter usually being an epoxy resin, polyamide or other 'plastic'. In general, composites tend to be as strong as the strongest metal alloys, bulk for bulk, whilst weighing much less than half as much. Often the fibres are costly, but the costs of manufacturing each component are much less because there are so few separate parts, whereas in today's airliners there may be hundreds of parts all joined with rivets, bolts and welds. So far, the most advanced airliners, such as the A320, have their entire tail made of composite materials, the most widely used being based on carbon fibre. There is no reason to doubt that the next generation of transports will have most of the wings, fuselage and engine nacelles made of composites, leaving high-strength steel in the landing gears and other metal parts in a few highly stressed joints and, of course, the engines.

Aluminium/lithium alloys were gradually introduced to jetliners, mainly by Boeing, from the early 1970s. Results have been well below expectation,

New Materials

☐ Primary structure and flight control surfaces
☐ Secondary structure

Left: The term 'composites' embraces a number of new materials that are non-metallic, such as carbon fibre or glass-reinforced plastic (GRP). Fabric-like in their qualities before being 'set', they can be used for a large variety of aircraft parts, as in this A320.

Below: The Embraer Brasilia, a product of the still-young Brazilian aircraft industry, provides a good example of the 'state-of-the-art' use of composites in the mid-eighties.

Below: The decade of the 'eighties has witnessed aircraft designers experimenting with many new ideas, made possible by such developments as non-metallic materials that offer great strength for low weight. The Beechcraft Starship is an example of the new configurations that are now gaining favour. It features monocoque wings with composite wingtip stabilisers, and variable geometry foreplanes.

Above: Noseplanes, or canards, have become popular on larger business aircraft in the mid-eighties, such as the Beechcraft Starship (shown below left) and the Piaggio Avanti (above)—the latter being unusual in having a tailplane also.

Left: Much interest is being generated in the airline business in the mid-eighties by the propfan or unducted fan (UDF) power plant, seen here on test on a Boeing 727. Propfans may be in airline service by 1992.

and even today, with several prolonged problems seemingly solved, these 'wonder metals' are no longer exciting. On the other hand, all bulk metals are made hundreds to thousands of times weaker than they could be because they are composed of astronomic numbers of strong crystals all jumbled together with very weak joints. If only a complete wing spar, for example, could be made from a single perfect crystal it could be made perhaps 99 per cent lighter than before without loss of strength. So far, a few small parts such as turbine blades can be made from single-crystal material, but there is not much hope of making a single-crystal metal aeroplane until well beyond 2000. For the present smaller gains must be sought from such improved manufacturing techniques as SPF/DB (superplastic forming and diffusion bonding), which in effect enables strong metals to be moulded like plastics into complex thin-walled shapes without joints.

Such features do not show externally, unlike major choices of configuration. The author has always hated traditional tailplanes (horizontal stabilizers) and elevators, which rotate the aircraft at take-off by forcing the tail down and in effect adding many tons to the weight at the most crucial point of the flight. It is much more sensible to use a canard surface, which achieves the same objective by lifting the nose, effectively taking part of the weight off the wing; but, whereas the highly unstable canard configuration is good for fighters, it is not quite so suitable for airliners. In the author's view the 21st-century passenger jet will nonetheless be a canard, at least with relaxed static stability.

There is no reason to doubt that traffic will continue to grow, which means that the unit size of vehicles will grow with it. There is still a little stretch left in the biggest current passenger carrier, the

Model 747-400, to a maximum of some 700 passengers with a full-length upper deck. At the start of the Model 747 project, Boeing looked carefully at twin-tube arrangements, either the traditional 'double bubble' with superimposed tubes comprising roughly equal upper and lower decks, or the radical parallel tube layout with left and right fuselages resulting in a cabin perhaps 40ft (12.2m) wide, with a row of pillars along the centreline to tie the upper and lower skins together against pressurization forces measured in thousands of tons. Many other design teams have looked at this arrangement, which would result in a wide body like nothing yet seen outside the biggest passenger ship lounge. It nevertheless looks unlikely to be adopted, and, while the Model 747-400 and future Model 747-500 versions of the Jumbo have adopted the superimposed double-bubble scheme because there is no alternative, tomorrow's 1,000-seater will adopt it because it looks the best layout. Certainly, the monster 1,000-seater will have two decks, despite the attractions of a near-circular fuselage with a floor 40ft (12.2m) wide.

It is perhaps worth noting that 40 years ago Northrop pioneered the all-wing aircraft which superficially seemed to be the most efficient shape possible. Certainly it seems attractive to eliminate the fuselage and tail, and bury the engines, but the fact remains that the most efficient transports ever built all have huge bodies and relatively small wings.

PROPULSION

Of all the subject headings considered, the most obvious revolution concerns that of propulsion. It is curious that, 40 years ago, the turbojet was thought applicable only to short-range aircraft, the turbofan (invented by Whittle in the 1930s) was ignored, and

for long ranges the only answer was thought to be the compound diesel or advanced turboprop. Today the turbofan has made possible all the range needed: for example, Boeing 747s of Cathay Pacific can take off with a full load from Hong Kong on a hot day and fly to London with no need for an intermediate stop. Tomorrow's big laminar aircraft will do London to Sydney or Melbourne, and many travellers would say they would even welcome a stop in order to stretch their legs. Current moves towards higher bypass ratios, notably by means of the propfan and unducted fan (UDF), which is discussed more fully in the chapter on engine technology, are aimed almost entirely at reducing fuel burn, not because of urgent need for greater range. Certainly there is no place in the world's airlines for the plain turbojet, but one can go too far in seeking higher propulsive efficiency. It would be possible to build a high-bypass engine with an overall pressure ratio of over 40 and a turbine entry temperature (TET) of 2,730°F (1,500°C). This might have an impressively low fuel consumption, provided one could tighten up the clearances and minimize air and gas leakage. Unfortunately it would also have a large number of extremely expensive blades, and its overall economics would probably look worse than a simpler engine with seemingly less-exciting design parameters. It cannot be too strongly emphasized that, certainly through 2000, airlines are looking to engine designers not so much for exciting performance as for absolute reliability and rock-bottom total costs over 25-year periods. Indeed, the world will continue to see a lot of the centrifugal compressor, which was derided by Whittle's critics 45 years ago as being completely passé!

Without trespassing on the previous chapter on engines, the timing of the introduction of UDF-type engines is currently a matter for much argument. Billions of dollars or pounds ride on who is believed. Boeing, at the time of writing, is urgently trying to stave off the A320, and persuade the world to wait for the UDF-engined Model 7J7. Like a more ambivalent McDonnell Douglas, Boeing stridently echoes General Electric in proclaiming that the UDF will be in airline service in early 1992. Perhaps it can be, but there are still several important unknowns, and considerable significance can be attached to the 1986 deal between Northwest and Airbus for up to 100 A320s. Admittedly, that deal allows the US carrier to cancel any of six sequential batches of 15 aircraft each after the first 10, but, once committed to a major type of equipment, airlines are reluctant to do an about-face, and the author expects by the mid-1990s to see all 100 A320s wearing the carrier's red tail. Moreover, this deal is influencing many waverers who had been agonizing over whether the traditional type of jet engine was really becoming outmoded.

By the late 1990s, the UDF and propfan are likely to be very important, and as well as providing higher cruise efficiency (compared with today's turbofans) will give relatively higher thrust on take-off, thus enabling maximum take-off weight to be increased for any given field length. To a first-order approximation, four UDF engines (much bigger than any yet designed) burning fuel at the same rate as the engines of a 1987 Model 747 would be well matched to an aircraft of 1,600,000lb (725,760kg) maximum take-off weight, double today's figure.

In the longer term it may be necessary to find an alternative to today's fuels, though scare stories about petroleum running out have been current for a long time. Quite a bit of flying has been done on liquefied natural gas (LNG), which burns cleanly and presents no severe problem, but this too is a finite (and thus presumably dwindling) supply. Eventually, but probably not before at least 2020, there seems little alternative to LH_2 (liquid hydrogen). This is a super fuel in many ways, and NASA in the USA has run aircraft engines on it for 30 years, starting with a J65 whose British Sapphire ancestry gave it vaporizing burners which needed few changes. The problems are that this liquid is almost the coldest thing known, though the background of experience with Rocketdyne and Pratt & Whitney rocket engines (among others) is so great that transfer of the technology to the airlines would 'merely' be a matter of investing a few tens of billions of dollars. The low density of LH_2 means that airliners would swell enormously, either with gigantic tanks at front and rear of the passenger/cargo area or, alternatively, with huge fuel pods on the outer wings. The latter might be preferred, because passengers might not like being sandwiched between colossal tanks of liquid at -453°F (-253°C). Among planemakers, Lockheed-California has had most to say about hydrogen, and despite the enormous bulk of tankage needed, the possible aircraft appear entirely plausible.

Of course, for basic reasons of cycle efficiency the SST (supersonic transport) engine beats all the subsonic ones, chiefly because of the tremendous overall pressure ratios that are attainable. It is simplicity itself to sketch attractive 350-seat SSTs with much better economics than those of Concorde, but the investment would be daunting. Unless for reasons of national prestige one (or both, in collaboration) of the superpowers decides this is a good thing to do, the author doubts that such investment will ever appear a profitable venture.

SYSTEMS

Systems can be discussed quite quickly, although this really is one of the most exciting of all areas. With the A320 the truly advanced all-digital aircraft (with totally integrated data bus networks linking every functioning item) has already been reached. There is no fundamental problem in switching from wire looms to fibre optics (so-called FBL, fly-by-light), and this would enable networks so reduced in weight that a man could carry one large enough to handle billions of bits of data each second, enough for the on-board management and maintenance logging of the biggest and most complex airliner. Thus, tomorrow's captain, seated in his simple cockpit with just the odd TV-type screen, could instantly check the pressures in all the tyres, the location of each member of cabin crew, the status of every latch on every door or hatch, and the temperature and temperature trend in any chosen part of the aircraft. There could even be inbuilt crack-detection for every unduplicated part of primary structure!

In the long term – not before 2000 – designers clearly must get away from the idea that all the propulsion system has to do is push the aircraft forwards. The best way of integrating the burning of fuel into useful lift, as well as thrust, has for many years seemed to be upper-surface blowing (USB), pioneered by NASA and Boeing, notably with the YC-14 and QSRA (Quiet Short-haul Research Aircraft). Today, Japan's Asuka is aimed at similar objectives, but with unimpressive brochure figures. There would be no difficulty in flying a short-haul 300-seater able to use a 1,000ft (305m) strip, with

acceptable environmental qualities, but the market hardly seems likely to support the investment needed.

As for helicopters, one of the few crystal-clear predictions that can be made is that there is no future in the large airline helicopter. The one thing the helicopter offers is the ability to hover. Airliners do not hover: they take off, fly from A to B, and land. To fly such missions with VTOL capability the obviously superior vehicle is the tilt-wing or tilt-rotor, now exemplified by the Bell/Boeing V-22 Osprey. This has a modest – but still marginally economic – size, with the ability to seat 28 to 30 passengers in a civil version, on 12,300hp (9,172kW). By 2005 it should be possible to have a next-generation 90-seater in 'scheduled service. The cruise efficiency, in terms of ton-miles per pound of fuel, is better than double that of a helicopter, quite apart from the cruising speed of over 340kts (628km/h; 390mph). The author wonders if today's helicopter builders have fully taken cognisance of the fact that, for simple A-to-B trucking jobs, the entire helicopter market will rapidly be taken over by the tilt-rotor. Civil certification authorities are already beginning to see if there are likely to be any deep problems; so far there are none that normal good engineering practice would not solve.

Below: Upper-surface blowing (USB) is one of several systems that have been studied as a means of deriving useful lift directly from the burning of fuel. It was given its first full-scale tests by Boeing and has a production application in the An-74. Japan's Asuka, here, uses the same idea.

Right: In 1985, Lockheed illustrated this concept for an airliner of the 21st century. With four jet engines burning liquid hydrogen, it is estimated that such an aircraft could carry 234 passengers at a speed of Mach = 2.7 over 4,000 naut mls (7,400km).

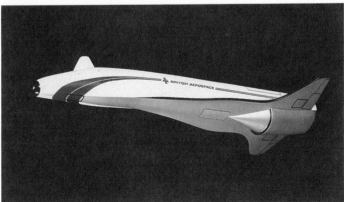

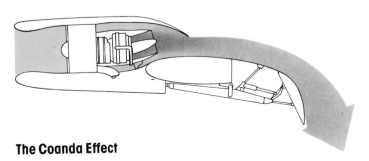

The Coanda Effect

Above: Bell's XV-15 tilt-rotor research prototypes of the late 'seventies showed that this concept is technically feasible. Civil applications may follow.

Right: The BAe HOTOL concept for a re-usable single-stage vehicle to place payloads into low-Earth orbits could be the basis for the design of hypersonic airliners.

Right: This diagram shows how upper-surface blowing works. Air that is ejected at high velocity from the turbofan engine remains 'attached' to the curved upper wing surface—as was discovered by Henri Coanda with his research into fluid flow—and provides lift when turned downwards.

In conclusion, there are many more unorthodox vehicles that one must consider when looking far ahead. One, very much a throwback to the distant past, is the airship. After lying dormant for 30 years, this suddenly attracted a lot of attention in the late 1960s, and various entrepreneurs tried to attract funds to build gigantic helium-filled ships made of carbon fibre, powered by highly efficient swivelling turboprops and able to hover over any factory in the world to pick up or set down standard 40ft (12.2m) containers. So far nothing like this has been built, and while it is doubtless possible – and the author would love to see it happen – not even the Soviet Union has yet reached the conclusion that the massive investment would yield a commercial return.

The other unorthodox vehicle is the semi-orbital aerospace plane. NASA and many US manufacturers are becoming increasingly strident in their search for Congressional funds to get started on something that could fly, say, 200 passengers to the other side of the globe in 60 to 90 minutes. As far as the author is concerned, the UK has the best answer of all in BAe's HOTOL vehicle with its very exciting Rolls-Royce RB.545 powerplant, which breathes air at lower altitudes and liquid oxygen in cruising flight. Very sadly, the UK simply lacks the will to support its big-time inventors.

THE AIRCRAFT

Year by year, the number of passengers travelling by air all over the world increases. From time to time, the rate at which air traffic grows suffers a set-back, such as occurred in 1986 because of tension in the Middle East and the threat of terrorism that deterred many would-be tourists. But the overall trend continues determinedly upwards — and air freight shows even more dramatic increases than passenger traffic.

Understandably, therefore, the design and production of aircraft for use by the world's airlines is an activity that attracts the attention of many of the world's largest aerospace manufacturing companies. Market surveys of the likely needs of the civil operators up to the end of the present century and beyond show that thousands of new aircraft will be bought.

Gathered together in this section are details and illustrations — in a consistent format to make possible direct comparisons — of the most important types of airliner to have appeared up to 1987. Thus, these types are the result of earlier market surveys, and their respective production totals give some indication of the success with which the aircraft makers judged the markets and met the requirements. They range from the largest of the 'jumbo' jetliners to small piston-engined twins, from the slow to the supersonic, from designs that trace their origins back to before World War II to those that were still taking shape on the drawing board (or, more accurately, on the computer screen) in 1987.

Although the products of numerous companies in many coutries are included in this section, the business of producing all but the smallest of airliners is now dominated by a few giants of the industry: Boeing and McDonnell Douglas in the US; Airbus, British Aerospace and Fokker in Europe. But there is no shortage of contenders for a share of the business at the smaller end of the size scale, and their products also receive proper attention in this section.

AEROSPATIALE/BAC CONCORDE FRANCE/UK

Having celebrated 10 years of successful revenue service in the hands of British Airways and Air France in January 1986, the Concorde has a history that goes back to 1955. In that year, member companies of the British aerospace industry and government agencies undertook preliminary design work that led to the establishment in 1956 of a Supersonic Transport Aircraft Committee (STAC) to study the feasibility of an SST. Among the project studies looked at by STAC was the Bristol Type 198 – a design number covering several different aircraft configurations, of which the most favoured came to be a slender delta-winged layout with eight engines and able to operate across the North Atlantic at Mach = 2.0. Through a process of continuous refinement, this evolved into the smaller Type 223, with four engines and 110 seats for a London to New York operation. While this work went on in the UK, a similar process was under way in France, leading by 1961 to evolution of a project called the Super Caravelle that was strikingly similar to the Bristol 223. At government behest, the British and French designers were merged into a single project, and a protocol of agreement was signed between the two governments on 29 November 1962. Principal airframe companies were BAC (which had absorbed Bristol) and Aérospatiale (incorporating Sud), and the engine companies were Rolls-Royce (which had meanwhile acquired the Bristol Siddeley engine company in which Concorde's Olympus engines originated) and SNECMA. The

Aérospatiale/BAC Concorde Cutaway Drawing Key

1 Variable geometry drooping nose
2 Weather radar
3 Spring pot
4 Visor jack
5 'A'-frame
6 Visor uplock
7 Visor guide rails and carriage
8 Droop nose jacks
9 Droop nose guide rails
10 Droop nose hinge
11 Rudder pedals
12 Captain's seat
13 Instrument panel shroud
14 Forward pressure bulkhead
15 Retracting visor
16 Multi-layer windscreen
17 Windscreen fluid rain clearance and wipers
18 Second pilot's seat
19 Roof panel
20 Flight-deck air duct
21 Third crew member's seat
22 Control relay jacks
23 First supernumerary's seat
24 Second supernumerary's folding seat (optional)
25 Radio and electronics racks (Channel 2)
26 Radio and electronics racks (Channel 1)
27 Plug-type forward passenger door
28 Slide/life-raft pack stowage
29 Cabin staff tip-up seat

49 Nosewheel actuating jacks
50 Underfloor air-conditioning ducts
51 Nosewheel door actuator
52 Nosewheel secondary (aft) doors
53 Fuselage frame (single flange)
54 Machined window panel
55 Underfloor forward baggage compartment (237cu ft/6.72m³)
56 Fuel lines
57 Lattice ribs
58 No 9 (port forward) trim tank
59 Single-web spar
60 No 10 (port forward) trim tank
61 Middle passenger doors (port and starboard)
62 Cabin staff tip-up seat
63 Toilets
64 Emergency radio stowage
65 Provision for VHF3
66 Overhead baggage racks (with doors)
67 Cabin aft section
68 Fuselage frame
69 Tank vent gallery
70 No 1 forward collector tank
71 Lattice ribs
72 Engine-feed pumps
73 Accumulator
74 No 5 fuel tank
75 Trim transfer gallery

92 Spraymat leading-edge de-icing panels
93 Leading-edge anti-icing strip
94 Spar-box machined girder side pieces
95 No 7 fuel tank
96 No 7a fuel tank
97 Static dischargers
98 Elevon
99 Inter-elevon flexible joint
100 Combined secondary nozzles/reverser buckets
101 Nozzle-mounting spigots
102 Cabin air delivery/distribution
103 Inspection panels
104 Cold-air unit
105 Fuel-cooled heat exchanger
106 Fuel/hydraulic oil heat exchanger
107 Fire-suppression bottles
108 Main spar frame
109 Accumulator
110 No 3 aft collector tank
111 Control linkage
112 'Z'-section spot-welded stringers
113 Riser to distribution duct
114 Anti-surge bulkheads

136 Honeycomb intake nose section
137 Spraymat intake lip de-icing
138 Ramp motor and gearbox
139 Forward ramp
140 Aft ramp
141 Inlet flap
142 Spill door actuator
143 Intake duct
144 Tank vent gallery
145 Engine front support links
146 Engine-mounting transverse equalizers
147 Oil tank
148 Primary heat exchanger
149 Secondary heat exchanger
150 Heat-exchanger exhaust air
151 Rolls-Royce/SNECMA Olympus 593 Mk 610 Turbojet
152 Outer wing fixing (340 high-tensile steel bolts)
153 Engine main mounting

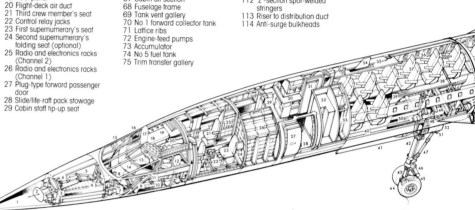

30 Forward galley units (port and starboard)
31 Toilets (2)
32 Coats (crew and passengers)
33 Twelve 26-man life-rafts
34 VHF1 antenna
35 Overhead baggage racks (with doors)
36 Cabin furnishing (heat and sound insulated)
37 Four-abreast one-class passenger accommodation
38 Seat rails
39 Metal-faced floor panels
40 Nosewheel well
41 Nosewheel main doors
42 Nosewheel leg
43 Shock absorber
44 Twin nosewheels
45 Torque links
46 Steering mechanism
47 Telescopic strut
48 Lateral bracing struts

76 Leading-edge machined ribs
77 Removable leading-edge sections
78 Expansion joints between sections
79 Contents unit
80 Inlet control valve
81 Transfer pumps
82 Flight-deck air duct
83 No 8 fuselage tank
84 Vapour seal above tank
85 Pressure-floor curved membranes
86 Pre-stretched integrally machined wing skin panels
87 No 8 wing tank
88 No 4 forward collector tank
89 No 10 starboard forward trim tank
90 No 9 starboard forward trim tank
91 Quick-lock removable inspection panels

115 No 6 (underfloor) fuel tank
116 Machined pressurised keel box
117 Fuselage frame
118 Double-flange frame/floor joint
119 Machined pressure-floor support beams
120 Port undercarriage well
121 Mainwheel door
122 Fuselage/wing attachments
123 Main spar frame
124 Mainwheel retraction link
125 Mainwheel actuating jack
126 Cross beam
127 Forked link
128 Drag strut
129 Mainwheel leg
130 Shock absorber
131 Pitch dampers
132 Four-wheel main undercarriage
133 Bogie beam
134 Torque links
135 Intake boundary layer splitter

154 Power control unit mounting
155 No 5a fuel tank
156 Tank vent
157 Transfer pump
158 Port outer elevon control unit fairing
159 Static dischargers
160 Honeycomb elevon structure
161 Flexible joint
162 Port middle elevon control hinge/fairing
163 Power control unit twin output
164 Control rod linkage
165 Nacelle aft support link
166 Reverser-bucket actuating screw jack
167 Retractable silencer lobs ('spades')
168 Primary (inner) variable nozzle
169 Pneumatic nozzle actuators
170 Nozzle-mounting spigots
171 Port inner elevon control hinge/fairing

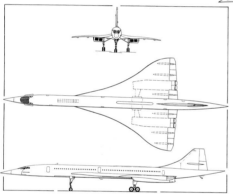

Above: Three-view drawing of the Anglo-French Concorde: an unmistakable shape in the sky thanks to its slender delta wing and long nose.

Below: The registration G-BOAG identifies the seventh Concorde in British Airways fleet. However, G-BOAF was actually the last Concorde to be built.

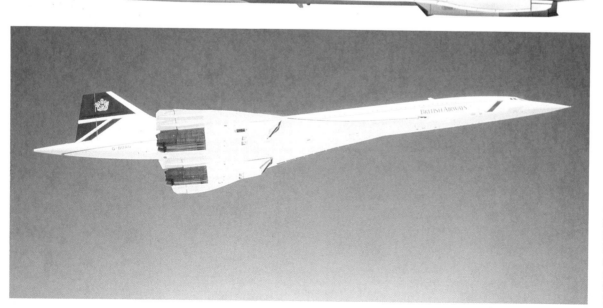

Left: Both British Airways and Air France – the only airlines operating Concorde – have adopted an overall white finish for their supersonic aircraft, with their respective liveries added. British Airways has several times changed its livery and logo style in the years that Concorde has been operating, the most recent being shown in this photograph. Thanks to the popularity of charter flights, BA Concordes are now seen, with greater or lesser regularity, in many parts of the world and not only in Europe and the USA.

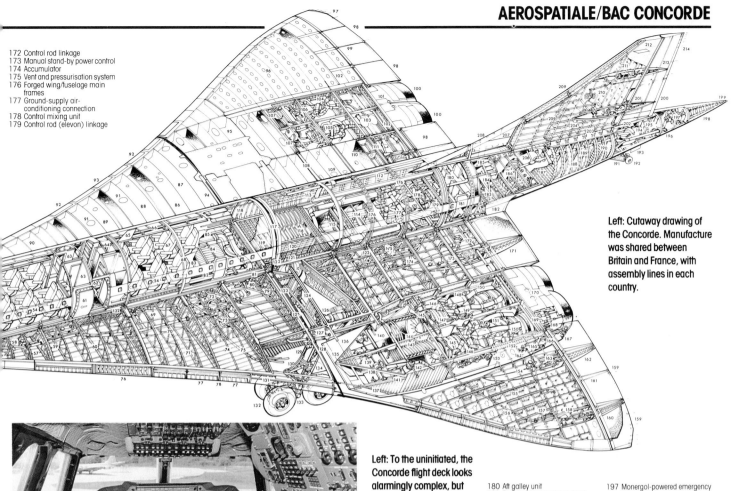

172 Control rod linkage
173 Manual stand-by power control
174 Accumulator
175 Vent and pressurisation system
176 Forged wing/fuselage main frames
177 Ground-supply air-conditioning connection
178 Control mixing unit
179 Control rod (elevon) linkage

Left: Cutaway drawing of the Concorde. Manufacture was shared between Britain and France, with assembly lines in each country.

Left: To the uninitiated, the Concorde flight deck looks alarmingly complex, but airline crews have found little difficulty in converting onto the supersonic transport from more conventional types of aircraft. As this photo shows, the Concorde is designed to be flown by a three-man crew, with a flight engineer's position to starboard behind the two pilots.

180 Aft galley unit
181 Rear emergency doors (port and starboard)
182 Wingroot fillet
183 Air-conditioning manual discharge valve
184 Automatic discharge/relief valve
185 First-aid oxygen cylinders
186 Rear baggage compartment (door to starboard)
187 Rear pressure bulkhead
188 Fin support frames
189 No 11 aft trim tank
190 Machined centre posts
191 Shock absorber
192 Retractable tail bumper
193 Tail bumper door
194 Nitrogen Dewar
195 Monergol tank (see 197)
196 Fuel jettison

197 Monergol-powered emergency power unit (pre-production aircraft only)
198 Tail cone
199 Rear navigation light
200 Rudder lower section
201 Servo control unit fairing (manual stand-by)
202 Fixed rudder stub
203 Multi-bolt fin-spar attachment
204 Fin construction
205 Fin spar
206 Air-conditioning ducting
207 HF antennae
208 Finroot fairing
209 Leading-edge structure
210 Servo unit threshold bellcrank
211 Servo control unit fairing
212 VOR antenna
213 Rudder upper section
214 Static dischargers

Concorde programme was handled in a number of stages, embracing the construction and testing of two prototypes, known as Concordes 001 and 002; two pre-production aircraft, originally known as Concordes 01 and 02 and subsequently as Concordes 101 and 102; and a production sequence commencing with Concorde 201. Production of an initial batch of 16 aircraft was authorized by the two governments and production of major airframe and engine components was divided between companies in the UK and France without duplication. Separate final assembly lines were set up at Toulouse and Filton, alternate aircraft being assembled in the UK and France. Concorde 001 made its first flight from Toulouse on 2 March 1969, its first supersonic flight on 1 October 1969, and its first excursion to Mach = 2 on 4 November 1970 (on its 102nd flight). Concorde 002 was the first to fly in the UK (at Filton) on 9 April 1969.

VARIANTS

Concordes 001 and 002 were slightly smaller than the production standard, which introduced lengthened front and rear fuselages, revised nose visors, changes to the wing geometry and uprated engines. These new features were progressively introduced on Concorde 101, first flown from Toulouse on 17 December 1971, and Concorde 102, flown at Filton on 10 January 1973. The more definitive production standard was represented by Concorde 201, flown at

Toulouse on 6 December 1973, and Concorde 202 flown at Filton on 13 February 1974. Production aircraft 203 to 216 flew alternately from the two assembly lines, the last two on 26 December 1978 and 20 April 1979 respectively.

SERVICE USE

Certification of the Concorde for full passenger-carrying operations was obtained on 13 October 1975 in France and on 5 December 1975 in the UK, leading to introduction into service by British Airways and Air France simultaneously on 21 January 1976. The routes, respectively, were London to Bahrein, and Paris to Rio de Janeiro (via Dakar). Services to Washington began on 24 May 1976 and to New York in December 1977. BA flew a service from London to Singapore (via Bahrain) jointly with Singapore Airlines in 1979/80, and in the same period Braniff leased aircraft time from Air France and BA to extend the Washington services to Dallas/Fort Worth. In 1985, BA introduced a service to Miami as an extension from Washington. For a time, Air France flew scheduled services to Caracas and to Mexico via Washington; many other destinations around the world have been served under an extensive programme of charters, primarily by BA aircraft. In 1987, seven aircraft each were available to Air France and to British Airways, and scheduled services were flown to New York from London and Paris, and to Washington and Miami from London.

SPECIFICATION

Power Plant: Four 38,050lb st (17,260kgp) Rolls-Royce/SNECMA Olympus 593 Mk 610 turbojets with silencers and reversers. Fuel capacity, 26,350 Imp gal (119,786l) in wing, fuselage and fin tanks.
Performance: Max cruising speed, 1,176kts (2,179km/h) at 51,300ft (15,635m); best range cruise, Mach = 2.02; initial rate of climb, 5,000ft/min (25.2m/sec); service ceiling, about 60,000ft (18,290m); take-off distance to 35ft (10.7m), 11,200ft (3,415m); landing distance from 35ft (10.7m), 7,300ft (2,225m); range with max payload, 3,360 naut mls (6,225km) at Mach = 2.02; range with max fuel and 19,500lb (8,845kg) payload, 3,550 naut mls (6,580km).
Weights: Operating weight empty, 173,500lb (78,700kg); typical payload, 25,000lb (11,340kg); max take-off weight, 408,000lb (185,065kg); max landing weight, 245,000lb (111,130kg); max zero-fuel weight, 203,000lb (92,080kg).
Dimensions: Span, 83ft 10in (25.56m); length, 203ft 9in (62.10m); height, 37ft 5in (11.40m); wing area, 3,856sq ft (358.25m²).
Accommodation: Cabin length, 129ft 0in (39.32m), max width, 8ft 7½in (2.63m), max height, 6ft 5in (1.96m). Maximum design accommodation, 144 passengers four-abreast at 32in (81cm) pitch, but standard layouts offer 128 seats at 34in (86cm) pitch and, in British Airways configuration, 100 seats. Baggage/freight compartments under floor and in rear fuselage, total volume, 697cu ft (19.74m³).

AEROSPATIALE (SUD-EST) CARAVELLE FRANCE

At the end of 1952, SNCA Sud-Est (one of the state-owned companies later merged to form Aérospatiale) was selected by the French air ministry to develop a twin-jet civil transport for short/medium-range operations. Designs had been submitted to meet the official specification drawn up in 1951, and covered a number of conventional layouts; that by Sud-Est selected for further development featured engines mounted on the rear fuselage – an innovative idea at that time, and one which had a number of attractions. Two prototypes were funded by the French government and made their first flight on 27 May 1955 and 6 May 1956, powered by Rolls-Royce Avon RA.26 Mk 521 engines. The first orders (from Air France and SAS) were obtained soon after the first flight, allowing Sud-Est to establish a production line at its Toulouse-Blagnac factory, where the Airbus is now assembled. Production continued until March 1973, with a total of 282 built, in addition to the prototypes – making the Caravelle at that time the most successful jet transport of European origin.

VARIANTS

The first production versions were the Caravelle I and IA with Avon RA.29 Mk 522 and Mk 526 turbojets respectively, initially flown on 14 May 1958 and 11 February 1960; 20 Srs I and 12 Srs IA aircraft were built. The Caravelle III, first flown on 30 December 1959, had Avon Mk 527s and increased weights; 78 were built and 31 Srs I/IAs were converted to this standard. A further change of Avon version (to the Mk 531) produced the Caravelle VI-N, first flown on 10 September 1960 and then, with thrust reversers on Avon 532R or 533R engines, the Caravelle VI-R; 53 and 56 were built respectively. First flown 18 January 1965, the Caravelle 10B1R or 10R was similar to the Srs VI-R but used Pratt & Whitney JT8D-1 or -7 engines; 20 were built. The Caravelle VII prototype with General Electric CJ805-23C engines, flown on 29 December 1960, led to the Caravelle 10A (also known as Caravelle Horizon or Caravelle Super A), with fuselage lengthened by 3ft 4in (1.0m), raised cabin window line and wing modifications. This prototype flew on 31 August 1962 and the Srs 10B3 (or Horizon B or Super B) was similar with JT8D-1, -7 or -9 engines; 22 were built, the first flight being on 3 March 1964. The Caravelle 11R was as the Srs 10B1R with JT8D-7 engines and a forward side cargo door for mixed cargo/passenger operations; the first of six flew on 21 April 1967. Final variant was the Caravelle 12, based on the Srs 10B3 with the fuselage lengthened a further 10ft 7in (3.23m). With JT8D-9 engines, its first flight was on 29 October 1970 and 12 were built.

SERVICE USE

Initial French certification was achieved on 2 April 1959, with American FAA endorsement following on April 8. The first customer delivery (apart from pre-certification deliveries for crew training) took place on 2 April 1959 to Air France, the first service being flown 6 May 1959. The first revenue service by SAS (using leased aircraft) was flown on 26 April 1959, and the first service in the USA (Srs VI-R of United Air Lines) followed on 14 July 1961. The Caravelle 10B1R (or 10R) was certificated on 23 May 1965 and entered service (Alia Royal Jordanian Airlines) on 31 July 1965. The Caravelle 12 was certificated on 12 March 1971 and entered service (Sterling Airways) on 20 March 1971. Orders for new-build Caravelles were placed by 33 airlines; more than 50 others have operated examples acquired in second-hand deals. Between 50 and 70 Caravelles of assorted marks were in service with about 20 airlines at the beginning of 1987.

SPECIFICATION
(Caravelle 10B3)

Power Plant: Two Pratt & Whitney JT8D-1 or -7 turbofans each rated at 14,000lb st (6,350kgp) for take-off and with a max continuous thrust of 12,600lb st (5,715kgp), or two JT8D-9 turbofans each rated at 14,500lb st (6,577kgp) for take-off. Fuel capacity, 4,180 Imp gal (19,000l) in four integral wing tanks and optional 660 Imp gal (3,000l) centre-section tank.

Performance: Max operating speed, 330kts (612km/h) IAS or Mach = 0.81; max cruise speed (JT8D-1 engines), 445kts (825km/h) at 25,000ft (7,620m); take-off balanced field length, 6,850ft (2,090m); landing distance from 50ft (15m), 5,180ft (1,580m); range with max payload, 1,450 naut mls (2,685km); range with max fuel and 16,340lb (7,410kg) payload, 1,965 naut mls (3,640km).

Weights: Basic operating weight, 66,259lb (30,055kg); max payload, 20,062lb (9,100kg); max take-off weight (JT8D-1), 114,638lb (52,000kg), later increased to 119,048lb (54,000kg) and (JT8D-9), 123,457lb (56,000kg); max landing weight, 109,127lb (49,500kg); max zero-fuel weight, 87,081lb (39,500kg).

Dimensions: Span, 112ft 6in (34.30m); overall length, 108ft 3½in (33.01m); overall height, 28ft 7in (8.72m); sweepback, 20 deg at quarter chord; wing area, 1,579 sq ft (146.7m²).

Accommodation: Cabin length, 76ft 11½in (23.45m), max width, 9ft 9½in (3.00m), max height, 6ft 7in (2.00m). Typical accommodation for 91 passengers in mixed-class layout, or 89 passengers in a single-class five-abreast layout at 35in (89cm) pitch, or up to 110 passengers in a five-abreast layout at 29in (74cm) pitch. Upper aft baggage compartment volume, 148cu ft (4.2m³). Normal flight crew of three.

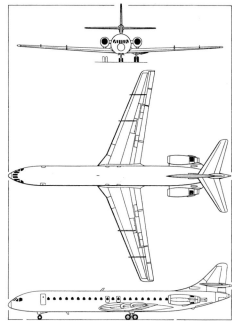

Above: Three-view drawing of the Aérospatiale Caravelle 12, the final production version.

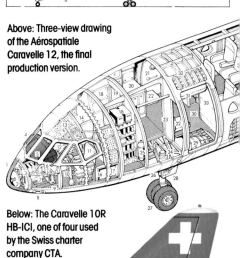

Below: The Caravelle 10R HB-ICI, one of four used by the Swiss charter company CTA.

Above: *Città di Tizzano*, one of the Caravelles operated by Altair Linee Aeree, an Italian airline that is partly owned by Pegasus Holidays, and operates chiefly between the UK and Mediterranean holiday resorts.

Above: The French charter operator Minerve began services in 1975 with a single Caravelle, and was still using two of the Srs VI aircraft in 1987. Illustrated is F-BRGU, previously used by JAT, the state-owned Yugoslav national airline.

Below: The cutaway drawing depicts the long-fuselage Super Caravelle or Caravelle 12.

Aérospatiale Super Caravelle Cutaway Drawing Key

1 Radome
2 Weather radar scanner
3 Front pressure bulkhead
4 Windscreen panels
5 Instrument panel shroud
6 Windscreen wipers
7 Rudder pedals
8 Landing/taxiing lamp
9 Cockpit floor level
10 Control column
11 Pilot's seat
12 Co-pilot's seat
13 Overhead systems switch panel
14 Flight engineer's position
15 Electrical system fuse panels
16 Crew baggage locker
17 Cockpit section joint frame
18 Radio and electrical equipment racks, port and starboard
19 Cockpit doorway
20 Galley
21 Service door/emergency exit
22 Cabin attendants' folding seats
23 Wardrobe
24 Nose undercarriage mounting frame
25 Oxygen cylinder
26 Nose undercarriage leg strut
27 Twin nosewheels
28 Nosewheel leg door
29 Hydraulic retraction jack
30 Entry lobby
31 Forward 'up-and-over' door
32 Door surround structure
33 Cabin bulkhead
34 Fuselage skin panelling
35 Frame and stringer fuselage construction
36 First-class 4-abreast seating
37 Overhead luggage racks
38 Curtained window panel
39 Cabin floor panels
40 Seat mounting rails
41 Forward underfloor cargo hold
42 Ventral cargo hold door
43 Removable cabin partition
44 Floor beam construction
45 Wing root fillet
46 Wing centre section carry-through
47 Skin panel centreline joint
48 Optional centre section fuel tank, capacity 600 Imp gal (3000l)
49 Front spar/fuselage attachment main frame
50 Starboard emergency exit windows
51 VHF aerial
52 Starboard wing inboard integral fuel tank
53 Inboard wing fence
54 Fuel pumps
55 Outboard wing fence
56 Outer wing fuel tank, total system capacity 4,180 Imp gal (19,000l)
57 Starboard navigation light
58 Wing tip fairing
59 Starboard aileron
60 Aileron balance weights
61 Aileron hydraulic jack
62 Starboard double slotted flap, down position
63 Flap screw jacks
64 Starboard spoilers, open
65 Airbrake, upper and lower surfaces, open
66 Spoiler hydraulic jack
67 Flap drive and interconnection shafts
68 Flap guide rails and carriage
69 Starboard main undercarriage mounting struts
70 Centre and rear spar/fuselage attachment frames
71 Anti-collision light
72 Centre fuselage construction
73 Pressure floor above wheel bay
74 Port emergency exit window
75 Fuselage centre keel
76 Port main undercarriage wheel bay
77 Hydraulic equipment compartment
78 Central flap drive motor
79 Aft underfloor cargo hold
80 Cabin wall trim panelling
81 Tourist-class five-abreast seating
82 Overhead luggage racks
83 Four-abreast rear seat row
84 Rear cabin bulkhead
85 Toilet compartments, port and starboard
86 Aft baggage compartment, port and starboard
87 Starboard engine intake
88 Detachable engine cowlings
89 Thrust reverser louvres
90 Fin root fillet
91 Wardrobe, port and starboard
92 Air conditioning system air intakes
93 Tailplane de-icing air ducting
94 Elevator hydraulic jack
95 Tailfin construction
96 Starboard tailplane
97 Starboard elevator
98 VOR aerial
99 Rudder horn balance
100 Rudder construction
101 Tailplane shock cone
102 Elevator torque shaft
103 Port elevator construction
104 Tailplane construction
105 APU ventral access door
106 Auxiliary power unit (APU)
107 Rudder lower segment
108 Tailplane support structure
109 Rudder hydraulic jack
110 Rear entry tunnel
111 Air system heat exchanger exhaust ducts
112 Air conditioning plant, port and starboard
113 Rear pressure bulkhead
114 Rear entry doorway
115 Primary heat exchanger
116 Thrust reverser louvres
117 Engine exhaust nozzle
118 Refractable airstairs
119 Thrust reverser actuator
120 Oil cooler air duct
121 Pratt & Whitney JT8D-7 turbofan engine
122 Engine mounting main frames
123 Bleed air ducting
124 Engine pylon construction
125 Port engine air intake
126 Ventral skin panelling
127 Fuel feed pipe
128 Trailing edge wing root fillet
129 Flap drive shaft
130 Main undercarriage wheel door
131 Main undercarriage leg pivot fixing
132 Flap shroud ribs
133 Inboard spoiler
134 Port double slotted flap, up position
135 Flap rib construction
136 Port airbrake
137 Inboard wing fence
138 Outboard spoiler
139 Spoiler honeycomb construction
140 Aileron construction
141 Aileron hydraulic jack
142 Wing tip fairing
143 Fuel system vent valve
144 Port navigation light
145 Outer wing fuel tank bay
146 Outboard wing fence
147 Three-spar wing torsion box construction
148 Wing rib construction
149 Corrugated double skin leading edge
150 Leading edge nose ribs
151 Wing skin plating
152 Four-wheel main undercarriage bogie
153 Main undercarriage leg strut
154 Hydraulic retraction jack
155 Inboard integral fuel tank bay
156 Wing stringers
157 Inboard tapered spar section
158 Leading edge de-icing air duct
159 Extended leading edge section

AEROSPATIALE 262 (and MOHAWK 298) FRANCE (USA)

This small regional airliner was evolved from a design by Max Holste, whose company flew on 20 May 1959 the prototype of a utility transport powered by Pratt & Whitney Wasp radial piston engines and based on a square-section fuselage. Known as the MH-250, this was followed by the MH-260 with Bastan turboprops, flown on 29 July 1960. A batch of 10 MH-260s was then built (for operation by Widerøes Flyveselskap and Air Inter) with the help of Nord Aviation. State-owned Nord (now merged into Aérospatiale) undertook further development of the basic design and produced as a result the Nord 262, which differed from the MH-260 primarily in having a pressurized circular-section cabin large enough for 24-26 passengers. A prototype flew on 24 December 1962 and was joined by three pre-production examples for the certification programme. These four aircraft were known as Nord 262Bs, the definitive production version being the Nord 262A, with Bastan VIC engines. This was the principal commercial variant, later developments being described below, and made its first flight on 8 July 1964.

VARIANTS

After the Nord 262A and 262B with Bastan VIC engines, the Nord 262C and Nord 262D were evolved with Bastan VIIC engines; data for this higher-powered version are given above. A re-engined airframe flew for the first time in July 1968 and certification was obtained on 24 December 1970, but most sales were in military guise as the Nord 262D Frégate to the Armée de l'Air. The designation Mohawk 298 was adopted for a variant developed in the USA, to allow the aircraft to perform more effectively under FAR 298 regulations that applied to regional or third-level airline operations. Development was instigated in 1974 by Allegheny Airlines – which had acquired a fleet of Nord 262As when it took over Lake Central Airlines – the major new feature being the

Above: The Nord 262 was one of the first of the smaller twin-turboprop transports designed for service with the regional airlines. Of the 110 built, more than half went straight to military users and by the beginning of 1987 only a score or so remained in commercial service.

Right: The Nord 262 is shown in this three-view drawing in its original Bastan-engined version. Based on an original design by Max Holste, the Nord 262 was later produced by Aérospatiale and known in some variants as the Frégate. The Mohawk 298 differed in engines and nacelles and is still used.

AIRBUS A330 AND A340 INTERNATIONAL

Right: The Airbus A330 proposal, shown in model form here, features the same cabin cross-section as the well-established A300 and A310, but introduces an advanced new wing with the now-standard winglets.

Below: The A330 is shown in this provisional three-view drawing, as planned early in 1987. The future of the A330 was at that time closely linked with that of the A340, with which it shares a common wing and a similar fuselage. The same power plant options as for the A310 will apply.

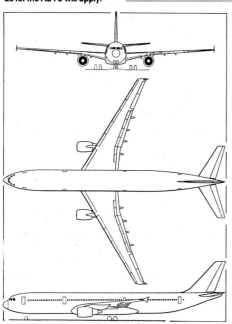

After studying a number of possible stretched versions and other derivatives of the basic A300 wide-body twin-jet, Airbus Industrie had by the mid-1980s narrowed down the choice to two. At the project stage, these were identified as the TA9, a medium-range large-capacity twin, and the TA11, a four-engined long-range variant of the same design. As the 'TA' designations indicated, these were twin-aisle designs, based on use of the basic A300 fuselage cross-section. By early 1986, Airbus had reached the conclusion that it needed to add both of these types to its product range in order to maintain its competitive position vis-a-vis the major US aerospace companies, and that the developing market would justify production of both for entry into service in the early 1990s. Signifying that these proposals had moved forward from project definition to the preliminary marketing phase (though still short of a formal launch decision), they were given the designations A330 and A340 respectively, and by late 1986 the two types had been closely integrated at design and engineering levels, while launch orders were being sought and the necessary

financial backing of the Airbus partner companies was being arranged.

VARIANTS

The Airbus proposal for the A330 and A340 is unusual, if not unique, in that it plans to use a single airframe, with basically the same fuselage, wing and tail unit, in both two- and four-engine versions. The fuselage uses the same cross-section as the A300 and A310, with a new and longer centre-section to mate with a new wing and provide about 17ft (5.2m) of extra length to increase the seating capacity. The wing is all-new for the A330 and A340 but is the same for both versions. Of advanced design, it has the highest aspect ratio of any large airliner planned to date, and is notable also for its use of variable camber, using an on-board computer to tailor the camber, through small movements of the trailing-edge flaps, to suit the weight, speed and altitude at which the aircraft is flying. Only small aerodynamic differences are necessary to allow for the variation in number of engines, and the structure is also identical except for some differences in skin thick-

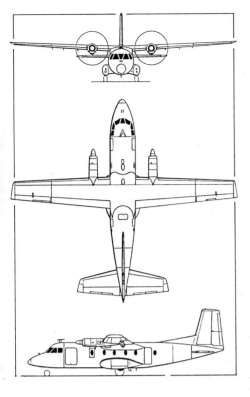

use of Pratt & Whitney Canada PT6A-45 turboprops in place of the Bastans. The modification programme was managed by Mohawk Air Services, and the work undertaken by Frakes Aviation at Cleburne, Texas: as well as the new engines, the nine aircraft received a Hamilton Standard air-conditioning system, an all-new Collins solid-state avionics system, new electrics and a revised cabin layout. The wing tips were new and increased the span slightly. The first flight of a converted aircraft was made on 7 January 1975. Production of the Nord 262 (also known later as the Aérospatiale 262), including those converted to Mohawk 298 standard, totalled 110.

SERVICE USE

The Nord 262B was certificated on 16 July 1964 and entered service with Air Inter. The definitive Nord 262A was certificated in March 1965 and entered service in August, and the Nord 262C/D was certificated on 24 December 1970. Commercial customers for the Nord 262A were Lake Central, Japan Domestic, Alisarda, Air Ceylon, Rousseau Aviation, Linjeflyg, Cimber Air, Krauss Interregional, Air Madagascar, Air Comores, Tunis Air and Air Alsace. Nord 262Cs were sold to users in Gabon, East Africa and Haute-Volta (now Burkina Faso). Some 20 Nord 262s remained in airline service at the beginning of 1987, with seven operators.

SPECIFICATION
(Nord 262C)

Power Plant: Two Turboméca Bastan VIIA turboprops each rated at 1,130shp (843kW) for take-off, with Ratier Forest four-blade propellers of 10ft 6in (3.2m) diameter. Fuel capacity, 440 Imp gal (2,000l) standard or 565 Imp gal (2,570l) with supplementary tanks.
Performance: Max operating speed, 214kts (397km/h) IAS; max cruising speed, 224kts (415km/h) at 20,000ft (6095m); typical cruising speed, 202kts (375km/h); initial rate of climb, 1,200ft/min (6.1m/sec); service ceiling, 23,500ft (7,160m); take-off distance to 35ft (10.7m), 2,690ft (820m); range with 26 passengers, 550 naut mls (1,020km).
Weights: Basic operating weight, 15,929lb (7,225kg); max payload, 6,781lb (3,075kg); max take-off weight, 23,810lb (10,800kg); max landing weight, 23,040lb (10,450kg); max zero-fuel weight, 22,710lb (10,300kg).
Dimensions: Span, 74ft 2in (22.60m); overall length, 63ft 3in (19.28m); height overall, 20ft 4in (6.21m); sweepback, nil; wing area, 592sq ft (55.0m²).
Accommodation: Cabin length, 34ft 10in (10.61m), width, 7ft 1in (2.15m), height, 5ft 11in (1.80m). Standard accommodation for 26 (or up to 29) passengers in a 2 + 1 arrangement at 33in (84cm) pitch. Baggage hold at front of cabin, volume, 159cu ft (4.50m³). Flight crew of two.

SPECIFICATION
(A330 and A340, provisional)

Power Plant: (A330) Two General Electric CF6-80C2 turbofans each rated at 64,000lb st (29,030kgp) for take-off or two Pratt & Whitney PW 4000 turbofans each rated at 60,000lb st (27,216kgp) for take-off, with thrust reversers. Fuel capacity, 24,500 Imp gal (111,380l).
Power Plant: (A340) Four CFM International CFM56-5S3 turbofans each rated at 30,600lb st (13,880kgp) for take-off, with thrust reversers.
Performance: (A330) Design range, about 5,000 naut mls (9,300km) with typical full two-class passenger payload.
Performance: (A340-200) Design range, about 7,650 naut mls (14,200km) with typical full three-class passenger payload; (A340-300) design range, 6,850 naut mls (12,700km) with 295 passengers.
Weights: Empty equipped weight, about 145,000lb (111,130kg); max take-off weight (A330), 450,000lb (204,000kg); (A340), about 542,300lb (246,000kg).
Dimensions: Span, (with wingtip fences) 190ft (58.0m); overall length, (A330), 205ft 4½in (62.6m); overall length (A340-200), 194ft 10in (59.38m); length (A340-300), 208ft 8in (63.6m); overall height, 55ft 11½in (16.8m); wing area, about 3,500 sq ft (325.2m²).
Accommodation: Cabin length, about 149ft 3in (45.5m), max width, 17ft 4in (5.28m), max height, 8ft 4in (2.54m). Typical two-class medium-range layout (A330) has 30 first-class seats six-abreast at 40in (102cm) pitch plus 275-298 economy-class eight-abreast at 33/34in (84/86cm) pitch, all with two aisles. Typical three-class long-range layout (A340-200) has 18 first-class six-abreast at 59/60in (150/152cm) pitch plus 74 business-class seven-abreast at 36in (91cm) pitch plus 170 in economy-class eight abreast at 34in (86cm) pitch, all with two aisles. Max single-class high-density arrangement for 375 seats nine abreast with two aisles.

Above: This model depicts the A340 as it was proposed towards the end of 1986, with four CFM56 turbofans.

Below: A provisional three-view drawing of the A340-200 in its 1986 configuration with CFM56 engines.

nesses and the engine attachments. Although the A340 will operate at slightly higher weights than the A330, wing bending moments are similar because of the extra relief provided by engine inertia, and the lighter, shorter-range A330 needs as much strength as the A340 because it will make more fatigue-inducing flights in a given number of hours. Both types use the same carbon fibre-reinforced plastic fins as the A310 and a CFRP tailplane trim-tank as in the A310-300. Cockpit and systems are based on those of the A320, with fly-by-wire controls, side-stick controllers and digital integrated displays. After giving consideration, in late 1986 and early 1987, to using the 28,600lb st (13,000kgp) CFM56-5-S2 and the 30,000lb st (13,600kgp) IAE SuperFan derivative of the V2500, Airbus announced on 8 April 1987 that it had selected the CFM56-S-S3 to power the A340 and a development of the General Electric CF6-80C2 for the A330.

SERVICE USE

The Airbus plan for the A330 and A340 was based on a launch decision in early 1987, based on orders being placed by a minimum of five airlines. The A340 is expected to be the first to enter service, not later than April 1992, followed about six months later by the A330. Lufthansa was one of the first airlines to indicate a positive interest in the A340, other airlines regarded as possible customers in-

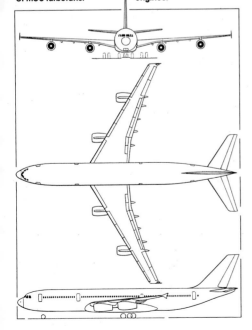

cluding Air France, Swissair, UTA, Singapore International and Thai International. Until firm orders are placed by these or other airlines, the precise timing of the development of these new Airbus projects remains uncertain, as does the final definition of the aircraft specifications.

AIRBUS A300 INTERNATIONAL

Product of a truly international programme of development and manufacture, the A300 was the first of the Airbus family of wide-body jet-liners that have challenged long-held US primacy in the production of transport aircraft. Design activity began in 1965 as an Anglo-French initiative to develop a large-capacity transport for BEA and Air France; West German participation dates from 1967, with signature of a memorandum of understanding by the three governments on 26 September 1967. The initial tri-nation project was for a 330,000lb (149,700kg) aircraft with two Rolls-Royce RB.207 engines, but this was scaled down after the British government withdrew on the grounds that a market could not be guaranteed, leaving Hawker Siddeley to maintain a British share on a privately-financed basis. The smaller A300B emerged in December 1968 with a 275,575lb (125,000kg) gross weight, two British or American engines each of about 45,000lb st (20,410kgp) and accommodation for 252 passengers. Two prototypes were built in this configuration: under the designation A300B1, these two aircraft first flew on 28 October 1972 and 5 February 1973 at Toulouse with General Electric CF6-50A turbofans. These had a fuselage length 8ft 8in (2.65m) less than that of the production models, as described under the Variants heading below. Production of the A300 family is shared between the Airbus partners, comprising Aérospatiale in France, MBB in West Germany, British Aerospace in the UK and CASA in Spain, with Fokker in the Netherlands as an associate in the programme. All final as-

sembly takes place at Toulouse, with major components ferried in from the other national production centres.

VARIANTS

Production began with the A300B2, later known as A300B2-100, with CF6-50C or C2 engines and first flown on 28 June 1973. The A300B2K (later A300B2-200) introduced wing-root leading-edge Krueger flaps for better field performance, and first flew 30 July 1976. Pratt & Whitney JT9D-59A engines were introduced on the A300B2-220 (and A300B2-320 with higher zero-fuel and landing weights), first flown 28 April 1979. The A300B4 (later A300B4-100 with CF6 engines, and A300B4-120 with JT9D engines) was introduced as a long-range version, with

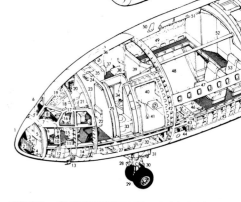

Above: Airbus Industrie, in vigorous competition with Boeing and MDC, has had considerable success selling the A300 in the Far East and Australia. Thai Airways International is one user in the area.

SPECIFICATION
(A300-600)

Power Plant: Two General Electric CF6-80C2 or Pratt & Whitney JT9D-7R4H1 turbofans each rated at 56,000lb st (25,402kgp). Fuel capacity, 13,836 Imp gal (62,900l) in integral tanks in wing, including centre section.
Performance: Max operating speed, 335kts (621km/h) IAS or Mach = 0.82; max cruising speed, 480kts (890km/h) at 31,000ft (9,450m); long-range cruise, 457kts (847km/h) at 35,000ft (10,670m); max operating altitude, 40,000ft (12,190m); take-off field length (FAR), 7,600ft (2,315m); landing field length (FAR), 5,025ft (1530m); range with max payload, 2,310 naut mls (4,285km); range with max fuel and 63,160lb (28,650kg) payload, 4,380 naut mls (8,120km).
Weights: Operating weight empty, 197,787lb (89,715kg); max payload, 88,813lb (40,285kg); max fuel, 111,331lb (50,499kg); max take-off weight, basic aircraft, 363,765lb (165,000kg); max take-off weights, optional, 375,880lb (170,500kg) or 308,640lb (140,000kg); max zero-fuel weight (for either take-off weight as quoted), 286,600lb (130,000kg).
Dimensions: Span, 147ft 1in (44.84m); overall length, 177ft 5in (54.08m); overall height, 54ft 6½in (16.62m); sweepback, 28 deg at quarter chord; wing area, 2,798.6sq ft (260.0m²).
Accommodation: Cabin length, 131ft 11in (40.21m), max width, 17ft 4in (5.28m), max height, 8ft 4in (2.54m). Basic accommodation for 267 passengers comprising 20 six-abreast at 38in (96.5cm) pitch and 247 eight-abreast at 34in (86.4cm) pitch; maximum one-class accommodation for 375 passengers six/seven/eight/nine-abreast with two aisles. Underfloor baggage/cargo volume, 5,205cu ft (147.40m³). Flight crew of two, plus two observer seats on flight deck.

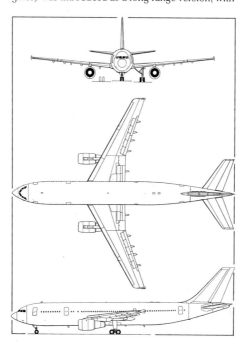

Above: The three-view drawing depicts the A300-600, the 1987 production version of the original Airbus, with winglets and the latest engines.

Below: Although Italy is not a partner in the Airbus consortium, the national airline Alitalia has eight A300B4s in its fleet, all with I-BUS- registrations.

Above: Airbus developed a Forward-Facing Crew Cockpit for the A300, in which the flight engineer, behind the two pilots, faces forwards.

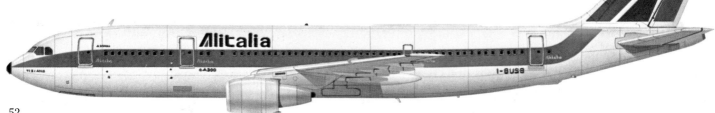

Airbus Industrie A300-600R Cutaway Drawing Key

1 Radome
2 Weather radar scanner
3 Scanner mounting and tracking mechanism
4 VOR localiser aerial
5 Front pressure bulkhead

30 Hydraulic steering jacks
31 Nosewheel leg doors
32 Nose undercarriage pivot fixing
33 Forward toilet compartment
34 Wash hand basin
35 Galley
36 Starboard entry/service door
37 Door mounted escape chute
38 Cabin attendant's folding seat
39 Curtained cabin divider
40 Forward main entry door
41 Door latch
42 Door surround structure
43 Underfloor avionics equipment racks
44 Runway turn-off light
45 Fuselage lower lobe frame and stringer construction
46 Floor beam construction
47 Cabin window panels
48 Forward freight hold door
49 Cabin wall trim panelling
50 VHF communications aerial
51 Overhead stowage bins
52 Curtained cabin divider
53 First class passenger seating, 26 seats
54 Underfloor air system ducting

72 Ventral air conditioning packs, 2
73 Wing centre box fuel tank
74 Three-spar wing centre-section construction
75 Centre-section floor beams
76 Front spar attachment main frame
77 Fuselage centre-section construction
78 Starboard wing inboard main fuel tank. Standard fuel capacity 13,628 Imp Gal (62,000l)
79 Outer wing skin panel joint strap
80 Fuel system piping
81 Pressure refuelling connection
82 Refuelling valves
83 Fuel feed tank and pumps
84 Fuel tank dividing ribs
85 Leading-edge slat drive shaft
86 Three-segment leading-edge slats, open
87 Wing fence

107 Wing root spoilers/lift dumpers (two)
108 Inboard flap segment
109 Cabin air system recirculation fan
110 Pressure floor above wheel bay
111 Rear spar attachment main frame
112 Starboard main undercarriage, retracted position
113 Undercarriage door jack
114 Equipment bay walkway
115 Undercarriage bay pressure bulkhead
116 Flap drive motor and gearbox
117 Hydraulic reservoir, triplex system
118 Eight-abreast tourist class passenger seating

Left: Shown in this cutaway drawing is the A300-600R, a long-range version which has a trimming fuel tank in the tailplane.

139 Glassfibre reinforced fin leading-edge
140 Fin rib construction
141 Fin tip fairing
142 Static dischargers
143 Carbon fibre rudder skin panelling
144 Honeycomb core construction
145 Rudder triplex hydraulic actuators
146 APU equipment bay
147 Garrett GTCP331-250 auxiliary power unit (APU)
148 Tailcone fairing
149 APU exhaust duct
150 Port elevator construction
151 Elevator triplex hydraulic actuators
152 Static dischargers
153 Port tailplane rib construction

176 Spoiler hydraulic jacks
177 Auxiliary spar
178 Main undercarriage side struts
179 Retractable ventral landing lamp, port and starboard
180 Hydraulic retraction jack
181 Main undercarriage pivot fixing
182 Inboard flap track mechanism
183 Aileron triplex hydraulic actuators
184 Port all-speed aileron construction
185 Port airbrakes/lift dumpers
186 Flap down position
187 Flap guide rails
188 Fuel jettison pipe
189 Flap track fairings
190 Roll control spoilers/lift dumpers
191 Fixed portion of trailing edge
192 Trailing-edge composite construction
193 Static dischargers
194 Tail navigation and strobe lights (white)
195 Port winglet
196 Wing tip fairing
197 Port navigation light (red)
198 Rear spar
199 Outer wing panel rib construction
200 Front spar
201 Port leading-edge slat segments
202 Slat screw jacks
203 Slat guide rails
204 Wing leading-edge de-icing air pipes
205 Telescopic de-icing air delivery ducts
206 Port wing integral fuel tank
207 Outer wing panel skin joint strap
208 Port main undercarriage four-wheel bogie
209 Main undercarriage leg strut
210 Nacelle pylon attachment joint
211 Engine pylon construction
212 Exhaust nozzle plug fairing
213 Core engine, hot stream, exhaust nozzle
214 Engine turbine section
215 Fan air, cold stream, exhaust duct
216 Reverser cascade, closed
217 Engine bleed air ducting
218 General Electric CF6-80C2-A1 turbofan
219 Engine fan blades
220 Noise attenuating intake lining
221 Intake cowling nose ring
222 Detachable engine cowling panels
223 Bleed air system pre-cooler
224 Inboard leading-edge slat
225 Bleed air delivery ducting
226 Inner wing panel three-spar construction
227 Inboard integral fuel tank
228 Inboard wing ribs
229 Wing root skin joint strap
230 Krueger flap actuator
231 Wing root Krueger flap, extended

6 Windscreen panels
7 Windscreen wipers
8 Instrument panel shroud
9 Control column
10 Rudder pedals
11 Cockpit floor level
12 ILS aerial
13 Pitot heads
14 Access ladder to lower deck
15 Captain's seat
16 Centre control pedestal
17 Direct vision opening side window panel
18 First officer's seat
19 Overhead systems switch panel
20 Maintenance side panel
21 Observer's seat
22 Folding fourth seat
23 Cockpit bulkhead
24 Air conditioning ducting
25 Crew wardrobe/locker
26 Nose undercarriage wheel bay
27 Hydraulic retraction jack
28 Taxying lamp
29 Twin nosewheels, forward retracting

55 Door mounted escape chute
56 Main cabin entry door
57 Overhead stowage bins
58 Central galley unit
59 Starboard General Electric CF6-80 engine nacelle
60 Pratt & Whitney JT9D-7R4H1 or PW4156 alternative engine installation
61 Common nacelle pylon beam
62 Pylon attachment links
63 Pylon tail fairing
64 Starboard wing engine pylon
65 Tourist class passenger cabin seating, 241 seats (267 seats total in mixed class layout)
66 Air system distribution ducting
67 Conditioned air delivery ducting
68 LD3 baggage container; 12 in forward hold
69 Water tank
70 Slat drive shaft motor and gearbox
71 Wing spar centre-section carry through

88 Slat screw jacks
89 Outer wing panel integral fuel tank
90 Fuel vent tank
91 Starboard navigation light (green)
92 Wing tip fairing
93 Starboard winglet
94 Tail navigation and strobe lights (white)
95 Static dischargers
96 Fixed portion of trailing edge
97 One-piece single slotted Fowler-type flap, down position
98 Flap guide rails
99 Fuel jettison pipe
100 Outboard roll-control spoilers/lift dumpers (two)
101 Inboard airbrakes/lift dumpers (three)
102 Spoiler/airbrake hydraulic jacks
103 Flap screw jacks
104 Flap drive shaft
105 Starboard all-speed aileron
106 Aileron triplex hydraulic actuators

119 Starboard Type 1 emergency exit door
120 Upper fuselage frame and stringer construction
121 Rear underfloor freight hold door
122 Freight/cargo compartment dividing bulkhead
123 Cabin wall insulating blankets
124 Cargo hold door
125 Cabin floor panelling
126 Seat mounting rails
127 Rear cabin air recirculation fan
128 ADF aerials
129 Fuselage skin panelling
130 Ceiling trim/lighting panels
131 Central overhead stowage bins
132 Rear galley
133 Fin root fairing
134 Fir spar attachment joints
135 Three-spar fin torsion box construction
136 Starboard trimming tailplane
137 Tailplane trim fuel tank, additional capacity 1,342 Imp Gal (6,100l)
138 Starboard elevator

154 Leading-edge nose ribs
155 Port tailplane integral fuel tank
156 Tailplane pivot fixing
157 Moving tailplane sealing plate
158 Tailplane centre-section carry-through
159 Tailplane trim screw jack
160 Fin support structure
161 Rear pressure bulkhead
162 Rear toilet compartments (four)
163 Cabin attendant's folding seat
164 Rear entry door
165 Rear cabin seven-abreast passenger seating
166 Cabin side-wall frames
167 Underfloor bulk cargo hold, volume 610cu ft (17.3m^3)
168 Cabin window panels
169 LD3 baggage containers, 10 in rear hold
170 Port Type-1 emergency exit door
171 Lower fuselage skin panelling
172 Wing root trailing-edge fillet
173 Port inboard single-slotted flap
174 Wing root spoilers/lift dumpers
175 Flap guide rail

more fuel capacity and higher weights; the first flight of this variant was made on 26 December 1974. A higher-weight option, with structural strengthening, is the A300B4-200, which could also have more fuel in the rear cargo hold. A two-man forward-facing cockpit distinguishes the A300B4-200FF, first flown on 6 October 1981. A convertible freighter version is designated A300C4, based on the B4 with a forward side-loading door and reinforced floor; the first example flew in mid-1979. The A300-600 was launched in 1980 as an advanced version of the B4, with a number of significant improvements including a rear fuselage of A310 profile, allowing two more seat rows in the cabin; use of composites and

simplified systems for reduced structure weight; and advanced engines as quoted above, or the 56,00lb st (25,402kgp) PW4156, 58,000lb st (26,309kgp) PW4158 or 53,000lb st (24,041kgp) RB.211-524D4A. The first A300-600 flew on 8 July 1983 with JT9D-7R4H1 engines, and an A300-600 with CF6-80C2 engines flew on 20 March 1985. The A300-600R introduced in 1986 has small wingtip fences, a trimming fuel tank in the tailplane and other new internal features.

SERVICE USE

French and West German certification of the A300B2 was obtained on 15 March 1974, and service use

began on 30 May 1974 with Air France. The first A300B2K was delivered to South African Airways on 23 November 1976. The A300B4 was certificated in France and West Germany on 26 March 1975, gained US approval 30 June 1976, and entered service with Germanair on 1 June 1975. The A300B4-200FF was certificated on 8 January 1982 and entered service with Garuda. The convertible A300C4 entered service with Hapag-Lloyd at the end of 1979. The first A300-600 was delivered to Saudi Arabian Airlines on 26 March 1984, and the first improved A300-600 to Thai Airways International in October 1985. At the beginning of 1987, sales of the A300 series totalled 282 to 36 customers.

SPECIFICATION
(A310-300)

Power Plant: Two Pratt & Whitney JT9D-7R4E1 turbofans each rated at 50,000lb st (22,680kgp) for take-off. Fuel capacity, 13,476 Imp gal (61,260l), plus optional 1,540 Imp gal (7,000l) in tanks in cargo hold.

Performance: Max operating speed, 360kts (667km/h) IAS or Mach = 0.84; max cruising speed, 484kts (897km/h) at 35,000ft (10,670m); long-range cruise, 463kts (858km/h) at 37,000ft (11,280m); take-off field length (FAR), 7,575ft (2,310m); landing field length (FAR), 5,000ft (1,525m); range with max payload, 3,750 naut mls (6,950km); range with max fuel and 52,825lb (23,960kg) payload, 5,240 naut mls (9,715km).

Weights: Operating weight empty, 169,842lb (77,040kg); max fuel weight, standard, 97,524lb (44,236kg) or optional, 109,023lb (49,452kg); max payload, 75,400lb (34,200kg); max take-off weight, basic, 330,690lb (150,000kg) or optional, 337,305lb (153,000kg); max landing weight (for both take-off weights as quoted) 271,170lb (123,000kg); max zero-fuel weight (for both take-off weights as listed), 249,120lb (113,000kg).

Dimensions: Span, 144ft 0in (43.90m); overall length, 153ft 1in (46.66m); overall height, 51ft 10in (15.81m); sweepback, 28 deg at quarter chord; wing area, 2,357sq ft (219.0m²).

Accommodation: Cabin length, 109ft 0¾in (33.24m), max width, 17ft 4in (5.28m), max height, 7ft 7¾in (2.33m). Typical accommodation for 218 passengers comprising 18 six-abreast at 38in (96.5cm) pitch and 200 eight-abreast at 34in (86cm) pitch; typical one-class accommodation for 236, and maximum one-class accommodation for 280 nine-abreast at 30in (76cm) pitch. Total underfloor baggage/cargo volume, 3,602cu ft (102m³). Flight crew of two, plus two observer seats on flight deck.

Shortly after the A300 had been launched, Airbus Industrie began to investigate a number of possible future derivatives of the basic aircraft. These acquired designations from A300B5 onwards, and by 1974 interest was centred upon the B9, a fuselage-stretched variant; the B10, a fuselage-shortened version; and the B11, with an enlarged wing and four engines. Of this trio, the B9 and B11 became the subject of further evolution under the TA9 and TA11 designations (now the A330 and A340), while the B10 was launched as the A310. Interest in a short/medium-range, medium-capacity transport crystalized in the mid-1970s as several European airlines indicated a need for such an aircraft for service from 1983 onwards. To achieve this timescale, Airbus made a marketing launch decision in July 1978, at which time 'pre-contracts' were obtained from Swissair, Lufthansa and Air France. The A310, as the A300B10 now became known, was not finally defined until the end of 1978, when the fuselage length was set at 13 frames less than the basic A300, but with some reprofiling of the rear fuselage to allow seating to extend farther aft. The wing was to remain structurally similar to that of the A300, but aerodynamically was completely new, taking advantage of extensive development work by British Aerospace at Hatfield. With government approval, British Aerospace (which had meanwhile absorbed the original Hawker Siddeley share in the

A300) became a full partner in Airbus Industrie on 1 January 1979, with a 20 per cent share, and this is reflected in the work-sharing on the A310, with participation by Aérospatiale, MBB, CASA and Fokker on a basis similar to that for the A300. The first A310 flew at Toulouse on 3 April and the second on 13 May 1983, both powered by JT9D-7R4 engines; the third aircraft, flown on 5 August 1982, had CF6-80A3 engines.

VARIANTS

Short- and medium-range versions of the A310 were at first designated A310-100 and A310-200, at maximum take-off weights of 266,755lb (121,000kg) and 291,010lb (132,000kg) respectively. The former version was dropped, however, and the A310-200 was developed to have optional higher weights of 305,560lb (138,600kg) and 313,055lb (142,000kg), with a fuel capacity of 12,077 Imp gal (54,900l) in all versions. To extend the range of the basic aircraft, the A310-300 was developed with a tailplane trim tank to increase fuel capacity, and optional underfloor tanks. The A310-300 is available at two weights as listed above, and has small wing tip fences, which also were retrospectively adopted for the A310-200. The first A310-300, with JT9D-7R4E engines, flew on 8 July 1985 and the second, with CF6-80C2 engines, on 6 September 1985. Engine options for the A310-200 include the JT9D-7R4D1 at 48,000lb st (21,773kgp), the JT9D-7R4E1 as detailed above, the CF6-80C2-A2 or -80A3 at 50,000lb st (22,680kgp) and the PW4150 at the same rating. Any of the 50,000lb st engines can be used in the A310-300. Convertible and all-freight variants are available as the A310C and A310F respectively.

SERVICE USE

The A310-200 was certificated in France and West Germany on 11 March 1983, in the UK in January 1984 and in the USA early in 1985. First deliveries to Swissair and Lufthansa were made on 29 March 1983, and the first revenue services were flown on 12 and 21 April 1983. The A310-300 with JT9D engines gained French and West German certification on 5 December 1985, and service use by Swissair began later that month. Sales of all versions of the A310 totalled 129 by January 1987, to 24 customers.

Airbus Industrie A 310 Cutaway Drawing Key

1. Radome
2. Weather radar scanner
3. Radar scanner mounting
4. VOR localiser aerial
5. Front pressure bulkhead
6. Windscreen panels
7. Windscreen wipers
8. Instrument panel shroud
9. Control column
10. Rudder pedals
11. Cockpit floor level
12. ILS aerial
13. Pitot tubes
14. Access ladder to lower deck
15. Captain's seat
16. Centre control pedestal
17. Opening side window panels
18. First officer's seat
19. Overhead systems control panel
20. Maintenance side panel
21. Observer's seat
22. Folding fourth seat
23. Cockpit bulkhead
24. Air conditioning ducting
25. Crew wardrobe/locker
26. Nose undercarriage wheel bay
27. Hydraulic retraction jack
28. Taxying lamp
29. Steering jacks
30. Nosewheel doors
31. Forward toilet
32. Wash hand basin
33. Galley
34. Starboard entry/service door
35. Door mounted escape chute
36. Cabin attendant's folding seat
37. Hand baggage locker/wardrobe
38. Port main entry door
39. Door latch
40. Door surround structure
41. Radio and electronics racks
42. Runway turn-off lights
43. Fuselage frame and stringer construction
44. Floor beam construction
45. Forward freight hold
46. Freight hold door
47. Cabin wall trim panels
48. VHF communications aerial
49. Overhead stowage bins
50. Curtained cabin divider
51. First-class passenger compartment, 18 seats
52. Air system ducting
53. Cabin window panels
54. Overhead baggage lockers
55. Galley unit
56. Air system circulation fan
57. Tourist-class seating, 193 seats
58. Air conditioning supply ducting
59. Water tank
60. LD3 baggage container (eight in forward hold)
61. Slat drive shaft gearbox
62. Wing span centre section carry-through
63. Ventral air conditioning packs (two)

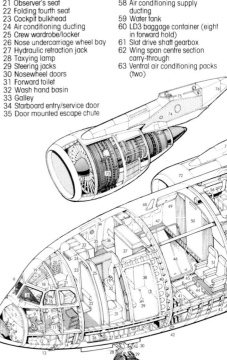

Left: The economy-class cabin of the A310 provides eight-abreast seating for 200 passengers. Twin aisles facilitate food service.

Below: Air India is among the early operators of the A310-300, with six in service.

64 Port overwing emergency exit door
65 Wing centre-box fuel tank, capacity 4,234 Imp gal (19,250l)
66 Centre section floor beams
67 Wing spar attachment main frame
68 Fuselage centre section construction
69 Starboard overwing emergency exit door
70 Starboard wing inboard fuel tank, capacity 3,066 Imp gal (13,937l)
71 Nacell pylon
72 Starboard Pratt & Whitney JT9D engine nacelle
73 Alternative General Electric CF6-80A1 turbofan engine
74 Common nacelle pylon beam
75 Pylon attachment points
76 Pylon tail fairing
77 Pressure refuelling connections
78 Slat screw jacks
79 Screw jack drive shaft
80 Leading edge slat segments
81 Fuel tank divider rib
82 Fuel pumps
83 Outboard fuel tank, capacity 866 Imp gal (3,938l)
84 Fuel system piping
85 Vent surge tank
86 Starboard navigation light
87 Wing tip fairing
88 Tail navigation and strobe lights
89 Static discharge wicks
90 Fixed portion of trailing edge
91 Outboard spoilers
92 Spoiler hydraulic jacks
93 Flap screw jacks
94 Flap carriage mechanism
95 Outboard single-slotted Fowler-type flap
96 Fuel jettison pipe
97 Centre spoilers/airbrakes
98 Flap drive shaft
99 Ailerion triplex hydraulic jacks
100 Starboard all-speed aileron
101 Inboard spoilers/lift dumpers
102 Inboard double slotted flap
103 Wing rear spar/fuselage main frame
104 Centre cabin air circulation fan
105 Pressure floor above wheel bay
106 Starboard main undercarriage, retracted position
107 Undercarriage door jack
108 Equipment by walkway
109 Undercarriage bay pressure bulkhead
110 Flap drive motor
111 Eight-abreast tourist class seating
112 Fuselage frame and stringer construction
113 Rear freight hold door
114 LD3 baggage container (six in rear hold)
115 Freight hold bulkhead
116 Cabin floor panels
117 Seat attachment rails
118 Rear cabin air circulation fan
119 ADF aerials
120 Fuselage skin plating
121 Central overhead stowage bins
122 Ceiling lighting panels
123 Starboard rear entry door
124 Galley units
125 Fin root fairing
126 Fin attachment bolted joints
127 Fin spars
128 Starboard tailplane
129 Starboard elevator
130 Tailfin construction
131 Glass-fibre reinforced leading edge
132 Fin tip fairing
133 Static discharge wicks
134 Carbon fibre rudder skin panels
135 Honeycomb rudder construction
136 Rudder triplex hydraulic jacks
137 APU equipment bay
138 Garrett GTCP 331-250 auxiliary power unit
139 Tailcone fairing
140 APU exhaust duct
141 Port elevator construction
142 Elevator triplex hydraulic jacks
143 Static discharge wicks
144 Port tailplane construction
145 Leading edge nose ribs
146 Tailplane pivot fixing
147 Moving tailplane sealing plate
148 Tailplane centre section
149 Tailplane trim screw jack
150 Fin support structure
151 Rear pressure bulkhead
152 Rear toilet compartment
153 Cabin attendant's folding seat
154 Rear entry door
155 Cabin window panel
156 Seven-abreast rear cabin seating
157 Cabin side wall frames
158 Freight hold skin panelling
159 Wing trailing edge fillet
160 Wing trailing edge fillet
161 Port inboard double slotted flap
162 Spoiler/lift dumpers
163 Undercarriage side struts
164 Main undercarriage pivot fixing
165 Inboard flap track mechanism
166 Aileron triplex hydraulic jacks
167 Port all-speed aileron construction
168 Port spoiler/airbrakes
169 Flap down position
170 Flap guide rails
171 Fuel jettison pipe
172 Flap track fairings
173 Fixed portion of trailing edge
174 Static discharges
175 Tail navigation and strobe lights
176 Wing tip fairing
177 Port navigation lights
178 Wing rear spar
179 Front spar
180 Port leading edge slats
181 Slat screw jacks
182 Slat guide rails
183 Leading edge de-icing air piping
184 Telescopic de-icing air duct
185 Wing skin joint strap
186 Wing stringer construction
187 Port wing integral fuel tank bays
188 Wing rib construction
189 Main undercarriage leg strut
190 Hydraulic retraction jack
191 Port main undercarriage four-wheel bogie
192 Nacelle pylon attachment joint
193 Engine mounting pylon
194 Hot stream exhaust nozzle
195 Fan air exhaust duct
196 Reverser cascade, closed
197 Bleed air ducting
198 Pratt & Whitney JT9D-7R4D turbofan engine
199 Engine fan blades
200 Intake ducting
201 Detachable engine cowlings
202 Bleed air system pre-cooler
203 Inboard leading edge slat
204 Bleed air delivery ducting
205 Inner wing integral fuel tank
206 Leading edge wing root fairing
207 Wing root Krueger flap

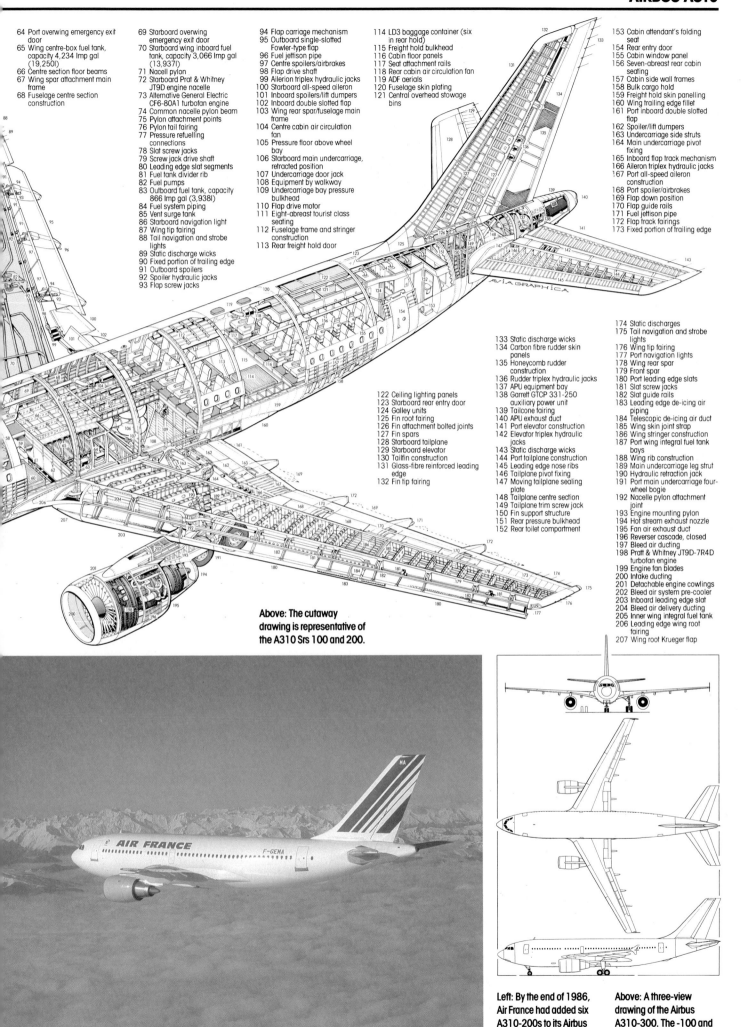

Above: The cutaway drawing is representative of the A310 Srs 100 and 200.

Left: By the end of 1986, Air France had added six A310-200s to its Airbus fleet.

Above: A three-view drawing of the Airbus A310-300. The -100 and -200 are similar.

AIRBUS A320 INTERNATIONAL

The 'decision in principle' to launch a short/medium-range jetliner in the 150-seat category was taken by Airbus Industrie in June 1981, and followed some 10 years of design activity in which all major European aircraft manufacturers had been either directly or indirectly involved, individually or in various collaborative groupings. Most directly a forerunner of the aircraft that became the A320 was the Aérospatiale AS-200 – actually a family of project designs that the French company studied in the mid-1970s. In 1977 Aérospatiale joined with British Aeros-pace, MBB and VFW-Fokker in the Joint European Transport (JET) study group, the objective of which was to provide a short/medium-range transport with 'a new order of quietness, fuel efficiency and operating economy'. The JET work was brought under Airbus Industrie direction when British Aerospace formally became an Airbus partner on 1 January 1979, and the studies continued under the SA (single-aisle) designation. The resulting SA-1, SA-2 and SA-3 had different fuselage lengths. The designation A320 was adopted early in 1981 as refinement of the design continued, while the optimum size remained under study. The aircraft was widely described as a '150-seater', this being the typical mixed-class capacity that was thought likely to be required by the airlines in the last decade of the present century. At the time of the marketing launch, however, there was still some interest in a

SPECIFICATION

Power Plant: Two CFM International CFM56-5 or International Aero Engines V2500 turbofans, each rated at 23,500-25,000lb st (10,660-11,340kgp) for take-off. Fuel capacity (A320-100), 3,380 Imp gal (15,365l) or (A320-200), 5,150 Imp gal (23,410l) with centre section tanks.
Performance: (A320-100) Max operating speed, 350kts (649km/h) IAS or Mach = 0.82; max cruising speed, 487kts (903km/h) at 28,000ft (8,535m); long-range cruising speed, 454kts (842km/h) at 37,000ft (11,280m); take-off field length (FAR), 5,630ft (1,715m); landing field length (FAR), 4,750ft (1,450m); range with max payload, 1,860 naut mls (3,450km); range with max fuel and 34,380lb (15,550kg) payload, 2,640 naut mls (4,895km).
Weights: (A320-100) Operating weight empty, 84,171lb (38,180kg); max fuel weight, 27,200lb (12,338kg); max payload, 41,535lb (18,840kg); max take-off weight, 145,503lb (66,000kg); max landing weight, 134,480lb (61,000kg); max zero-fuel weight, 125,662lb (57,000kg).
Weights: (A320-200) Operating weight empty, 85,604lb (38,830kg); max fuel weight, 41,460lb (18,806kg); max payload, 40,125lb (18,200kg); max take-off weight, 158,730lb (72,000kg); max landing weight, 138,890lb (63,000kg); max zero-fuel weight, 130,072lb (59,000kg).
Dimensions: Span, 111ft 3in (33.91m); overall length, 123ft 3in (37.58m); overall height, 38ft 7in (11.76m); sweepback, 24.96 deg at quarter chord; wing area, 1,317.5sq ft (122.40m²).
Accommodation: Cabin length, 90ft 3in (27.51m), max width, 12ft 1½in (3.696m), max height, 7ft 4in (2.22m). Typical mixed-class accommodation for 150, comprising 12 four-abreast at 36in (91.5cm) pitch and 138 six-abreast at 32in (81cm) pitch; max one-class accommodation, 179 six-abreast at 30in (76cm) pitch.

somewhat larger capacity, so A320-100 and A320-200 projects were on offer with one-class accommodation at 32in (81cm) pitch, 154- and 172-seat capacities being provided by different fuselage lengths. Air France was the first to announce an intention to purchase the A320, in both these versions, but before Airbus was able to announce a full launch, with the necessary financial backing, in March 1984, the decision had been made to concentrate on a single body size to accommodate 162 passengers, but still at two different weights, with different fuel capacities, to which the -100 and -200 designations now referred. The A320 is a wholly new design, the structure of which is based on well-proven principles used in the A300 and A310. Much use is made of the latest materials (including composites) and of advanced technology features in systems and equipment, with a quadruplex fly-by-wire control system, sidestick controllers for the two pilots, computerized control functions, an electronic flight instrument system (EFIS) and electronic centralized aircraft monitor. Development and construction of the A320 are shared between the Airbus Industrie partners in the same way as those of the A300 and A310, with British Aerospace (24 per cent of the work share) responsible for the wing, Aérospatiale (34 per cent) for the forward fuselage and nose, Deutsche Airbus (35 per cent) for the centre and rear fuselage, CASA (5 per cent) for rear fuselage panels and tailplane, and Belairbus (2 per cent) for the wing leading edge.

VARIANTS

The first two announced variants of the A320, as noted above, are the A320-100 and A320-200, which have the same overall dimensions but different fuel capacities and operating weights. The initial choice of engines is between the CFM56-5 produced by the General Electric/SNECMA partnership under the CFM International marketing organization, and the V2500 produced by the International Aero Engines consortium.

SERVICE USE

First flight of the company-owned A320 prototype, with CFM56-5 engines, was made on 22 February 1987. Certification and flight testing, using four aircraft, all with CFM56 engines initially but one to be retrofitted with V2500s at a later date, are designed to allow entry into service by March 1988, with Air France the

Above: This mock-up of the cockpit of the Airbus A320 shows its many advanced features, including the six identical electronic displays – two for each pilot giving primary flight and navigation information, and two (vertically) between the pilots to provide engine instrumentation details and aircraft monitoring data.

Right: An early cutaway drawing of the A320-200, showing the two engine options.

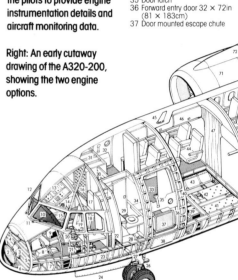

first operator followed by BCal and Air Inter. The first firm orders for the A320 were placed by Air France, Air Inter, BCal, Inex Adria, Cyprus Airways, Pan American, Lufthansa, Ansett, TAA (now known as Australian Airlines) Alia, All Nippon Airways and Northwest Airlines, as well as the US leasing company GATX. Total orders by the end of 1986 amounted to 256 from 15 customers, with 141 more on option.

Below: An impression of the A320 in Air France livery, as it will enter service in 1988. Twenty-five have been ordered by the French airline.

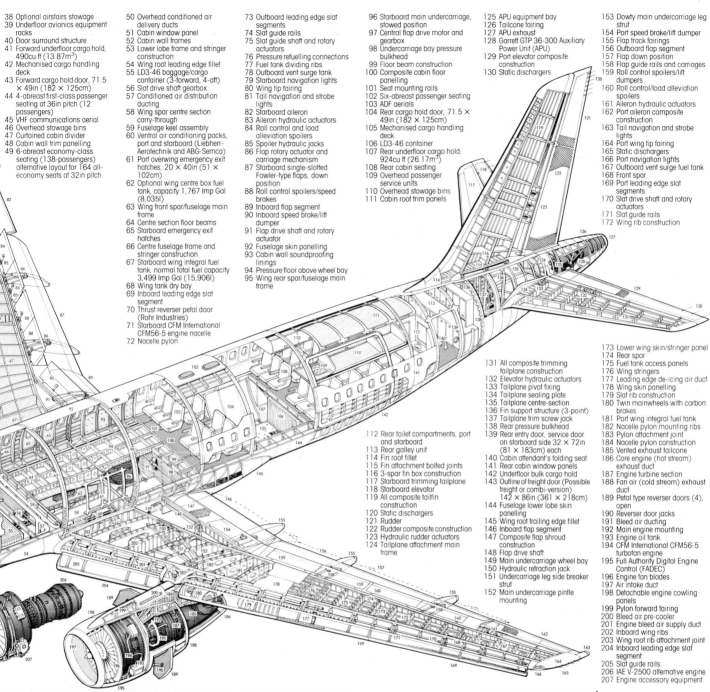

38 Optional airstairs stowage
39 Underfloor avionics equipment racks
40 Door surround structure
41 Forward underfloor cargo hold, 490cu ft (13.87m³)
42 Mechanised cargo handling deck
43 Forward cargo hold door, 71.5 × 49in (182 × 125cm)
44 4-abreast first-class passenger seating at 36in pitch (12 passengers)
45 VHF communications aerial
46 Overhead stowage bins
47 Curtained cabin divider
48 Cabin wall trim panelling
49 6-abreast economy-class seating (138-passengers) alternative layout for 164 all-economy seats at 32in pitch

50 Overhead conditioned air delivery ducts
51 Cabin window panel
52 Cabin wall frames
53 Lower lobe frame and stringer construction
54 Wing root leading edge fillet
55 LD3-46 baggage/cargo container (3-forward, 4-aft)
56 Slat drive shaft gearbox
57 Conditioned air distribution ducting
58 Wing spar centre section carry-through
59 Fuselage keel assembly
60 Ventral air conditioning packs, port and starboard (Liebherr-Aerotechnik and ABG-Semca)
61 Port overwing emergency exit hatches, 20 × 40in (51 × 102cm)
62 Optional wing centre box fuel tank, capacity 1,767 Imp Gal (8,035l)
63 Wing front spar/fuselage main frame
64 Centre section floor beams
65 Starboard emergency exit hatches
66 Centre fuselage frame and stringer construction
67 Starboard wing integral fuel tank, normal total fuel capacity 3,499 Imp Gal (15,906l)
68 Wing tank dry bay
69 Inboard leading edge slat segment
70 Thrust reverser petal door (Rohr Industries)
71 Starboard CFM International CFM56-5 engine nacelle
72 Nacelle pylon

73 Outboard leading edge slat segments
74 Slat guide rails
75 Slat guide shaft and rotary actuators
76 Pressure refuelling connections
77 Fuel tank dividing ribs
78 Outboard vent surge tank
79 Starboard navigation lights
80 Wing tip fairing
81 Tail navigation and strobe lights
82 Starboard aileron
83 Aileron hydraulic actuators
84 Roll control and load alleviation spoilers
85 Spoiler hydraulic jacks
86 Flap rotary actuator and carriage mechanism
87 Starboard single-slotted Fowler-type flaps, down position
88 Roll control spoilers/speed brakes
89 Inboard flap segment
90 Inboard speed brake/lift dumper
91 Flap drive shaft and rotary actuator
92 Fuselage skin panelling
93 Cabin wall soundproofing linings
94 Pressure floor above wheel bay
95 Wing rear spar/fuselage main frame

96 Starboard main undercarriage, stowed position
97 Central flap drive motor and gearbox
98 Undercarriage bay pressure bulkhead
99 Floor beam construction
100 Composite cabin floor panelling
101 Seat mounting rails
102 Six-abreast passenger seating
103 ADF aerials
104 Rear cargo hold door, 71.5 × 49in (182 × 125cm)
105 Mechanised cargo handling deck
106 LD3-46 container
107 Rear underfloor cargo hold, 924cu ft (26.17m³)
108 Rear cabin seating
109 Overhead passenger service units
110 Overhead stowage bins
111 Cabin roof trim panels

112 Rear toilet compartments, port and starboard
113 Rear galley unit
114 Fin root fillet
115 Fin attachment bolted joints
116 3-spar fin box construction
117 Starboard trimming tailplane
118 Starboard elevator
119 All composite tailfin construction
120 Static dischargers
121 Rudder
122 Rudder composite construction
123 Hydraulic rudder actuators
124 Tailplane attachment main frame

125 APU equipment bay
126 Tailcone fairing
127 APU exhaust
128 Garrett GTP 36-300 Auxiliary Power Unit (APU)
129 Port elevator composite construction
130 Static dischargers

131 All composite trimming tailplane construction
132 Elevator hydraulic actuators
133 Tailplane pivot fixing
134 Tailplane sealing plate
135 Tailplane centre-section
136 Fin support structure (3-point)
137 Tailplane trim screw jack
138 Rear pressure bulkhead
139 Rear entry door, service door on starboard side 32 × 72in (81 × 183cm) each
140 Cabin attendant's folding seat
141 Rear cabin window panels
142 Underfloor bulk cargo hold
143 Outline of freight door (Possible freight or combi-version) 142 × 86in (361 × 218cm)
144 Fuselage lower lobe skin panelling
145 Wing root trailing edge fillet
146 Inboard flap segment
147 Composite flap shroud construction
148 Flap drive shaft
149 Main undercarriage wheel bay
150 Hydraulic retraction jack
151 Undercarriage leg side breaker strut
152 Main undercarriage pintle mounting

153 Dowty main undercarriage leg strut
154 Port speed brake/lift dumper
155 Flap track fairings
156 Outboard flap segment
157 Flap down position
158 Flap guide rails and carriages
159 Roll control spoilers/lift dumpers
160 Roll control/load alleviation spoilers
161 Aileron hydraulic actuators
162 Port aileron composite construction
163 Tail navigation and strobe lights
164 Port wing tip fairing
165 Static dischargers
166 Port navigation lights
167 Outboard vent surge fuel tank
168 Front spar
169 Port leading edge slat segments
170 Slat drive shaft and rotary actuators
171 Slat guide rails
172 Wing rib construction

173 Lower wing skin/stringer panel
174 Rear spar
175 Fuel tank access panels
176 Wing stringers
177 Leading edge de-icing air duct
178 Wing skin panelling
179 Slat rib construction
180 Twin mainwheels with carbon brakes
181 Port wing integral fuel tank
182 Nacelle pylon mounting ribs
183 Pylon attachment joint
184 Nacelle pylon construction
185 Vented exhaust tailcone
186 Core engine (hot stream) exhaust duct
187 Engine turbine section
188 Fan air (cold stream) exhaust duct
189 Petal type reverser doors (4), open
190 Reverser door jacks
191 Bleed air ducting
192 Main engine mounting
193 Engine oil tank
194 CFM International CFM56-5 turbofan engine
195 Full Authority Digital Engine Control (FADEC)
196 Engine fan blades
197 Air intake duct
198 Detachable engine cowling panels
199 Pylon forward fairing
200 Bleed air pre-cooler
201 Engine bleed air supply duct
202 Inboard wing ribs
203 Wing root rib attachment joint
204 Inboard leading edge slat segment
205 Slat guide rails
206 IAE V-2500 alternative engine
207 Engine accessory equipment

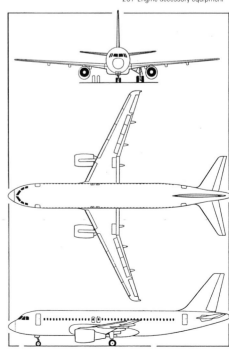

Left: When it began its flight test programme in February 1987, the first A320 was finished in Airbus style as depicted here. Certification was expected to take approximately one year, using four aircraft, all fitted with the General Electric/SNECMA CFM56 engine in the first instance.

Right: The three-view drawing depicts the A320 in its initial production form, with the CFM56 engines. Both the -100 and -200 are externally similar, differing only in fuel capacities and operating weights. The IAE V2500 engine installation will differ slightly from that shown here.

AIRTECH (CASA-NURTANIO) CN-235 SPAIN/INDONESIA

Left: Designed with the needs of commuter airlines in mind, the Airtech CN-235 provides straight-through four-abreast seating for 40 passengers at 32in (81cm) pitch. By having the wing centre-section located wholly above the fuselage, the cabin does not suffer the common inconvenience, in high-wing aircraft, of main spars interrupting the ceiling line where they pass through the fuselage.

Airtech CN-235 Cutaway Drawing Key

1 Radome
2 Weather radar scanner
3 ILS glideslope aerial
4 Front pressure bulkhead
5 Pitot tube, port and starboard
6 Radar transmitter and receiver
7 Rudder pedals
8 Nosewheel bay
9 Taxying lamps (2)
10 Nosewheel doors
11 Forward-retracting single nosewheel
12 Underfloor control linkages
13 Cockpit floor level
14 Control column
15 Instrument panel
16 CRT cockpit displays
17 Instrument panel shroud
18 Windscreen wipers
19 Windscreen panels
20 Stand-by compass
21 Overhead systems switch panels
22 Co-pilot's seat
23 Cockpit roof frames
24 Direct vision opening side window
25 Nosewheel steering control
26 Document stowage case
27 Pilot's seat
28 Cockpit bulkhead
29 Control cable duct
30 Radio and electronics equipment racks
31 Crew oxygen bottle
32 Galley unit
33 Toilet compartment
34 VHF aerial
35 Starboard side forward entry door and airstairs
36 Control cable runs
37 Cabin attendant's folding seat
38 Front passenger-seat row
39 Passenger cabin floor panelling
40 Emergency exit hatch
41 Seat mounting rails
42 Cabin window panels
43 Four-abreast passenger seating (39-seat layout)
44 Cabin wall trim panels
45 ATC aerial

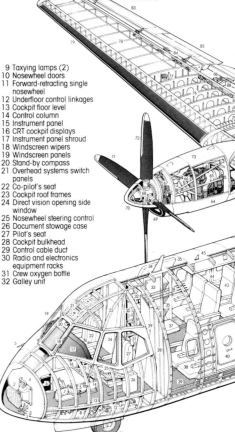

etails of the CN-235 were made public in June 1981, when Construcciones Aeronauticas SA (CASA) in Spain and P T Nurtanio in Indonesia announced their intention to develop and produce the aircraft on an equally-shared basis for both commercial and military applications. Subsequently, a company known as Aircraft Technology Industries (Airtech) was set up in Madrid to handle the programme. With accommodation for up to 44 passengers or 48 troops, the CN-235 entered what appeared to be an overcrowded marketplace for aircraft of approximately the same capacity, but it differed noticeably from its several competitors in being designed as much for military use as commercial application, as indicated in particular by the provision of a large rear ventral loading and supply-dropping ramp/door, and the retractable tandem-wheel main landing gear units suitable for rough-field operations. The size of the cabin in the circular cross-section fuselage was such as to offer a high degree of comfort in commuter airline layouts; at the same time, the military aspects of the design made the aircraft potentially useful also for mixed-traffic and quick-change operations or as a pure commercial freighter able to carry, for example, 18 passengers and two LD3 containers, or four standard LD3s or five LD2s. As indicated by the payload/range figures quoted above, the CN-235 has been designed primarily for very short ranges, with provision to operate a number of short sectors without refuelling: four stages of 100 naut mls (185 km) each can be flown, with standard airline reserves, on a full fuel load. The agreement between CASA and Nurtanio provided for each company to be responsible for 50 per cent of the development and production of the CN-235, without duplication of manufacturing effort but with final assembly lines at the CASA works in Madrid and those of IPTN (previously Nurtanio) at the Husein Sastranegara Air Force Base at Bandung in Indonesia. So far as manufacture is concerned, CASA is responsible for the forward and centre portions of the fuselage, the wing centre section and inboard flaps. IPTN produces the rear fuselage section, outer wings complete with flaps and ailerons, and the entire tail unit. Both companies make extensive use of numerical control machines in manufacturing components and subassemblies. Preliminary design activities concerned with the CN-235 began in January 1980, with manufacture of two prototypes commencing in May 1981 and final assembly starting in 1983. Simultaneously, the two prototypes were rolled out on 10 September 1983, one in Madrid and the other at Bandung. First to fly was the CASA-assembled aircraft (ECT-100) on 11 November 1983, the Indonesian PK-XNC following on 30 December of the same year. Early flight testing revealed a number of problems, particularly in respect of drag, which was higher than predicted, and test hours built up only slowly during 1984 and 1985 to reach a combined total of about 500 hours by the

end of the latter year. Modifications were made progressively to the CASA prototype in the course of this testing, and were later applied to PK-XNC to bring that aircraft up to the same standard. The first production example (ECT-135) flew in Spain on 19 August 1986.

VARIANTS

Civil and military variants are described in the foregoing paragraph, and have similar overall dimensions and weights. Provision was made at an early stage in the design of the CN-235 to allow the fuselage to be stretched, increasing accommodation to about 60 passengers, and such a version was being studied, primarily by IPTN, as the N-260.

SERVICE USE

The CN-235 is certificated to FAR Parts 25 and 36 and to the European JAR 25. FAA certification was granted on 3 December 1986. Early airline customers, whose orders were subject to confirmation after certification of the CN-235, included Spain's Aviaco, with an option on 16, and the Indonesian Merpati Nusantara Airlines, with an order for 15, plus options taken by Bouraq (10), Dirgantara (10), Deraya Air Taxi (5) and Mandala (5). Two have been ordered for airways calibration duties in Spain.

SPECIFICATION

Power Plant: Two General Electric CT7-7A turboprops each rated at 1,700shp (1,268kW) for take-off with Hamilton Standard 14-RF11 four-blade constant-speed, reversing and feathering propellers of 10ft 10in (3.3m) diameter. Fuel capacity, 1,159 Imp gal (5,268l) in integral main and auxiliary tanks in wing and wing centre section.

Performance: Max operating speed, 230kts (426km/h) IAS; max cruising speed, 244kts (452km/h) at 15,000ft (4,570m); initial rate of climb, 1,527ft/min (7.75m/sec); service ceiling, 26,000ft (7,925m); take-off distance to 50ft (15m), 2,165ft (660m); landing distance from 50ft (15m), 1,920ft (585m); range with max payload, 208 naut mls (386km); range with max fuel, 2,110 naut mls (3,912km).

Weights: Operating weight empty, 20,723lb (9,400kg); max fuel, 9,039lb (4,100kg); max passenger payload, 9,259lb (4,200kg); max cargo payload, 11,023lb (5,000kg); max take-off weight, 31,746lb (14,400kg); max landing weight, 31,305lb (14,200kg); max zero-fuel weight, 29,982lb (13,600kg).

Dimensions: Span, 84ft 8in (25.81m); overall length, 70ft 0¾in (21.35m); overall height, 26ft 10in (8.18m); sweepback, 3 deg 52 min at quarter chord; wing area, 645.8sq ft (60.0m²).

Accommodation: Cabin length, 31ft 8in (9.65m), max width, 8ft 10½in (2.70m), max height, 6ft 2¾in (1.90m). Typical layout provides 40 seats four-abreast with central aisle, at 32in (81cm) pitch; max seating, 44 at 30in (76cm) pitch. Baggage compartment volume, 247.2cu ft (7.0m³). Flight crew of two and one flight attendant.

Below: The three-view of the CN-235 shows the aircraft configuration as initially certificated, with small ventral fins and other changes from the prototype.

Above: The cutaway of the CN-235 gives an indication of the passenger seating in the civil version and shows provision for an optional baggage container on the ramp.

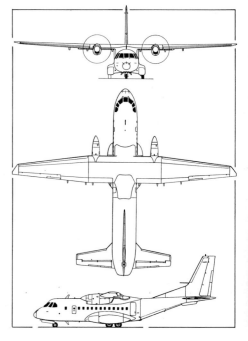

46 Overhead stowage bins
47 DME aerial
48 Fire extinguisher bottles
49 Fuselage frame-and-stringer construction
50 Floor beam construcion
51 Heat exchanger air intake
52 Overhead passenger service unit duct
53 Heat exchanger air exhaust
54 Wing spar attachment fuselage main frames
55 Spar attachment joints
56 Wing mounting drag strut
57 Centre wing panel rib construction
58 Engine bleed air ducting
59 Air conditioning plant, port and starboard
60 Composite wing root fairing construction
61 Starboard wing inboard fuel tank (227 Imp Gal/1,030l)
62 Leading edge engine control runs
63 Engine exhaust duct
64 Starboard engine nacelle
65 Intake particle separator air duct

66 General Electric CT-7-7 turboshaft engine
67 Propeller reduction gearbox
68 Propeller hub pitch change mechanism
69 Engine air intake
70 Propeller spinner
71 Hamilton Standard 14RF-3 four bladed variable-pitch reversible propeller
72 Leading edge de-icing boot (optional)
73 Engine cowling panels
74 Engine mounting wing ribs
75 Outer wing panel bolted joint
76 Starboard wing outboard fuel tank (334 Imp Gal/1,520l)
77 Fuel filler cap
78 Starboard outer wing panel
79 Leading edge de-icing boot (optional)
80 Wing tip fairing
81 Starboard navigation light
82 Static dischargers
83 Starboard aileron
84 Aileron hinge control mechanism
85 Aileron tab
86 Flap screw jacks
87 Screw jack drive shaft
88 Flap guide rails
89 Two-segment single-slotted flaps (down position)
90 Flap track fairings

91 Retractable ventral landing lamp
92 Inboard aileron cable pulleys
93 Central flap drive motor
94 Starboard side aft emergency exit hatch
95 Rear seat row
96 Cabin rear bulkhead
97 Trailing edge wing root fairing
98 Tailcone/baggage bay access doorway
99 Tail control cables
100 Rear fuselage skin panelling
101 HF aerial cable
102 Composite construction fin root fillet

103 Tailplane leading edge de-icing (optional)
104 Starboard tailplane
105 Starboard elevator
106 Tailfin construction
107 Fin leading edge de-icing (optional)

108 VOR aerial
109 Anti-collision light
110 Rudder horn balance
111 Static dischargers
112 Rudder
113 Servo tab
114 Rudder composite construction
115 Rudder trim tab
116 Rudder hinge control
117 Tailcone composite construction
118 Tail navigation light
119 Elevator trim tab
120 Servo tab
121 Elevator composite construction

122 Elevator horn balance
123 Tailplane construction
124 Elevator hinge control
125 Fin/tailplane attachment bulkheads
126 Tailplane leading edge root extension
127 Ventral strake, port and starboard
128 Rear pressure bulkhead
129 Cargo ramp door, open
130 Ramp door hydraulic jack
131 Tailcone frame construction
132 Baggage/cargo loading ramp (down position)
133 Ramp hydraulic jack
134 Optional baggage container
135 Wardrobe compartment
136 Rear passenger entry doorway
137 Cabin attendant's folding seat
138 Port single-slotted flap segments

139 Retractable ventral landing lamp
140 Flap shroud ribs
141 Flap composite construction
142 Aileron tab
143 Aileron composite construction
144 Static dischargers
145 Port navigation light
146 Glass-fibre wing tip fairing
147 Leading edge de-icing boot (optional)
148 Leading edge nose ribs
149 Outboard wing panel rib construction
150 Rear spar
151 Fuel filler cap
152 Port outboard integral fuel tank
153 Rear entry door/airstairs, open
154 Machined wing skin/stringer panels
155 Front spar
156 Port outer wing panel bolted joint
157 Engine exhaust nozzle fairing
158 Engine mounting struts
159 Nacelle mounting bulkhead
160 Oil cooler
161 Front bearer struts
162 Engine forward mounting ring frame
163 Port propeller spinner
164 Intake lip de-icing
165 Main undercarriage sponson fairing

166 Runway turn-off light
167 Electrical system equipment bay
168 Batteries
169 Undercarriage mounting frame
170 Main undercarriage pivot mounting
171 Hydraulic retraction jack
172 Main undercarriage leg struts
173 Leg strut interconnecting link
174 Shock absorber strut
175 Twin mainwheels
176 Hydraulic equipment bay
177 Position of pressure refuelling connection on starboard side

Above: First flown on 11 November 1986 the CASA-built prototype of the CN-235 at first had the large dorsal fin shown in this profile drawing, without ventral fins or tailplane leading-edge extensions. Named 'Infanta Elena', it has been flown in several colour schemes.

Left: CASA flew the first production CN-235 from the Spanish assembly line on 19 August 1986, in time for it to be shown at the Farnborough Air Show, where this photograph was taken. The Indonesian airline Merpati Nusantara took delivery of the first Indonesian CN-235 in December 1986.

ANTONOV AN-24 SOVIET UNION (CHINA)

The design bureau headed by the late Oleg K. Antonov began the development in 1958 of a twin-turboprop transport intended to replace the large numbers of piston-engined twins (such as the Lisunov Li-2 and the Ilyushin Il-12 and Il-14) used on internal routes in the Soviet Union. First flown in April 1960, the An-24 is a conventional high-wing monoplane, comparable in size and configuration to the Handley Page Herald and Fokker F27, both of which had been designed a few years earlier. As first projected, the An-24 was to have seated 32 to 40 passengers, but Aeroflot revised its requirements during prototype construction and the size of the cabin was enlarged to its final 44/52-passenger size. A second prototype and five pre-production airframes were built, two of the latter being for static and fatigue testing, and flight testing and certification were completed during 1963, by which time full production had been initiated. One of the first generation of turbine-engine transports for civil use developed in the Soviet Union, the An-24 joined the earlier An-12 and the Ilyushin Il-18 in an important modernization programme for Aeroflot, and also became one of the most widely exported of Soviet post-war transports.

VARIANTS

The standard 50-seat production version of the Antonov transport was designated An-24V (often appearing in cyrillic characters on the side of the aircraft as *AH-24B*) and was powered by 2,550shp (1,902kW) AI-24 engines. It was followed in production by the An-24V Seriiny II (Series 2) which had improved AI-24A engines (with water injection), increased chord on the wing centre section, and

larger flaps. For aircraft operating in 'hot and high' conditions, 2,820shp (2,103kW) AI-24T engines could be fitted. The designation An-24T referred to a specialized all-freight variant which incorporated a loading door in the rear of the cabin floor, hinged to open upwards into the rear fuselage. To allow both the An-24V and An-24T to carry bigger payloads out of 'difficult' airfields, an optional installation was an RU-19-300 auxiliary turbojet in the starboard engine nacelle in the An-24RV and An-24RT versions (*AH-24PB* and *AH-24PT* in cyrillic). Developed in 1971, the An-24P was a special firefighting version, with provision to drop firefighters and equipment by parachute. Primarily intended for military duties, the An-26 was based on the An-24RT and, first seen in public in 1969, incorporated a completely new rear fuselage with a 'beaver tail' and a unique rear door which could either hinge down conventionally as a loading ramp or slide forward under the fuselage to provide a clear exit for parachuting. A specialized version of the An-24 for aerial survey duties is designated An-30, and appeared in 1973. This differs from the An-24 primarily in having a raised cockpit and a more bulbous, largely transparent nose to give the navigator a wide field of view. In May 1977 details became known of another derivative of the basic aircraft, designated An-32 and in effect a 'hot and high' version of the An-26. With the same rear fuselage and loading ramp arrangement as the latter, and also intended primarily for military use as a personnel or supplies transport, the An-32 is powered by AI-20M engines of 4,195shp (3,128kW) or, for even better field performance, 5,180shp (3,862kW) AI-20DM turboprops. In China, a version of the An-24 was put into production at the State Aircraft Factory in Xian, and is known as the Y-7 or Yun-7. After nine pre-production examples had been built, the first full production Y-7 flew early in 1984, and production is continuing at a rate of six per year. The Y-7 has Shanghai-built Wojiang-5A-1 engines based on the AI-24A. In 1984, Hong Kong Aircraft Engineering Co. completed the first Y-7-100, featuring a modernized flight deck and cabin, winglets and other new features, to establish a new production standard for the Xian factory, which is also working on a more extensively modified Y-7-200.

SERVICE USE

The An-24 entered service with Aeroflot in September 1963 on the routes between Moscow, Voronezh and Saratov. It became widely used in the Soviet Union, and was also exported (for airline use) to some 14 other airlines, including most of those of the Soviet bloc nations. Production ended in the Soviet Union in 1978, with about 1,100 reported to have been built. CAAC in China was one of the airlines which acquired An-24s in the early 1970s, and in 1984 CAAC began to put into service the locally-built Y-7 versions.

Below: Polish Airlines LOT is among the several East European airlines that uses the An-24V. Sixteen were still in service with LOT in 1986.

SPECIFICATION
(Antonov An-24V)

Power Plant: Two Ivchenko AI-24A turboprops each rated at 2,550ehp (1,902kW) for take-off, plus (in An-24RV) one RU-19-300 auxiliary turbojet rated at 1,984lb st (900kgp) in starboard nacelle. Fuel capacity, 1,221 Imp gal (5,550l) in integral wing tanks.
Performance: Normal cruising speed, 243kts (450km/h) at 19,685ft (6,000m); long-range cruising speed, 243kts (450km/h) at 22,965ft (7,000m); initial rate of climb, 375ft/min (1.9m/sec); service ceiling, 27,560ft (8,400m); take-off field length 5,645ft (1,720m); landing distance from 50ft (15m), 5,215ft (1,590m); range with max payload, 296 naut mls (550km); range with max fuel, 1,293 naut mls (2,400km).
Weights: Empty weight, 29,321lb (13,300kg); max fuel weight, 9,821lb (4,455kg); max payload, 12,125lb (5,500kg); max take-off and landing weight, 46,296lb (21,000kg).
Dimensions: Span, 95ft 9½in (29.20m); overall length, 77ft 2½in (23.53m); overall height, 27ft 3½in (8.32m); sweepback, 6 deg 50 min on outer panels at quarter chord; wing area, 807.1sq ft (74.98m²).
Accommodation: Cabin length, 31ft 9½in (9.69m), max width, 9ft 1in (2.76m), max height, 6ft 3in (1.91m). Standard layout for 52 passengers in paired seats four-abreast with central aisle, at 28.3in (72cm) pitch. Alternative layouts for 44-46 passengers or mixed passenger/freight loads with 36 passengers and a 495cu ft (14m³) forward hold. Rear baggage hold (all versions) volume, 99cu ft (2.8m³), above floor; no underfloor stowage. Flight crew of two plus one cabin attendant.

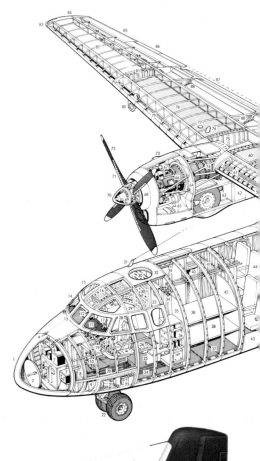

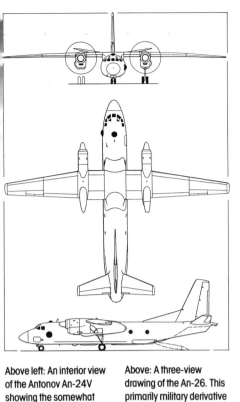

Antonov An-24V Series II Cutaway Drawing Key

1 Radome
2 Weather radar scanner
3 Scanner tracking mechanism
4 Radome hinges
5 ILS glideslope aerial
6 VOR localiser aerial
7 Radar transmitters and receivers
8 Forward pressure bulkhead
9 Nose undercarriage wheel bay
10 Rudder pedals
11 Instrument panel shroud
12 Radar display
13 Curved windscreen panels
14 Windscreen wipers
15 Cockpit eyebrow windows
16 Overhead systems switch panel
17 Co-pilot/Navigator/Radio Operator's seat
18 Instrument panel
19 Control column
20 Cockpit floor level
21 Nose undercarriage pivot fixing
22 Twin steerable nosewheels, forward retracting
23 Lower electrical equipment bay, port and starboard
24 Underfloor control runs
25 Space provision for Radio Operator
26 Side console panel

27 Pilot's seat
28 Opening (direct vision) side window panel
29 Space provision for Flight Engineer
30 Circuit breaker panels
31 Aerial lead-in
32 Cockpit roof escape hatch, interchangeable with jettisonable astrodome observation hatch
33 Cockpit doorway
34 Control linkage
35 Cockpit rear bulkhead
36 Radio and electronics equipment racks
37 Baggage compartment
38 Baggage loading shelving
39 Starboard side 'up-and-over' baggage door
40 Crew wardrobe
41 Curtained cabin doorway
42 Passenger cabin front bulkhead
43 Fuselage skin doubler in line with propellers
44 Four-abreast passenger seating, 50-seat all-tourist-class layout
45 Cabin window panels
46 Passenger cabin floor panelling
47 VHF aerial
48 Seat mounting rails
49 Emergency exit window hatch
50 Floor beam construction
51 Cabin wall trim panelling
52 Curtained window panels
53 Centre fuselage frame and stringer construction

54 D/F loop aerial
55 Air supply ducting
56 Wing root fillet
57 Leading-edge de-icing air duct
58 Cabin air supply duct
59 Fuel filler cap
60 Inboard bag-type fuel tanks
61 Leading-edge engine control runs
62 Starboard nacelle
63 Starboard main undercarriage, stowed position
64 Fireproof bulkhead
65 Air conditioning system, hot air supply
66 Ivchenko AI-24A turboprop engine
67 Engine auxiliary equipment
68 Hot air de-iced intake lip
69 Propeller hub pitch change mechanism
70 Spinner
71 Propeller blade root electric de-icing
72 AV-72 four-bladed, constant speed propeller
73 Engine cowling panels
74 Exhaust duct, exhausts on outboard side of nacelle
75 Wing panel joint rib
76 Fuel vent
77 Fuel filler cap
78 Outer wing panel integral fuel tank; total system capacity 1220 Imp gal (5550l)
79 Leading edge de-icing air duct
80 Retractable landing/taxying lamp
81 Outer wing panel joint rib
82 Anhedral outer wing panel
83 Starboard navigation light
84 Wing tip fairing
85 Starboard two-segment aileron
86 Aileron tabs
87 Outboard double-slotted Fowler-type flap, down position

88 Flap guide rails and screw jacks
89 Nacelle tail fairing
90 TG-16 tubine starter/generator, starboard side only
91 Inboard double-slotted flap segment, down position
92 Flap guide rails
93 Flap screw jacks
94 Optional long-range fuel tanks (four), capacity 228 Imp gal (1,037l)
95 Central flap drive electric motor
96 Wing/fuselage attachment main rib
97 Wing attachment joints
98 Control access panels
99 Wing root trailing edge fillet
100 Cabin roof lighting panels
101 Overhead light luggage racks
102 Detachable ceiling panels, systems access
103 Cabin warm air ducting
104 Galley/buffet unit
105 Cabin attendant's folding seat
106 Toilet compartment
107 Coat rails
108 Tailplane de-icing air duct
109 Fin root fillet construction
110 HF notch aerial

111 Starboard tailplane
112 Starboard elevator
113 Fin leading-edge de-icing
114 Fin rib and stringer construction
115 HF aerial cable
116 De-icing air exit louvres
117 Static discharger
118 Rudder construction
119 Rudder tabs
120 Tail navigation light
121 Elevator tab
122 Port elevator rib construction
123 Static discharger
124 Tailplane leading-edge de-icing
125 Tailplane rib construction
126 Elevator hinge control
127 Radar altimeters
128 Rudder torque shaft
129 Ventral fin
130 Fin tailplane attachment main frame
131 Tailcone construction
132 Tailplane control rods
133 Rear pressure bulkhead
134 Emergency flare chutes, port and starboard
135 Tailcone access door
136 Rear baggage/wardrobe compartment
137 Sliding main entry door, open
138 Folding airstairs
139 Entry doorway
140 Passenger cabin rear bulkhead
141 Cabin fresh air supply duct
142 Cot, port and starboard, infant accommodation
143 Rear cabin passenger seating
144 Port inboard double-slotted Fowler-type flap
145 Flap screw jacks
146 Engine mounting main ribs
147 Control access panels
148 Nacelle tail fairing construction
149 Port outer double-slotted flap
150 Flap shroud ribs
151 Flap rib construction
152 Rear spar
153 Aileron tabs
154 Port two-segment aileron construction
155 Wing tip fairing
156 De-icing air outlet louvres
157 Port navigation light
158 Outer wing panel rib construction
159 Aileron segment interconnection
160 Leading-edge corrugated inner skin panel, de-icing air ducts
161 Front spar
162 Outer wing panel joint rib
163 Port wing integral fuel tank bay
164 Retractable landing/taxying lamp
165 Wing stringers
166 Wing skin panelling
167 Hydraulic reservoir
168 Main undercarriage pivot fixing
169 Hydraulic retraction jack
170 Port engine exhaust pipe
171 Mainwheel leg doors
172 Main undercarriage leg strut
173 Twin mainwheels, forward retracting
174 Main undercarriage, front strut
175 Mainwheel doors, closed after cycling of undercarriage leg
176 Mainwheel bay
177 Engine bearer struts
178 Inboard leading-edge de-icing air ducting
179 Inner wing panel fuel tank bays
180 Wing attachment fuselage main frames
181 Port engine cowling panels
182 Fireproof bulkhead
183 Main engine mounting ring frame
184 Forward engine mounting struts
185 Cabin air system cold air and pressurising supply
186 Oil cooler
187 Engine annular air intake
188 Propeller spinner
189 Oil cooler and air system intake
190 Intake lip hot air de-icing

Above left: An interior view of the Antonov An-24V showing the somewhat spartan 52-seat layout with four-abreast seating and open baggage rack running the full length of the cabin each side.

Above: A three-view drawing of the An-26. This primarily military derivative of the An-24 differs in the design of the rear fuselage, which as shown incorporates a rear-loading ramp and door.

Above: A cutaway drawing of the Antonov An-24V Srs II, which introduced uprated AI-24A engines.

Right: The Antonov An-24V CU-T877 is one of the first of these transports to have entered service with Cubana, which also has An-24RV and An-26 freighters in its fleet. Most exports of Soviet airliners have been to Eastern European countries, but some operators in the Middle East rely heavily upon Antonov, Ilyushin and Tupolev types, as does the Cuban airline, Cubana, with its 60-aircraft fleet (in 1986).

ANTONOV AN-28 SOVIET UNION

The An-28 appeared in September 1969, at which time it was known as the An-14M, indicating its relationship to the An-14 piston-engined light transport. The latter had flown for the first time on 15 March 1958 and was intended as a successor for the ubiquitous An-2 biplane, offering a higher standard of comfort and performance but comparable short take-off and landing capabilities. Known as the Pchelka (little bee), the An-14 underwent a lengthy period of flight development and proving trials before entering production, but several hundred were eventually built, primarily for use by Aeroflot. Versions included, in addition to the basic passenger carrier, a five-seat executive transport, a light freighter, geological survey and photographic models, and an ambulance capable of accommodating six casualty stretchers and a medical attendant. A braced high-wing monoplane with an all-metal semi-monocoque pod-and-boom fuselage and two-spar wing carrying full-span leading-edge slats and double-slotted trailing-edge flaps, the An-14 was intended for single-pilot operation. With a similar overall configuration, including the provision of an aft loading ramp/door in the rear fuselage, the An-28 was considerably larger, with almost twice the capacity in the cabin. The new design, which was evaluated alongside the Beriev Be-30 and Be-32 (of generally similar size and configuration apart from a single fin and rudder), did not at first prove wholly satisfactory in relation to the stringent requirements that had been laid down by Aeroflot, and the prototype appears to have undergone progressive changes, as indicated by photographs released in the Soviet Union. These show that modifications were made to the wing and its high-lift devices, to the tail assembly and to the stub wings

Below: The Antonov An-28 has a simple, functional layout, as shown here when the aircraft was being tested in sub-arctic conditions at Komi.

Right: A Polish-built example of the An-28 as operated by Aeroflot, for whom it is now in large-scale production at the PZL Mielec factory.

ANTONOV AN-72 and AN-74 SOVIET UNION

An-72 appears to have been developed as much for military duty (tactical battlefield support transport) as for commercial use, although all the examples displayed to date, or illustrated in the Soviet Union, bear Aeroflot markings. It is unique as a production aircraft for its use of upper surface blowing (USB) as a means of increasing lift and thus providing STOL performance. Before the appearance of the An-72, this configuration had been applied experimentally to several other aircraft, in particular by Boeing on its YC-14 prototypes built for the USAF's AMST programme. Like the YC-14, the An-72 has two high-bypass turbofans mounted in nacelles that project well ahead of the high-positioned wing. This location allows the engine exhaust to be discharged directly over the wing centre section, through suitably-shaped orifices, producing a 'Coanda' effect that causes the airflow to attach itself to the wing surface, even when the large-area trailing-edge flaps are deflected downwards. The lift of the wing is enhanced as a result of the airflow remaining attached to the upper surface, and low-speed performance is consequently improved to produce a good STOL capability. The large-area vertical and horizontal tail surfaces are in turn required to maintain control of the aircraft at the low speeds made possible by the high wing lift coefficient. Other features of the An-72, including its multi-leg main landing gear contained in fuselage-side blisters and its rear-loading provisions, are indicative of the military applications and the requirement for the aircraft to operate from unprepared surfaces, whether in military or civil guise. Three prototypes of the An-72 are reported to have been built, of which one was for static trials. The first of the flying prototypes was airborne for the first time on 22 December 1977. In late 1983, a series of flights made in an An-72 set a total of 17 records under conditions specified by the FAI, for aircraft in classes C1 and C1k, these being for take-off weights up to 25,000kg (55,115lb) and up to 35,000kg

SPECIFICATION
(Antonov An-72)

Power Plant: Two Lotarev D-36 high-bypass turbofans each rated at 14,330lb st (6,500kgp) for take-off. Fuel carried in integral tanks between outer wing spars.
Performance: Max speed, 410kts (760km/h); max cruising speed, 388kts (720km/h); service ceiling, 36,090ft (11,000m); normal operating altitude, 26,245 to 32,800ft (8,000 to 10,000m); take-off run, 1,540ft (470m); take-off run, one engine out, 3,935ft (1,200m); range with max payload, 540 naut mls (1,000km); range with max fuel and 30-minute reserve 2,050 naut mls (3,800km).
Weights: Max payload for normal operations, 22,045lb (10,000kg); payload for STOL operation, 7,715lb (3,500kg); max take-off weight (unrestricted runway), 72,750lb (33,000kg); max take-off weight from 3,935ft (1,200m) runway, 67,240lb (30,500kg); max take-off weight from 3,280ft (1,000m) runway, 58,420lb (26,500kg).
Dimensions: Span, 84ft 9in (25.83m); overall length, 87ft 2¼in (26.58m); overall height, 27ft 0¼in (8.24m); sweepback, about 12 deg at quarter chord; wing area, about 969sq ft (90.0m²).
Accommodation: Cabin length, 29ft 6¼in (9.00m), width at floor level, 6ft 10¾in (2.10m), overall height, 7ft 2½in (2.20m). Typical accommodation for up to 32 passengers on sideways-facing seats along cabin sides, or 24 casualties on stretchers; cargo loads carried on pallets up to 6ft 3in by 7ft 11in by 4ft 9½in (1.90m by 2.42m by 1.46m) or in containers up to 6ft 3in by 8ft by 4ft 9½in (1.90m by 2.44m by 1.46m). Flight crew of three (pilot, co-pilot/navigator and flight engineer).

(77,160lb) respectively. At the lower weight the aircraft set time-to-height records that included 18 minutes 1.2 seconds to 12,000m (39,370ft), an absolute height record of 13,440m (44,095ft), and a payload-to-height record of 3,528kg (7,778lb) to 2,000m (6,562ft). At the higher weight, records included a time of 27 minutes 25.4 seconds to 12,000m (39,370ft), an absolute altitude of 12,400m (40,682ft), and a payload of 8,064kg (17,778lb) lifted to 2,000m (6,562ft). The An-72 has the NATO reporting name 'Coaler'.

VARIANTS

During its flight development, the An-72 was flown with several changes to the profile of the rear fuselage. As first illustrated, it had two large ventral fins, canted out on each side of the ramp-door in the rear fuselage, with two petal-type airbrakes forming the end of the fuselage. Later, a beaver-tail rear fairing appeared, with revised ramp and door, but the latest and presumably production form of the An-72 incorporates a door arrangement similar to that of the An-26, with a ramp that can be hinged down when the aircraft is on the ground, to permit easy loading and unloading of supplies, but which can also move down and forwards to lie flush under the rear fuselage so that trucks can be backed up to link with the cabin floor for the man-handling of smaller items of freight. In 1984, official reference was made in the Soviet press to the An-74 as an aircraft specifically developed to operate in Arctic and Antarctic regions, with wheel/ski landing gear. According to the Soviet report the An-74 is equipped for all-weather operations in polar regions, where its duties include ferrying personnel and supplies for scientific stations on ice floes, air-dropping supplies to expedition teams, and icefield reconnaissance. When first seen outside the Soviet Union in 1986, the An-74 revealed a number of differences from the prototypes of the An-72, and these changes may also apply to the definitive production version of the latter. Overall dimensions are increased to a span of 104ft 7½in (31.89m) and length of 85ft 6⅓in (28.07m), and gross weight is increased to 76,058lb (34,500kg). With the same D-36 engines as the An-72, the An-74 has a reported maximum speed of 380kts (705km/h) and cruises at 297kts (550km/h).

carrying the main units of the landing gear. Initially, all three members of the landing gear were retractable, the main members retracting into fairings at the base of the fuselage and the nosewheel folding into a bay in the fuselage nose, but all examples of the An-28 subsequent to the first have featured fixed, levered-suspension landing gear. Like the An-14, the An-28 has double-slotted flaps extending from root to tip and incorporating single-slotted ailerons. Spoilers in the wing upper surfaces ahead of the ailerons are automatically operated in an Antonov patented system so that in the event of an engine

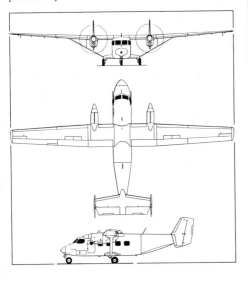

SPECIFICATION

Power Plant: Two PZL Rzeszow TVD-10S turboprops each rated at 960shp (716kW) for take-off, with PZL three-blade feathering and reversing propellers. Fuel capacity, 431 Imp gal (1,960l) in integral tanks in outer wing panels.
Performance: Max cruising speed, 189kts (350km/h) at 9,845ft (3,000m); economical cruising speed, 181kts (335km/h) at 9,845ft (3,000m); initial rate of climb, 2,315ft/min (11.7m/sec); service ceiling, more than 19,685ft (6,000m); take-off distance to 35ft (11.7m), 1,180ft (360m); landing distance from 50ft (15m), 1,035ft (315m); range with max payload and no reserves, 302 naut mls (560km); range with max fuel, 2,205lb (1,000kg) payload and 30-minute fuel reserve, 736 naut mls (1,365km).
Weights: Empty weight, equipped, 8,267lb (3,750kg); max fuel load, 3,454lb (1,567kg); max payload, 4,409lb (2,000kg); max take-off and landing weight, 14,330lb (6,500kg).
Dimensions: Span, 72ft 5in (22.07m); overall length, 42ft 11¾in (13.10m); overall height, 16ft 1in (4.90m) sweepback, nil; wing area, 427.5sq ft (39.72m²).
Accommodation: Cabin length, 17ft 3in (5.26m), max width, 5ft 8½in (1.74m), max height, 5ft 3in (1.60m). Standard layout for 17 passengers, basically three-abreast (2+1) with offset aisle, at 28in (72cm) pitch. Flight crew of two.

Left: Three-view drawing of the An-28, showing the final arrangement of the landing gear, tail unit and wings, after modifications had been made to the prototypes used for initial flight testing.

failure, the 'opposite' spoiler opens to limit the wing-drop that would otherwise occur. The An-28 is said to be unstallable because of the action of the automatic slots; there is also a patented, fixed leading-edge slat on the tailplane. The An-28 has the NATO reporting name 'Cash'.

VARIANTS
The prototype and at least one pre-production An-28 had 810shp (604kW) Isotov TVD-850 turboprops, but these were then replaced by 960shp (716kW) Glushenkov TVD-10 engines, which also power the production aircraft in the Polish-built equivalent.

SERVICE USE
The An-28 was awarded a temporary Soviet type certificate on 4 October 1978, based on testing of prototypes and pre-production examples. Under an agreement concluded in February 1978, all subsequent production has become the responsibility of the PZL Mielec factory in Poland, where the first of a pilot-batch of 15 (including one for static testing) flew on 22 July 1984. Initial deliveries were made to Aeroflot during 1985. After completing five aircraft in 1984, the Mielec factory delivered 30 An-28s in 1985 and the production tempo continued to build up towards a planned peak of 200 per year. The production plan provides for a total of 1,200 An-28s to be built by 1990, some of which are likely to be adapted for military tasks, as was the An-14. The An-28 is also expected to see service in many of the Comecon nations.

ANTONOV AN-72 and AN-74

A payload of 11,023lb (5,000kg) can be carried over a distance of 1,780 naut mls (3,300km), or twice that load (which is the maximum payload) a distance of 620 naut mls (1,150km). Maximum range is 2,537 naut miles (4,700km).

SERVICE USE
All examples of the An-72 and An-74 seen to date operate in Aeroflot markings. Announced Aeroflot re-equipment plans have made reference to the expected use of the An-72, but it is likely that this is for special duties, for example in the development of remote areas of Siberia, rather than on scheduled domestic air services.

Below left: A three-view drawing of the Antonov 74, which differs substantially in detail from the An-72, whilst sharing the same overall configuration.

Below: The Antonov An-72 seen here was displayed in Britain during 1984. Bearing the registration CCCP-7200, it was believed to be a pre-production example.

Right: The late Oleg K Antonov is seen (left) in the pilot's seat of the An-72, with his chief designer Yakob G Orlov to the right. The flight deck appears to be relatively simple and uncluttered in its layout. Not visible here is the map display for the Doppler-based automatic navigation system that the aircraft carries as part of its avionics system.

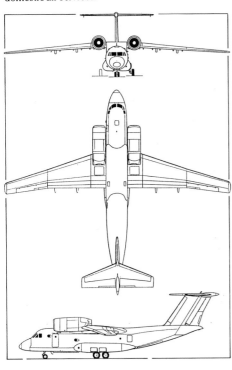

The Avions de Transport Régional organization was set up on 5 February 1982 under French law as a Groupement d'Intérêt Economique (GIE) to manage the programme of development, production and management of a regional airliner known as the ATR 42. The aircraft in question had been launched some three months earlier, on 29 October 1981, as a joint product of Aérospatiale in France and Aeritalia in Italy, in continuation of a preliminary accord reached by the two companies in July 1980. Before that time, both companies had been studying the market for a regional airliner with 30-40 seats and had produced project designs under the designations Aérospatiale AS-35 and Aeritalia AIT 320. These projects were of generally similar configuration, and the ATR 42 was a continuation of the same theme, with a high wing, two turboprop engines, fuselage-side blisters for the main landing gear units, and a T-tail. Sizing of the aircraft was a matter for careful study, with 42 seats eventually adopted as the norm, a few more than in the earlier independent project designs (as their designations indicated). From the start of development, however, there has been some pressure to increase the seating capacity, and a stretched version was eventually launched some four years after the go-ahead for the ATR 42 itself, as noted below. The division of labour between the two companies provides for Aérospatiale to manufacture the wing while Aeritalia produces the fuselage and tail unit. The Italian company is also responsible for the hydraulic, air-conditioning and pressurization systems, while the French partner looks after the flight deck and cabin, the power plant, and the electrical and flight-control systems. Civil passenger versions of the ATR 42 are assembled and test flown at Toulouse; the ATM 42-R military cargo version and any civil freighters with rear loading ramp are assembled at Naples. Flight testing of the ATR 42 began on 16 August 1984, the second development aircraft being flown on 31 October of that year and the first production ATR 42 on 30 April 1985.

VARIANTS

The designations ATR 42-100 and ATR 42-200 were at first applied to versions with gross weights of 32,848lb (14,900kg) and 34,722lb (15,750kg) respectively, the latter having a redesigned interior that allowed accommodation to be increased from 42 to 50 without any change in external dimensions. By the time production deliveries began, the ATR 42-200 had become the standard aircraft, with the ATR 42-300 available as a high gross weight option at 35,604lb (16,150kg), with a range of 890 naut mls (1,650km) carrying the full passenger payload. In 1985 the ATR 72 was launched, featuring a fuselage lengthened by 14ft (4.27m) to provide up to 74 seats at a pitch of 30in (76cm). There is also an increase in wing span, of 8ft 1½in (2.48m), and the engines are 2,400shp (1,790kW) PW124s. For deliveries starting at the end of 1988, the ATR 72 has a maximum take-off weight of 44,070lb (19,990kg), a maximum payload of 15,432lb (7,000kg) and a range with 70 passengers of 900 naut mls (1 669km). Other designated variants of the basic aircraft include the ATR 42-F commercial freighter and the ATM 42 military freighter, the latter with a rear-loading ramp.

SPECIFICATION
(ATR 42-200)

Power Plant: Two Pratt & Whitney Canada PW120 turboprops each flat-rated at 1,800shp (1,342kW) for take-off, with Hamilton Standard 14SF four-blade constant-speed reversing and feathering propellers of 13ft 0in (3.96m) diameter. Fuel capacity 1,254 Imp gal (5,700l) in integral tanks in wing torsion box.
Performance: Max operating speed, 250kts (463km/h) CAS or Mach = 0.55; max cruising speed, 268kts (497km/h) at 17,000ft (5,180m); initial rate of climb, 2,100ft/min (10.6m/sec); cruising ceiling, 25,000ft (7,620m); take-off field length, 3,575ft (1,090m); landing field length, 3,150ft (960m); range with max passenger payload, 645 naut mls (1,195km); range with max fuel, 2,490 naut mls (4,615km).
Weights: Operating weight empty, 21,986lb (9,973kg); max fuel, 9,921lb (4,500kg); max payload, 9,980lb (4,527kg); max take-off weight, 34,722lb (15,750kg); max landing weight, 34,171lb (15,500kg); max zero-fuel weight, 31,966lb (14,500kg).
Dimensions: Span, 80ft 7½in (24.57m); overall length, 74ft 4½in (22.67m); overall height, 24ft 10¾in (7.59m); sweepback, nil; wing area, 586.6sq ft (54.5m²).
Accommodation: Cabin length, 45ft 5¼in (13.85m), max width, 8ft 5¼in (2.57m), max height, 6ft 3¼in (1.91m). Standard layouts provide for 42 passengers four-abreast with central aisle at 32in (81cm) pitch, or up to 50 at 30in (76cm) pitch. Baggage/freight compartments at front and rear of cabin with max combined volume of 321.4cu ft (9.1m³). Flight crew of two (with optional third seat).

SERVICE USE

Certification of the ATR 42-200 and ATR 42-300 was obtained in France on 24 September 1985, and immediately ratified in Italy, in accordance with the joint European JAR standards. US certification to FAR 25 was confirmed on 25 October 1985. Deliveries began on 3 December 1985, to Air Littoral, and the first revenue services were flown on 9 December 1985, by that company. Subsequent deliveries were to Cimber Air in December 1985, and to Holland Air and Command Airways in January 1986, the latter becoming the first US operator of the type in March 1986. By early 1987 some 75 ATR 42s were on firm order, with 25 on option; orders and options for the stretched-fuselage ATR 72 totalled 24. Thirty ATR 42s had been delivered to a total of 15 airlines by the end of 1986.

Avions de Transport Régional ATR 42 Cutaway Drawing Key

1 Radome
2 Weather radar scanner
3 Scanner tracking mechanism
4 ILS glideslope aerial
5 Front pressure bulkhead
6 Pitot heads
7 Twin nosewheels, forward retracting
8 Nosewheel leg doors
9 Taxying lamps
10 Nose undercarriage wheel bay
11 Rudder pedals
12 Static ports
13 Instrument panel (Electronic Flight Instrument System)
14 Windscreen wipers
15 Instrument panel shroud
16 Windscreen panels
17 Overhead systems switch panels
18 Co-pilot's seat
19 Emergency equipment stowage
20 Centre control pedestal
21 Control column handwheel
22 Side console panel
23 Cockpit floor level
24 Underfloor control linkage
25 Pilot's flight bag stowage
26 Oxygen bottle
27 Angle of attack transmitter
28 Pilot's seat
29 Avionics equipment racks
30 Central Observer's folding seat
31 Electrical equipment racks
32 Cockpit roof escape hatch
33 Cockpit doorway
34 VHF aerial
35 Control cable runs
36 Baggage restraint net
37 Main cabin doorway
38 Forward baggage/cargo compartment
39 Baggage loading floor
40 External power socket
41 Baggage/cargo door, open
42 Door latch
43 Wing inspection light
44 Main cabin bulkhead (moveable to suit internal layout)
45 Four-abreast passenger seating, 46-seat layout (48 and 50-seat alternative configurations)
46 Emergency escape window hatch, port and starboard
47 Recirculating air fans
48 Floor beam construction
49 Underfloor conditioned air distribution ducting
50 Fuselage skin panel doubler/propeller debris guard
51 Fuselage frame and stringer construction
52 Cabin wall trim panelling
53 ADF loop aerials
54 Fuselage skin panelling
55 Cabin wall soundproofing lining
56 Cabin roof lighting panels
57 Overhead stowage bins
58 Passenger service units
59 Cabin air distribution duct
60 Conditioned air delivery duct risers
61 Engine bleed air duct to conditioning plant
62 Wing/fuselage attachment main frames
63 Spar attachment joints
64 Wing centre section rib construction
65 Centre section dry bay
66 Control cable runs to engines
67 Wing leading edge fillet framing
68 Honeycomb leading edge fillet panels
69 Fuel pumps
70 Starboard wing integral fuel tank, total fuel capacity 1254 Imp gal (5,700l)

Right: A cutaway drawing of the ATR 42. This is representative of both the Srs 200 and Srs 300, which differ in their operating weights.

Below: The stylish interior of an ATR 42, featuring one-class, four-abreast seating, with full length luggage lockers.

Below: Simmons Airlines in the USA uses its ATR 42s to operate services linked to the American Airlines network, wearing the American Eagle livery depicted here.

71 Detachable leading edge honeycomb panel
72 Engine bleed air ducting
73 Ventral exhaust nozzle
74 Starboard engine nacelle
75 Pratt & Whitney Canada PW120 turboprop engine
76 Engine accessory equipment gearbox
77 Digital engine controller
78 Particle separation intake air duct
79 Ventral oil cooler
80 Propeller reduction gearbox
81 Hamilton Standard four-bladed variable pitch, reversible propeller
82 Spinner
83 Propeller hub pitch change mechanism
84 Detachable engine cowling panels
85 Outer wing panel multi-bolt attachment joint
86 Outboard integral fuel tank
87 Fuel system piping
88 Pressure refuelling connection
89 Gravity fuel filler cap

90 Upper wing skin access panel
91 Aileron control linkage
92 Outer wing panel ribs
93 Leading edge pneumatic de-icing boot
94 Starboard navigation (red) and strobe (white) lights
95 Aileron horn balance
96 Static dischargers
97 Port aileron
98 Aileron tabs
99 Carbon-fibre aileron skin panelling
100 Starboard spoiler, open
101 Outboard double-slotted flap, down position
102 Flap hydraulic jack
103 Ventral flap hinge fairings
104 Flap slot closure panels
105 Inboard double-slotted flap segment, down position
106 Inboard flap jack
107 Wing root trailing edge fillet
108 Fillet honeycomb construction
109 Aileron central control linkage
110 Engine fire extinguisher bottles, port and starboard
111 Overhead stowage bins
112 Rear cabin seating
113 Curtained wardrobe
114 Galley unit
115 Passenger cabin rear bulkhead
116 Starboard side service/emergency exit door
117 Rear baggage compartment door
118 Cabin attendant's control panel
119 Interphone

120 Cabin attendant's folding seat
121 Toilet compartment door
122 Starboard side rear baggage/cargo compartment
123 Rear pressure bulkhead
124 Glass-fibre fin root fillet
125 Kevlar/Nomex honeycomb extended chord fin root section
126 Fin spar attachment joints
127 Elevator control rods
128 Three-spar tailfin construction
129 VOR aerial
130 Fin leading edge
131 Tailplane attachment joints
132 Starboard tailplane
133 Tailplane leading edge pneumatic de-icing boot
134 Starboard elevator
135 Rudder horn balance
136 Anti-collision light
137 Static dischargers
138 Rudder
139 Elevator hinge control
140 Elevator tab
141 Port elevator honeycomb construction
142 Elevator horn balance
143 Port tailplane construction
144 Leading edge nose ribs
145 Rudder honeycomb construction
146 Rudder tab
147 Tailcone transparency
148 Tail navigation and strobe lights (white)
149 Composite tailcone construction
150 Rudder hinge control
151 Tailcone vent
152 Autopilot controller
153 Tailcone rear bulkhead

154 Fin spar attachment main frames
155 Ventral access hatch
156 Crashproof cockpit voice and data recorders
157 Cabin pressurisation valves
158 Toilet compartment
159 Water tank
160 Wash basin
161 Folding handrail
162 Counterbalance spring
163 Rear passenger entry door/airstairs
164 Entry lobby
165 Rear fuselage frame and stringer construction
166 Cabin window panels
167 Port inboard double-slotted flap
168 Honeycomb flap shroud panel
169 Inboard flap hydraulic jack
170 Flap vanes
171 Flap honeycomb core construction
172 Outboard double-slotted flap
173 Port spoiler
174 Spoiler hydraulic jack
175 Aileron spring tab
176 Port aileron rib construction
177 Aileron trim tab
178 Static dischargers
179 Aileron horn balance

180 Port navigation (red) and strobe (white) lights
181 Outer wing panel rib construction

182 Leading edge pneumatic de-icing boot
183 Fuel tank end rib
184 Fuel filler cap

185 Port wing integral fuel tank
186 Pneumatic de-icing valve
187 Port wing rib construction
188 Rear spar
189 Outer wing panel bolted joint
190 Front spar
191 Ventral engine exhaust nozzle
192 Port engine nacelle
193 Fireproof bulkhead
194 Sponson mounted hydraulic reservoirs and filters, port and starboard
195 Engine mounting frame bearer struts
196 Main engine mounting frame
197 Twin mainwheels, inward retracting
198 Levered suspension axle beam
199 Mainwheel doors
200 Shock absorber strut
201 Main undercarriage pivot fixing
202 Hydraulic retraction jack
203 Forward engine mounting/gearbox support struts
204 Fuselage sponson mounted air conditioning plant, port and starboard
205 Oil cooler air intake
206 Engine air intake
207 Air conditioning system ram air intake
208 Port landing lamp
209 Fuselage sponson fairing

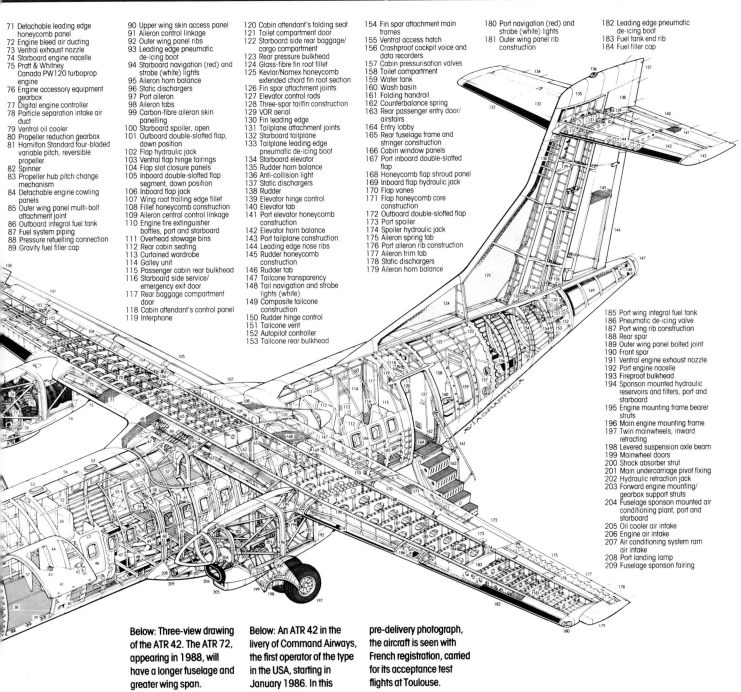

Below: Three-view drawing of the ATR 42. The ATR 72, appearing in 1988, will have a longer fuselage and greater wing span.

Below: An ATR 42 in the livery of Command Airways, the first operator of the type in the USA, starting in January 1986. In this pre-delivery photograph, the aircraft is seen with French registration, carried for its acceptance test flights at Toulouse.

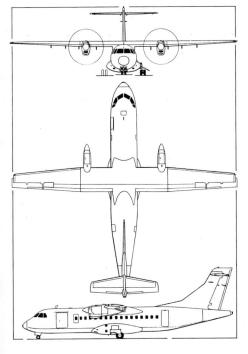

BEECHCRAFT C99 AIRLINER USA

Beech Aircraft entered the commuter airliner market in 1965 with a decision to evolve a small transport aircraft based on its experience with the Queen Air, a piston-engined twin then in production for corporate and air taxi use. Using a wing similar to that of the Queen Air (and the later King Air and Super King Air series), the new aircraft was identified as the Beechcraft Model 99, and designed to carry 15 passengers. A standard feature of the design was an airstair incorporated in the main cabin door, but a wide cargo-loading door was offered as an option to facilitate use of the aircraft in mixed passenger/cargo operations, this door being adjacent to the main passenger door. Beech flew a development airframe in the form of a long-fuselage Queen Air in December 1965, with piston engines, and in July 1966 this prototype began a new series of trials with Pratt & Whitney Canada PT6A-20 turboprops. In this form, it represented the Model 99 in all major respects and provided the basis for certification to be obtained on 2 May 1968. The Beechcraft 99 is a conventional cantilever low-wing monoplane of all-metal construction, magnesium being used for the ailerons. The single-slotted trailing-edge flaps are of aluminium alloy construction, and pneumatic de-icing boots on the leading edges are optional. Landing gear and brakes are hydraulically operated, and there is a freon air-conditioning system for the cabin and cockpit, engine bleed air being used for heating. To supplement the baggage space provided in the nose and in a compartment at the rear of the cabin (access to both of which is through external doors), the Beechcraft 99 can carry a large baggage/cargo pod under the fuselage: this has an internal length of 10ft 10½in (3.31m).

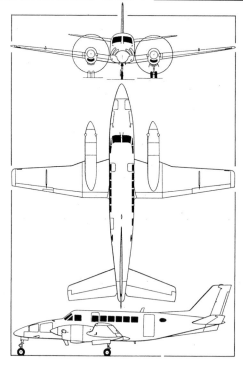

Left: A three-view drawing of the Beechcraft C99 Airliner, which was the final production version of this commuter aircraft. Production had begun about 20 years earlier, in the original Model 99 form, and was resumed in 1979 after a five-year pause. Some 227 Beechcraft 99s were produced, in four principal series; all were externally similar.

Right: A Beechcraft B99 in service with Baron Air, a Swedish air taxi operator. Most of the later production aircraft, in the C99 version, were delivered to, and in 1987 are still operated by, commuter airlines in the USA. The smaller but similar King Air is shown on page 174.

VARIANTS
The first production version, the Beechcraft 99, was powered by 550shp (410kW) PT6A-20 engines. When 680shp (507kW) PT6A-27 engines were introduced, the designation changed to A99, although these engines were flat-rated to the same power as the PT6A-20s originally used. The Beechcraft 99 and A99 each have a maximum take-off weight of 10,400lb (4,717kg); most were delivered for airline use, but Executive versions with 8-17 seats were also available. In the B99, with the same PT6A-27 engines, the maximum weight went up to 10,900lb (4,944kg). Production of the Model 99 ended in 1974 when 164 had been built, but a new version, announced as the Commuter C99, was included in Beech Aircraft's plan to re-enter the commuter air-

BEECHCRAFT 1900 AIRLINER USA

Having stopped production of the Beechcraft 99 in 1975, and thus separated itself from the developing market for small commuterliners and regional airliners, Beech Aircraft announced in 1979 its intention to develop one or more new types of aircraft suitable for this portion of the market. Design studies were already in hand for a pressurized aircraft in the 30/40-seat category – an aircraft which, had it been built, would have been the largest Beechcraft to date – but to provide a more immediate entry into the regional airliner market place, variants of the Super King Air 200 were projected. One such, tentatively known as the Model 1300, would have used the same airframe as its progenitor with a cabin arranged to seat 13 passengers (hence the designation), whilst the Model 1900 was to have a lengthened fuselage (for 19 passengers) and uprated engines. With indications of airline interest, development of the Model 1900 was continued and in 1981 work began on three flying prototypes, a static test airframe and a fuselage for pressure-cycle testing. The first two flying prototypes made their maiden flights on 3 September and 30 November 1982. The third, after being used for function and reliability testing, equipment certification and demonstration, was refurbished for customer delivery. Before the first flight of the prototype, testing of the PT6A-65 engine began in a Super King Air flying test bed on 30 April 1981. Based as it is on the Super King Air 200, the Model 1900 has the same fuselage cross section, the parallel section of the fuselage being lengthened by some 14ft (4.27m). Most other major components, including the wing centre section and the tail unit, are dimensionally similar to those of the Super King Air, but strengthened structurally where necessary to permit operations at higher weights. The PT6A-65B engines are flat-rated in order to provide constant power in elevated ambient temperatures. An unusual feature of the Beechcraft 1900 is its use of auxiliary horizontal fixed tail surfaces, known to Beech as stabilons, on each side of the rear fuselage just forward of the tailplane, which is mounted atop the fin. Small 'taillet' vertical fins are also mounted beneath each tailplane half, near the tips.

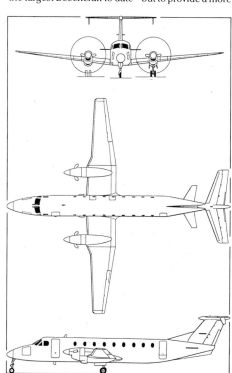

Left: Three-view drawing of the Beechcraft 1900 Airliner, some 60 of which were in service by the end of 1986. The stabilons on the rear fuselage and tailets on the tailplane are an unusual feature of the design.

Below: A view, looking forward, towards the cockpit, inside the Beechcraft 1900. Single seats are located each side of a central aisle, in which a step is produced by the wing spar, as is visible in this photograph.

VARIANTS
The basic 19-seat commuterliner is the Model 1900 Airliner (also known as the 1900C), and incorporates an upward-hinged cargo-loading door in the port rear fuselage side. The Model 1900 Executive has a standard-sized door in this position and seats anything between 12 and 18 passengers. At one time, this was to have been known as the Model 1200. A 'wet' wing has also been developed for the Model 1900, with integral tankage replacing the five bladder tanks in the original design. This increases fuel capacity by some 60 per cent and results in the

SPECIFICATION

Power Plant: Two Pratt & Whitney Canada PT6A-36 turboprops each rated at 715shp (533kW), with Hartzell three-blade feathering and reversing propellers. Fuel capacity, 310 Imp gal (1,412l) in rubber tanks in wings.
Performance: Max level speed, 268kts (497km/h) at 8,000ft (2,440m); cruising speed, 245kts (454km/h) at 16,000ft (4,875m); initial rate of climb, 2,221ft/min (11.1m/sec); service ceiling, 28,080ft (8,560m); range with max payload, 578 naut mls (1,072km); range with max fuel, 910 naut mls (1,687km).
Weights: Operating weight empty, 6,494lb (2,946kg); max fuel weight, 2,466lb (1,119kg); max payload, 3,250lb (1,474kg); max take-off and landing weights, 11,300lb (5,126kg).
Dimensions: Span, 45ft 10½in (13.98m); overall length, 44ft 6¾in (13.58m); overall height, 14ft 4¼in (4.37m); sweepback, nil; wing area, 279.7sq ft (25.98m²).
Accommodation: Cabin length (including flight deck and aft baggage compartment), 25ft 4½in (7.73m), max width, 4ft 7in (1.40m), max height, 4ft 9in (1.45m). Max seating for 15 passengers in individual seats with central aisle. Nose and aft baggage compartment volume, 60.9cu ft (1.72m³), plus provision for underfuselage baggage/cargo pod of 59.4cu ft (1.68m³).

liner market in May 1979, at which time development of the larger Commuter 1900 was launched. With a generally updated structure and systems, the C99 had the same overall dimensions and characteristics as the B99, but maximum take-off weight was again increased, this time to 11,300lb (5,126kg), and the engines were flat-rated 715shp (533kW) PT6A-36s. The prototype C99 was a converted B99 airframe, first flown at Wichita on 20 June 1980. The company's approved designation was later changed from Commuter C99 to C99 Airliner.

SERVICE USE

Following certification of the original Model 99, deliveries began in May 1968, the first customer being Commuter Airlines Inc. A few of the production run of 164 Beechcraft 99, A99 and B99 versions were delivered to military users, notably the Chilean air force. The C99 variant was certificated in July 1981 and the first deliveries were made on 30 July, with initial aircraft going to Christman Air System and Sunbird Airlines. A total of 63 Beech C99s was sold, production coming to an end in 1985, at which time the price of a new aircraft was just under $2 million.

extension of the Beechcraft 1900's maximum range by some 85 per cent.

SERVICE USE

The Model 1900 Airliner was certificated under FAR Part 41C regulations on 22 November 1983, with simultaneous approval for single-pilot operations under FAR 135. Deliveries for airline use began in February 1984 and the first Model 1900 Executive was delivered in July 1985. For its commuter role, the Model 1900 is designed for multi-stop operations without intermediate refuelling, and with the maximum landing weight matching the maximum take-off weight, there is no minimum distance to be flown before the first stop can be made. Typically, a range of 406 naut mls (752km) can be achieved, assuming a cruising altitude of 10,000ft (3,050m) and a 45-minute fuel reserve, with four intermediate stops. Sales of the Beechcraft 1900 in all variants totalled 60 by January 1987.

SPECIFICATION

Power Plant: Two Pratt & Whitney Canada PT6A-65B turboprops each flat-rated at 1,100shp (820kW) for take-off, with Hartzell four-blade feathering and reversing propellers. Fuel capacity 358 Imp gal (1,627l) in integral and bladder tanks in the wing.
Performance: Max cruising speed, typical cruising weight, 256kts (475km/h) at 8,000ft (2,440m), 253kts (469km/h) at 16,000ft (4,875m) and 235kts (436km/h) at 25,000ft (7,620m); initial rate of climb, 2,330ft/min (11.8m/sec); certificated ceiling, 25,000ft (7,620m); take-off distance to 50ft (15m), 3,260ft (995m); landing distance from 50ft (15m), 2,540ft (775m); range with max fuel and 45-minute reserve, 596 naut mls (1,105km) at 8,000ft (2,440m) or 794 naut mls (1,472km) at 25,000ft (7,620m).
Weights: Empty weight, 8,700lb (3,946kg); max fuel weight, 2,848lb (1,292kg); max payload, 5,300lb (2,404kg); max take-off weight, 16,600lb (7,530kg); max landing weight, 16,100lb (7,303kg); max zero-fuel weight, 14,000lb (6,350kg).
Dimensions: Span, 54ft 5¾in (16.61m); overall length, 57ft 10in (17.63m); overall height, 14ft 10¾in (4.54m); sweepback, nil; wing area, 303.0sq ft (28.15m²).
Accommodation: Cabin length (including flight deck and baggage compartments), 39ft 5½in (12.02m), max width, 4ft 6in (1.37m), max height, 4ft 9in (1.45m). Standard commuter configuration provides 19 single seats in cabin, with centre aisle; executive layouts provide 12-18 seats. Nose, forward and rear cabin baggage compartments, total volume 105.5cu ft (2.99m³). Flight crew of one or two depending on certification status adopted by operator, FAR Pt 91 or FAR Pt 135 respectively.

Left: The N1900J registration shows that this 1900 is one of the aircraft used for development and certification, prior to the start of deliveries.

BOEING 707 USA

The first of the company's jetliners and first US jet transport to enter service, the Boeing 707 had its origins in the design studies conducted by the company in the late 1940s and early 1950s for a new tanker for the USAF as a successor to the C-97/KC-97 family. From a number of turboprop and turbojet designs studied, Boeing selected its Model 367-80 for prototype construction and this aircraft, which later became best known simply as the 'Dash 80', made its first flight on 15 July 1954 at Renton, powered by four Pratt & Whitney JT3C turbojets. The Model 367-80 successfully demonstrated its potential to the USAF, which subsequently purchased many hundred KC-135A tankers and related reconnaisance and special-purpose variants, similar in size and configuration to the prototype. For airline use, however, Boeing decided that the cross-section of the fuselage should be increased so that more comfortable six-abreast seating could be provided, and the new commercial project became identified as the Model 707. With 13,000lb st (5,897kgp) JT3C-6 engines, the Model 707 was offered in 'short-body' and 'long-body' versions, and the latter was chosen by Pan American when it placed a launching order on 13 October 1955 (more than three years after the de Havilland Comet had become the world's first jet airliner in service). The first two Boeing 707s, used for certification, were flown on 20 December 1957 and 3 February 1958, and Boeing adopted a series of designation suffixes by which the first number of a three-numerical group indicated the model variant and the second and third numbers, in combination, served as a means of identifying the particular customer.

VARIANTS

Most early orders were for the so-called 'long-body' variant of the Boeing 707-120; only Qantas ordered the 'short-body' version of the -120 (this being the Model 707-138, with '38' referring to the customer, Qantas). With the same fuselage length as the 'long-body' -120, the Model 707-220 introduced 15,800lb st (7,167kgp) JT4A-3 or -5 engines for 'hot and high' performance but was specified only by Braniff, the first flight being made on 11 June 1959. These same engines – or the 16,800lb st (7,620kgp) JT4A-9 or 17,500lb st (7,938kgp) JT4A-11 – were then adopted for the third model, the Model 707-320. This was the intercontinental version of the aircraft, whereas the -120 was the transcontinental model, and it had the fuselage lengthened enough to accommodate up to 189 passengers, and a larger wing to cope with the higher weights. The first Model 707-320 flew on 11 January 1959, and was followed on 20 May 1959 by the first Model 707-420, which featured 16,500lb st (7,484kgp) Rolls-Royce Conway 505 engines. In 1957 Boeing offered a short/medium-range version of the basic aircraft as the Model 720, featuring a fuselage 1ft 8in (0.51m) longer than that of the short-body Model 707-120 used by Qantas, a lightened structure, lower fuel capacity, 12,000lb st

SPECIFICATION
(Boeing 707-320C)

Power Plant: Four Pratt & Whitney JT3D-7 turbofans each rated at 19,000lb st (8,618kgp), or JT8D-3 turbofans each rated at 18,000lb st (8,165kgp). Fuel capacity, 19,863 Imp gal (90,299l) in integral tanks in wing and centre section.

Performance: Max operating speed, 375kts (695km/h) IAS or Mach = 0.90; max cruising speed, 525kts (973km/h) at 25,000ft (7,620m); long-range cruise, 464kts (860km/h) at 35,000ft (10,670m); initial rate of climb, 4,000ft/min (20.3m/sec); service ceiling, 39,000ft (11,885m); take-off field length (FAR), 10,020ft (3,055m); landing field length (FAR), 6,400ft (1,950m); range with max fuel, 5,000 naut mls (9,270km); range with 80,000lb (36,287kg) cargo payload, 3,150 naut mls (5,840km).

Weights: Operating weight empty, 146,400lb (66,406kg); max payload, 52,593lb (23,856kg); max cargo payload, 93,098lb (42,229kg); max fuel weight, 159,560lb (72,375kg); max take-off weight, 333,600lb (151,315kg); max landing weight, 247,000lb (112,037kg); max zero-fuel weight, 230,000lb (104,330kg).

Dimensions: Span, 145ft 9in (44.42m); overall length 152ft 11in (46.61m); overall height, 42ft 5in (12.93m); sweepback, 35 deg at quarter chord; wing area, 3,050sq ft (283.4m²).

Accommodation: Cabin length 111ft 4in (33.93m), max width, 11ft 8in (3.55m), max height, 7ft 8in (2.34m). Typical mixed-class layout for 14 first-class four-abreast plus a four-seat lounge, and 133 tourist-class six-abreast; max one-class layout for 189 six-abreast at 32in (81cm) pitch. Upper deck cargo volume, 5,693cu ft (161.21m³); underfloor cargo/baggage volume, 1,700cu ft (48.15m³). Flight crew of three.

(5,443kgp) JT3C-7 engines and extended chord on the inboard wing leading edges. The Model 720 first flew on 23 November 1959. In 1960 Boeing introduced versions of the Models 707 and 720 with the newly-developed JT3D turbofan engines, identified by a 'B' designation suffix: the Model 707-120B, with the aerodynamic refinements of the Model 720, first flew on 22 June 1960, and the first Model 720B flew on the 6 October 1960. The turbofan-engined Model 707-320B, which first flew on 31 January 1962, also had new low-drag wing tips with a span increase of 3ft 3½in (1.0m), slotted leading-edge flaps and improved trailing-edge flaps. The passenger/cargo convertible version, with side-loading cargo door, was designated Model 707-320C and flew on 19 February 1963. One Model 707 was flown (starting on 27 November 1979) with CFM56 turbofans, but a proposed retrofit programme for these engines did not proceed, and variants, some with lengthened fuselages, designated up to Model 707-820, also remained in the project stage.

SERVICE USE

The first model of the Boeing 707 was certificated on 23 September 1958 and revenue service was inaug-

Boeing 707-320C
Cutaway Drawing Key

1 Nose cone
2 Weather radar scanner
3 Glideslope aerial
4 Forward pressure bulkhead
5 Pitot head
6 Nose frames
7 Windscreen panels
8 Eyebrow windows
9 Overhead console
10 First officer's seat
11 Captain's seat
12 Forward frame
13 Twin nosewheels
14 Nosewheel doors
15 Nosewheel box
16 Drag struts
17 Navigator's table
18 Observer's seat
19 Navigator's seat
20 Navigator's overhead panel
21 Flight engineer's seat
22 Flight engineer's instrument panels
23 Flight deck entry door
24 Crew coat closet
25 Crew toilet
26 Crew galley/buffet
27 Spare life vest stowage
28 Radio (emergency) transmitter
29 Life raft stowage (2)
30 VHF aerial
31 Smoke and fume-proof curtain
32 Forward entry door, 24in (61cm) by 72in (183cm)
33 Escape slide stowage
34 Forward underfloor freight hold
35 Cabin floor level
36 Six cargo pallets, total volume 4,424cu ft (125.3m³)
37 Ball transfer mat (five segments)
38 Door actuator rams
39 Main cargo door (raised)
40 Engine intakes
41 Secondary inlet doors
42 Turbocompressor intakes
43 Turbocompressor outlets
44 Nacelle pylons
45 Leading-edge wing flaps
46 Main tank No 3, capacity 3,388 Imp gal (15,403l)
47 Fuel system dry bay
48 Vortex generators
49 Main tank No 4, capacity 1,934 Imp gal (8,793l)
50 Reserve tank, capacity 366 Imp gal (1,662l)
51 Vent surge tank
52 Starboard wingtip
53 Starboard outboard aileron
54 Aileron balance tab
55 Staboard outboard spoiler (extended)
56 Starboard outboard flap
57 Flap tracks
58 Aileron/spoiler actuator linkage
59 Starboard inboard aileron
60 Control tab
61 Starboard inboard flap
62 Starboard inboard spoiler (extended)
63 Life raft stowage (4)
64 Escape straps
65 Escape hatches/emergency exits, 20in (51cm) by 38in (97cm) (4)
66 Life raft attachment clips
67 Inter-cabin movable bulkhead
68 Access door (port walkway)
69 Fuselage frames
70 87-passenger tourist class cabin configuration, 34in (86cm) seat pitch
71 Four-abreast seating row (emergency exit stations)

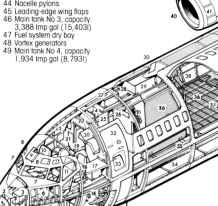

Above: Three-view drawing depicting the Boeing 707-320B fitted with Comtran hush-kits to comply with current noise regulations.

Left: The cockpit of a Boeing 707, showing the typical three-man layout with a sideways-facing seat for the flight engineer. Notice the array of controls and switches on the overhead panel.

urated by Pan American on 26 October across the North Atlantic. Key dates for other variants were: Model 707-220 certificated on 5 November 1959 and first service by Braniff on 20 December 1959; Model 707-320 certificated on 15 July 1959 and first service by Pan American on 10 October 1959; Model 707-420 certificated on 12 February 1960 and first service by BOAC in May 1960; Model 720 certificated on 30 June 1960 and first service by United on 5 July 1960; Model 707-120B certificated on 1 March 1961 and Model 720B on 3 March 1961, first services by American Airlines on 12 March 1961; and Model 707-320B certificated on 31 May 1962 and first services by Pan American in June 1963. Boeing built a total of 917 Model 707s (excluding airframes for the E-3 and E-6 military programmes), made up of 63 -120, 78 -120B, five -220, 69 -320, 174 -320B, 337 -320C, 37 -420, 65 -720 and 89 -720B variants.

Right: In service with Zambia Airways, the Boeing 707-351C 9J-AEB is typical of the aircraft of this type that have changed hands several times since new. The customer number gives a clue to the purchaser of the aircraft when built—in this case, '51' shows that it was Northwest Orient Airlines.

72 Ceiling air-conditioning
73 Passenger amenities
74 Rear cabin single-row seating
75 Cabin windows
76 Coat closet
77 Life raft stowage (2)
78 Spare life vests (and machete)
79 First-aid kit
80 Aft service door (starboard) 24in (61cm) by 84in (122cm)
81 Fin fillet
82 Starboard tailplane
83 VOR antenna
84 Removable fin leading edge
85 Rudder control linkage

86 Tailfin construction
87 Rudder 'Q' bellows
88 HF probe antenna
89 LORAN antenna
90 Rudder
91 Rudder control tab
92 Rudder anti-balance tab
93 Internal balance panel
94 Rudder flutter damper
95 Elevator torque tube
96 Rudder trim tab
97 Tail cone
98 Tailplane actuator tab
99 Elevator control tab
100 Port elevator
101 Port tailplane

102 Internal balance panel
103 Elevator linkage
104 Crank assembly
105 Elevator quadrant
106 Autopilot elevator servo
107 Tailfin spar/fuselage joints
108 Rear pressure bulkhead
109 Aft toilets (2)
110 Coat closet
111 Aft entry door
112 Escape slide stowage
113 Vestibule
114 Fuselage skinning
115 Aft underfloor freight hold
116 Wingroot fairing
117 Fillet flap

118 Landing gear trunnion
119 Undercarriage shock strut
120 Main undercarriage well
121 Side strut
122 Torsion links
123 Fuel tank end rib
124 Wing rear spar/fuselage pick-up point
125 Inboard wing stringers
126 Wing front spar/fuselage pick-up point
127 Fuselage centre tank forward face
128 Landing lights
129 Front spar
130 Four-wheel main landing gear

140 Starter
141 Primary thrust reverser cascade vanes
142 Wing anti-ice check valve
143 Wing anti-ice shut-off valve
144 Duct temperature sensor
145 Leading-edge wing flap
146 Dimpled inner skin
147 Rear spar
148 Leading-edge thermal anti-icing duct
149 Integral wing fuel tanks
150 Port inboard aileron
151 Control tab
152 Port outboard spoilers
153 Port outboard flap

Below: A cutaway drawing of the Boeing 707-320C, showing the forward side door of the convertible ('C') passenger/freight variant. The -320B was similar but did not have this door.

131 Port inboard spoilers
132 Port inboard flap
133 Vortex generators
134 Nacelle pylon
135 Turbocompressor
136 Engine intake
137 Pratt & Whitney JT3D turbofan
138 Fan thrust reverser doors
139 Engine fuel pump

154 Engine access doors (port and starboard)
155 Nacelle nose cowl
156 Nacelle structure
157 Strut/pylon attachment
158 Exhaust
159 Pylon/wing joint
160 Tab
161 Leading-edge anti-ice supply manifold
162 Port outboard aileron
163 Wing skinning
164 Port wingtip

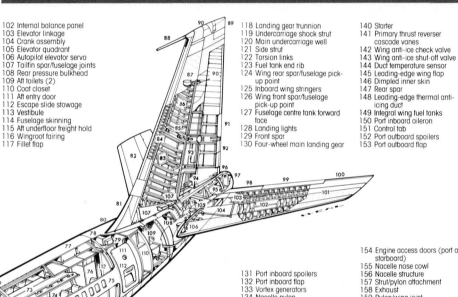

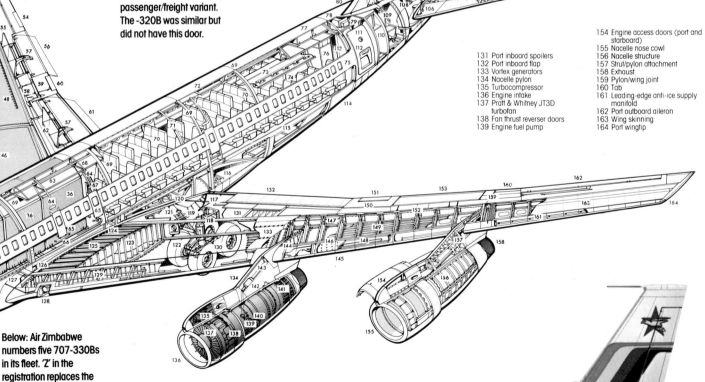

Below: Air Zimbabwe numbers five 707-330Bs in its fleet. 'Z' in the registration replaces the 'VP' used by Rhodesia.

BOEING 727-200 USA

SPECIFICATION

Power Plant: Three Pratt & Whitney JT8D turbofans, each rated at (-9A) 14,500lb st (6,577kgp) or (-11) 15,000 st (6,804kgp) or (-15) 15,500lb st (7031kgp) or (-17) 16,000lb st (7258kgp) or (-17R) 16,400lb st (7,439kgp) plus 1,000lb st (454kgp) through automatic performance reserve. Fuel capacity, 6,736Imp gal (30,623l) plus up to 546Imp gal (9,387l) in auxiliary fuel tanks.

Performance: Max operating speed, 350kts (649km/h) IAS or Mach = 0.88; max cruising speed, 530kts (983km/h) at 25,000ft (7,620m), long-range cruise, 467kts (866km/h) at 33,000ft (10,060m); initial cruising altitude, 33,000ft (10,060m); take-off distance (FAR, max weight option), 9,950ft (3,035m); landing distance (FAR), 4,900ft (1,495m); range with max payload, 2,140 naut mls (3,967km); range with max fuel and 27,500lb (12,474kg) payload 2,400 naut mls (4,449km).

Weights: Typical operating weight empty, 101,773lb (46,164kg); max fuel weight, 59,750lb (27,102kg); max payload, 41,000lb (18,598kg); max take-off weight, basic, 184,800lb (83,820kg); max take-off weight, optional, 190,500lb (86,405kg) or 209,500lb (95,027kg); max landing weight (first two take-off weights), 154,500lb (70,081kg) or (max optional take-off weight), 161,000lb (73,028kg); max zero-fuel weights for three take-off weights quoted, 138,000lb (62,595kg), 140,000lb (63,500kg) and 144,000lb (65,315kg).

Dimensions: Span, 108ft 0in (32.92m); overall length, 153ft 2in (46.69m); overall height, 34ft 0in (10.36m); sweepback, 32 deg at quarter chord; wing area, 1,700sq ft (157.9m²).

Accommodation: Cabin length, 92ft 8in (28.24m); max width, 11ft 8in (3.55m); max height, 6ft 11in (2.11m). Basic layout provides for 14 first-class passengers (four-abreast) and 131 tourist-class (six-abreast); max one-class layout for 189 passengers, six-abreast. Flight crew of 3.

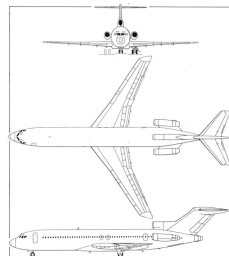

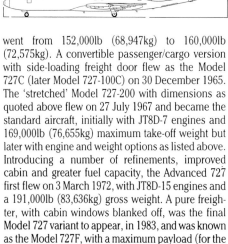

Above: Conceived only a few years after the Boeing 707, the 727's flight deck is only a little more advanced (unless modernised since delivery). As this photo shows, the three-man layout was retained.

Left: Three-view of the Boeing 727-200. Most of the 1,832 Boeing 727s were of this overall configuration, the -100 having a shorter fuselage and the final 15 Srs 200Fs having no windows.

Boeing Advanced 727-200 Cutaway Drawing Key

1 Radome
2 Radar dish
3 Radar scanner mounting
4 Pressure bulkhead
5 Windscreen panels
6 Instrument panel shroud
7 Back of instrument panel
8 Rudder pedals
9 Radar transmitter and receiver
10 Pitot tube
11 Cockpit floor control ducting
12 Control column
13 Pilot's seat
14 Cockpit eyebrow windows
15 Co-pilot's seat
16 Engineer's control panel
17 Flight engineer's seat
18 Cockpit door
19 Observer's seat
20 Nosewheel bay
21 Nosewheel doors
22 Twin nosewheels
23 Retractable airstairs (optional)
24 Handrail
25 Escape chute pack
26 Front entry door
27 Front toilet
28 Galley
29 Starboard galley service door
30 Cabin bulkhead
31 Closet
32 Window frame panel
33 Radio and electronics bay
34 First class passenger cabin, 18 seats in mixed layout
35 Cabin roof construction
36 Seat rails
37 Cabin floor beams
38 Cargo door
39 Anti-collision light
40 Air conditioning supply ducting
41 Forward cargo hold
42 Cargo hold floor
43 Baggage pallet container
44 Tourist class passenger cabin, 119 seats in mixed layout
45 Communications antenna
46 Fuselage frame and stringer construction

The Model 727 was the second member of the Boeing jet family to appear, design work on a 'junior partner' for the Boeing 707/720 series having begun a full two years before the first Model 707 entered service. Many possible configurations were studied before Boeing decided to adopt the tri-jet arrangement with one engine in the rear fuselage and the other two on the sides of the rear fuselage in pods. By the autumn of 1959 the design had been frozen, based on three Allison-built Rolls-Royce Speys (which had also been specified for the Hawker Siddeley Trident, launched in 1958 with a near-identical layout). By the time a launch decision was made on 5 December 1960, however, with orders for 40 aircraft each placed by Eastern and United Air Lines, Pratt & Whitney JT8D engines had been chosen, and these were destined to be used, in progressively more powerful versions, in every Model 727 built. The new airliner was designed to have as much commonality as possible with the Model 707, and this applied in particular to the entire upper lobe of the fuselage (from the cabin floor up), thus permitting closely-similar cabin layouts and fitments to be used. At the time of its launch, the Model 727 had the most advanced aerodynamics of any commercial aircraft, with greater wing sweepback than was then and is now common, and a combination of high-lift devices on the leading and trailing edges to ensure reasonable field performance. The first flight of the Model 727 was made on 9 February 1963, the second aircraft following on 12 March 1963.

VARIANTS

The original Model 727 production aircraft had an overall length of 133ft 2in (40.59m) and were later designated Model 727-100; engine options were the 14,000lb st (6,350kgp) JT8D-1 or -7, and the 14,500lb st (6,577kgp) JT8D-9, and maximum take-off weight

went from 152,000lb (68,947kg) to 160,000lb (72,575kg). A convertible passenger/cargo version with side-loading freight door flew as the Model 727C (later Model 727-100C) on 30 December 1965. The 'stretched' Model 727-200 with dimensions as quoted above flew on 27 July 1967 and became the standard aircraft, initially with JT8D-7 engines and 169,000lb (76,655kg) maximum take-off weight but later with engine and weight options as listed above. Introducing a number of refinements, improved cabin and greater fuel capacity, the Advanced 727 first flew on 3 March 1972, with JT8D-15 engines and a 191,000lb (83,636kg) gross weight. A pure freighter, with cabin windows blanked off, was the final Model 727 variant to appear, in 1983, and was known as the Model 727F, with a maximum payload (for the Federal Express 'small package' operation) of 58,750lb (26,650kg).

SERVICE USE

FAA Type Approval of the Model 727-100 was obtained on 24 December 1963, and the first revenue services were flown by Eastern on 1 February and by United on 6 February 1964. The first operator outside the USA was Lufthansa, on 16 April 1964. The Model 727C was certificated on 13 January 1966 and entered service with Northwest on 23 April 1966. Boeing obtained certification of the Model 727-200 on 29 November 1967, and Northwest flew the first service on 14 December, while All Nippon Airways was the first to fly the Advanced 727 in July 1972 following certification on 14 June. The first Model 727 with ATR on its JT8D-17R engines flew with Hughes Airwest on 27 May 1976, and Federal Express took delivery of the last Model 727 built, on 18 September 1984, bringing total production to 1,832 of all variants: 408 Srs 100 (including one test aircraft not delivered to a customer), 164 Srs 100C and QC (Quick Change), 1,245 Srs 200 and 15 Srs 200F.

47 Cabin window frame panels
48 Air conditioning system intake
49 Air conditioning plant
50 Overhead air ducting
51 Main fuselage frames
52 Escape hatches, port and starboard
53 Wing centre section No. 2 fuel tank
54 Centre section stringer construction
55 Cabin floor construction
56 Starboard wing No. 3 fuel tank
57 Inboard Krueger flaps
58 Krueger flap hydraulic jack
59 Leading edge fence

60 Outboard leading edge slat segments
61 Slat hydraulic jacks
62 Fuel vent surge tank
63 Navigation lights
64 Starboard wing tip
65 Fuel jettison pipe
66 Static dischargers
67 Outboard, low speed, aileron
68 Aileron balance tab
69 Outboard spoilers
70 Outboard slotted flap
71 Flap screw jack mechanism
72 Inboard, high speed, aileron
73 Trim tab
74 Inboard spoilers
75 Inboard slotted flap

76 Fuselage centre section construction
77 Pressurised floor over starboard main undercarriage bay
78 Auxiliary power unit (APU)
79 Port main undercarriage bay
80 Tourist class, six-abreast, passenger seating
81 Overhead hand baggage stowage bins
82 Cabin trim panels
83 Rear cargo door
84 Aft cargo compartment floor
85 Passenger overhead service panels
86 Starboard service door/rear emergency exit
87 Aft galleys
88 Closet
89 Toilets, port and starboard
90 Cabin rear entry door
91 Starboard engine cowling
92 Centre engine intake
93 Noise-attenuating intake lining
94 Intake S-duct
95 Duct de-icing

96 Fin root fairing construction
97 Fin construction
98 VOR aerial
99 Elevator control cables
100 Tailplane trim jack
101 Starboard tailplane
102 Elevator horn balance
103 Static dischargers
104 Starboard elevator
105 Elevator tab
106 Fin bullet fairing
107 VHF aerial boom
108 Elevator control jack
109 Port elevator
110 Tailplane construction
111 Port tailplane
112 Rudder upper section
113 Rudder control jacks

114 Rudder lower section
115 Lower section trim jack
116 Centre engine mounting pylon
117 Centre engine exhaust pipe
118 Thrust reverser
119 Centre engine
120 Rear fuselage construction
121 Side engine thrust reverser
122 Engine pylon fairing
123 Rear pressure bulkhead
124 Bleed air system pipes
125 Pratt & Whitney JT8D-9A trubofan engine
126 Detachable cowlings
127 Rear entry ventral airstairs
128 Engine air intake
129 Port rear service door/ emergency exit
130 Lower lobe fuselage frame construction

131 Trailing edge fillet
132 Inboard flap
133 Flap track fairings
134 Flap track mechanism
135 Inboard spoilers
136 Main undercarriage leg pivot
137 Retraction mechanism
138 Rear spar
139 Wing rib construction
140 Front spar
141 Leading edge construction
142 Landing and taxying lamp
143 De-icing air duct
144 Inboard Krueger flap segments
145 Landing lamp
146 Main undercarriage leg
147 Twin mainwheels
148 Wing stringer construction
149 Inboard, high speed, aileron
150 Aileron trim tab
151 Flaps down position
152 Outboard spoilers
153 No 1 wing integral fuel tank, total capacity 6,816 Imp gal (30,984l)
154 Re-fuelling connectors
155 Leading edge fence
156 Leading edge slat segments
157 Slat hydraulic jacks
158 Slat track mechanism
159 Outboard slotted trailing edge flap
160 Flap track fairings
161 Outboard flap track mechanism
162 Aileron balance tab
163 Outboard, low speed, aileron
164 Aileron control jack
165 Fuel vent surge tank
166 Port navigation lights
167 Static dischargers
168 Fuel jettison pipe

Above: Cutaway drawing of the Boeing 727-200 in its standard all-passenger configuration.

Above: Spain's national airline Iberia is one of more than 100 that purchased Boeing 727s during the 20 years the type was in production. Many users of the 727 have introduced new liveries — as shown here on Iberia's EC-DCC, one of 35 727-256s used by this operator in 1986.

Left: United Air Lines was one of the two US airlines whose orders placed in December 1960 launched the Boeing 727 into production. More than 150 were in the United fleet in 1986, including original short-body 727-22s, 727-222s and, as illustrated here in the revised United livery, Advanced 727-222s with improved interiors.

BOEING 737-200 USA

The Model 737 is the 'baby' of the Boeing jet-liner family and the third of the series of commercial jet transports to appear from the Seattle company. Boeing announced its intention to develop a twin jet with 80-100 seats in November 1964, by which time two other new types in a similar category, the BAC One-Eleven and the Douglas DC-9, were already well advanced. By contrast with its two rear-engined competitors, however, the Boeing design featured a more conventional layout with underwing engines and a low tailplane position; for commonality with the Models 707 and 727, Boeing also chose to use the same basic cabin cross-section (from the floor up), allowing comfortable six-abreast seating and interchangeability for passenger facilities, galley equipment, etc, for airlines using more than one of the Boeing jetliner types. Named Model 737 to continue the Boeing family of designations that had begun with the Model 707, the new type won a launch order from Lufthansa on 19 February 1965 – the first time that a non-US airline had been in the position of ordering a new American airliner that was not already in production for at least one major US operator. As launched, the Model 737 was sized for 100 seats and powered by 14,000lb st (6,350kgp) Pratt & Whitney JT8D-1 engines. The first flight, by a company-owned prototype, was made on 9 April 1967.

VARIANTS

Only 30 aircraft were built in the original Model 737-100 configuration, this version quickly being superseded by the Model 737-200, with a fuselage 'stretch' of 6ft (1.82m) to allow basic accommodation for 119 and, eventually, a maximum of 130. United Airlines was the first to order this variant, and the fifth example of the Model 737 to fly, on 8 August 1967, was the first stretched Model 737-200. Engine options for the -200 are shown in the data panel. A passenger/cargo convertible version, with a forward side door similar to that of the Model 727-200C, was flown in August 1968 and designated Model 737-200C. Aircraft from no.135 onwards introduced a series of modifications to the thrust reversers (switching from clamshell to target type) and wing flaps, and another series of changes to the leading-edge and trailing-edge devices, nacelle mountings and other items led to the introduction of the Advanced 737, whose first flight was made on 15 April 1971. The Model 737-200 first appeared at a maximum take-off weight of 97,000lb (43,999kg), but this has been progressively increased to the values quoted above. As noise regulations at airports became more stringent, Boeing introduced in 1973 a Quiet Nacelle modification, and an optional gravel runway kit was offered, including deflection shields on the main and nosewheel legs, fuselage abrasion protection, flap protection, blow-away jets beneath the engine intakes and other special features. Several schemes for stretching the Boeing 737 were studied during the late 1970s, eventually leading to the launch of the Model 737-300 as described separately. Several Model 737s have been sold as corporate or executive transports and the designation 77-32 is now used for aircraft in this role.

SERVICE USE

The Boeing 737-100 was certificated on 15 December 1967, and this variant entered service with

SPECIFICATION

Power Plant: Two Pratt & Whitney JT8D turbofans each rated at (-7) 14,000lb st (6,350kgp) or (-9) 14,500lb st (6,577kgp) or (-15/15A) 15,500lb st (7,031kgp) or (-17/17A) 16,000lb st (7,258kgp) or (-17R) 16,400lb st (7,439kgp) plus 1,000lb st (454kgp) with automatic thrust reserve. Standard fuel capacity, 4,297 Imp gal (19,532l) in integral tanks in wing and centre section; optional high weight versions have capacities of 4,621 Imp gal (21,009l) or 4,971 Imp gal (22,598l) with auxiliary tanks in aft underfloor cargo compartment.
Performance: Max operating speed, 350kts (649km/h) IAS or Mach = 0.84; max cruising speed, 488kts (905km/h) at 25,000ft (7,620m); long-range cruise, 420kts (779km/h) at 35,000ft (10,670m); take-off field length (FAR), 6,000ft (1,830m); landing field length (FAR), 4,430ft (1,350m); range with standard fuel and 115 passengers, 1,855 naut mls (3,439km); range, max high gross weight version (128,100lb, 58,106kg) with 115 passengers, 2,530 naut mls (4,690km).
Weights: Operating weight empty, 60,210lb (27,310kg); max payload, 34,790lb (15,781kg); max take-off weight, standard aircraft, 115,500lb (52,391kg); max take-off weight, optional high gross weight versions, 117,000lb (53,071kg) or 124,500lb (56,473kg) or 128,100lb (58,106kg); max landing weight, standard aircraft, 103,000lb (46,720kg); max landing weight, optional high gross weight versions, 105,000lb (47,627kg) or 107,000lb (48,534kg); max zero-fuel weight, 95,000lb (43,091kg); max zero-fuel weight option, -200 only, 99,000lb (44,906kg).
Dimensions: Span, 93ft 0in (28.35m); overall length, 100ft 2in (30.53m); height overall, 37ft 0in (11.28m); sweepback, 25 deg at quarter chord; wing area, 1,098sq ft (102.0m²).
Accommodation: Cabin length, 68ft 6in (20.88m), max width, 11ft 7in (3.53m), max height, 7ft 0in (2.13m). Basic arrangements provide seating for 115 passengers six-abreast at 34in (86cm) seat pitch, or 130 passengers at 30in (76cm) pitch. Underfloor freight/baggage holds volume, 875cu ft (24.78m³). Flight crew of two.

Lufthansa on 10 February 1968. Type Approval for the Model 737-200 followed quickly, on 21 December 1967, and United operated the first services on 28 April 1968. Wien Consolidated was the first operator of the Model 737-200C towards the end of 1968, after certification in October. The Advanced 737-200 gained its Type Approval on 3 May 1971, allowing all Nippon Airways to become the first operator of this model in June 1971; the first example with a 'wide look' interior was operated by Air Algeria in January 1972, and Eastern Provincial Airways was first to receive the Quiet Nacelle modification in October 1973. By the beginning of 1987, Boeing had sold 1,746 Model 737s of all variants, this total including 30 Srs 100 and 1,101 Srs 200 made up of 978 passenger aircraft and 104 Srs 200C convertibles for commercial and non-commercial customers, plus 19 T-43A navigation trainers. The price of a new Boeing 737-200 is currently in excess of $20 million.

Right: Cutaway drawing of the Boeing 737-200 showing some optional features – such as the gravel deflector on the nose wheel and vortex dissipator below the engine air intakes.

Below: The Boeing 737 serves a wide spectrum of airlines, some of which have 100+ fleets of the type while others, such as Air Pacific, have but a single example of the 'baby Boeing' in operation.

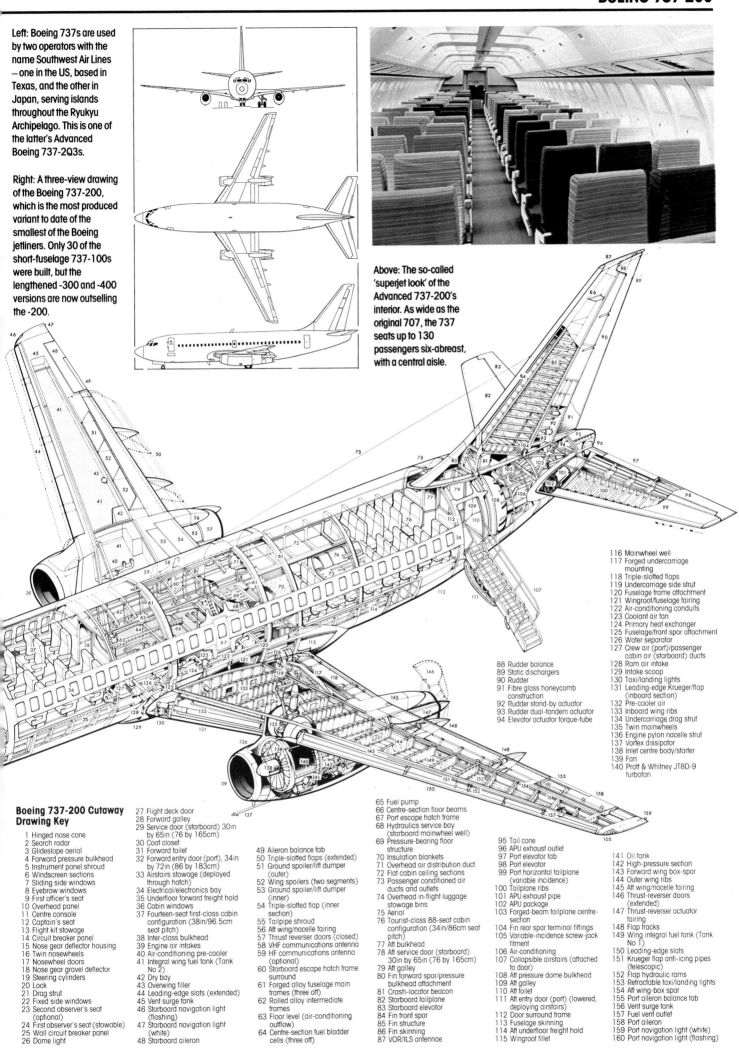

Left: Boeing 737s are used by two operators with the name Southwest Air Lines — one in the US, based in Texas, and the other in Japan, serving islands throughout the Ryukyu Archipelago. This is one of the latter's Advanced Boeing 737-2Q3s.

Right: A three-view drawing of the Boeing 737-200, which is the most produced variant to date of the smallest of the Boeing jetliners. Only 30 of the short-fuselage 737-100s were built, but the lengthened -300 and -400 versions are now outselling the -200.

Above: The so-called 'superjet look' of the Advanced 737-200's interior. As wide as the original 707, the 737 seats up to 130 passengers six-abreast, with a central aisle.

Boeing 737-200 Cutaway Drawing Key

1 Hinged nose cone
2 Search radar
3 Glideslope aerial
4 Forward pressure bulkhead
5 Instrument panel shroud
6 Windscreen sections
7 Sliding side windows
8 Eyebrow windows
9 First officer's seat
10 Overhead panel
11 Centre console
12 Captain's seat
13 Flight kit stowage
14 Circuit breaker panel
15 Nose gear deflector housing
16 Twin nosewheels
17 Nosewheel doors
18 Nose gear gravel deflector
19 Steering cylinders
20 Lock
21 Drag strut
22 Fixed side windows
23 Second observer's seat (optional)
24 First observer's seat (stowable)
25 Wall circuit breaker panel
26 Dome light
27 Flight deck door
28 Forward galley
29 Service door (starboard) 30in by 65in (76 by 165cm)
30 Coat closet
31 Forward toilet
32 Forward entry door (port), 34in by 72in (86 by 183cm)
33 Airstairs stowage (deployed through hatch)
34 Electrical/electronics bay
35 Underfloor forward freight hold
36 Cabin windows
37 Fourteen-seat first-class cabin configuration (38in/96.5cm seat pitch)
38 Inter-class bulkhead
39 Engine air intakes
40 Air-conditioning pre-cooler
41 Integral wing fuel tank (Tank No 2)
42 Dry bay
43 Overwing filler
44 Leading-edge slats (extended)
45 Vent surge tank
46 Starboard navigation light (flashing)
47 Starboard navigation light (white)
48 Starboard aileron
49 Aileron balance tab
50 Triple-slotted flaps (extended)
51 Ground spoiler/lift dumper (outer)
52 Wing spoilers (two segments)
53 Ground spoiler/lift dumper (inner)
54 Triple-slotted flap (inner section)
55 Tailpipe shroud
56 Aft wing/nacelle fairing
57 Thrust reverser doors (closed)
58 VHF communications antenna
59 HF communications antenna (optional)
60 Starboard escape hatch frame surround
61 Forged alloy fuselage main frames (three off)
62 Rolled alloy intermediate frames
63 Floor level (air-conditioning outflow)
64 Centre-section fuel bladder cells (three off)
65 Fuel pump
66 Centre-section floor beams
67 Port escape hatch frame
68 Hydraulics service bay (starboard mainwheel well)
69 Pressure-bearing floor structure
70 Insulation blankets
71 Overhead air distribution duct
72 Flat cabin ceiling sections
73 Passenger conditioned air ducts and outlets
74 Overhead in-flight luggage stowage bins
75 Aerial
76 Tourist-class 88-seat cabin configuration (34in/86cm seat pitch)
77 Aft bulkhead
78 Aft service door (starboard) 30in by 65in (76 by 165cm)
79 Aft galley
80 Fin forward spar/pressure bulkhead attachment
81 Crash-locator beacon
82 Starboard tailplane
83 Starboard elevator
84 Fin front spar
85 Fin structure
86 Fin skinning
87 VOR/ILS antennae
88 Rudder balance
89 Static dischargers
90 Rudder
91 Fibre glass honeycomb construction
92 Rudder stand-by actuator
93 Rudder dual-tandem actuator
94 Elevator actuator torque-tube
95 Tail cone
96 APU exhaust outlet
97 Port elevator tab
98 Port elevator
99 Port horizontal tailplane (variable incidence)
100 Tailplane ribs
101 APU exhaust pipe
102 APU package
103 Forged-beam tailplane centre-section
104 Fin rear spar terminal fittings
105 Variable-incidence screw-jack fitment
106 Air-conditioning
107 Collapsible airstairs (attached to door)
108 Aft pressure dome bulkhead
109 Aft galley
110 Aft toilet
111 Aft entry door (port) (lowered, deploying airstairs)
112 Door surround frame
113 Fuselage skinning
114 Aft underfloor freight hold
115 Wingroot fillet
116 Mainwheel well
117 Forged undercarriage mounting
118 Triple-slotted flaps
119 Undercarriage side strut
120 Fuselage frame attachment
121 Wingroot/fuselage fairing
122 Air-conditioning conduits
123 Coolant air fan
124 Primary heat exchanger
125 Fuselage/front spar attachment
126 Water separator
127 Crew air (port)/passenger cabin air (starboard) ducts
128 Ram air intake
129 Intake scoop
130 Taxi/landing lights
131 Leading-edge Krueger/flap (inboard section)
132 Pre-cooler air
133 Inboard wing ribs
134 Undercarriage drag strut
135 Twin mainwheels
136 Engine pylon nacelle strut
137 Vortex dissipator
138 Inlet centre body/starter
139 Fan
140 Pratt & Whitney JT8D-9 turbofan
141 Oil tank
142 High-pressure section
143 Forward wing box-spar
144 Outer wing ribs
145 Aft wing/nacelle fairing
146 Thrust-reverser doors (extended)
147 Thrust-reverser actuator fairing
148 Flap tracks
149 Wing integral fuel tank (Tank No 1)
150 Leading-edge slats
151 Krueger flap anti-icing pipes (telescopic)
152 Flap hydraulic rams
153 Retractable taxi/landing lights
154 Aft wing-box spar
155 Port aileron balance tab
156 Vent surge tank
157 Fuel vent outlet
158 Port aileron
159 Port navigation light (white)
160 Port navigation light (flashing)

BOEING 737-300 USA

SPECIFICATION

Power Plant: Two CFM International CFM56-3B1 turbofans each rated at 20,000lb st (9,072kgp) or CFM56-3B2 turbofans each rated at 22,000lb st (9,980kgp) for take-off. Fuel capacity, 4,422 Imp gal (20,104l) in integral tanks in wings and centre section, with optional capacity of 674 Imp gal (3,066l) in tanks in aft underfloor cargo bay.
Performance: Max operating speed, 340kts (630km/h) IAS or Mach = 0.82; max cruising speed, 491kts (908km/h) at 26,000ft (7,925m); long-range cruising speed, 429kts (794km/h) at 35,000ft (10,670m); take-off field length (FAR), 6,360ft (1,940m); landing field length (FAR), 4,580ft (1,395m); range with max payload, 950 naut mls (1,760km); range with 141 passengers, standard fuel and US domestic reserves, 1,390 naut mls (2,570km); range with 141 passengers, max optional fuel and US domestic reserves, 2,350 naut mls (4,353km).
Weights: Operating weight empty, 69,580lb (31,561kg); max payload, 35,420lb (16,067kg); max take-off weight, basic aircraft, 124,500lb (56,473kg); max take-off weight, optional, 135,000lb (61,235kg); max landing weight; 114,000lb (51,710kg); max zero fuel weight (for two take-off weights quoted), 105,000lb (47,628kg) and 106,500lb (48,308kg).
Dimensions: Span, 94ft 9in (28.88m); overall length, 109ft 7in (33.40m); overall height, 36ft 6in (11.13m); sweepback, 25 deg at quarter chord; wing area, 1,135sq ft (105.4m²).
Accommodation: Cabin length, 77ft 2in (23.52m), max width, 11ft 4in (3.45m), max height, 7ft 0in (2.13m). Typical mixed-class layout for eight passengers four-abreast and 120 tourist six-abreast at 32in (81cm) pitch, or one-class layout for 141 passengers six-abreast at 32in (81cm) pitch or maximum of 149 six-abreast at 30in (76cm) pitch. Underfloor baggage/freight volume 1,068cu ft (30.24m³). Flight crew of two.

Development of a stretched version of the Boeing 737 began in 1979, when market studies began to show the need for what Boeing was later to describe as 'a longer-bodied version of the popular 737 twinjet, designed to burn less fuel per passenger and provide reduced noise levels for the short-haul markets of 1985 and beyond'. As has been the case with many programmes to 'stretch' an existing aircraft, the exact degree of lengthening that was desirable remained open to question for some time, as airline reactions were studied and launch customers sought. By early 1980, the Model 737-300 designation had been adopted for the proposal and, when details were published by Boeing in the course of the Farnborough Air Show later that year, a stretch of 84in (2.13m) was indicated, compared with earlier studies that provided for a lengthening of only 40in (1.02m). However much the aircraft was lengthened, engines more advanced and more powerful than the JT8Ds used in the Model 737-200 were needed, with fuel efficiency and low noise levels the two most important characteristics. As plans for the Model 737-300 were confirmed, it became clear that the choice of engine lay between the CFM56, which could be developed in a version of suitable thrust, or the RJ500, a proposed new engine which Rolls-Royce in the UK and JAE in Japan hoped to launch, based on Rolls-Royce's earlier work on the RB.432. When the RJ500 itself became submerged in the V2500 turbofan under develop-

ment by IAE, a consortium in which both Rolls-Royce and JAE became members, the CFM56 became the only engine that could be available for the Model 737-300 in the proposed timescale. The latter, based on launch orders announced in March 1981 from US Air and Southwest Airlines, was established with an entry into service date of late 1984. By the time of the launch, the fuselage had grown again, by a further 20in (0.51m), with a 44in (1.12m) plug ahead of the wing and a 60in (1.52m) plug aft of it. This allowed the maximum seating to be increased to 149 and gave the Model 737-300 some 21 more seats than the Model 737-200 in a comparable all-tourist layout. Apart from (and to some extent because of) the higher weights at which the Model 737-300 was to operate, some airframe modifications were made, including wing tip extensions that added 9in (23cm) to each tip, some changes to the leading-edge slots, revised trailing-edge 'flipper' flaps and flap track fairings, an addition to the dorsal fin area, and a lengthened nosewheel leg to provide adequate ground clearance for the engines. To fit the larger-diameter CFM56 engines under the wings, their accessory drives were located on the sides of the engines, resulting in a somewhat unusual flat-bottomed nacelle shape. The first Model 737-300, destined for delivery eventually to US Air, flew at Seattle on 24 February 1984, with second and third aircraft flying on 2 March and 4 May.

VARIANTS
The Model 737-300 is available at two maximum weights, the higher weight being required when the optional fuel tanks are carried in the aft cargo bay. Uprated CFM56-3B2 engines are available for operation in 'hot and high' conditions. Corporate/executive versions of the stretched aircraft carry the designation 77-33. Since launching the Model 737-300, Boeing has considered a number of ways of extending the market for the Model 737, including further stretches of the fuselage. At the project stage, these included a Model 737-500 (also known at one stage as the Model 737-300L) with extra fuselage length to seat another 17 passengers, and a Model

737-400 (sometimes known as the Model 737-100L) which was to be a shortened version with CFM56-3B4 engines. The latter was intended particularly to meet a US Air requirement, and when this airline ordered Fokker 100s, the Model 737-400 designation was switched to the lengthened derivative, for which a launch order was obtained from Piedmont Airlines on 4 June 1986. As then defined, the Model 737-400 has a 9ft 6in (2.9m) fuselage stretch to offer an all coach-class layout for 156 passengers. With 22,000lb st (9,979kgp) CFM56-3B2 engines, the Model 737-400 has a gross weight of 150,000lb (68,040kg), and other changes include a tail-down rubbing strip under the rear fuselage, new Krüger flaps outboard of the engine nacelles, extra emergency exits and some changes in the galley layout. The date of the Model 737-400's first flight was set for January 1988, with deliveries to Piedmont to start in September 1988.

SERVICE USE
FAA certification of the Model 737-300 was obtained on 14 November 1984, and Boeing began delivering the new variant on the 28th day of that month, when US Air accepted its first aircraft, followed two days later by Southwest Airlines, first acceptance. The latter operator flew the first revenue services on 7 December 1984, with US Air following on 18 December. The first delivery to a non-US customer was made to Orion Airways in the UK on 29 January 1985, with service entry on 22 February, and Pakistan Airlines took delivery of the first Model 737-300 with the uprated -3B2 engines on 31 May 1985, for first service on 1 July. By early 1987, Boeing had sold 549 of the Model 737-300 model to 36 customers. Sales of the 737-400 totalled 66. The price is in the bracket of $25 to $30 million.

Right: The Boeing 737-300 differs from the 737-200 in having a lengthened fuselage and more powerful CFM International CFM56 engines.

Above: The flight deck of the Boeing 737-300 has been designed to take advantage of 'eighties technology and Boeing's experience in developing the 757 and 767 for two-crew operation. A fully-integrated flight management system is fitted.

Below: Texas-based Southwest Airlines began operating in 1971 with Boeing Advanced 737-200s. Since then, its fleet of -200s has grown to 46, to which the company has recently added more than 30 of the -300 variants.

Boeing 737-300 Cutaway Drawing Key

1 Radome
2 Weather radar scanner
3 Scanner tracking mechanism
4 Lightning conductor strips
5 ILS glideslope aerial
6 Front pressure bulkhead
7 Rudder pedals
8 Control column
9 Instrument panel
10 Instrument panel shroud
11 Windscreen wipers
12 Windscreen panels
13 Overhead systems switch panel
14 Co-pilot's seat
15 Cockpit eyebrow windows
16 Pilot's seat
17 Nosewheel steering control
18 Flight bag stowage
19 Nose undercarriage wheel bay
20 Nosewheel doors
21 Twin nosewheels
22 Torque scissor links
23 Nosewheel steering jacks
24 Nose undercarriage pivot fixing
25 Pitot heads (2)
26 Crew wardrobe
27 Observer's folding seat
28 Cockpit doorway
29 Forward galley unit
30 Starboard side service door
31 Toilet compartment
32 Forward entry door, open
33 Door latch
34 Escape chute stowage
35 Retractable airstairs
36 Folding handrail
37 Entry lobby
38 Cabin attendant's folding seat
39 First-class cabin, four-abreast seating (eight-passengers)
40 Overhead stowage bins
41 Curtained cabin divider
42 Passenger emergency oxygen bottles
43 Underfloor avionics equipment bay
44 Cabin window panels
45 Seat rail support structure
46 Lower VHF aerial
47 Forward underfloor freight/baggage hold, capacity 425cu ft (12.03m³)
48 Forward freight hold door
49 Overhead air conditioning distribution ducting
50 Tourist class cabin, six-abreast seating (114 to 120 passengers)
51 Air system ducting
52 Wing inspection light
53 Conditioned air riser
54 Wing root leading edge fillet
55 Ventral air conditioning intake
56 Landing and taxying lamps
57 Wing panel/fuselage bolted root joint
58 Ventral air conditioning pack, port and starboard
59 Centre section fuel tanks
60 Floor beam construction
61 Front spar/fuselage main frame
62 Anti-collision light
63 Starboard nacelle pylon
64 Starboard engine nacelle
65 Engine air intake
66 Hinged cowling panels
67 Pressure refuelling connection
68 Starboard wing integral fuel tank. Total system capacity 4,422 Imp gal (20,104l)
69 Fuel venting channels
70 Overwing fuel filler cap
71 Vortex generators
72 Leading-edge slat segments, open
73 Slat drive shaft
74 Screw jacks
75 Guide rails
76 Vent surge tank
77 Wing tip fairing
78 Starboard navigation light (green) and strobe light (white)
79 Tail navigation light (white)
80 Starboard aileron
81 Aileron hinge control
82 Aileron tab
83 Outboard triple-slotted Fowler-type flap, down position
84 Flap guide rails
85 Screw jacks
86 Flap track fairings
87 Outboard (flight) spoilers, open
88 Spoiler hydraulic jacks
89 Nacelle tail fairing
90 Inboard flap screw jack
91 Inboard (ground) spoiler, open
92 Fuselage skin panelling
93 Upper VHF aerial
94 Centre fuselage frame and stringer construction
95 Emergency exit window hatches, port and starboard
96 Pressure floor above starboard wheel bay
97 Cabin soundproofing lining
98 Rear spar/fuselage main frame
99 Overhead stowage bins
100 Passenger service units
101 Cabin roof lighting panels
102 Rear freight hold door
103 Cockpit voice recorder
104 Cabin wall trim panelling
105 Cabin roof frames
106 Rear cabin tourist class seating
107 Starboard side rear galley unit
108 Fin root fillet construction
109 Fin spar attachment joints
110 Optional flush HF aerial
111 Starboard tailplane
112 Starboard elevator mass balance
113 Fin rib construction
114 VOR aerial
115 Fin tip aerial fairing
116 Rudder mass balance
117 Static dischargers
118 Rudder
119 Honeycomb rudder panel construction
120 Rudder hydraulic actuators
121 Tailcone
122 Rear position light (white)
123 Elevator tab
124 Port elevator honeycomb construction
125 Elevator mass balance
126 Static dischargers
127 Port tailplane construction
128 APU exhaust duct
129 Elevator hinge control
130 Trimming tailplane pivot fixing
131 Garrett GTCP85-129(C) Auxiliary Power Unit (APU)
132 Fin/tailplane support main frame
133 Tailplane trim screw jack
134 APU intake duct
135 Rear pressure dome
136 Rear toilet compartments, port and starboard
137 Rear entry and service doors, port and starboard
138 Cabin attendant's folding seat
139 Wardrobe/closet
140 Rear cabin window panels
141 Rear underfloor freight/baggage hold, capacity 643cu ft (18.21m³)
142 Rear fuselage frame and stringer construction
143 DME aerial
144 Wing root trailing-edge fillet
145 ADF sense aerial
146 Central flap drive hydraulic motor
147 Port main undercarriage wheel bay
148 Main undercarriage mounting beam
149 Hydraulic retraction jack
150 Spoiler hydraulic jack
151 Inboard (ground) spoiler
152 Inboard triple-slotted Fowler-type flap
153 Flap guide rails and screw jacks
154 Flap down position
155 Flap thrust gate segments
156 Nacelle tail fairing
157 Outboard triple-slotted Fowler-type flap
158 Outboard flap screw jacks and guide rails
159 Outboard four-segment (flight) spoilers
160 Flap track fairings
161 Flap down position
162 Aileron tab
163 Port aileron
164 Fixed portion of trailing-edge
165 Static dischargers
166 Tail navigation light (white)
167 Port navigation light (red) and strobe light (white)
168 Leading-edge slat segments, open
169 Slat screw jacks
170 Guide rails
171 Telescopic de-icing air ducts
172 Front spar
173 Port wing integral fuel tank
174 Wing rib construction
175 Rear spar
176 Wing stringers
177 Wing skin panelling
178 Engine pylon mounting ribs
179 Twin mainwheels
180 Main undercarriage leg strut
181 Undercarriage leg-pivot mounting
182 Inboard wing rib construction
183 Engine bleed air ducting
184 Krueger flap jacks
185 Inboard two-segment Krueger flaps, open
186 Nacelle strake
187 Nacelle pylon construction
188 Intake lip de-icing air duct
189 Port engine air intake
190 CFM International CFM56-3 turbofan engine
191 Engine fan casing
192 Laterally mounted accessory equipment gearbox
193 Thrust reverser cascades
194 Engine turbine section
195 Fan air (cold stream) exhaust duct
196 Core engine (hot stream) exhaust duct
197 Tailcone fairing
198 Cowling open position to expose reverser cascades

Below: A 737-300 in service with Lufthansa, who helped to launch the original Boeing 737.

Right: A three-view drawing of the 737-300. The -400 will have a longer fuselage with the same engines.

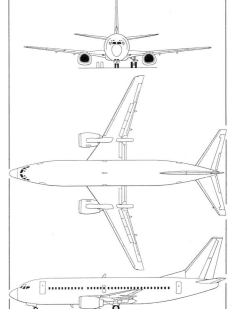

Boeing's development of its fourth individual jetliner design, and the largest built to date, began in the early 1960s as a by-product, in the first instance, of the work done on a large military logistics transport, the CH-X. When Lockheed won the military order with the C-5A Galaxy, Boeing studied civil alternatives of its military project, with 'double-bubble' fuselage arrangements and a mid-wing layout, but eventually adopted a more orthodox Model 707-type configuration, though at much larger scale. The design that became the Model 747 then evolved around the concept of a single main deck, wide enough over most of its length for 10-abreast seating with two aisles, whilst the flight deck was at a higher level, with a small passenger cabin in the fuselage behind it and reached by a spiral staircase from the main deck. By 1965, the basic concept of this very large jetliner, with seating for up to 500 passengers, had been settled and the all-new Pratt & Whitney JT9D turbofan chosen to power it. The launch order, from Pan American, came on 14 April 1966, and the production go-ahead was given in July after orders were placed by Lufthansa and JAL. The first flight was made on 9 February 1969 at Everett, Washington, where Boeing established a completely new production facility for the massive new transport, which soon became known as the Jumbo Jet. Subsequent evolution of the design has produced a number of variants as set out below, most of which have retained the same external dimensions and shapes of the original. The Model 747-300 with a longer upper deck, the Model 747-400 with this same upper deck plus an extended wing and winglets, and possible further stretches of the basic Model 747, are described separately.

VARIANTS

The original Boeing 747 was introduced with JT9D-1 or -3 engines at 43,500lb st (19,732kgp) and a certificated gross weight of 710,000lb (322,050kg). Other engines used were the JT9D-3A, -3W, -7 and -7W, and higher gross weights were approved in due course. These early variants all became the Model 747-100 when the designation Model 747-200 was adopted for a version first flown on 11 October 1970 as the Boeing 747B, with increased weight, more fuel and uprated engines. A reduced gross weight,

shorter-range version introduced in 1973 as the Model 747SR later became the Model 747-100B and is used primarily in Japan. Versions of the Model 747-200 were developed as pure freighters (Model 747F) or convertible passenger/freighter (Model 747C) with upward-hinged nose for straight-in freight loading; the first Model 747F flew on 30 November 1971, and the first Model 747C on 23 March 1973. A version with a large side-loading freight door aft of the wing appeared in 1974 as the Model 747M Combi, sometimes combined with the nose-loading door. All the foregoing Model 747 variants are dimensionally similar, but the Model 747SP (Special Performance), first flown on 4 July 1975, has a fuselage shortened by 48ft (14.6m) for a typical mixed-class accommodation of 288, and a taller fin and rudder, together with other less obvious changes. Retaining the full tankage of the basic aircraft, the Model 747SP achieves a full-payload range of 5,750 naut mls (10,660km). There have been a number of increases in the maximum permitted weights of the basic Model 747-200, hand-in-hand with the introduction of more powerful engines, including the options quoted above. Other engine variants applicable have included the JT9D-7J, -7Q, -7AW and -7O, the CF6-50D, -50E and -45AZ, and the RB.211-524B2 and -524C2.

SERVICE USE

The Model 747 was originally certificated on 30 December 1969, and Pan American put the 'jumbo' into service across the North Atlantic on 21 January 1970. The Model 747-200 was certificated on 23 December 1970 and entered service with KLM early in 1971. Type Approval of the Model 747F was obtained on 7 March 1972 and service use by Lufthansa began on 19 April 1972; and the Model 747C convertible with nose-loading door entered service with World Airways after certification on 24 April 1973, while Sabena was first to operate the Model 747M Combi in 1974. The 'lightweight' Model 747SR entered service with Japan Air Lines on 9 October 1973, and the short-body Model 747SP with Pan American in May 1976. By early 1987, sales of these variants totalled 635, comprising 176 -100/-100B, 27 -100SR, 243 -200, 13 -200C, 58 -200F, 74 -200M and 44 Model 747SP aircraft.

SPECIFICATION

Power Plant: Four Pratt & Whitney JT9D-7R4G2 turbofans each rated at 54,750lb st (24,835kgp), or General Electric CF6-50E2 turbofans each rated at 52,500lb st (23,814kgp), or Rolls-Royce RB.211-524D4 turbofans each rated at 53,110lb st (24,091kgp). Fuel capacity, 43,641 Imp gal (198,390l) in integral tanks in wings and centre section, plus 1,312 Imp gal (5,966l) in two optional outboard reserve tanks, plus 1,432 Imp gal (6,511l) in optional fuselage tank.
Performance: Max operating speed, 375kts (695km/h) IAS or Mach = 0.92; max cruising speed, 507kts (940km/h) at 35,000ft (10,670m); long-range cruise, 484kts (897km/h) at 35,000ft (10,670m); cruise ceiling, 45,000ft (13,715m); take-off field length (FAR), 10,400ft (3,170m); landing field length (FAR), 6,950ft (2,120m); range with full passenger payload, 6,150 naut mls (11,402km); range with max fuel, 7,100 naut mls (13,163km).
Weights: Operating weight empty, 375,170lb (170,180kg); max fuel, 353,760lb (160,463kg); max payload, 151,500lb (68,719kg); max take-off, basic aircraft, 800,000lb (362,875kg); max take-off, optional, 820,000lb (371,945kg) or 833,000lb (377,840kg); max landing, for take-off weights quoted above, 564,000lb (255,825kg), or 585,000lb (265,350kg) or 630,000lb (285,765kg) respectively; max zero-fuel weight, all options, 526,500lb (238,815kg).
Dimensions: Span, 195ft 8in (59.64m); overall length, 231ft 10in (70.66m); overall height, 63ft 5in (19.33m); sweepback, 37 deg 30 min at quarter chord; wing area, 5,500sq ft (510.95m²).
Accommodation: Cabin length, 187ft 0in (57.00m), max width, 20ft 1½in (6.13m), max height, 8ft 4in (2.54m). Basic layout provides 32 first-class and 420 economy-class seats including 32 on upper deck; alternative one-class layouts for 447 nine-abreast or 516 10-abreast, all with twin aisles. Underfloor baggage/cargo volume, 5,190cu ft (146.96m³). Flight crew of three.

Below: Air Canada is one of some 70 airlines around the world now operating the Boeing 747. Three early 747-100s (as illustrated here) have been joined by a pair of 747-233B Combis.

Left: Japanese Air Lines has provided a major market for Boeing, with the 747 and smaller types. Shown here is the first 747-200 acquired by All Nippon Airways, which already had 20 747-100s and freighters in service.

Left: About five per cent of all Boeing 747s built to date have been of the SP (Special Performance) version, featuring a shorter fuselage than the standard -100 and -200 variants. This illustration shows one of the four SPs acquired by China's Civil Aviation Administration in 1980. A similarly-shortened version of the advanced 747-400 was under study by Boeing in 1987, to compete with the McDonnell Douglas MD-11.

Right: Three-view drawing of the Boeing 747-200. The -100 variants are externally similar and the SP has the same wing.

Boeing 747-200 Combi Cutaway Drawing Key

1 Radome
2 Weather radar scanner
3 Forward pressure bulkhead
4 Radar scanner mounting
5 Nose visor cargo door
6 First class passenger cabin
7 Typically, 32 seats in forward cabin
8 Nose visor hydraulic jack
9 Visor hinge fixing
10 Rudder pedals
11 Control column
12 Instrument panel shroud
13 Curved windscreen panels
14 Co-pilot's seat
15 Flight engineer's control panel
16 Cockpit doorway
17 Observers' seats (2)
18 Captain's seat
19 Cockpit floor level
20 First class bar unit
21 Window panel
22 Nose undercarriage wheel bay
23 Nosewheel doors
24 Twin nosewheels, forward retracting
25 Steering hydraulics jacks
26 Underfloor avionics equipment racks
27 Circular staircase between decks
28 Upper deck crew door, port and starboard
29 Cockpit air conditioning
30 First class galley
31 First class toilet
32 Plug-type forward cabin door, No. 1
33 First class passenger seating
34 Cabin dividing bulkhead
35 Upper deck window panel
36 Upper deck toilet
37 Anti-collision light
38 Cabin roof construction
39 Upper deck galley
40 Upper deck passenger seating, up to 32 seats
41 Air conditioning supply ducts
42 Forward fuselage frame construction
43 Baggage pallet containers
44 Forward underfloor freight compartment
45 Air conditioning system ram air intake
46 Wing root fairing
47 Ventral air conditioning plant, port and starboard
48 No. 2 passenger door, port and starboard
49 Lower deck forward galley
50 Upper deck galley
51 Meal trolley elevator
52 Communications aerial
53 Forward tourist-class cabin, typically 141 seats
54 Fuselage frame and stringer construction
55 Cabin floor beam construction
56 Centre-wing section skin/stringer panel
57 Fresh water tanks
58 Wing spar bulkhead
59 Wing centre-section fuel tank, capacity 14,154 Imp gal (64,345l)
60 Front spar attachment fuselage main frame
61 Air conditioning cross-feed ducts
62 Air distribution duct
63 Risers to distribution ducts
64 Wing centre spar attachment main frame
65 Satellite navigation aerial
66 Fuselage skin panelling
67 Starboard wing inboard fuel tank, capacity 10,240 Imp gal (46,555l)
68 Fuel pumps
69 Engine bleed air supply duct
70 Krueger flap operating jacks
71 Inboard Krueger flap
72 Starboard inner engine nacelle
73 Inboard engine pylon
74 Leading edge Krueger flap flap segments
75 Krueger flap drive shaft
76 Ventral refueling panel
77 Krueger flap motors
78 Starboard wing outboard fuel tank, capacity 3,680 Imp gal (16,730l)
79 Starboard outer engine nacelle
80 Outboard engine pylon
81 Outboard Krueger flap segments
82 Krueger flap drive mechanism
83 Extended range fuel tank, capacity 666 Imp gal (3,028l)
84 Surge tank
85 Wing tip fairing
86 Starboard navigation light
87 VHF aerial boom
88 Fuel vent
89 Static dischargers
90 Outboard, low-speed, aileron
91 Outboard spoilers
92 Outboard slotted flaps
93 Flap drive mechanism
94 Inboard, high-speed, aileron
95 Trailing edge beam
96 Inboard spoilers/lift dumpers
97 Inboard slotted flap
98 Flap screw jack
99 Centre fuselage construction
100 Pressure floor above starboard wheel bay
101 Wing-mounted main undercarriage wheel bay
102 Central flap drive motors
103 Undercarriage mounting beam
104 No. 3 passenger door, port and starboard
105 Fuselage-mounted main undercarriage wheel bay
106 Hydraulic retraction jack
107 Wheel bay pressure bulkhead
108 Cargo net
109 Rear underfloor freight hold
110 Freight and baggage container, LD-1
111 Cargo loading deck
112 Roller conveyor floor tracks
113 Cabin wall trim panelling
114 Rear cabin air supply duct
115 Control cable runs
116 Rear fuselage frame and stringer construction
117 Upper deck freight containers, M1
118 Rear toilet compartments
119 Fin root fairing
120 Starboard tailplane
121 Static dischargers
122 Starboard elevator
123 Fin leading edge construction
124 Fin spar construction
125 Fin tip fairing
126 VOR aerial
127 Static dischargers
128 Upper rudder segment
129 Lower rudder segment
130 Rudder hydraulic jacks
131 Tailcone fairing
132 APU exhaust
133 Auxiliary Power Unit (APU)
134 Port elevator inner segment
135 Elevator outer segment
136 Static dischargers
137 Tailplane construction
138 Elevator hydraulic jacks
139 Tailplane sealing plate
140 Tailcone fram construction
141 Fin attachment joint
142 Tailplane centre section
143 Trimming tailplane screw jack
144 APU air duct
145 No. 5 passenger door, port and starboard
146 Stowage lockers, port and starboard
147 Rear fuselage window panel
148 Side loading cargo door, open
149 Cargo doorway 10ft (3.05m) x 11ft 2in (3.4m)
150 No. 4 passenger door, port and starboard
151 Fuselage lower lobe frame and stringer construction
152 Trailing edge wing root fillet
153 Fuselage mounted main undercarriage pivot fixing
154 Trailing edge beam
155 Port inboard slotted flap
156 Flap tracks
157 Flap track fairings
158 Inboard spoilers/lift dumpers
159 Flap drive shaft
160 Flap down position
161 Fuselage-mounted four-wheel main undercarriage bogie
162 Wing spar and rib construction
163 Wing root bolted attachment joint
164 Front spar
165 Engine bleed air supply duct
166 Leading-edge ribs
167 Upper Krueger flap
168 Inboard Krueger flap
169 Krueger flap motor and drive
170 Wing-mounted main undercarriage leg strut
171 Four-wheel main undercarriage bogie
172 Mainwheel leg side brace
173 Wing-mounted undercarriage hydraulic retraction jack
174 Wing skin panelling
175 Wing stringer construction
176 Inboard engine mounting rib
177 Pylon attachment strut
178 Inboard engine pylon
179 Pylon construction
180 Detachable engine cowling panels
181 Engine air intake
182 General Electric CF6-50 turbofan engine
183 Engine accessory equipment gearbox
184 Fan air, cold-stream, exhaust duct
185 Engine turbine section
186 Core engine, hot-stream, exhaust nozzle
187 Port wing integral fuel tankage
188 Inboard, high-speed aileron
189 Aileron hydraulic actuator
190 Outboard slotted flap
191 Flap track fairing
192 Outboard flap, down position
193 Outboard spoilers
194 Flap tracks
195 Flap track mounting beams
196 Wing spar and rib construction
197 Leading air rib construction
198 Krueger flap segments
199 Krueger flap hinge mechanism
200 Outboard engine mounting rib
201 Port outer engine pylon
202 Outer engine cowling panels
203 Thrust reverser cascades
204 Thrust reverser cowling door, open
205 Door operating jacks
206 Outboard Krueger flap segments
207 Krueger flap hinge mechanism
208 Outer wing panel construction
209 Aileron hydraulic actuators
210 Outboard, low-speed, aileron
211 Static dischargers
212 Fuel vent
213 Wing tip fairing
214 Port navigation light
215 VHF aerial boom

Above: A cutaway of the 747-200 Combi with freight door behind the wing.

BOEING 747-300 USA

Having launched the Model 747 in 1966, Boeing soon turned its attention to the possibility of 'stretching' the basic aircraft in a number of possible ways. Increasing engine power, fuel capacity and operating weights enhanced the aircraft's economics and broadened its operational spectrum, as indicated in the account of the earlier Model 747 variants, but plans to increase the passenger-carrying ability matured more slowly. Two possible 'stretches' were studied during the 1970s: one by adding fuselage plugs ahead of and behind the wing to bring the seating capacity up to 600, the other by providing an upper deck over the entire length of the fuselage, to allow the aircraft to carry 1,000 or so passengers. In the event, the downturn in the air transport market at the beginning of the 1980s made both of these proposals appear over-optimistic, and a more modest stretch proposal emerged in 1980, in which the upper passenger deck, behind the flight deck, was extended aft by 23ft 4in (7.11m), effectively doubling the 'upstairs' seating area. This proposed new variant was identified at first as the Model 747SUD (stretched upper deck), later as the Model 747EUD (extended upper deck) and finally as the Model 747-300. The importance of the upper deck seating area as a revenue-earner for the airlines is indicated by its progressive development, since initial certification of the Model 747 allowed only eight fare-paying passengers to be carried in that cabin. First, a smoke barrier increased the limit to 16; then a straight staircase in place of the original spiral allowed seating to in-

crease to 24; then the addition of a second type emergency exit/door made it possible to seat 32 (special staircase) or 45 (straight staircase), and finally extending the upper deck fairing aft made the cabin large enough for 69 seats in the Model 747-300 and later models. Boeing formally launched the Model 747-300 on the basis of an order from Swissair that included both passenger and -300M Combi versions, the latter with side-loading freight door. The first -300 flew on 5 October 1982, with JT9D-7R4G2 engines, and the second on 10 December 1982 with CF6-50E2 engines.

VARIANTS
The Model 747-300 is available with engine and gross weight options similar to those of the Model 747-200, and as set out above. The Model 747-300M Combi has the rear side freight door and provision for mixed passenger/freight loads and the Model 747-300SR is a short-range variant designed, like the SR version of the Model 747-100, to operate at lower weights in order to achieve a higher ratio of flights to flight hours. At least one Model 747-300 has been completed in VIP configuration for a Middle East head of state and carries the designation Model 77-43 in line with Boeing practice for its corporate aircraft. As a further development of the stretched upper deck aircraft, Boeing launched the Model 747-400 in October 1985, on the basis of an order for 10 aircraft placed by Northwest Airlines; this was followed by a 14-aircraft order from Singapore Airlines in March 1986. The Model 747-400 differs from the -300 in having extensive changes to the structure and system; an advanced two-crew flight deck; extended wing tips plus winglets that increase overall span to 212ft 2in (64.67m), and a choice of advanced technology, lean-burn engines such as the 56,000lb st (25,402kgp) Pratt & Whitney PW4056, the 59,000lb st (26,762kgp) General Electric CF6-80C2 and the 56,000lb st (25,402kgp) Rolls-Royce RB.211-524D4. The first Model 747-400 is to enter service in November 1988. The Model 747-500 is a projected derivative with a stretched fuselage, lengthened upper deck, UDF engines and the ability to fly 500 passengers (in mixed-class layout) over ranges of up to 7,825 naut mls (14,500km).

SERVICE USE
The Model 747-300 was certificated on 7 March 1963 and entered service with Swissair on 28 March, with JT9D engines. The first operator with CF6-50E2 engines was UTA, starting on 1 April 1983, and the first with RB.211-524D4 engines was Qantas, starting on 25 November 1984. By early 1987, 15 airlines had ordered 67 of the -300 variants, including 15 Combi and two SR aircraft, and eight airlines had ordered 59 of the Model 747-400 variant.

SPECIFICATION

Power Plant: Four Pratt & Whitney JT9D-7R4G2 turbofans each rated at 54,750lb st (24,834kgp), or General Electric CF6-50E2 turbofans each rated at 52,500lb st (23,814kgp), or CF6-80C2 turbofans each rated at 59,000lb st (26,762kgp), or Rolls-Royce RB.211-524D4 turbofans each rated at 53,110lb st (24,090kgp). Fuel capacity, 43,641 Imp gal (198,390l) in integral tanks in wings and centre section, plus 1,312 Imp gal (5,966l) in two optional outboard reserve tanks, plus 1,432 Imp gal (6,511l) in optional fuselage tank.
Performance: Max operating speed, 375kts (695km/h) IAS or Mach = 0.92; max cruising speed, 507kts (940km/h) at 35,000ft (10,670m); long-range cruise, 490kts (908km/h) at 35,000ft (10,670m); cruising ceiling, 45,000ft (13,715m); take-off field length (FAR), 10,450ft (3,185m); landing field length (FAR), 6,920ft (2,110m); range with full passenger payload, 5,650 naut mls (10,475km).
Weights: Operating weight empty, 384,480lb (174,400kg); max fuel, 353,760lb (160,463kg); max passenger payload, 151,000lb (68,492kg); max payload, 747-300M Combi, 181,000lb (82,100kg); max take-off, basic aircraft, 800,000lb (362,875kg); max take-off, options, 820,000lb (371,945kg) or 833,000lb (377,840kg); max landing, for take-off weights quoted above, 574,000lb (260,360kg) or 585,000lb (263,350kg) or 630,000lb (285,765kg) respectively; max zero-fuel weight, passenger aircraft, 535,000lb (242,670kg); max zero-fuel weight, 747-300M Combi, 565,000lb (256,280kg).
Dimensions: Span, 195ft 8in (59.64m); overall length, 231ft 10in (70.66m); overall height, 63ft 5in (19.33m); sweepback, 37 deg 30 min at quarter chord; wing area, 5,500sq ft (510.95m²).
Accommodation: Cabin length, 187ft 0in (57.00m), max width, 20ft 1½in (6.13m), max height, 8ft 4in (2.54m). Typical layout provides 18 first-class seats at 62in (1.57m) pitch, 52 business-class seats at 36in (91cm) pitch, 397 economy-class seats at 34in (86cm) pitch all on main deck, plus 69 economy-class or 52 business-class or 38/26 first-class on extended upper deck. Max passenger capacity, 624 high-density in -300SR short-range version. Underfloor baggage/cargo volume, 5,190cu ft (147m³). Flight crew of three.

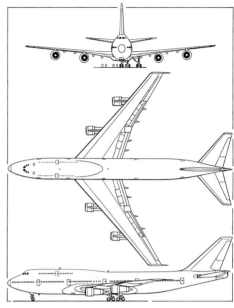

Left: Stairs leading to the extended upper deck of the 747-300 are adjacent to the No 2 passenger doors ahead of the wing.

Below: A three-view drawing of the 747-300 in its basic version. The Combi variant has a freight-loading door in the rear port side.

Boeing 747-300 Cutaway Drawing Key
1 Radome
2 Weather radar scanner
3 Front pressure bulkhead
4 Scanner tracking mechanism
5 Wardrobe
6 First class cabin; 18 "sleeper" seats typical, at 62in (157cm) pitch
7 Nose undercarriage wheel bay
8 Nosewheel doors
9 Twin nosewheels
10 Hydraulic steering jacks
11 Nose undercarriage pivot fixing
12 Underfloor avionics equipment racks
13 Cabin window panel
14 First class bar unit
15 Flight deck floor level
16 Rudder pedals
17 Control column
18 Instrument panel shroud
19 Windscreen panels
20 Overhead systems switch panel
21 First officer's seat
22 Captain's seat
23 Flight engineer's station
24 Observers' seats (2)
25 Cockpit doorway
26 Upper deck toilet compartment, port and starboard
27 Upper deck window panel
28 Air distribution ducting
29 Forward lower deck galley
30 Plug-type forward cabin door, No 1, port and starboard
31 Business-class passenger seating; 52-seats eight-abreast typical at 36in (91cm) pitch
32 Fuselage lower lobe skin panelling
33 Baggage/cargo pallet containers
34 Forward underfloor cargo hold, capacity 2,768cu ft (78.4m³)
35 Forward fuselage frame and stringer construction
36 Upper deck doorway, port and starboard
37 Cabin roof frames
38 Anti-collision light
39 No 1 UHF communications aerial
40 Economy-class seating; 69-seats, six-abreast typical at 34in (86cm) pitch (alternative layouts for 42 business-class or 38 or 26 first-class)
41 Lower deck toilet compartments
42 No 2 passenger door, port and starboard
43 Air conditioning system intake ducting
44 Ventral flush air intakes
45 Wing-root leading-edge fillet
46 Ventral air conditioning packs, port and starboard
47 Wing spar bulkhead
48 Economy-class seating
49 Staircase to upper deck
50 Fresh water tanks

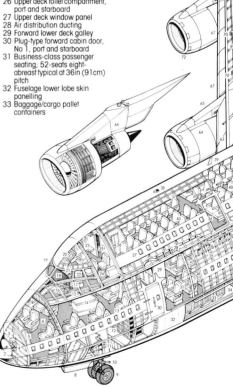

Left: Swissair was the launch customer for the Boeing 747-300, the extended upper deck of which is clearly shown here.

Below: KLM was an early customer for the 747-300, with an order for three of the Combi version with CF6-50E2 engines.

Below: Cutaway drawing of the Boeing 747-300, showing the engine options.

51 Wing centre section fuel tankage, capacity 14,292 Imp gal (64,973l)
52 Centre section stringer construction
53 Floor beam construction
54 Front spar/fuselage main frame
55 Upper deck lobby area
56 Closet/storage locker
57 Curtained bulkhead
58 Galley units
59 Starboard wing inboard main fuel tank, capacity 10,447 Imp gal (47,492l)
60 Fuel pumps
61 Engine bleed air supply ducting
62 Krueger flap operating mechanism
63 Inboard Krueger flap segments
64 Starboard inner Rolls-Royce RB.211 engine nacelle
65 Inboard nacelle pylon
66 Pratt & Whitney JT9-7R4G2 turbofan, alternative engine installation
67 Leading-edge Krueger flap segments

68 Pressure refuelling connections, port and starboard
69 Krueger flap drive shaft
70 Krueger flap rotary actuators
71 Starboard wing outboard main fuel tank, capacity 3.732 Imp gal (16,966l)
72 Starboard outer engine nacelle
73 Outboard nacelle pylon
74 Wing dry bay
75 Outboard Krueger flap
76 Krueger flap drive mechanism
77 Extended range fuel tank (optional), capacity 656 Imp gal (2,983l)
78 Vent surge tank
79 Starboard wing tip fairing
80 Starboard navigation lights
81 VHF aerial boom
82 Fuel vent
83 Static dischargers
84 Outboard, low-speed, aileron
85 Outboard four-segment spoilers
86 Outboard triple-slotted Fowler-type flap, down position
87 Flap screw jacks and segment linkages
88 Flap drive shaft
89 Inboard, high-speed, aileron
90 Inboard triple slotted flap, down position

95 Extended upper deck rear bulkhead
96 Upper deck floor beam construction
97 Air system cross-feed ducting
98 Conditioned air risers
99 Machined wing spar attachment main frames
100 Central flap drive motors
101 Wing mounted, outboard, main undercarriage wheel bay
102 Undercarriage mounting beam
103 Nr 3 passenger door, port and starboard
104 Pressure floor above wheel bay
105 Centre fuselage frame and stringer construction
106 No 2 UHF communications aerial
107 Cabin wall trim panelling
108 Seat mounting rails
109 Main cabin floor panelling
110 Fuselage mounted, inboard, main undercarriage wheel bay
111 Hydraulic retraction jack
112 Cabin window panel

113 Overhead conditioned air distribution ducting
114 Economy-class seating; 397-seats typical at 34in (86cm) pitch
115 No 4 passenger door, port and starboard
116 Centre cabin galley
117 Overhead stowage bins
118 Rear cabin air supply ducting
119 Rear cabin galley
120 Rear cabin passenger seating

121 Nine-abreast economy-class passenger seating
122 Central overhead stowage bins
123 Cabin roof panels
124 Control cable runs
125 Rear fuselage frame and stringer construction
126 Rear cabin seating
127 Cabin bulkhead

128 Door mounted escape chute, all doors
129 Rear toilet compartments
130 Wardrobes, port and starboard
131 Rear pressure bulkhead
132 Fin root fillet
133 Starboard trimming tailplane
134 Static dischargers
135 Starboard elevator
136 Fin leading-edge construction
137 Two-spar fin box construction
138 Fin tip fairing
139 VOR aerial
140 Static dischargers
141 Upper rudder segment
142 Lower rudder segment
143 Rudder hydraulic actuators
144 Tailcone fairing
145 APU exhaust
146 Auxiliary power unit (APU)
147 Port elevator inboard segment
148 Port elevator outboard segment

149 Static dischargers
150 Port trimming tailplane construction
151 Elevator hydraulic actuators
152 Tailplane sealing plate
153 Aft fuselage frames
154 Fin root attachment joint
155 Tailplane centre section
156 Tailplane trim screw jack
157 APU high pressure air supply duct
158 No 5 passenger door, port and starboard
159 Rear fuselage window panel
160 Underfloor bulk cargo hold, capacity 1,000cu ft (28.3m³)
161 Rear fuselage baggage/cargo hold, capacity 2,422cu ft (68.6m³)
162 Baggage/cargo pallet
163 Fuselage lower lobe frame and stringer construction
164 Wing root trailing-edge fillet
165 Fuselage-mounted main undercarriage pivot fixing
166 Trailing-edge auxiliary spar
167 Undercarriage leg breaker strut

168 Wing-mounted main undercarriage pivot fixing
169 Hydraulic retraction jack
170 Four-wheel inboard main undercarriage bogie
171 Flap drive shaft
172 Flap guide rails
173 Inboard spoilers/lift dumpers
174 Port inboard triple-slotted flap
175 Flap track fairings
176 Flap down position
177 Aileron hydraulic actuator
178 Inboard, high-speed, aileron
179 Outboard triple-slotted flap
180 Outboard flap tracks
181 Outboard spoilers

182 Flap track fairings
183 Flap down position
184 Outboard, low-speed, aileron
185 Aileron hydraulic actuators
186 Static dischargers
187 Fuel vent
188 VHF aerial boom
189 Wing-tip fairing
190 Port navigation lights
191 Outboard leading edge Krueger flap segments
192 Krueger flap drive mechanism
193 Outer wing panel rib construction
194 Lower wing skin access panels
195 Rear spar
196 Outboard engine pylon mounting rib
197 Port outer nacelle pylon
198 Pre-cooler exhaust duct
199 Thrust reverser cowling door, open

200 Cowling door screw jack
201 Reverser cascades
202 Outboard engine nacelle
203 Central leading-edge Krueger flap segments
204 Krueger flap drive mechanism
205 Leading-edge rib construction
206 Wing panel spar and rib construction
207 Flap track mounting beams
208 Port wing integral fuel tanks
209 Inner engine pylon mounting rib
210 Wing stringers
211 Wing skin panelling
212 Wing mounted main undercarriage leg strut
213 Pylon attachment strut
214 Four-wheel outer main undercarriage bogie
215 Nacelle pylon construction
216 Bleed air pre-cooler
217 Core engine, hot stream, exhaust duct
218 Fan air, cold stream, exhaust duct
219 Engine accessory equipment gearbox
220 Rolls-Royce RB.211-524D4 turbofan engine
221 Engine intake

91 Inboard two-segment spoilers/lift dumpers
92 Flap screw jack
93 Auxiliary trailing-edge wing spar
94 Cabin air distribution ducting

222 Detachable engine cowling panels
223 Inboard Krueger flap segments
224 Krueger flap motor and drive shaft
225 Three-spar wing torsion box construction
226 Inboard wing ribs
227 Bolted wing root attachment joint strap
228 Front spar
229 Engine bleed air ducting
230 Leading-edge nose ribs
231 Twin landing lamps
232 General-Electric CF6-50E2 alternative engine installation

AVIAGRAPHICA

BOEING 757 USA

SPECIFICATION

Power Plant: Two Rolls-Royce RB.211-535C or RB.211-535E4 turbofans each rated at 37,400lb st (16,965kgp) or 40,100lb st (18,189kgp) respectively for take-off, or two Pratt & Whitney PW2037 turbofans each rated at 38,200lb st (17,328kgp) for take-off. Fuel capacity, 9,370 Imp gal (42,597l).
Performance: Max operating speed, 350kts (649km/h) IAS or M = 0.86; max cruising speed, 505kts (936km/h) at 31,000ft (9,450m); long-range cruise, 459kts (851km/h) at 39,000ft (11,885m); initial cruising altitude, about 38,000ft (11,580m) according to engine; take-off field length (FAR), 5,380 to 5,960ft (1,640 to 1,815m) according to engine at basic max take-off weight, 6,400 to 7,760ft (1,950 to 2,365m) according to engine at highest optional max take-off weight; landing field length (FAR), 4,600ft (1,400m) at max landing weight; range with max payload, 3,180 naut mls (5,895km) with 535E4 engines at max optional take-off weight; range with max fuel, 4,570 naut mls (8,475km) with 37,920lb (17,200kg) payload.
Weights: Operating weight empty, 126,250lb (57,267kg); max payload, 57,530lb (26,096kg); basic max take-off weight, 220,000lb (99,792kg); optional medium-range and max take-off weights, 230,000 and 240,000lb (104,328 and 108,864kg) respectively; max landing weight, 198,000lb (89,813kg); max zero-fuel weight, 184,000lb (83,462kg).
Dimensions: Span, 124ft 10in (38.05m); overall length, 155ft 3in (47.32m); overall height, 44ft 6in (13.56m); sweepback, 25 deg at quarter chord; wing area, 1,994sq ft (185.25m²).
Accommodation: Cabin length, 118ft 5in (36.09m), max width, 11ft 7in (3.53m), max height, 7ft 0in (2.13m). Standard layouts available range from 178 to 239 passenger seats, e.g. 16 first-class four-abreast at 38in (96.5cm) pitch plus 170 tourist-class six-abreast at 34in (86cm) pitch, or 239 six-abreast at 32in (81cm) pitch. Flight crew of two and five-seven cabin attendants.

The Boeing 757, launched in mid-1978, is essentially a 'big brother' for the Model 727 which, up to the mid-1980s, retained its position as the best-seller among the Western world's jetliners. During the 1970s Boeing devoted much time and effort to studying possible stretches of the Model 727, with particular attention to the advantages to be gained from the use of more modern engines. In the end, the Model 757 emerged as a wholly new design. Although attempts were made to retain commonality with the Model 727, the switch from a configuration using three rear-mounted engines to one with a pair of engines in underwing pods made this difficult, and with a new wing and a low-mounted tailplane the Model 757 retained little of the Model 727 other than the same basic fuselage cross section, which was therefore similar to that also used in the Models 707 and 737. Even the original intention of using a flight deck with Model 727 features was eventually abandoned in favour of achieving the best possible commonality with the Boeing 767, and as finally built the Model 757 has more in common with the latter than the former, to the extent that it is possible for pilots to obtain a single flight rating that allows them to fly either the Model 757 or the Model 767. Of the several advanced high by-pass ratio turbofans under development, the RB.211-535 was chosen as one of the most suitable for the Model 757, with the General Electric

CF6-32C1 rated at 36,500lb st (16,566kgp) as an alternative. Until the launch of the new aircraft, on 31 August 1978, two alternative fuselage lengths were on offer, as the Model 757-100 and Model 757-200; the two launch customers, British Airways and Eastern Airways, both chose the -200 with Rolls-Royce engines, and the -100 was eventually dropped as an option. Also dropped, by General Electric's decision not to proceed with its development, was the CF6-32 engine option, after Pratt & Whitney had entered the market with the PW2000 family, and a version of the latter has become the alternative to the RB.211 in the Model 757. Flight testing began on 19 February 1982 at the Boeing factory at Renton, with four more aircraft used in the flight development programme. The first flight with PW2037 engines was made on 14 March 1984.

VARIANTS

The Model 757 is available at three different gross weights, and with three different engine options, as noted above. In 1986, the first sale was made of a freighter version, designated Model 757PF (package freighter), with a large cargo door in the forward fuselage port side, a single crew entry door and no cabin windows. The same large loading door is used in the Model 757 Combi, also introduced in 1986, which retains the standard features for passenger-carrying and can be used to accommodate mixed cargo/passenger loads in varying combinations. The designation Model 77-52 is used to identify corporate/executive versions of the 757.

SERVICE USE

Following its certification by the FAA on 21 December 1982 and the CAA (in the UK) on 14 January 1983, Boeing 757 deliveries to Eastern Airlines began on 22 December 1982 and to British Airways on 25 January 1983. These two airlines started revenue service with the type on 1 January and 9 February 1983 respectively. The Model 757 with PW2037 engines was certificated in October 1984, and deliveries to Delta Air Lines began on 5 November that year, with the first service flown on 28 November. The first Model 757 with the uprated RB.211-535E4 engines was delivered to Eastern on 10 October 1984. By the beginning of 1987, a total of 204 Boeing 757s had been ordered by 18 airlines. The Boeing 757 price is in the region of $45 million.

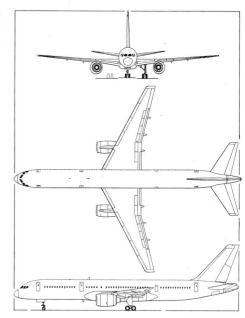

Above: A three-view drawing of the Boeing 757-200. The designation derives from the choice of fuselage lengths initially projected, but the shorter -100 was not put into production and all 757s built to date have the same overall configuration.

Below: Cutaway drawing of the Boeing 757-200 in its standard form. Shown in this drawing are the Rolls-Royce RB.211-535 engines that have been specified for more than half of all the 757s ordered up to the end of 1986. Others have PW 2037 turbofans.

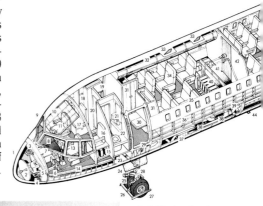

Left: The interior of a Boeing 757 showing the use of varying fabrics to break up the 'long thin tube' appearance of such layouts.

Below: Singapore Airlines, one of 13 operators of the 757 in 1986, uses Pratt & Whitney PW 2037 engines, as illustrated here.

Boeing 757-200 Cutaway Drawing Key

1 Radome
2 Weather radar scanner
3 VOR localiser aerial
4 ILS glideslope aerials
5 Front pressure bulkhead
6 Rudder pedals
7 Windscreen wipers
8 Instrument panel shroud
9 Windscreen panels
10 Cockpit roof systems control panels
11 First officer's seat
12 Centre console
13 Captain's seat
14 Cockpit floor level
15 Crew baggage locker
16 Observer's seat
17 Optional second observer's seat
18 Coat locker
19 Forward galley
20 Cockpit door
21 Wash basin
22 Forward toilet compartment
23 Nose undercarriage wheel bay
24 Nosewheel leg doors
25 Steering jacks
26 Spray deflector
27 Twin nosewheels
28 Taxying and runway turn-off lamps
29 Forward entry door
30 Cabin attendants' folding seats
31 Closets, port and starboard
32 Overhead stowage bins
33 DABS aerials
34 First-class cabin four-abreast seating, 16 seats
35 Cabin window panels
36 Fuselage frame and stringer construction
37 Underfloor radio and electronics compartment
38 Negative pressure relief valves
39 Electronics cooling air ducting
40 Radio racks
41 Forward freight door
42 Curtained cabin divider
43 Tourist-class six-abreast seating, 162 seats

44 Ventral VHF aerial
45 Underfloor freight hold
46 Passenger entry door, port and starboard
47 Door mounted escape chutes
48 Upper VHF aerial
49 Overhead air conditioning distribution ducting
50 LD-W cargo container, (seven in forward hold)
51 Graphite composite wing root fillet
52 Landing lamp
53 Air system recirculating fan
54 Air distribution manifold
55 Conditioned air risers
56 Wing spar centre-section carry-through
57 Front spar/fuselage main frame
58 Ventral air conditioning plant, port and starboard
59 Centre section fuel tank
60 Floor beam construction
61 Centre fuselage construction
62 Centre wing integral fuel tank; total system capacity 9,060 Imp gal (41,185l)
63 Dry bay
64 Bleed air system pre-cooler
65 Thrust reverser cascade doors, open
66 Starboard engine nacelle
67 Nacelle pylon
68 Fuel venting channels
69 Fuel system piping

70 Pressure refuelling connections
71 Leading edge slat segments, open
72 Slat drive shaft
73 Guide rails
74 Overwing fuel filler cap
75 Vent surge tank
76 Starboard navigation light (green) and strobe light (white)
77 Tail navigation strobe light (white)
78 Starboard aileron
79 Aileron hydraulic jacks
80 Spoiler sequencing control mechanism
81 Outboard double-slotted flaps, down
82 Flap guide rails
83 Screw jacks
84 Outboard spoilers, open
85 Spoiler hydraulic jacks
86 Inboard flap outer single-slotted segment
87 Inboard spoilers

88 Starboard main undercarriage mounting beam
89 Cabin wall trim panels
90 Rear spar/fuselage main frame
91 Flap-drive hydraulic motor (electric motor back-up)
92 Port mainwheel bay
93 Pressure floor above wheel bay
94 DF loop aerials
95 Cabin roof lighting panels

96 Port overhead stowage bins, passenger service units beneath
97 Mid-section toilet compartments (two port, one starboard)
98 Emergency exit doors, port and starboard
99 Rear freight door
100 APU battery and controls
101 Rear cabin seating
102 Overhead stowage bins
103 Starboard rear galley unit
104 Fin root fillet
105 Fin construction
106 Fin 'logo' spotlight
107 Starboard tailplane
108 Starboard elevator
109 HF aerial couplers
110 Leading edge HF aerial
111 Fin tip aerial fairing
112 Tail VOR aerials
113 Static dischargers
114 Rudder
115 Rudder hydraulic jacks
116 Honeycomb rudder panel construction
117 APU intake plenum
118 Tailcone
119 APU exhaust
120 AiResearch GTCP 331-200 auxiliary power plant (APU)

121 Port elevator
122 Elevator hydraulic jacks
123 Honeycomb panel construction
124 Static dischargers
125 Tailplane construction
126 Fin 'logo' light
127 Tailplane sealing plate
128 Fin support frame
129 Tailplane centre-section
130 Tailplane trim control jack
131 Rear pressure bulkhead
132 Aft galley
133 Rear entry door, port and starboard
134 Underfloor freight hold
135 LD-W cargo containers, (six in rear hold)
136 Ventral VHF aerial
137 Roller tray cargo handling floor
138 Graphite composite wing root fillet
139 Port inboard double slotted flap
140 Main undercarriage mounting beam
141 Undercarriage leg side strut
142 Hydraulic retraction jack
143 Inboard spoilers
144 Flap hinge linkage
145 Inboard flap single slotted outer segment

146 Flaps down position
147 Flap track fairings
148 Outboard double slotted flap
149 Outboard spoilers
150 Aileron hydraulic jacks
151 Port aileron honeycomb construction
152 Tail navigation strobe light (white)
153 Port navigation light (red) and strobe light (white)
154 Vent surge tank
155 Port leading edge slat segments
156 Slat guide rails
157 Drive shaft
158 Port wing dry bay
159 Ventral access panels
160 Port wing integral fuel tank
161 Wing rib construction
162 Wing stringers
163 Wing-skin plating
164 Four-wheel main undercarriage bogie
165 Main undercarriage leg strut
166 Inboard wing ribs
167 Bleed air ducting
168 Inboard leading edge slat
169 Engine mounting pylon
170 Detachable engine cowlings
171 Port engine intake
172 Intake de-icing air duct
173 Rolls-Royce RB.211-535C turbofan engine (PW2037 turbofans optional fit)
174 Engine accessory gearbox
175 Oil cooler
176 Fan air exhaust duct
177 Hot stream exhaust nozzle

Below: Following British Airways' launch order for the 757, independent operator Air Europe was an early customer for the type, and now has four in service.

BOEING 767-200 USA

Boeing conducted many studies during the early and mid 'seventies with a view to providing a new medium-range aircraft of large capacity, in order to maintain its competitive position vis-à-vis Airbus Industrie, which was at the same time projecting an aircraft of similar size. For much of the time, the project was known as the 7X7, and its precise size and overall configuration remained uncertain until the first airline orders were obtained. As finally launched, the Boeing 767 is a twin-aisle aircraft, breaking away from the constant cabin cross section used by Boeing for the 707/727/737/757 narrow-body series and having a fuselage that is 4ft 1in (1.24m) wider. This allowed an eight-abreast layout with two aisles (2+4+2) and no passenger more than one seat away from an aisle. Initially, Boeing planned to use a three-man flight deck, with a two-pilot arrangement offered later as an option, but airline preference led to adoption of the two-man flight deck as standard before deliveries began, although this called for modification of a number of aircraft already completed. Much use was made in the design of advanced materials, including new alloys as well as composites, and the avionics included an advanced digital flight management system with electronic flight instrument systems (EFIS) – one of the first to be applied as standard to a commercial transport. Two variants of the basic aircraft were planned at first as the 767-100 and 767-200 with different fuselage lengths, but all early orders were for the larger-capacity version and the 767-100 has not been continued. The Boeing-owned 767-200 prototype made its first flight at Everett, Washington, on 26 September 1981 with Pratt & Whitney engines, followed by three in United Airlines configuration on 4 November, 28 December and 30 December 1982. The fifth aircraft was the first with General Electric engines, in Delta Air Lines configuration, and was flown on 19 February 1982. The first prototype is being used to test-fly a US Army sensor system.

VARIANTS

The basic variant is the 767-200 at a max take-off weight of 300,000lb (136,097kg); a so-called medium range variant operates at a weight of 282,000lb (127,915kg), with a reduced max fuel capacity, and a high gross weight variant carries additional fuel in the centre section and has a max weight of 315,000lb (142,880kg). A version designated 767-200ER carries a further 3,750 US gal (14,195l) in a second centre section tank and is available at max weights of 345,000lb (156,489kg) or 351,000lb (159,211kg). All variants offered with the 47,8000lb st (21,680kgp) JT9D-7R4D, 47,900lb st (21,730kgp) CF6-80A, or 50,000lb st (22,680kgp) JT9D-7R4E or

E4 or CF6-80AZ engines. A corporate/executive version of the 767 carries the designation Boeing 77-62.

SERVICE USE

Initial certification of 767-200 by the FAA obtained on 30 July 1982 (JT9D-7R4D engine) and on 30 September 1982 (CF6-80A engines). First customer delivery with CF6-80A engines, to Delta, on 25 October 1982 and first service flown 15 December. First 767-200ER, with JT9D-7RE4 engines, delivered to Ethiopian Airlines on 18 May 1984 and entered service 6 June. First delivery with JT9D-7R4E4 engines (-200-ER) to CAAC, 8 October 1985. Total sales confirmed to end -1986, 220 to 22 customers worldwide.

SPECIFICATION

Power Plant: Two Pratt & Whitney JT9D-7R4D or General Electric CF6-80A turbofans each rated at 48,000lb st (21,770kgp). Fuel capacity, 13,900 Imp gal (63,216l).

Performance: (A330) Max operating speed, 360kts (667km/h) IAS or Mach=0.86; max cruising speed, 484kts (897km/h) at 39,000ft (11,887m); long-range cruising speed, 459kts (850km/h) at 39,000ft (11,887m), equivalent to Mach=0.80, at a weight of 260,000lb (117,935kg); take-off field length (FAR), 5,650ft (1,720m); landing field length (FAR), 4,750ft (1,450m); range with max payload, 2,495 naut mls (4,620km); range with full tanks, 6,210 naut mls (11,500km) with 11,530lb (5,230kg) payload.

Weights: Standard aircraft operating weight empty, 176,200lb (79,923kg); max fuel, 112,725lb (51,131kg); max payload, 71,800lb (32,570kg); max take-off, basic 300,000lb (136,078kg); max take-off, medium range, 282,000lb (127,913kg); max take-off, optional, 315,000lb (142,881kg); max landing (for three max take-off weights as listed, respectively), 270,000lb (122,470kg), 257,000lb (116,573kg), 272,000lb (123,377kg); max zero fuel (for three max take-off weights as listed respectively), 248,000lb (112,491kg), 242,000lb (109,769kg), 250,000lb (113,398kg).

Dimensions: Span, 156ft 1in (47.57m); overall length, 159ft 2in (48.51m); overall height, 52ft 0in (15.85m); sweepback, 31.5 deg at quarter chord; gross wing area, 3,050sq ft (283.3m²).

Accommodation: Cabin length, 111ft 4in (33.93m); max width, 15ft 6in (4.72m), max height, 9ft 5in (2.87m). Basic accommodation for 220 passengers comprising 18 six-abreast at 38-in (96.5cm) pitch and 202 seven-abreast at 33in (84cm) seat pitch; maximum one-class 255 seven-abreast, or 290 eight-abreast with extra emergency exits fitted. Total underfloor baggage/cargo volume, 3,930cu ft (111,3m³). Flight crew of two with optional third position on flight deck.

Boeing 767-200 Cutaway Drawing Key

1 Radome
2 Radar scanner dish
3 VOR localiser aerial
4 Front pressure bulkhead
5 ILS glideslope aerials
6 Windscreen wipers
7 Windscreen panels
8 Instrument panel shroud
9 Rudder pedals
10 Nose undercarriage wheel bay
11 Cockpit air conditioning duct
12 Captain's seat
13 Opening cockpit side window
14 Centre console
15 First officer's seat
16 Cockpit roof systems control panels
17 Flight engineer's station
18 Observer's seat
19 Pitot tubes
20 Angle of attack probe
21 Nose undercarriage steering jacks
22 Twin nosewheels
23 Nosewheel doors
24 Waste system vacuum tank
25 Forward toilet compartment
26 Crew wardrobe
27 Forward galley
28 Starboard overhead sliding door
29 Entry lobby
30 Cabin divider
31 Port entry door
32 Door control handle
33 Escape chute stowage
34 Underfloor electronics racks
35 Electronics cooling air system
36 Skin heat exchanger
37 Fuselage frame and stringer construction
38 Cabin window panel
39 Six-abreast first class seating compartment (18 seats)
40 Overhead stowage bins
41 Curtained cabin divider
42 Sidewall trim panels
43 Negative pressure relief valves
44 Forward freight door
45 Forward underfloor freight hold
46 LD-2 cargo containers, 12 in forward hold
47 Centre electronics rack
48 Anti-collision light
49 Cabin roof frames
50 VHF aerial
51 Seven-abreast tourist class seating (193 seats)
52 Conditioned air riser
53 Air conditioning distribution manifolds
54 Wing spar centre section carry through
55 Floor beam construction
56 Overhead air conditioning ducting
57 Front spar/fuselage main frame
58 Starboard emergency exit window
59 Starboard wing integral fuel tank; total system capacity 12,955 Imp gal (58,895l)
60 Thrust reverser cascade door, open
61 Starboard engine nacelle
62 Nacelle pylon
63 Fixed portion of leading edge
64 Leading edge slat segments, open
65 Slat drive shaft
66 Rotary actuators
67 Fuel system piping
68 Fuel venting channels
69 Vent surge tank
70 Starboard navigation light (green)
71 Anti-collision light (red)
72 Tail navigation strobe light (white)
73 Static dischargers
74 Starboard outer aileron
75 Aileron hydraulic jacks

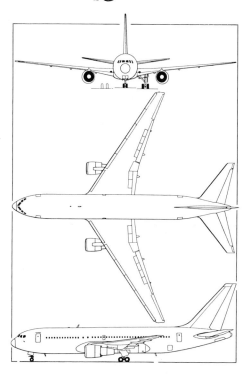

Left: This flight deck, which is common to both the Boeing 757 and 767, was designed to meet the needs of airline crews up to the year 2000. The main panel is dominated by CRT-type displays. The most prominent of these are the Engine Indication and Crew Alerting Systems (EICAS) in the centre, the Attitude Director Indicator (ADI) at upper left and right, and the Horizontal Situation Indicator (below the ADI displays on both sides of the cockpit). The HSI can display a visual map with the aircraft position indicated.

Above: Three-view drawing of the Boeing 767-200, the basic 220-passenger configuration of this series of aircraft. It can be easily distinguished from the newer 300 Series aircraft because the latter have a fuselage that is 21ft (6.4m) longer to accommodate another 49 passenger seats.

76 Single slotted outer flap, down
77 Flap hinge fairings
78 Flap hinge control links
79 Outboard spoilers, open
80 Spoiler hydraulic jacks
81 Rotary actuator
82 Flap drive shaft
83 Aileron hydraulic jacks
84 Inboard aileron
85 Inboard double slotted flap, down
86 Flap hinge control linkage
87 Fuselage centre section construction
88 Mid-cabin toilet compartments
89 Cabin attendant's folding seat
90 Port emergency exit window
91 Ventral air conditioning plant, port and starboard
92 Mainwheel doors
93 Door jack
94 Wheel bay pressure bulkhead

95 Starboard wheel bay hydraulic reservoir
96 Rear spar/fuselage main frame
97 Pressure floor above starboard wheel bay
98 Cabin floor panels
99 Seat mounting rails
100 Overhead stowage bins
101 Cabin roof lighting panels
102 Centre stowage bins
103 VOR aerials
104 Fuselage skin plating
105 Negative pressure relief valves
106 Rear freight door
107 Seven-abreast tourist class seating
108 Rear toilet compartments
109 Cabin attendant's folding seat
110 Rear galleys
111 Overhead sliding door counterbalance
112 Rear pressure dome
113 Fin root fillet
114 Tailfin construction
115 Fin 'logo' spotlight
116 Starboard tailplane

117 Leading edge HF aerial
118 HF aerial coupler
119 Television aerial
120 Fin tip aerial fairing
121 Tail VOR aerials
122 Static dischargers
123 Rudder

124 Rudder hydraulic jacks
125 Balance weights
126 Rudder honeycomb construction
127 Tailplane centre section
128 APU intake plenum
129 Gas turbine auxiliary power unit (APU)
130 Tailcone
131 AFU exhaust
132 Two-segment elevator
133 Elevator hydraulic jacks

134 Honeycomb control surface construction
135 Static dischargers
136 Tailplane construction
137 Fin 'logo' spotlight
138 Tailplane sealing plate
139 Fin attachment frames
140 Tailplane trim control jack
141 Rear fuselage frame and stringer construction
142 Port rear galley unit
143 Curtained cabin divider
144 Door operating handle
145 Rear entry door
146 Pressurisation outflow valve
147 Bulk cargo door
148 Rear underfloor freight hold, ten LD-2 containers
149 Air turbine driven hydraulic pump
150 Trailing edge wing root fillet
151 Inboard flap rotary actuator
152 Inboard double slotted flap
153 Main undercarriage mounting beam

154 Retraction jack
155 Inboard spoilers
156 Flap hinge control link
157 Hinge link fairing
158 Port inner aileron
159 Flap 'down' position
160 Outer single slotted flap
161 Outboard spoilers
162 Flap hinge link fairings
163 Honeycomb control surface construction
164 Port outer aileron
165 Tail navigation strobe light (white)
166 Anti-collision light (red)
167 Port navigation light
168 Port vent surge tank
169 Rear spar
170 Wing rib construction
171 Front spar
172 Leading edge slat segments

173 Slat guide rails
174 Rotary actuators
175 Slat operating links
176 Pressure refuelling connectors
177 Port wing integral fuel tank
178 Wing stringers
179 Wing skin plating
180 Four-wheel main undercarriage bogie
181 Mainwheel leg
182 Undercarriage leg side struts
183 Port wing dry bay
184 Inboard auxiliary fuel tank
185 Engine bleed air ducting
186 Slat drive motor
187 Landing and taxying lamps
188 Inboard leading edge slat
189 Slat open position
190 Port engine cowlings
191 Intake de-icing air duct
192 Port engine intake
193 Pratt & Whitney JT9D-7R4 turbofan engine (General Electric CF6-80A optional fit)
194 Engine mounting pylon
195 Oil tank
196 Fan air exhaust duct
197 Hot stream exhaust nozzle

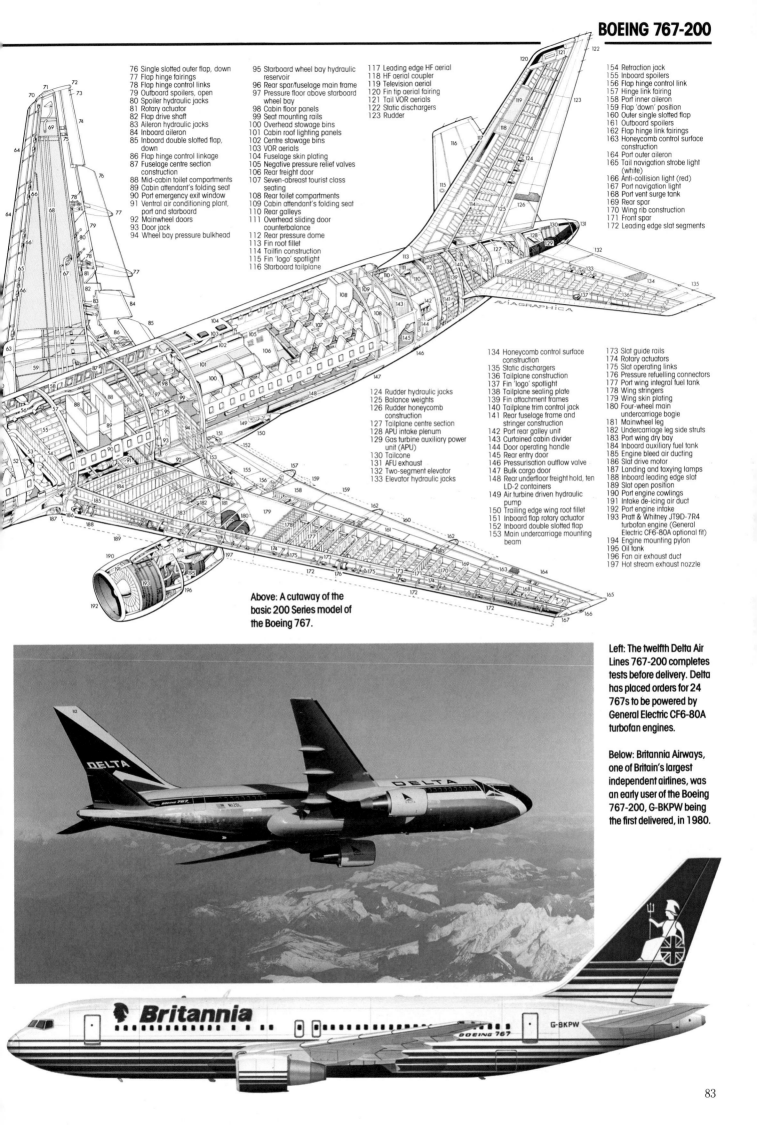

Above: A cutaway of the basic 200 Series model of the Boeing 767.

Left: The twelfth Delta Air Lines 767-200 completes tests before delivery. Delta has placed orders for 24 767s to be powered by General Electric CF6-80A turbofan engines.

Below: Britannia Airways, one of Britain's largest independent airlines, was an early user of the Boeing 767-200, G-BKPW being the first delivered, in 1980.

BOEING 767-300 USA

SPECIFICATION

Power Plant: Two Pratt & Whitney JT9D-7R4E or General Electric CF6-80A2 turbofans each rated at 50,000lb st (22,680kgp). Fuel capacity, 13,900 Imp gal (63,216l).

Performance: Max operating speed, 360kts (667km/h) IAS or Mach = 0.86; max cruising speed, 484kts (897km/h) at 39,000ft (11,885m); long-range cruising speed, 459kts (850km/h) at 39,000ft (11,885m), equivalent to Mach = 0.80, at a weight of 260,000lb (117,936kg); take-off field length (FAR), 7,900ft (2,410m); landing field length (FAR), 5,600ft (1,705m); range with max payload, 2,820 naut mls (5,220km); range with full tanks and 43,480lb (19,720kg) payload, 5,220 naut mls (9,670km).

Weights: Standard operating weight empty, 188,800lb (85,638kg); max fuel weight, 112,725lb (51,131kg); max payload, 89,200lb (40,460kg); max take-off weight, basic aircraft, 345,000lb (156,489kg); max take-off weight, optional, 352,200lb (159,755kg); max landing weight (for either take-off weight as quoted), 300,000lb (136,078kg); max zero-fuel weight (for either take-off weight as quoted), 278,000lb (126,098kg).

Dimensions: Span, 156ft 1in (47.57m); overall length, 180ft 3in (54.94m); overall height, 52ft 0in (15.85m); sweepback, 31.5 deg at quarter chord; gross wing area, 3,050sq ft (283.3m^2).

Accommodation: Cabin length, 132ft 5in (40.36m), max width, 15ft 6in (4.72m), max height, 9ft 5in (2.87m). Standard accommodation for 269 passengers in mixed-class layout; maximum of 290 passengers seven-abreast or 330 when extra emergency exits are fitted. Total underfloor baggage/cargo volume, 5,190cu ft (147.0m^3).

Right: Japan Air Lines was the first airline to order the stretched -300 version of the Boeing 767, and therefore also the first to put the new type into regular service, in October 1986. In the US, Delta Air Lines began using the 767-300 on 1 December 1986, in this case with CF6 engines.

BOEING 7J7 USA

From the early 1980s an evolving market for substantial numbers of a short/medium-range airliner in the 150-seat category increasingly attracted the attention of the 'big three' jetliner manufacturers. Airbus Industrie, with no type already in production in this size bracket, could meet the requirement only by launching a new design: hence the A320. Both Boeing and McDonnell Douglas were better placed to respond to the market demand, at least in the near term, with development of a new variant of the Boeing 737 and McDonnell Douglas MD80 respectively, while they prepared and studied new aircraft projects that could be launched at what appeared to be the optimum moment to catch a substantial share of the market in the 1990s. While project studies continued, neither of the US companies had reached a definitive stage in their planning for a 150-seat new technology aircraft by the time the major engine manufacturers made known their projected time-scale for the introduction of ultra-high-bypass (UHB) or propfan engines with dramatic reductions in specific fuel consumption compared with conventional turbofans available in the same period.

To take advantage of these new-technology engines and a number of other new technologies expected to be ready for commercial application by the early 1990s, Boeing decided during 1985 to set aside the turbofan-engined 150-seat projects then under study, preferring to meet any interim demand with existing or derivative types. McDonnell Douglas took a similar view, although it foresees an all-new UHB-engined aircraft entering production a couple of years later than Boeing's forecast, with fuel prices having a decisive effect upon timing.

Boeing established 1992 as the year in which its new aircraft, known during the development phase as the Model 7J7, should be introduced. This conclusion was based partly on market considerations, partly on technological opportunity. So far as market conditions are concerned, Boeing notes that the dominant 150-seat aircraft at present is the Model 727-200, of which some 1,200 were in service in 1986. Many of these will be approaching their time for replacement by the beginning of the 1990s, but airlines will need to be persuaded that the price, operating economics and marketing advantages of an alternative, brand new, aircraft offer compelling reasons for its purchase. The Model 7J7 is being designed to offer just such a combination of attractions for the airlines, taking advantage of the new technologies that will be available by 1992. These advances apply not just to the structures and systems incorporated in the aircraft itself, but also to the way in which it is designed and built.

Propulsion is the most obvious single technology that allows Boeing to claim major improvements for the Model 7J7. Up to the end of 1986, Boeing indicated that the Model 7J7 would be powered by two UHB engines, mounted on the rear fuselage of a low-wing-monoplane design with a T-tail. These engines were expected to show a reduction of about 25 per cent over the latest turbofans available for airline use by 1992, and would meet US and ICAO

Below: After several years of uncertainty, Boeing confirmed early in 1987 that it was concentrating on a twin-aisle design for the 7J7, here depicted as it would appear with General Electric UDF engines.

Right: The Boeing 7J7 as projected in late 1986 is shown in this artist's impression, with UDF engines. In parallel, Boeing had studied in 1987 a similar design with IAE SuperFans underwing.

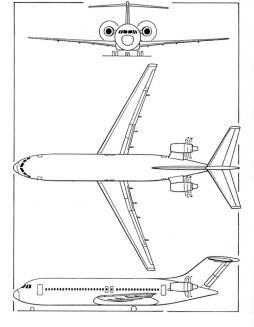

The Boeing 767-300 was announced in February 1983 as a fuselage-stretched addition to the Model 767 family. Using the same basic airframe as the Model 767-200ER, the Model 767-300 incorporates fuselage plugs fore and aft of the wing, with lengths of 10ft 1in (3.07m) and 11ft (3.35m) respectively, and has strengthened main and nose gear legs and some thickening of wing skins. The Model 767-300 made its first flight on 30 January 1986, powered by JT9D-7R4D engines each rated at 48,000lb st (21,773kgp). The second aircraft, with CF6-80A2 turbofans, joined the programme in March 1986.

VARIANTS

The basic Model 767-300 is offered with the same fuel capacity as the basic Model 767-200, and with the same engine options. It has the same maximum take-off weight as the Model 767-200, with an optional high gross weight variant at 352,200lb (159,755kg) as shown in the data panel. A long-range version, the Model 767-300ER, introduces additional centre-section fuel tanks to bring the capacity to 20,026 Imp gal (91,039l) and has a further weight increase, to 380,000lb (172,365kg) in the first instance and later to 400,000lb (181,440kg), with certification of these two variants scheduled for August 1987 and early 1988 respectively. To maintain airfield performance and operating economics at these higher weights, the engine options for the Model 767-300ER include the 59,000lb st (26,762kgp) General Electric CF6-80C2 and the Pratt & Whitney PW4059 of similar power. In 1986, Boeing was projecting a further stretch of the Model 767 to produce the Model 767-400 which would have two more fuselage plugs, of 11ft (3.35m) ahead of the wing and 10ft 1in (3.07m) aft of it. This would bring the basic mixed-class seating to about 300, and the maximum one-class accommodation to some 370. Maximum take-off weight would be limited to the same values as for the basic Model 767-300ER, with the same engine options as the latter; weights higher than about 380,000lb (172,365kg) would be unacceptable because of the limit on aircraft rotation angle at take-off resulting from the increased length of fuselage behind the main wheels.

SERVICE USE

The Model 767-300 was first ordered on 29 September 1983, by Japan Air Lines, with JT9D-7R4D engines. The airline took delivery of its first stretched Model 767 on 25 September 1986, this being the third aircraft off the line, following certification on 22 September based on the programme flown by the first two aircraft. Further deliveries in October and December 1986 and June 1987 complete the initial JAL order for four aircraft, and service was inaugurated on 20 October, on domestic routes in Japan, for which the aircraft were arranged to have 16 first-class 'superseats' and 254 economy-class seats. Other orders had been placed, by early 1987, by Delta, for nine aircraft with CF6-80A2 engines and delivery starting in October 1986, and by All Nippon Airways, for 15 aircraft and delivery from October 1987 onwards.

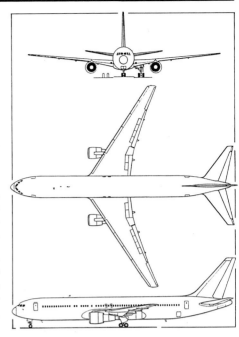

Above: The Boeing 767-300, as shown in this three-view drawing, differs from the basic -200 variants externally only in its overall length, which is increased by 21ft (6.42m).

Left: The flight deck of the 767-300 differs in no significant respect from that of the earlier Boeing 767 variants and, as shown here, features electronic displays for flight and navigation information.

noise requirements. One such engine is the ungeared General Electric GE-36, the first flight of which occurred on 20 August 1986 with the engine on the port rear side of a Boeing 727-100, in a joint General Electric/Boeing programme. A Pratt & Whitney/Allison 528-DX was to be similarly tested on the Boeing 727 during 1987, but in January of that year Boeing said that the General Electric UDF was 'one of the leading contenders to power the 7J7'. This was confirmed in February 1987 when Boeing selected the 25,000lb st (11,340kgp) GE36-B22A version of the General Electric UDF for the 7J7, after also having given consideration to the IAE SuperFan in an underwing installation.

Another area where new technology will benefit the Model 7J7 as proposed by Boeing, is the use of lightweight structural materials to improve fuel economy. Aluminium-lithium alloys have the potential to save about 8 per cent over conventional alloys, and composites such as graphite/epoxy have already demonstrated savings of up to 25 per cent in secondary structures. Applications in primary structures are planned for the Model 7J7, together with greater use of thermoplastic composites. Advanced computer simulation techniques are also being used by Boeing to facilitate the application of new aerodynamic ideas to wing design.

The flight deck of the Model 7J7 will feature multi-colour flat-panel displays in place of contemporary CRT displays, needing reduced space, weight and power, and offering better reliability. Data bus techniques are being adapted in Boeing's Digital Autonomous Terminal Access Communications (DATAC) system to link aircraft systems and transfer necessary data. The flight-control system will use fly-by-wire and fibre optic systems.

Boeing's timescale for the Model 7J7 was based on offering airlines a basic specification by mid-1987, with a production commitment expected by mid-1988 and first delivery of a certified aircraft in early 1992. At the end of 1986, consideration had been given to a smaller, 100/110 seat Model 7J7-110 as well as the baseline Model 7J7-150, but by early 1987 Boeing had decided again to concentrate on the 150-seat 7J7 while offering new versions of the 737 for the 100-seat market. The twin-aisle 7J7 has an outside fuselage diameter of 188in (4.78m). Depending on the engine choice and location, the overall length would be 139ft 10in (42.62m) or 120ft 6in (36.73m), and the wingspan 120ft 0in (36.58).

BRITISH AEROSPACE 748 UK

S eeking to diversify its product line as it was aware that orders for military aircraft, upon which it was then heavily dependant, were likely to dwindle, the Avro company began to explore commercial aircraft designs in the late 1950s. Efforts soon after World War II to enter the civil aircraft market with the Tudor had not been successful, and by the mid-1950s all Avro's design and production activity related to defence contracts. Following the 1957 decision to re-enter the commercial field, attention was focussed upon the small short-haul turboprop category of aircraft, as a replacement for such piston twins as the Douglas DC-3 and Vickers Viking and a competitor for the Fokker F27, by then already in flight test. Early studies under the Avro 748 designation were for a 20-seat, high-wing, twin-engined aircraft with a gross weight of only 18,000lb (8,165kg), but analysis of airline reaction to this proposal, and of other market studies, led to the development of a new low-wing design with a gross weight of 33,000lb (14,968kg), two Rolls-Royce Darts and 36 seats. Features of this design, which was launched into prototype construction in January 1959, included a high-aspect-ratio wing with a novel type of single slotted flap to enhance field performance, and the use of fail-safe principles in structural design. Known at first as the Avro 748, this aircraft later became the H.S.748 when Avro was absorbed into the Hawker Siddeley Group, and then as the British Aerospace 748 after HSA's nationalization. The 748 remained in production from 1961 to 1986, and provided the basis for development of the British Aerospace ATP, which then succeeded it. The two prototypes entered flight testing on 24 June 1960 and 10 April 1961 respectively.

VARIANTS

The prototype and first production batch, to Srs 1 standard, had 1,880ehp (1,402kW) Rolls-Royce RDa6 Dart Mk 514 engines. The Srs 2, first flown 6 November 1961, introduced 2,105ehp (1,570kW) RDa7 Dart Mk 531 engines and was superseded in 1967 by the Srs 2A with uprated Darts, usually the 2,280ehp (1,700kW) Mk 535-2 (originally designated Mk 532-2S), but some with the Mk 534-2 (originally Mk 532-2L) and nine special-purpose aircraft with RDa8 variants. The Srs 2C, first flown 31 December 1971, was as Srs 2A fitted with large freight door in rear port fuselage side. The Srs 2B introduced a number of refinements and improvements, including a 4ft (1.22m) span increase with new wingtips, modified tail surfaces and Dart Mk 536-2 engines, plus a hush-kit option; the first production Srs 2B flew on 22 June 1979. The final variant was the BAe Super 748, similar to the Srs 2B but with a new flight deck, Dart Mk 552 engines with hush kit and automatic water-methanol injection options, new cabin interior design, and other improvements. The Super 748 first flew on 30 July 1984. Military variants of the 748 were also produced, either similar to the Srs 2B but cleared to operate at higher weights, or with a new rear fuselage incorporating clamshell doors and a loading ramp; in the latter form, the type was named Andover. The name

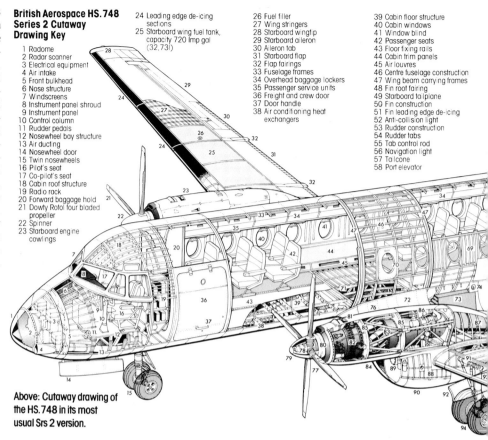

British Aerospace HS.748 Series 2 Cutaway Drawing Key

1 Radome
2 Radar scanner
3 Electrical equipment
4 Air intake
5 Front bulkhead
6 Nose structure
7 Windscreens
8 Instrument panel shroud
9 Instrument panel
10 Control column
11 Rudder pedals
12 Nosewheel bay structure
13 Air ducting
14 Nosewheel door
15 Twin nosewheels
16 Pilot's seat
17 Co-pilot's seat
18 Cabin roof structure
19 Radio rack
20 Forward baggage hold
21 Dowty Rotol four bladed propeller
22 Spinner
23 Starboard engine cowlings
24 Leading edge de-icing sections
25 Starboard wing fuel tank, capacity 720 Imp gal (3,273l)
26 Fuel filler
27 Wing stringers
28 Starboard wingtip
29 Starboard aileron
30 Aileron tab
31 Starboard flap
32 Flap fairings
33 Fuselage frames
34 Overhead baggage lockers
35 Passenger service units
36 Freight and crew door
37 Door handle
38 Air conditioning heat exchangers
39 Cabin floor structure
40 Cabin windows
41 Window blind
42 Passenger seats
43 Floor fixing rails
44 Cabin trim panels
45 Air louvres
46 Centre fuselage construction
47 Wing beam carrying frames
48 Fin root fairing
49 Starboard tailplane
50 Fin construction
51 Fin leading edge de-icing
52 Anti-collision light
53 Rudder construction
54 Rudder tabs
55 Tab control rod
56 Navigation light
57 Tailcone
58 Port elevator

Above: Cutaway drawing of the HS.748 in its most usual Srs 2 version.

SPECIFICATION
(Super 748)

Power Plant: Two Rolls-Royce Dart Mk 552 (RDa7) turboprops each rated at 2,280ehp (1,700kW) for take-off, with Dowty Rotol four-blade constant-speed fully-feathering propellers of 12ft 0in (3.66m) diameter. Fuel capacity, 1,440 Imp gal (6,500l) in integral wing tanks.
Performance: Cruising speed at 38,000lb (17,236kg) gross weight, 245kts (454km/h); initial rate of climb, 1,420ft/min (7.2m/sec); service ceiling, 25,000ft (7,620m); take-off field length (BCAR), 4,525ft (1,380m); landing field length, 3,360ft (1,025m); range with max payload and typical reserves, 1,007 naut mls (1,865km); range with max fuel and 7,921lb (3,593kg) payload, 1,650 naut mls (3,055km); ferry range, 1,905 naut mls (3,528km).
Weights: Operating weight empty, 27,059lb (12,274kg); max fuel weight, 11,520lb (5,225kg); max payload, 11,441lb (5,189kg); max take-off weight, 46,500lb (21,092kg); max landing weight, 43,000lb (19,504kg); max zero-fuel weight, 38,500lb (17,463kg).
Dimensions: Span, 102ft 6in (31.24m); overall length, 67ft 0in (20.42m); overall height, 24ft 10in (7.57m); sweepback, 2 deg 54 min at quarter chord; wing area, 828.87sq ft (77.00m²).
Accommodation: Cabin length, 46ft 6in (14.17m), max width, 8ft 1in (2.46m), max height, 6ft 3½in (1.92m). Standard layouts for 40-58 passengers four-abreast with central aisle. Freight/baggage volume, 316cu ft (8.95m³). Flight crew of two.

Coastguarder was applied to a variant equipped for maritime patrol and surveillance and first flown on 18 February 1977.

SERVICE USE

The 748 Srs 1 was certificated on 7 December 1961 and entered service with Skyways in 1962. The Srs 2 was certificated in October 1962 and entered service with BKS Air Transport. Deliveries of the Srs 2B began in January 1980, to Air Madagascar. Deliveries of the Super 748 began in 1984, to LIAT. Production of the 748 up to the beginning of 1987 totalled 377. This figure included two prototypes and 18 Series 1s; 31 military Andover C.Mk 1s built for the RAF; approximately 52 Srs 2/2A aircraft sold to military users, of which 18 had the Srs 2B-type side freight door; and 89 sets of components supplied to India for assembly by Hindustan Aeronautics Ltd, 72 of these being for the Indian Air Force and 17 for Indian Airlines. Some 50 airlines around the world were operating a total of about 160 HS.748s at the beginning of 1987. The major users are Dan-Air, Bouraq Indonesia, and Philippine Airlines.

Below: The first of six HS. 748 Srs 2Bs acquired by German regional operator DLT, which was formed in 1974 and flies several routes for Lufthansa which has a 26% shareholding.

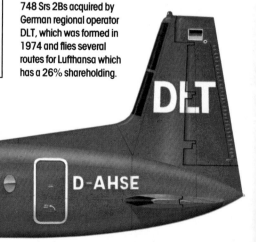

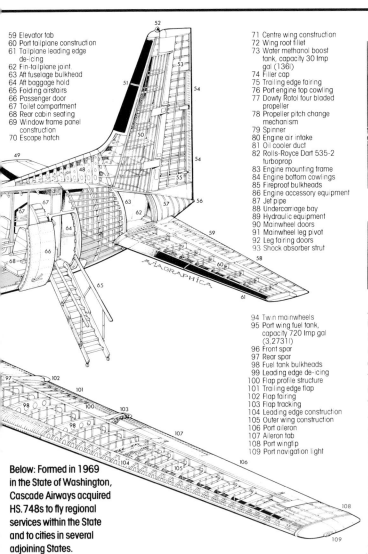

59 Elevator tab
60 Port tailplane construction
61 Tailplane leading edge de-icing
62 Fin-tailplane joint
63 Aft fuselage bulkhead
64 Aft baggage hold
65 Folding airstairs
66 Passenger door
67 Toilet compartment
68 Rear cabin seating
69 Window frame panel construction
70 Escape hatch

71 Centre wing construction
72 Wing root fillet
73 Water methanol boost tank, capacity 30 Imp gal (136l)
74 Filler cap
75 Trailing edge fairing
76 Port engine top cowling
77 Dowty Rotol four bladed propeller
78 Propeller pitch change mechanism
79 Spinner
80 Engine air intake
81 Oil cooler duct
82 Rolls-Royce Dart 535-2 turboprop
83 Engine mounting frame
84 Engine bottom cowlings
85 Fireproof bulkheads
86 Engine accessory equipment
87 Jet pipe
88 Undercarriage bay
89 Hydraulic equipment
90 Mainwheel doors
91 Mainwheel leg pivot
92 Leg fairing doors
93 Shock absorber strut

94 Twin mainwheels
95 Port wing fuel tank, capacity 720 Imp gal (3,273l)
96 Front spar
97 Rear spar
98 Fuel tank bulkheads
99 Leading edge de-icing
100 Flap profile structure
101 Trailing edge flap
102 Flap fairing
103 Flap tracking
104 Leading edge construction
105 Outer wing construction
106 Port aileron
107 Aileron tab
108 Port wingtip
109 Port navigation light

Above: Since its introduction, the HS.748 has undergone several major updates of systems and equipment, including the cabin interior. This illustration shows the four-abreast seating in a 48-seat layout, with enclosed overhead lockers, of a late-production HS.748.

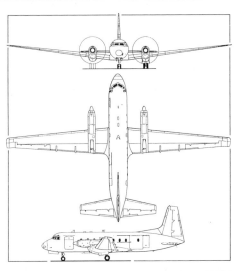

Right: Three-view drawing of the British Aerospace 748 Srs 2B, with the optional freight door in the rear port side of the fuselage.

Below: Formed in 1969 in the State of Washington, Cascade Airways acquired HS.748s to fly regional services within the State and to cities in several adjoining States.

BRITISH AEROSPACE ATP UK

The idea of stretching the original Avro/Hawker Siddeley 748 feederliner dates back at least to 1961 when an Avro 748E was projected, with a 6ft (1.83m) fuselage extension and the uprated 2,400ehp (1,790kW) RDa10 Dart engines. Market forecasts for this project indicated that it was premature and it did not proceed beyond the paper stage. Twenty years or so were to elapse, in fact, before the need for an enlarged derivative of the 748 could be clearly demonstrated, and it was not until 1980 that serious work on such a possibility was resumed at the Manchester works of what had by then become British Aerospace. Although conceived in essence as a stretched and modernized 748, the new aircraft became known as the Advanced Turboprop, shortened to ATP, in preference to BAe 846, its official type number in the drawing office. Several possible stretches of the 748 fuselage were considered, and were evaluated alongside a wholly new aircraft designed to offer the same capacity of about 60-65 seats and similar payload/range performance. From the studies and market contracts in the early 1980s it emerged that an all-new aircraft would be expensive to develop, thus putting a strain on BAe resources when expenditure on the Airbus A320 was peaking; on the other hand, a simple stretch of the 748 to add 8-12 passengers did little to enhance the economics or airline appeal of the aircraft. The 'middle course' that emerged as the best way to go was to aim for a capacity of 60-70 seats and to combine the best features of the Super 748 with new fuel-efficient engines. This provided BAe with an opportunity to minimize the launch costs and to offer an aircraft that in terms of operating economics could compete with all other types known or expected in the market place through the late 1980s and early 1990s. The 'marketing launch' was announced in September 1982 on this basis, the ATP being designed to use PW124 engines on the basic 748 wing, with a lengthened version of the 748 fuselage (retaining

SPECIFICATION

Power Plant: Two Pratt & Whitney Canada PW124 turboprops each rated at 2,150shp (1,604kW) for normal take-off, with automatic emergency reserve to increase output to 2,400shp (1,790kW) or (PW125 variant) 2,570shp (1,916kW), with BAe/Hamilton Standard six-blade propellers of 13ft 9in (4.19m) diameter. Fuel capacity, 1,400 Imp gal (6,365l) in integral wing tanks.
Performance: Max operating speed, 225kts (417km/h) IAS; typical cruising speed, 265kts (491km/h); long-range cruising speed, 240kts (444km/h) at 23,000ft (7,010m); typical rate of climb, 1,370ft/min (6.96m/sec); max operating altitude, 25,000ft (7,620m); range with max payload, 575 naut mls (1,065km); range with 64 passengers, 985 naut mls (1,825km); range with max fuel, and 8,000lb (3,629kg) payload, 1,860 naut mls (3,444km).
Weights: Typical operating weight empty, 29,970lb (13,594kg); max fuel weight, 11,200lb (5,080kg); max payload, 14,830lb (6,727kg); max take-off weight, 49,500lb (22,453kg); max landing weight, 48,000lb (21,773kg); max zero-fuel weight, 44,300lb (20,094kg).
Dimensions: Span, 100ft 6in (30.63m); overall length, 85ft 4in (26.01m); height, 23ft 5in (7.14m); sweepback, 2 deg 54 min at quarter chord; wing area, 843sq ft (78.30m²).
Accommodation: Cabin length, 63ft 0in (19.20m), max width, 8ft 1in (2.46m), max height, 6ft 4in (1.92m). Standard configuration provides 64 seats four-abreast at 31in (79cm) pitch; alternative layouts available for up to 72 passengers. Baggage/freight compartments at front and rear of cabin, total volume, 390cu ft (11.04m³). Flight crew of two and two cabin attendants.

Below: The prototype of the British Aerospace ATP made its first flight at Manchester on 6 August 1986, within a few minutes of a target day and time that had been set some three years earlier. This photograph shows the ATP on its first flight, in a BAe livery. British Midland is the launch customer.

British Aerospace ATP Cutaway Drawing Key
1 Radome
2 Weather radar scanner
3 Scanner mounting
4 Batteries
5 Front pressure bulkhead
6 Static port
7 Nose undercarriage wheel bay
8 Nosewheel doors
9 Pitot head
10 Cockpit floor level
11 Rudder pedals
12 Instrument panel, Electronic Flight Instrument Display
13 Instrument panel shroud
14 Windscreen panels
15 Windscreen wipers
16 Cockpit roof framing
17 Overhead systems switch panel
18 Co-pilot's seat
19 Direct vision opening side window panel
20 Control column handwheel
21 VOR/ILS aerial
22 Chart case
23 Nose undercarriage pivot fixing
24 Nosewheel leg strut
25 Twin nosewheels, forward retracting
26 Nosewheel leg door
27 Radio and avionics equipment rack
28 Pilot's seat
29 Cockpit eyebrow window
30 Electrical distribution panel
31 Starboard side baggage door
32 Toilet compartment
33 Main entry door, open position
34 Door latch
35 Retractable airstairs
36 Folding handrail
37 Entry lobby
38 Cabin attendant's folding seat
39 Starboard side forward baggage compartment
40 Airstairs stowage space
41 Passenger wardrobe and hand baggage locker
42 Conditioned air riser ducts
43 Passenger compartment forward bulkhead

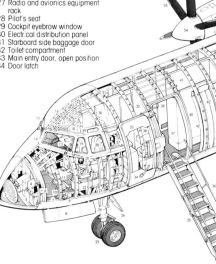

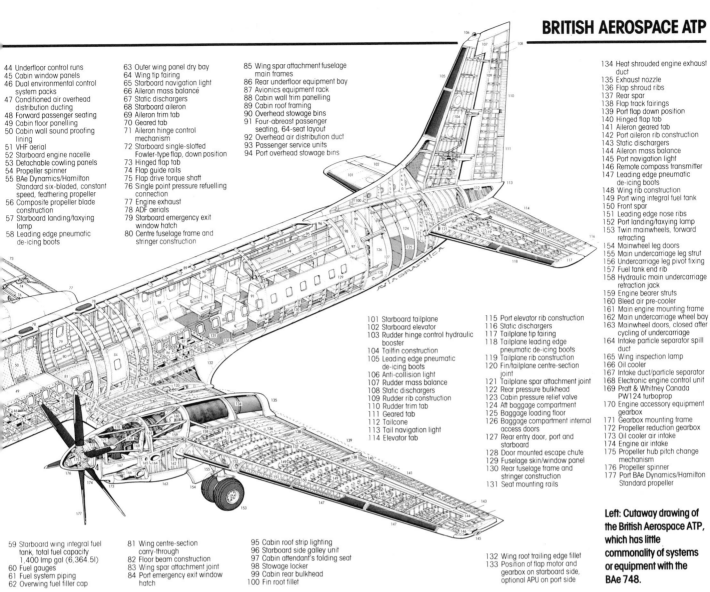

44 Underfloor control runs
45 Cabin window panels
46 Dual environmental control system packs
47 Conditioned air overhead distribution ducting
48 Forward passenger seating
49 Cabin floor panelling
50 Cabin wall sound proofing lining
51 VHF aerial
52 Starboard engine nacelle
53 Detachable cowling panels
54 Propeller spinner
55 BAe Dynamics/Hamilton Standard six-bladed, constant speed, feathering propeller
56 Composite propeller blade construction
57 Starboard landing/taxying lamp
58 Leading edge pneumatic de-icing boots

63 Outer wing panel dry bay
64 Wing tip fairing
65 Starboard navigation light
66 Aileron mass balance
67 Static dischargers
68 Starboard aileron
69 Aileron trim tab
70 Geared tab
71 Aileron hinge control mechanism
72 Starboard single-slotted Fowler-type flap, down position
73 Hinged flap tab
74 Flap guide rails
75 Flap drive torque shaft
76 Single point pressure refuelling connection
77 Engine exhaust
78 ADF aerials
79 Starboard emergency exit window hatch
80 Centre fuselage frame and stringer construction

85 Wing spar attachment fuselage main frames
86 Rear underfloor equipment bay
87 Avionics equipment rack
88 Cabin wall trim panelling
89 Cabin roof framing
90 Overhead stowage bins
91 Four-abreast passenger seating, 64-seat layout
92 Overhead air distribution duct
93 Passenger service units
94 Port overhead stowage bins

101 Starboard tailplane
102 Starboard elevator
103 Rudder hinge control hydraulic booster
104 Tailfin construction
105 Leading edge pneumatic de-icing boots
106 Anti-collision light
107 Rudder mass balance
108 Static dischargers
109 Rudder rib construction
110 Rudder trim tab
111 Geared tab
112 Tailcone
113 Tail navigation light
114 Elevator tab

115 Port elevator rib construction
116 Static dischargers
117 Tailplane tip fairing
118 Tailplane leading edge pneumatic de-icing boots
119 Tailplane rib construction
120 Fin/tailplane centre-section joint
121 Tailplane spar attachment joint
122 Rear pressure bulkhead
123 Cabin pressure relief valve
124 Aft baggage compartment
125 Baggage loading floor
126 Baggage compartment internal access doors
127 Rear entry door, port and starboard
128 Door mounted escape chute
129 Fuselage skin/window panel
130 Rear fuselage frame and stringer construction
131 Seat mounting rails

134 Heat shrouded engine exhaust duct
135 Exhaust nozzle
136 Flap shroud ribs
137 Rear spar
138 Flap track fairings
139 Port flap down position
140 Hinged flap tab
141 Aileron geared tab
142 Port aileron rib construction
143 Static dischargers
144 Aileron mass balance
145 Port navigation light
146 Remote compass transmitter
147 Leading edge pneumatic de-icing boots
148 Wing rib construction
149 Port wing integral fuel tank
150 Front spar
151 Leading edge nose ribs
152 Port landing/taxying lamp
153 Twin mainwheels, forward retracting
154 Mainwheel leg doors
155 Main undercarriage leg strut
156 Undercarriage leg pivot fixing
157 Fuel tank end rib
158 Hydraulic main undercarriage retraction jack
159 Engine bearer struts
160 Bleed air pre-cooler
161 Main engine mounting frame
162 Main undercarriage wheel bay
163 Mainwheel doors, closed after cycling of undercarriage
164 Intake particle separator spill duct
165 Wing inspection lamp
166 Oil cooler
167 Intake duct/particle separator
168 Electronic engine control unit
169 Pratt & Whitney Canada PW124 turboprop
170 Engine accessory equipment gearbox
171 Gearbox mounting frame
172 Propeller reduction gearbox
173 Oil cooler air intake
174 Engine air intake
175 Propeller hub pitch change mechanism
176 Propeller spinner
177 Port BAe Dynamics/Hamilton Standard propeller

Left: Cutaway drawing of the British Aerospace ATP, which has little commonality of systems or equipment with the BAe 748.

59 Starboard wing integral fuel tank, total fuel capacity 1,400 Imp gal (6,364.5l)
60 Fuel gauges
61 Fuel system piping
62 Overwing fuel filler cap

81 Wing centre-section carry-through
82 Floor beam construction
83 Wing spar attachment joint
84 Port emergency exit window hatch

95 Cabin roof strip lighting
96 Starboard side galley unit
97 Cabin attendant's folding seat
98 Stowage locker
99 Cabin rear bulkhead
100 Fin root fillet

132 Wing root trailing edge fillet
133 Position of flap motor and gearbox on starboard side, optional APU on port side

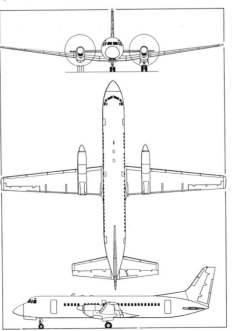

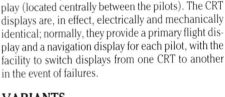

the same cross section) and a swept-back fin and rudder, adopted to give the aircraft a more modern appearance. By the time the full launch decision was made, on 1 March 1984, the original concept of 'minimum change' from the 748 had been modified to one of 'maximum change', in order to give operators the most modern systems and equipment available in the second half of the 1980s. Thus the ATP now offers a wholly new, variable frequecy AC electrical system; a new environmental control system; a revised hydraulic system; carbon brakes;

a completely new avionics suite based on a digital data bus; and an advanced flight deck. The latter incorporates a Smiths electronic flight instrument system (EFIS) with four cathode ray tube displays (two for each pilot) and a Bendix multi-function display (located centrally between the pilots). The CRT displays are, in effect, electrically and mechanically identical; normally, they provide a primary flight display and a navigation display for each pilot, with the facility to switch displays from one CRT to another in the event of failures.

VARIANTS

The basic ATP is certificated in accordance with the US FAR Pt25 and the equivalent Joint Airworthiness Requirements (JAR25) in Europe. The latter permits a higher engine operating temperature than FAR Pt25 allows in the emergency power reserve case. Consequently, aircraft operating with a JAR25 certificate have PW125 engines and a 420shp (313kW) power reserve that is available automatically if one engine fails during take-off. The PW124 engines used in aircraft operating under FAR Pt25 certification have a 250shp (186.4kW) power reserve.

SERVICE USE

Flight testing of the ATP began at Woodford on 6 August 1986, the second flight development aircraft joining the programme some months later. The certification target date of 30 July 1987 allows deliveries to begin at that time to British Midland, which has ordered three with two more on option; these are for operation by British Midland itself and two of its associated operators, Manx Airlines and Loganair. The second customer, LIAT Caribbean Airlines, will take delivery of two ATPs in 1988.

Above: A view of the ATP flight deck, by night, showing the four CRT displays of the Smiths Electronic Flight Instrumentation System, two for each pilot, with a fifth, central, display for the Bendix MFD.

Left: LIAT, the successor to Leeward Islands Air Transport, is one of the first to buy the ATP.

Right: A three-view drawing of the ATP, showing both its similarities to, and differences from, the British Aerospace 748. The fuselage, of the same cross section, is longer by some 18ft, and the fin and rudder are swept back to improve the appearance. Pratt & Whitney PW124 engines replace the Rolls-Royce Darts that powered all versions of the BAe 748.

British Aerospace 146-100 Cutaway Drawing Key

1 Radome
2 Weather radar scanner
3 Radar mounting
4 ILS aerial
5 Oxygen bottle, capacity 400 Imp gal (1,812l)
6 Sloping front pressure bulkhead
7 VOR flush aerial
8 Nose undercarriage wheel bay
9 Nosewheel leg strut
10 Twin nosewheels
11 Pitot tube
12 Rudder pedals
13 Instrument panel
14 Windscreen wipers

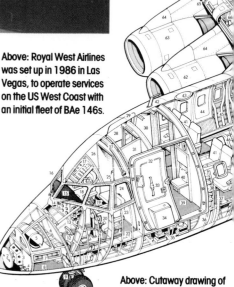

The history of the British Aerospace 146 goes back to the 1960s and to the design studies initiated by the then-independent de Havilland Aircraft Company for a small turboprop-engined feederliner designated D.H.123. This was a twin-engined, high-wing design, but further studies, which were continued at Hatfield after de Havilland had been absorbed in the Hawker Siddeley Aviation company, favoured low-wing layouts with turbofan engines mounted on the rear fuselage. These studies culminated in the H.S.144 project, but lack of a suitable engine led the designers in April 1971 to revert to a high-wing layout using four smaller turbofans, such as the Avco Lycoming ALF 502. In this form, as the H.S.146, the project was formally launched on 29 August 1973, in partnership with the British government. But the economic recession of 1974 – 75 resulted in the termination of the programme in October 1974, when the H.S.146 reverted to project design status. In substantially the same form as originally planned, the aircraft was re-launched on 10 July 1978 by British Aerospace, into which HSA had meanwhile been nationalized, once again with government financial assistance, and an initial production batch was put in hand at Hatfield. From the start of development two fuselage lengths were planned for models identified as the Srs 100 and Srs 200 (see Variants section below), and construction, development and flight testing proceeded in parallel. The first Srs 100 flew on 3 September 1981, followed by a second and third on 25 January and 2 April 1982, and the first Srs 200 (the fourth airframe completed) flew on 1 August 1982. Production of the BAe 146 has been spread within BAc factories in the UK, and also internationally on a risk-sharing basis. In particular, Avco Aerostructures in the USA produces the main wing torsion box, and Saab Scania in Sweden is responsible for the tailplane and all moving control surfaces. Pods for the ALF 502 turbofans are produced in Northern Ireland by Short Brothers. All final assembly takes place at Hatfield.

VARIANTS

The initial variant is the BAe 146-100, with an overall length of 85ft 11in (26.19m), providing for 82 passengers at 33in (84cm) pitch, or up to a maximum of 93. This has the same power plant as the 146-200 indicated in the data panel, but a maximum take-off weight of 84,000lb (38,102kg). The 146-200, developed in parallel with the 146-100, differs only in length of fuselage and operating weights, with associated structural and system changes. A freighter version of the 146-200 has been developed, with an upward-hinged door (in the rear fuselage port side) measuring 6ft 6in (1.98m) in height by 10ft 10in (3.30m) in width. Under a 1986 agreement with BAe the Dothan Division of Hayes International Corporation in the USA is responsible for the detail design, manufacture and installation of the freight door and freight handling equipment, plus necessary structural changes to the aircraft, which are flown for this purpose as 'green' airframes from Hatfield to the Hayes facility at Dothan, Alabama. The 146-200 Freighter, which first flew on 21 August 1986, can accommodate six standard LD3 freight containers and carry a 22,000lb (9,980kg) payload. Military versions of the BAe 146 are also being studied in conjunction with Lockheed-Georgia Company. In September 1984 BAe announced that it was launching a 146-300, featuring a further lengthening of the fuselage to increase the standard seating to 122 at 32in (81cm) pitch, or 130 at 29in (74cm) pitch. This plan was modified during 1986, when the decision was made to proceed with conversion of the original Srs 100 prototype to Srs 300 standard, with the 'stretch' set at 7ft 10in (2.38m) on the Srs 200 length, and gross weight limited initially to 93,000lb (48,184kg), using the same ALF 502R-5 engines as the Srs 200. In this form, the Srs 300 will provide comfortable five-abreast seating for 100 passengers, and will offer operating economics comparable to those of the Srs 200. Weights of up to 104,000lb (47,174kg) are expected to be possible later.

SERVICE USE

Certification of the BAe 146-100 was achieved on 20 May 1983, and Dan-Air put the type into revenue service on 27 May. The Srs 200 was certificated in June 1983 in the UK and USA, allowing Air Wisconsin to become the first operator of the type on 27 June. Orders by January 1987 totalled 81; customers for the Srs 100 include AirPac of Alaska, Aspen Airways, British Caribbean Airways, CAAC in China, Dan-Air, the government of Mali, Royal West Airlines, TABA in Brazil, and The Queen's Flight in the UK. The Srs 200 has been ordered by Air Wisconsin, AirCal, Ansett, Hawaiian Airlines, Pacific Southwest Airlines, TNT and Pelita. Air Wisconsin is expected to be the first operator or the Srs 300.

Above: Royal West Airlines was set up in 1986 in Las Vegas, to operate services on the US West Coast with an initial fleet of BAe 146s.

Above: Cutaway drawing of the BAe 146 Srs 100.

SPECIFICATION
(BAe 146-200)

Power Plant: Four Avco Lycoming ALF 502R-5 turbofans each rated at 6,970lb st (3,162kgp) for take-off. Fuel capacity, 2,580 Imp gal (11,728l) in integral tanks in wing and wing centre section; optional auxiliary tankage can be carried in wing root fairings with maximum capacity of 258 Imp gal (1,173l).

Performance: Max operating speed, 295kts (547km/h) IAS or Mach = 0.70; max cruising speed, 423kts (784km/h) at 24,000ft (7,315m); economical cruising speed, 381kts (706km/h) at 31,000ft (9,450m); take-off field length (FAR), 4,950ft (1,510m); landing field length (FAR), 3,790ft (1,155m); range with max payload and typical reserves, 1,176 naut mls (2,179km); range with max fuel, and payload of 14,500lb (6,575kg), 1,476 naut mls (2,733km).

Weights: Operational weight empty, 50,500lb (22,861kg); standard fuel weight, 20,640lb (9,362kg); max fuel weight, 22,704lb (10,298kg); max payload, 23,100lb (10,478kg); max take-off weight, 93,000lb (42,184kg); max landing weight, 81,000lb (36,741kg); max zero-fuel weight, 73,500lb (33,339kg).

Dimensions: Span, 86ft 5in (26.34m); overall length, 93ft 10in (28.60m); overall height, 28ft 3in (8.61m); sweepback, 15 deg at quarter chord; wing area, 832sq ft (77.30m²).

Accommodation: Cabin length, 50ft 7in (15.42m), max width, 11ft 1in (3.38m), max height, 6ft 7½in (2.02m). Typical one-class accommodation for 96 passengers six-abreast at 33in (84cm) pitch, or a maximum of 109 six-abreast at 29in (74cm) pitch. Underfloor baggage/freight hold volume, 645cu ft (18.3m³). Flight crew of two and two or three cabin attendants.

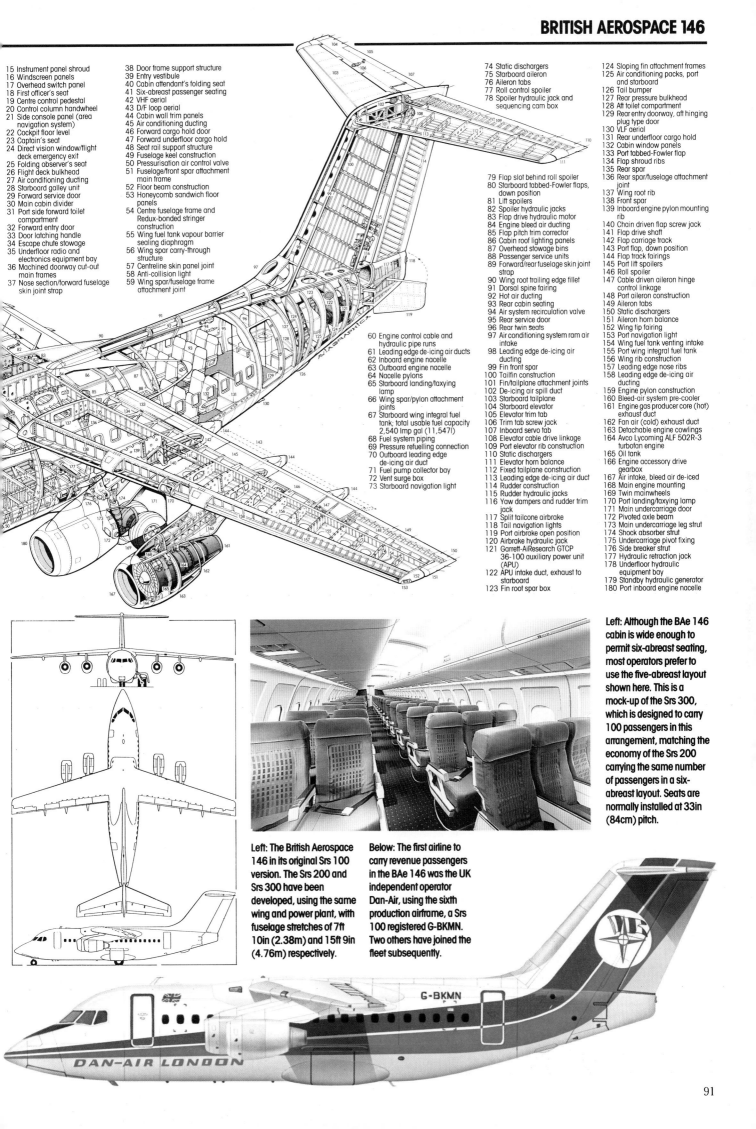

15 Instrument panel shroud
16 Windscreen panels
17 Overhead switch panel
18 First officer's seat
19 Centre control pedestal
20 Control column handwheel
21 Side console panel (area navigation system)
22 Cockpit floor level
23 Captain's seat
24 Direct vision window/flight deck emergency exit
25 Folding observer's seat
26 Flight deck stowage
27 Air conditioning ducting
28 Starboard galley unit
29 Forward service door
30 Main cabin divider
31 Port side forward toilet compartment
32 Forward entry door
33 Door latching handle
34 Escape chute stowage
35 Underfloor radio and electronics equipment bay
36 Machined doorway cut-out main frames
37 Nose section/forward fuselage skin joint strap

38 Door frame support structure
39 Entry vestibule
40 Cabin attendant's folding seat
41 Six-abreast passenger seating
42 VHF aerial
43 D/F loop aerial
44 Cabin wall trim panels
45 Air conditioning ducting
46 Forward cargo hold door
47 Forward underfloor cargo hold
48 Seat rail support structure
49 Fuselage keel construction
50 Pressurisation air control valve
51 Fuselage/front spar attachment main frame
52 Floor beam construction
53 Honeycomb sandwich floor panels
54 Centre fuselage frame and Redux-bonded stringer construction
55 Wing fuel tank vapour barrier sealing diaphragm
56 Wing spar carry-through structure
57 Centreline skin panel joint
58 Anti-collision light
59 Wing spar/fuselage frame attachment joint

60 Engine control cable and hydraulic pipe runs
61 Leading edge de-icing air ducts
62 Inboard engine nacelle
63 Outboard engine nacelle
64 Nacelle pylons
65 Starboard landing/taxiing lamp
66 Wing spar/pylon attachment joints
67 Starboard wing integral fuel tank; total usable fuel capacity 2,540 Imp gal (11,547l)
68 Fuel system piping
69 Pressure refuelling connection
70 Outboard leading edge de-icing air duct
71 Fuel pump collector bay
72 Vent surge box
73 Starboard navigation light

74 Static dischargers
75 Starboard aileron
76 Aileron tabs
77 Roll control spoiler
78 Spoiler hydraulic jack and sequencing cam box
79 Flap slot behind roll spoiler
80 Starboard tabbed-Fowler flaps, down position
81 Lift spoilers
82 Spoiler hydraulic jacks
83 Flap drive hydraulic motor
84 Engine bleed air ducting
85 Flap pitch trim corrector
86 Cabin roof lighting panels
87 Overhead stowage bins
88 Passenger service units
89 Forward/rear fuselage skin joint strap
90 Wing root trailing edge fillet
91 Dorsal spine fairing
92 Hot air ducting
93 Rear cabin seating
94 Air system recirculation valve
95 Rear service door
96 Rear twin seats
97 Air conditioning system ram air intake
98 Leading edge de-icing air ducting
99 Fin front spar
100 Tailfin construction
101 Fin/tailplane attachment joints
102 De-icing air spill duct
103 Starboard tailplane
104 Starboard elevator
105 Elevator trim tab
106 Trim tab screw jack
107 Inboard servo tab
108 Elevator cable drive linkage
109 Port elevator rib construction
110 Static dischargers
111 Elevator horn balance
112 Fixed tailplane construction
113 Leading edge de-icing air duct
114 Rudder construction
115 Rudder hydraulic jacks
116 Yaw dampers and rudder trim jack
117 Split tailcone airbrake
118 Tail navigation lights
119 Port airbrake open position
120 Airbrake hydraulic jack
121 Garrett-AiResearch GTCP 36-100 auxiliary power unit (APU)
122 APU intake duct, exhaust to starboard
123 Fin root spar box

124 Sloping fin attachment frames
125 Air conditioning packs, port and starboard
126 Tail bumper
127 Rear pressure bulkhead
128 Aft toilet compartment
129 Rear entry doorway, aft hinging plug type door
130 VLF aerial
131 Rear underfloor cargo hold
132 Cabin window panels
133 Port tabbed-Fowler flap
134 Flap shroud ribs
135 Rear spar
136 Rear spar/fuselage attachment joint
137 Wing root rib
138 Front spar
139 Inboard engine pylon mounting rib
140 Chain driven flap screw jack
141 Flap drive shaft
142 Flap carriage track
143 Port flap, down position
144 Flap track fairings
145 Port lift spoilers
146 Roll spoiler
147 Cable driven aileron hinge control linkage
148 Port aileron construction
149 Aileron tabs
150 Static dischargers
151 Aileron horn balance
152 Wing tip fairing
153 Port navigation light
154 Wing fuel tank venting intake
155 Port wing integral fuel tank
156 Wing rib construction
157 Leading edge nose ribs
158 Leading edge de-icing air ducting
159 Engine pylon construction
160 Bleed-air system pre-cooler
161 Engine gas producer core (hot) exhaust duct
162 Fan air (cold) exhaust duct
163 Detachable engine cowlings
164 Avco Lycoming ALF 502R-3 turbofan engine
165 Oil tank
166 Engine accessory drive gearbox
167 Air intake, bleed air de-iced
168 Main engine mounting
169 Twin mainwheels
170 Port landing/taxiing lamp
171 Main undercarriage door
172 Pivoted axle beam
173 Main undercarriage leg strut
174 Shock absorber strut
175 Undercarriage pivot fixing
176 Side breaker strut
177 Hydraulic retraction jack
178 Underfloor hydraulic equipment bay
179 Standby hydraulic generator
180 Port inboard engine nacelle

Left: Although the BAe 146 cabin is wide enough to permit six-abreast seating, most operators prefer to use the five-abreast layout shown here. This is a mock-up of the Srs 300, which is designed to carry 100 passengers in this arrangement, matching the economy of the Srs 200 carrying the same number of passengers in a six-abreast layout. Seats are normally installed at 33in (84cm) pitch.

Left: The British Aerospace 146 in its original Srs 100 version. The Srs 200 and Srs 300 have been developed, using the same wing and power plant, with fuselage stretches of 7ft 10in (2.38m) and 15ft 9in (4.76m) respectively.

Below: The first airline to carry revenue passengers in the BAe 146 was the UK independent operator Dan-Air, using the sixth production airframe, a Srs 100 registered G-BKMN. Two others have joined the fleet subsequently.

BRITISH AEROSPACE JETSTREAM UK

The Jetstream was launched in 1965, at which time it was a product of Handley Page Ltd, designated the HP.137 and destined to be the last aircraft type produced by that company before its demise in 1969. The Jetstream was intended, when launched, to serve as an executive transport and to have applications in the air-taxi, feederline and military markets. Despite some vicissitudes along the way, the Jetstream has made good in all these respects and, since its relaunch by British Aerospace as the Jetstream 31, has been selling steadily as a commuterliner, particularly in the USA. Handley Page flew the first of several Jetstream prototypes on 18 August 1967, at which time the favoured engines were Turboméca Astazou XIV free-shaft turboprops; later prototypes represented the Jetstream Mk 2 with Astazou XVIs and Jetstream Mk 3 with Garrett TPE331s, which had been specified by the USAF when it ordered 11 Jetstream 3Ms as C-10As. Five prototypes and 35 production Jetstreams (with Astazou engines) had been completed when all work ceased at Radlett on 27 February 1970, and four more were completed from existing components under the initiative of Terravia Trading Service Ltd. Rights in the Jetstream were subsequently acquired by Scottish Aviation, which built 26 as navigation trainers for the RAF. In the USA some of the original HP-built Jetstreams were modified, by the Riley company, to have Pratt & Whitney Canada PT6A-41 engines; others were brought up to Jetstream 200 standard with Astazou XVIs; and still more became Century III Jetstreams with TPE331 engines, retrofitted by Volpar for Apollo Airways. Scottish Aviation having been absorbed into British

Aerospace upon the latter's formation, the Jetstream became part of the BAe civil aircraft product range, but it was not until December 1978 that the decision to launch an updated version of the Jetstream was announced, backed up in January 1981 with a full production commitment. In its reincarnation, the aircraft became the Jetstream 31, as a close relative of the Mk 3 that Handley Page had built with Garrett TPE331 engines. These engines, and some structural changes, allowed the gross weight of the Mk 3 to be increased to 14,500lb (6,577kg), compared with 12,500lb (5,670kg) for the earlier version, and this became the starting weight for the Jetstream 31 (since increased, as shown in the data panel). BAe introduced new advanced-technology propellers, a DC (in place of AC) electrical system, a revised air-conditioning system, a changed hydraulic pump, a totally revised cockpit layout, and a range of new interior options. No significant changes were made to the external appearance or the structure of the Jetstream 31, the prototype of which (modified from a Mk 1) flew at Prestwick on 28 March 1980.

VARIANTS
The Jetstream 31 has benefited from some small increases in operating weights since being first produced, but there have been no important variations in production standard in the first 100 or so aircraft produced up to 1987. Differences centre upon interior layouts, which are designed to meet the needs of the regional airline or the corporate owner. For the latter, there is a useful executive shuttle interior, making the Jetstream 31 particularly suitable for use on regular flights transporting personnel between company-owned sites. In its airline role, the Jetstream can carry a ventral cargo pack, and several special-role variants have been proposed for such duties as airfield calibration, resources survey and protection. The Jetstream 31EZ has a 360-degree scan radar installation and is intended for offshore patrol and surveillance of exclusive economic zones. Under study in 1986 were a Jetstream 31 variant with a small fuselage stretch to allow a forward entrance door and extra rear baggage space, and a Jetstream 41 with a greater fuselage lengthening to allow 26-28 seats.

SERVICE USE
The Jetstream 31 was certificated in the UK on 29 June 1982, using the prototype and the first production aircraft, which had flown on 18 March 1982. US certification was obtained on 30 November 1982. The first customer delivery was made on 15 December 1982 to Contactair in Stuttgart, followed on 30 December by the first to a UK operator, Peregrine Air Services. Sales of the Jetstream 31 totalled 148 by the beginning of 1987 with 32 more on option.

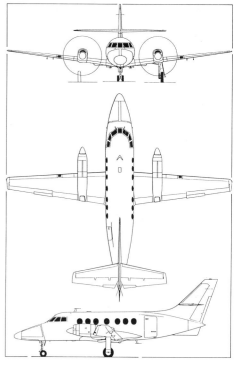

Above: Three-view drawing of the Jetstream 31, which retains the same overall dimensions as the original Handley Page aircraft, but features Garrett TPE331 turboprops in place of the Astazous first used.

Below: Cutaway drawing of the British Aerospace Jetstream 31, which has enjoyed considerable sales success among US commuter airlines since it was re-launched in its present form in 1982.

SPECIFICATION

Power Plant: Two Garrett TPE331-10UF turboprops each rated at 940shp (701kW) for take-off, with Dowty Rotol four-blade variable-pitch reversing and fully-feathering propellers. Fuel capacity, 378 Imp gal (1,718l) in integral wing tanks.
Performance: Max operating speed, 223kts (413km/h) IAS; max cruising speed, 263kts (488km/h) at 15,000ft (4,570m); economical cruising speed, 230kts (426km/h) at 25,000ft (7,620m); initial rate of climb, 2,080ft/min (10.6m/sec); certificated operational ceiling, 25,000ft (7,620m); take-off field length (FAR), 3,200ft (975m); landing field length (FAR), 3,820ft (1,165m); range with 18 passengers and IFR reserves, 675 naut mls (1,250km); range with nine passengers and IFR reserves, 1,065 naut mls (1,975km).
Weights: Operating weight empty, 9,570lb (4,341kg); max fuel weight, 3,024lb (1,372kg); max payload, 3,980lb (1,805kg); max take-off weight, 15,212lb (6,900kg); max landing weight, 14,550lb (6,600kg); max zero-fuel weight, 13,889lb (6,300kg).
Dimensions: Span, 52ft 0in (15.85m); overall length, 47ft 1½in (14.37m); overall height, 17ft 5½in (5.32m); sweepback, 0 deg 34 min at quarter chord; wing area, 271.3sq ft (25.20m²).
Accommodation: Cabin length, 24ft 3in (7.39m), max width, 6ft 1in (1.85m), max height, 5ft 11in (1.80m). Standard commuter arrangement provides 18 or 19 seats three-abreast, with offset aisle, at 30-31in (76-79cm) pitch; optional layouts include 12-seat executive shuttle or 8/10-seat full executive interiors, with a quick-change provision between commuter and executive shuttle arrangements. Flight crew of two.

Below: The German operator Contactair Flugdienst of Stuttgart, founded in 1972, was one of the first to order the Jetstream 31, and the first customer to take delivery, in December 1982. D-CONE was the first of three acquired by the company.

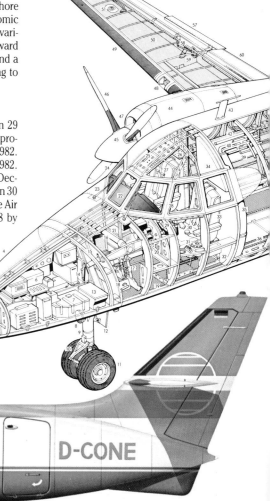

D-CONE

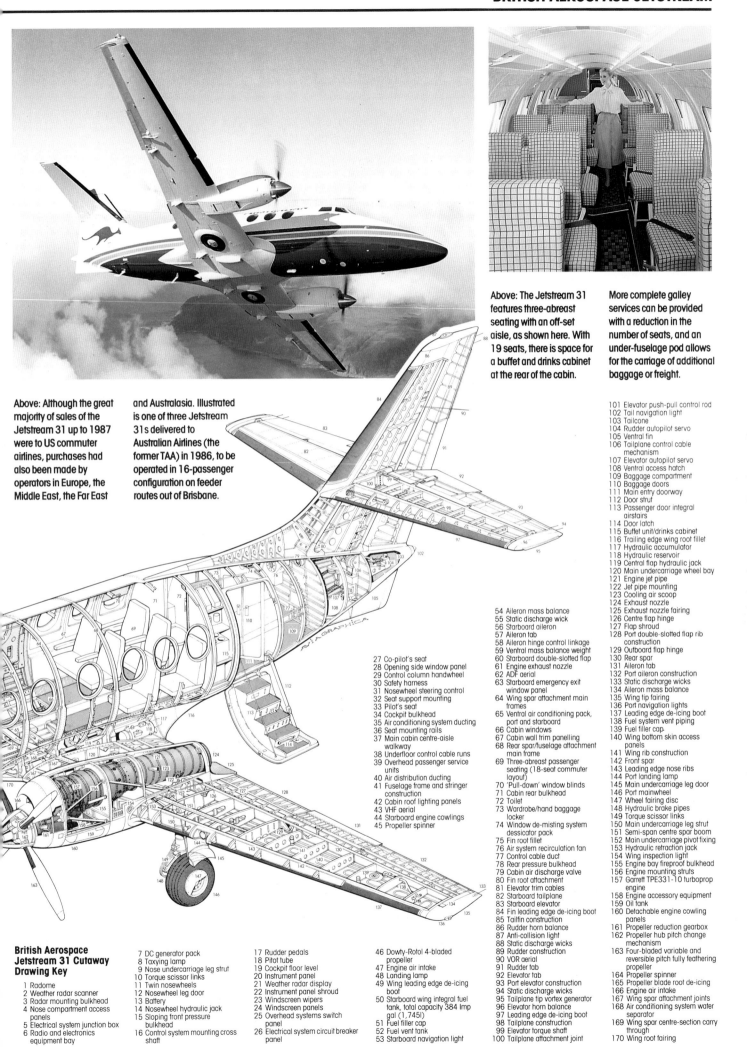

Above: The Jetstream 31 features three-abreast seating with an off-set aisle, as shown here. With 19 seats, there is space for a buffet and drinks cabinet at the rear of the cabin.

More complete galley services can be provided with a reduction in the number of seats, and an under-fuselage pod allows for the carriage of additional baggage or freight.

Above: Although the great majority of sales of the Jetstream 31 up to 1987 were to US commuter airlines, purchases had also been made by operators in Europe, the Middle East, the Far East and Australasia. Illustrated is one of three Jetstream 31s delivered to Australian Airlines (the former TAA) in 1986, to be operated in 16-passenger configuration on feeder routes out of Brisbane.

British Aerospace Jetstream 31 Cutaway Drawing Key

1 Radome
2 Weather radar scanner
3 Radar mounting bulkhead
4 Nose compartment access panels
5 Electrical system junction box
6 Radio and electronics equipment bay
7 DC generator pack
8 Taxying lamp
9 Nose undercarriage leg strut
10 Torque scissor links
11 Twin nosewheels
12 Nosewheel leg door
13 Battery
14 Nosewheel hydraulic jack
15 Sloping front pressure bulkhead
16 Control system mounting cross shaft
17 Rudder pedals
18 Pitot tube
19 Cockpit floor level
20 Instrument panel
21 Weather radar display
22 Instrument panel shroud
23 Windscreen wipers
24 Windscreen panels
25 Overhead systems switch panel
26 Electrical system circuit breaker panel
27 Co-pilot's seat
28 Opening side window panel
29 Control column handwheel
30 Safety harness
31 Nosewheel steering control
32 Seat support mounting
33 Pilot's seat
34 Cockpit bulkhead
35 Air conditioning system ducting
36 Seat mounting rails
37 Main cabin centre-aisle walkway
38 Underfloor control cable runs
39 Overhead passenger service units
40 Air distribution ducting
41 Fuselage frame and stringer construction
42 Cabin roof lighting panels
43 VHF aerial
44 Starboard engine cowlings
45 Propeller spinner
46 Dowty-Rotol 4-bladed propeller
47 Engine air intake
48 Landing lamp
49 Wing leading edge de-icing boot
50 Starboard wing integral fuel tank, total capacity 384 Imp gal (1,745l)
51 Fuel filler cap
52 Fuel vent tank
53 Starboard navigation light
54 Aileron mass balance
55 Static discharge wick
56 Starboard aileron
57 Aileron tab
58 Aileron hinge control linkage
59 Ventral mass balance weight
60 Starboard double-slotted flap
61 Engine exhaust nozzle
62 ADF aerial
63 Starboard emergency exit window panel
64 Wing spar attachment main frames
65 Ventral air conditioning pack, port and starboard
66 Cabin windows
67 Cabin wall trim panelling
68 Rear spar/fuselage attachment main frame
69 Three-abreast passenger seating (18-seat commuter layout)
70 'Pull-down' window blinds
71 Cabin rear bulkhead
72 Toilet
73 Wardrobe/hand baggage locker
74 Window de-misting system dessicator pack
75 Fin root fillet
76 Air system recirculation fan
77 Control cable duct
78 Rear pressure bulkhead
79 Cabin air discharge valve
80 Fin root attachment
81 Elevator trim cables
82 Starboard tailplane
83 Starboard elevator
84 Fin leading edge de-icing boot
85 Tailfin construction
86 Rudder horn balance
87 Anti-collision light
88 Static discharge wicks
89 Rudder construction
90 VOR aerial
91 Rudder tab
92 Elevator tab
93 Port elevator construction
94 Static discharge wicks
95 Tailplane tip vortex generator
96 Elevator horn balance
97 Leading edge de-icing boot
98 Tailplane construction
99 Elevator torque shaft
100 Tailplane attachment joint
101 Elevator push-pull control rod
102 Tail navigation light
103 Tailcone
104 Rudder autopilot servo
105 Ventral fin
106 Tailplane control cable mechanism
107 Elevator autopilot servo
108 Ventral access hatch
109 Baggage compartment
110 Baggage doors
111 Main entry doorway
112 Door strut
113 Passenger door integral airstairs
114 Door latch
115 Buffet unit/drinks cabinet
116 Trailing edge wing root fillet
117 Hydraulic accumulator
118 Hydraulic reservoir
119 Central flap hydraulic jack
120 Main undercarriage wheel bay
121 Engine jet pipe
122 Jet pipe mounting
123 Cooling air scoop
124 Exhaust nozzle
125 Exhaust nozzle fairing
126 Centre flap hinge
127 Flap shroud
128 Port double-slotted flap rib construction
129 Outboard flap hinge
130 Rear spar
131 Aileron tab
132 Port aileron construction
133 Static discharge wicks
134 Aileron mass balance
135 Wing tip fairing
136 Port navigation lights
137 Leading edge de-icing boot
138 Fuel system vent piping
139 Fuel filler cap
140 Wing bottom skin access panels
141 Wing rib construction
142 Front spar
143 Leading edge nose ribs
144 Port landing lamp
145 Main undercarriage leg door
146 Port mainwheel
147 Wheel fairing disc
148 Hydraulic brake pipes
149 Torque scissor links
150 Main undercarriage leg strut
151 Semi-span centre spar boom
152 Main undercarriage pivot fixing
153 Hydraulic retraction jack
154 Wing inspection light
155 Engine bay fireproof bulkhead
156 Engine mounting struts
157 Garrett TPE331-10 turboprop engine
158 Engine accessory equipment
159 Oil tank
160 Detachable engine cowling panels
161 Propeller reduction gearbox
162 Propeller hub pitch change mechanism
163 Four-bladed variable and reversible pitch fully feathering propeller
164 Propeller spinner
165 Propeller blade root de-icing
166 Engine air intake
167 Wing spar attachment joints
168 Air conditioning system water separator
169 Wing spar centre-section carry through
170 Wing root fairing

BRITISH AEROSPACE TRIDENT UK

The Trident owes its evolution to a requirement of British European Airways drawn up in July 1956, for an aeroplane to operate over routes that were mostly less than 870 naut mls (1,610km) in length. It was to be BEA's first pure-jet airliner, replacing the Vickers Viscounts and Vanguards then in service, and drew proposals from Avro (Type 540), Bristol (Type 200) and de Havilland. The last-mentioned company at first projected the four-engined D.H.119, then studied a project that might have met (in two variants of the same D.H.120 design) the needs of both BEA and of BOAC (which needed greater range), and then reverted in the D.H.121 to an aircraft specifically intended for BEA. To meet political requirements, de Havilland entered into an arrangement with the Hunting and Fairey companies to set up the Airco consortium, and the latter was successful in gaining a preliminary order for 24 D.H.121s in February 1958. As then ordered, the D.H.121 was powered by three 13,790lb st (6,255kgp) Rolls-Royce RB.141/3 Medway turbofans, had 111 seats and a maximum range of 1,800 naut mls (3,337km). BEA changed its specification, however, and by 1959 the new transport had been redesigned around three RB.163 Spey engines of 9,850lb st (4,468kgp), to carry 97-103 passengers over a range of only 810 naut mls (1,500km). Although this satisfied BEA, it made the D.H.121 considerably less attractive to airlines elsewhere, as the subsequent sales record showed. Production of the D.H.121 went ahead under Hawker Siddeley direction, after the Airco consortium had been dissolved and DH acquired by the Hawker Siddeley Group. The D.H.121, duly named Trident, was configured to have three rear-mounted engines, in keeping with a vogue for rear-engined T-tailed aircraft, and the 35-degree sweepback was as large an angle as used on any commercial aircraft. The configuration was closely matched by that of the Boeing 727, launched some months later, but the much larger fuel capacity of the US aircraft allowed it to meet the needs of many airlines that the Trident could not satisfy. Flight testing of the Trident began at Hatfield on 9 January 1962, using production aircraft; no prototypes were built.

VARIANTS

The initial variant for BEA was the Trident 1, with Spey Mk 505s and a gross weight of 115,000lb (52,165kg); 24 were built for the state airline. Six other airlines between them bought 15 Trident 1Es, which differed in having 11,400lb st (5,171kgp) Spey Mk 511s, gross weight increased to 128,000lb (58,060kg) and span increased from 89ft 10in (27.41m) to 95ft (28.95m); maximum accommodation was also increased to 140, seated six-abreast. Production for BEA continued with the Trident Two (known as the Trident 2E to HSA), which had a further small increase of span to 98ft (29.9m), increased fuel capacity, 11,960lb st (5,425kgp) Spey Mk 512-5W engines and higher weights (see data panel); maximum seating went up to 149. The first Trident 2E flew on 27 July 1967, and sales of this variant were made to Cyprus Airways and CAAC in China as well as to BEA, bringing the total of Trident 2Es built to 50. The final variant was the Trident Three (maker's designation Trident 3B), with the fuselage lengthened by 16ft 5in (5.00m) to increase accommodation to 180 for BEA's use on short high-density routes. To allow the maximum weight to increase to 150,000lb (68,040kg), a fourth or 'booster' engine was added in the base of the fin above the rear fuselage, this being a 5,250lb st (2,381kgp) RB.162-86. The first Trident Three flew on 11 December 1969. The two Super Trident 3Bs built for CAAC differed in having increased weights, including a take-off weight of 158,000lb (71,667kg), more fuel and changed cabin layouts; the first flew on 9 July 1975. During their service with BEA, Trident Twos and Threes had their wing span reduced by 3ft (91cm) to reduce bending moments and improve fatigue life. This modification was brought about because fatigue cracks were discovered in several of the Tridents in BEA's fleet.

SERVICE USE

The Trident 1 entered BEA service on 11 March 1964, the Trident Two on 18 April 1968 and the Trident Three on 1 April 1971. In May 1973, BEA began operating its Trident Threes to Cat IIIA standards, with landings using Smiths Autoland equipment when

runway visual range was 885ft (270m) combined with a decision height of 12ft (3.66m). All Trident services with British Airways ended 31 December 1985, leaving some Trident 2Es and two 3Bs operating in China and four ex-BEA Trident Threes in the hands of Air Charter Service in Zaire. The total of 117 Tridents built comprised 24 Srs 1, 15 Srs 1E, 50 Srs 2E, 26 Srs 3 and two Super 3B aircraft.

Below: The flight-deck of the Trident 2E, as arranged for CAAC, for whom this was the first example built. The Trident was the first airliner equipped and certificated to operate in Cat IIIA weather.

Below: Other than Air Charter Service in Zaire, China's Civil Aviation Administration (CAAC) is now the only airline using the HSA (BAe) Trident. This aircraft is on pre-delivery trials.

SPECIFICATION
(Trident 2E)

Power Plant: Three Rolls-Royce RB.163-25 Spey Mk 512-5W turbofans each rated at 11,960lb st (5,425kgp) for take-off. Fuel capacity, 6,400 Imp gal (29,094l) in integral tanks in wings and centre section.
Performance: Typical max cruising speed, 525kts (972km/h) at 27,000ft (8,230m); economical cruising speed, 518kts (959km/h) at 30,000ft (9,145m); take-off field length, aircraft loaded for 868 naut ml (1,610km) stage length with 21,378lb (9,697kg) payload, 6,400ft (1,950m); range with typical payload, 2,140 naut mls (3,965km); range with max fuel and 16,520lb (7,493kg) payload, 2,171 naut mls (4,025km).
Weights: Operating weight empty, 73,200lb (33,203kg); max payload, 26,800lb (12,156kg); max take-off weight, 144,000lb (65,315kg); max landing weight, 113,000lb (51,261kg); max zero-fuel weight, 100,000lb (45,359kg).
Dimensions: Span, 98ft 0in (29.87m); overall length, 114ft 9in (34.97m); overall height, 27ft 0in (8.23m); sweepback, 35 deg at quarter chord; wing area, 1,462sq ft (135.82m²).
Accommodation: Cabin length, 67ft 1½in (20.46m), max width, 11ft 3½in (3.44m), max height, 6ft 7½in (2.02m). Typical mixed-class layout provides 12 first-class seats four-abreast and 79 tourist-class seats six-abreast; all-tourist class layout provides 97 seats and max high-density layout seats 132. Forward and rear underfloor freight holds, total volume, 760cu ft (21.53m³). Flight crew of three.

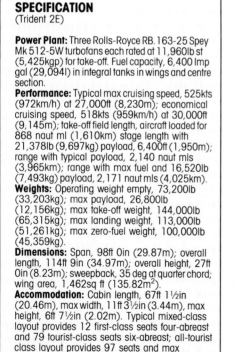

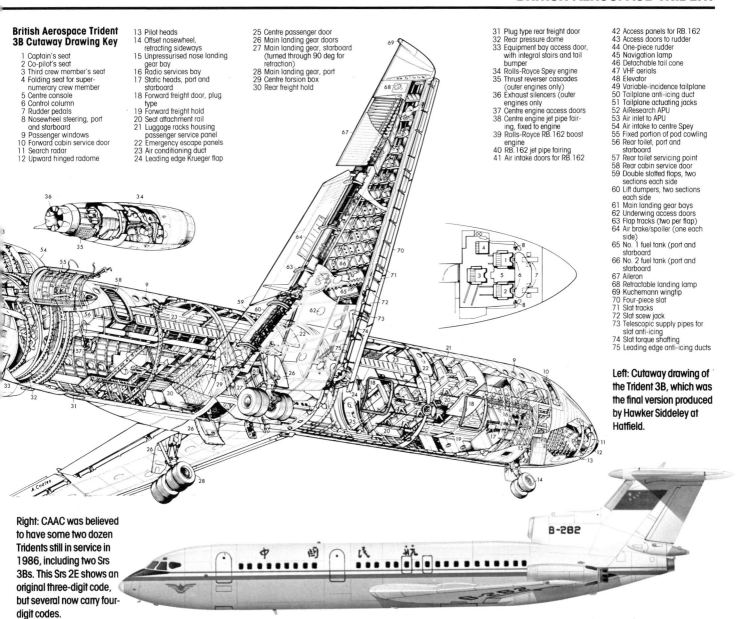

British Aerospace Trident 3B Cutaway Drawing Key

1 Captain's seat
2 Co-pilot's seat
3 Third crew member's seat
4 Folding seat for super-numerary crew member
5 Centre console
6 Control column
7 Rudder pedals
8 Nosewheel steering, port and starboard
9 Passenger windows
10 Forward cabin service door
11 Search radar
12 Upward hinged radome
13 Pilot heads
14 Offset nosewheel, retracting sideways
15 Unpressurised nose landing gear bay
16 Radio services bay
17 Static heads, port and starboard
18 Forward freight door, plug type
19 Forward freight hold
20 Seat attachment rail
21 Luggage racks housing passenger service panel
22 Emergency escape panels
23 Air conditioning duct
24 Leading edge Krueger flap
25 Centre passenger door
26 Main landing gear doors
27 Main landing gear, starboard (turned through 90 deg for retraction)
28 Main landing gear, port
29 Centre torsion box
30 Rear freight hold
31 Plug type rear freight door
32 Rear pressure dome
33 Equipment bay access door, with integral stairs and tail bumper
34 Rolls-Royce Spey engine
35 Thrust reverser cascades (outer engines only)
36 Exhaust silencers (outer engines only)
37 Centre engine access doors
38 Centre engine jet pipe fairing, fixed to engine
39 Rolls-Royce RB.162 boost engine
40 RB.162 jet pipe fairing
41 Air intake doors for RB.162
42 Access panels for RB.162
43 Access doors to rudder
44 One-piece rudder
45 Navigation lamp
46 Detachable tail cone
47 VHF aerials
48 Elevator
49 Variable-incidence tailplane
50 Tailplane anti-icing duct
51 Tailplane actuating jacks
52 AiResearch APU
53 Air inlet to APU
54 Air intake to centre Spey
55 Fixed portion of pod cowling
56 Rear toilet, port and starboard
57 Rear toilet servicing point
58 Rear cabin service door
59 Double slotted flaps, two sections each side
60 Lift dumpers, two sections each side
61 Main landing gear bays
62 Underwing access doors
63 Flap tracks (two per flap)
64 Air brake/spoiler (one each side)
65 No. 1 fuel tank (port and starboard)
66 No. 2 fuel tank (port and starboard)
67 Aileron
68 Retractable landing lamp
69 Kuchemann wingtip
70 Four-piece slat
71 Slat tracks
72 Slat scew jack
73 Telescopic supply pipes for slat anti-icing
74 Slat torque shafting
75 Leading edge anti-icing ducts

Left: Cutaway drawing of the Trident 3B, which was the final version produced by Hawker Siddeley at Hatfield.

Right: CAAC was believed to have some two dozen Tridents still in service in 1986, including two Srs 3Bs. This Srs 2E shows an original three-digit code, but several now carry four-digit codes.

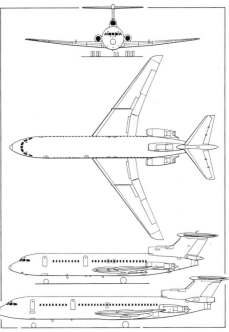

Above: A three-view drawing of the Trident 2E, which is now the most-used variant, together with a side view (bottom) of the Trident 3B, which introduced a lengthened fuselage and an extra small jet engine to boost its performance when taking off at maximum weights.

Now produced only in Romania, the One-Eleven had its origins in a design known as the Hunting H.107, projected in the mid-1950s by Hunting Aircraft Ltd as a 48-seat (four-abreast) short-range jet transport. Proposed engines in the period 1956-59, when wind-tunnel testing and mock-up construction continued, were the Bristol Siddeley Orpheus turbojet, and the BS.61 or BS.75 turbofans, but after Hunting had been acquired by British Aircraft Corporation (BAC) in 1960, the design was enlarged to provide five-abreast seating for about 65 passengers, and Rolls-Royce Speys were adopted. In this form, the aircraft became the BAC One-Eleven and a decision to put the type into production was taken in March 1961. A prototype/company demonstrator first flew on 20 August 1963, with Spey Mk 505 engines, 73,500lb (33,340kg) gross weight and a maximum of 79 seats. The One-Eleven design followed the fashion of its day in having rear-mounted engines and a T-tail, a configuration that led to the loss of the prototype on 22 October 1963 after it entered a deep stall during high angle of attack investigation. This revealed a hitherto unsuspected characteristic of the layout, calling for the development of protective systems and causing a delay in certification and production. After building more than 200 One-Elevens in the variants described below, British Aerospace (into which BAC had meanwhile merged) concluded in 1979 an agreement with the National Centre of the Romanian Aircraft Industry (CNIAR), providing for the latter to establish a One-Eleven production line in Romania. This deal provided for BAe to supply three complete aircraft and 22 kits from the UK production line, the latter in progressively less complete stages of construction, for final assembly in a plant in Bucharest. The first aircraft assembled in this way flew at Bucharest on 18 September 1982 and deliveries of components from the UK under this agreement ended in 1986.

VARIANTS

The first production version of the One-Eleven was designated Srs 200, with 10,330lb st (4,686kg) RB.168-25 Spey Mk 506 engines and a maximum weight of 79,000lb (35,833kg). The Srs 300 was generally similar but had 11,400lb st (5,171kgp) Spey Mk 511 engines, increased fuel in centre section tank and structural modification for a gross weight

of 87,000lb (39,462kg). The Srs 400, first flown on 13 July 1965, was based on the Srs 300 but optimized for US operators. A stretched version, the Srs 500, was developed primarily to meet BEA requirements, and used the Srs 300/400 airframe with a fuselage lengthened by 13ft 6in (4.1m) and span increased by 5ft (1.52m) at the wingtips. More powerful engines matched the higher weights of this version (see data panel). The Srs 500 prototype (a converted Srs 400) flew on 30 June 1967, and the first production example for BEA flew on 7 February 1968, initially with Spey Mk 511 engines and a gross weight of 92,483lb (41,950kg). To provide an aircraft with improved field performance and the ability to operate from unprepared surfaces, the wings and power plant of the Srs 500 were combined with the fuselage of the Srs 400 to produce the Srs 475, flown in prototype form on 27 August 1970 and in production guise on 5 April 1971. The Srs 670 flew as a prototype only, and had some aerodynamic refinements to the wing to improve the field performance in line with Japanese requirements. Romanian production versions of the Srs 475 and 500 are designated Srs 495 and 560 respectively. A forward side freight-loading door was developed for Srs 475 aircraft in military service. In 1986, the Dee Howard company in the USA announced plans to fit Rolls-Royce Tay turbofans in place of Speys in a One-Eleven and, after certification, to offer this as a retrofit, applicable to Srs 200s (mostly in corporate use) and to Srs 400s and Srs 500s used by airlines.

SERVICE USE

The One-Eleven 200 was certificated on 6 April 1965 and entered service with the first customer, British United, on 9 April, followed on 25 April by the first services by Braniff in the USA, where FAA certification was obtained on 20 April. The Srs 400 was approved in the US on 22 November 1965 and by ARB on 10 December 1965, American Airlines being the first user. The Srs 500 was certificated at the initial BEA gross weight on 18 August 1968, and entered revenue service on 17 November. The Srs 475 was certificated in July 1975 and the first example was delivered to Faucett in Peru during the same month. Production of the One-Eleven totalled 230 in the UK, made up of 56 Srs 200, nine Srs 300, 69 Srs 400, nine Srs 475 and 87 Srs 500 aircraft; kits for a further 22 have been supplied to Romania.

Above: British Airways was one of the largest users of the One-Eleven in 1987, with five Srs 400s and 18 Srs 500s in service.

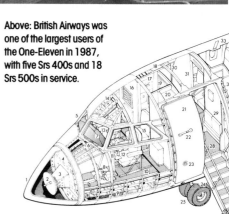

SPECIFICATION
(One-Eleven 500)

Power Plant: Two Rolls-Royce Spey Mk 512DW turbofans each rated at 12,550lb st (5,692kgp) for take-off. Fuel capacity, 3,085 Imp gal (14,024l) in integral wing and centre section tanks; provision for optional underfloor tanks of 350 Imp gal (1,591l) or 700 Imp gal (3,182l) capacity.
Performance: Max operating speed, 336kts (623km/h) IAS or Mach = 0.78; max cruising speed, 470kts (871km/h) at 21,000ft (6,400m); best economy cruising speed, 400kts (742km/h) at 25,000ft (7,620m); initial rate of climb, 2,280ft/min (11.6m/sec); max operating altitude, 35,000ft (10,670m); take-off field length, 7,300ft (2,225m); range with typical capacity payload, 1,480 naut mls (2,744km); range with max fuel, 1,880 naut mls (3,484km).
Weights: Operating weight empty, 54,582lb (24,758kg); max payload, 26,418lb (11,983kg); max take-off weight, 104,500lb (47,400kg); max landing weight, 87,000lb (39,462kg); max zero-fuel weight, 81,000lb (36,741kg).
Dimensions: Span, 93ft 6in (28.50m); overall length, 107ft 0in (32.61m); overall height, 24ft 6in (7.47m); sweepback, 20 deg at quarter chord; wing area, 1,031sq ft (95.78m²).
Accommodation: Cabin length, 70ft 4in (21.44m), max width, 10ft 4in (3.16m), max height, 6ft 6in (1.98m). Standard layout provides up to 119 one-class seats, five-abreast, at 29in (74cm) pitch. Forward and aft underfloor baggage/freight holds, total volume, 510cu ft (14.44m³). Flight crew of two.

British Aerospace (BAC) One-Eleven 670 Cutaway Drawing Key

1 Radome
2 Weather radar scanner
3 Radar scanner mounting
4 Pressure bulkhead
5 Windscreen panels
6 Windscreen wipers
7 Instrument panel shroud
8 Rudder pedals
9 Nose equipment bay
10 Cockpit floor level
11 Control column
12 Pilot's seat
13 Co-pilot's seat
14 Cockpit roof construction
15 Supernumerary crew seat
16 Cockpit bulkhead
17 Radio rack
18 Starboard galley
19 Cockpit door
20 Port galley
21 Forward entry door
22 Entry door handle
23 Wing icing inspection light
24 Nosewheel doors
25 Twin nosewheels
26 Retractable airstairs
27 Folding handrail
28 Entry lobby
29 Cabin attendants' folding seats
30 Starboard service door
31 Cabin bulkhead
32 Wardrobe
33 Communications aerials
34 Forward cabin seating
35 Window panel skin doubler plate
36 Freight hold door
37 Forward freight hold
38 Fuselage frame and stringer construction
39 ADF loop aerials
40 Floor beam support structure
41 Air conditioning distribution ducting
42 Forward/centre fuselage joint frame
43 Front wing spar main frame
44 Ventral air conditioning plant
45 Port emergency exit
46 Wing centre section fuel tank
47 Seat rail support beams
48 Starboard emergency exit window
49 Fuselage skin plating
50 Wing fence
51 Leading edge de-icing air duct
52 Starboard wing fuel tanks
53 Starboard navigation lights
54 Extended wing tip
55 Static dischargers
56 Starboard aileron
57 Aileron tab
58 Aileron hinge control mechanism
59 Spoilers open position

60 Spoiler jacks
61 Flap screw jacks and gearboxes
62 Flap track fairings
63 Starboard outboard slotted flaps, open position
64 Aerial cable
65 Cabin window trim panels

66 Rear wing spar main frame
67 Cabin floor panels
68 Centre/rear fuselage joint frame
69 Starboard three-abreast passenger seats
70 Overhead luggage lockers
71 Passenger overhead service unit
72 Fresh air delivery duct
73 Rail type aerial
74 Starboard engine nacelle
75 Cabin rear bulkhead
76 Starboard toilet
77 Rear entry door
78 Aft pressure bulkhead
79 Ejector cowl, closed
80 Eight lobe exhaust nozzle
81 Fin leading edge de-icing
82 Fin construction
83 VOR aerial
84 Twin pitot tubes
85 Tailplane bullet fairing
86 Tailplane trimming screw jack
87 Starboard tailplane
88 Static dischargers
89 Elevator tab
90 Starboard elevator
91 Communications aerial
92 Elevator control rods
93 Tail navigation light
94 Port aileron tabs
95 Port aileron construction
96 De-icing air outlet louvres
97 Tailplane construction
98 Leading edge de-icing

99 Rudder upper hinge
100 Rudder construction
101 Hydraulic rudder jacks
102 APU exhaust duct
103 Auxiliary power unit (APU)
104 Fireproof bulkhead
105 Fin mounting sloping frames
106 Engine nacelle pylon
107 Ejector cowl, open position
108 Cowl screw jack
109 Eight-lobe exhaust nozzle
110 Thrust reverser cascades
111 Reverser operating jacks
112 Rear ventral airstairs

113 Detachable engine cowlings
114 Engine bleed air ducting
115 Rolls-Royce Spey 25 Mk512-14DW turbofan engine
116 Engine accessories
117 Engine mounting frame
118 Fire extinguisher bottles
119 Wash basin
120 Port toilet compartment
121 Engine intake
122 Port two-abreast passenger seats
123 Window panels
124 Rear freight hold
125 Trailing edge root fillet
126 Hydraulic reservoir
127 Flap operating motor and gearbox
128 Main undercarriage wheel well
129 Undercarriage retraction linkage
130 Main undercarriage pivot mounting
131 Automatic ground spoiler
132 Inboard slotted flap
133 Flap track fairings
134 Flaps down position
135 Flap shroud construction
136 Outboard flight spoilers
137 Flap guide rails
138 Aileron hinge control mechanism
139 Aileron tab
140 Port aileron
141 Static dischargers
142 Extended wing tip construction
143 Port navigation lights
144 Leading edge construction
145 Front spar
146 Fuel system piping
147 Centre spar
148 Port wing integral fuel tank
149 Rear spar
150 Wing fence/leading edge fillet
151 Machined wing skin panels
152 Main undercarriage leg strut
153 Automatic wheel brakes
154 Twin mainwheels
155 Leading edge de-icing air duct
156 Wing attachment joint strap
157 Wing root ventral fairing

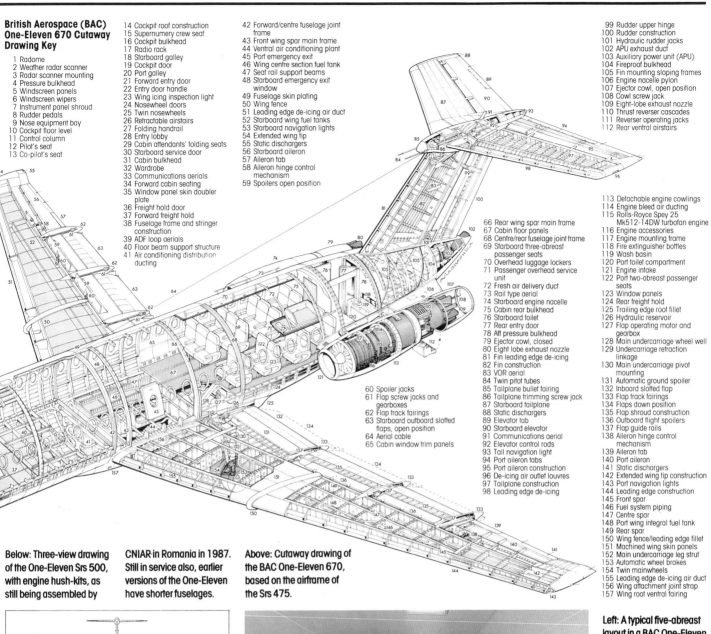

Below: Three-view drawing of the One-Eleven Srs 500, with engine hush-kits, as still being assembled by CNIAR in Romania in 1987. Still in service also, earlier versions of the One-Eleven have shorter fuselages.

Above: Cutaway drawing of the BAC One-Eleven 670, based on the airframe of the Srs 475.

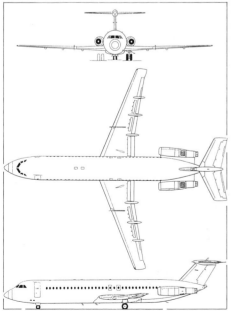

Left: A typical five-abreast layout in a BAC One-Eleven 500. As this photograph graphically illustrates, it is difficult to avoid a 'long, thin tube' appearance in aircraft of this size. The One-Eleven 500 can carry up to 119 passengers in this configuration.

Below: YR-BCK identifies this as one of the BAC One-Eleven 525s supplied from the UK production line to the Romanian airline TAROM in 1977. Similar Srs 561s have been delivered to TAROM since 1982 from the CNIAR assembly line.

CASA C-212 AVIOCAR SPAIN

Development of the C-212 began in the late 1960s to meet the requirements of the Spanish air force for a small tactical transport and multi-role aircraft, and prototypes were built in military guise. Layout and construction followed conventional practice for an aircraft of the type, with a high wing, fixed landing gear with the main units attached on each side of the fuselage with sponson-type fairings over the mountings, and a rear loading ramp providing straight-in loading to the box-section cabin. Prototypes were first flown on 26 March and 23 October 1971, and the Aviocar entered production against Spanish air force orders, the first production example flying on 17 November 1972. As intended, the Aviocar was able to perform in a number of roles, and it has replaced the CASA-built Junkers Ju 52/3m, Douglas DC-3 and CASA 207 Azor in Spanish service, to operate as a personnel and cargo transport, ambulance, photo-survey aircraft and specialized crew trainer. The C-212 was subsequently developed for civil use as a 19-seat commuterliner, whose initial sale was made to Pertamina in Indonesia. An agreement was then concluded with P T Nurtanio (now IPTN) for the licence production (also in Indonesia) of the Aviocar as a means, in particular, of providing access to a substantial market for this type of aircraft in that country and the Pacific basin generally.

VARIANTS

The initial production aircraft were powered by the 776ehp (579kW) TPE331-5-251C engine and had a gross weight of 12,500lb (5,675kg) in the first C-212CA civil variant, increased to 13,890lb (6,300kg) in the C-212CB. In 1977 a further increase was made in the gross weight, to 14,332lb (6,500kg), and a year later CASA introduced the more powerful TPE331-10-501C engine, which allowed the gross weight to be increased again, to 16,424lb (7,450kg), as indicated in the data panel. At this stage, the aircraft with the different engine versions were designated as the C-212-5 and C-212-10 respectively, but this nomenclature was quickly changed to C-212 Srs 100 and C-212 Srs 200. The first aircraft with -10 engines, serving as prototypes of the Srs 200, were the 138th and 139th Aviocars built, and made their first flights

SPECIFICATION
(C-212 Series 200)

Power Plant: Two Garrett TPE331-10R-511C turboprops each rated at 900shp (671kW) for take-off, with Dowty Rotol R-313 four-blade constant-speed feathering and reversing propellers of 9ft 0in (2.74m) diameter. Fuel capacity, 449 Imp gal (2,040l) in integral tanks in outer wings.
Performance: Max operating speed, 202kts (374km/h) IAS; max cruising speed, 197kts (365km/h) at 10,000ft (3,050m); economical cruising speed, 187kts (346km/h) at 10,000ft (3,050m); initial rate of climb, 1,555ft/min (7.9m/sec); take-off field length (FAR Pt 25), 2,000ft (610m); landing distance, (FAR Pt 25), 1,805ft (550m); range with max payload, 220 naut mls (408km); range with max fuel, 950 naut mls (1,760km).
Weights: Empty weight, 8,333lb (3,780kg); max fuel weight, 3,527lb (1,600kg); max payload, 6,107lb (2,770kg); max take-off weight, 16,424lb (7,450kg); max landing weight, 16,204lb (7,350kg); max zero-fuel weight, 15,542lb (7,050kg).
Dimensions: Span, 62ft 4in (19.00m); overall length, 49ft 9in (15.16m); overall height, 20ft 8in (6.30m); sweepback, nil; wing area, 430.56sq ft (40.00m²).
Accommodation: Cabin length, 21ft 4in (6.50m), max width, 6ft 10¾in (2.10m), max height, 5ft 11in (1.80m). Standard layout provides up to 28 seats four-abreast at 28.5in (72cm) pitch; provision for mixed passenger/cargo arrangements with quick-change facility. Baggage compartment volume, 102.4cu ft (2.9m³). Flight crew of two.

on 30 April and 20 June 1978 respectively. In 1984, CASA announced the availability of the C-212 Srs 300, with 900shp (671kW) TPE331-10R-512C engines and Dowty Rotol propellers of a more recent type than those which had replaced Hartzell propellers in Srs 200 aircraft in July 1983. The Srs 300 has redesigned wing tips, a modified nose with larger baggage compartment, and a gross weight of 16,975lb (7,700kg). It also has, as an option, a rear fuselage fairing in place of the loading ramp, allowing 28 passengers to be carried at the increased seat pitch of 29.5in (75cm). The new wing tips widen the span to 66ft 11¼in (20.40m), resulting in a wing area of 441.3sq ft (41.00m²).

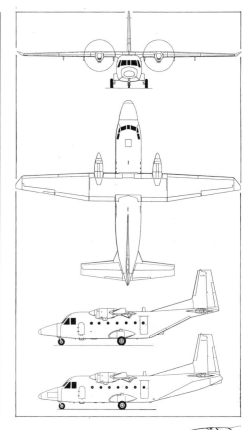

Above: The three-view shows the CASA C-212M with rear-loading ramp and the extra side-view (bottom) depicts the civil C-212 Srs 300.

SERVICE USE

More than 400 Aviocars had been sold by the end of 1986, of which approximately half were for commercial use. Civil operations in Indonesia make up the largest single group of airlines flying the C-212C in its Srs 100 and Srs 200 form. The Srs 300 was certificated at the end of 1985.

Left: The prototype C-212 Srs 300 demonstrating at Farnborough. Note the upturned wingtips and rear underfuselage fairing.

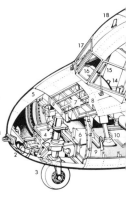

CASA 212 Aviocar Cutaway Drawing Key

1 Glide path (ILS) antenna
2 Triple landing/taxying light cluster
3 Steerable nosewheel (mechanical/hydraulic steering)
4 Nosewheel oleo
5 Hinged nose cone (hydraulic and wiring access)
6 Brake regulator valve
7 Forward stringers

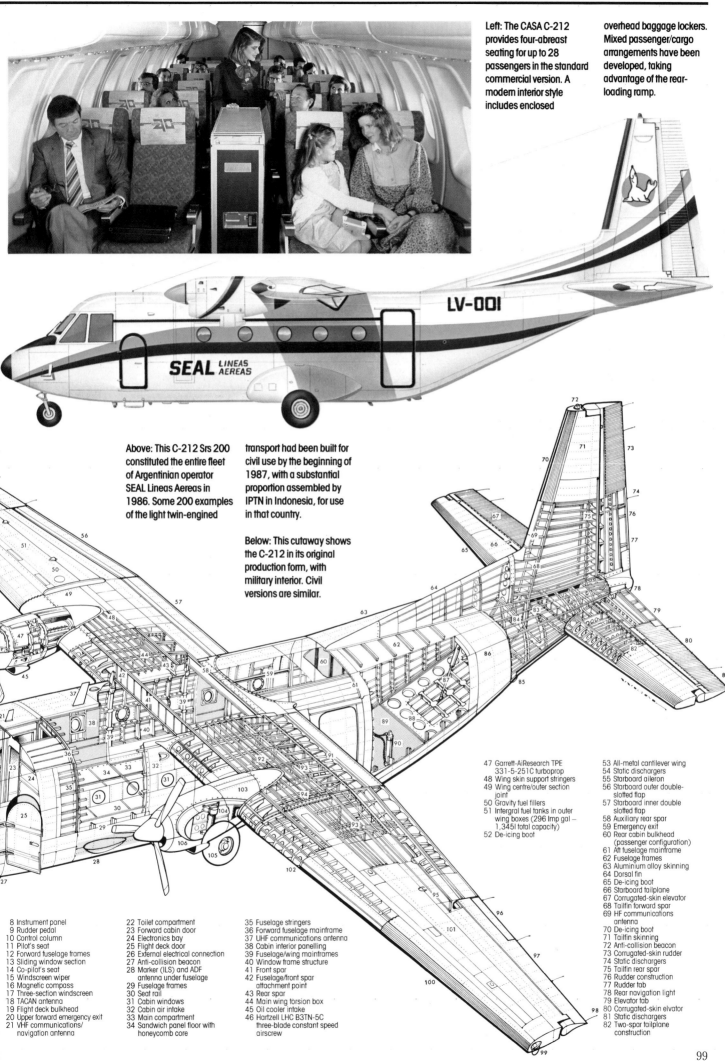

Left: The CASA C-212 provides four-abreast seating for up to 28 passengers in the standard commercial version. A modern interior style includes enclosed overhead baggage lockers. Mixed passenger/cargo arrangements have been developed, taking advantage of the rear-loading ramp.

Above: This C-212 Srs 200 constituted the entire fleet of Argentinian operator SEAL Lineas Aereas in 1986. Some 200 examples of the light twin-engined transport had been built for civil use by the beginning of 1987, with a substantial proportion assembled by IPTN in Indonesia, for use in that country.

Below: This cutaway shows the C-212 in its original production form, with military interior. Civil versions are similar.

8 Instrument panel
9 Rudder pedal
10 Control column
11 Pilot's seat
12 Forward fuselage frames
13 Sliding window section
14 Co-pilot's seat
15 Windscreen wiper
16 Magnetic compass
17 Three-section windscreen
18 TACAN antenna
19 Flight deck bulkhead
20 Upper forward emergency exit
21 VHF communications/ navigation antenna
22 Toilet compartment
23 Forward cabin door
24 Electronics bay
25 Flight deck door
26 External electrical connection
27 Anti-collision beacon
28 Marker (ILS) and ADF antenna under fuselage
29 Fuselage frames
30 Seat rail
31 Cabin windows
32 Cabin air intake
33 Main compartment
34 Sandwich panel floor with honeycomb core
35 Fuselage stringers
36 Forward fuselage mainframe
37 UHF communications antenna
38 Cabin interior panelling
39 Fuselage/wing mainframes
40 Window frame structure
41 Front spar
42 Fuselage/front spar attachment point
43 Rear spar
44 Main wing torsion box
45 Oil cooler intake
46 Hartzell LHC B3TN-5C three-blade constant speed airscrew
47 Garrett-AiResearch TPE 331-5-251C turboprop
48 Wing skin support stringers
49 Wing centre/outer section joint
50 Gravity fuel fillers
51 Intergral fuel tanks in outer wing boxes (296 Imp gal – 1,345l total capacity)
52 De-icing boot
53 All-metal cantilever wing
54 Static dischargers
55 Starboard aileron
56 Starboard outer double-slotted flap
57 Starboard inner double slotted flap
58 Auxiliary rear spar
59 Emergency exit
60 Rear cabin bulkhead (passenger configuration)
61 Aft fuselage mainframe
62 Fuselage frames
63 Aluminium alloy skinning
64 Dorsal fin
65 De-icing boot
66 Starboard tailplane
67 Corrugated-skin elevator
68 Tailfin forward spar
69 HF communications antenna
70 De-icing boot
71 Tailfin skinning
72 Anti-collision beacon
73 Corrugated-skin rudder
74 Static dischargers
75 Tailfin rear spar
76 Rudder construction
77 Rudder tab
78 Rear navigation light
79 Elevator tab
80 Corrugated-skin elevator
81 Static dischargers
82 Two-spar tailplane construction

CONVAIR 240, 340 and 440 USA

Left: The smart airline-style livery on this Convair 440-75 is deceptive, for it is not operated by Metropolitan but by a Norwegian enthusiasts' organisation, the Metropolitan Klubb, dedicated to preserving an airworthy example of the Convair piston-twin. In fact, several dozen examples of the Convairliner in its 240, 340 and 440 versions still fly with small airlines in North and South America in 1987, but none remains in service in Europe. For the most part, those airlines that do still fly the type have only one or two each, the exception being Air Resorts Airlines with a fleet of 14.

Convair, the successor to the Consolidated-Vultee company that had been responsible during World War II for the B-24 Liberator bomber and the PBY Catalina flying-boat, was one of several companies to respond to an American Airlines invitation early in 1945 to develop a medium-sized twin-engined aircraft with a range of about 865 naut mls (1,600km). Envisaged as a 'DC-3 replacement', the new type was wanted by American to complement the longer-range four-engined types then becoming available from Boeing, Lockheed

and Douglas. Encouraged by discussions with American, Convair produced a prototype of its 30-seat Model 110, which flew for the first time on 8 July 1946, but American had by then decided it required a larger twin, and had placed an order with Convair for 75 of its Model 240, based on the Model 110 but large enough to seat 40. Soon known as the Convairliner, the Convair 240 first flew at San Diego on 16 March 1947, and was, for its day, a conventional low-wing monoplane in both design and construction, with a high-aspect-ratio wing in keeping with

the preferences of I.M. Laddon, who had designed the B-24 and was still in charge of the team designing the Model 240. The Convairliner (a name that also applied to the Models 340 and 440, described under the Variants heading below) proved an effective transport and certainly the most successful, until the advent of the turboprop generation, of the several types launched as 'DC-3 replacements'. It also proved amenable to modification to fit turboprops, the three programmes of this kind being described below.

CONVAIR 580, 600 and 640 USA

During the 1950s and early 1960s the Convair 240, 340 and 440 family of twin-engined transports became the subject of several conversion programmes to fit turboprop engines. In all, about 175 of the original airframes were converted in this way, making the Convair the most successful of several contemporary schemes to apply turbo-

prop power to what had been designed as piston-engined transports. The first programme aimed at airline application was initiated by the Napier engine company in the UK in 1954, and a Convair 340 with 3,060ehp (2,288kW) Eland NEl.1 turboprops flew on 9 February 1955. Six more of these conversions were made, and the type entered airline service in July 1959; in addition, Canadair in Canada built 10 new airframes (using original Convair jigs) with Eland engines, for military use. The second turboprop conversion scheme was set up by the Allison company and was handled by Pacific Airmotive. Either the Model 340 or Model 440 could be converted in this scheme to produce a new variant known as the Convair 580, or sometimes the Super Convair, with Allison 501-D13 engines (as described in the data panel). The first conversion was flown on 19 January 1960, and this proved to be the most successful of the three turboprop Convair programmes with 130 aircraft being converted eventually, the majority for airline use. The added power of the turboprops required increases in the span and area of the tailplane, and in the height and area of the fin. The fuselage and wing remained substantially unchanged, apart from the engine installation, but considerable changes were made internally to the fuel, hydraulic, air-conditioning and pressurization, electric, starting, fire extinguishing and anti-icing systems. The flight deck was modernized, and soundproofing in the cabin was improved. Third and last of the turboprop Convairs was the scheme initiated by the original manufacturer, as the Convair Division of General Dynamics. This scheme introduced a pair of Rolls-Royce RDa10 Dart Mk 542-4 engines with Rotol 13ft (3.96m) diameter four-bladed propellers, and was applicable to all models of the piston-engined transport. When modified, Model 240s became Model 600s (at first Model

240Ds), while Model 340s and 440s became known as Model 640s with Darts (after initially being designated Models 340D and 440D respectively). The first Model 600 flew at San Diego on 20 May 1965, and the first Model 640 later in the same year.

VARIANTS

In addition to the basic turboprop conversion schemes described above, the Super 580 Aircraft Company was set up in the early 1980s as a division of Flight Trails Inc. to develop an improved version of the Allison-engined Convair 580. As the Super 580

SPECIFICATION
(Convair 580)

Power Plant: Two Allison 501-D13H turboprops each rated at 3,750shp (2,796kW) for take-off, with Aeroproducts four-blade constant-speed feathering and reversing propellers of 13ft 6in (4.11m) diameter. Fuel capacity, 1,440 Imp gal (6,546l), or 1,732 Imp gal (7,874l) with modified integral wing tanks plus optional 666 Imp gal (3,027l) in additional inboard tanks.
Performance: Cruising speed, 297kts (550km/h) at 20,000ft (6,095m); initial rate of climb, more than 2,200ft/min (11.2m/sec); take-off field length (CAR), 4,700ft (1,435m); landing field length, 4,160ft (1,270m); range with 5,000lb (2,270kg) payload, 1,970 naut mls (3,650km); range with max fuel, 2,577 naut mls (4,773km).
Weights: Operating weight empty, 30,275lb (13,732kg); max fuel weight, 13,887lb (6,299kg); max payload, 8,870lb (4,023kg); max take-off weight, normal 53,200lb (24,130kg); max take-off weight, optional, 58,140lb (26,371kg); max landing weight, 50,670lb (22,985kg).
Dimensions: Span, 105ft 4in (32.12m); overall length, 81ft 6in (24.84m); overall height, 29ft 2in (8.89m); wing area, 920sq ft (85.5m²).
Accommodation: Cabin length, 36ft 7in (11.1m), max width, 9ft 5in (2.87m), max height, 6ft 7in (2.0m). Typical one-class layout for 52 seats at 35in (89cm) pitch or 56 seats at 32in (81cm) pitch, four-abreast with central aisle. Two above-floor baggage/freight holds, total volume, 436cu ft (12.35m³) and one underfloor hold, volume, 78cu ft (2.21m³). Flight crew of two.

VARIANTS

The Convair 240 was followed in 1951 by the Model 340, first flown on 5 October that year at San Diego. Designed to improve upon the Model 240's characteristics, the Model 340 had a fuselage stretch of 4ft 6in (1.38m) and a revised wing of greater span and area. The new fuselage could accommodate four more passengers at the maximum seat pitch, and many examples were later flown with up to 52 seats. On 6 October 1955 Convair flew the first Model 440, known as the Metropolitan by some operators, mostly in Europe. This was dimensionally the same as the Model 340 but had redesigned engine nacelles and a number of other refinements to improve performance and passenger comfort. Most Model 440s were fitted with weather radar, requiring a further lengthening of the front fuselage by 2ft 4in (70cm). As well as their sales to the airlines, the Models 240, 340 and 440 achieved considerable success in military roles, including training and freight and personnel transport – some with suitably enlarged side freight doors.

SERVICE USE

The Convair 240 was put into service by American Airlines on 1 June 1948. The Convair 340 entered service on 28 March 1950, and Continental Airlines put the Convair 440 into service in February 1956. Production totals for airline use were: CV-240 176, CV-340 212, and CV-440 153; in addition, 520 were built for military use. Many of these (of both commercial and military models) were converted to have turboprop engines, as described below. At the beginning of 1987 fewer than 50 of the piston-engined Convair twins remained in airline service.

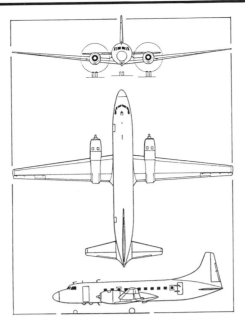

Above: The three-view here depicts the Convair 440 Metropolitan, which was the last of the piston-engined airliners produced by the Convair company. The configuration of the CV-240, 340 and 440 was similar but the original Convair 240 of 1948 was shorter by 6ft (1.83m) and had a wing span that was 13ft 7in (4.15m) less. More immediately obvious when viewing the aircraft was the longer nose of the CV-440 (and CV-340) containing a weather radar installation. The high aspect ratio of the wing – for long a feature of Convair designs – is apparent.

SPECIFICATION
(Convair 440)

Power Plant: Two Pratt & Whitney R-2800-CB17 18-cylinder two-row radial piston engines each rated at 2,500hp (1,864kW) for take-off, with Hamilton Standard or Curtiss Electric three-blade fully-feathering and reversing constant-speed propellers of 13ft 6in (4.15m) diameter. Fuel capacity, 1,440 Imp gal (6,546l) in integral tanks in wings and centre section.
Performance: Max operating speed, 260kts (481km/h) IAS up to 12,200ft (3,720m); max cruising speed, 261kts (483km/h) at 13,000ft (3,960m); best economy cruising speed, 251kts (465km/h) at 20,000ft (6,095m); initial rate of climb, 1,260ft/min (6.4m/sec); service ceiling 24,900ft (7,590m); range with max payload, 248 naut mls (459km); range with max fuel and 5,220lb (2,368kg) payload, 1,677 naut mls (3,106km).
Weights: Typical operating weight empty, 33,314lb (15,110kg); max fuel weight, 10,380lb (4,708kg); max payload, 12,836lb (5,820kg); max take-off weight, 49,700lb (22,544kg); max landing weight, 47,650lb (21,614kg); max zero-fuel weight, 47,000lb (21,320kg).
Dimensions: Span, 105ft 4in (32.12m); overall length, 81ft 6in (24.84m); overall height, 28ft 2in (8.59m); sweepback, nil; wing area, 920sq ft (85.5m²).
Accommodation: Cabin length, 36ft 7in (11.1m), max width, 9ft 5in (2.87m), max height, 6ft 7in (2.0m). Typical layouts provide 44 seats at 38in (97cm) pitch or 52 seats at 35in (89cm) pitch or 56 seats at 32in (81cm) pitch, all four-abreast with central aisle. Two above-floor baggage/freight holds, total volume, 436cu ft (12.35m³) and one underfloor hold, volume, 78cu ft (2.21m³). Flight crew of two.

Left: Operating in Canada's 'golden triangle' of routes linking Montreal, Quebec and Toronto, Air Ontario is the successor to Great Lakes Airlines. Its fleet in 1986 comprised 11 Convair 580s such as this. At least three other airlines, all in the US, had even larger fleets of the Allison-engined conversion of the Convair 440 Metropolitan.

Right: The three-view drawing depicts the Convair 580 with its distinctive nacelles housing Allison 501-D13H turboprops. The Rolls-Royce Dart installation in the Convair 600 and 640 is rather more streamlined in appearance, but the CV-580 achieved greater success.

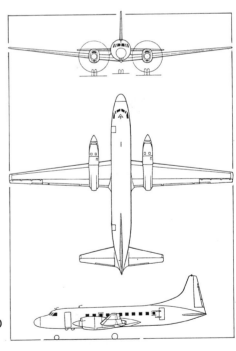

this had 4,000shp (2,983kW) Allison 501-D22G turboprops in place of the earlier -D13 engines, with Hamilton Standard propellers and a number of additional systems changes including a Garrett auxiliary power unit and a redesigned flight deck. Either piston-engined Model 340s and 440s or turboprop-powered Model 580s could be converted. A prototype Super 580 conversion made by Hamilton Aviation flew on 21 March 1984 and a similar conversion by Super 580 Aircraft Co. flew on 20 November 1984. A version with a ventral installation of a Westinghouse APG-66S radar was proposed as the Super

580 Falcon for anti-drug smuggling patrols. An alternative conversion was proposed by the Allison company itself as the Turbo Flagship ATF, featuring a fuselage stretch of 14ft 3in (4.34m) in order to increase capacity to 72-78 passengers or, with a rear side cargo door, 9-12 standard LD3 containers. With 4,300shp (3,207kW) 501-D22G Srs 3 engines, this conversion, also known as the Convair 580S, was to have a gross weight of 63,000lb (28,580kg) and Tracor Aviation was responsible for the actual work of conversion of a prototype, which was underway in 1986.

SERVICE USE

The Convair 580 was certificated by the FAA on 21 April 1960 and entered service with Frontier Airlines in June 1964, earlier deliveries having been for corporate owners. The Convair 600 was certificated on 18 November 1965 and entered airline service on 30 November, with Central Airlines. The Convair 640 was certificated on 7 December 1965 and entered service with Caribair on 22 December. By the beginning of 1987, some 75-80 Convair 580s remained in airline service, almost entirely in North and South America, and 30-odd Convair 600s and 640s were also still in use.

DASSAULT-BREGUET MERCURE FRANCE

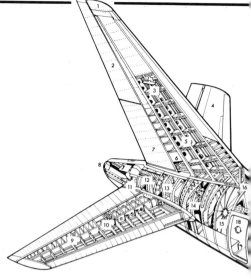
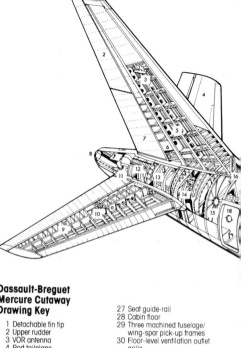

The Mercure is the largest aircraft produced by the Dassault company to date, and its only attempt to enter the airliner market. The attempt did not succeed, and only 12 examples of the Mercure were built, including two prototypes. Technically the aircraft was sound and it has performed well in service, but its payload/range characteristics appear to have restricted its appeal to airline operators in general, and marketing efforts may also have been hampered by airline conservatism, which led to the Dassault company being regarded with some suspicion for its lack of experience in building and supporting a commercial transport aircraft. Before launching the Mercure (and indeed since that time) Dassault has depended heavily upon military aircraft production for its success, but it has also been responsible, since 1962, for the development, design, manufacture and after-sales support of a popular series of business-jet aircraft: the Mystère/Falcon 10, 20, 50 and 900. It was an attempt to broaden this portion of the company's business in the civil field that led Dassault to embark upon the Mercure in the late 1960s. A lengthy series of studies of the potential market led to the preparation of several projects under the title Mystère 30 or Mercure, ranging in size from 30 to 150 seats. These market studies led the company to conclude that there was potential for the sale of up to 1,500 large-capacity short-range transports in the period from 1973 to 1981, and design of the Mercure was optimized for 150 seats over a range of up to 810 naut mls (1,500km). This put the Mercure into the same class as the Boeing 737, although it was limited to considerably shorter ranges than the American aircraft; in configuration also the Dassault aircraft was comparable to the Model 737, with its low wing, 25-degree sweepback and JT8D turbofans close-fitted under the wings. Dassault obtained the backing of the French government to help launch the Mercure, in the form of a loan covering 56 per cent of the launching costs (to be repaid from a levy on sales) and a further 30 per cent was obtained by signing risk-sharing agreements with Aeritalia, CASA, SABCA, F + W and Canadair. While major new production and assembly facilities were built up by Dassault, which was itself responsible for 14 per cent of the launching costs, the construction of two prototypes were put in hand at the company's Bordeaux works. There, the first flight was made on 28 May 1971, using 15,000lb st (6,804kgp) JT8D-11 engines. The definitive JT8D-15 engines were first used on the 21st flight, on 7 September 1971, and dihedral was introduced at the tailplane to improve handling, the type first flying in this form on 18 November. The second protoype flew from the factory at Istres on 7 September 1972, with new leading-edge slats.

VARIANTS

The short production run of the Mercure embraced no variants; flight testing of the prototypes had already led to the introduction of such small innovations as dihedral on the tailplane and leading-edge slats.

SERVICE USE

Air Inter, the French domestic airline, placed an order for 10 Mercures on 29 January 1972, and production was launched on the basis of this single order; no further sales were achieved. The first production Mercure flew at Istres on 17 July 1973 and French certification was obtained on 12 February 1974, based on Cat II operations. Delivery of the first two aircraft to Air Inter was made on 16 May and 11 June 1974 respectively, and the first commercial service was flown on 4 June. With a Bendix autopilot and Thomson-CSF head-up display, the Mercure was certificated on 30 September 1974 for Cat III

SPECIFICATION

Power Plant: Two Pratt & Whitney JT8D-15 turbofans each rated at 15,500lb st (7,030kgp) for take-off. Fuel capacity, 4,048 Imp gal (18,400l).

Performance: Max operating speed, 380kts (704km/h) EAS or Mach = 0.85; max cruising speed, 500kts (926km/h) at 20,000ft (6,095m); best economy cruising speed, 463kts (858km/h) at 30,000ft (9,145m); initial rate of climb, 3,300ft/min (16.7m/sec) at 7,000ft (2,135m) at 100,000lb (45,360kg) weight; take-off field length (FAR Pt25) 8,900ft (2,715m); landing distance (FAR Pt121), 6,050ft (1,845m); range with max payload, 600 naut mls (1,110km); range with 150 passengers at Mach = 0.78 at 33,000ft (10,060m), 1,115 naut mls (2,070km); range with max fuel, 1,750 naut mls (3,240km).

Weights: Operating weight empty, 70,107lb (31,800kg); max fuel weight, 32,520lb (14,750kg); max payload, 35,715lb (16,200kg); max take-off weight, 124,560lb (56,500kg); max landing weight, 114,640lb (52,000kg); max zero-fuel weight, 105,820lb (48,000kg).

Dimensions: Span, 100ft 3in (30.55m); overall length, 114ft 3½in (34.84m); overall height, 37ft 3¼in (11.36m); sweepback, 25 deg at quarter chord; wing area, 1,249sq ft (116.0m²).

Accommodation: Cabin length, 83ft 7in (25.50m), max width, 11ft 11in (3.66m), max height, 7ft 2¾in (2.20m). Typical mixed-class layout for 12 first-class passengers four-abreast at 38in (96.5cm) pitch and 108 tourist-class passengers six-abreast at 34in (86.5cm) pitch; alternative single-class layouts for 135 at 34in (86.5cm) or 150 at 32in (81.5cm) pitch six-abreast. Baggage/freight underfloor holds fore and aft, total volume, 1,200cu ft (34.0m³). Flight crew of two.

Dassault-Breguet Mercure Cutaway Drawing Key

1 Detachable fin tip
2 Upper rudder
3 VOR antenna
4 Port tailplane
5 Two/three-spar fin box structure
6 Hydraulic rudder servo
7 Lower rudder
8 APU exhaust
9 Two-spar tailplane
10 Hydraulic servo unit
11 Garrett GTCP 85 auxiliary power unit in tail cone
12 APU intake grille
13 VI tailplane pivot frame
14 Horizontal tailplane trim motor and screw jack
15 Rear pressure dome
16 Front fin spar torque link
17 Two aft toilets
18 Aft cabin and service doors (starboard and port)
19 Cabin entry vestibule
20 Inward-opening door to underfloor baggage compartment
21 Rear two seat-rows staggered (three starboard, two port)
22 Flexible riser pipes for cabin ventilation
23 Constant pitch notched frame structure (fail safe)
24 Air conditioning diffusers
25 Polarised windows
26 Outward-opening rear freight hold door
27 Seat guide-rail
28 Cabin floor
29 Three machined fuselage/ wing-spar pick-up frames
30 Floor-level ventilation outlet grille
31 Built-up floor grid
32 Integrally-machined window surround panels
33 Undercarriage and hydraulic bay
34 Central wing box
35 Over-wing longitudinal machined floor-support frame
36 Air-conditioning bay beneath wing centre box
37 Main air ducts
38 Air mixing chamber

operations, permitting landings to be made with a runway visual range of 500ft (150m) and decision height of 50ft (15m). The first four aircraft, already in service with Air Inter, were subsequently brought up to this definitive standard. Later, the second prototype also was brought up to full delivery standard and was put into service by Air Inter, which has continued to operate the Mercure fleet with some financial backing from the French government.

Below: The cockpit of the Dassault-Breguet Mercure, which is flown by a two-pilot crew. One of the first commercial transports to be fitted with a head-up display, the Mercure is certificated to operate in Category III weather conditions, when the visibility is no more than 500ft (150m).

Right: The Dassault-Breguet Mercure is used by Air Inter, the French domestic airline, on a number of its medium-density routes within France.

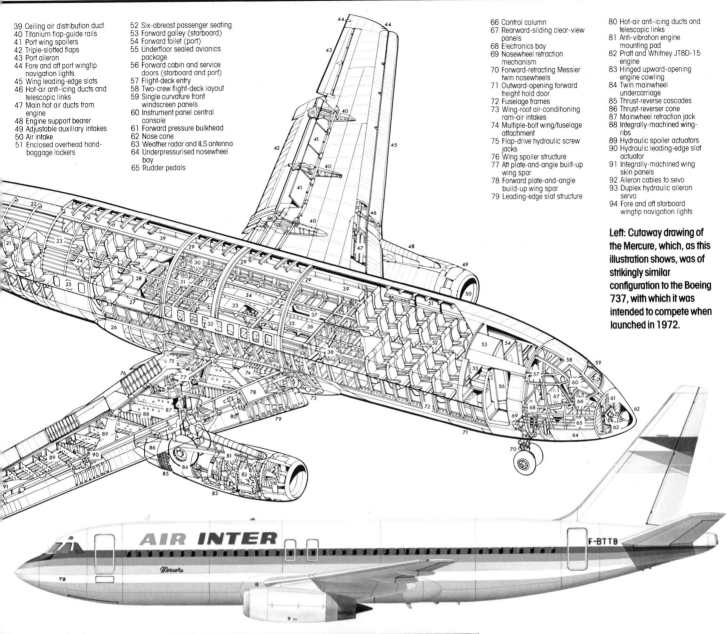

39 Ceiling air distribution duct
40 Titanium flap-guide rails
41 Port wing spoilers
42 Triple-slotted flaps
43 Port aileron
44 Fore and aft port wingtip navigation lights
45 Wing leading-edge slats
46 Hot-air anti-icing ducts and telescopic links
47 Main hot air ducts from engine
48 Engine support bearer
49 Adjustable auxiliary intakes
50 Air intake
51 Enclosed overhead hand-baggage lockers

52 Six-abreast passenger seating
53 Forward galley (starboard)
54 Forward toilet (port)
55 Underfloor sealed avionics package
56 Forward cabin and service doors (starboard and port)
57 Flight-deck entry
58 Two-crew flight-deck layout
59 Single curvature front windscreen panels
60 Instrument panel central console
61 Forward pressure bulkhead
62 Nose cone
63 Weather radar and ILS antenna
64 Underpressurised nosewheel bay
65 Rudder pedals

66 Control column
67 Rearward-sliding clear-view panels
68 Electronics bay
69 Nosewheel retraction mechanism
70 Forward-retracting Messier twin nosewheels
71 Outward-opening forward freight hold door
72 Fuselage frames
73 Wing-root air-conditioning ram-air intakes
74 Multiple-bolt wing/fuselage attachment
75 Flap-drive hydraulic screw jacks
76 Wing spoiler structure
77 Aft plate-and-angle built-up wing spar
78 Forward plate-and-angle build-up wing spar
79 Leading-edge slat structure

80 Hot-air anti-icing ducts and telescopic links
81 Anti-vibration engine mounting pad
82 Pratt and Whitney JT8D-15 engine
83 Hinged upward-opening engine cowling
84 Twin mainwheel undercarriage
85 Thrust-reverse cascades
86 Thrust-reverser cone
87 Mainwheel retraction jack
88 Integrally-machined wing-ribs
89 Hydraulic spoiler actuators
90 Hydraulic leading-edge slat actuator
91 Integrally-machined wing skin panels
92 Aileron cables to sevo
93 Duplex hydraulic aileron servo
94 Fore and aft starboard wingtip navigation lights

Left: Cutaway drawing of the Mercure, which, as this illustration shows, was of strikingly similar configuration to the Boeing 737, with which it was intended to compete when launched in 1972.

Above: The second production Mercure in the Air Inter livery. The fleet is registered F-BTTA to F-BTTK and (second prototype) F-BTTX.

Below: Three-view drawing of the Mercure in its sole production version. The first prototype lacked the leading-edge slats on the wing.

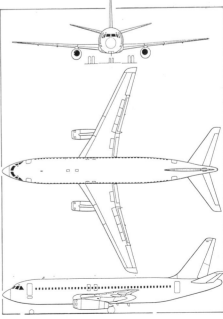

DE HAVILLAND CANADA TWIN OTTER CANADA

The de Havilland Aircraft of Canada Ltd has had a variety of owners since its foundation in 1928 as a subsidiary of the then-independent de Havilland Aircraft company in the UK. The latter eventually became part of the Hawker Siddeley Group, which transferred ownership of the Canadian subsidiary to Canada's federal government in 1974. At the end of January 1986, DHC, as the Canadian company is frequently known, was purchased by The Boeing Co. and is now operating as a subsidiary of Boeing of Canada Ltd. Despite these changes of ownership, the DHC product policy has changed little over the years, with the emphasis upon light transport aircraft with STOL capabilities. After successfully developing the DHC-2 Beaver for Canadian 'bush' type operations, and the large but generally similar DHC-3 Otter, the company gained twin-engine experience with the DHC-4 Caribou and DHC-5 Buffalo, both of which were intended primarily for military operation, thus combining the company's experience of the needs of the smaller civil operator (flying in less-developed areas of the world) with the possibilities of achieving STOL performance with twin-engined transport aircraft. DHC began in January 1964 to design a twin-engined derivative of the Otter. Appropriately named the Twin Otter, this DHC-6 project was intended specifically for the commercial operator, especially in the role of commuter airliner with short-field capabilities. The design objective was to use as much of the Otter as possible, and the DHC-6 emerged with the same basic fuselage cross-section as its single-engined forebear, and the same basic

SPECIFICATION
(Twin Otter Series 300)

Power Plant: Two Pratt & Whitney Canada PT6A-27 turboprops each rated at 620shp (462kW) for take-off, with Hartzell three-blade reversible and feathering propellers of 8ft 6in (2.59m) diameter. Fuel capacity, 319 Imp gal (1,446l) in two underfloor tanks, with optional auxiliary tankage of 74 Imp gal (337l).
Performance: Max operating speed, 170kts (315km/h) IAS; max cruising speed, 182kts (338km/h) at 10,000ft (3,050m); long-range cruising speed, 145kts (269km/h) at 10,000ft (3,050m); initial rate of climb, 1,600ft/min (8.13m/sec); service ceiling, 26,700ft (8,140m); take-off field length (CAR Pt 3), 1,500ft (455m); landing field length (CAR Pt 3), 1,940ft (590m); range with 2,500lb (1,134kg) payload, 700 naut mls (1,297km).
Weights: Typical operating weight empty, 7,415lb (3,363kg); max fuel weight, 2,583lb (1,171kg); max payload, 4,280lb (1,941kg); max take-off weight, 12,500lb (5,670kg); max landing weight, land plane, 12,300lb (5,579kg); max landing weight, floatplane, 12,500lb (5,670kg); max zero-fuel weight, 12,300lb (5,670kg).
Dimensions: Span, 65ft 0in (19.81m); overall length, 51ft 9in (15.77m); overall height, 19ft 6in (5.94m); sweepback, nil; wing area, 420sq ft (39.02m²).
Accommodation: Cabin length, 18ft 6in (5.64m), max width, 5ft 3¼in (1.61m), max height, 4ft 11in (1.50m). Standard accommodation for up to 20 seats in cabin three-abreast, with offset aisle, at 30in (76cm) pitch. Baggage compartments in nose and rear of cabin, total volume, 126cu ft (4.37m³). Flight crew of two.

wing section though of longer span. The cabin length was extended, and new nose and tail assemblies were introduced. Fixed tricycle landing gear was adopted, and following experience with the Caribou and Buffalo, STOL performance was achieved solely by aerodynamic means, using double-slotted full-span trailing-edge flaps, the outboard portions of which also operated differentially as ailerons. In November 1964, DHC put in hand the construction of an initial batch of five Twin Otters, and the first of these flew at the Downsview, Ontario, plant on 20 May 1965.

VARIANTS
The first three Twin Otters were powered by 579shp (432kW) PT6A-6 turboprops, after which a switch was made to the similarly-rated but improved PT6A-20 as the definitive power plant. Retrospectively, this initial production version became known as the Twin Otter Srs 100, superseded after 115 aircraft had been built by the Twin Otter Srs 200. The latter differed in having a lengthened nose fairing with increased baggage capacity. Production of the Srs 200 also totalled 115, after which the Twin Otter Srs 300 became the standard production model, with up-rated PT6A-27 engines (see data panel) and maximum take-off weight increased by 921lb (418kg) to the present figure, with corresponding benefit to the payload/range performance. During 1974 six aircraft with the designation Twin Otter Srs 300S were used for the Airtransit experiment conducted by Air Canada for the Canadian government. This was an evaluation of the practicability of using suitably adapted aircraft to operate to and from city-centre STOLports which – in this case at Montreal and Ottawa – comprised 2,000ft (610m) paved strips 100ft (30m) wide. The 11-passenger Twin Otter Srs 300S was equipped with upper wing spoilers to facilitate steep approach angles; high-capacity brakes and an anti-skid braking system; emergency brakes; improved fire protection for the engines; a sophisticated instrument flight rules (IFR) avionics package; and other changes. Float and combination wheel/ski landing gear are available for the Twin Otter, and a ventral pod has also been developed, with a capacity of up to 600lb (272kg) of baggage or freight. Military derivatives of the basic type are designated DHC-6-300M or -300MR.

SERVICE USE
The Twin Otter was first certificated (to FAR 23 Pt 135 standards) in May 1966, allowing customer deliveries to start in July. Deliveries of the Srs 200 began in April 1968 and of the Srs 300 in the spring of 1969. Sales exceeded 820, including 115 each of the Srs 100 and Srs 200. The majority of all variants has been delivered for commercial use, in the designed role of third-level airliner, but about 70 were sold for military use in a dozen countries and others have been specially equipped for such tasks as photographic and geological surveys, firefighting and oil-spill dispersal. The standard aircraft price was a little over $2million in 1986.

Below: NorOntair, a division of the Ontario Northland Transportation Commission, operates nine Twin Otter 300s on a network throughout Northern Ontario.

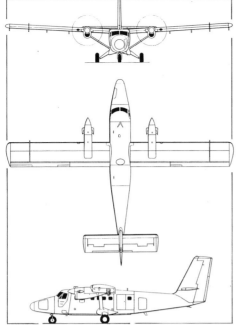

Above: The national airline of the Republic of Mali operates this Twin Otter in a mixed fleet of five aircraft of five types.

Above: Three-view of the de Havilland Canada Twin Otter 300. The Srs 200 is externally identical; Srs 100 had a short nose.

Below: Cutaway drawing of the Twin Otter Srs 300, which has been the standard production version since 1969.

Above: A view looking aft in a Twin Otter, showing the three-abreast seating with an off-set aisle. This layout provides 20 seats, although most Twin Otters in commuter airline use operate with only 19 seats, or fewer if the aircraft is fitted with a galley.

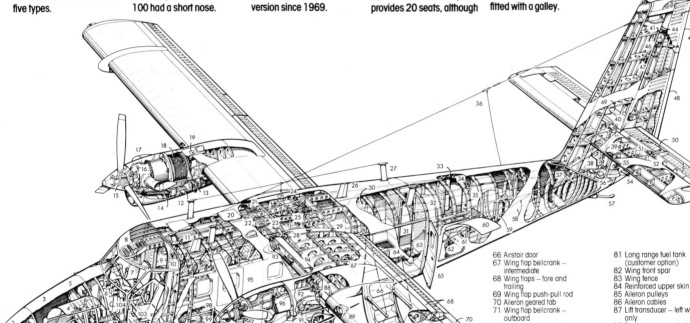

DHC-6 Twin Otter Cutaway Drawing Key

1 Lightning protection rod – not used when weather radar is fitted
2 Weather radar (customer option)
3 Baggage compartment – forward
4 Forward baggage compartment door
5 Avionics equipment
6 Instrument panel – pilot and co-pilot
7 Control columns – pilot and co-pilot
8 Engine power and propeller levers
9 Door to passenger cabin
10 Pulleys and cables – elevator and rudder tabs
11 Engine and propeller control cables
12 Airflow duct
13 Oil cooler
14 Air intake deflector
15 Hartzell constant speed, reverse pitch, fully feathering propeller
16 Pratt & Whitney Canada PT6A-27 turboprop
17 Engine exhaust nozzles
18 Engine air inlet
19 Engine oil tank filler
20 ADF loop antenna (two places, customer option)
21 Engine and propeller control cables
22 Engine and propeller control pulleys
23 Aileron control quadrant
24 Flap/elevator trim interconnect screw jack
25 Wing flap actuator and control quadrants
26 VHF antennæ (two places, customer option)
27 ADF sense antennæ (two places, customer option)
28 Wing/fuselage attachment – forward
29 Wing/fuselage attachment – aft

30 Cabin door – right
31 Door to aft baggage compartment
32 Baggage compartment – aft
33 Passenger oxygen cylinder – customer option
34 Pulleys and cables – elevator and rudder trim tabs
35 Aft baggage compartment extension
36 HF antenna – customer option
37 Rudder control pulleys
38 Elevator control quadrant
39 Elevator control rod
40 Elevator torque tube
41 VOR/ILS antenna (customer option)
42 Anti-collision light and lightning protection horn
43 Rudder
44 Rudder attachment point
45 Rudder trim tab
46 Rudder trim tab screw jack
47 Rudder trim cables
48 Rudder geared tab

49 Elevator/flap interconnect trim tab
50 Elevator trim tab
51 Elevator trim tab screw jack
52 Elevator attachment point
53 Elevator
54 Rudder lever
55 Rudder geared tab geabox
56 Rudder control pulleys
57 Tail bumper
58 Rudder and elevator cables
59 No. 1 and No. 2 static inverters
60 Aft baggage compartment door
61 Oxygen recharging point – (customer option)
62 Rudder and elevator pulleys
63 28-volt battery
64 Air conditioning unit – (customer option)
65 Cabin door – left

66 Airstair door
67 Wing flap bellcrank – intermediate
68 Wing flaps – fore and trailing
69 Wing flap push-pull rod
70 Aileron geared tab
71 Wing flap bellcrank – outboard
72 Adjustable push-pull rod-wing flap

73 Aileron control pulley
74 Aileron push-pull rod
75 Aileron
76 Aileron trim tab actuator
77 Aileron trim tab – left wing only
78 Position light and lightning protection horn
79 Position light visual indicator
80 Long range fuel pressure pump and transfer valve (customer option)

81 Long range fuel tank (customer option)
82 Wing front spar
83 Wing fence
84 Reinforced upper skin
85 Aileron pulleys
86 Aileron cables
87 Lift transducer – left wing only
88 Engine power control pulleys
89 Landing light – both wings
90 Main landing gear leg
91 Main landing gear shock absorber
92 Wing strut attachment point at fuselage
93 Engine power and propeller control cables
94 Hinged leading edge
95 Emergency door – both sides
96 Engine attachment point – 3 places
97 Engine air intake
98 Fuel cells – 315 Imp gallons (1,432l) usable fuel, or with long range tanks 392 Imp gallons (1,782l)
99 Interconnecting fuel vent lines
100 Fuel filler
101 Pulleys and cables – aileron control
102 Hydraulic reservoir and recharging panel
103 Aileron trim console
104 Centre pedestal
105 Rudder pedals
106 Taxi light (customer option)
107 Nosewheel leg
108 Nosewheel torque links
109 Nosewheel steering acuator
110 Crew oxygen cylinder
111 Glideslope antenna (customer option)

In pursuance of its policy of specializing in the production of small/medium-capacity transport aircraft with STOL capability, de Havilland Aircraft of Canada conducted an extensive market survey of short-haul transport requirements in the early 1970s. Based on the results of this survey, design definition was finalized for a STOL aircraft in the 50-seat category and, with the backing of the Canadian government, prototype construction was put in hand in late 1972. The DHC-7, or Dash 7 as it soon became known, was de Havilland's first four-engined aircraft, but its configuration followed earlier practice, with a high-wing, T-tail layout and an aerodynamic high-lift system. The latter made use of double-slotted flaps over some 80 per cent of the wing span, operating in the slipstream from the propellers. The flaps operate mechanically for take-off and hydraulically for landing, and are supplemented by two outboard spoilers in each wing that can be operated symmetrically or, to supplement the ailerons, differentially. Pratt & Whitney Canada worked with DHC to develop a new variant of the PT6A turboprop, matched to new slow-running five-blade propellers to achieve the lowest possible noise levels, both externally and internally in the cabin. Special attention was given to the aircraft's noise characteristics and the noise 'footprint' since it was expected that the type would be applicable to planned intercity services using close-in downtown airports or STOLports. Such operations have developed less rapidly than DHC anticipated, however, and sales of the Dash 7 have suffered accordingly; many regional airlines requiring an aircraft of Dash 7 size have continued (for commercial or regulatory reasons) to use out-of-town airports where STOL performance and ultra-low noise levels are less significant than the lower first costs and operating costs offered by the Dash 7's principal competitors. The Dash 7 development programme made use of four airframes: one for static testing, one fatigue test specimen and two for flight test and certification. The last made their first flights at Downsview on 27 March and 26 June 1975 respectively.

VARIANTS

The basic production model is the Dash 7 Srs 100, as described in the data panel. An all-cargo or mixed passenger/cargo variant is designated Dash 7 Srs 101 and incorporates a large forward freight door in the port side of the fuselage. The Dash 7 Srs 150 has an increased take-off weight of 47,000lb (21,319kg), the maximum landing weight being 45,000lb (20,411kg), and provision is made for an extra 912 Imp gal (4,145l) of fuel in the wings, bringing the maximum fuel load up to 17,500lb (7,938kg). With this extra fuel, the maximum range of the Srs 150 increases to 2,525 naut mls (4,679km). The all-cargo or mixed passenger/cargo version of the Srs 150 is designated Dash 7 Srs 151 and, like the Srs 101, this can carry up to five standard pallets in the all-cargo role. Projected developments of the type included the Dash 7 Srs 200 with 1,230shp (918kW) PT6A-55 engines and the same weights as the Srs 150, and the Dash 7 Srs 300 with the fuselage stretched to increase the maximum seating to about 70. The advent of such aircraft as the British Aerospace ATP and the ATR-72, combined with the reduced opportunities for STOL operations, led DHC to suspend development of these projects in the early 1980s, however, and after the company had been acquired in 1986 by Boeing, attention has focussed on stretched versions of the Dash 8.

SERVICE USE

Canadian certification of the Dash 7 was obtained (to FAR Pt 25 standards) on 2 May 1977, based on the flight test and development of the two prototypes. The first production aircraft flew on 30 May 1977 and the second production aircraft entered service with Rocky Mountain Airways in the USA on 3 February 1978. Srs 150 aircraft became available for commercial use in 1986, after the first had been completed for the Canadian Department of the Environment, with special features for ice reconnaissance. This aircraft was designated Dash 7IR. By early 1987, sales of the Dash 7 totalled 108; the new aircraft price was of the order of $9 million.

SPECIFICATION
(Dash 7 Series 100)

Power Plant: Four Pratt & Whitney PT6A-50 turboprops each flat-rated at 1,120shp (835kW) for take-off, with Hamilton Standard four-blade constant-speed feathering and reversing propellers of 11ft 3in (3.43m) diameter. Fuel capacity, 1,232 Imp gal (5,602l) in integral wing tanks.
Performance: Max operating speed, 231kts (427km/h) IAS; max cruising speed, 227kts (420km/h) at 15,000ft (4,575m); long-range cruising speed, 215kts (399km/h) at 20,000ft (6,095m); en route rate of climb, 1,220ft/min (6.2m/sec); service ceiling, 21,000ft (6,400m); take-off field length, 2,250ft (685m); landing field length, 2,160ft (660m); range with 50 passengers, 690 naut mls (1,279km); max range with 6,500lb (2,948kg) payload, 1,170 naut mls (2,168km).
Weights: Operating weight empty, 27,690lb (12,560kg); max fuel weight, 10,060lb (4,563kg); max payload, 11,310lb (5,130kg); max take-off weight, 44,000lb (19,958kg); max landing weight, 44,000lb (19,958kg); max zero-fuel weight, 39,000lb (17,690kg).
Dimensions: Span, 93ft 0in (28.35m); overall length, 80ft 6in (24.54m); overall height, 26ft 2in (7.98m); sweepback, 3.2 deg at quarter chord; wing area, 860sq ft (79.9m²).
Accommodation: Cabin length, 39ft 6in (12.04m), max width, 8ft 6¼in (2.60m), max height, 6ft 4½in (1.94m). Standard layout provides 50 seats four-abreast, with central aisle, at 32in (81cm) pitch; max seating 54 at 29in (74cm) pitch. Baggage compartment in rear fuselage, volume 240cu ft (6.8m³). Flight crew of two.

Left: One of the smaller airliners to have four engines, the Dash 7 necessarily has a crowded flight deck. Primary flight instruments and engine controls are conventionally located, with navigation and communications consoles between the two pilots.

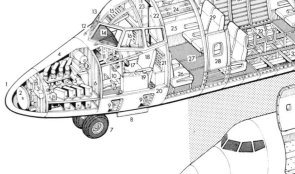

Above: Cutaway drawing of the de Havilland Canada Dash 7 Srs 100, with an inset sketch of the cargo door designed for the Srs 101.

De Havilland Canada Dash 7 Cutaway Drawing Key

1 Radome
2 Weather radar scanner
3 Radar transmitter and receiver units
4 Nose electronics compartment
5 Radio and electronics racks
6 Front pressure bulkhead
7 Twin nosewheels
8 Nosewheel doors
9 Control runs beneath cockpit floor
10 Rudder pedals
11 Instrument panel
12 Windscreen wipers

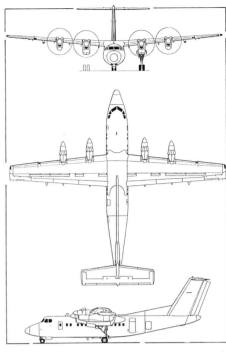

Above: More than 50 years old, Wideroe's Flyveselskap is today Norway's oldest airline. It operates an extensive scheduled network of domestic routes, for which it uses a fleet exclusively of de Havilland Canada origin, including eight Dash 7 Srs 100s as well as a dozen smaller Twin Otters.

Above: Three-view drawing of the Dash 7 in its basic Srs 100 form. The heavier Srs 150 is externally the same; Srs 101 and 151 have a forward freight door.

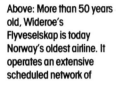

13 Windscreen panels
14 Instrument panel shroud
15 Overhead switch panel
16 Co-pilot's seat
17 Control column handwheel
18 Pilot's seat
19 Nosewheel steering control
20 Pitot tubes
21 Circuit breaker panel
22 Cockpit bulkhead
23 Electrical distribution panel
24 Cabin roof control runs
25 Cabin trim panels
26 Rearward facing seat row
27 Seat attachment rails
28 Emergency exit window panel, port and starboard
29 Four-abreast passenger seating, 50 seats
30 VHF aerial
31 Fuselage frame and stringer construction
32 Floor beam construction
33 Underfloor air conditioning ducting
34 Overhead stowage bins
35 Wing root fairing construction
36 Main undercarriage wheel doors
37 Air system water separators
38 Wing spar box centre section
39 Skin panel joint strap
40 Wing stringers
41 Starboard air conditioning plant

42 Main undercarriage wheel bay
43 Engine compartment firewall
44 Intake debris separator
45 Engine air intake
46 Hamilton Standard four-bladed, reversible pitch propellers
47 Glass-fibre propeller blades
48 Blade root de-icing boots
49 Propeller hub pitch change mechanism
50 Pratt & Whitney Canada PT6A-50 turboprop
51 Engine intake screen
52 Exhaust stubs
53 Engine support link
54 Bleed air piping
55 Starboard wing fuel tanks; total aircraft fuel capacity 1,232 Imp gal (5,602l)
56 Overwing fuel filler caps
57 Engine cowling panels
58 Leading edge de-icing boots
59 Landing lamp
60 Wing fence
61 Starboard navigation light
62 Compass flux valve
63 Starboard aileron
64 Geared tab
65 Aileron trim tab
66 Starboard double slotted flaps, down position
67 Roll control spoilers
68 Ground spoilers
69 Flap screw jacks
70 Wing root trailing edge fillet
71 Fuel transfer pipe fairing
72 Starboard service door
73 Rear seat row

74 Buffet unit
75 Starboard baggage door (open)
76 Fin root fillet
77 Refuelling/defuelling pipe
78 Emergency locator transmitter aerial
79 Fin leading edge
80 Fin construction
81 VOR aerial
82 Elevator control rods
83 Tailplane/fin attachment spar box
84 Upper position light
85 Anti-collision light
86 Tailplane leading edge de-icing boots
87 Starboard tailplane
88 Static discharge wicks
89 Elevator trim tabs
90 Elevator spring tab
91 One-piece elevator
92 Elevator horn balance
93 Tailplane construction
94 Rudder hydraulic jacks
95 Trailing rudder
96 Fore-rudder
97 Tail navigation light
98 Rear fuselage vent
99 Tailcone access door
100 Retractable tail bumper
101 Cockpit voice recorder
102 Sloping fin attachment frames
103 Ventral pressure refuelling connection
104 Rear pressure bulkhead
105 Baggage compartment
106 Baggage restraint net
107 Toilet compartment
108 Wash basin
109 Passenger door upper segment
110 Trailing edge wing root fillet
111 Inboard flap track
112 Wing spar/fuselage main frame attachment joint
113 Flap shroud ribs
114 Port wing integral fuel tank bays

115 Lower passenger door segment/airstairs
116 Handrail
117 Nacelle tail fairing
118 Port double slotted flaps
119 Roll control spoilers
120 Port aileron construction
121 Aileron geared tab
122 Static discharge wicks
123 Aileron horn balance
124 Compass flux valve
125 Port navigation light
126 Wing rib construction
127 Leading edge nose ribs
128 Wing fence
129 Wing tank outboard end rib
130 Landing lamp
131 Leading edge de-icing boots
132 Outboard nacelle hydraulics bay
133 Engine nacelle construction
134 Twin mainwheels
135 Engine air intake
136 Front engine mounting
137 Undercarriage breaker strut
138 Main undercarriage leg strut
139 Hydraulic retraction jack
140 Main undercarriage pivot mounting frame
141 Wing tank inboard end rib
142 Bleed air piping
143 Port air conditioning plant
144 Port inner nacelle construction
145 Propeller spinner
146 Oil cooler
147 HF aerial rail
148 Quick-change passenger/cargo version
149 Cargo door
150 'Ballmat' heavy duty cargo handling floor

Below: One of three Dash 7s used by Brymon Airways in the UK.

DE HAVILLAND CANADA DASH 8 CANADA

A s interest in commuter aircraft with a capacity of 30-40 seats grew at the end of the 1970s, de Havilland Aircraft of Canada chose this portion of the airline market for its project to follow the Dash 7. The DHC-8, or Dash 8, that resulted from this decision neatly filled the gap between the 19-seat Twin Otter and the 50-seat Dash 7, but it also came into competition with the new aircraft of similar capacity being developed in a similar timescale by CASA/Nurtanio, Embraer, Shorts and Saab-Fairchild. In keeping with DHC policy and experience, the Dash 8 was designed to have particularly good field performance, and its configuration was that of a scaled-down Dash 7, with a high wing, a T-tail, a two-element rudder, and powerful single-slotted flaps supplemented by roll control spoilers. Once again, with the Dash 8, de Havilland designers avoided the use of movable leading-edge devices as a means of achieving high lift for good field performance, believing that such devices were prone to damage in the type of operations for which the aircraft was designed. To power the Dash 8, the company selected the newest engine type offered by Pratt & Whitney Canada, a turboprop developed under the PT7 designation but put into production as the PW100 family. Under a new P&W designating procedure, the individual variants of this basic engine were identified as to their power by the last two digits in the designation: thus the 2,000shp (1,491kW) model for the initial production version of the Dash 8 became the PW120, and the uprated

SPECIFICATION
(Dash 8 Series 100)

Power Plant: Two Pratt & Whitney Canada PW120A turboprops each rated at 1,800shp (1,432kW) for take-off, with automatic power reserve of 200shp (149kW) for use in case of one engine failure, with Hamilton Standard four-blade constant-speed feathering and reversing propellers of 13ft (3.96m) diameter. Fuel capacity, 695 Imp gal (3,160l) in integral wing tanks, with optional auxiliary tankage of 549 Imp gal (2,496l).
Performance: Max operating speed, 245kts (454km/h) IAS; max cruising speed, 265kts (554km/h) at 25,000ft (7,620m); long-range cruising speed, 237kts (439km/h) at 25,000ft (7,620m); initial rate of climb, 2,070ft/min (10.5m/sec); take-off field length (FAR Pt 25), 3,110ft (950m); landing field length (FAR Pt 25), 3,150ft (960m); range with max passenger payload, 1,150 naut mls (2,130km); range with max cargo payload, 150 naut mls (278km).
Weights: Operating weight empty, 21,590lb (9,793kg); standard fuel weight, 5,678lb (2,576kg); max fuel weight, 10,160lb (4,609kg); max passenger payload, 7,824lb (3,549kg); max cargo payload, 9,410lb (4,268kg); max take-off weight, 34,500lb (15,649kg); max landing weight, 33,900lb (14,923kg); max zero-fuel weight, 31,000lb (14,062kg).
Dimensions: Span, 85ft 0in (25.91m); overall length, 73ft 0in (22.25m); overall height, 24ft 7in (7.49m); sweepback, 3.03 deg at quarter chord; wing area, 585sq ft (54.4m²).
Accommodation: Cabin length, 30ft 2in (9.19m), max width, 8ft 2in (2.49m), max height, 6ft 2in (1.88m). Standard layout for 36 passengers four-abreast, with central aisle, at 31in (79cm) pitch, or up to a maximum of 40. Baggage compartment at rear of cabin, volume, 300cu ft (8.5m³). Flight crew of two and one cabin attendant.

engine for later variants is the PW123. When the decision to launch the Dash 8 was reached during 1980, the company proceeded, with the help of government financing, to lay down production tooling, with jigs and fixtures to allow production of up to eight aircraft a month – a decision reflecting confidence in the design but also influenced by the competitiveness of 30/40-seat market, which made it essential to have aircraft available as soon as any of the alternative types. Four pre-production aircraft were assigned to the test flying and certification programme, the first of these flying on 20 June 1983. The second followed on 26 October 1983, the third in November 1983 and the fourth (the first to be fitted with definitive PW120 engines) in early 1984. The fifth aircraft, which introduced a fully-furnished production interior, flew in June 1984.

VARIANTS
The basic production variant is the Dash 8 Srs 100, as described in the data panel. It is available as a 36-seat regional airliner, or with a corporate interior with layouts for 17-24 passengers and optional additional fuel tankage that brings the total capacity up to 1,036 Imp gal (4,709l) and allows the aircraft to fly up to 2,000 naut mls (3,706km) with a 1,200lb (544kg) payload. A projected Srs 200, with higher operating weights, was superseded by the Dash 8 Srs 300, development of which was put in hand in 1985 and continued after Boeing had acquired DHC in January 1986. The Srs 300 has a fuselage 'stretch' of 11ft 3in (3.43m), and the span is increased by 5ft (1.52m), with accommodation going up to a maximum of 56 at a seat pitch of 29in (74cm). Powered by 2,380shp (1,776kW) PW123 turboprops, the Dash 8-300 has the same fuel capacity as the -100, and a maximum take-off weight of 41,000lb (18,598kg). Military versions of the basic aircraft are designated Dash 8M and are available with equipment for a variety of different missions. Specially-equipped commercial versions have been produced for such duties as airways calibration and medevac.

Above: De Havilland Canada has achieved a light and spacious appearance in the interior of the Dash 8, shown here in its Series 100 form. The seat pitch in this 36-seat layout is 31in (79cm), which is quite adequate for the stages normally flown.

Right: Cutaway drawing of the Dash 8 Series 100, which follows de Havilland Canada practice in its structural design. Notably, the Dash 8 does not rely upon leading-edge flaps to achieve its short take-off and landing capability.

SERVICE USE
The Dash 8 was certificated in Canada to the standards of FAR Pts 25 and 36, and SFAR No. 27, on 28 September 1984, shortly followed by FAA approval in the USA. Deliveries began on 23 October 1984, the second production aircraft going to NorOntair, and this company put the type into revenue service on 19 December 1984. By early 1987, sales of the Dash 8 totalled 109 Srs 100 and 23 Srs 300, with a further 48 on option. The basic price of a standard airline version was then of the order of $6 million.

Below: City Express – an early user of the Dash 8 – is one of Canada's newer airlines, operating low-cost services from Toronto's close-in Island Airport to Ottawa and Montreal.

40 Cockpit roof escape hatch
41 Starboard side toilet compartment
42 VHF aerial
43 Starboard side service door/emergency exit
44 Buffet/drinks unit
45 Main cabin doorway
46 Wardrobe compartment
47 Cabin attendant's folding seat
48 Interphone
49 External inspection light
50 Radio and electronics racks
51 Airstairs external handle
52 Passenger entry door/airstairs
53 Folding handrail
54 Entry lobby
55 Four-abreast passenger seating, 36 seats
56 Cabin wall trim panels
57 Fuselage frame and stringer construction
58 Floor beam construction
59 Cabin window panels
60 Navigation system electronics equipment
61 Underfloor air conditioning ducting

62 External floodlights
63 Main cabin honeycomb floor panels
64 Seat mounting rails
65 Emergency exit window panels, port and starboard
66 Overhead stowage bins
67 Wing attachment fuselage main frames
68 Centre wing panel rib construction
69 De-icing control valve
70 Kevlar honeycomb wing root fairing
71 Engine bleed air ducting
72 Engine control runs
73 Starboard main undercarriage leg struts
74 Starboard engine nacelle
75 Pratt & Whitney Aircraft of Canada PW120 turboprop engine
76 Engine accessory equipment
77 Propeller reduction gearbox
78 Engine air intake
79 Hamilton Standard four-bladed variable pitch reversible propeller
80 Spinner
81 Propeller hub pitch change mechanism
82 Engine accessory equipment access panels
83 Twin landing lamps
84 Outer wing panel joint rib

85 Starboard wing integral fuel tank; total fuel capacity 720 Imp gal (3,271l)
86 Leading-edge stall strip
87 Wing access panels
88 Fuel filler cap
89 Pneumatic leading edge de-icing boot
90 Starboard navigation light
91 Wing tip fairing
92 Static dischargers
93 Starboard aileron
94 Aileron trim tab
95 Aileron spring tab
96 Aileron hinge control
97 Outboard differential roll control spoilers, open
98 Flap track fairings
99 Starboard single slotted flap, down position
100 Flap guide rail
101 Outboard ground spoiler/lift dumper, open
102 Flap screw jack
103 Starboard engine exhaust duct
104 Exhaust shroud
105 Pressure refuelling connection
106 Main undercarriage wheel bay
107 Inboard ground spoiler/lift dumper, open
108 Inboard flap segment
109 Trailing-edge wing root fairing
110 Control cable linkages
111 Flap hydraulic motor
112 Fire extinguisher bottles
113 Port inboard ground spoiler
114 Flap screw jack housing

115 Flap drive shaft
116 Port inboard single-slotted flap segment
117 Overhead passenger service units
118 Rear seat row
119 Cabin rear bulkhead
120 Up-and-over baggage/cargo door, open
121 Bleed air supply duct to air conditioning
122 Fin root fillet
123 Heat exchanger flush air intake
124 Emergency location transmitter
125 Emergency location transmitter aerial
126 Fin leading edge flush HF aerial
127 Tailfin construction
128 Rudder hydraulic actuators

129 Fin skin panels
130 Elevator cable pulley
131 Elevator control rods
132 Tailplane centre section attachment
133 Upper position light
134 Anti-collision light
135 Tailplane pneumatic leading edge de-icing boot
136 Starboard tailplane
137 Starboard elevator
138 Elevator trim tabs
139 Elevator spring tabs
140 Port elevator rib construction
141 Static dischargers
142 Elevator horn balance
143 Tailplane construction
144 Two segment rudder construction

145 Fore rudder
146 Trailing rudder
147 Lower position light
148 Heat exchanger exhaust duct
149 Tailcone
150 Ventral access hatch
151 Sloping fin attachment frames
152 Flight data and cockpit voice recorders
153 Rear fuselage frame and stringer construction
154 Air conditioning plant
155 Rear pressure bulkhead
156 Baggage restraint net
157 Baggage/cargo bay floor
158 Baggage door guards
159 Port nacelle tail fairing
160 Exhaust duct shroud
161 Port engine exhaust pipe
162 Port outer ground spoiler
163 Honeycomb trailing edge shroud panels
164 Port outer single slotted flap
165 Flap down position
166 Flap rib construction
167 Port roll control spoilers
168 Aileron hinge control
169 Aileron spring tab
170 Port aileron rib construction
171 Static dischargers
172 Aileron mass balance
173 Glass-fibre wing tip fairing
174 Port navigation and strobe lights
175 Leading edge de-icing
176 Leading edge honeycomb skin panels
177 Rear spar
178 Fuel filler cap
179 Wing rib construction
180 Port wing integral fuel tank
181 Front spar
182 Pneumatic de-icing valves
183 Leading edge stall strip
184 Hydraulic equipment bay
185 Outer wing panel joint rib
186 Main undercarriage upper yoke
187 Mainwheel leg doors
188 Main undercarriage faired leg strut
189 Twin mainwheels
190 Hydraulic brake pipes
191 Faired forward V-strut
192 Main leg breaker strut
193 Twin landing lamps
194 Undercarriage mounting frame
195 Engine oil cooler
196 Engine bay firewall
197 Intake snow and debris ejector
198 Wing inspection lamp
199 Engine bearer struts
200 Intake duct
201 Forward engine mounting ring frame
202 Port propeller spinner
203 Intake lip de-icing

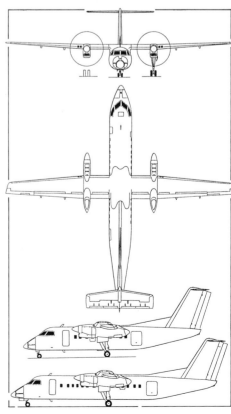

Left: An affiliate of Metro Airlines of Houston, Eastern Metro Express uses Dash 8s (together with Twin Otters and Jetstream 31s) to feed Eastern Airlines at its Atlanta, Georgia, hub. The development of hub-type operations by most of the major US airlines in the early 'eighties opened up a useful market for the commuter airlines using such types as the Dash 8.

Right: The three-view drawing shows the de Havilland Canada Dash 8 in its basic Series 100 version, sales of which had surpassed 100 by the start of 1987. The lower side view shows the Series 300, which has a fuselage 'stretch' of 11ft 3in (3.43m) and more powerful engines. To make its first flight in 1988, the Dash 8 Series 300 will carry a maximum of 56 passengers.

DORNIER 228 FEDERAL REPUBLIC OF GERMANY

Development of the Dornier 228 began with the work that the company undertook, under a government-funded research contract, to evolve a 'new technology wing' (*Tragflugels Neuer Technologie*, or TNT). An example of this wing, featuring the Do A-5 supercritical section and unusual planform with raked tips, flew for the first time on a converted Do 28D-2 Skyservant on 14 June 1979. Associated with the TNT wing was a new power plant installation, two Garrett TPE331-5 turboprops in conventional wing nacelles replacing the Skyservant's sponson-mounted piston engines. To take full advantage of the performance and economic gains possible with the TNT, Dornier designed a new fuselage to provide an aircraft able to fulfil a range of missions, among which commuter passenger operations were to be the most important. Although some of the structural philosophy of the Skyservant was retained, the aircraft was completely new, a fact that the original designation (Do 28E) did little to emphasize. In 1980, Dornier redesignated its range of light transport aircraft and the new type, then still under development, became the Dornier 228. Two versions, with different fuselage lengths, had already been proposed as the Do 28E-1 and Do 28E-2: to carry 15 or 19 passengers respect-

ively, these became the Dornier 228-100 and 228-200, and work on the pair proceeded in parallel. The new fuselage, in the shorter of its two forms, was some 12ft (3.5m) longer than that of the Dornier 128-2 (as the Do 28D-2 had meanwhile become), whilst the 228-200's fuselage was 5ft (1.52m) longer than that of the 228-100. The prototypes made their first flights on 28 March and 9 May 1981 respectively. On 29 November 1983, Dornier concluded a licence agreement with Hindustan Aeronautics Ltd providing for the construction of up to 150 Dornier 228s in India to meet local military and commercial requirements, and the first aircraft assembled in India (using components supplied by Dornier) was flown at Kanpur on 31 January 1986.

VARIANTS
The Dornier 228-100 and 228-200 differ from each other in fuselage length, as already described. The Dornier 228-100 has the same take-off and landing weights as the 228-200, but can carry approximately 300lb (136kg) more payload, and has more than twice the range of the 228-200 with maximum passenger payload. In 1984, Dornier introduced new versions designated Dornier 228-101 and 228-202, with a maximum take-off weight of 13,183lb (5,980kg) and ranges of 939 naut mls (1,740km) and 593 naut mls (1,000km) respectively with maximum payloads. For delivery from the autumn of 1987, the Dornier 228-202 has a maximum take-off weight of 13,668lb (6,200kg) and maximum landing weight of 13,448lb (6,100kg), together with increased max cruising speed, and take-off and climb performance. At the end of 1986, development of the 30-passenger Dornier 328 was approved. Several military configurations have been evolved, for such duties as maritime surveillance, and the support of search and rescue missions as well as the basic personnel and freight transport.

SERVICE USE
The Dornier 228-100 was certificiated in West Germany, in accordance with FAR Pt 23 requirements, on 18 December 1981 and deliveries began in February 1982 to the first commercial operator, Norving Flyservice in Norway. The 228-200 was certificated on 6 September 1982. British and US certification was obtained on 17 April and 11 May 1984 respectively. Deliveries from the Hindustan Aeronautics assembly line at Kanpur began on 22 March 1986, when the Indian domestic airline Vayudoot received the first of a batch of five Indian-built examples. Sales of Dornier 228s in all versions totalled 110 by January 1987, and the prices of the short- and long-fuselage versions were then about $2 million and $2.5 million respectively.

SPECIFICATION
(Dornier 228-200)

Power Plant: Two Garrett TPE331-5-252D turboprops each rated at 715shp (533kW) for take-off, with Hartzell four-blade constant-speed feathering and reversing propellers of 8ft 11½in (2.73m) diameter. Fuel capacity, 525 Imp gal (2,386l) in integral tanks in wing box.
Performance: Max cruising speed, 231kts (428km/h) at 10,000ft (3,050m) and 199kts (370km/h) at sea level; initial rate of climb, 2,025ft/min (10.3m/sec); service ceiling, 29,600ft (9,020m); take-off distance to 50ft (15m), 1,945ft (590m); landing distance from 50ft (15m), 1970ft (600m); range with max passenger payload, 323 naut mls (600km); range with max fuel, 1,460 naut mls (2,704km).
Weights: Operating weight empty, 7,820lb (3,547kg); max payload, 4,394lb (1,993kg); max take-off weight, 12,566lb (5,700kg); max landing weight, 12,566lb (5,700kg); max zero fuel weight, 11,900lb (5,400kg).
Dimensions: Span, 55ft 8in (16.97m); overall length, 54ft 3in (16.55m); overall height, 15ft 11½in (4.86m); sweepback, nil; wing area, 344.3sq ft (32.0m²).
Accommodation: Cabin length, 23ft 2¾in (7.08m), max width, 4ft 5in (1.35m); max height, 5ft 1in (1.55m). Standard layout provides 19 single passenger seats with central aisle at 30in (76cm) pitch. Baggage compartments in nose and rear of cabin, total volume, 123.2cu ft (3.49m³).

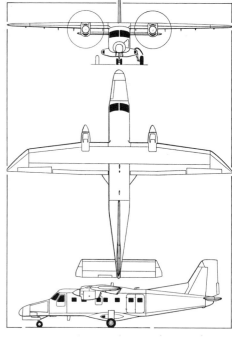

Above: This three-view drawing shows the short-fuselage Series 100 version of the Dornier 228. The 228-200 is identical except for the fuselage length. Note the distinctive planform of the Dornier New Technology Wing.

Right: The registration of this Dornier 228-201 gives the only clue to its owner, the commuter operator Fischer Brothers Aviation. It has six Dornier 228s and since February 1986 has served as a Northwest Airlines Airlink company.

Dornier 228-200 Cutaway Drawing Key

1 Glassfibre radome
2 Weather radar scanner (optional)
3 Radar mounting bulkhead
4 Nosewheel doors, closed after cycling of undercarriage
5 Ground power socket
6 Battery
7 Pitot heads
8 Nose compartment construction
9 Forward baggage compartment, 31.4cu ft (0.89m³)
10 Nose undercarriage pivot fixing
11 Nosewheel leg strut
12 Twin nosewheels, forward retracting
13 Torque scissor links
14 Hydraulic retraction jack
15 Baggage door
16 Baggage loading floor
17 Cockpit front bulkhead
18 Rudder pedals
19 Instrument panel
20 Instrument panel shroud
21 Stand-by compass
22 Windscreen wipers
23 Curved windscreen panels
24 Overhead systems switch panels
25 Folding sun visors
26 Co-pilot's seat
27 Centre control pedestal
28 Control column
29 Cockpit floor level
30 Underfloor control linkages
31 Boarding step
32 Lower VHF aerial
33 Pilot's seat mounting
34 Crew entry door
35 External door latch
36 Safety harness
37 Pilot's seat
38 Electrical equipment racks
39 Cockpit rear bulkhead
40 Radio and avionics equipment racks
41 Curtained doorway to main cabin

42 Fuselage skin panelling
43 Cabin wall trim panelling
44 Cabin roof frames
45 Forward passenger seats, 19-seat layout

Left: The Dornier 228 provides a good level of comfort for passengers on the relatively short flights that are typical of commuter operators, with a 30in (76cm) seat pitch for 15 or 19 passengers in single seats, depending on the variant concerned. The -200 is 5ft (1.52m) longer than the -100.

Right: Cutaway drawing of the Dornier 228-200, which is designed for a long structure life combined with ease of maintenance and for operations independent of ground equipment.

Left: By the end of 1986, Dornier had sold 110 examples of the Model 228 in all its variants, not counting the planned production in India of at least 150 under licence by Hindustan Aeronautics. The first 100 deliveries had by then taken the Dornier 228 to many parts of the world, principally to serve with smaller companies and in small numbers with each operator. Japan Air Commuter, typically, had two 228-200s in service, in the Amami Islands.

46 Cabin window panel
47 Forward fuselage frame and stringer construction
48 Seat mounting rails
49 Underfloor control runs
50 Floor beam construction
51 Hydraulic equipment module
52 Port emergency exit window panel
53 Wing spar attachment fuselage
54 Wing joint frame drag member
55 Passenger cabin ceiling lighting and trim panels
56 Front spar attachment light
57 Wing panel centre section construction

58 Front spar
59 Wing mounting main ribs
60 Cabin heater
61 Heater air intake
62 Kevlar composite leading-edge fillet
63 Starboard inboard main fuel tank. Total fuel capacity 525 Imp Gal (2,386l)
64 Fuel tank access panels
65 Leading-edge engine control runs
66 Starboard engine nacelle
67 Garrett TPE331-5-252D turboprop
68 Propeller reduction gearbox
69 Propeller hub pitch change mechanism
70 Hartzell four-bladed constant speed, fully feathering and reversible propeller
71 Spinner
72 Propeller blade root de-icing (optional)
73 Oil cooler air intake
74 Oil radiator
75 Engine accessory equipment

76 Main engine bearers
77 Wing skin panelling
78 Outer wing panel skin joint strap
79 Fuel filler cap
80 Outer wing panel integral fuel tank
81 Leading-edge de-icing boot (optional)
82 Raked wing-tip fairing
83 Starboard navigation light
84 Static dischargers
85 Aileron external hinge
86 Aileron mass balance weight
87 Aileron hinge control
88 Starboard drooping aileron
89 Aileron Kevlar skin panelling
90 Starboard single-slotted Fowler-type flap
91 Flap hinge fittings

92 Trailing-edge hinged links
93 Central flap drive motor
94 Wing rear spar
95 Kevlar composite flap shroud panel
96 Starboard rear emergency exit window hatch
97 Anti-collision light
98 Upper VHF aerial
99 Trailing-edge fairing corrugated skin panel

100 Aerial lead-in
101 Rear cabin passenger seating
102 Door frame structure
103 UHF aerial
104 Passenger cabin rear bulkhead
105 Whip aerial
106 Rear baggage compartment, 91.8cu ft (2.60m³)
107 Baggage compartment rear bulkhead

108 Fin root fillet construction
109 Composite fin leading-edge panel
110 Tailplane leading-edge de-icing boot (optional)
111 Starboard trimming tailplane
112 Carbon fibre tip fairing
113 Starboard elevator
114 HF aerial cable
115 Fin leading-edge de-icing boot (optional)
116 Fin front spar
117 Corrugated fin skin panelling
118 Fin rib construction
119 VOR aerial
120 Glassfibre fin tip panelling
121 Rudder horn balance
122 Fin rear spar
123 Rudder rib construction
124 Static dischargers
125 Rudder trim tab
126 Elevator hinge control
127 Tail navigation light
128 Elevator rib construction
129 Static dischargers
130 Elevator horn balance
131 Leading edge de-icing boot

132 Tailplane rib construction
133 Trimming tailplane spar pivot joint
134 Tailplane control access panel
135 Fin spar attachment main frame
136 Tail control run
137 Rear fuselage frame and stringer construction
138 Baggage compartment door
139 Baggage loading floor
140 Freight door, closed
141 Two-segment passenger and freight doorway
142 Rear three-abreast seat row
143 External door latches
144 Folding handrail
145 Passenger door/airstairs, open
146 Port single-slotted flap
147 Flap rib construction

148 Port aileron
149 Aileron external hinges
150 Static dischargers
151 Port navigation light
152 Carbon-fibre wing tip fairing
153 Port leading-edge de-icing boot (optional)
154 Outer wing panel lattice ribs
155 Fuel tank end rib
156 Leading-edge nose ribs
157 Integral machined wing skin/ stringer panel
158 Port outboard integral fuel tank
159 Fuel filler cap
160 Outer wing panel joint rib
161 Inboard engine mounting rib
162 Port inboard integral fuel tank
163 Inboard leading-edge ribs
164 Engine bearer ribs
165 Main undercarriage retraction hydraulic jack
166 Main engine mounting frame
167 Oil cooler air intake
168 Port propeller spinner
169 Main undercarriage sponson fairing
170 Engine air intake
171 Intake lip de-icing (optional)
172 Port engine nacelle
173 Landing/taxying lamps
174 Main undercarriage leg pivot fixing
175 Torque scissor links
176 Port mainwheel, inward retracting
177 Composite mainwheel leg door

DORNIER DO 128 FEDERAL REPUBLIC OF GERMANY

The origins of the Do 128 go back to 1959, when the Dornier company, re-established in West Germany by members of the family of Claudius Dornier of pre-war fame, developed the Do 28 as a twin-engined version of the Do 27. The latter was itself a derivative of the single-engined Do 25, the first post-war design for which Dornier was responsible, although built only in Spain (by CASA, as the C-127). Between 1956 and 1966, Dornier built 571 Do 27s at its works near Munich, and in this period evolved the Do 28 using basically the same fuselage with a new nose fairing, a similar high-mounted wing but of increased span, and two piston engines carried in nacelles at the ends of stub wings cantilevered off the fuselage sides. Between 1961 and 1971, Dornier built 60 each of the Do 28A and Do 28B versions of this design. Then, in 1965, with financial aid from the Federal Ministry of Research and Technology, Dornier embarked upon the construction of a further derivative which had been projected as the P350 but became the Do 28D when put into active development. The objective with the P350 was to evolve an aircraft of generally similar configuration but of larger capacity and greater utility. This was achieved by adopting more powerful engines and a new, more angular, fuselage with greater cross-section, large enough to accommodate 13 passengers plus the pilot. The 380hp (283kW) Lycoming IGSO-540 engines were mounted at the end of stub wings, as on the earlier Do 28, and the wing remained little changed in size or structure, although the remainder of the Do 28D was almost all new. Named the Skyservant, the Do 28D made its first flight on 23 February 1966, and obtained its certification on 24 February 1967. Six more Do 28Ds were followed by the Do 28D-1, which

Below: The Dornier Do 28 Skymaster is seen here in its turboprop-engined version, the 128-6, which was introduced in 1980.

Sometimes known as the Turbo, this variant sold more for military than primarily civil use up to the end of 1986.

DOUGLAS DC-6 and DC-7 USA

Prevented, by wartime exigencies, from exploiting fully the commercial potential of its first four-engined airliner, the DC-4, Douglas embarked in the early 1940s upon the design of an enlarged successor to the DC-4. Future military needs, as well as prospective airline demand, were kept in mind as the DC-6 took shape, and prototype construction was in fact launched on the basis of a USAAF contract for a single example designated XC-112. Using substantially the same wing as the DC-4, the DC-6, as the type became known in civil guise, had a fuselage lengthened by 81in (2.06m) to increase the basic passenger capacity to 52. The fuselage was pressurized, and more powerful engines and improved systems were introduced. The XC-112 first flew on 15 February 1946, but no production took place for the military (other than one presidential transport, the C-118 *Independence*). Orders from American Airlines and United Airlines established the DC-6 in production, however, as the Douglas company's first significant post-war commercial aircraft, a total of 174 being built by 1951. Subsequent evolution of the type brought a further lengthening of the fuselage to produce the all-cargo DC-6A (74 built) and passenger-carrying DC-6B (288 built). When another redesign of the fuselage was undertaken, coupled with the introduction of Wright R-3350 Cyclone engines in place of the DC-6B's Pratt & Whitney Double Wasps, the designation was changed to DC-7. The wing of the DC-4 remained little changed until the DC-7C emerged in December 1955, with wing-root extensions adding 10ft (3.05m) to the span. Production of all DC-7 variants totalled

SPECIFICATION
(DC-6B)

Power Plant: Four Pratt & Whitney R-2800-CB17 Double Wasp 18-cylinder two-row air-cooled radial piston engines each rated at 2,500hp (1,864kW) for take-off, with Hamilton Standard Hydromatic three-blade constant-speed and feathering propellers of 13ft 6in (4.11m) diameter. Fuel capacity, 4,580 Imp gal (20,820l) in eight integral and six bag type tanks in wings and centre section.

Performance: Max (never exceed) speed, 312kts (578km/h) IAS; max cruising speed, 275kts (509km/h); typical cruising speed, 235kts (435km/h) at 20,000ft (6,095m); initial rate of climb, 1,120ft/min (6.2m/sec); take-off field length, 6,150ft (1,875m); landing field length, 5,000ft (1,525m); range with max payload, 1,650 naut mls (3,058km); range with max fuel, 2,320 naut mls (4,300km).

Weights: Operating weight empty, about 62,000lb (28,123kg); max fuel weight, 32,950lb (14,946kg); max payload, 24,565lb (11,143kg); max take-off weight, 107,000lb (48,534kg); max landing weight, 88,200lb (40,000kg); max zero-fuel weight, 83,200lb (37,740kg).

Dimensions: Span, 117ft 6in (35.81m); overall length, 105ft 7in (32.18m); overall height, 29ft 3in (8.92m); wing area, 1,463sq ft (135.9m²).

Accommodation: Cabin length, 68ft 9in (20.96m), max width, 9ft 0½in (2.76m), max height, 7ft 9in (2.36m). Typical one-class layout for 82 passengers, five-abreast, at 34in (86cm) pitch; maximum high-density accommodation 102. Baggage holds above and below floor, total volume, 886cu ft (25.1m³). Flight crew of four.

Below: Three-view drawing of the Douglas DC-6B, some 60 examples of which are still in airline service, primarily in the Americas. The longer, but generally similar, DC-7, is now virtually out of service.

Below right: Although it bears no company name, this Douglas DC-6A was in service with Seagreen Air Transport in Antigua. This Caribbean operator was also using two DC-7CFs in 1986.

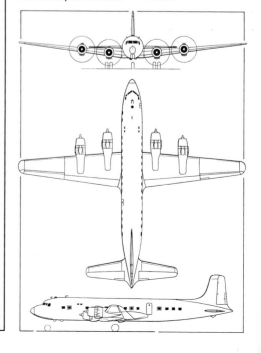

had a small increase in wing span. Then, with effect from the 50th aircraft, the Do 28D-2 became the standard Skyservant production model, with increased gross weight, internal redesign to lengthen the cabin by 6in (15cm), increased fuel capacity, aerodynamic changes to the wing and tailplane, and numerous other small changes. In its civil guise, the Do 28D-2 Skyservant normally carried 10 passengers

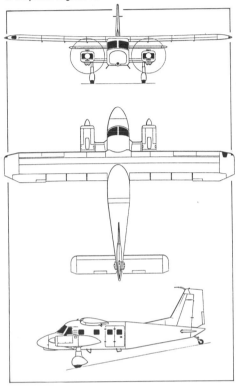

Below: Three-view drawing of the piston-engined Do 128-2 Skyservant in its standard form.

with two pilots, various other interior arrangements being possible for special roles. Of more than 260 built, fewer than half were for civil use, however, and only a small proportion of these could be regarded as for airline operation. The Do 28D-3, with tricycle landing gear in place of the standard tailwheel type, did not proceed beyond the project stage; nor did the Do 28D-4, a proposal to meet a Portuguese air force requirement by fitting Allison 250 turboprops. The latter proposal was, however, only one of several studies to replace the Lycoming piston engine with turboprops, and on 9 April 1978 Dornier flew the prototype Do 28D-5 TurboSky, one of the original Do 28s fitted with Avco Lycoming LTP101-600 turboprops. The substitution of turboprops for piston engines was achieved relatively easily thanks to the location of the engines in independent nacelles at the ends of the stub wings, and when flight testing and marketing of the Do 28-5X proved disappointing, Dornier proceeded to the Do 28D-6 version with PT6A-110 turboprops in place of the LTP101s. The prototype, which was the Do 28-5X re-engined, first flew on 4 March 1980. Apart from the engine installation and strengthened landing gear, the Do 28D-6 differed little from the Do-28D-2 Skyservant, and it retained the same split, two-section door in the port rear side of the cabin, to provide for the loading of freight as well as passengers. The designation was changed, for production aircraft, to Do 128-6 when the Do 228 was launched; the name Skyservant was not used for this version.

VARIANTS
The Do 128-6 was produced only in one basic variant, options being restricted, in commercial versions, to cabin layouts. As an alternative to the basic 10-passenger layout, the aircraft could be arranged to carry five stretchers as well as five seated passengers, or stripped of passenger amenities for

freight carrying. One military variant carried Marec radar under the nose for maritime patrol duties, and a single example of the Do 128-6, with combination wheel/ski landing gear, weather radar and other special equipment, participated in the 1983-84 German Antarctic expedition.

SERVICE USE
The Do 128-6 was certificated in Germany in March 1981 and the first aircraft was delivered to Lesotho Airways in July 1981. Production ended in 1985.

SPECIFICATION

Power Plant: Two Pratt & Whitney Canada PT6A-110 turboprops each rated at 400shp (298kW) for take-off, with Hartzell three-blade constant-speed and feathering propellers of 7ft 9in (2.36m) diameter. Fuel capacity, 196.5 Imp gal (893l) in tanks in rear of engine nacelles.
Performance: Max speed, 183kts (339km/h); max cruising speed, 178kts (330km/h) at 10,000ft (3,050m); max range cruising speed, 140kts (259km/h) at 10,000ft (3,050m); initial rate of climb, 1,260ft/min (6.4m/sec); service ceiling, 32,600ft (9,935m); take-off distance to 50ft (15m), 1,820ft (555m); landing distance from 50ft (15m), 1,650ft (505m); range with max fuel, 985 naut mls (1,825km); range with 1,774lb (805kg) payload, 788 naut mls (1,460km).
Weights: Empty weight, 5,600lb (2,540kg); max payload, 2,806lb (1,273kg); max take-off weight, 9,590lb (4,350kg); max landing weight, 9,127lb (4,140kg).
Dimensions: Span 52ft 0in (15.85m); overall length, 37ft 5¼in (11.41m); overall height, 12ft 9½in (3.90m); sweepback, nil; wing area, 312.1sq ft (29.00m²).
Accommodation: Cabin length, 13ft 0½in (3.97m), max width, 4ft 6in (1.37m), max height 4ft 11¼in (1.52m). Standard cabin layout provides 10 individual seats with central aisle. Baggage compartment volume, 31.8cu ft (0.90m³). Flight crew of two.

DOUGLAS DC-6 and DC-7

336, and brought the era of piston-engined 'Douglas Commercials' to an end.

VARIANTS
The DC-6 had a fuselage length of 100ft 2in (30.53m); both the DC-6A and DC-6B had a 5ft (1.52m) 'stretch', as indicated in the data panel. The DC-6C designation referred to a DC-6A variant with a

convertible passenger/freight interior. A few examples of the DC-6B were later converted for freighting with DC-6A style side-loading doors, and a few were modified (by Sabena) to swing-tail freighters. The DC-7 emerged with a fuselage length of 109ft 0in (33.22m) and the DC-7B was similar but carried more fuel. The length of the DC-7C increased to 112ft 6in (34.29m) and span to 127ft 6in (38.86m).

SERVICE USE
The DC-6 was first flown in production, civil, guise in June 1946, and deliveries began in November 1946 to American and United. The first commercial service was flown on 27 April 1947, and the DC-6 became widely used on US trunk routes and, with foreign airlines, on regional routes throughout the world. Subsequent variants, with their enlarged passenger loads and greater ranges, reinforced the status of the Douglas transports in this type of service, with the DC-7s adding transatlantic and nonstop US transcontinental capability. Relative merits of the Pratt & Whitney (DC-6) and Wright (DC-7) engines led to a more rapid withdrawal from service of the latter type, however, with scarcely any in airline use in 1986, when some 60 DC-6 variants continued to fly commercially.

Below: Indonesian cargo charter airline Bayu Indonesia Air PT had two DC-6As (and two Canadair CL-44s) in service in 1986 on schedules to Singapore, Australia and Brunei.

DOUGLAS DC-3 USA

A product of the 1930s, the DC-3 soldiers on in the 1980s, with an unequalled record of world-wide service to the airlines and military operators over more than half a century. Evolution of this ubiquitous twin began in 1932, primarily to meet a TWA requirement for an aircraft to compete with the Boeing 247s that had newly entered service with United Air Lines. Responding to that requirement, Douglas – under the guiding influence of the company's founder, Donald Douglas, Snr – produced the DC-1, a twin-engined low-wing monoplane of similar configuration to the Boeing 247, with a retractable landing gear and a number of 'state-of-the-art' technical innovations. First flown on 1 July 1933, the DC-1 entered production in slightly developed form as the DC-2, which first flew on 11 May 1934. TWA's successful operation of DC-2s led American Airlines to ask Douglas to produce a further improved and somewhat enlarged version, which emerged as the DC-3 (or DST, for Douglas Sleeper Transport) to fly on 17 December 1935 – the 27th anniversary of the Wright brothers' first successful powered flight in 1908. Compared with the DC-2, the DC-3 had a wider fuselage, larger wing and tail areas, and increased power and weights. It was intended to seat 24 passengers or carry 16 sleeping berths – hence the DST appellation. Up to the time that the USA became involved in World War II some 430 examples of the DC-3 had been built for civil use, including almost 100 for export; after the war ended in 1945, another 28 were delivered to the commercial market. Wartime requirements, however, saw the production of about 10,200 of the Douglas twin-engined transports for military use – mostly under the USAAF designation C-47 Skytrain or the RAF name Dakota. Post-war, substantial num-

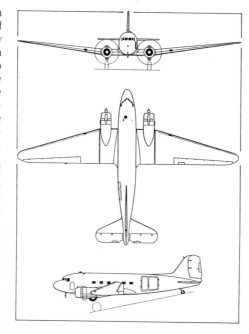

bers of these ex-military machines reached the airlines, often being known as C-47s or Dakotas rather than DC-3s. Indeed, in the period from 1945 to the mid-1960s, these aircraft became the true workhorses of the world's airline industry, and few companies operating in that period did not have at least one example in their fleet at some time, while not a few built their business exclusively on the revenues generated by a Dakota or two.

VARIANTS

Initial production versions of the DC-3 were powered by 920hp (686kW) Wright GR-1820-G5 Cyclone engines, but 1,000hp (746kW) Pratt & Whitney R-1830 Twin Wasps were soon offered as alternatives in the DST-A and DC-3A, whilst 1,100hp (820kW) Wright Cyclone G-102s distinguished the DC-3B. Production for and use by the military accounted for numerous other variants (and several different USAAF and USN designations, including C-53, C-117 and R4D). After World War II several schemes were developed, by Douglas and other companies, to improve the performance and standard of passenger comfort. This led to the appearance of some modified airframes in Super DC-3 guise. Several other schemes have involved the replacement of the original piston engines with turboprops of various types, including one three-engined variant. In the Soviet Union, the DC-3 was built under a pre-war licensing agreement, with the designation Lisunov Li-2; these had Shvetsov M-62IR or M-36R engines and numerous differences from the US version.

SERVICE USE

The DC-3 obtained its first civil airworthiness certificate on 21 May 1936 and entered service with American Airlines on 25 June 1936. From total production (excluding Soviet versions) of 10,926, several thousand have seen airline use since 1945. Numbers are now declining steadily but some 350 were still in airline use during 1986.

Above left: Three-view drawing of the Douglas DC-3 showing the military-style double-door used by passengers and freight.

Above: The cockpit of the Douglas DC-3 and its military equivalent was 'classically functional' and posed few problems for pilots converting onto the transport from smaller types of aircraft.

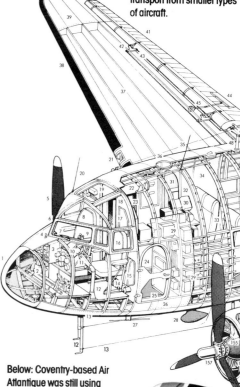

Below: Coventry-based Air Atlantique was still using five DC-3s in 1986 for its ad hoc cargo and passenger operations. Most surviving DC-3s fly in the Americas.

SPECIFICATION

Power Plant: Two Pratt & Whitney R-1830-92 Twin Wasp 14-cylinder two-row air-cooled radial piston engines each rated at 1,200hp (895kW) for take-off, with Hamilton Standard Hydromatic three-blade constant-speed and feathering propellers of 11ft 6in (3.50m) diameter. Fuel capacity, 670 Imp gal (3,046l) in metal cell tanks in wing and centre section.

Performance: Max (never-exceed) speed, 206kts (381km/h) IAS; max speed, 187kts (346km/h); high-speed cruising speed, 169kts (312km/h) at 5,000ft (1,525m); economical cruising speed, 143kts (266km/h) at 6,000ft (1,830m); initial rate of climb, 1,070ft/min (5.4m/sec); service ceiling, 21,900ft (6,675m); range with max payload, 305 naut mls (563km); range with max fuel, 1,312 naut mls (2,430km).

Weights: Operating weight empty, 17,720lb (8,030kg); max fuel weight, 4,820lb (2,186kg); max payload, 6,600lb (2,994kg); max take-off weight (US, passenger operation), 25,200lb (11,430kg); max take-off weight (British C of A, freighter) 28,000lb (12,700kg).

Dimensions: Span, 95ft 0in (28.96m); overall length, 64ft 6in (19.66m); overall height, 16ft 11½in (5.16m); wing area, 987sq ft (91.69m²).

Accommodation: Cabin length, 30ft 0in (9.14m), max width, 7ft 8in (2.34m), max height, 6ft 7in (2.0m). Typical layouts for 28 or 32 passengers four-abreast, with central aisle, at 38in (97cm) pitch. Baggage compartments above cabin floor, volume 123cu ft (3.48m³). Flight crew of two.

Above: More than 50 years have passed since the Douglas company completed the prototype DC-3—known at the time of its first flight as the DST (Douglas Sleeper Transport) since it was designed to carry passengers in sleeping berths on night flights across the US. No-one could guess, in 1935, that in the ensuing 10 years, more than 10,000 would be built for military use throughout the world.

Below: In this cutaway of the Douglas DC-3, an indication is given of a typical passenger-carrying interior, with four-abreast seating. The integral airstairs in the door were a post-war option.

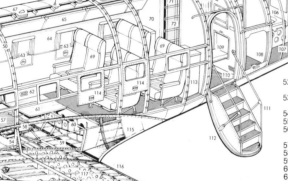

Douglas DC-3 Cutaway Drawing Key

1 Hinged nose cone, access to instruments and controls
2 Rudder pedals
3 Instrument panels
4 Windscreen de-icing
5 Starboard propeller
6 Windscreen panels
7 Windscreen wipers
8 Co-pilot's seat
9 Engine throttle levers
10 Trim control handwheel
11 Control column
12 Cockpit floor level
13 Access panels to control cable runs
14 Adjustable seat mountings
15 Propeller de-icing fluid tank
16 Pilot's seat
17 Electrical fuse panel
18 Cockpit bulkhead
19 Cockpit roof escape hatch
20 Whip aerial
21 Starboard landing/taxiying lamp
22 Windscreen and carburettor de-icing fluid tank
23 Starboard baggage/freight compartment
24 Entry lobby
25 Crew entry doorway
26 Skin doubler plate in way of propeller
27 Dipole aerial
28 ADF loop aerial housing
29 Radio and electronics equipment racks
30 Life jacket stowage
31 Main cabin doorway
32 Passenger cabin front bulkhead
33 Forward passenger seat row
34 Cabin wall trim panelling
35 Whip aerial
36 Astro-hatch observation window
37 Starboard outer wing panel
38 Leading edge pneumatic de-icing boot
39 Wing skin panelling
40 Starboard navigation light
41 Starboard aileron
42 Hinge control linkage
43 Aileron operating cables
44 Aileron tab
45 Trim tab control jack
46 Flap torque shaft
47 Starboard outboard split trailing edge flap
48 ILS aerial mast
49 Fuselage frame and stringer construction
50 Centre fuselage main frames
51 Centre wing section corrugated inner skin
52 Port main fuel tank, capacity 175 Imp Gal (794l)
53 Port auxiliary fuel tank, capacity 167 Imp Gal (760l)
54 Wing spar attachment joints
55 Cabin window panels
56 Cabin wall insulating and soundproofing lining
57 Corrugated flap shroud panel
58 Flap hydraulic jack
59 Centre section flap
60 Floor beam construction
61 Plywood floor panel
62 Cabin warm air distribution duct
63 Starboard emergency exit window hatches
64 Curtained window panels
65 Coat rack
66 VHF aerials
67 Cabin roof air vents
68 Anti-collision light
69 4-abreast passenger seating, 32-seat layout
70 Passenger cabin rear bulkhead
71 Starboard side baggage/freight hold
72 Baggage restraint net
73 Baggage bay curtain
74 Toilet compartment doorway
75 Access door to tail compartment
76 Fin root fillet construction
77 Starboard tailplane
78 Starboard elevator
79 Fin leading edge pneumatic de-icing boot
80 Tailfin construction
81 HF aerial cables
82 Rudder aerodynamic balance
83 Hinge post
84 Rudder rib construction
85 Fabric covered rudder framework
86 Rudder trim tab
87 Trim tab control gear
88 Rudder elevator control horns
89 Fuselage tail fairing
90 Tail navigation light
91 Elevator trim tab
92 Port elevator construction
93 Fabric covered elevator
94 Leading edge pneumatic de-icing boot
95 Tailplane multi-spar and rib construction
96 Tailplane attachment joint strap
97 Rudder stop cables
98 Tailplane centre-section
99 Fixed castoring tailwheel
100 Shock absorber leg strut
101 Tailwheel mounting plate
102 Tailwheel strut
103 Rudder and elevator control cables
104 Tail fuselage joint frame
105 Cabin rear bulkhead
106 Toilet compartment
107 Port baggage bay
108 Baggage loading door
109 Cabin attendant's folding seat
110 Rear entry lobby
111 Folding handrail
112 Passenger entry door/airstairs, open
113 Stowage bins, port and starboard
114 Port emergency exit window hatches
115 Wing root trailing edge fillet
116 Inboard split trailing edge flap
117 Flap shroud construction
118 Fuel filler caps
119 Outer wing panel bolted joint
120 Wing panel joint capping strip
121 Outer split trailing edge flap
122 Port aileron
123 Aileron fabric covering
124 Detachable wing tip joint rib
125 Port navigation light
126 Leading edge pneumatic de-icing boot
127 Wing stringers
128 Rear spar
129 Centre spar
130 Wing rib construction
131 Front spar
132 Leading edge nose ribs
133 Leading edge stringers
134 Port landing/taxiying lamp
135 Port mainwheel
136 Main undercarriage drag strut
137 Shock absorber leg strut
138 Undercarriage leg knee joint
139 Exhaust pipe
140 Undercarriage bungee cables
141 Engine nacelle tail fairing
142 Oil tank, capacity 24 Imp Gal (109l)
143 Main undercarriage hydraulic retraction jack
144 Mainwheel well
145 Engine bay fireproof bulkhead
146 Engine accessory equipment
147 Engine bearer struts
148 Oil cooler
149 Detachable engine cowling panels
150 Cooling air exhaust flaps
151 Exhaust collector pipe
152 Carburettor air intake
153 Ventral cabin air intake duct
154 Pratt & Whitney R-1830-92 air cooled 14-cylinder two-row radial engine
155 Propeller reduction gearbox
156 Cowling nose ring/cooling air intake
157 Propeller hub pitch change mechanism
158 Hamilton Standard three-blade constant speed propeller

DOUGLAS DC-8 USA

The decision to launch development of a four-jet medium/long range jetliner was taken by Douglas Aircraft Company in June 1955, almost a year after Boeing had flown its Dash 80 prototype from which the Model 707 family emerged. As the DC-8, the new aircraft was the first Douglas commercial jet and a successor for the DC-7C. It also closely resembled the Boeing 707 in overall configuration, although with slightly less sweepback on the wing. Subject of a launch order from Pan American on 13 October 1955, the DC-8 quickly attracted further orders from US and foreign airlines, and 142 were on order by the time the prototype made its first flight on 30 May 1958. Powered by JT3C turbojets, the prototype represented the medium-range domestic version; other variants were already in production, as detailed below under the Variants heading.

VARIANTS

Subsequent to its introduction, the initial version of the DC-8 was designated the DC-8 Srs 10, distinguishing it from the long-range DC-8 Srs 30 which, with JT4A engines, first flew on 21 February 1959. For airlines requiring enhanced take-off performance in the domestic variant, the DC-8 Srs 20 had the JT4A engines, but operated at the lower Srs 10 weights, and was first flown on 29 November 1958 (being the second DC-8 to fly). As an alternative to the Pratt & Whitney JT4As, Douglas offered to fit Rolls-Royce Conways in the DC-8 Srs 40, first flown on 23 July 1959. During the DC-8's production life, several different versions of the JT4A were fitted in the airliner, with ratings ranging from 15,500lb st (7,167kgp) to 17,500lb st (7,945kgp), and the intercontinental Srs 30 and Srs 40 featured extended wing tips and the so-called 'four per cent' wing, the leading edge being modified to increase chord by this amount. The advent of a turbofan adaptation of the JT-3C in the form of the JT-3D led to the appearance of the DC-8 Srs 50, first flown on 20 December 1960, and this was also the basis for the Jet Trader (DC-8 Srs 55) with a side-loading freight door, re-

SPECIFICATION
(DC-8 Srs 73)

Power Plant: Four CFM International CFM56-2-C5 turbofans each rated at 22,000lb st (9,980kgp) or 24,000lb st (10,886kgp) for take-off. Fuel capacity, 20,213 Imp gal (91,890l) in wing and centre section integral tanks; provision for up to three auxiliary tanks in the underfloor baggage holds.

Performance: Max operating speed, 352kts (652km/h) IAS or Mach=0.88; max cruising speed, 479kts (887km/h) at mid-cruise weight at 39,000ft (11,890m); economical cruising speed, 459kts (850km/h) at mid-cruise weight at 39,000ft (11,890m); take-off distance, 10,000ft (3,050m); landing distance, 6,500ft (1,980m); initial cruising altitude, 32,800ft (10,000m); range with max passenger payload, 4,830 naut mls (8,950km).

Weights: Operating weight empty, 166,500lb (75,500kg); max fuel weight, 162,642lb (73,773kg); max payload, 64,500lb (29,257kg); max take-off weight, 355,000kg (161,025kg); max landing weight, 258,000lb (117,000kg); max zero-fuel weight, 231,000lb (104,780kg).

Dimensions: Span, 148ft 5in (45.20m); overall length, 187ft 5in (57.12m); overall height, 43ft 0in (13.11m); sweepback, 30.6 deg at quarter chord; wing area, 2,927sq ft (271.9m²).

Accommodation: Cabin length, 138ft 9in (42.29m), max width, 11ft 6in (3.50m), max height, 7ft 3in (2.21m). Standard accommodation for up to a maximum of 269 passengers, six-abreast, with central aisle at 30in (76cm) pitch in all-tourist layout. Underfloor baggage and cargo holds, total volume 2,500cu ft (70.80m³). Flight crew of three.

McDonnell Douglas/Cammacorp DC-8-Super 71 Cutaway Drawing Key

1 Radome
2 Weather radar scanner
3 Air conditioning system ram air intake
4 Pitot tubes
5 Air conditioning units, port and starboard
6 Front pressure bulkhead
7 Rudder pedals
8 Instrument panel
9 Windscreen rain dispersal air ducts
10 Windscreen panels
11 Overhead systems switch panels
12 Co-pilot's seat
13 Cockpit eyebrow window
14 Pilot's seat
15 Cockpit floor level
16 Air system heat exchanger exhausts
17 Nosewheel doors, closed after cycling of undercarriage
18 Landing/taxiing lamps
19 Nosewheel steering jacks
20 Twin nosewheels, forward retracting
21 Nosewheel leg door
22 Nose undercarriage leg pivot point
23 Navigator's station
24 Supernumary crew seat
25 Flight engineer's station
26 Engineer's instrument panels
27 Cockpit bulkhead
28 Avionics equipment racks
29 Forward entry door, open
30 Cabin attendant's folding seat
31 Toilet compartments (2)

37 Outline of freight door (Super 71CF variant) 85in by 140in (216cm by 356cm)
38 Cabin window panels
39 Fuselage lower lobe frame construction
40 Underfloor freight compartment, volume 1,290cu ft (36.53m³)
41 Floor beam construction
42 Starboard side freight door, 54in by 63in (137cm by 160cm)
43 Cabin wall trim panelling
44 Seat mounting rails
45 Main cabin floor panelling
46 Six-abreast passenger seating, 251-seat single class layout
47 Forward cabin emergency exit doors, port and starboard
48 Cabin air distribution ducting
49 Bulk cargo door, 36in by 44in (91cm by 112cm)
50 Cabin wall soundproof lining
51 Optional auxiliary power unit (APU) installation, port and starboard
52 Fuselage skin panelling
53 Fuselage frame and stringer construction
54 Wing inspection light
55 APU exhaust
56 Runway turn-off lamp
57 Forward cargo bay pressure bulkhead
58 Recirculated air ducting
59 Wing attachment fuselage main frames
60 Wing root joint strap

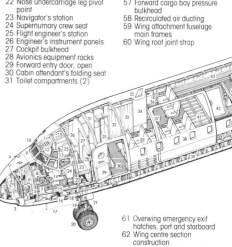

61 Overwing emergency exit hatches, port and starboard
62 Wing centre section construction
63 Pressure floor above wing carry-through
64 Fuselage centre section construction
65 Fuel system piping
66 Variable leading edge slot operating mechanism

32 Wardrobes (2)
33 Forward cabin seating
34 Galley unit
35 VHF aerial
36 Starboard side service door/emergency exit

Below: Here seen in United Airlines livery, the DC-8 Srs 71 is a conversion of the long-body Srs 61, with CFM56-2 turbofans to provide improved operating economy. United used 29 Srs 71s, out of a total of 110 DC-8s so converted.

Right: Cutaway drawing of the DC-8 Srs 71. The airframe is structurally unchanged from the Srs 61 in most respects other than the new powerplant, but some systems updating was also part of the conversion programme.

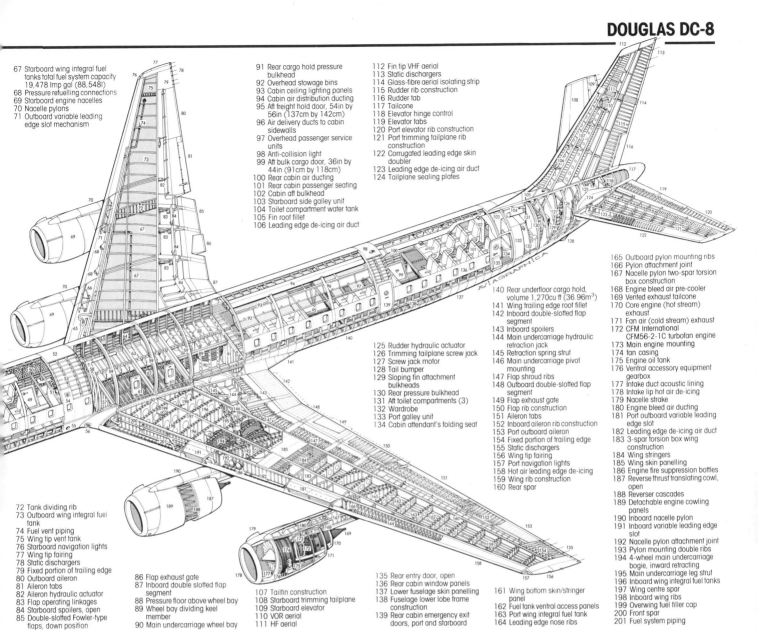

67 Starboard wing integral fuel tanks total fuel system capacity 19,478 Imp gal (88,548l)
68 Pressure refuelling connections
69 Starboard engine nacelles
70 Nacelle pylons
71 Outboard variable leading edge slot mechanism

91 Rear cargo hold pressure bulkhead
92 Overhead stowage bins
93 Cabin ceiling lighting panels
94 Cabin air distribution ducting
95 Aft freight hold door, 54in by 56in (137cm by 142cm)
96 Air delivery ducts to cabin sidewalls
97 Overhead passenger service units
98 Anti-collision light
99 Aft bulk cargo door, 36in by 44in (91cm by 118cm)
100 Rear cabin air ducting
101 Rear cabin passenger seating
102 Cabin aft bulkhead
103 Starboard side galley unit
104 Toilet compartment water tank
105 Fin root fillet
106 Leading edge de-icing air duct

112 Fin tip VHF aerial
113 Static dischargers
114 Glass-fibre aerial isolating strip
115 Rudder rib construction
116 Rudder tab
117 Tailcone
118 Elevator hinge control
119 Elevator tabs
120 Port elevator rib construction
121 Port trimming tailplane rib mounting
122 Corrugated leading edge skin doubler
123 Leading edge de-icing air duct
124 Tailplane sealing plates

140 Rear underfloor cargo hold, volume 1,270cu ft (36.96m^3)
141 Wing trailing edge root fillet
142 Inboard double-slotted flap segment
143 Inboard spoilers
144 Main undercarriage hydraulic retraction jack
145 Retraction spring strut
146 Main undercarriage pivot mounting
147 Flap shroud ribs
148 Outboard double-slotted flap segment
149 Flap exhaust gate
150 Flap rib construction
151 Aileron tabs
152 Inboard aileron rib construction
153 Port outboard aileron
154 Fixed portion of trailing edge
155 Static dischargers
156 Wing tip fairing
157 Port navigation lights
158 Hot air leading edge de-icing
159 Wing rib construction
160 Rear spar

125 Rudder hydraulic actuator
126 Trimming tailplane screw jack
127 Screw jack motor
128 Tail bumper
129 Sloping fin attachment bulkheads
130 Rear pressure bulkhead
131 Aft toilet compartments (3)
132 Wardrobe
133 Port galley unit
134 Cabin attendant's folding seat

165 Outboard pylon mounting ribs
166 Pylon attachment joint
167 Nacelle pylon two-spar torsion box construction
168 Engine bleed air pre-cooler
169 Vented exhaust tailcone
170 Core engine (hot stream) exhaust
171 Fan air (cold stream) exhaust
172 CFM International CFM56-2-1C turbofan engine
173 Main engine mounting
174 fan casing
175 Engine oil tank
176 Ventral accessory equipment gearbox
177 Intake duct acoustic lining
178 Intake lip hot air de-icing
179 Nacelle strake
180 Engine bleed air ducting
181 Port outboard variable leading edge slot
182 Leading edge de-icing air duct
183 3-spar torsion box wing construction
184 Wing stringers
185 Wing skin panelling
186 Engine fire suppression bottles
187 Reverse thrust translating cowl, open
188 Reverser cascades
189 Detachable engine cowling panels
190 Inboard nacelle pylon
191 Inboard variable leading edge slot
192 Nacelle pylon attachment joint
193 Pylon mounting double ribs
194 4-wheel main undercarriage bogie, inward retracting
195 Main undercarriage leg strut
196 Inboard wing integral fuel tanks
197 Wing centre spar
198 Inboard wing ribs
199 Overwing fuel filler cap
200 Front spar
201 Fuel system piping

72 Tank dividing rib
73 Outboard wing integral fuel tank
74 Fuel vent piping
75 Wing tip vent tank
76 Starboard navigation lights
77 Wing tip fairing
78 Static dischargers
79 Fixed portion of trailing edge
80 Outboard aileron
81 Aileron tabs
82 Aileron hydraulic actuator
83 Flap operating linkages
84 Starboard spoilers, open
85 Double-slotted Fowler-type flaps, down position

86 Flap exhaust gate
87 Inboard double slotted flap segment
88 Pressure floor above wheel bay
89 Wheel bay dividing keel member
90 Main undercarriage wheel bay

107 Tailfin construction
108 Starboard trimming tailplane
109 Starboard elevator
110 VOR aerial
111 HF aerial

135 Rear entry door, open
136 Rear cabin window panels
137 Lower fuselage skin panelling
138 Fuselage lower lobe frame construction
139 Rear cabin emergency exit doors, port and starboard

161 Wing bottom skin/stringer panel
162 Fuel tank ventral access panels
163 Port wing integral fuel tank
164 Leading edge nose ribs

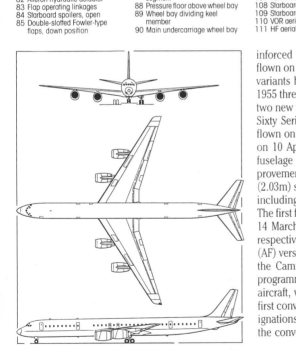

Above: Three-view drawing of the DC-8 Srs 73, similar to the Srs 71 but with some aerodynamic improvements.

The Srs 71, 72 and 73 are Sixty Series aircraft that have been retrofitted with CFM56 turbofans

inforced floor and cargo-handling provisions, first flown on 29 October 1962. Up to this point, all DC-8 variants had the same fuselage length, but in April 1955 three new variants were launched, introducing two new fuselage lengths. Known generically as the Sixty Series, these comprised the DC-8 Srs 61 first flown on 14 March 1966, the DC-8 Srs 63 first flown on 10 April 1967 with the same 36ft 8in (11.18m) fuselage stretch but a number of aerodynamic improvements, and the DC-8 Srs 62 with only a 6ft 8in (2.03m) stretch but the same aerodynamic changes, including an increase of 6ft (1.83m) in wing span. The first flights of the Srs 61, 62 and 63 were made on 14 March 1966, 29 August 1966 and 10 April 1967 respectively, and convertible (CF) and all-freight (AF) versions of all three were later offered. In 1979, the Cammacorp company launched a conversion programme to fit CFM56 turbofans to the Sixty Series aircraft, with substantial benefit to economics. The first conversion flew on 15 August 1981 and the designations DC-8 Srs 71, 72 and 73 were adopted for the converted aircraft.

Below: This drawing of a Quebecair DC-8 Srs 63 shows the original P & W JT3D engine installation of

this variant, one of the original Super Sixty Series versions of the DC-8. Many Srs 63 later became Srs 73.

SERVICE USE

The DC-8 Srs 10 was certificated on 31 August 1959, and United Air Lines and Delta Airlines flew the first revenue services on 18 September. The DC-8 Srs 30 was certificated on 1 February 1960 and was in service with KLM and Pan American on transatlantic services in April. Certification of the DC-8 Srs 40 on 24 March 1960 allowed TCA (now Air Canada) to put this version into operation in April. The DC-8 Srs 50 was certificated on 10 October 1961, and the DC-8 Srs 55 Jet Trader on 29 January 1963. Certification dates for the Sixty Series were 2 September 1966, 27 April 1967 and 30 June 1967, and entry into service dates were 25 February, 22 May and 27 July respectively. The DC-8 Super 71, 72 and 73 were certificated in April, June and September 1982. Production of the DC-8 totalled 556 and ended in May 1972, including 263 of the Super Sixty series, of which 110 had been converted to Super Seventy series when the Cammacorp programme came to an end in March 1986. About 230 DC-8s of Srs 50, 60 and 70 versions were in service in early 1987.

EMBRAER EMB-110 BANDEIRANTE BRAZIL

The EMB-110 Bandeirante (pioneer) has played a key role in the successful foundation of a Brazilian aircraft industry of international status, having been in production for the entire lifespan (to date) of Embraer (Empresa Brasileira de Aeronautica). Development of the Bandeirante began in the late 1960s at the Institute for Research and Development under the direction of French engineer Max Holste, and to meet a specific requirement of the Brazilian air force for a multi-role transport/trainer. Three prototypes were built by the IRD, making their first flights on 26 October 1968, 19 October 1969 and 26 June 1970 respectively, these aircraft being slightly smaller than the later production type and having circular 'port hole' type windows and PT6A-20 engines. To handle production of the aircraft, primarily for the Brazilian air force in the first instance, Embraer was founded in August 1969, and from the new facilities set up at São Paulo, the first production Bandeirante flew on 9 August 1972 with PT6A-27 engines, slightly lengthened fuselage with 'square' windows and redesigned nacelles. A domestic requirement for a version of the Bandeirante rapidly emerged, and Embraer set about meeting this need as soon as the initial demands of the air force had been met. This gave the company, which was still a largely unknown quantity outside Brazil, an opportunity to build up its experience of civil operations and the confidence subsequently to launch into the export business, in which it has enjoyed a substantial success. The 200th Bandeirante was delivered on 18 December 1978 and the 400th on 23 April 1982; about one third of total production has been for military users and the balance for commercial operation in more than 30 countries.

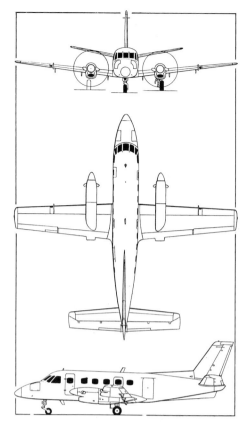

SPECIFICATION
(EMB-110 P1/41)

Power Plant: Two Pratt & Whitney Canada PT6A-34 turboprops each rated at 750shp (559kW) for take-off, with Hartzell three-blade constant-speed feathering and reversing propellers of 7ft 9in (2.36m) diameter. Fuel capacity, 378 Imp gal (1,720l) in integral wing tanks.
Performance: Max operating speed, 230kts (426km/h) IAS; max cruising speed, 221kts (410km/h) at 10,000ft (3,050m); long-range cruising speed, 181kts (356km/h) at 10,000ft (3,050m); initial rate of climb, 1,640ft/min (8.3m/sec); service ceiling, 21,500ft (6,555m); take-off field length, 4,000ft (1,220m); landing field length, 4,400ft (1,340m); range with max fuel, 1,060 naut mls (1,964km).
Weights: Operational weight empty, 8,565lb (3,855kg); max fuel weight, 2,883lb (1,308kg); max passenger payload, 3,443lb (1,561kg); max cargo payload, 3,774lb (1,712kg); max take-off weight, 13,010lb (5,900kg); max landing weight, 12,566lb (5,700kg); max zero-fuel weight, 12,015lb (5,450kg).
Dimensions: Span, 50ft 3½in (15.33m); overall length, 49ft 6½in (15.10m); overall height, 16ft 1¾in (4.92m); sweepback, 0 deg 19.5 sec at quarter chord; wing area, 313.23sq ft (29.10m²).
Accommodation: Cabin length, 31ft 3¼in (9.53m), max width, 5ft 3in (1.60m), max height, 5ft 3in (1.60m). Accommodation for up to 18 passengers three-abreast, with offset aisle, at 31in (79cm) pitch. Baggage compartment at rear of cabin, volume, 70.6cu ft (2.0m³). Flight crew of two.

Above: Three-view drawing of the EMB-110P1A, showing the dihedral tailplane that identifies it.

Below: Air Ecosse, based in Aberdeen, Scotland, was one of several companies that held Post Office contracts for overnight mail distribution services, for which this Bandeirante was used for a time.

Embraer EMB-110 Bandeirante Cutaway Drawing Key

1 Nose cone
2 Radar array (Bendix RDR-1200 or RCA AVQ-47
3 Nosewheel well
4 Nosewheel doors (close after activation)
5 Pitot probe

19 Second pilot's seat
20 Clear vision panel
21 Pilot's adjustable seat
22 Control column
23 Rudder pedals
24 ADF antenna
25 Forward/centre fuselage join
26 Port cloaks/stores
27 Aerial mast
28 Starboard equipment rack

40 Double slotted flap
41 Aerial
42 Starboard cabin-air trunking
43 Seven cabin windows (starboard)
44 Emergency exit window (starboard only)
45 Five-a-side cabin seating
46 Riveted aluminium sheet fuselage skin

58 Port cabin-air trunking
59 Fin fairing
60 Cabin-air inlet
61 Front fin spar/fuselage join

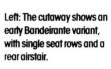

Left: The cutaway shows an early Bandeirante variant, with single seat rows and a rear airstair.

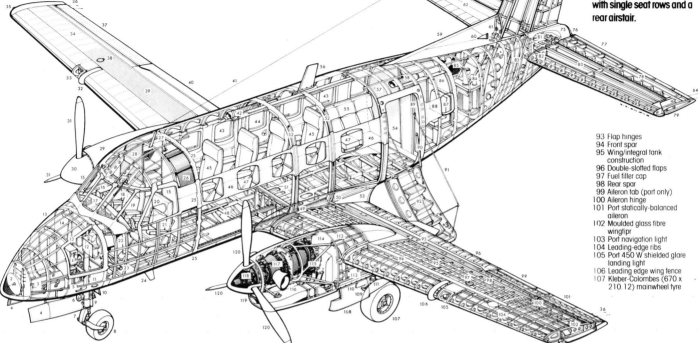

93 Flap hinges
94 Front spar
95 Wing/integral tank construction
96 Double-slotted flaps
97 Fuel filler cap
98 Rear spar
99 Aileron tab (port only)
100 Aileron hinge
101 Port statically-balanced aileron
102 Moulded glass fibre wingtip
103 Port navigation light
104 Leading-edge ribs
105 Port 450 W shielded glare landing light
106 Leading edge wing fence
107 Kleber-Colombes (670 x 210.12) mainwheel tyre

6 250W taxi light
7 Nosewheel fork
8 Goodyear 6.50 x 8 nose-wheel tyre
9 Nosewheel oleo (by ERAM)
10 Nosewheel oleo flap
11 External power socket
12 Avionics bay
13 Avionics bay access doors (upward hinged)
14 Bulkhead
15 Plexiglass windscreen side panels
16 13-mm stressed acrylic windscreen centre panels
17 Instrument panel shroud
18 Variable speed wipers

29 Starboard nacelle
30 Spinner
31 Hartzell HC-B3TN-3C/T10178H-8R constant speed propeller
32 Leading-edge wing fence
33 Starboard 450 W shielded glare landing light
34 Riveted aluminium sheet wing skin
35 Starboard navigation light
36 Aileron static dischargers
37 Starboard statically-balanced aileron
38 Fuel filler cap
39 Two wing integral fuel tanks each side (total capacity 370 Imp gal/1,690l)

47 Five cabin windows (port)
48 Floor support structure (stressed for cargo)
49 Front spar/fuselage steel join
50 Rear spar/fuselage steel join
51 Centre box structure
52 Main fuselage frames
53 Wingroot fairing
54 Entry door with integral steps
55 Three-place bench seat (C-95: optional cargo space)
56 Dorsal antenna
57 Cabin rear bulkhead (cargo compartment)

62 Starboard tailplane
63 Elevator balance
64 Elevator static dischargers
65 Starboard elevator
66 All-metal cantilever fin
67 Fin leading-edge
68 Anti-collision beacon
69 Rudder balance
70 Rudder hinges
71 Rudder static dischargers
72 Rudder structure
73 Rudder tab (upper)
74 Rudder tab (lower)
75 Tail cone
76 Rear navigation light
77 Elevator tab
78 Port elevator
79 Elevator balance

80 All-metal cantilever tailplane
81 Tailplane centre-section structure
82 Tailplane/fuselage join
83 Angled fuselage frames
84 Air trunking
85 Aircycle air-conditioning plant
86 Aft cabin bulkhead
87 Aft window (port and starboard)
88 Rear single seat (C-95: optional cargo space)
89 Entry door frame
90 Door actuating cylinder
91 Handrails
92 Entry steps

108 Mainwheel door (closes after activation)
109 Mainwheel fork
110 Mainwheel oleo flap
111 Mainwheel oleo leg (by ERAM)
112 Mainwheel well
113 Nacelle structure
114 Firewall
115 Engine bearers
116 Exhaust trunk
117 Pratt & Whitney (Canada) PT6A-27 turboprop
118 Propeller auto-feather/reverse pitch
119 Air intake
120 Hartzell three-blade propeller

Left: Skypower Express Airways was the operating name of a newly-formed company in Nigeria that acquired five of the EMB-110P1A versions of the Bandeirante in 1986 to provide postal services in the West African state—one of 34 countries where the type operates.

Below: Typical for aircraft of its size and class, the Bandeirante provides three-abreast seating, with an offset aisle. Up to 18 seats can be provided in such arrangements, with a toilet, rear baggage compartment, curtains at the front of the cabin and a flight attendant's seat.

VARIANTS

The first version of the Bandeirante intended specifically for commercial use, as a 15-passenger feederliner operated by Brazilian third-level airlines, was the EMB-110C. It was followed by the EMB-110P, developed more specifically for export markets, with PT6A-27 engines and accommodation for up to 18 passengers; the maximum weight of this version was 12,345lb (5,600kg). After a lengthened version of the Bandeirante had been developed for military use as a cargo carrier (the EMB-110K1) with a 2ft 9½in (0.85m) fuselage plug and upward-opening freight-loading door aft of the wing, this same longer fuselage was adopted for the EMB-110P1 and EMB-110P2 commercial versions, the former being for mixed or all-cargo operations with the same door as the K1 and quick-change facilities, and the latter being a dedicated airliner with up to 21 seats. The EMP-110P2, which became the major civil variant, first flew on 3 May 1977, and in 1981 was joined by the EMB-110P2/41, which was certificated at a maximum take-off weight of 13,010lb (5,900kg), an increase of 510lb (230kg), in accordance with the provisions of the US SFAR Pt 41 regulations. The EMB-110P1/41 was the equivalent quick-change version. In 1983, after 438 Bandeirantes had been delivered, a series of changes was introduced to improve passenger comfort and handling; the most obvious external change concerned the tailplane, which acquired 10 degrees of dihedral. The com-mercial versions previously described, but with these new features, were then designated EMB-110P1A, EMB-110P2A and EMB-110P2A-41. The designation EMB-110E(J) applied to a seven-seat corporate transport version of the Bandeïrante, and the EMB-110S1 was a geophysical survey version, with provision for wing-tip tanks similar to those developed for the EMB-111, a maritime patrol version. Embraer projected in the early 1980s a pressurized version of the Bandeirante, which would have had 1,173shp (875kW) PT6A-65 engines and a T-tail, accommodation for 19 passengers and a maximum take-off weight of 15,432lb (7,000kg). Development of this EMB-110P3 version was discontinued before a prototype had flown.

SERVICE USE

The original EMB-110 military transport version was certificated to FAR Pt 23 standards, providing a basis for the subsequent approval of individual variants. The civil EMB-110C entered airline service on 16 April 1973, with Transbrasil, and the EMB-110P entered service with TABA, also in Brazil, early in 1976. The first EMB-110P1/41 was delivered to Provincetown-Boston Airlines in the USA during the spring of 1981, and this operator was also the first to receive the EMB-110P1A variant, in December 1983. Total sales of the Bandeirante were approaching the 500 mark early in 1987, and the price of a new aircraft was, typically, a little under $2 million.

EMBRAER EMB-120 BRASILIA BRAZIL

Very soon after the Bandeirante had been established in production by the newly-founded Embraer organization, a series of related projects was drawn up under EMB-12X designations. These grew out of a wish to produce a pressurized version of the Bandeirante, and the three projects shared a common fuselage diameter, with different lengths; the smallest was the EMB-121 Xingu, which made use of the Bandeirante's wing (with slightly reduced span) and was intended as a business transport. Production of the Xingu eventually proceeded (about 100 being built), but neither the EMB-120 Araguaia nor the EMB-123 Tapajos was developed in the form projected in 1975, with 20 and 10 seats respectively, a 'Xingu-diameter' fuselage and a new supercritical wing with tip tanks. The concept of a pressurized regional airliner somewhat larger than the Bandeirante continued to interest the Brazilian design team, however, and by 1979 market surveys had convinced the company that its next step should be to develop a regional airliner in the 30-seat category. Development was launched officially in September 1979 and a first flight target date of July 1983 was established, it being realized that the new aircraft was entering a highly competitive portion of the commuter market. The EMB-120 designation was retained for the new project, which was named Brasilia in due course, and which retained the same overall configuration as the earlier Araguaia: it was thus a twin-engined low-wing monoplane with a circular-section fuselage and a T-tail. To power the Brasilia, Embraer turned once again to Pratt & Whitney in Canada, selecting that company's new turboprop that was then being developed as the PT7A-1 and would enter production as the PW100 series. In the 1,500shp (1,119kW) version originally selected for the Brasilia, this engine was designated PW115 and began flight test on 27 February 1982 in the nose of Pratt & Whitney's Vickers Viscount test-bed in a representative Brasilia nacelle. With deposit-paid options taken on 100 or so aircraft by the time the first Brasilia was ready to fly, Embraer was well justified in establishing a production line right from the start of the programme, and this it did at its facilities at Sao José

Above: The German regional airline DLT was the first European-based operator to place the EMB-120 in service, starting in January 1986. As of early 1987, it had placed orders and options for 20 aircraft.

Left: Like its smaller compatriot the Bandeirante, the Brasilia features three-abreast seating, but offers 20in (50cm) greater width, with an aisle wide enough to permit trolley service of food and drink.

SPECIFICATION

Power Plant: Two Pratt & Whitney Canada PW118 turboprops each flat-rated at 1,800shp (1,343kW) for take-off, with Hamilton Standard four-blade constant-speed feathering and reversing propellers of 10ft 6in (3.20m) diameter. Fuel capacity, 734 Imp gal (3,340l) in integral wing tanks.

Performance: Max operating speed, 270kts (500km/h) IAS; max cruising speed, 300kts (556km/h) at 22,000ft (6,705m); long-range cruising speed, 260kts (482km/h) at 25,000ft (7,620m); initial rate of climb, 2,120ft/min (10.8m/sec); service ceiling, 29,800ft (9,085m); take-off field length (FAR Pt 25), 4,660ft (1,420m); landing field length (FAR Pt 135), 4,495ft (1,370m); range with 30 passengers, 945 naut mls (1,750km); range with max fuel, 1,610 naut mls (2,982km).

Weights: Operating weight empty, 15,163lb (6,878kg); max fuel weight, 5,510lb (2,500kg); max payload, 7,650lb (3,470kg); max take-off weight, 25,353lb (11,500kg); max landing weight, 24,802lb (11,250kg); max zero-fuel weight, 23,148lb (10,500kg).

Dimensions: Span, 64ft 10¾in (19.78m); overall length, 65ft 7in (20.00m); overall height, 20ft 10in (6.35m); sweepback, nil; wing area, 424.46sq ft (39.43m²).

Accommodation: Cabin length, 30ft 8in (9.35m), max width, 6ft 10¾in (2.10m), max height, 5ft 9¼in (1.76m). Standard accommodation for 30 passengers three-abreast, with off-set aisle, at 31in (79cm) pitch. Baggage compartment at rear of cabin, volume, 226cu ft (6.40m³). Flight crew of two.

Embraer EMB-120 Brasilia Cutaway Drawing Key

1 Radome
2 Weather radar scanner
3 ILS glideslope aerial
4 Radar mounting bulkhead
5 Nose compartment construction
6 Avionics equipment bay
7 Access doors from wheel bay
8 Nose undercarriage wheel bay
9 Cooling air scoop
10 Radio and electronics racks
11 Nosewheel hydraulic retraction jack
12 Nosewheel leg doors
13 Nose undercarriage leg strut
14 Twin nosewheels
15 Torque scissor links
16 Hydraulic steering jacks
17 Taxiing lamps (2)
18 Battery
19 Cooling air outlet grille
20 Front pressure bulkhead
21 Windscreen wipers
22 Curved windscreen panels
23 Instrument panel shroud
24 Instrument panel CRT displays
25 Angle of attack vane
26 Rudder pedals

27 Ground power supply socket
28 Pitot tube
29 Temperature probe
30 Underfloor control linkages

31 Cockpit floor level
32 Nosewheel steering control
33 'Rams-horn' control column
34 Co-pilot's seat
35 Overhead systems switch panel
36 Cockpit roof framing
37 Cockpit/passenger cabin doorway

38 Cockpit rear bulkhead
39 Pilot's seat
40 Safety harness
41 Opening side window panel
42 Cabin attendant's folding seat
43 Entry lobby
44 Main entry door (open)
45 Integral airstairs
46 Folding handrail
47 Fuselage frame-and-stringer construction
48 Fuselage skin panelling
49 Cabin window panels
50 Forward cabin seating (30-seat layout)
51 VHF aerial

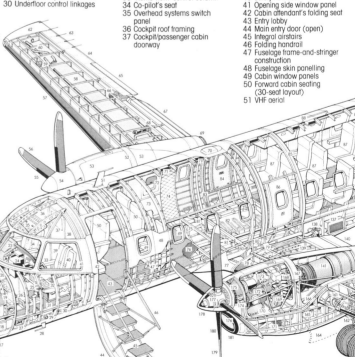

dos Campos, near São Paulo. There, metal was cut for the first aircraft on 6 May 1981, and final assembly of major components began in August 1982 in a large new building erected for the purpose. Six airframes were put in hand for the development, test and certification of the Brasilia: of these, one was for static testing and one was a fatigue test airframe; the sixth was to become a demonstrator, and three were the flying prototypes. First flights were made by these three aircraft on 27 July 1983, 21 December 1983 and 9 May 1984.

VARIANTS

The basic Brasilia is a 30-passenger regional airliner, but cargo and mixed-traffic versions are expected to be made available, the latter with 24-26 passenger seats and up to 1,984lb (900kg) of cargo in an enclosed rear baggage compartment. Executive and military interiors have also been designed, and the Brazilian air force is among the customers for the Brasilia. Installation of a Garrett auxiliary power unit in the tail cone is an optional extra, and was featured in the second and third prototypes. Early production aircraft had PW115 engines, as noted, and a maximum take-off weight of 23,810lb (10,800kg), but the more powerful PW118 was adopted in 1986 to improve the performance at higher weights then being introduced, as set out in the data panel.

SERVICE USE

The Brasilia was certificated by the Brazilian CTA on 16 May 1985, followed by FAA approval (to FAR Pt 25) on July 9. British certification was confirmed in April 1986. The second prototype was the subject of a formal handover to the first customer, Atlantic Southeast Airlines of Atlanta, Georgia, on 1 June 1985 during the Paris Air Show, but this was for crew training purposes only and the first production aircraft for ASA was delivered in August 1985. Two early-standard aircraft were delivered to DLT in Germany in October 1985, and in 1986 the first 18-seat corporate version of the Brasilia was handed over to United Technologies Corporation. By early 1987, Embraer had delivered 28 aircraft, against total firm orders for 89 with a further 115 on option. The basic price is quoted as about $5.5 million.

Below: The first of the 10 Embraer Brasilias acquired by Altantic Southeast Airlines of Georgia.

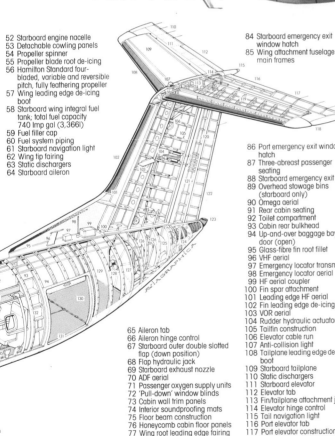

52 Starboard engine nacelle
53 Detachable cowling panels
54 Propeller spinner
55 Propeller blade root de-icing
56 Hamilton Standard four-bladed, variable and reversible pitch, fully feathering propeller
57 Wing leading edge de-icing boot
58 Starboard wing integral fuel tank; total fuel capacity 740 Imp gal (3,366l)
59 Fuel filler cap
60 Fuel system piping
61 Starboard navigation light
62 Wing tip fairing
63 Static dischargers
64 Starboard aileron

65 Aileron tab
66 Aileron hinge control
67 Starboard outer double slotted flap (down position)
68 Flap hydraulic jack
69 Starboard exhaust nozzle
70 ADF aerial
71 Passenger oxygen supply units
72 'Pull-down' window blinds
73 Cabin wall trim panels
74 Interior soundproofing mats
75 Floor beam construction
76 Honeycomb cabin floor panels
77 Wing root leading edge fairing
78 Extended chord wing root section
79 Bleed air ducting from engine
80 Wing spar attachment joints
81 Underfloor air conditioning ducting
82 Wing centre-section carry-through
83 Centre fuselage construction

84 Starboard emergency exit window hatch
85 Wing attachment fuselage main frames

86 Port emergency exit window hatch
87 Three-abreast passenger seating
88 Starboard emergency exit door
89 Overhead stowage bins (starboard only)
90 Omega aerial
91 Rear cabin seating
92 Toilet compartment
93 Cabin rear bulkhead
94 Up-and-over baggage bay door (open)
95 Glass-fibre fin root fillet
96 VHF aerial
97 Emergency locator transmitter
98 Emergency locator aerial
99 HF aerial coupler
100 Fin spar attachment
101 Leading edge HF aerial
102 Fin leading edge de-icing
103 VOR aerial
104 Rudder hydraulic actuators
105 Tailfin construction
106 Elevator cable run
107 Anti-collision light
108 Tailplane leading edge de-icing boot
109 Starboard tailplane
110 Static dischargers
111 Starboard elevator
112 Elevator tab
113 Fin/tailplane attachment joint
114 Elevator hinge control
115 Tail navigation light
116 Port elevator tab
117 Port elevator construction
118 Elevator horn balance
119 Tailplane construction
120 Two-segment rudder construction
121 Fore rudder
122 Trailing rudder/trimmer
123 APU exhaust duct
124 Optional Garrett GTCP36-150(A) auxiliary power unit (APU)
125 APU bay firewall
126 Sloping fin attachment frames
127 Rear pressure bulkhead
128 Cabin air outlet and pressure relief valves

129 Baggage compartment
130 Baggage loading floor
131 Baggage loading doorway
132 Galley unit
133 Overhead passenger service units
134 Air conditioning delivery ducts
135 Floor level ventilating air ducts
136 Trailing edge root fillet
137 Heat exchanger
138 Port air conditioning plant
139 Port wing inboard integral fuel tank
140 Inboard double-slotted flap
141 Jet pipe
142 Exhaust nozzle
143 Nacelle 'Flapette'
144 Port outer double-slotted flap
145 Flap hydraulic jack
146 Honeycomb flap shroud panel
147 Flap rib construction
148 Aileron tab
149 Port aileron rib construction
150 Static dischargers
151 Compass flux valve
152 Glass-fibre wing tip fairing
153 Port navigation light
154 Leading edge de-icing boot
155 Fuel filler cap
156 Wing rib construction
157 Leading edge honeycomb construction
158 Port wing outboard integral fuel tank
159 Three-spar wing torsion box assembly
160 Main undercarriage pivot fixing
161 Landing lamp (port and starboard)
162 Main undercarriage leg strut
163 Twin mainwheels
164 Mainwheel doors (closed after cycling of undercarriage leg)
165 Mainwheel bay
166 Engine nacelle construction
167 Main engine mounting ring frame
168 Pratt & Whitney Canada PW115 turboprop
169 Engine integral oil tank
170 Particle separator intake air duct
171 Oil cooler
172 Electronic engine control units
173 Engine accessory equipment
174 Gearbox mounting
175 Propeller reduction gearbox
176 Engine air intake
177 Propeller hub pitch change mechanism
178 Port propeller spinner
179 Port Hamilton Standard 4-bladed propeller
180 Propeller blade root de-icing
181 Engine intake lip de-icing system

Left: The cutaway drawing of the EMB-120 Brasilia shows the conventional structure of this latest product from the Embraer organization, centre of the developing Brazilian aircraft industry.

Below: Three-view drawing of the EMB-120 Brasilia, only the one basic version of which had appeared up to the beginning of 1987, albeit with some slightly different engine options on offer.

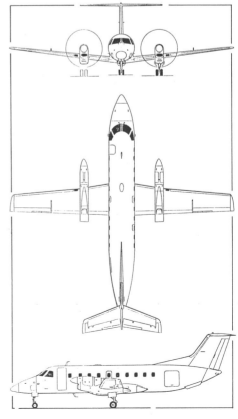

FAIRCHILD METRO USA

The Metro has its origins with the company formed by Ed Swearingen, which used the Beechcraft Queen Air as the basis of a family of business aircraft known as the Merlin I, II and IIB. By continuous refinement and development, Swearingen eventually replaced all major components of the Queen Air to produce the Metro, a 19-seat commuter transport, with a parallel version for the corporate market known as the Merlin III. The Metro first flew on 26 August 1969 and production was well under way by the time the Swearingen company was taken over in November 1971, by the Fairchild Industries Corporation. As Fairchild Swearingen, the company continued to produce the Metro at its San Antonio plant, and to develop new variants. The Swearingen name was later dropped, the Texas branch of Fairchild Industries then becoming the Fairchild Aircraft Corporation. With more than 350 Metros delivered by the end of 1986, this has proved to be one of the most successful of the 19-seat regional airliners – a size limit that was dictated by the US regulations that required a cabin attendant to be carried if 20 or more passengers were embarked.

VARIANTS

The original Metro was followed in 1974 by the Metro II, which introduced some internal changes, 'square' cabin windows and the optional installation of a small rocket unit in the tail to improve take-off performance in hot and high conditions as encountered in many areas where the Metro was likely to operate. Like the initial model, the Metro II was restricted to a gross weight of 12,500lb

SPECIFICATION
(Metro III)

Power Plant: Two Garrett TPE331-11U-611G turboprops each rated at 1,000shp (746kW) for take-off or 1,100shp (820kW) using water injection, with Dowty Rotol four-blade constant-speed fully-feathering and reversing propellers. Fuel capacity, 540 Imp gal (2,452l) in integral tanks.
Performance: Max operating speed, 248kts (459km/h) CAS or Mach=0.52; max cruising speed, 278kts (515km/h) at 12,500ft (3,810m); long-range cruising speed 256kts (475km/h) at 25,000ft (7,620m); initial rate of climb 2,350ft/min (11.9m/sec); service ceiling 27,500ft (8,380m); take-off field length, 3,250ft (990m); landing field length, 2,805ft (855m); range with max passenger payload, 869 naut mls (1,610km).
Weights: Operating weight empty, 8,737lb (3,963kg); max fuel weight, 4,342lb (1,969kg); max payload, 4,880lb (2,214kg); max take-off weight, 14,500lb (6,577kg); max landing weight, 14,000lb (6,350kg); max zero-fuel weight, 12,500lb (5,670kg).
Dimensions: Span, 57ft 10in (17.37m); overall length, 59ft 4¼in (18.09m); overall height, 16ft 8in (5.08m); sweepback, 0 deg 54 min at quarter chord; wing area, 309sq ft (28.71m²).
Accommodation: Cabin length, 25ft 5in (7.75m), max width, 5ft 2in (1.57m), max height, 4ft 9in (1.45m). Standard layout provides 19 or 20 individual seats, with centre aisle, at 30in (76cm) pitch. Pressurized rear baggage compartment and unpressurized nose baggage compartment, total volume, 181cu ft (5.12m³). Flight crew of two and one cabin attendant.

Above: Passengers in the Fairchild Metro occupy single seats on each side of a central aisle, which allows service to be offered by an attendant.

Fairchild Metro II Cutaway Drawing Key

1 Radome
2 Weather radar scanner
3 Oxygen bottle
4 Radio and electronics equipment
5 Nosewheel door
6 Baggage restraint net
7 Baggage doors, forward opening
8 Fuselage nose construction
9 Nose baggage hold
10 Landing and taxi lamp
11 Nosewheel leg
12 Twin nosewheels
13 Torque scissors
14 Pitot tube
15 Cockpit pressure bulkhead
16 Windscreen panels
17 Instrument panel shroud
18 Curved centre panel
19 Windscreen wipers
20 Rudder pedals
21 Control column
22 Co-pilot's seat
23 Cockpit roof construction
24 Cockpit bulkhead
25 Electrical panels
26 Pilot's seat
27 Pilot's side control panel
28 Passenger door
29 Airstairs
30 Handrails
31 Entry doorway
32 Cabin centre aisle floor
33 Air conditioning duct louvre
34 Forward fuselage frame construction
35 Starboard engine cowlings
36 Engine intake
37 Hartzell three-bladed constant-speed reversing and feathering propeller
38 Propeller de-icing boot
39 Leading edge de-icing
40 Starboard wing fuel tank, capacity 270 Imp gal (1,226l)
41 Starboard navigation light
42 Fuel filler cap
43 Starboard aileron
44 Static dischargers
45 Starboard flap
46 Tailpipe exhaust duct
47 Fuselage frames
48 Cabin interior trim panels
49 Passenger seats
50 Window side panel
51 Cabin floor construction
52 Seat rails
53 Air trunking
54 Cabin windows
55 Starboard emergency escape hatches
56 Main fuselage frames
57 Centre box construction
58 Port emergency escape hatch
59 Starboard seating, 10 passengers

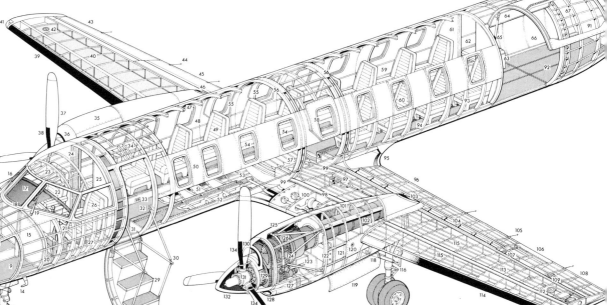

Right: Cutaway drawing of the Fairchild Metro II, one of the earliest and now most successful of the 19-seaters.

90 Fin attachment frame
91 Cargo hold rear bulkhead
92 Baggage/cargo hold floor
93 Rear fuselage frames
94 Seat fixing rails
95 Trailing edge root fillet
96 Port flap
97 Fuel pumps

98 Wing main spar
99 Wing spar attachment
100 Air conditioning plant
101 Engine cowling construction
102 Tailpipe
103 Engine exhaust duct
104 Double slotted flap construction
105 Static dischargers
106 Aileron trim tab
107 Trim tab hinge control
108 Port aileron
109 Aileron hinge control
110 Port wing-tip
111 Port navigation light
112 Fuel tank filler cap
113 Wing rib construction
114 Leading edge de-icing
115 Port wing fuel tank, 270 Imp gal (1,226l)
116 Main undercarriage leg
117 Twin mainwheels
118 Retraction strut
119 Mainwheel door
120 Leading edge ice inspection light
121 Main undercarriage wheel bay
122 Hydraulic system reservoir
123 Engine oil tank, capacity 3.3 Imp gal (15l)
124 Engine bearers
125 Detachable engine cowlings
126 Garrett AiResearch TPE 331-3UW-303G turboprop
127 Oil cooler
128 Oil cooler intake
129 Propeller gearbox
130 Engine intake
131 Propeller reversing and feathering hub mechanism
132 Spinner
133 Hartzell three-bladed propeller
134 Propeller blade de-icing boots

60 Port seating, nine passengers
61 Cabin rear bulkhead
62 Toilet compartment door
63 Toilet
64 Rear cargo door
65 Door actuator
66 Rear cargo and baggage compartment
67 Fuselage frame and stringer construction
68 Fin root fillet
69 Tailplane electric trim jacks
70 Starboard tailplane
71 Leading edge de-icing
72 Elevator horn balance
73 Starboard elevator
74 Static dischargers
75 Fin construction
76 Rudder balance
77 Antenna
78 Anti-collision light
79 Rudder trim tab
80 Trim tab control jack
81 Rudder construction
82 Elevator hinge control
83 Port elevator
84 Static dischargers
85 Tailplane construction
86 Tail navigation light
87 Ventral fin
88 Rudder hinge control
89 Tailplane control cables

(5,670kg) to comply with US regulations for commuter airliners. When this restriction was lifted, by Special Federal Aviation Regulation (SFAR) 41, Fairchild introduced in 1980 the Metro IIA at a gross weight of 13,100lb (5,941kg), and followed this with further improvements in the Metro III at 14,000lb (6,350kg). Structural changes and uprated engines made the increased operating weights possible, and the standard aircraft was subsequently approved for 14,500lb (6,577kg), with an option at 16,000lb (7,257kg). Other changes distinguishing the Metro III from the Metro II included an extension of 10ft (3.05m) in wing span, with conical cambered wing tips to reduce drag; new landing gear doors; more streamlined nacelle cowlings; and Dowty Rotol four-blade propellers. Large loading doors in the rear fuselage, a reinforced cabin floor, reduced empty weight and the high gross weight option allow an all-cargo version of the Metro, known as the Expediter, to carry a cargo payload of 5,000lb (2,268kg). The high gross weight version also provides the basis for projected quasi-military variants, carrying search radar and other sensors for maritime surveillance, anti-submarine patrol and similar duties, with the name Air Sentry. For operators wishing to standardize on the Pratt & Whitney PT6A engine, Fairchild developed the Metro IIIA with 1,000shp (746kW) PT6A-45Rs, first flown on 31 December 1981.

SERVICE USE

The Metro entered service in early 1971, the first major commuter airline operator being by Air Wisconsin. The Metro III was certificated to SFAR 41 standards (the first to be so approved by the FAA) on 23 June 1980. The Expediter was first operated by

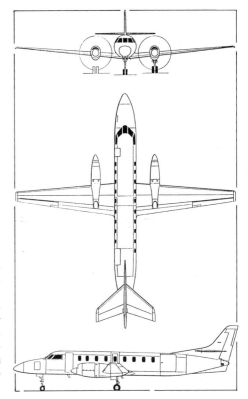

SAT-AIR, on behalf of United Parcel Service. A Metro III delivered on 27 December 1984 was the 600th turboprop transport built by Fairchild, and brought total deliveries of the Metro series to more than 300, since increased to over 350 with production continuing in 1986 at a rate of four per month.

FOKKER F27 FRIENDSHIP THE NETHERLANDS

E urope's best-selling turboprop transport, the F27 emerged as Fokker's first post-war commercial aircraft, designed at the beginning of the 1950s to provide airlines with a 'DC-3 replacement'. Among several project studies, the P.275 of August 1950 became the basis for further development, taking shape by the end of 1952 as a high-wing monoplane with a pressurized circular-section fuselage, two Rolls-Royce Dart turboprops and accommodation for up to 40 passengers. The full payload range was to be only 260 naut mls (482km), restricting the aircraft to the short-haul market, and attention was given to providing good field performance. With Netherlands government backing, two prototypes of the F27, as the project now became known, were launched in 1953, and these made their first flights on 24 November 1955 and 29 January 1957 respectively, the second having a lengthened fuselage to increase basic seating from 32 to 36. Increases in fuel capacity were made later to give the F27 greater operational flexibility. Production of the F27, for which the name Friendship was later adopted, was initiated both by Fokker and, under licence agreements, by Fairchild in the USA. The first production aircraft flew at Schiphol on 23 March 1958 and at Hagerstown, Md, on 12 April 1958, and a Fairchild-built example became the first to operate revenue services by the type. Subsequent developments by Fokker and Fairchild are described below.

VARIANTS

The first Fokker production variant was the F27 Mk 100 with Dart Mk 511 (RDa6) engines, matched by

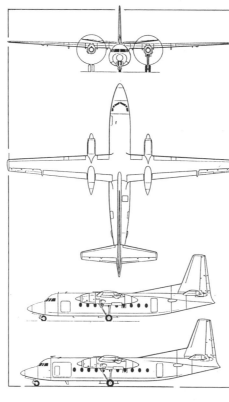

Above: Three-view of the F27 Mk 200 plus a side-view (bottom) of the longer F27 Mk 500, showing the larger door in the front port side of the latter.

Fokker F27 Friendship Mk 500 Cutaway Drawing Key

1 Radome
2 Weather radar
3 Glideslope aerial
4 Nosewheel doors
5 Taxying lamp
6 Nosewheel forks
7 Steerable nosewheel
8 Nose undercarriage pivot fixing
9 Nosewheel well
10 Radar transmitter/receiver
11 Nosewheel retraction jack
12 Brake reservoirs
13 Front pressure bulkhead
14 Windscreen wipers
15 Windscreen panels
16 Instrument panel shroud
17 Overhead switch panel
18 Co-pilot's seat
19 Electrical equipment switch panel
20 Instrument panel
21 Rudder pedals
22 Cockpit floor level
23 Side console panel
24 Control column handwheel
25 Pilot's seat
26 Fire extinguisher
27 Cockpit bulkhead
28 Radio and electronics equipment rack
29 Control runs
30 HF aerial cable
31 Aerial lead-in
32 Control cable duct
33 Cargo door operating jack
34 Pneumatic system air bottles
35 Crew entry door/emergency exit
36 Port cargo stowage area
37 Starboard cargo stowage area
38 Cargo/baggage restraint net
39 Main cabin bulkhead
40 Door locking handle
41 Cargo door, 92in by 72in (234cm by 183cm) (open position)
42 Forward fuselage frames
43 UHF aerial
44 Upper fuselage unpressurised (outer) skin/control duct
45 Pressurised (inner) skin panelling
46 Curtained cabin window panelling
47 Cabin wall trim panels
48 Main cabin flooring
49 Door surround structure
50 Twin keel beams
51 Floor beam construction
52 Cabin window panels
53 Forward cabin four-abreast seating
54 Wing/fuselage joint drag strut
55 Wing spar/fuselage attachment joint
56 Centre section spar
57 Glassfibre wing root fairing
58 Optional wing bag tanks, increasing fuel capacity by 504 Imp gal (2,289l)
59 Inboard leading edge de-icing boot
60 Fuel system collector tank
61 Engine fire extinguisher bottles
62 Starboard main undercarriage front strut
63 Engine cowling panels
64 Propeller spinner
65 Dowty-Rotol four-bladed, variable pitch propeller
66 Oil cooler intake
67 Oil cooler exhaust
68 Centre wing panel inner corrugated skin
69 Outer wing panel bolted joint

Above: Cutaway drawing of the F27 Mk 500, which was one of the final production versions.

Left: An F27 Mk 500 in service with Air Wisconsin, which acquired 12 of the long-fuselage variants of the Friendship between 1983 and 1986.

Right: An interior view of a late-production Fokker F27, with updated cabin fittings, including the enclosed overhead lockers.

Below: NLM Cityhopper, a KLM subsidiary, uses a mix of the Mk 200, 400 and 500 F27s, one of the latter variants being depicted in this colour profile.

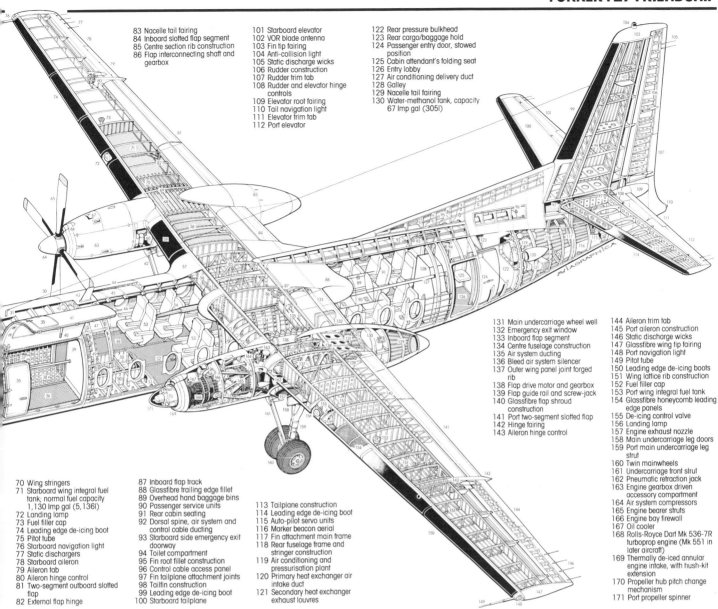

83 Nacelle tail fairing
84 Inboard slotted flap segment
85 Centre section rib construction
86 Flap interconnecting shaft and gearbox

101 Starboard elevator
102 VOR blade antenna
103 Fin tip fairing
104 Anti-collision light
105 Static discharge wicks
106 Rudder construction
107 Rudder trim tab
108 Rudder and elevator hinge controls
109 Elevator root fairing
110 Tail navigation light
111 Elevator trim tab
112 Port elevator

122 Rear pressure bulkhead
123 Rear cargo/baggage hold
124 Passenger entry door, stowed position
125 Cabin attendant's folding seat
126 Entry lobby
127 Air conditioning delivery duct
128 Galley
129 Nacelle tail fairing
130 Water-methanol tank, capacity 67 Imp gal (305l)

131 Main undercarriage wheel well
132 Emergency exit window
133 Inboard flap segment
134 Centre fuselage construction
135 Air system ducting
136 Bleed air system silencer
137 Outer wing panel joint forged rib
138 Flap drive motor and gearbox
139 Flap guide rail and screw-jack
140 Glassfibre flap shroud construction
141 Port two-segment slotted flap
142 Hinge fairing
143 Aileron hinge control

144 Aileron trim tab
145 Port aileron construction
146 Static discharge wicks
147 Glassfibre wing tip fairing
148 Port navigation light
149 Pitot tube
150 Leading edge de-icing boots
151 Wing lattice rib construction
152 Fuel filler cap
153 Port wing integral fuel tank
154 Glassfibre honeycomb leading edge panels
155 De-icing control valve
156 Landing lamp
157 Engine exhaust nozzle
158 Main undercarriage leg doors
159 Port main undercarriage leg strut
160 Twin mainwheels
161 Undercarriage front strut
162 Pneumatic retraction jack
163 Engine gearbox driven accessory compartment
164 Air system compressors
165 Engine bearer struts
166 Engine bay firewall
167 Oil cooler
168 Rolls-Royce Dart Mk 536-7R turboprop engine (Mk 551 in later aircraft)
169 Thermally de-iced annular engine intake, with hush-kit extension
170 Propeller hub pitch change mechanism
171 Port propeller spinner

70 Wing stringers
71 Starboard wing integral fuel tank; normal fuel capacity 1,130 Imp gal (5,136l)
72 Landing lamp
73 Fuel filler cap
74 Leading edge de-icing boot
75 Pitot tube
76 Starboard navigation light
77 Static dischargers
78 Starboard aileron
79 Aileron tab
80 Aileron hinge control
81 Two-segment outboard slotted flap
82 External flap hinge

87 Inboard flap track
88 Glassfibre trailing edge fillet
89 Overhead hand baggage bins
90 Passenger service units
91 Rear cabin seating
92 Dorsal spine, air system and control cable ducting
93 Starboard side emergency exit doorway
94 Toilet compartment
95 Fin root fillet construction
96 Control cable access panel
97 Fin tailplane attachment joints
98 Tailfin construction
99 Leading edge de-icing boot
100 Starboard tailplane

113 Tailplane construction
114 Leading edge de-icing boot
115 Auto-pilot servo units
116 Marker beacon aerial
117 Fin attachment main frame
118 Rear fuselage frame and stringer construction
119 Air conditioning and pressurisation plant
120 Primary heat exchanger air intake duct
121 Secondary heat exchanger exhaust louvres

the Fairchild F27. The F27 Mk 200, first flown on 20 September 1962, and F27A introduced uprated Dart RDa7 engines, used in a number of sub-variants including the Mk 528, 532 and 552 turboprops; associated with these engines were progressive increases in gross weight. The F27 Mk 300 Combiplane and F27B had RDa6 engines and a side-loading freight door in the forward fuselage for mixed passenger/freight operations. The F27 Mk 400 (and similar

F27M Troopship) first flown on 24 April 1965, combined the freight door and freight floor with RDa7 engines, while the Mk 600, flown on 28 November 1968, was similar but lacked the former's special all-metal watertight freight floor. Fairchild's F27F was an F27A with Dart Mk 529s for corporate users, while the F27J and F27M had Dart Mk 532-7 and Mk 532-7N engines respectively. In all, Fairchild built 128 of its F27 variants, ending in 1970. Fairchild also developed a stretched-fuselage variant, the FH-227, with a 6ft (1.83m) plug, and built several sub-variants with different weights and Dart ratings. The first FH-227 flew on 27 January 1966 and production totalled 79. Fokker's stretched F27 Mk 500, in the project stage for several years, flew on 15 November 1967, and remained in production, with the F27 Mk 200, through 1986. By the time production of these variants was phased out in favour of the Fokker 50, sales of the F27 had totalled 579 from the Dutch production line, including 85 F27 Mk 100 and 13 F27 Mk 300/300M aircraft. The last F27 was delivered early in 1987.

SERVICE USE

The Fairchild F27 was certificated on 16 July 1958 and entered service on 27 November 1958 with West Coast Airlines. The first Fokker-built F27 entered service with Aer Lingus in December 1958. The fairchild F27B was certificated 25 October 1958 and first entered service with Northern Consolidated. The F27F was certificated on 24 February 1961, the F27J on 3 August 1965 and the F27M on 12 June 1969.

SPECIFICATION
(F27 Friendship Mk 200)

Power Plant: Two Rolls-Royce RDa7 Dart Mk 522 turboprops each rated at 2,280ehp (1,700kW) for take-off, with Dowty Rotol four-blade constant-speed fully-feathering propellers of 11ft 6in (3.50m) diameter. Fuel capacity, 1,130 Imp gal (5,136l) in integral wing tanks plus optional 503.5 Imp gal (2,289l) in wing bag tanks.

Performance: Max operating speed, 227kts (419km/h) IAS; cruising speed at 38,000lb (17,237kg) weight, 259kts (480km/h) at 20,000ft (6,095m); initial rate of climb, 1,480ft/min (7.5m/sec) at 40,000lb (18,143kg) weight; service ceiling, 29,500ft (8,990m); take-off field length, 3,240ft (990m) at 40,000lb (18,143kg) weight; landing field length, 3,290ft (1,005m) at 36,000lb (16,329kg) weight; range with max payload, 1,117 naut mls (2,070km); range with max fuel, 1,193 naut mls (2,211km).

Weights: Empty weight, 22,696lb (10,295kg); operating weight empty, 24,600lb (11,159kg); max payload, 10,340lb (4,690kg); max take-off weight, 45,000lb (20,410kg); max landing weight, 41,000lb (18,600kg); max zero-fuel weight, 39,500lb (17,917kg).

Dimensions: Span, 95ft 2in (29.00m); overall length, 77ft 3½in (23.56m); overall height, 27ft 11in (8.51m); sweepback, nil; wing area, 753.5sq ft (70.00m²).

Accommodation: Cabin length, 47ft 5in (14.46m), max width, 8ft 2in (2.49m), max height, 6ft 4in (1.93m). Standard layout provides 44 seats four-abreast at 30in (76cm) pitch. Baggage hold volume 300cu ft (8.50m³). Normal flight crew of two and one cabin attendant.

P lans to develop a short/medium-haul jet transport partner for its F27 turboprop twin were made by Fokker at the beginning of the 1960s, the first details of this F28 Fellowship being published in April 1962. Projected to carry about 50 passengers over 1,000 naut mls (1,650km), the F28 was at first studied with Bristol Siddeley BS.75 engines, but the eventual selection was a lightened and simplified version of the Rolls-Royce Spey, known at first as the Spey Junior. In configuration, the F28 was similar to the BAC One-Eleven and Douglas DC-9, with a moderately swept wing, engines mounted on the sides of the rear fuselage and a T-tail, but it was smaller than either of those types, although the basic capacity of the initial version grew to 60 and eventually to 65. To help establish production of the F28, Fokker concluded risk-sharing agreements with several companies, including Shorts in the UK (for the wings), and HFB and VFW (now MBB) in West Germany for fuselage sub-assemblies. Three prototypes of the F28 were built, making their first flights on 9 May, 3 August and 20 October 1967 respectively, and production went ahead on the basis of a launch order placed by LTU, a German inclusive-tour charter operator, in November 1965. The first production F28, the fourth aircraft completed, flew on 21 May 1968.

VARIANTS

The initial production version of the F28 became known as the F28 Mk 1000 after a stretched-fuselage variant was introduced as the F28 Mk 2000 in 1970. The Mk 1000 is basically a 65-seater (one-class) aircraft, the gross weight of which was initially 62,000lb (28,123kg), but subject to subsequent increases. With a side-loading freight door and provision for mixed passenger/freight loads, the designation is F28 Mk 1000-C. The F28 Mk 2000 has a 7ft 3in (2.21m) longer fuselage and seats up to 79 passengers in a one-class arrangement. It first flew on 28 April 1971. In 1972, Fokker introduced the F28 Mk

5000 (short fuselage) and F28 Mk 6000 (long fuselage), whose new features were an increase of 6ft 11½in (1.57m) in wing span, with leading-edge slats added, and improved Spey Mk 555-15H engines with additional noise reduction features. A Mk 6000 prototype flew on 27 September 1973, but the take-off performance bestowed by the flaps proved to be an unwanted luxury for most airlines and the F28 Mk 3000 (short fuselage) and F28 Mk 4000 (long fuselage) became the preferred versions, with the extra span and new engines, but without the slats. Interior redesign also took the maximum seating up to 85 in the Mk 4000, which flew for the first time on 20 October 1976. The Mks 3000 and 4000 remained the only types in production in 1986, at a rate of one per month until the end of the year.

SERVICE USE

The F28 Mk 1000 was certificated by the Dutch authorities on 24 February 1969 and entered service with LTU immediately after. The first F28 Mk 2000 went to Nigeria Airways in October 1972, two months after certification. The F28 Mk 6000 was certificated on 27 September 1973, but was not produced. The F28 Mk 4000 entered service with Linjeflyg of Sweden late in 1976, and the first operator of the F28 Mk 3000 was Garuda in Indonesia. Sales of the F28 totalled 241 by the end of 1986, when production ended.

Below: Three-view drawing of the Fokker F28 Mk 4000, which was the final version in production in 1986. The similar Mk 3000 has a shorter fuselage.

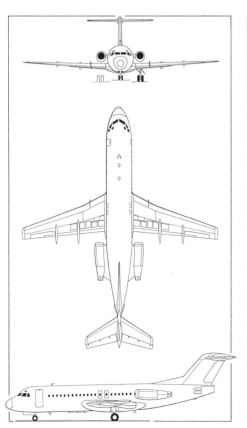

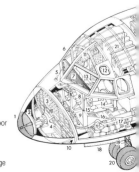

SPECIFICATION
(F28 Fellowship Mk 4000)

Power Plant: Two Rolls-Royce RB.183-2 Spey Mk 555-15P turbofans each rated at 9,900lb st (4,490kgp) for take-off, and not fitted with thrust-reversers. Fuel capacity, 2,143 Imp gal (9,740l) in integral wing tanks, plus optional 726 Imp gal (3,300l) in bladder tanks in wing centre section.
Performance: Max operating speed, 330kts (612km/h) EAS or Mach = 0.75; max cruising speed, 436kts (808km/h) at 33,000ft (10,060m); long-range cruising speed, 354kts (656km/h) at 30,000ft (9,145km/h); max cruising altitude, 35,000ft (10,675m); take-off field length (FAR), 5,200ft (1,585m); landing field length, 3,495ft (1,065m); range with 85 passengers, 1,125 naut mls (2,085km).
Weights: Operating weight empty, 38,900lb (17,645kg); standard fuel weight, 17,240lb (7,820kg); max fuel weight, 23,080lb (10,469kg); max payload, 23,100lb (10,478kg); max take-off weight 73,000lb (33,113kg); max landing weight 69,500lb (31,525kg); max zero-fuel weight 62,000lb (28,123kg).
Dimensions: Span, 82ft 3in (25.07m); overall length, 97ft 1¾in (29.61m); overall height, 27ft 9½in (8.47m); sweepback, 16 deg at quarter chord; wing area, 850sq ft (79.00m²).
Accommodation: Cabin length, 50ft 3in (15.31m), max width, 10ft 2in (3.10m), max height, 6ft 7¼in (2.02m). Layouts for up to 85 passengers, five-abreast, at 29in (74cm) seat pitch. Underfloor freight holds, total volume, 479cu ft (13.54m³). Flight crew of two.

Fokker F28 Fellowship Mk 4000 Cutaway Drawing Key
1 Radome
2 Weather radar scanner
3 Front pressure bulkhead
4 Radar equipment mounting
5 Windscreen wipers
6 Windscreen frame
7 Instrument panel shroud
8 Back of instrument panel
9 Rudder pedals
10 Ram air intake
11 Cockpit roof control panel
12 Overhead window
13 Co-pilot's seat
14 Pilot's seat
15 Control column
16 Pilot's side console
17 Air conditioning plant
18 Nosewheel doors
19 Nose undercarriage leg
20 Twin nosewheels
21 Cockpit roof construction
22 Radio and electronics rack
23 Radio rack cooling duct
24 Galley
25 Stewardess' seat
26 Curtained doorway to passenger cabin
27 Handrail
28 Entrance vestibule
29 Entry stairway
30 VHF aerial
31 Main passenger door
32 Upper VHF aerial
33 Air conditioning duct
34 Forward cabin passenger seating
35 Seat rails
36 Freight and baggage hold door
37 ADF loop aerials
38 Fuselage frame and stringer construction
39 Soundproofing panels
40 Underfloor freight and baggage hold
41 Window panels
42 Cabin floor construction
43 Hot air duct
44 Wing centre section front spar
45 HF aerial fixing
46 Leading edge fence
47 Starboard wing integral fuel tank
48 Fuel filler
49 Starboard navigation light
50 Static discharge wicks
51 Starboard aileron
52 Aileron tab
53 Flap mechanism fairings
54 Starboard outer flaps
55 Outboard spoilers (open)
56 Starboard inboard flaps
57 Inboard spoilers (open)
58 Centre section main fuselage frames
59 Air distribution duct
60 Wing centre section construction
61 Emergency escape windows
62 Mainwheel well pressurized cover

Below left: An F28 Mk 4000 in service with Empire Airlines which, with 17 F28s in its fleet, is the largest operator of the type in the United States. Empire was acquired by Piedmont Airlines in early 1986 and its aircraft are being progressively integrated into the Piedmont fleet. Note the open airbrakes.

Below: This is one of three F28 Mk 1000 transports used for domestic and regional service by Aero Peru, the national flag carrier of Peru.

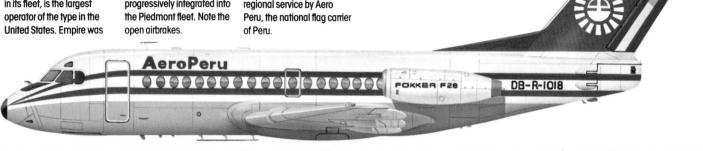

Above: The flight deck of the F28 shows good contemporary practice, with nav/comm between the pilots and systems controls overhead. A foldaway third seat is provided for an observer.

63 Port mainwheel well
64 Cabin window trim panels
65 Rear cabin seating
66 Passenger overhead service panels
67 Overhead luggage rack
68 Cabin rear bulkhead
69 Starboard engine cowling
70 Toilet
71 Wash basin
72 Air intake to APU
73 Fin root fairing
74 Fuselage sloping frames
75 De-icing air duct
76 HF aerials
77 Fin leading edge de-icing
78 Fin construction
79 Tailplane hydraulic jacks
80 Tailplane de-icing air duct
81 Anti-collision light
82 Starboard tailplane
83 Starboard elevator
84 Tailplane pivot fairing
85 Elevator hinge controls
86 Tailcone fairing
87 Tail navigation light
88 Port elevator
89 Tailplane construction
90 Leading edge de-icing
91 Tailplane pivot
92 Rudder
93 Rudder hydraulic jack
94 Port airbrake (open)
95 Airbrake jack housing
96 Rear fuselage construction
97 Hydraulic accumulators
98 Exhaust silencer nozzle
99 Engine pylon fairing
100 Bleed air ducting
101 Rolls Royce Mk 555-15 Spey Junior turbofan
102 Engine mountings
103 Engine cowlings
104 Auxiliary power unit (APU)
105 Engine mounting beam
106 Air intake
107 Five-abreast passenger seating
108 Underfloor air duct
109 Trailing edge wing root fairing
110 Inboard flap track fairing
111 Port inboard spoilers
112 Port flaps
113 Flap mechanism fairings
114 Port outboard spoilers
115 Flap construction
116 Aileron tab
117 Port aileron
118 Static discharge wicks
119 Port wingtip
120 Port navigation light
121 Outer wing rib construction
122 Leading edge de-icing air ducts
123 Leading edge construction
124 Lattice ribs
125 Wing integral fuel tanks
126 Twin mainwheels
127 Main undercarriage leg
128 Leading edge fence
129 Undercarriage retraction jack fixing
130 Wing panel bolted joint
131 Corrugated inner wing skin
132 Wing spar attachment frame
133 Leading edge de-icing air duct

Left: Cutaway drawing of the F28 Mk 4000, which is typical also of the earlier variants.

FOKKER 50 THE NETHERLANDS

The Fokker 50 was announced in November 1983, on the occasion of a celebration in Amsterdam of the 25th anniversary of airline service with the F27 Friendship, which the Fokker 50 is designed to succeed. After prolonged studies of possible stretched derivatives of the F27, Fokker concluded that the size of the aircraft was about right for that portion of the regional airline market it sought to fill. Nevertheless, and despite an ongoing programme of product improvement since the F27 had first appeared in 1957, there was much room to introduce the benefits of new technology in the structure and system of the basic aircraft, and this is the keynote of Fokker's approach to the design of the Fokker 50. The most obvious change is in respect of the power plant, a switch being made from the Rolls-Royce Dart of the F27 family to the more modern Pratt & Whitney Canada PW124 with significant gains in fuel economy. Less obvious but more extensive changes have been made under the skin, to the extent that 80 per cent of the Fokker 50's component parts are new or modified by comparison with those of the F27. Thus, apart from the engines with their new nacelles and six-blade propellers, the Fokker 50 has a hydraulic instead of pneumatic system for landing gear and flap operation; a new Hamilton Standard air-conditioning system with a Garrett digital cabin pressure-control system; and Sundstrand integrated drive generators on each engine to supply the electric system. The F27's much-appreciated (by passengers) large cabin windows have given way to a larger number of smaller windows, in the interest of greater flexibility of cabin layout, and the cabin itself is wholly redesigned, with large overhead stowage bins and the main passenger access door at the front instead of the rear, with the F27's forward baggage/cargo loading

door deleted. The flight deck is extensively redesigned, with an all-new avionics fit including an electronic flight instrument system (EFIS). A small airframe change is made with the addition of the wingtips or 'Foklets' (a variation of the larger winglets that serve a similar purpose) and extensive use is made throughout the airframe of carbon, aramid and glass fibre composites. Flight development of the Fokker 50 began on 28 December 1985, using an F27 airframe with the new power plants; a second prototype flown on 30 April 1986 had more

representative Fokker 50 systems. Both these aircraft made use of F27 fuselages, and the first true Fokker 50 was first flown on 13 February 1987.

VARIANTS

The Fokker 50 is offered at two gross weights, as indicated in the data panel. Fokker also has illustrated a possible later development with a stretched fuselage for up to 66 passengers at the basic 32in (81cm) pitch, but no decision has been taken to launch such a version.

FOKKER 100 THE NETHERLANDS

In its search for a programme to maintain its share of the regional airliner market through the 1990s, Fokker evaluated a number of possible derivative versions of its F28. These included projects variously identified as the Super F28, the F29 and (in collaboration with McDonnell Douglas) the MDF-100. Finally, in November 1983, the company announced that it was going ahead with a derivative known as the Fokker 100, with backing from the Netherlands government; the designation was chosen to reflect the basic seating capacity (actually 107), in the same way that the improved F27 – announced simultaneously – was renamed the Fokker 50. To achieve the Fokker 100, the original F28 Mk 4000 fuselage was extended by 18ft 10in (5.74m) in two 'plugs', one ahead of and one behind the wing, producing an aircraft that seemed to fit well with the forecast needs of regional airlines, and which was also well sized for the power offered by Rolls-Royce for its reformed Spey Junior engine that is named Tay. Although Fokker studied, through extensive wind tunnel testing, the potential of completely new wing aerofoil sections, the final decision favoured retention of the basic F28 wing box unchanged. However, aerodynamic efficiency was improved by changes at the leading and trailing edges, with increased leading-edge chord resulting in the F28's prominent leading-edge 'kink' being virtually eliminated. The changes in the aerofoil brought about by the new leading edge resulted, according to Fokker, in a 30 per cent improvement in aerodynamics efficiency, an increase in the high-speed buffet limit and a reduction in drag at both high and low speeds. New trailing-edge flaps were adopted, and the landing gear was strengthened for the higher operating weights. Wing span was increased, at the tips, by 9ft

SPECIFICATION

Power Plant: Two Rolls-Royce Tay Mk 620-15 turbofans each rated at 13,320lb st (6,042kgp) for take-off and fitted with thrust-reversers. Standard fuel capacity, 2,868 Imp gal (13,040l) in integral wing tanks.

Performance: Max operating speed, 320kts (592km/h) IAS or Mach = 0.75; max cruising speed, 432kts (800km/h) at 35,000ft (10,670m); long-range cruising speed, 404kts (747km/h) at 35,000ft (10,670m); max cruising altitude, 35,000ft (10,670m); take-off field length, 5,970ft (1,820m); landing field length, 4,430ft (1,350m); range with full passenger payload, 1,200 naut mls (2,224km).

Weights: Operating weight empty, 51,260lb (23,250kg); max fuel weight, 23,070lb (10,460kg); max payload, 25,353lb (11,500kg); max take-off weight, 91,500lb (41,500kg); max landing weight, 84,500lb (38,330kg); max zero-fuel weight, 76,500lb (34,700kg).

Dimensions: Span, 92ft 1½in (28.08m); overall length, 115ft 10¼in (35.31m); overall height, 27ft 10½in (8.50m); sweepback, 17 deg 45 min at quarter chord; wing area, 1,014.7sq ft (94.30m²).

Accommodation: Cabin length, 64ft 6¼in (21.19m), max width, 9ft 9in (2.97m), max height, 6ft 7¼in (2.01m). Standard layout provides 107 seats five-abreast, with off-set aisle, at 32in (82cm) pitch; alternative layouts for 12 first-class four-abreast at 36in (91cm) pitch and 85 economy-class at 32in (81cm), or 55 business-class five-abreast at 34in (86cm) and 50 economy class at 32in (81cm) pitch, or up to a maximum of 119 one-class passengers at 29in (74cm) pitch. Underfloor baggage/cargo compartments (two), total volume, 618.8cu ft (17.52m³). Flight crew of two, with three cabin attendants.

9½in (3.0m), and tailplane span by 4ft 7in (1.4m). Considerable use is made of composites in the structure, for such items as the nosecone, wing/fuselage fairings, cabin floor panels, etc. Cabin redesign gives the Fokker 100 a new look, by comparison with the F28, and on the flight deck, digital electronics are introduced to provide a state-of-the-art presentation and equipment fit, with a four-screen electronic flight instrument system (EFIS). The digital autoflight control system provides for Cat II oper-

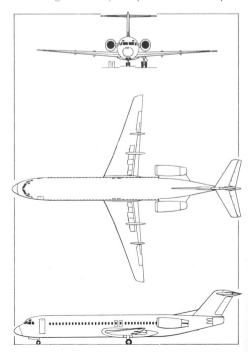

SPECIFICATION

Power Plant: Two Pratt & Whitney Canada PW124 turboprops each rated at 2,150shp (1,603kW) for take-off, with Dowty Rotol six-blade constant-speed feathering and reversing propellers of 12ft 0in (3.66m) diameter. Standard internal fuel capacity, 1,130 Imp gal (5,136l) in integral wing tanks.

Performance: Max operating speed, 227kts (419km/h) IAS or Mach = 0.507; max cruising speed, 278kts (515km/h) at 21,000ft (6,400m); long-range cruising speed, 245kts (454km/h) at 25,000ft (7,620m); max operating altitude, 25,000ft (7,620m); take-off field length, 5,770ft (1,760m); landing field length, 3,490ft (1,065m); range with 50 passengers at standard weight, 750 naut mls (1,390km); range with 50 passengers at optional high gross weight, 1,610 naut mls (2,983km).

Weights: Operating weight empty (typical), 27,850lb (12,633kg); max fuel weight, 9,090lb (4,123kg); max payload, 12,700lb (5,760kg); max take-off weight, standard, 41,865lb (18,990kg); max take-off weight, optional, 45,900lb (20,820kg); max landing weight, standard, 41,865lb (18,990kg); max landing weight, optional, 43,500lb (19,731kg); max zero-fuel weight, 40,350lb (18,303kg).

Dimensions: Span, 95ft 1¾in (29.00m); overall length, 82ft 10in (25.25m); overall height, 28ft 7in (8.60m); sweepback, nil; wing area, 754sq ft (70.00m²).

Accommodation: Cabin length, 52ft 4in (15.96m), max width, 8ft 2in (2.49m), max height, 6ft 5¼in (1.96m). Standard layout for 50 passengers, four-abreast, at 32in (81cm) seat pitch; alternatively, 46 business-class passengers at 34in (86cm) pitch or a maximum of 58 passengers at 30in (76cm) pitch. Baggage volume, 310cu ft (8.78m³) in main compartment plus 29cu ft (0.82m³) in carry-on compartment. Flight crew of two and two cabin attendants.

Above left: The registration PH-OSO identifies this as the first of two prototypes of the Fokker 50. Fitted with the new Pratt & Whitney PW124 turboprops, these two aircraft had the small windows planned for the Fokker 50, but used stock F27 airframes and lacked many Fokker 50 features.

Above: The flight deck of the Fokker 50 showing the two CRT displays for the Sperry electronic flight instrument system (EFIS) provided for each of the two pilots. Space for a multifunction display is provided between the pilots, as can be seen here, ahead of the throttle console.

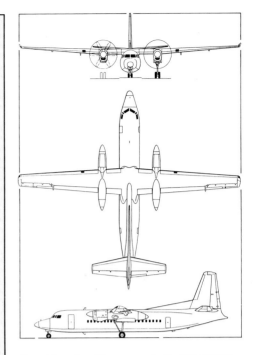

Above: Three-view of the Fokker 50 in its initial production form, showing the 'Foklet' wingtips.

SERVICE USE

The launch order for the Fokker 50 was placed by Ansett Transport Industries and was for 15 aircraft, with deliveries starting in early 1987. Subsequent orders placed by DLT, Busy Bee, Corsair of the USA, Austrian Airlines and Maersk Air of Denmark took the total of aircraft ordered to 39, with 12 options, by the beginning of 1987.

FOKKER 100

ation, with operators having the option to upgrade to Cat III if an autothrottle is fitted. Manufacture of the Fokker 100 is distributed round Europe in a fashion similar to that for the F28. The first F100 flew on 30 November 1986.

VARIANTS

When the Fokker 100 was announced, Fokker indicated that an optional high gross weight version was under study, at a take-off weight of 95,000lb (43,090kg). Subsequent airline interest indicated that this might become the definitive variant, probably powered by uprated versions of the Rolls-Royce Tay. The effect of this increase is to give the Fokker 100 a range of about 1,500 naut mls (2,414km). The heavier variant was specified by US Air together with some other changes, the design and introduction of which delayed the first flight of the Fokker 100 by some five months beyond the original July 1986 date which had been the target.

SERVICE USE

Launch customer Swissair expects to have the Fokker 100 in service by the end of 1987, about 10 to 12 months after the first flight of the first of two prototypes. Other orders have been placed by KLM and US Air, the latter a significant victory for the Dutch company over Boeing, which was offering a light-weight version of the Model 737. Orders totalled 88 (with 91 more on option) by the beginning of 1987.

Above: The interior of the Fokker 100, shown in mock-up form, with single-class five-abreast seating for 107 passengers.

Left: Three-view of the Fokker 100, which has a lengthened version of the F28 fuselage, and the new Rolls-Royce Tay engines.

Right: Flight testing of the Fokker 100 began at Amsterdam on 30 November 1986 using this prototype. With a second aircraft joining the programme in 1987, certification was to be completed by the autumn to allow Swissair to operate the aircraft before year-end.

Development of a small utility transport suitable for military or civil roles began at Australia's Government Aircraft Factories (GAF) during the mid-1960s. As the N2, this project took shape as a strutted high-wing monoplane having a slab-sided fuselage of almost square cross section, large side-loading doors and retractable landing gear with stub wings, carrying nacelles into which the main wheels retracted. Prototypes of this N2 design flew on 23 July and 5 December 1971, respectively. The name Nomad was adopted for the production version, and several variants were developed, as noted below. Production ended in late 1984 with a total of 170 built, of which 20 to 25 had not, at that time, been sold.

VARIANTS

The Nomad went into production as the N22, with a gross weight of 8,000lb (3,629kg). This was later increased to 8,500lb (3,855kg) in the N22B, which became the standard short-fuselage variant for commercial use, with up to 12 passengers. Meanwhile, GAF had 'stretched' the Nomad's fuselage by 3ft 9in (1.14m) to produce, in 1976, the N24, with seating increased from 12 to a maximum of 17. With the

same power plant as the N22, the N24 was introduced at a gross weight of 8,500lb (3,855kg), but this was increased to 9,400lb (4,263kg) in the definitive N24A. Production of the long-fuselage version accounted for about one-third of the Nomad total. In May 1985, GAF recertificated the N22B at increased gross weight of 8,950lb (4,060kg) as the N22C, this version also featuring a force-feed oil filter system. During 1979, a version of the N22B was certificated as a seaplane, fitted with a pair of Wipaire (of Minnesota) aluminium floats, and in the following year an amphibious variant was also certificated, using Wipaire floats incorporating Cessna wheels and tyres in a retractable installation. Approximately half of the total production of Nomads has been in military versions of the short-fuselage N22. These fall into three categories, named as the Missionmaster, Searchmaster B and Searchmaster L. The Missionmaster is the utility transport and forward area support version, special features of which include load-bearing drop doors in the cabin floor; four wing strongpoints for pylons to carry supply packs, flares, etc; improved transparencies in the cockpit roof for better visibility from the flight deck; military avionics; and specific role equipment to

Above: Typically for aircraft of its size and class, the Nomad provides single seats for its passengers on each side of the cabin, with a central aisle. Cabin dimensions did not allow the Nomad to have the customary overhead baggage rack or lockers.

Government Aircraft Factories N24A Nomad Cutaway Drawing Key

1 Nose cone
2 Optional weather radar
3 Radar transmitter/receiver
4 Glassfibre nose skinning
5 Enlarged forward baggage compartment
6 Baggage door
7 Landing/taxying lamps
8 Nosewheel
9 Nose undercarriage leg strut
10 Front bulkhead
11 Windscreen panels
12 Windscreen wipers
13 Instrument panel shroud
14 Rudder pedals
15 Forward fuselage longeron
16 Control system linkages
17 Entry steps

18 Radio and electronics racks
19 Pilot's floor level
20 Cockpit entry door
21 Control column handwheel
22 Pilot's seat
23 Safety harness
24 Sliding window panel
25 Engine throttle and propeller control levers
26 Co-pilot's seat
27 Fuel cock controls
28 Glassfibre honeycomb cockpit roof panel (or optional transparency)
29 Sliding doorway to main cabin
30 Cockpit rear bulkhead
31 Cabin window panels

32 Heater distribution ducting
33 Floor beam construction
34 Passenger cabin floor level (seat mounting and freight lashing rails)
35 Passenger seats: up to 16 in commuter version
36 Fresh air distribution ducting

37 Forward emergency exit window
38 Fuselage frame and stringer construction
39 Wing spar root joints
40 Wing/fuselage mounting double frames
41 Communications antenna
42 Additional inboard de-icing boot
43 Hinged leading edge section (engine control run access)
44 Starboard wing fuel tankage
45 Fuel filler caps
46 Oil cooler
47 Allison 250-B-17B turboshaft engine
48 Exhaust stub
49 Engine intake
50 Propeller hub pitch control mechanism

51 Hartzell three-bladed, constant speed, reversible pitch propeller
52 Propeller blade root de-icing
53 Engine oil tank, capacity 1.9 Imp gal (8.6l)
54 Starboard wing bracing strut
55 Leading edge stall strip

56 Stall warning transmitter
57 Leading edge de-icing boot
58 Leading edge nose ribs
59 Wing stringers
60 Wing skin plating
61 Optional long-range fuel tank
62 Starboard navigation light
63 Slot-lip aileron
64 Outer double slotted flap section (used as aileron when flaps are up)
65 Flap hinge bracket
66 Inboard double slotted flap section
67 Corrugated flap shroud skinning
68 Flap operating electric motor and control shaft
69 D/F loop aerial

70 Aft emergency exit window
71 Cabin roof frames
72 Rear fuselage joint frame
73 Baggage restraint net
74 Aft baggage compartment
75 Control cable runs
76 Extended fin root construction
77 Tailplane mass balance weight

78 Aerial cable
79 N22B Floatmaster version
80 Additional ventral fin
81 Starboard one-piece flying tailplane
82 Tailfin construction
83 Rudder horn balance
84 Anti-collision light
85 Corrugated rudder skin plating
86 Rudder trim tab
87 Tailplane tab
88 Tailplane construction
89 Tailplane control mechanism
90 N22B Searchmaster L version
91 Radar operator's station
92 Tactical navigator's station
93 Observer's seat

94 Floor hatch
95 Life raft stowage
96 Oven and food locker
97 Optional additional internal fuel tankage
98 Toilet
99 Litton APS-504 360-deg scanning radome

100 Observation bubble window
101 Aft baggage door
102 Aft passenger seating
103 Rear freight/passenger door, folds down to form entry steps
104 Forward opening rear door upper segment
105 Forward freight/passenger door
106 Port wing fuel tankage
107 Corrugated flap shroud skinning
108 Port inboard double slotted flap
109 Flap/aileron mixer linkage
110 Rear spar
111 Wing rib construction
112 Aileron control links
113 Port slot lip aileron

114 Outboard double slotted flap
115 Mass balance weight
116 Wing tip fairing
117 Port navigation light
118 Port long range ferry tank
119 Main spar
120 Leading edge nose ribs
121 Stall warning
122 Leading edge de-icing boots
123 Outer wing panel spar joint
124 Strut attachment
125 Port wing bracing strut
126 Twin-wheel port main undercarriage
127 Main undercarriage wheel well and pre-closing door
128 Battery

129 Port undercarriage pod
130 Stub wing extension
131 Electric undercarriage jack motor
132 Port engine nacelle
133 Engine air intake
134 Oil cooler intake
135 Leading edge de-icing air ducting

Below: The cutaway shows the Nomad N24A, with insets depicting some of the optional versions.

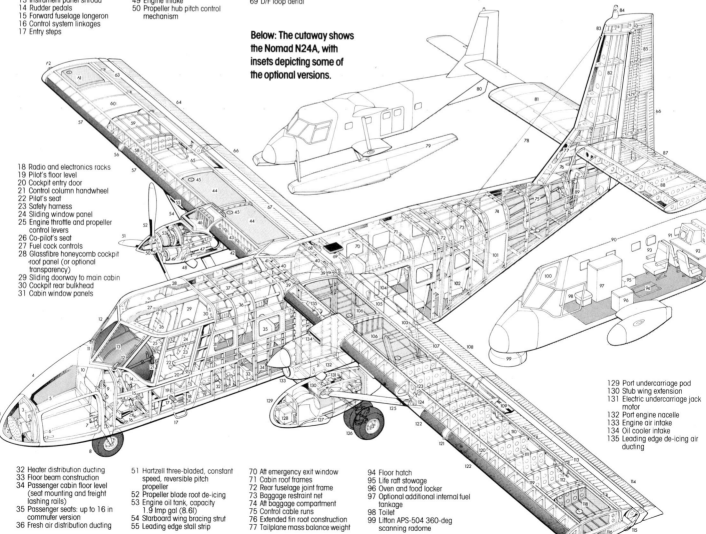

SPECIFICATION
(Nomad N22B)

Power Plant: Two Allison 250-B17C turboprops each rated at 420shp (313kW) for take-off, with Hartzell three-blade constant-speed fully-feathering and reversible propellers. Fuel capacity, 224 Imp gal (1,018l) in flexible bag tanks, plus optional integral tanks in wing tips, total capacity 147.4 Imp gal (670l).

Performance: Max operating speed, 169kts (313km/h); normal cruising speed 165kts (311km/h) at 10,000ft (3,050m); long-range cruising speed 140kts (260km/h) at 10,000ft (3,050m); initial rate of climb, 1,460ft/min (7.4m/sec); service ceiling, 21,000ft (6,400m); take-off distance (FAR Pt 23), 1,180ft (360m); landing distance (FAR Pt 23), 1,340ft (410m); max range, 580 naut mls (1,074km).

Weights: Operating weight empty, 5,436lb (2,446kg); standard fuel weight, 1,770lb (803kg); max fuel weight, 2,350lb (1,066kg); max payload, 3,714lb (1,685kg); max take-off weight, 8,500lb (3,855kg); max landing weight, 8,500lb (3,855kg); max zero-fuel weight, 8,250lb (3,742kg).

Dimensions: Span, 54ft 2in (16.51m); overall length, 41ft 3in (12.57m); overall height, 18ft 2in (5.54m); sweepback, nil; wing area, 324.0sq ft (30.10m²).

Accommodation: Cabin length, 17ft 6in (5.33m), max width, 4ft 3in (1.30m), max height, 5ft 2½in (1.58m). Individual seats for up to 12 passengers, with central aisle, at 29in (74cm) pitch. Nose baggage compartment, volume, 27cu ft (0.76m³). Flight crew of two, but certificated for single-pilot operation.

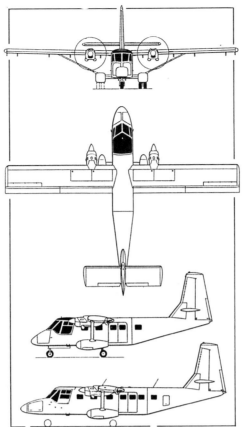

meet customer needs. The Searchmaster B is a basic coastal patrol and offshore surveillance variant, carrying Bendix search radar in the nose and operated by a crew of four. Some civil operators, such as Queensland Air and Northern Territory Air Work, purchased this version. Of more specific interest to armed services and government agencies, the Searchmaster L had Litton APS-504(V) search radar in a radome under the nose for 360-degree search, and an operating crew of five. Underwing pylons were an option, as on the Missionmaster.

SERVICE USE

GAF obtained certification of the basic N2 on 11 August 1972, and the N22 went into service on 18 December 1975 with Aero Pelican, after certification of the production version on 29 April 1975. The N22B was certificated in August 1975 and gained US FAR Pt 135 (Appendix A) certification in December 1978. The N22C was approved in May 1985. Certification of the N24 was obtained in October 1977 and of the N24A in May 1978, with FAR Pt 135 (Appendix A) approval gained in December 1978.

Left: The three-view drawing shows the GAF Nomad 22, which was the basic version of the Australian feeder-liner. The lengthened N24A is depicted in the extra side-view, bottom.

Below: Alaska Central was an early user of the GAF Nomad N24A.

Below: Standard (background) and long-fuselage versions of the Nomad formate over an Australian landscape.

HANDLEY PAGE HERALD UK

Above: The Handley Page Herald was one of the first of the turboprop-engined feeder-liners to enter service, in 1960, but the slow development of the market for this class of aeroplane combined with the financial difficulties encountered by the makers led to a premature ending of production. Only a dozen or so Heralds were in service in 1987.

The design of a medium-sized, short-range feederliner with a pressurized fuselage was begun by the Handley Page company in the early 1950s, and its detailed design was made the responsibility of the company's Reading-based subsidiary (the former Miles Aircraft company at Woodley). As the HPR 3, the new airliner emerged as a high-wing monoplane of conventional design, powered by four Alvis Leonides Major piston radial engines. Two prototypes were built in this configuration, with the first flight made on 25 August 1955, but early commitments for the purchase of some 29 aircraft, mostly for Australian operators, were not made good and it became clear to Handley Page that the HPR 3 could not hold its own in the new era of the turboprop. Consequently, in May 1957, the company announced that a version of the Herald would be offered with two Darts in place of the four piston engines, and the latter variant was subsequently dropped. Both prototypes were converted to have Dart RDa.7 engines, flying for the first time in this form on 11 March and 17 December 1958 respectively. The first production HPR 7 Herald flew on 30 October 1959, and three more followed to the same standard before a switch was made to the slightly lengthened, definitive model as noted below. Production of the Herald continued, at a low rate, throughout the 1960s with final assembly transferred from Woodley to the parent company's plant at Radlett before Handley Page Ltd collapsed in 1968. At that time, six more Heralds were in various stages of construction in advance of firm orders, but these were not completed.

VARIANTS

The initial production standard was the Herald Srs 100, with a fuselage length of 71ft 11in (21.92m) and a maximum take-off weight of 39,000lb (17,690kg). Of four built, three were delivered to British

HARBIN Y-12 PEOPLE'S REPUBLIC OF CHINA

Right: The Harbin Y-12, which is of typical configuration for a small turboprop twin designed for feeder-line use, is notable as the first civil aircraft wholly of Chinese design and construction to achieve quantity production. The Y-12-2 had entered small-scale service by late-1986

Below: The cockpit of the Harbin Y-12, which is provided with full dual controls for the two pilots and a conventional arrangement of the flight instruments. Radio and navigation controls and engine instruments are in the centre of the front panel, with legends in Chinese characters.

The Y-12 (Y indicates 'Yunshuji' or Transport aircraft, and the designation is sometimes rendered as Yun-12) is a product of the Harbin aircraft factory in Heilongjiang province, one of the 10 major centres of aerospace activity known to be active in China. Known as the Harbin Aircraft Manufacturing Corporation, the factory was set up in 1952, and for six years was concerned only with aircraft repair. It then progressed to the licence production of Soviet aircraft, building some 1,000 examples of the Mil Mi-4 helicopter (as the Z-5) and about 500 examples of the Ilyushin Il-28 light bomber (as the H-5). Its earliest design activity dates from 1975 when work began on the Y-11 utility transport, a high-wing monoplane with two piston engines, in the same general category as the Britten-Norman Islander. Although the designation indicated that this was the 11th transport design in a series, the Y-11 was one of the first modern aircraft of wholly Chinese design and construction when it made its first flight, in the second half of the 1970s. Powered by a pair of locally-produced 285hp (213kW) HS-6A nine-cylinder radials derived from the Soviet Ivchenko AI-14RF, the seven-seat Y-11 was certificated in 1981, by which time a pre-production batch was under way. Eventually, 40 Y-11s were built, to be used for a variety of environmental support duties. From the Y-11, with which it shared the configuration but little else, the Y-12 was developed. The first of three prototypes flew on 14 July 1982. Picking the Pratt & Whitney PT6A to power the Y-12, Harbin adopted such new features

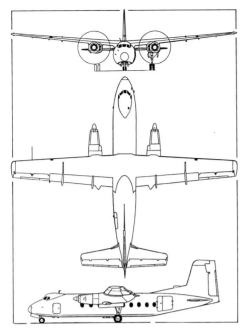

Above: A three-view of the Herald in its Series 200 form, which was the most-produced variant. The initial Series 100 had a shorter fuselage but only four were built before the lengthened version appeared. Variants up to Series 800 were built or projected, but all the surviving Heralds in use in 1987 were of the basic Series 200 type.

European Airways (BEA) for use on the Scottish Highlands and Islands routes. The Herald Srs 200 featured a 3ft 7in (1.09m) lengthening of the fuselage to give two more seat rows, and higher weights. After the second prototype HPR 7 had flown in Srs 200 configuration on 8 April 1961, the first production example flew on 13 December 1961, and 36 of this variant were delivered. In addition, the company built eight Herald Srs 400s as military transports for the Royal Malaysian Air Force. The Herald Srs 300 designation referred to the Srs 200 with small modifications to meet US certification requirements. Unbuilt projects were the Srs 500, another military transport variant similar to the Srs 400; the Srs 600 with a 5ft (1.5m) lengthening of the fuselage for 68 passengers, with 2,320ehp (1,831kW) Dart RDa.9 engines, more fuel and higher weights; the Srs 700 combining the Srs 200 size fuselage with Srs 600 features to provide a high-density layout for 60 passengers at 28-in (71-cm) seat pitch; and the Srs 800 which combined the Srs 400 military fuselage with Srs 600 features.

SERVICE USE

The Herald Srs 100 obtained British certification on 25 November 1959 and entered service with BEA early in 1960. The Srs 200 was certificated on 1 June 1961 and entered service with Jersey Airlines early in 1962. Production totals were four Srs 100, 36 Srs 200 and eight Srs 400, plus two prototypes. About a dozen remained current in 1987, mostly with European operators.

SPECIFICATION
(Herald Series 200)

Power Plant: Two Rolls-Royce Dart Mk 527 (RDa.7) turboprops each rated at 2,105ehp (1,570kW) for take-off, with Rotol four-blade constant-speed fully-feathering propellers of 12ft 6in (3.81m) diameter. Fuel capacity, 1,080 Imp gal (4,910l) in integral and flexible tanks in the wings.
Performance: Max cruising speed, 239kts (443km/h) at 15,000ft (4,575m); best economy cruising speed, 230kts (426km/h) at 23,000ft (7,010m); initial rate of climb, 1,805ft/min (9.2m/sec); service ceiling, 27,900ft (8,505m); take-off distance to 35ft (10.7m), 2,700ft (823m); landing distance from 50ft (15.2m), 1,900ft (580m); range with max payload, 608 naut mls (1,127km); range with max fuel, 1,530 naut mls (2,830km).
Weights: Empty equipped weight, 25,800lb (11,703kg); max payload, 11,700lb (5,307kg); max take-off weight, 43,000lb (19,505kg); max landing weight, 39,500lb (17,915kg); max zero-fuel weight, 37,500lb (17,010kg).
Dimensions: Span, 94ft 9in (28.88m); overall length, 75ft 6in (23.01m); overall height, 24ft 1in (7.34m); sweepback, 0.38 deg at quarter chord; wing area, 886sq ft (82.31m²).
Accommodation: Cabin length, 54ft 0in (16.46m), max width, 8ft 8¼in (2.65m), max height, 6ft 4in (1.93m). Standard one-class layout for 50 passengers four-abreast with central aisle at 36-in (91-cm) seat pitch, or maximum of 56 passengers at 34-in (86-cm) pitch. Two above-floor baggage holds, total volume, 285cu ft (8.07m³). Flight crew of two.

HARBIN Y-12

(compared with the Y-11) as a NASA GAW supercritical aerofoil section, bonded construction in place of rivets, and integral in place of bag fuel tanks. Two prototypes and a static test airframe (at first known as Y-11T1s but then as Y-12-1s) were followed by three Y-12-2 (originally Y-11T2) development aircraft, used to obtain certification in compliance with US FAR Pt 23 and Pt 135 standards. The first of the Y-12-2s flew in 1983. Under an agreement between Harbin and the Hong Kong Aircraft Engineer-

ing Co. (HAECO), the latter installed Western avionics and interior in the sixth Y-12 to help 'westernize' the aircraft for export, and Lockheed provided flight test support for Y-12 certification. The Chinese government has also concluded an agreement with Pratt & Whitney to allow assembly of PT6A engines in China.

VARIANTS

The basic production version is the Y-12-2, which introduced PT6A-27 engines after lower-rated PT6A-11s had been used in the two Y-12-1s. The latter were fitted with magnetic anomaly detection equipment, after completing flight tests, for geological survey work in the Harbin area. Production aircraft have no leading-edge slats (as fitted to the prototypes) and a larger dorsal fin, with taller fin, than at first used.

SERVICE USE

The Y-12-2 was certificated in China in December 1985. Full international certification should be achieved by 1988. About a dozen Y-12s had been completed by the end of 1986.

SPECIFICATION
(Y-12-2)

Power Plant: Two Pratt & Whitney Canada PT6A-27 turboprops each rated at 620shp (462kW) for take-off, with Hartzell three-blade variable-pitch fully-feathering and reversing propellers. Fuel capacity, 352 Imp gal (1,600l) contained in wing torsion box.
Performance: Max speed, 163kts (302km/h) at 9,845ft (3,000m); cruising speed, 129kts (240km/h) at 9,845ft (3,000m); initial rate of climb, 1,575ft/min (8m/sec); normal cruising altitude, 9,845ft (3,000m); service ceiling, 22,965ft (7,000m); take-off field length (FAR Pt 23), 1,395ft (425m); landing field length (FAR Pt 23), 2,135ft (650m); range with 17-passenger payload, 221 naut mls (410km).
Weights: (Y-12-1) Operating weight empty, 6,614lb (3,000kg); max fuel weight, 2,645lb (1,200kg); max payload, 3,748lb (1,700kg); max take-off weight, 11,684lb (5,300kg); max landing weight, 11,023lb (5,000kg); max zero-fuel weight, 10,362lb (4,700kg).
Dimensions: Span, 56ft 6½in (17.235m); overall length 48ft 9in (14.86m); overall height, 17ft 3¾in (5.275m); sweepback, nil; wing area, 368.88sq ft (34.27m²).
Accommodation: Cabin length, 16ft 1in (4.90m), overall width, 4ft 9½in (1.46m), overall height, 5ft 7in (1.70m). Standard accommodation for up to 17 passengers, three-abreast with offset aisle, at 31.5in (80cm) seat pitch. Baggage compartments in nose and at rear, total volume 93.95cu ft (2.66m³). Flight crew of two.

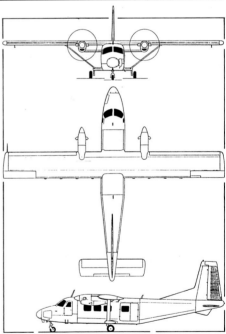

Above: A three-view of the Harbin Y-12-2 in its definitive production form, with a larger dorsal fin than was used on the first prototypes.

Left: Although only slightly wider than the GAF Nomad (see previous spread), the Harbin Y-12 provides three-abreast seating for its 17 passengers, with a narrow, off-set aisle. Indirect roof lighting is a feature.

IAI ARAVA ISRAEL

Israel's indigenous aircraft industry, now centred upon the Israel Aircraft Industries complex at Lod, outside Tel Aviv, had its origins in 1953 when the Bedek Aircraft Company was formed. Changing its name to Israel Aircraft Industries in April 1967, the company was at first exclusively engaged in providing maintenance and engineering support for the Israeli air force. Production activities began in the late 1950s, at first with licence-manufacture of the Fouga CM-170 Magister, and at about the same time design work began on aircraft of wholly Israeli origin. The first IAI design, the B-101C, was for a nine-seat corporate jet transport, and reached the mock-up stage but proceeded no further, whilst a second design, for a six-seat corporate jet, was also abandoned when IAI acquired the design and manufacturing rights for the Rockwell Jet Commander, which it went on to develop and produce as the Westwind. Attention then switched, in the project office, to a light STOL transport, for which there seemed to be a large world-wide market, both military and civil. Design work began in 1965 and led to a project for a high-wing twin-turboprop transport with STOL performance characteristics. The most unusual feature of the design was the twin-boom layout, combined with a circular-section fuselage having a hinged tail cone for straight-in loading of vehicles or cargo. Like most other aircraft in its class, the new transport, which took the designation IAI-101, was designed to meet the American FAR Pt 23 regulations; which established the maximum take-off weight at 12,500lb (5,670kg) for civil operations. The first prototype of the IAI-101 flew on 27 November 1969 and the second on 8 May 1971, but thereafter the emphasis of early production and development switched to the heavier IAI-201 military variant. The name Arava was adopted for both civil and military types.

VARIANTS

The original Arava was designed around a pair of Turboméca Astazou turboprops, but PT6A-27s were adopted instead for the IAI-101 prototypes, switching to the 783shp (584kW) PT6A-34 for the IAI-101 initial production standard, later identified as the IAI-102. This was matched by the IAI-201 military version, which had a maximum weight of 15,000lb (6,804kg). The IAI-101B, which is the current commercial version, has PT6A-36 engines and improved performance in hot and high conditions, as well as a better cabin interior. An all-cargo version, with a 5,200lb (2,360kg) payload, is known as the Cargo Commuterliner in the USA. The IAI-202 is a modified version with PT6A-36 engines, winglets and a lengthened fuselage.

SERVICE USE

The IAI-101 was certificated with PT6A-27 engines in April 1972, and the IAI-101A with PT6A-34 engines in August 1973. The IAI-102 was type-approved by the Israeli authorities in April 1976, and was the first commercial version to go into service. FAA certification of the IAI-101B was obtained on 17 November 1980 to SFAR Pt 41 provision, and in October 1982 to the upgraded SFAR Pt 41C. Of about 80 Aravas built to date, some 20 were for commercial operators.

SPECIFICATION
(IAI-101B)

Power Plant: Two Pratt & Whitney Canada PT6A-36 turboprops each rated at 750shp (559kW) for take-off, with Hartzell three-blade variable-pitch fully-feathering and reversing propellers. Fuel capacity, 366 Imp gal (1,663l) in integral wing tanks.
Performance: Max operating speed, 170kts (315km/h) IAS; max cruising speed, 172kts (308km/h) at 10,000ft (3,050m); long-range cruising speed, 140kts (259km/h) at 10,000ft (3,050m); initial rate of climb, 1,290ft/min (6.5m/sec); service ceiling, 25,000ft (7,620m); take-off distance to 50ft (15m), 2,450ft (745m); landing distance from 50ft (15m), 2,150ft (655m); range with max payload, 237 naut mls (440km); range with max fuel, 740 naut mls (1,370km).
Weights: Operating weight empty, 8,818lb (4,000kg); max payload, 5,182lb (2,350kg); max take-off weight, 15,000lb (6,804kg); max landing weight, 15,000lb (6,804kg); max zero-fuel weight, 14,000lb (6,350kg).
Dimensions: Span, 68ft 9in (20.96m); overall length, 42ft 9in (13.05m); overall height, 17ft 1in (5.21m); sweepback, nil; wing area, 470sq ft (43.7m²).
Accommodation: Cabin length, 12ft 8in (3.87m), max width, 7ft 8in (2.33m), max height, 5ft 9in (1.75m). Standard accommodation for up to 19 seats, in four-abreast layout with central aisle, at 30in (76cm) pitch. Baggage compartment, volume, 91.8cu ft (2.60m³) plus 113cu ft (3.20m³) available in tail cone. Flight crew of two, with provision for single-pilot operation, should this be necessary.

ILYUSHIN IL-18 SOVIET UNION

SPECIFICATION
(Il-18D)

Power Plant: Four Ivchenko AI-20M turboprops each rated at 4,250shp (3,169kW) for take-off, with AV-68I four-blade constant-speed feathering and reversing propellers. Fuel capacity, 6,599 Imp gal (30,000l) in integral tanks in outboard wing panels and bag-type tanks in inboard wing panels and centre section.
Performance: Max cruising speed (at max take-off weight), 364kts (675km/h); economical cruising speed, 337kts (625km/h); normal operating altitude, 26,250 to 32,820ft (8,000 to 10,000m); take-off run, 4,265ft (1,300m); landing run, 2,790ft (850m); range with max payload and one-hour fuel reserve, 1,997 naut mls (3,700km); range with max fuel and one-hour fuel reserve, 3,508 naut mls (6,500km).
Weights: Empty, equipped (90-seat configuration), 77,160lb (35,000kg), max payload, 29,750lb (13,500kg); max take-off weight, 141,100lb (64,000kg).
Dimensions: Span, 122ft 8½in (37.40m); overall length, 117ft 9in (35.90m); overall height, 33ft 4in (10.17m); sweepback, nil; wing area, 1,507sq ft (140.0m²).
Accommodation: Cabin length, about 79ft 0in (24.0m), max width, 10ft 7in (3.23m), max height, 6ft 6in (2.00m). Standard layout provides 110 seats in forward, main and rear cabins, mostly six-abreast, reducing to five-abreast for the three rows in the rear cabin; maximum capacity, 122; alternative layouts include 90 seats all five-abreast and 65 seats in mixed four-abreast and five-abreast arrangements. Flight crew of five comprising two pilots, flight engineer, navigator and wireless operator.

The Il-18 first flew in July 1957 as one of the first of a new generation of airliners developed after World War II to meet the needs of Aeroflot and to take advantage of then-new technology including gas turbine engines. Named *Moskva*, the prototype was followed by two pre-production aircraft and a service trials batch of 20, of which some were powered by the Kuznetsov NK-4 engine and others by the AI-20. The latter was adopted as the standard power plant on the basis of early service results and, with maximum take-off weight increased from 126,100lb (57,200kg) to 130,514lb (59,200kg), the Il-18B became the first major production version, with 84 seats. The Il-18 soon became Aeroflot's 'workhorse', supplementing the Tupolev Tu-104 twin-jet which was used for prestige routes, domestically and internationally. Once Aeroflot's initial needs had been met, the Il-18 was widely exported to commercial operators in countries within the Soviet sphere of influence. Between 700 and 800 examples of the Il-18 are believed to have been built, including some for use by military agencies, mostly as staff and VIP transports. The design provided the basis for development of the

Right: The Ilyushin Il-18, which was one of the first turboprop transports to be developed in the Soviet Union, has also been one of the more successful in the field of exports. Examples still fly in the fleets of many airlines that are in the Soviet sphere of influence, among them Cubana, as illustrated.

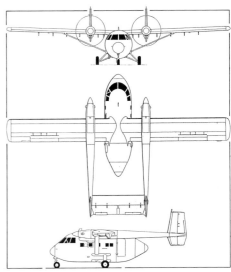

Left: The Israeli-developed Arava has found more application in military roles than for commercial use, thanks in part to its good field performance, which is seen here being demonstrated. A score or so of Aravas have been bought for use by small commuter airlines, mostly in the US and Israel.

Above: The distinctive layout of the IAI Arava is shown in this three-view drawing of the basic IAI-201 variant, which has a side-hinged rear fuselage cone to facilitate cargo loading. The IAI-202, with a lengthened fuselage, winglets and other changes, flew only in the form of a prototype.

ILYUSHIN IL-18

Il-38 anti-submarine/maritime patrol aircraft and versions equipped for Elint (electronic intelligence gathering) also appeared later, these probably being original commercial airframes modified after being phased out of service by Aeroflot. The Il-18 has the NATO reporting name 'Cub'.

VARIANTS
The original standard Il-18B, noted above, was followed in production in 1961 by the Il-18V, with AI-20K engines rated at 4,000ehp (2,983kW) each, fuel capacity of 5,213 Imp gal (23,700l) and standard layouts for 90 or 110 passengers. In 1964, the more powerful A1-20M engine was introduced (see data panel). Some internal redesign of the cabin, with the deletion of the rear cargo hold and extension aft of the pressurized section, made it possible to increase accommodation to 110 or, by omitting coat stowage space during summer, a maximum of 122. With these changes the designation became Il-18E (or Il-18Ye in a more accurate transliteration of the cyrillic), but this was swiftly followed by the Il-18D, in which fuel capacity was increased by nearly 27 per cent, with extra bag tanks in the centre section.

Some Il-18s were modified as cargo carriers after being retired from passenger service, with a large freight door in the rear fuselage side.

SERVICE USE
The Il-18 entered service with Aeroflot on 20 April 1959, followed by the Il-18V in 1961, and by the Il-18D and Il-18E in 1965. Between 150 and 200 still in service in 1986 were operated by Aeroflot, Air Guinea, Air Mali, Balkan Bulgarian, CAAC, Choson Minhang, CSA, Cubana, Interflug, Hang Khong Vietnam, LOT, Malev and Tarom.

Above: The Ilyushin Il-18's flight deck is cluttered and complicated when compared with contemporary Western practice, but dates from the mid 'fifties. This example is one of several Il-18s adapted for Antarctic operations, for which a weather radar scope has been provided.

Right: A three-view of the Il-18. This drawing is representative of the various production variants described in the text, all externally similar.

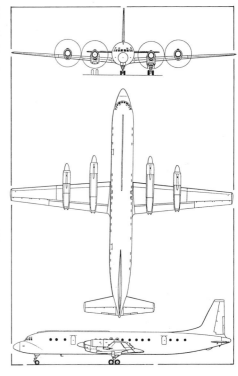

ILYUSHIN IL-62 SOVIET UNION

The Il-62 made its first flight in January 1963, having been developed to provide Aeroflot with a long-range jet transport comparable in comfort and performance to the equipment already in service with Western airlines. Soviet design bureaux matched Western products in most categories of airliner, both turboprop and turbojet, with the notable exception of a four-jet design featuring podded engines on the wing, as exemplified by the Boeing 707/Douglas DC-8/Convair 880 generation. Instead, when the first Soviet four-jet design was developed by the Ilyushin bureau, a rear-engined, high-tail layout was chosen, closely matching the configuration of the Vickers VC-10. In common with Western designs of similar layout, the Il-62 required lengthy flight development to overcome the tendency of this type to enter a deep stall from which recovery was impossible. An additional complication resulted from the tardy development of an engine suitable for the Il-62, the first example(s) of which flew with 16,535lb st (7,500kgp) Lyulka AL-7 turbojets. The 23,150lb st (10,500kgp) Kuznetsov NK-8-4 turbofans were introduced later in the programme, which involved two prototypes and three pre-production aircraft. The Il-62 has the NATO reporting name 'Classic'.

VARIANTS

The Il-62 entered production with NK-8-4 turbofans, and was normally furnished to accommodate 168 passengers in a single-class layout, although up to 186 could be carried. This version had cascade-type thrust-reversers on the outer engines only. By 1971 Ilyushin had produced the Il-62M, in which Soloviev D-30KU engines replaced the Kuznetsov engines. The improved specific fuel consumption of this new engine was combined with increased fuel capacity (through the introduction of a tank in the fin) to give the Il-62M considerably better payload/range performance, thus overcoming one of the failings of the original version. A number of internal changes were made, with a revised layout of the flight deck, new avionics to allow routine operation in Cat II conditions (with provision to extend to Cat III), and a

ILYUSHIN IL-86 SOVIET UNION

With responsibility for almost all non-military flying activities within the Soviet Union, Aeroflot is the sponsoring agency for a wide range of aircraft types, ranging from agricultural biplanes through helicopters and Arctic support aircraft to the turboprop and turbojet/turbofan airliners with which to maintain airline services both within the Soviet Union and internationally to destinations throughout the world. The upper end of the range of aircraft operated in Aeroflot colours is represented at present by the Il-86, a product of the Ilyushin design bureau that is not only the largest Soviet airliner to date, but also the first to provide a 'widebody' cabin and the first to have its engines in wing-mounted pods, all previous Soviet jet transports either having their engines rear-mounted on the fuselage or buried in the wing roots. Even so, it is interesting to record that the first published illustration of the Il-86 design showed a rear-engined configuration. The Il-86 design dates back to the early 1970s, the first of two prototypes having made its initial flight from a Moscow airfield on 22 December 1976. To power the Soviet 'airbus', the Kuznetsov bureau developed a new engine, the NK-86, although it is believed that Soloviev turbofans were in view from the outset, and these have now been adopted in the Il-96 derivative, noted below. Flight development of the Il-86 appears to have proceeded relatively smoothly, and the third aircraft, described as the first production example, flew on 24 October 1977 at Voronezh, where the final assembly line has been set up. A substantial contribution to Il-86 production is made by the Polish aircraft industry, which manufactures the fin and tailplane, engine pylons and wing slats at the PZL Mielec plant. One of the interesting features of the Il-86, and related to the limited support facilities available at many airports served by Aeroflot, is that entry to the cabin is by way of airstairs incorporated in three doors at ground level in the lower fuselage. From the lower deck vestibules, where heavy winter overcoats can be stowed, stairs lead up to the main cabin, making the aircraft independent of airport loading stairs. The type has the NATO reporting name 'Camber'.

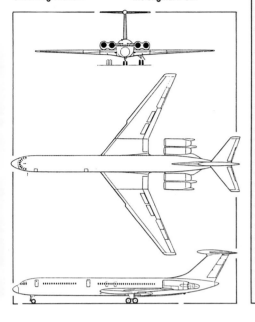

Below left: The national airline of Czechoslovakia, CSA, makes use of 10 Ilyushin Il-62s (illustrated) and Il-62Ms. The 'OK Jet' logo is derived from the Czech registration.

Below: A three-view of the Ilyushin Il-62M, which was the principal version of this four-jet transport produced in the 'seventies. Engine details distinguish it from the original Il-62.

SPECIFICATION
(Il-62M)

Power Plant: Four Soloviev D-30KU turbofans each rated at 24,250lb st (11,000kgp) for take-off, with thrust reversers on outboard engines only. Fuel capacity, 23,162 Imp gal (103,500l) in integral tanks in wing, centre section and fin.
Performance: Max cruising speed, 496kts (920km/h) at 26,245ft (8,000m); long-range cruising speed, 442kts (820km/h) at 36,090ft (11,000m); take-off field length, 10,830ft (3,300m); landing distance, 8,200ft (2,500m); range with max payload, 4,210 naut mls (7,800km); range with 22,046lb (10,000kg) payload, 5,400 naut mls (10,000km).
Weights: Operating weight empty, 157,520lb (71,600kg); max payload, 50,700lb (23,000kg); max take-off weight, 363,760lb (165,000kg); max landing weight, 231,500lb (105,000kg); max zero-fuel weight, 208,550lb (94,600kg).
Dimensions: Span, 141ft 9in (43.20m); overall length, 174ft 3½in (53.12m); overall height, 40ft 6¼in (12.35m); sweepback, 32 deg 30 min at quarter chord; wing area, 3,009sq ft (279.55m²).
Accommodation: Cabin max height, 6ft 11½in (2.12m), max width, 11ft 5¼in (3,49m). Standard aircraft have single-class layouts for 186 passengers, six-abreast, at 34in (86cm) pitch; mixed-class arrangements include four-abreast and five-abreast seating. Four cargo holds have total volume of 1,695cu ft (48.0m³). Flight crew of up to five, comprising two pilots, navigator, radio operator and flight engineer.

change in the wing spoiler control system to permit the spoilers to be used differentially for better roll control. A further variant appeared in 1978 as the Il-62MK, with the same engines as the Il-62M, but with structural, landing gear and control system changes to permit operation at the higher take-off and landing weights of 368,170lb (167,000kg) and 242,500lb (110,000kg) respectively. Maximum accommodation increased to 195, with an interior redesign featuring a 'widebody' look and enclosed overhead baggage lockers. Clamshell-type thrust reversers were used on the D-30KU engines.

SERVICE USE
The Il-62 entered service with Aeroflot on 15 September 1967, on the Moscow-Montreal route, after a period of providing flights within the Soviet Union. It replaced the Tu-114 on the Moscow-New York route in July 1968 and subsequently became standard equipment on most of Aeroflot's long-distance routes, internationally and domestically. The Il-62M entered service on the Moscow-Havana route in 1974. Production of the Il-62 in all versions is thought to exceed 200, of which about 150 have been for Aeroflot, with the balance going to nations in the Soviet sphere of influence, for airline use by CAAC (China), Interflug (East Germany), Balkan Bulgarian, LOT (Poland), Tarom (Romania), CSA (Czechoslovakia), Cubana, LA Mozambique and Choson Minhang (North Vietnam).

SPECIFICATION

Power Plant: Four Kuznetsov NK-86 turbofans each rated at 28,660lb st (13,000kgp) for take-off, with thrust reversers. Fuel capacity, between 15,400 and 17,600 Imp gal (70,000 and 80,000l) in integral tanks.
Performance: Max cruising speed, 512kts (950km/h); long-range cruising speed 485kts (900km/h); normal operating altitude, 29,525 to 36,090ft (9,000 to 11,000m); take-off field length, up to 8,530ft (2,600m); range with 88,185lb (40,000kg) payload, 1,945 naut mls (3,600km); range with max fuel, 2,480 naut mls (4,600km).
Weights: Max payload, 92,600lb (42,000kg); max fuel weight, 189,600lb (86,000kg); max take-off weight, sub-standard runways, 418,875lb (190,000kg); alternative max take-off weight, unrestricted runways, 454,150lb (206,000kg); max landing weight, 385,800lb (175,000kg).
Dimensions: Span, 157ft 8¼in (48.06m); overall length, 195ft 4in (59.54m); overall height, 51ft 10½in (15.81m); sweepback, 35 deg at quarter chord; wing area, 3,444sq ft (320.0m²).
Accommodation: Cabin max width, about 18ft 8½in (5.70m), max height 8ft 7in (2.61m). Basic cabin layout provides up to 350 seats, nine-abreast with two aisles; alternative mixed class layout provides 28 seats six-abreast in front cabin and 206 seats eight-abreast in centre and rear cabins. Lower deck provides access from ground level via airstairs and internal stairways, with stowage for hand baggage and outer coats, plus lower deck cargo holds to accommodate up to 16 standard LDS containers. Flight crew of three (two pilots and flight engineer) plus provision for a navigator if required.

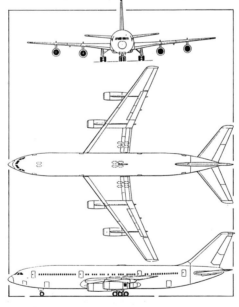

VARIANTS
Since going into production, the Il-86 has undergone routine improvement and updating, in the course of which the gross weight has been increased to a maximum permitted 458,560lb (208,000kg). As early as 1981 reports were appearing that a longer-range derivative of the Il-86 was under development, and by 1986 this was known to have been redesignated Il-96 (also often quoted in the Soviet press as Il-96-300, indicating the number of seats) as described overleaf.

SERVICE USE
The Il-86 entered service on 26 December 1980, operating between Moscow and Tashkent. Many other domestic destinations were added to the Il-86 network during 1981, and the first international service, between Moscow and East Berlin, was flown on 3 July 1981. Between 50 and 80 Il-86s are believed to have been delivered to Aeroflot by early 1987, although Polish sources claim to have delivered 130 sets of Mielec-built components by mid-1985.

Left: The Ilyushin Il-86 appeared in the late 'seventies as the Soviet Union's first 'wide-body' large-capacity transport. Only Aeroflot uses the Il-86, but CSA and LOT are among airlines that may later acquire examples.

Above right: The three-view depicts the Il-86, only one version of which has appeared to date.

Right: A 'fish-eye' view of the nine-abreast seating in the main cabin of the Il-86, with two aisles.

SPECIFICATION

Power Plant: Four high-bypass-ratio turbofans of unspecified type (probably Soloviev) each rated at 35,300lb st (16,000kgp) for take-off, with thrust reversers.

Performance: Maximum cruising speed, 486kts (900km/h) at 39,370ft (12,000m); economical cruising speed, 459kts (850km/h); take-off distance, 10,500ft (3,200m); max operating altitude, 42,650ft (13,000m); range, 4,860 naut mls (9,000km) with 66,150lb (30,000kg) payload, and 4,050 naut mls (7,500km) with 33,070lb (15,000kg) payload.

Weights: Empty equipped weight, 257,940lb (117,000kg); max payload, 88,180lb (40,000kg); max take-off weight, 507,060lb (230,000kg).

Dimensions: Span (excluding winglets), 189ft 2in (57.66m); overall length, 181ft 7in (55.35m); overall height, 57ft 7¾in (17.57m); sweepback, 30 deg at quarter chord; wing area, 3,767sq ft (350.0m²).

Accommodation: Cabin max width, about 18ft 7in (5.66m), max height, 8ft 6½in (2.60m). Typical mixed-class layout for 22 first-class, 40 business-class and 173 tourist-class passengers at 41½-in (102-cm) to 34¼-in (87-cm) pitch; maximum one-class arrangement for 300 passengers, basically nine-abreast in triple seats with two aisles. Underfloor holds with capacity for 16 standard 1,653lb (750kg) containers. Flight crew of three.

The Il-96 (also known as the Il-96-300 in its basic 300-seat form) is an obvious derivative of the Il-86, although described as an almost wholly new design. Compared with its predecessor, the Il-96 has a shorter fuselage, though of the same cross-section, and a wing of greater span and area but reduced sweepback (about 30 deg), with the addition of large winglets at the tips. The wing changes result in modification of the control surfaces, with increased aileron span. New engines, of uncertain origin at the time of writing, will make a major contribution to the expected 27 per cent reduction in fuel consumption compared with that of the Il-86. Structurally, the Il-96 makes use of newer materials to reduce weight, and systems have been modernized, with the introduction of a 'glass' cockpit featuring six displays (three for each pilot) for presentation of all performance and system status information. Equipment is of a standard to allow operation in Cat III weather minima, but modernization has not been taken so far as to allow two-crew operation and a flight engineer's position is retained on the flight deck. The Il-96 is designed for a 60,000-hour/12,000-landing life over a 20-year period.

VARIANTS

At the time of writing there are no known variants of the basic design.

SERVICE USE

The Il-96 is expected to enter flight testing in 1990, as one of the key types on which modernization of Aeroflot is likely to proceed during the 1990s.

Above: This three-view of the Il-96-300 shows both its similarities to and differences from the Il-86. The fuselage has the same cross section and length but the wing is all-new, with greater chord, less sweepback and winglets.

Left: An impression of the Ilyushin Il-96-300, which is expected to enter service with Aeroflot in the early 'nineties.

LET L-410 TURBOLET CZECHOSLOVAKIA

The state-run aircraft manufacturing industry in Czechoslovakia includes three principal factories concerned with aircraft production, each perpetuating the name of one of the (originally privately-owned) companies that built sound reputations between the two world wars. Of these three, the works at Kunovice are named Let National Corporation after the pre-war Let company. After some years of licence-production of Soviet types, the Kunovice works began in 1966 the design and development of a small twin-engined light transport intended to meet the needs of East European nations in general (including the Soviet Union) as well as Czechoslovakia in particular. A high-wing monoplane of conventional appearance, this aircraft emerged as the XL-410 in 1969, making its first flight on 16 April 1969. New turboprop engines under development by Motorlet at the Walter works were not ready, so prototypes and early production aircraft were fitted with imported Pratt & Whitney engines.

Production of the L-410 was at a rate of 8-10 per month in the mid-1980s, and the total requirement was expected to exceed 1,000 aircraft, including several hundred for use in the Soviet Union.

VARIANTS

The initial production version of the Turbolet, as the aircraft came to be known, was the L-410A, with 715shp (533kW) PT6A-27 engines. Thirty-one were built, including four prototypes, one of which later

ILYUSHIN IL-114 SOVIET UNION

Designed to be a successor to the Antonov An-24 on Aeroflot routes with ranges of up to 540 naut mls (1,000km), the Il-114 is one of the three types of Soviet airliner reported to be under development for introduction during the 1990s. The designation appears to be intended to link this new turboprop-twin with the piston-engined Il-14, although there is no real connection between the two types; alternatively, as a design-bureau number, Il-114 may be a sequential allocation. Equipped to operate in weather minima down to ICAO Cat II standard, the Il-114 makes considerable use of composite materials and advanced metal alloys, including titanium, in its structure. It has a striking resemblance, in configuration, size and performance, to the British Aerospace ATP, for the purchase and/or licence manufacture of which the Soviet authorities had shown some interest in the mid-1980s. The engines, whose designation or design bureau remained unrevealed at the time of writing, are likely to be advanced turboprops offering better fuel consumption figure than previous Soviet power plants, and modern-technology propellers are known to be under development for the Il-114 at the PZL-Okecie factory in Poland, with a minimum of six blades. The Polish aircraft industry will also contribute the Il-114's landing gear from the PZL-Krosno works.

VARIANTS

There are as yet no known variants.

SERVICE USE

The Il-114 is likely to enter flight test in 1990.

Right: This provisional three-view drawing of the Ilyushin Il-114 is based on information published in the Soviet Union during 1986. It shows that the new turboprop-twin for Aeroflot has a superficial resemblance to the British Aerospace ATP, which is in the same class in terms of engine power and seating.

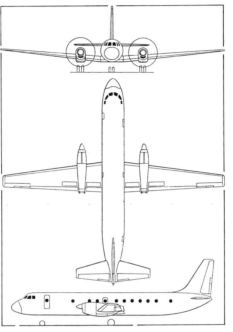

Left: An artist's impression of the Il-114, based on early information. This new product from the Ilyushin design bureau, which is now headed by G. Novozhilov, is expected to make its first flight no later than 1990, and to enter service with Aeroflot in 1991/1992. If successful in meeting its design objectives, the Il-114 is also likely to find a useful export market.

SPECIFICATION

Power Plant: Two turboprops of unspecified type, each rated at 2,465shp (1840kW) for take-off, with advanced-technology six- or eight-blade constant-speed feathering and reversing propellers of 11ft 9¾in (3.60m) diameter.
Performance: Max cruising speed, 270kts (500km/h) at 24,600ft (7,500m); operating altitude, 19,658 to 26,245ft (6,000 to 8,000m); take-off distance, 4,600ft (1,400m) from concrete, or 5,415ft (1,650m) from natural surface; range, 540 naut mls (1,000km) with 11,905lb (5,400kg) payload, or 1,390 naut mls (2,850km) with 7,715lb (3,500kg) payload.
Weights: Empty weight equipped, 28,660lb (13,000kg); max payload, 13,230lb (6,000kg); max take-off weight, 44,645lb (22,250kg).
Dimensions: Span, 98ft 5in (30.00m); overall length, 83ft 6½in (25.46m); overall height, 28ft 2½in (8.60m); sweepback, nil; wing area, 796.6sq ft (74.0m²).
Accommodation: Fuselage outside diameter, 9ft 4½in (2.86m). Standard layout provides 60 seats four-abreast with central aisle, at 29.5in (75cm) seat pitch. Baggage stowage at front and rear, within pressure shell; no underfloor compartments. Flight crew of two and one cabin attendant.

LET L-410 TURBOLET

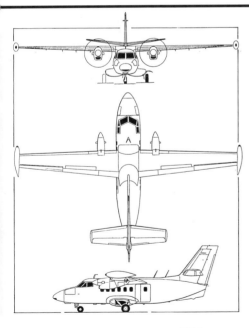

Above left: An early example of the L-410 Turbolet, with Pratt & Whitney PT6A-27 engines. The major production run has made use of the locally-developed Motorlet M601 engine, in several variants of the basic airframe.

Above: The 1986 production version of the Turbolet, was the L-410 UVP-E. The most obvious external feature of this variant was the provision of wing-tip tanks, but a number of internal changes were made to improve economy.

became L-410AB when test-flown with Hartzell four-blade (in place of the original three-blade) propellers. One L-410AF was built (for Hungary) with a revised, glazed, nose compartment and was equipped for the aerial survey role. The L-410AS was equipped with a Soviet avionics fit. In 1973 the Motorlet M 601 engine became available, and the L-410M entered production with the 550shp (410kW) M 601A, soon superseded by the L-410MA with the more powerful M 601B. The L-410MU included equipment specified by Aeroflot, and production of all 'M' variants totalled 110. To overcome Soviet criticism of handling characteristics, the L-410UVP, first flown on 1 November 1977, introduced increased wing span and vertical tail area, dihedral on the tailplane, spoilers, automatic bank-control flaps and numerous other systems and equipment changes. Soviet certification of the L-410UVP was obtained in 1980. Generally similar to this variant, the L-410UVP-E first flew in late 1984 and introduced five-blade propellers, tip tanks and more powerful engines.

SERVICE USE

The L-410A entered service on Czech domestic routes operated by Slov-Air in late 1971. The L-410 began deliveries in 1976, followed by the L-410 UVP after certification in 1979. Aeroflot took delivery of its 500th L-410 in March 1985, at which time about 80-100 more had been built for other operators, including some as military transports by the air forces of Czechoslovakia and East Germany. An aerial survey version has also been developed.

SPECIFICATION
(L-410 UVP)

Power Plant: Two Motorlet (Walter) M 601 B turboprops each rated at 730shp (554kW) for take-off, with Avia V 508 three-blade constant-speed fully-feathering and reversing propellers of 8ft 2½in (2.50m) diameter. Fuel capacity, 284 Imp gal (1,290l) in bag tanks in wings.
Performance: Max cruising speed, 197kts (365km/h) at 9,845ft (3,000m); economical cruising speed, 162kts (300km/h); initial rate of climb, 1,495ft/min (7.75m/sec); max operating altitude, 19,685ft (6,000m); take-off distance (Soviet NLGS-2 certification), 3,115ft (950m); landing distance from 30ft (9m), 2,655ft (810m); range with max payload and 30-minute fuel reserve, 210 naut mls (390km); range with max fuel, 1,874lb/850kg payload and 30-minute fuel reserve, 561 naut mls (1,040km).
Weights: Empty weight, equipped, 8,378lb (3,800kg); max fuel weight, 2,205lb (1,000kg); max payload, 2,888lb (1,310kg); max take-off weight, 12,786lb (5,800kg); max landing weight, 12,125lb (5,500kg); max zero-fuel weight, 11,398lb (5,170kg).
Dimensions: Span, 63ft 10¾in (19.48m); overall length, 47ft 5½in (14.47m); overall height, 19ft 1½in (5.83m); sweepback, nil on front spar; wing area, 378.67sq ft (35.18m²).
Accommodation: Cabin length, 20ft 9½in (6.34m), max width, 6ft 4¾in (1.95m), max height, 5ft 5¼in (1.66m). Standard layout provides 15 seats, in a three-abreast (2+1) arrangement, at 30in (76cm) pitch. Rear baggage compartment, volume 27.2cu ft (0.77m³). Flight crew of two, with provision for single-pilot operation.

LET L-610 CZECHOSLOVAKIA

The Let National Corporation began development of the L-610 in the mid-1980s primarily in response to a Soviet specification for a regional airliner with about 40 seats to operate over stage lengths of about 216-324 naut mls (400-600km). Similar in configuration to the L-410 and resembling an enlarged derivative of that type, the L-610 is in fact an entirely new design, for which Vlastimil Mertl is responsible as chief designer at Kunovice. Using new, more powerful engines from the Motorlet works in Prague, the L-610 introduces a pressurized cabin, allowing the aircraft to cruise at higher altitudes, giving a 7,875ft (2,400m) equivalent at 23,620ft (7,200m). An auxiliary power unit has been installed in the rear fuselage to provide ground operation of the systems, and to serve as an emergency hydraulic and electric power source in the air. The high wing is a two-spar structure and has integral tanks, whereas the L-410 has bag tanks. A change of configuration puts the fixed-incidence, three-spar tailplane high on the fin, which is built integrally with the unpressurized portion of the rear fuselage. Operation of the flight controls is classically conventional, with no power boosting, using push-pull rods; the rudder is spring loaded, and twin tabs are incorporated in the elevators. The wing incorporates single-slotted flaps and spoilers, the latter, which are used also as lift dumpers during the landing run, being automatically activated with manual override. The duplicated hydraulic system operates the flaps, spoilers, landing gear, brakes, nosewheel steering and windscreen wipers. Wing, tail and intake de-icing are all pneumatic, with electric anticing for the windscreen, pitot head and propellers. The L-610 is equipped to operate in Cat I weather minima in the first instance, with provision for upgrading to Cat II, and for the installation of an electronic flight instrument system (EFIS). The new M 602 engine used in the L-610 is a three-shaft unit with a two-stage axial compressor and a two-stage free turbine. Cruising at 23,620ft (7,200m), the M 602 has an output of 938shp (700kW), in which conditions the specific fuel consumption is 0.975lb/shp (0.33kg/kW).

VARIANTS

There are as yet no variants of the L-610.

SERVICE USE

The L-610 was under development in 1986 with a view to first flight of the prototype being made by early 1988. This will allow for a two-year development and certification period, leading to introduction into service in 1990. Initial service use is expected to be in the hands of Aeroflot, for which development of the L-610 has been primarily undertaken. The Czech state airline CSA and its domestic-operating associate Slov-Air are likely to operate the L-610, and other airlines in the East European bloc will be primary prospects for other export sales.

SPECIFICATION

Power Plant: Two Motorlet (Walter) M 602 turboprops each rated at 1,822shp (1,360kW) for take-off and 896shp (1,200kW) maximum cruise, with Avia V518 five-blade constant-speed fully-feathering and reversing propellers of 11ft 6in (3.5m) diameter. Fuel capacity, 770 Imp gal (3,500l) in integral tanks in the wing.
Performance: Max cruising speed, 265kts (490km/h); economical cruising speed, 216kts (400km/h); cruising altitude, 23,620ft (7,200m); take-off field length, 2,870ft (875m) from concrete or 3,380ft (1,030m) from grass; range with max passenger payload and 45-minute fuel reserve 656 naut mls (1,216km); range with max fuel, 1,295 naut mls (2,400km).
Weights: Operating weight empty, 19,840lb (9,000kg); max fuel weight, 5,842lb (2,650kg); max payload, 7,936-8,377lb (3,600-3,800kg); max take-off weight, 30,864lb (14,000kg); max landing weight, 29,762lb (13,500kg); max zero-fuel weight, 28,220lb (12,800kg).
Dimensions: Span, 84ft 0in (25.60m); overall length, 70ft 2½in (21.40m); overall height, 24ft 11½in (7.60m); sweepback, nil; wing area, 602.8sq ft (56.0m²).
Accommodation: Cabin floor width, 6ft 7½in (2.02m), cabin max height, 6ft 0in (1.83m). Standard layout provides 40 seats, four-abreast with central aisle, at 29.5in (75cm) seat pitch; optional mixed cargo/passenger or all-cargo arrangements possible. Baggage compartment, volume, 151.85cu ft (4.3m³). Flight crew of two.

LOCKHEED ELECTRA USA

The trigger for initial design activity by Lockheed's Burbank, California, company was a 1954 specification produced by American Airlines for a short/medium-range transport to operate on its US domestic routes. The specification indicated that turboprop engines were preferred, but the passenger capacity was greater than could be carried in the Vickers Viscount, which was emerging at that time as the world's foremost turboprop transport. Initial attempts (by Lockheed and Vickers amongst others) were unsuccessful in satisfying American Airlines, but a revision of the requirement in 1955 allowed Lockheed to amend its L-188 project and to obtain, in June of that year, launch orders from American and Eastern Airlines for a combined total of 75 aircraft. Broadly, the design was for a 100-seater with a range of some 2,000 naut mls (3,700km), grossing about 110,000lb (49,900kg). It was the first US-originating airliner to feature turboprop power, and was destined to be the only such aircraft to achieve production status in the USA. The first of four prototype/flight test Electras flew on 6 December 1957 and the fifth, which was to be the first delivered for airline service, flew on 19 May 1958. Orders for the Electra quickly accumulated in the period between launch and entry into service, when the turboprop engine still appeared to offer marked advantages over the turbojet on medium ranges. But experience was soon to show that turbojet types could compete effectively over the stage lengths for which the Electra was destined, and the market for both the Lockheed product and its primary competitor, the Vickers Vanguard, evaporated. Confidence in the Electra was also shaken, within the first 15 months of airline service, by two fatal accidents that occurred in similar circumstances and were found, after painstaking research, to be attributable to structural failures occuring in an unforeseen chain reaction after damage to the power plant mounting that could be caused, for example, by a heavy landing. A major structural modification programme was put in hand by Lockheed after all Electras had been made the subject of

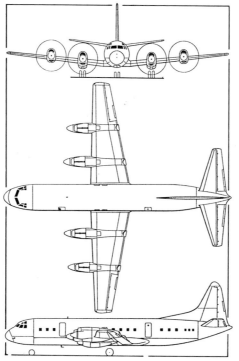

Above: The Lockheed Electra appeared in only one version, so far as external appearance was concerned, and as depicted in this three-view. Some aircraft now have a cargo door.

Right: Canadian operator Nordair, based in Quebec, has two Electras in its fleet to fly ice-reconnaissance patrols under contract to the government.

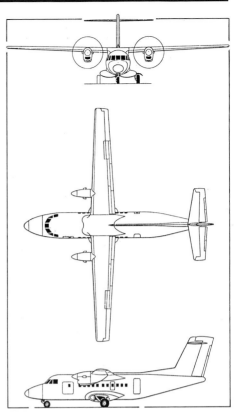

Above: Building on the success it has achieved with the L-410, the LET National Corporation at Kunovice is developing the larger L-610, with first flight expected early in 1988.

This artist's impression of the L-610 shows that it has the same overall configuration as the L-410, although it is larger, with a maximum seating capacity of 40 passengers.

Right: As this three-view drawing of the L-610 shows, all the principal features of the L-410 have been carried forward into the new design with the exception of the tailplane, which is mounted high on the fin of the L-610. Single-slotted flaps are used on the wing, but there are no leading-edge devices to contribute to the aircraft's field performance.

LOCKHEED ELECTRA

Left: Many Electras have now been modified for cargo-carrying, with a large side-loading door and reinforced floor. The largest fleet of Electras in 1986 was operated by the scheduled and charter cargo airline Zantop with 21 in service.

strict flight limitation by the FAA in March 1960, and a modified aircraft obtained an unrestricted certificate of airworthiness from the FAA on 5 January 1961. Electras have flown since that time without any recurrence of the problem.

VARIANTS
The initial production version of the Electra was the L-188A, described above. For customers requiring greater range (initially Northwest and Western) the L-188C provided extra fuel capacity and operated at higher weights. As a post-production modification, Lockheed Aircraft Service Co. (LAS) developed a cargo door for installation in the port side of the fuselage ahead of the wing, together with appropri-

ate cargo-carrying features in the cabin. Maximum zero-fuel weight was increased, in this conversion, to 90,000lb (40,823kg).

SERVICE USE
The L-188A obtained FAA certification on 22 August 1958 and entered service with Eastern Airlines on 12 January 1959, followed by American Airlines on 23 January 1959. Ansett-ANA in Australia was the first non-US airline to operate the type, in March 1959. Production, which ended in 1962, totalled 170, of which 55 were of the L-188C variant. By 1987, the number remaining in service had dwindled to below 80, almost wholly in North and South America, and many for cargo services.

SPECIFICATION
(L-188A Electra)

Power Plant: Four Allison 501D-13 turboprops each rated at 3,750shp (2,800kW) for take-off, or 501D-15 turboprops each rated at 4,050shp (3,022kW) for take-off, with Aeroproducts or Hamilton Standard four-blade reversing and feathering propellers of 13ft 6in (4.11m) diameter. Fuel capacity, 4,596 Imp gal (20,895l) in integral wing tanks; provision for additional tankage of 833 Imp gal (3,785l) in L-188C.
Performance: Max operating speed, 324kts (600km/h) IAS or Mach = 0.615; max cruising speed 352kts (652km/h) at 22,000ft (6,700m) at average weight; best economy cruising speed, 325kts (602km/h); initial rate of climb, 1,670ft/min (8.5m/sec); service ceiling, 27,000ft (8,230m); take-off field length, 4,720ft (1,440m); landing field length, 4,300ft (1,310m); range with max payload, 1,910 naut mls (3,540km); range with max fuel, 2,180 naut mls (4,040km).
Weights: Typical operating weight empty, 61,500lb (27,895kg); max fuel weight, 37,500lb (17,010kg); max payload, 26,500lb (12,020kg); max take-off weight, 116,000lb (52,664kg); max landing weight, 95,650lb (43,385kg); max zero-fuel weight, 86,000lb (39,010kg).
Dimensions: Span, 99ft 0in (30.18m); overall length, 104ft 6in (31.81m); overall height, 32ft 10in (10.0m); sweepback, nil; wing area, 1,300sq ft (120.8m^2).
Accommodation: Cabin length, 76ft 5in (23.29m), max width, 10ft 6in (3.20m), max height, 7ft 0½in (2.15m). Typical mixed-class layout provides 16 first-class seats four-abreast and 51 tourist-class seats five-abreast, all at 38in (96.5cm) pitch; alternative one-class layouts provide for 85 five-abreast or 98 six-abreast at 38in (96.5cm) pitch. Underfloor baggage/cargo holds, total volume 528cu ft (14.95m^3). Flight crew of three.

LOCKHEED TRISTAR USA

SPECIFICATION
(L-1011-500)

Power Plant: Three Rolls-Royce RB.211-524B4 turbofans each rated at 50,000lb st (22,680kgp) for take-off, and fitted with thrust-reversers. Fuel capacity, 26,347 Imp gal (119,774l) in integral wing and centre-section tanks.

Performance: Max operating speed, 375kts (695km/h) IAS or Mach=0.90; max cruising speed, 518kts (959km/h) at mid-cruise weight at 33,000ft (10,060m); economical cruising 483kts (895km/h) at mid-cruise weight at 33,000ft (10,060m); initial rate of climb, 2,820ft/min (14.3m/sec); service ceiling, 43,000ft (13,100m); take-off field length, 9,200ft (2,800m); landing field length, 6,770ft (2,065m); range with max passenger payload, 5,345 naut mls (9,905km); range with max fuel, 6,090 naut mls (11,286km).

Weights: Operating weight empty, 245,400lb (111,312kg); max payload, 92,253lb (41,845kg); max take-off weight, 510,000lb (231,330kg); max landing weight, 368,000lb (166,920kg); max zero-fuel weight, 338,000lb (153,315kg).

Dimensions: Span, 164ft 4in (50.09m); overall length, 164ft 2½in (50.05m); overall height, 55ft 4in (16.87m); sweepback, 35 deg at quarter chord; wing area, 3,541sq ft (329.0m²).

Accommodation: Cabin length, 122ft 5in (37.31m), max width, 18ft 11in (5.77m), max height, 7ft 11in (2.41m). Typical mixed-class layout for 24 first-class seats, six-abreast, and 222 tourist-class seats nine-abreast; maximum 330 passengers 10-abreast at 30/33in (76/83cm) pitch. Baggage/cargo underfloor holds, total volume, 4,200cu ft (118.9m³). Flight crew of three.

market projections and production was ended by Lockheed in 1984, leaving the company without a commercial jet transport programme.

VARIANTS

The original TriStar, with a fuselage length of 177ft 8½in (54.17m) and up to 400 seats, was the L-1011-1, with a gross weight of 430,000lb (195,045kg). This was followed in 1974 by the L-1011-200 with RB.211-524 engines rated at 48,000-50,000lb st (21,772-22,680kgp) and maximum take-off weight of up to 477,000lb (216,363kg) depending on fuel capacity. With the same higher operating weights and increased fuel capacities but the lower-rated -22B engines the aircraft was designated L-1011-100. The first flight of a TriStar with -524 engines was made on 12 August 1976. In 1976 Lockheed launched the L-1011-500, which combined higher weights and enlarged fuel capacity with a shorter fuselage (see data panel) to achieve very long ranges. Advanced aerodynamic features were also introduced in the L-1011-500, including active controls, resulting in a 9ft (2.74m) increase in wing span and a reduction in tailplane area. The first L-1011-500 flew in October 1978, with 50,000lb st (22,700kgp) -524B engines but without the extended wingtips, which were first flown in November 1979. The designation L-1011-250 applies to conversions of the L-1011-1 to have the same -524B4 engines as used in the L-1011-500, allowing maximum take-off weight to be increased to 496,000lb (224,985kg). Fuel capacity is also increased. Conversion of six L-1011-1s to -250 standard for Delta Airlines began in 1986.

SERVICE USE

The L-1011-1 was certificated on 14 April 1972, and Eastern Airlines flew the first revenue service on 26 April, with TWA flying its first service on 25 June 1972. The L-1011-200 was certificated on 26 April 1977 and entered service with Saudia. The L-1011-500 entered service with British Airways on 7 May 1979, and with extended wings and active controls, was introduced by Pan American in 1980. Production of the TriStar totalled 250, including a small number built as stock and still unsold in 1986, when some 230 remained in service.

L
ike the Electra, Lockheed's TriStar owes its origins to an American Airlines specification – but contrary to the case of the Electra, this airline did not in the end become a launch customer for the Lockheed jetliner. The 1966 specification was for a short/medium-range large-capacity transport, and to meet it Lockheed and Douglas produced very similar project designs, the most notable feature of which was the combination of podded engines on the wing with a third at the rear of the aircraft. Lockheed obtained launch orders for its L-1011 design on 29 March 1968, from TWA and Eastern Airlines, after American had opted for the Douglas competitor. From the big new turbofan engines offered by Pratt & Whitney, General Electric and Rolls-Royce, Lockheed chose – with the full approval of its initial customers – the RB.211, a decision that committed Rolls-Royce to a programme of development and production that led it into bankruptcy in February 1971, placing not only the TriStar but the whole of the Lockheed company in jeopardy. The first L-1011 had flown, meanwhile, on 17 November 1970, with four more required for the certification programme following by 2 December 1971. With the future of Rolls-Royce assured through its nationalization, Lockheed was able to proceed with the TriStar, using the RB.211-22 at its initial rating of 42,000lb st (19,050kgp), the first flight with engines of this standard being made on 8 September 1971. Production and development proceeded throughout the 1970s, but sales of the TriStar failed to match

Lockheed TriStar 500 Cutaway Drawing Key

1 Radome
2 VOR localiser aerial
3 Radar scanner dish
4 ILS glideslope aerial
5 Front pressure bulkhead
6 Curved windscreen panels
7 Windscreen wipers
8 Instrument panel shroud
9 Rudder pedals
10 Cockpit floor level
11 Ventral access door
12 Forward underfloor radio and electronics bay
13 Pitot tubes
14 Observer's seat
15 Captain's seat
16 First officer's seat
17 Overhead panel
18 Flight engineer's station
19 Cockpit roof escape hatch
20 Air conditioning ducting
21 Forward galley units
22 Starboard service door
23 Forward toilet compartments
24 Curtained cabin divider
25 Wardrobe
26 Forward passenger door
27 Cabin attendant's folding seat
28 Nose undercarriage wheel bay
29 Ram air intake
30 Heat exchanger
31 Nose undercarriage leg strut
32 Twin nosewheels
33 Steering jacks
34 Nosewheel doors
35 Air conditioning plant, port and starboard
36 Cabin window panel
37 Six-abreast first class seating, 24 seats
38 Forward underfloor freight hold
39 Forward freight door
40 VHF aerial
41 Curtained cabin divider
42 Overhead stowage bins
43 Nine-abreast tourist class seating, 222 seats
44 Baggage/freight containers, twelve LD3 containers forward
45 Fuselage frame and stringer construction
46 Wing root fillet
47 Taxying lamp
48 Bleed air system ducting
49 Escape chute and life raft stowage
50 Mid-section entry door
51 Centre section galley units
52 Fuselage centre section construction
53 Wing centre section carry-through structure
54 Dry bay
55 Centre section fuel tanks, capacity 6,711 Imp gal (30,510l)
56 Floor beam construction
57 Fuselage/front spar attachment main frame
58 Anti-collision lights
59 Starboard inboard fuel tank bay, capacity 6,649 Imp gal (30,226l)
60 Thrust reverser cascade, open
61 Starboard engine nacelle
62 Nacelle pylon
63 Fixed portion of leading edge
64 Fuel surge box and boost pump reservoir
65 Fuel system piping
66 Outboard fuel tank bay, capacity 3,169 Imp gal (14,407l)
67 Pressure refuelling connections
68 Screw jack drive shaft
69 Slat screw jacks
70 Leading-edge slat segments, open
71 Extended wing tip fairing
72 Starboard navigation light
73 Wing tip strobe light
74 Static dischargers
75 Starboard 'active control' aileron
76 Aileron hydraulic jacks
77 Fuel jettison pipe
78 Outboard spoilers
79 Outboard spoilers/speedbrakes
80 Flap screw jacks
81 Flap track fairings
82 Outboard double slotted flap, down
83 Inboard aileron

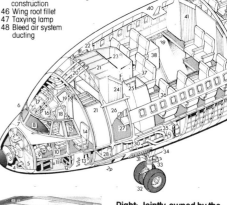

Above: As one of the first 'wide-body' airliners in service, the Lockheed TriStar offered some innovative cabin ideas when it was introduced. A nine-abreast twin-aisle arrangement is shown.

Right: Jointly-owned by the states of Bahrain, Qatar, Oman and the United Arab Emirates, Gulf Air has been a TriStar operator since 1973, having in its fleet examples of the L-1011-1 and L-1011-100, as well as eight Rolls-Royce-engined L-1011-200s, as illustrated. A white finish and bright colours are in keeping with Gulf Air's sunny location.

Below: One of the last airlines to order new TriStars from Lockheed before production ended in 1984 was TAP Air Portugal, which had five of the long-range L-1011-500 version in service in 1986.

AIR PORTUGAL

CS-TEE

L1011

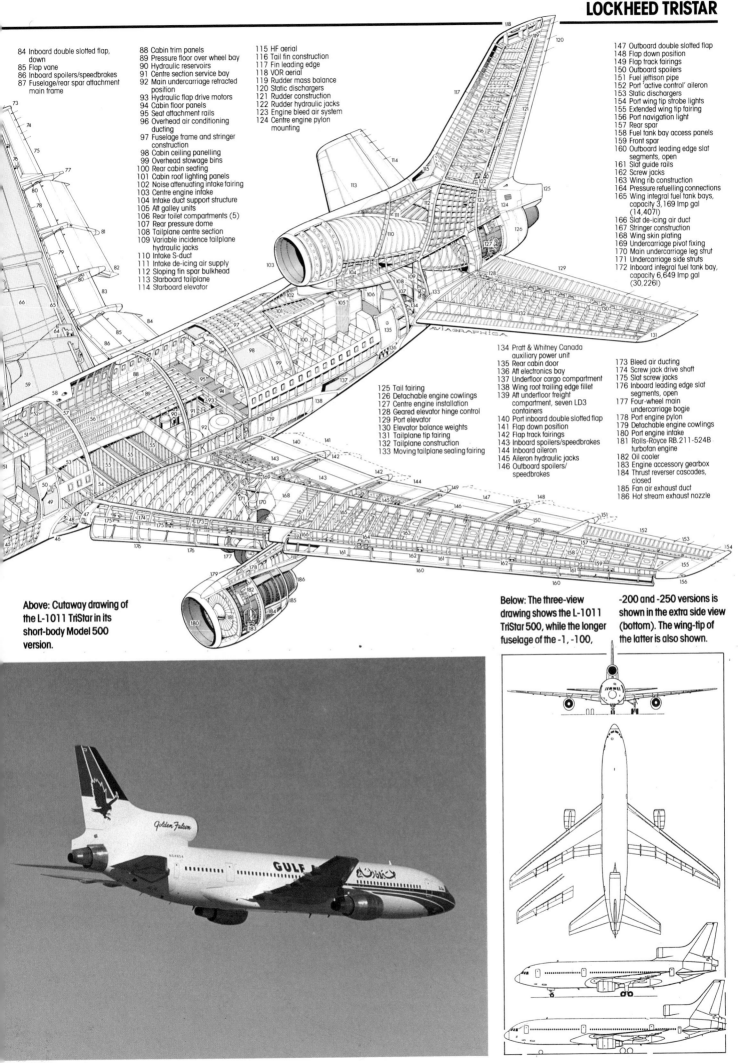

84 Inboard double slotted flap, down
85 Flap vane
86 Inboard spoilers/speedbrakes
87 Fuselage/rear spar attachment main frame
88 Cabin trim panels
89 Pressure floor over wheel bay
90 Hydraulic reservoirs
91 Centre section service bay
92 Main undercarriage retracted position
93 Hydraulic flap drive motors
94 Cabin floor panels
95 Seat attachment rails
96 Overhead air conditioning ducting
97 Fuselage frame and stringer construction
98 Cabin ceiling panelling
99 Overhead stowage bins
100 Rear cabin seating
101 Cabin roof lighting panels
102 Noise attenuating intake fairing
103 Centre engine intake
104 Intake duct support structure
105 Aft galley units
106 Rear toilet compartments (5)
107 Rear pressure dome
108 Tailplane centre section
109 Variable incidence tailplane hydraulic jacks
110 Intake S-duct
111 Intake de-icing air supply
112 Sloping fin spar bulkhead
113 Starboard tailplane
114 Starboard elevator
115 HF aerial
116 Tail fin construction
117 Fin leading edge
118 VOR aerial
119 Rudder mass balance
120 Static dischargers
121 Rudder construction
122 Rudder hydraulic jacks
123 Engine bleed air system
124 Centre engine pylon mounting

125 Tail fairing
126 Detachable engine cowlings
127 Centre engine installation
128 Geared elevator hinge control
129 Port elevator
130 Elevator balance weights
131 Tailplane tip fairing
132 Tailplane construction
133 Moving tailplane sealing fairing

134 Pratt & Whitney Canada auxiliary power unit
135 Rear cabin door
136 Aft electronics bay
137 Underfloor cargo compartment
138 Wing root trailing edge fillet
139 Aft underfloor freight compartment, seven LD3 containers
140 Port inboard double slotted flap
141 Flap down position
142 Flap track fairings
143 Inboard spoilers/speedbrakes
144 Inboard aileron
145 Aileron hydraulic jacks
146 Outboard spoilers/speedbrakes

147 Outboard double slotted flap
148 Flap down position
149 Flap track fairings
150 Outboard spoilers
151 Fuel jettison pipe
152 Port 'active control' aileron
153 Static dischargers
154 Port wing tip strobe lights
155 Extended wing tip fairing
156 Port navigation light
157 Rear spar
158 Fuel tank bay access panels
159 Front spar
160 Outboard leading edge slat segments, open
161 Slat guide rails
162 Screw jacks
163 Wing rib construction
164 Pressure refuelling connections
165 Wing integral fuel tank bays, capacity 3,169 Imp gal (14,407l)
166 Slat de-icing air duct
167 Stringer construction
168 Wing skin plating
169 Undercarriage pivot fixing
170 Main undercarriage leg strut
171 Undercarriage side struts
172 Inboard integral fuel tank bay, capacity 6,649 Imp gal (30,226l)

173 Bleed air ducting
174 Screw jack drive shaft
175 Slat screw jacks
176 Inboard leading edge slat segments, open
177 Four-wheel main undercarriage bogie
178 Port engine pylon
179 Detachable engine cowlings
180 Port engine intake
181 Rolls-Royce RB.211-524B turbofan engine
182 Oil cooler
183 Engine accessory gearbox
184 Thrust reverser cascades, closed
185 Fan air exhaust duct
186 Hot stream exhaust nozzle

Above: Cutaway drawing of the L-1011 TriStar in its short-body Model 500 version.

Below: The three-view drawing shows the L-1011 TriStar 500, while the longer fuselage of the -1, -100, -200 and -250 versions is shown in the extra side view (bottom). The wing-tip of the latter is also shown.

MARTIN 4-0-4 USA

SPECIFICATION

Power Plant: Two Pratt & Whitney R-2800-CB-16 Double Wasp air-cooled two-row radial piston engines each rated at 2,400hp (1,791kW) for take-off, with Hamilton Standard Hydromatic three-blade fully-feathering and reversing constant-speed propellers of 13ft 1in (3.99m) diameter. Fuel capacity, 1,345 US gal (5,091l) in bag tanks between spars in outer wing panels.

Performance: Max cruising speed, 271kts (502km/h) at 14,500ft (4,420m); typical cruising speed, 240kts (444km/h) at 16,000ft (4,877m); initial rate of climb, 1,905ft/min (9.6m/sec); service ceiling, 29,000ft (8,845m); take-off balanced field length, 4,360ft (1,330m); landing field length, 4,100ft (1,250m); range with max payload and representative reserves, 270 naut mls (499km); range with max fuel, 930 naut mls (1,722km).

Weights: Typical operating weight empty, 31,100lb (14,107kg); fuel weight, 8,070lb (3,660kg); max payload, 9,900lb (4,491kg); max take-off weight, 44,900lb (20,385kg); max landing weight, 43,000lb (19,522kg); max zero-fuel weight, 41,000lb (18,598kg).

Dimensions: Span, 93ft 3½in (28.44m); overall length, 74ft 7in (22.75m); overall height, 28ft 2in (8.61m); sweepback, nil; wing area, 864sq ft (79.89m²).

Accommodation: Cabin length, 37ft 11in (11.56m), max width, 9ft 2in (2.79m), max height, 6ft 5½in (1.97m). Typical layouts for 40 passengers four-abreast with a central aisle at seat pitch of 40 in (102cm), or 48 or 52 passengers in high-density layouts. Underfloor hold volume, 107cu ft (3.03m³) plus two above-floor holds with combined capacity, 237cu ft (6.7m³). Flight crew of two or three.

Turning from its military activities in World War II and seeking to re-establish its pre-war reputation as a manufacturer of commercial aircraft, the Glenn L Martin Co of Baltimore, Maryland, announced in November 1945 its plan to produce a twin-engined 40-seat transport of modern design, offering a substantial performance advance over the pre-war types such as the Douglas DC-3 and Curtiss CW-20 (C-46) on which the world's airlines were heavily dependent. The US domestic airlines made up the market of most immediate interest to Martin (as it did also to Convair, whose Model 240 was a direct competitor), and early success in meeting the needs of this market appeared to have been achieved when Martin recorded orders for its Model 2-0-2 (as the new design was styled) from Eastern Air Lines for 50, Northwest for 40, Pen-Central for 35, Colonial for 20, TWA for 12 and smaller quantities for several other operators. Powered by 2,400hp (1,790kW) Double Wasp R-2800-CA18 engines, the first 2-0-2 flew on 23 November 1946 and was a conventional low-wing monoplane of stressed-skin light-alloy construction, having an unpressurized fuselage and a relatively high aspect ratio (10.0:1) wing that was notable for its considerable dihedral angle and large double-slotted flaps. Featuring tricycle landing gear, the 2-0-2 had several design innovations aimed at the needs of airlines with short stage lengths and quick turnarounds. In particular, passenger access to the cabin was by way of a ventral airstair under the tail so that engines could remain at ground idle during short stops; a door in the front fuselage side was intended for galley and cabin servicing, but not for passenger use. Service

use of the 2-0-2 began less than a year after the first flight (as noted below) but early production delays were encountered by the company and the 2-0-2's reputation suffered a blow in 1948 when an accident was attributed to structural failure in the wing, and the type was grounded for remedial action, returning to service only in 1950 after modification to 2-0-2A standard.

VARIANTS

The Martin 2-0-2A introduced a number of product improvements found desirable in the light of early operational experience with the 2-0-2, in addition to structural strengthening necessary to obtain approval for the type to be used in commercial service after the 1948 grounding of the 2-0-2. The second 2-0-2 served as the vehicle for development of the 2-0-2A, and first flew as such in July 1950. On 20 June 1947, a Martin 3-0-3 prototype was flown, this being in effect a pressurized version of the 2-0-2, but the difficulties encountered with the original model led to the cancellation of production plans for the 3-0-3. Instead, Martin proceeded to develop a more-extensively modified and improved variant as the 4-0-4, whose first flight was made on 21 October 1950. A little larger than the 2-0-2, the Martin 4-0-4 was ordered by Eastern and TWA, and of just over 100 built a handful remained in service in 1987, demonstrating a longevity that made up for the early setbacks suffered by the type's progenitor.

SERVICE USE

The Martin 2-0-2 was awarded its US Approved Type Certificate (ATC No. 795) on 13 August 1947, nine

McDONNELL DOUGLAS DC-9 USA

Douglas project studies in the early 1950s for an aircraft to complement the then recently-launched DC-8 concentrated upon a scaled-down version of that type to operate over medium ranges. Intensive market studies over a period of several years led the company to extend the time-scale for the launch of this new type, and to initiate a wholly original design rather than attempt to use DC-8 components. As the DC-9, the new jetliner was firmed up in 1963 and was formally launched on 8 April of that year as a short/medium range aircraft with about 75 seats in typical mixed-class arrangement. In configuration the DC-9 closely resembled the BAC One-Eleven, with rear-mounted engines and a T-tail. Delta Air Lines became the launch airline with an order for 15, and the first of five aircraft for the certification programme flew on 25 February 1965. From the outset, Douglas planned to offer a variety of fuselage lengths and fuel capacities, with appropriate engine powers and operating weights, and this policy has helped to keep the DC-9 in production for more than 22 years, with the very latest variants designated as the MD-80 series (treated seperately) and yet more derivatives still in prospect in the MD-90 series.

VARIANTS

With 12,000lb st (5,443kgp) Pratt & Whitney JT8D-5 engines, the DC-9 Srs 10 had an overall length of 104ft 4¾in (31.82m) and up to 90 seats. The DC-9 Srs 20 was similar with more powerful JT8D-9 or -11 engines and the increased wing span of the Srs 30 with full-span leading-edge slats, for 'hot and high' performance. It first flew on 18 September 1968, preceded by the first DC-9 Srs 30 on 1 August 1966, with fuselage lengthened by 14ft 11in (4.6m) to seat up to 115 passengers. To meet the needs of SAS, the Srs 30 was further evolved in the mid-1960s to produce the DC-9 Srs 40 with another stretch of 6ft 4in (1.87m)

and up to 125 seats. This version first flew on 28 November 1967. Yet another fuselage stretch was announced in July 1973 when Swissair ordered the DC-9 Srs 50, longer than the Srs 40 by 6ft 4in (1.87m) at an overall length of 133ft 7½in (40.72m). The Srs 50 introduced the uprated -15 or -17 versions of the JT8D engine and several other engineering improvements, these engines later becoming options for the Srs 30 and 40. With a forward port-side freight loading door and appropriate cabin arrangements, convertible (C) or all-freight (F) versions of the DC-9 Srs 10 and Srs 30 have also been delivered. The final DC-9 variant emerged in 1979 as the Super 80 but was subsequently redesignated McDonnell Douglas MD-80 and is separately described as such.

Below: Longest of the DC-9 family is the Series 50, this example being in the colourful livery of BWIA, the airline of Trinidad and Tobago.

SERVICE USE

The DC-9 Srs 10 was approved by the FAA on 23 November 1965 and entered service with Delta Air Lines on 8 December. The DC-9 Srs 30 was certificated on 19 December 1966 and entered service with Eastern Airlines in early 1967. The DC-9 Srs 20 was bought only by SAS, entering service on 27 January 1969, and SAS was also first to use the DC-9 Srs 40, starting on 12 March 1968 after certification on 27 February. The DC-9 Srs 50 gained FAA approval in 1975, to enter service with Swissair on 24 August of that year. Continental Airlines was the first to receive the convertible DC-9C Srs 10 on 7 March 1966; Overseas National received the first convertible Srs 30 in October 1967 and Alitalia accepted the first all-cargo DC-9 Srs 30 on 13 May 1968. Production of all DC-9 variants up to and including the Srs 50 totalled 976 (including 43 for military customers); of these, all but about 100 remain in service in 1987.

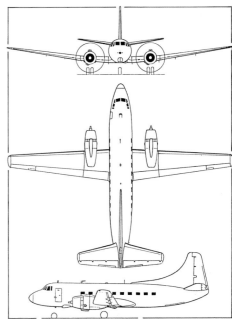

months after first flight, and flew its first revenue service in October 1947 with LAN Chile, the first US operator, Northwest, following in November. After modification, the first 2-0-2A entered service with TWA on 1 September 1950, and this same airline put the 4-0-4 into service on 5 October 1951. Martin built 43 of the Model 2-0-2s and 103 of the Model 4-0-4s. About a dozen of the latter were still in revenue airline service in 1987.

Above: Users of the few remaining Martin 4-0-4 piston-engined transports could be counted on the fingers (and thumb) of one hand in 1986, all of them in North or South America. These aircraft tended to change hands rapidly

between smaller airlines that found low first cost and running costs advantageous in markets where more modern types did not represent a competitive threat. The Martin 4-0-4s are more than 35 years old.

Above: The three-view drawing depicts the Martin 4-0-4, which was built only in this single version, just over 100 being produced by the Glenn L Martin Company at Baltimore. Developed from the Martin 2-0-2, which was

generally similar but a little smaller in overall dimensions, the 4-0-4 was the last airliner designed and built by the Martin company, which was one of the first to suffer the effects of the post-war rundown in the USA.

McDONNELL DOUGLAS DC-9

Below: The three-view drawing depicts the DC-9 in its Series 50 form, which entered service with Swissair in 1975. This version was the result of progressive development of the basic aircraft, which first flew in February 1965. Steps in this evolution are shown in the drawings (below right), depicting from top to bottom the original Srs 10 and 20; the Srs 30; the Srs 30CF and military C-9A with cargo door; the Srs 40, the Srs 50 and the Srs 80, now the MD-80 (next page).

Left: The flight deck of the DC-9 in its Srs 50 form. Progressive updating has kept the DC-9 abreast of state-of-the-art improvements in flight deck design and equipment, but as this

photo shows, the Srs 50 still relied solely on clock-style instruments for the presentation of flight, engine and systems information. CRT displays and 'glass' cockpits arrived with the MD-80.

SPECIFICATION
(DC-9 Srs 30)

Power Plant: Two Pratt & Whitney JT8D-9, -11, -15 or -17 turbofans each rated at 14,500lb st (6,580kgp), 15,000lb st (6,800kgp), 15,500lb st (7,030kgp) or 16,000lb st (7,257kgp) respectively for take-off, with target-type thrust-reversers. Fuel capacity, 3,063 Imp gal (13,925l) in integral wing tanks.
Performance: Max operating speed, 350kts (648km/h) IAS or Mach=0.84; max cruising speed, 490kts (907km/h) at 25,000ft (7,620m); long-range cruising speed, 431kts (798km/h) at 35,000ft (10,670m); initial rate of climb, 2,900ft/min (14.7m/sec); take-off field length, 5,530ft (1,685m); landing field length, 4,290ft (1,310m); range with 80 passengers, 1,670 naut mls (3,095km) at 30,000ft (9,145m).
Weights: Operational weight empty, 57,190lb (25,940kg); max payload, 31,000lb (14,060kg); max take-off weight, 121,000lb (54,885kg); max landing weight, 110,000lb (49,895kg); max zero-fuel weight, 98,500lb (44,678kg).
Dimensions: Span, 93ft 5in (28.47m); overall length, 119ft 3½in (36.37m); overall height, 27ft 6in (8.38m); sweepback, 24 deg at quarter chord; wing area, 1,000.7sq ft (92.97m²).
Accommodation: Cabin max width, 10ft 1in (3.07m), max height, 6ft 9in (2.06m). Maximum seating for 115 passengers five-abreast, with offset aisle, at 32in (81cm) pitch. Underfloor baggage/freight holds, total volume, 895cu ft (25.3m³). Flight crew of two.

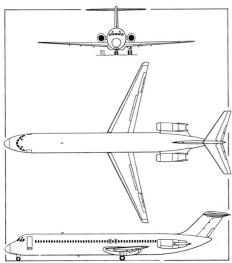

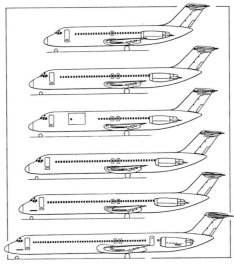

Power Plant: Two Pratt & Whitney JT8D turbofans each rated at 18,500lb st (8,391kgp) for take-off, plus emergency thrust reserve of 750lb st (340kgp) each. Standard fuel capacity, 4,812 Imp gal (21,876l) in integral wing tanks.
Performance: Max operating speed, 340kts (630km/h) IAS or Mach=0.84; max cruising speed, 499kts (924km/h) at 27,000ft (8,230m); long-range cruising speed, 439kts (813km/h) at 35,000ft (10,670m); take-off field length, 7,250ft (2,195m); landing field length, 4,860ft (1,480m); range with 155 passengers, 1,563 naut mls (2,896km).
Weights: Operating weight empty, 78,420lb (35,570kg); max fuel weight, 39,128lb (17,748kg); max payload 39,579lb (17,953kg); max take-off weight 140,000lb (63,503kg); max landing weight, 128,000lb (58,060kg); max zero-fuel weight, 118,000lb (53,524kg).
Dimensions: Span, 107ft 10in (32.87m); overall length, 147ft 10in (45.06m); overall height, 29ft 8in (9.04m); sweepback, 24.5 deg at quarter chord; wing area, 1,270sq ft (118.0m²).
Accommodation: Cabin length, 101ft 0in (30.78m), max width, 10ft 1in (3.09m), max height, 6ft 9in (2.06m). Accommodation for up to 172 passengers five-abreast at 31in (78cm) pitch. Underfloor baggage/cargo holds, total volume, 1,253cu ft (35.48m³). Flight crew of two.

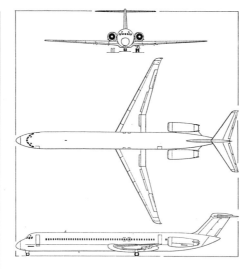

Above: This three-view drawing is representative of the basic members of the McDonnell Douglas MD-80 family, comprising the MD-81, MD-82, MD-83 and MD-88. All of these have the same overall dimensions and external configuration, and differ primarily in their fuel capacities, weights, power plants and flight deck equipment standards. Later aircraft have a revised tail cone.

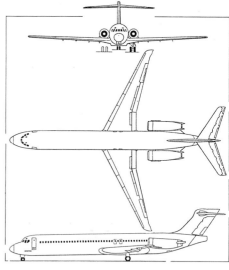

Above: First flown at Long Beach, California, in December 1986, the MD-87 is the first member of the basic MD-80 family to differ in size. Designed to meet the needs of some airlines for an MD-80-style aircraft of smaller capacity, it has a fuselage of the same length as the DC-9 Srs 50 and other changes that include a taller fin and a blunt tail cone. The latter is to become standard on all versions of the MD-80.

From 1975 onwards, Douglas Aircraft Company (a division of McDonnell Douglas) studied a number of possible derivatives of the DC-9 that would take advantage of the refanned versions of the Pratt & Whitney JT8D engine. An early example of this engine, the JT8D-109, was flown on a DC-9 starting on 9 January 1975, to gain data on the new engine, which went into production as the JT8D-209. DC-9 variants identified as the Srs 50RS, Srs 60, Srs 50-17R and DC-9SC were among those studied with this or other engines and with such innovations as a supercritical wing and/or fuselage extensions. Market surveys eventually led to the launch, in October 1977, of what was then known as the DC-9 Super 80, with a fuselage 14ft 3in (4.34m) longer than that of the Srs 50, JT8D-209 engines and other new features. Swissair, Austrian Airlines and Southern Airways became the launch customers for what would prove to be the most successful of all DC-9 variants. Three Super 80s required for certification made their first flights on 18 October 1979, 6 December 1979 and 29 February 1980.

VARIANTS

Three subvariants of the Super 80 were offered, all with the same overall dimensions but with different engine powers, fuel capacities and operating weights. These were the DC-9 Srs 81 as initially developed; the DC-9 Srs 82 with 20,000lb st (9,072kgp) JT8D-217s (plus emergency thrust reserve) and the same fuel as the Srs 82; and the DC-9 Srs 83 with 21,000lb st (9,526kgp) JT8D-219s and an extra 966 Imp gal (4,390l) of fuel in cargo compartment tanks. First flights were made of the MD-82 on 8 January 1981 and of the MD-83 on 17 December 1984. In 1984, the designation of the DC-9 Super 80 was changed to MD-80 and the three production variants became the MD-81, MD-82 and MD-83. In 1985, the MD-87 was announced, featuring a fuselage reduced in length by 16ft 5in (5.0m), 20,000lb st (9,072kgp) JT8D-217B engines and a standard fuel capacity of 4,863 Imp gal (22,106l), plus optional auxiliary tanks. The MD-87 was ordered first by Finnair and Austrian Airlines, and made its first flight on 4 December 1986. A 10in (25.4cm) extension of the fin above the tailplane was introduced on the MD-87 to balance the shorter moment arm. A fifth member of the family was launched early in 1986

when Delta Airlines ordered the MD-88, a close relative of the MD-82 with JT8D-217C engines, a 160,000lb (72,575kg) gross weight and a number of systems and equipment refinements. Late in 1987, MD-88s were to be delivered with a Sperry electronic flight instrument system (EFIS) in the cockpit, combined with a flight-management system and an inertial reference system. Provision is made in the design of the MD-88 for an eventual retrofit of propfan engines. Other engine options studied by Douglas include the CFM56-5 and the IAE V2500, which could be used on the MD-89 or MD-90 with another stretch to increase maximum seating to 173 or 180.

SERVICE USE

The MD-81 gained FAA certification on 26 August 1980 and entered service with Swissair on 5 October 1980. Certificated on 30 July 1981, the MD-82 entered service with Republic Airlines in August, followed in 1982 by the higher gross weight option at 149,500lb (67,812kg) with JT8D-217A engines to provide a significant increase in range with maximum payload. The MD-83 was certificated late in 1985 and entered service with Finnair before the end of that year. By the beginning of 1987, McDonnell Douglas had recorded 555 orders and 275 conditional orders and options for the MD-80 family.

Above: Keeping pace with innovations in cabin design and the availability of new materials, Douglas redesigned the interior of the MD-80 in 1982, introducing enlarged baggage racks and a simplified ceiling, the lines of which helped to give the aircraft a 'wide-body' look.

McDonnell Douglas MD-81 Cutaway Drawing Key

1 Radome
2 Weather radar scanner
3 Front pressure bulkhead
4 Pitot tube
5 Radio and electronics bay
6 Nosewheel well
7 Twin nosewheels
8 Rudder pedals
9 Instrument panel
10 Instrument panel shroud
11 Windscreen wipers
12 Windscreen panels
13 Cockpit eyebrow windows
14 First officer's seat
15 Overhead switch panel
16 Captain's seat
17 Nosewheel steering control
18 Underfloor electrical and electronics bay
19 Nose strake
20 Retractable airstairs
21 Door mounted escape chute
22 Forward passenger door, open
23 Entry lobby
24 Starboard service door
25 Forward galley
26 Toilet compartment
27 Wash hand basin
28 First class seating compartment, 12 passengers four-abreast
29 D/F loop aerials
30 VHF aerial
31 Curtained cabin divider
32 Cabin window panel
33 Pressurization valves
34 Fuselage lower lobe frame construction
35 Wardrobe
36 Tourist class seating, 125 passengers five-abreast
37 Overhead stowage bins
38 Cabin roof frames
39 Air conditioning ducting
40 Cabin roof trim panels
41 Floor beam construction
42 Forward freight hold, capacity 849cu ft (24.04m³)

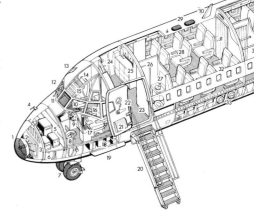

Above: Italian flag carrier Alitalia is a major user of the DC-9 and MD-80, with 40 in use and more on order. This is one of the Alitalia MD-82s.

Left: Cutaway drawing of the MD-80 in its initial production form, the MD-81. The MD-82 and MD-83 are similar in most respects but have different fuel loads and engine ratings. The MD-88, with the same overall dimensions, introduces a 'glass' cockpit.

Below: Swissair was one of the three airlines whose orders placed in October 1977 led McDonnell Douglas to launch production of the MD-80 (then known as the DC-9 Super 80). The Swiss airline bought the MD-81 variant, as shown here, to add to its smaller DC-9 Srs 32s and Srs 51s.

43 Forward freight hold rear door
44 Port overhead stowage bin rack
45 Fuselage frame and stringer construction
46 Leading edge slat central hydraulic jack control
47 Wing panel centreline joint
48 Floor beam construction
49 Centre fuselage construction
50 Cable drive to leading edge slats
51 Starboard wing integral fuel tank; total system capacity 4,812 Imp gal (21,876l)
52 Fuel system piping
53 Ventral wing fence (vortilon)
54 Pressure refuelling connections
55 Leading edge slat segments, open
56 Overwing fuel filler cap
57 Starboard navigation lights
58 Extended wing tip
59 Rear navigation and strobe lights
60 Static dischargers
61 Starboard aileron
62 Aileron tabs
63 Starboard outer double slotted flap, down position
64 Flap hydraulic jacks
65 Flap hinge brackets
66 Outboard spoilers
67 Inner double-slotted flap, down position
68 Inboard spoiler
69 Starboard emergency exit windows
70 Pressure floor above wheel bay
71 Port emergency exit windows
72 Hydraulic reservoir
73 Main undercarriage wheel well
74 Rear cabin tourist class seats
75 Cabin attendant's folding seat
76 Rear service door/emergency exit
77 Rear underfloor freight hold door
78 Cabin wall trim panels
79 Overhead stowage bins
80 Starboard engine intake
81 Detachable engine cowlings
82 Cabin rear bulkhead
83 Rear galleys, port and starboard
84 Toilet compartments, port and starboard
85 Rear pressure bulkhead
86 Rear entry door
87 Engine thrust reverser, open position
88 Fin root fillet
89 Air conditioning ram air intake
90 Fin construction
91 VOR aerials
92 Rudder feel system pressure sensor
93 Tailplane trim jack
94 Starboard tailplane
95 Elevator horn balance
96 Starboard elevator
97 Elevator tabs
98 Tailplane bullet fairing
99 Elevator hinge controls
100 Tailplane pivot mounting
101 Port elevator
102 Tailplane construction
103 Rudder construction
104 Rudder tab
105 Static dischargers
106 Tailcone, jettisonable for emergency exit
107 Air conditioning louvres
108 Sloping fin attachment frames
109 Tailplane de-icing air duct
110 Rear entry airstairs tunnel
111 Air conditioning plant
112 Engine pylon
113 Port engine thrust reverser doors, closed
114 Radial lobe engine silencer
115 Nacelle strake
116 Bleed air piping
117 Pratt & Whitney JT8D-209 turbofan engine
118 Engine accessory gearbox
119 Port engine intake
120 Rear underfloor freight hold, capacity 445cu ft (12.60m³)
121 Wing root trailing edge fillet
122 Port inner double-slotted flap
123 Flap rib construction
124 Flap vane
125 Main undercarriage mounting
126 Main undercarriage leg strut
127 Inboard spoiler
128 Flap down position
129 Outer double-slotted flap
130 Outboard spoilers
131 Aileron tabs
132 Port aileron
133 Fixed portion of trailing edge
134 Static dischargers
135 Rear navigation and strobe lights
136 Retractable landing lamp
137 Port navigation lights
138 Leading edge slat segments, (fully open position)
139 Slat guide rails
140 Front spar
141 Wing rib construction
142 Port wing integral fuel tank
143 Rear spar
144 Wing stringers
145 Ventral wing fence ('vortilon')
146 Wing skin plating
147 Twin mainwheels
148 Slat de-icing air duct
149 Air supply duct
150 Wing root fillet
151 Taxying lamp

Above: Malaysian Airline System (MAS), as the national airline of Malaysia, had three DC-10 Srs 30s in its fleet in 1986. In common with the majority of DC-10 operators, MAS specified CF6-50 engines.

With the DC-8 in production and the DC-9 recently entering service, the Douglas Aircraft Company (not then merged with McDonnell), turned its attention in March 1966 to the so-called 'Jumbo Twin' specification prepared by American Airlines. Subsequent discussions between the company and the airline, and an assessment of broader market needs, led to the final proposal becoming a three-engined wide-body type of larger capacity than first planned, and in this form, the type became the DC-10 as ordered by American Airlines on 19 February 1968. A full production launch was achieved in April, when United Airlines also placed an order. The configuration and size closely matched that of the TriStar which Lockheed launched in March 1968, the most significant difference being that the rear engine of the DC-10 was located in an individual nacelle above the fuselage, on a short pylon, with the fin and rudder carried above this nacelle. All early versions of the DC-10 were powered by General Electric CF6-50 engines, the Pratt & Whitney JT9D being offered as an option at a later time, and the flight test programme began on 29 August 1970, with the second and third aircraft, in American and United colours respectively, following on 24 October and 23 December 1970.

VARIANTS
The launch version of the DC-10 was aimed at providing non-stop US transcontinental range and, after the subsequent introduction of longer-range versions, this initial model became known as the DC-10 Series 10. This had CF6-6D or 6D1 engines of 40,000lb st or 41,000lb st (18,144kgp or 18,598kgp) respectively and 410,000lb (185,976kg) or, later, 455,000lb (206,388kg) gross weight. The DC-10 Srs 15 introduced CF6-50C2F engines at 46,500lb st (21,092kgp) for high-temperature, high-altitude operations by Mexican airlines, and first flew on 8 January 1981. Both these variants had the original DC-10 wing with a span of 155ft 4in (47.35m). For long-range operations, Douglas developed centre-section and fuselage (underfloor) fuel tanks, and a 10ft (3.05m) increase in wing span to allow for higher weights; a third main landing gear leg was

also introduced, on the fuselage centreline. With CF6-50 engines, this variant was the DC-10 Srs 30, first flown on 21 June 1972. With JT9D-20 engines, it was at first the DC-10 Srs 20, later changed to DC-10 Srs 40, first flown on 28 February 1972; the first Srs 40 with JT9D-59 engines flew on 25 July 1975. Progressive increases in certificated weights and fuel capacities were made once the Srs 30 and 40 were in production, and in 1980 the designation DC-10 Srs 30ER was adopted for the extended-range variants. A convertible freighter version with a forward side cargo door was introduced as the DC-10 Srs 30CF, first flown on 28 February 1973, and a maximum take-off weight of 590,000lb (267,620kg) was certificated for this variant. Some DC-10 Srs 10CFs were also built. A windowless pure freighter, the DC-10 Srs 30F, appeared in 1985 to meet the requirements of Federal Express and could accommodate up to 36 standard containers. A number of fuselage-stretched variants of the DC-10 was studied under the Srs 50 and 60 designations and as the MD-100, leading eventually to the MD-11.

SERVICE USE
The DC-10 Srs 10 was certificated on 29 July 1971, and entered service on 5 August 1971 with American Airlines. The Srs 15 was certificated on 12 June 1981 for service with Mexicana and Aero Mexico. The Srs 30 was certificated 21 November 1972, with first deliveries to KLM and Swissair. The first Srs 30ER deliveries were made to Swissair, and the first Srs 30ER with maximum supplementary tankage was delivered to Finnair. The Srs 40 was certificated on 20 October 1972, with the first delivery following to Northwest Orient Airlines. The Srs 30CF was first delivered to TIA and ONA on 19 April and 21 April 1973 respectively. The first Srs 30F was delivered to Federal Express on 24 January 1986. DC-10 production and sales total 442 by early 1987, including 60 KC-10A tanker transports for the USAF.

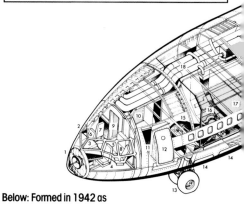

Below: Formed in 1942 as a subsidiary of the Canadian Pacific Railway, and known for some time as CP Air, Canadian Pacific was taken over in 1986 by Pacific Western, creating the second largest Canadian airline. Canadian Pacific's 12 DC-10 Srs 30s had emerged in this new livery shortly before.

McDonnell Douglas DC-10 Series 30 CF Cutaway Drawing Key

1 Weather radar
2 Windshield
3 Instrument console
4 Flight deck
5 Captain's seat (Aircraft Mechanics Inc)
6 First officer's seat (ditto)
7 Flight engineer's position
8 Supernumary crew seat
9 Flight deck door
10 Forward starboard toilet
11 Forward port toilet
12 Crew passenger forward entry door
13 Twin wheel nose gear (Abex or Dowty Rotol; Goodyear tyres)
14 Air conditioning access doors
15 Forward cargo bulkhead
16 Air conditioning bay (Garrett AiResearch equipment)
17 Forward lower galley area (used for containerized cargo)
18 Air conditioning trunking
19 Cargo deck lateral transfer area (omni-caster rollers)
20 Cargo deck pallet channels (rollers)
21 Main cargo door (fully open position)
22 VHF antenna
23 Frame-and-stringer fuselage construction
24 Main deck cargo (ten 88 x 125in, 2.23 x 3.17m (pallets), capacity 4,958 cu ft (140.4m³)
25 Passenger door
26 Forward lower compartment (five 88 x 125in, 2.23 x 3.17m (pallets), capacity 1,890 cu ft 53.5m³)
27 Centre-section fuselage main frame
28 Centre-section front beam
29 Sheer-web floor support over centre-section fuel tank
30 Cargo/passenger compartment dividing bulkhead
31 Starboard engine pod (Rhor subcontract)
32 Engine intake
33 Nacelle pylon
34 Leading-edge slats
35 Integral wing fuel tank
36 Starboard navigation lights
37 Low-speed outboard aileron
38 Fuel ventpipe
39 Wing spoilers/lift dumpers
40 Double-slotted flaps
41 All-speed inboard drooping aileron
42 Passenger doors
43 Centre-section fuselage mainframe
44 Cabin air ducts
45 Centre undercarriage bay
46 Keel box structure
47 Fuselage/wing attachment points
48 Wing torsion-box construction
49 Leading-edge structure
50 Nacelle pylon
51 Engine intake
52 General Electric CF6-50 turbofan
53 Exhaust outlet
54 Four-wheel main undercarriage (Menasco Manufacturing; Goodyear tyres and brakes)
55 Leading-edge slats
56 Outboard slat extended
57 Port navigation lights
58 Low-speed outboard aileron
59 Fuel vent pipe
60 Outboard flap hinge fairings
61 Fuel pipes
62 All-speed inboard drooping aileron
63 Inboard flap hinge actuator and fairing
64 Undercarriage support structure
65 Flap construction
66 Wing root fairing
67 Fuselage-attached flap track
68 Centre cargo compartment, capacity 1,280 cu ft (36.25m³)
69 Cabin floor support
70 Overhead luggage lockers
71 Eight-abreast coach-class seating (147 passengers)
72 Baggage containers
73 Bulk cargo hold door
74 Rear passenger door (port and starboard)
75 Rear toilet (port and starboard)
76 Three toilets/washrooms
77 Underfloor bulk cargo hold capacity 805 cu ft (22.79m³)
78 Rear pressure bulkhead
79 Tailplane centre-section
80 Tailplane leading-edge
81 Tailplane construction (LTV subcontract)
82 Elevator actuators
83 Dual elevators (LTV subcontract)
84 Tail cone (Mitsubishi subcontract)
85 Exhaust outlet
86 General Electric CF6-50 turbofan
87 Intake trunking
88 Intake hot-air duct
89 Engine intake
90 Starboard tailplane
91 Dual elevators
92 Tailfin leading-edge
93 Rudder actuator
94 Tailfin torsion box construction
95 VOR
96 Upper rudder sections (Aerfer subcontract)
97 Lower rudder sections
98 Tail pylon

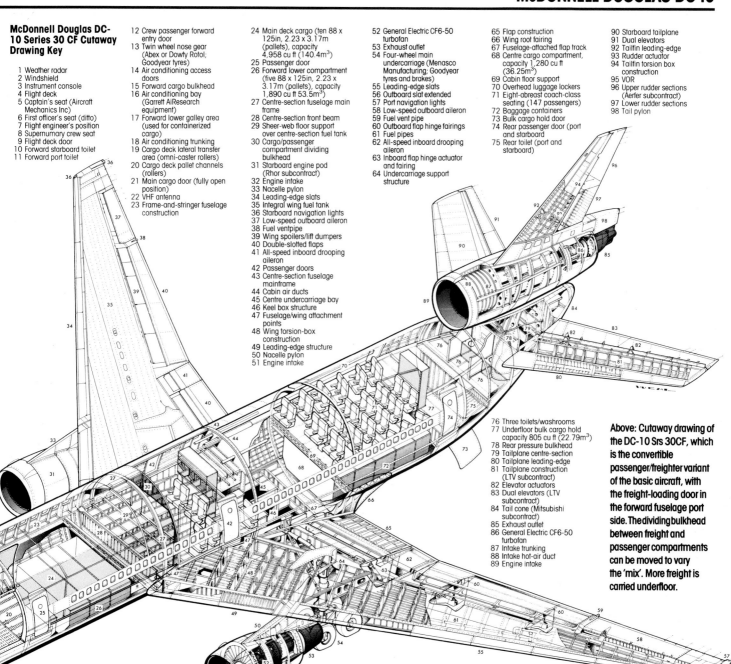

Above: Cutaway drawing of the DC-10 Srs 30CF, which is the convertible passenger/freighter variant of the basic aircraft, with the freight-loading door in the forward fuselage port side. The dividing bulkhead between freight and passenger compartments can be moved to vary the 'mix'. More freight is carried underfloor.

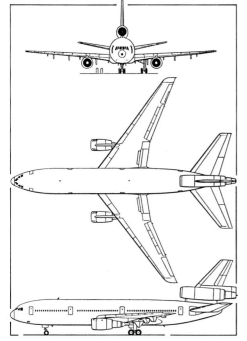

Left: The three-view drawing shows the Series 30 version of the DC-10, which has proved to be the most numerous variant among the 442 DC-10s sold by early 1987. The Srs 30CF and Srs 40 were externally similar.

Right: The flight deck of the DC-10, which was laid out from the start for a crew of three, with the flight engineer facing to starboard behind the first officer. The basic flight instruments for the two pilots are of conventional mechanical type, arranged in the orthodox fashion. For the MD-11, derived from the DC-10, a two-man 'glass' cockpit has been designed.

McDONNELL DOUGLAS MD-11 USA

For at least the past 15 years, stretched (and in some cases 'shrunk') versions of the DC-10 have been studied by the Douglas Aircraft Company under a number of different designations, while production of the DC-10 itself continued in a form little changed from that in which it was launched. As noted in its own entry, the DC-10 was produced in only three principle series, all having

fundamentally the same fuselage length and differing primarily in weights, fuel capacities and engine type and power. Almost from the start of the design, however, possible stretched-fuselage versions were being considered and in the early 1970s, for example, a 42ft (12.8m) lengthening was considered a possibility, to allow the DC-10 to carry 365 passengers for 3,600 naut mls (6,680km). At the same time, a DC-10 twin was being studied, with the tail engine removed and the fuselage shortened by 10ft (3.05m). Stretched versions of the Srs 10, Srs 30 and Srs 40 continued under study throughout the 1970s and by the end of the decade the designations Srs 61, Srs 62 and Srs 63 were being used, with stretches of 26ft (7.9m) or 40ft (12.2m) and varying weights. No market was found for these projects, which were followed in the early 1980s by a DC-10 Super 10 proposal combining the Srs 30 wing with a slightly shortened Srs 10 fuselage and the latter's lighter structure and two-leg main landing gear. New power plants, such as the RB.211-535 and PW2037, were now being considered, and two-crew cockpits with digital instruments and CRT displays were under review. When McDonnell Douglas de-

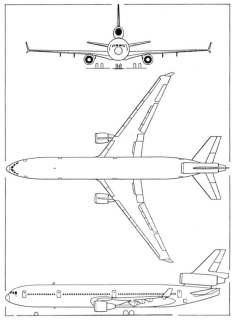

Above: The McDonnell Douglas MD-11 is closely related to the DC-10, as this three-view clearly shows. A longer fuselage and the winglets identify the MD-11.

Above right: An impression of the MD-11, which was launched in December 1986 with 12 customers.

Left: Designed for two-pilot operations, the MD-11 has one of the most advanced flight decks to date, with six electronic displays.

McDONNELL DOUGLAS MD-91/94 USA

The MD-91 and 94 designations identify a series of projects under study by the Douglas Aircraft Company in 1986, based upon the use of the forthcoming ultra-high-bypass or propfan engines. No commitment had been made by the company to launch any of these projects up to the time this volume went to press. Before any decision was taken, the company planned to gather further data on UHB engines in a test programme using an MD-80 (one of the original test aircraft, built as a DC-9 Super Eighty). The term ultra-high-bypass was adopted by McDonnell Douglas to cover the new family of engines of which the General Electric GE36, known to its manufacturer as an unducted fan (UDF) was the first example to fly. To ensure that it remained abreast of this evolving technology, Douglas set up a UHB Technology Readiness Program in April 1985, establishing a group of engineers to oversee the flight test programme and to define the type(s) of prop fan-powered aircraft that might most readily be developed to meet market needs. Under an agreement between McDonnell Douglas and General Electric, a GE-36 was to be installed on the port side of the MD-80 test bed, replacing the JT8D in that position, for a 3/4-month flight test programme based at Mojave, where General Electric has its Flight Test Center. This was the second GE-36 flight test engine, differing from the first (which first flew in the Boeing 727-100 test-bed in August 1986) in having 10 blades instead of eight in the front row,

and some other changes to reduce noise levels. Testing of the MD-80 was to begin in April 1987 and the GE-36 was then to be replaced by a Pratt & Whitney/Allison 578-DX propfan, at the end of 1987, for a similar test programme. Both engines have four blades with a diameter of about 11ft 6in (3.50m), but differ in particular in that the GE-36 has no gearbox, whereas the 578-DX does. Both engine designs are potentially able to produce the power that would be required for a twin-engined short-range transport.

VARIANTS

Studies by the UHB Technology Readiness Program group led to the conclusion that the first application of UHB engines could be made to a variant of the existing MD-80 airframe, rather than to an all-new design. With market research indicating that there is a developing opportunity for an aircraft of about 100-seat capacity and a range of up to 1,500 naut mls (2,780km), the MD-91X was projected as a 'shrunk' MD-80, having a fuselage shortened by 28ft 6in (8.69m) to bring it back to the size of the DC-9 Srs 30. Wing span would similarly be reduced to the original Srs 30 dimensions, but the tail unit would be akin to that of the MD-87, with its 10in (25.4cm) extension above the tailplane, and the recently adopted redesigned tail cone would also be used. The MD-91X, planned for service availability as early as 1991 should the market require, would be as advanced as the latest MD-80 in terms of structural

materials, furnishing, equipment and avionics. The combined effect of the MD-80 refinements, lower empty weight and reduced specific fuel consumption of the new engines is to reduce the fuel cost on a typical 350-naut ml (648 km) stage, with a full payload, by as much as 50 per cent, compared with a DC-9 Srs 30 operation. Either in parallel with or a little later than, the MD-91X, Douglas planned to of-

cided, in late 1982, to replace the famous 'DC' series of designations with a new 'MD' series, this project became the MD-100, but it was discontinued in November 1983 when all work on projected new commercial aircraft was temporarily suspended by the parent company. In 1984, work resumed, with a high priority, on a stretched derivative of the DC-10 with the designation MD-11, and on 29 December 1986 this was formally launched into production in the form illustrated here.

VARIANTS

Based on a close study of the prospective market, the MD-11 evolved between 1984 and 1986 as a very-long-range large-capacity transport, using the basic DC-10 fuselage cross section, with an 18ft 7in (5.66m) stretch. The wing has a 10ft (3.05m) increase in span and outward-canted winglets that

add another 4ft 4in (1.32m), plus other new features such as a smaller tailplane containing fuel that can be used to assist aircraft trimming, carbon brakes, revised tail cone, greater use of composites and advanced metals, a two-man cockpit and digital FMS and EFIS on the flight deck. The basic version, seats up to 405 passengers, as indicated in the accompanying data panel. Further evolution will lead to all-freight and Combi versions, the former with a 180,000lb (81,650kg) cargo payload and the latter able to accommodate for example, six pallets on the main deck, loaded through a side door aft of the wing, plus 214 passengers. Another option is the MD-11M, which would be a 'lightweight' MD-11 with reduced fuel capacity and the third, centreline, main leg removed in order to fly with the same passenger loads over shorter ranges at improved economy, using re-rated engines. Alternatively (or

in addition) an MD-11ER could have a shorter fuselage, achieving still greater ranges with fewer passengers, and, somewhat later, the MD-11ADV (Advanced) is in prospect, with a larger fuselage, new wing, updated systems and new technology engines such as the Rolls-Royce Contrafan or unducted UHB.

SERVICE USE

The MD-11 was committed to full-scale development on 29 December 1986, at which time 12 companies had placed orders for 52 aircraft with 40 more on option. Principal airline customers included British Caledonian, which is expected to be first to operate the MD-11 in the Spring of 1990 following first flight in March 1989; SAS; Swissair; Alitalia; Varig; Thai Airways; Korean Air; Federal Express; JAT and Dragonair.

McDONNELL DOUGLAS MD-91/94

fer the MD-92X, using a longer fuselage to provide a 155-seat cabin. Airline needs were expected to decide priorities for development, but an MD-80 with UHB engines seemed likely in the Douglas view to be more attractive to the airlines, on economic grounds, than an all-new aircraft unless or until fuel costs rose considerably above their 1986 level. Meanwhile, project studies continued under the

MD-94X designation for just such an all-new aircraft, in the 150-seat category. This project had an overall configuration similar to that of the MD-80 with a very high aspect ratio supercritical wing, but could introduce – (depending on timing and cost factors) – such advanced concepts as canard noseplanes, laminar and turbulent boundary layer control, fibre optics in the flight control system, side-stick con-

trollers, flight control active stability augmentation and aluminium-lithium computers in the structure.

SERVICE USE

No commitment to buy any variant of the MD-90. Specific designations are intended by the manufacturer to indicate the expected year of entry into service, ie MD-91X available in 1991.

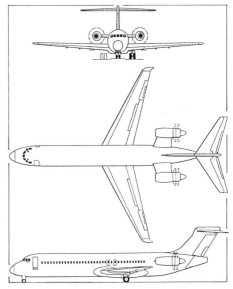

Left: A model of the MD-94X, one of the projects that McDonnell Douglas was studying in 1987 to take advantage of the forthcoming prop-fan engines. Of similar layout to the MD-80, the MD-94X would have a new wing and 150-seat capacity.

Right: Projected for service in an earlier timescale than the MD-94X (left), the MD-91X is proposed as a variant of the MD-80, of similar size to the original DC-9 Srs 30 but with a pair of General Electric or Pratt & Whitney/Allison propfan engines on the rear fuselage.

NAMC YS-11 JAPAN

Encouraged by the Ministry of International Trade and Industry, six Japanese companies (Mitsubishi, Kawasaki, Fuji, Shin Meiwa, Showa and Japan Aircraft Manufacturing) began during 1956 to study the design of a short/medium-range civil airliner as a wholly indigenous project, primarily with a view to meeting the requirements of Japanese domestic airlines. The design emerged as a relatively large twin turboprop, for whose construction the six companies set up Nihon Aircraft Manufacturing Co Ltd (NAMC) in May 1957. The de-

velopment programme embraced four airframes: two flying prototypes and two structural test specimens. The first flights were made on 30 August and 28 December 1962 respectively, by which time plans had been completed to launch production of the aircraft known as the YS-11.

VARIANTS

After production of 48 YS-11s, the first of which flew on 23 October 1964, NAMC developed the YS-11A with higher operating weights and increased

payload. First flown on 27 November 1967, the YS-11A was offered in three versions which became known as the Srs 200, 300 and 400, the original YS-11s then becoming Srs 100 aircraft by implication. The YS-11A-200 was the basic 60-passenger aircraft with a 2,700lb (1,350kg) increase in payload over that of the Srs 100, and 92 were built. With the same overall weights as the Srs 200, the YS-11A-300 was a mixed-traffic version featuring a side-loading cargo door in the forward side of the fuselage and able to carry 46 passengers plus 540cu ft (15.3m³) of cargo.

Right: Originally developed primarily to meet the special requirements of Japanese domestic airlines, the NAMC YS-11 twin-turboprop transport is still serving in Japan in quite large numbers, with nearly 70 owned by four airlines there in 1986. Outside of Japan, the biggest operator is Mid Pacific Air, based in Hawaii. One of this operator's YS-11s is illustrated here at Honolulu, in service on routes linking the Hawaiian islands. As well as using YS-11s on its own routes, Mid Pacific Air leases some of its fleet to other airlines.

PILATUS BRITTEN-NORMAN ISLANDER UK

SPECIFICATION
(BN-2T Turbine Islander)

Power Plant: Two Allison 250-B17C turboprops each rated at 400shp (298kW) thermal capacity and flat-rated at 320shp (238.5kW), with Hartzell three-blade constant-speed, fully-feathering propellers of 6ft 8in (2.03m) diameter. Fuel capacity, standard, 108 Imp gal (492l).
Performance: Max operating speed, 152kts (285km/h) IAS; max cruising speed, 170kts (315km/h) at 10,000ft (3,050m) and 154kts (285km/h) at sea level; cruising speed at 72 per cent power, 150kts (278km/h) at 10,000ft (3,050m) and 142kts (263km/h) at 5,000ft (1,525m); initial rate of climb, 1,050ft/min (5.3m/sec); service ceiling, over 25,000ft (7,620m); take-off distance to 50ft (15.2m), 1,250ft (380m); landing distance from 50ft (15.2m), 1,115ft (340m); range with max payload, no reserves, 141 naut mls (261km); range with max fuel, IFR reserves, 590 naut mls.
Weights: Empty equipped weight, 4,040lb (1,832kg); max payload, 2,454lb (1,113kg); payload with max fuel, 1,340lb (608kg); max take-off weight, 7,000lb (3,175kg); max landing weight, 6,800lb (3,084kg); max zero-fuel weight, 6,300lb (2,857kg).
Dimensions: Span, standard tips, 49ft 0in (14.94m) or, extended tips with fuel tankage, 53ft 0in (16.15m); overall length, standard nose, 35ft 7¾in (10.87m) or, with weather radar nose, 36ft 3¾in (11.07m); overall height, 13ft 8¾in (4.18m); sweepback, nil; wing area, standard tips, 325.0sq ft (30.19m²) or, with extended tips, 337.0sq ft (31.31m²).
Accommodation: Cabin length, 10ft 0in (3.05m), max width 3ft 7in (1.09m); max height, 4ft 2in (1.27m). Accommodation for up to 10 occupants (including pilot), on two individual side-by-side seats and four bench-type seats, with no aisle; access to each seat row through individual doors. Up to 49cu ft (1.39m³) of baggage volume, plus optional nose compartment with 22cu ft (0.62m³) capacity; maximum cabin freight capacity (no passenger seats), 166cu ft (4.70m³).

Left: A three-view drawing of the Islander in its BN-2B piston-engined form, with the optional long nose to provide extra baggage space, and standard wing-tips without the fuel-tank extensions.

Right: In flight over the Bembridge, Isle of Wight, airfield where the Islander is assembled, this example shows the standard, short nose and the extended, fuel-carrying wing tips. The registration G-TWOB is based on the BN-2B designation of the Islander and is an example of the 'personalized' registrations now used by some British aircraft.

The Islander was conceived in the early 1960s by the original Britten-Norman company founded by John Britten and Desmond Norman, in an effort to produce a very simple, light twin-engined transport for third-level and commuter airlines. The company had a 25 per cent interest in Cameroon Air Transport and the BN-2, as the new twin was designated, was designed specifically to meet the needs of that company, which was regarded as typical of many throughout the world which needed an aircraft with 6-10 seats, good take-off performance, low purchase cost, low operating costs and easy maintenance. Featuring a high-mounted, untapered and strutted wing, fixed landing gear and unusual 'wall-to-wall' seating in the fuselage, with

three access doors (two to port and one to starboard), the BN-2 prototype was powered by a pair of 210hp (157kW) Continental IO-360-B engines and flew on 13 June 1965. With a span of 45ft (13.7m) and gross weight of 4,750lb (2,155kg), it was later fitted with 260hp (194kW) Lycoming O-540-E engines, with which it flew on 17 December 1965, the span then being increased to 49ft (14.9m) and gross weight to 5,700lb (2,585kg). A production prototype to similar specification flew on 20 August 1966. After it had encountered financial difficulties in 1972, the Britten-Norman company was acquired by the Fairey Group, but the latter also went into receivership in 1977, whereafter the Britten-Norman designs and facilities at Bembridge in the Isle of Wight were

The YS-11A-300, which first flew on 17 September 1969, was an all-cargo variant, with the cargo door (larger than that of the Srs 300) in the forward fuselage side and providing 2,860cu ft (81m³) of cargo volume. The nine YS-11A-400s built were all for Japanese military use, as were a few of the earlier models. With an increase in maximum take-off weight of 1,105lb (500kg) to 55,115lb (25,000kg), the YS-11A-500, 600 and 700 were otherwise similar, respectively, to the Srs 200, 300 and 400. Production of four Srs 500 and five Srs 600 aircraft brought the YS-11A programme to an end.

SERVICE USE

Japanese certification of the YS-11 was obtained on 25 August 1964, followed by FAA Type Approval on 7 September 1965. Deliveries of the YS-11 began in March 1965, the first aircraft going to the Japan Civil Aviation Bureau. Passenger services were inaugurated in April 1965 by Toa Airways (now TDA), followed in May by Japan Domestic Airlines (JDA) and in July by All Nippon Airlines. The YS-11A was approved by the JLAB in January 1968 and by the FAA on 3 April 1968, with deliveries beginning later in the year to Piedmont Aviation in the USA. Following delivery of the last YS-11 in 1973, NAMC was progressively put into liquidation, gradually transferring responsibility for spares production and after-sales support to its constituent companies. Mitsubishi is now primarily responsible for customer support and reported in mid-1986 that 159 YS-11s were then in operation (67 with Japanese airlines, 51 with foreign airlines, and 41 with government agencies) out of a total production of 182.

SPECIFICATION
(YS-11A-200)

Power Plant: Two Rolls-Royce Dart Mk 542-10K (RDa.10/1) turboprops, each rated at 3,060ehp (2,284kW) for take-off, with Rotol four-blade constant-speed, feathering and reversing propellers of 14ft 6in (4.42m) diameter. Fuel capacity, 1,600 Imp gal (7,270l) in integral tanks in outer wing panels and bag tanks in inner wing panels.

Performance: Max cruising speed, 253kts (469km/h) at 15,000ft (4,575m); economical cruising speed, 244kts (452km/h) at 20,000ft (6,095m); initial rate of climb, 1,220ft/min (6.2m/sec); service ceiling, 22,900ft (6,980m); take-off field length (SR422B), 3,650ft (1,110m); landing distance (SR422B), 2,170ft (660m); range (no reserves) with max payload, 590 naut mls (1,090km); range with max fuel, 1,736 naut mls (3,215km).

Weights: Operating weight empty, 33,993lb (15,419kg); max payload, 14,508lb (6,581kg); max take-off weight, 54,010lb (24,500kg); max landing weight, 52,910lb (24,000kg); max zero-fuel weight, 48,500lb (22,000kg).

Dimensions: Span, 104ft 11¾in (32.00m); overall length, 86ft 3½in (26.30m); overall height, 29ft 5½in (8.98m); sweepback, 3 deg 11 min at quarter chord; wing area, 1,020.4sq ft (94.8m²).

Accommodation: Cabin length, 44ft 1in (13.44m); max width, 8ft 10in (2.70m), max height, 6ft 6in (1.99m). Standard one-class layout provides 60 seats four-abreast with central aisle at 34-in (86-cm) pitch. Underfloor baggage compartment volume, 70cu ft (1.98m³) and above-floor baggage compartments volume, 307cu ft (8.69m³).

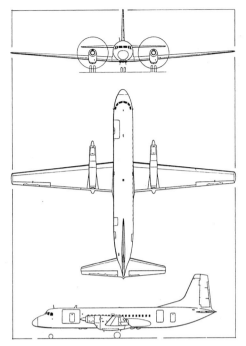

Above: Three-view of the NAMC YS-11, showing the freight door in the forward port side that was a feature of the Srs 300 and Srs 600, versions that were built mostly for military use. The passenger-carrying Srs 100, 200 and 500 were externally similar but lacking the freight door, as did the Srs 400. Differences between the variants were principally concerned with operating weights.

PILATUS BRITTEN-NORMAN ISLANDER

Above: The interior of the Islander is of necessity somewhat basic, although adequate for the short journeys typically flown by these aircraft. As shown here, there are four bench-type seats, access to which is, alternately, through doors in opposite sides of the fuselage (two port, one starboard).

acquired by Pilatus, part of the Swiss Oerlikon-Bührle manufacturing group.

VARIANTS

The first production standard of Islander, as the BN-2, was similar to the prototype in its modified form, the first aircraft flying on 24 April 1967. In June 1969, the production standard became the BN-2A, with a number of product improvements, a further change to BN-2B being made in 1978 with higher landing weight and improved interior design. Both the BN-2A and BN-2B were made available in a number of subvariants, the most significant options being 300hp (224kW) Lycoming IO-540-K1B5 engines in place of the original standard O-540-E4C5s (first flown on 30 April 1970); Riley-Rajay superchargers on standard O-540 engines; extended-span wing tips containing extra fuel tankage; and a long-nosed BN-2S with two more seats in the cabin, replacing baggage stowage space that was provided, instead, in the nose (first flown 22 August 1972). A series of suffix numbers added to the BN-2A and BN-2B designations indicated these and other options, such as revised wing leading-edge camber to meet US certification requirements, drooped flaps for better single-engined climb, and (the -20 series) a higher gross weight. On 6 April 1977, the BN-2A-40 prototype flew with 600shp (448kW) Lycoming LTP 101 turboprops, but a switch was made to Allison 250 engines for the production BN-2T Turbine Islander. The BN-2T prototype first flew on 2 August 1950 and many of the previously described options are also available on this model. Specifically military versions are known as Defenders.

SERVICE USE

The BN-2 Islander received British certification on 10 August 1967 and first deliveries were made on 13 and 15 August respectively, to Glosair and Loganair. FAA approval on 19 December 1967 was followed by first deliveries to the USA in January 1968. The BN-2T Turbine Islander obtained UK certification in May 1981 and US approval (to FAR Pt 23) on 15 July 1982. By 1987, the production total for all Islander variants was approaching 1,100.

PILATUS BRITTEN-NORMAN TRISLANDER UK/USA

The uniquely-configured Trislander resulted from the effort that began in 1968 to 'stretch' the Islander to carry more passengers. The first result of this activity was a long-fuselage Islander (converted from the original BN-2 production prototype), which first flew on 14 July 1968. Consideration of the flight test results obtained with this aircraft led the Britten-Norman company to conclude that additional power was needed to match the higher operating weights that were, in their turn, required to allow the full potential of a stretched aircraft to be achieved. Rather than redesign the wing to accept engines of greater power, the designers decided to fit a third engine of the same type as already used in the Islander, and chose to locate this extra power plant in a nacelle at the top of the fin. A redesigned, enlarged tailplane was fitted in line with the propeller of the third engine for maxi-

mum effectiveness; the fuselage cross section was unchanged, as was the wing geometry, but a little strengthening was required for the higher weights. Known as the BN-2A Mk III, this three-engined derivative of the Islander was sensibly named the Trislander and made its first flight at Bembridge on 11 September 1970. Flight testing revealed the need to make some adjustments to the shape and area of the tail unit (the upper portion of the fin not being fitted at the time of the first flight). Production of the Trislander was initiated in 1970 by the original Britten-Norman company and continued under Fairey and then Pilatus ownership. On 5 June 1982, International Aviation Corporation in Florida acquired a licence to produce the Trislander in the USA, under the new name of Tri-Commutair, for which purpose Pilatus Britten-Norman would transfer all jigs and tools, following the assembly by IAC of an initial

batch of 12 aircraft from components built by the British company.

VARIANTS

The BN-2A Mk III entered production with a gross weight of 9,350lb (4,245kg), this being increased in the BN-2A Mk III-1 version to 10,000lb (4,540kg). A further change was then made by adopting as standard the long nose (with extra baggage capacity) that had been developed for the BN-2S version of the Islander. This first flew on a Trislander on 18 August 1974 and resulted in the designation BN-2A Mk III-2.

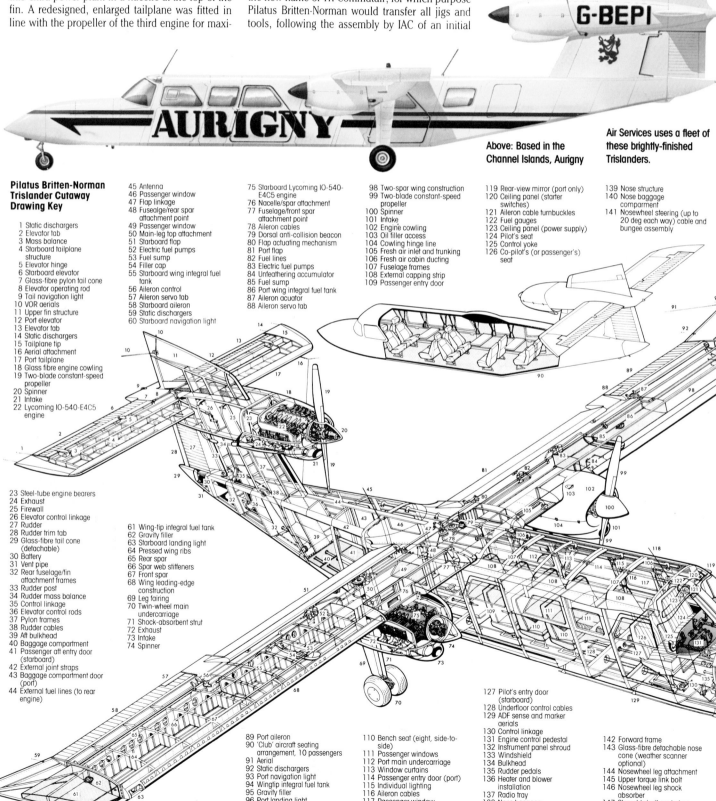

Above: Based in the Channel Islands, Aurigny Air Services uses a fleet of these brightly-finished Trislanders.

Pilatus Britten-Norman Trislander Cutaway Drawing Key

1 Static dischargers
2 Elevator tab
3 Mass balance
4 Starboard tailplane structure
5 Elevator hinge
6 Starboard elevator
7 Glass-fibre pylon tail cone
8 Elevator operating rod
9 Tail navigation light
10 VOR aerials
11 Upper fin structure
12 Port elevator
13 Elevator tab
14 Static dischargers
15 Tailplane tip
16 Aerial attachment
17 Port tailplane
18 Glass fibre engine cowling
19 Two-blade constant-speed propeller
20 Spinner
21 Intake
22 Lycoming IO-540-E4C5 engine

23 Steel-tube engine bearers
24 Exhaust
25 Firewall
26 Elevator control linkage
27 Rudder
28 Rudder trim tab
29 Glass-fibre tail cone (detachable)
30 Battery
31 Vent pipe
32 Rear fuselage/fin attachment frames
33 Rudder post
34 Rudder mass balance
35 Control linkage
36 Elevator control rods
37 Pylon frames
38 Rudder cables
39 Aft bulkhead
40 Baggage compartment
41 Passenger aft entry door (starboard)
42 External joint straps
43 Baggage compartment door (port)
44 External fuel lines (to rear engine)

45 Antenna
46 Passenger window
47 Flap linkage
48 Fuselage/rear spar attachment point
49 Passenger window
50 Main-leg top attachment
51 Starboard flap
52 Electric fuel pumps
53 Fuel sump
54 Filler cap
55 Starboard wing integral fuel tank
56 Aileron control
57 Aileron servo tab
58 Starboard aileron
59 Static dischargers
60 Starboard navigation light

61 Wing-tip integral fuel tank
62 Gravity filler
63 Starboard landing light
64 Pressed wing ribs
65 Rear spar
66 Spar web stiffeners
67 Front spar
68 Wing leading-edge construction
69 Leg fairing
70 Twin-wheel main undercarriage
71 Shock-absorbent strut
72 Exhaust
73 Intake
74 Spinner

75 Starboard Lycoming IO-540-E4C5 engine
76 Nacelle/spar attachment
77 Fuselage/front spar attachment point
78 Aileron cables
79 Dorsal anti-collision beacon
80 Flap actuating mechanism
81 Port flap
82 Fuel lines
83 Electric fuel pumps
84 Unfeathering accumulator
85 Fuel sump
86 Port wing integral fuel tank
87 Aileron acuator
88 Aileron servo tab

89 Port aileron
90 'Club' aircraft seating arrangement, 10 passengers
91 Aerial
92 Static dischargers
93 Port navigation light
94 Wingtip integral fuel tank
95 Gravity filler
96 Port landing light
97 Magnesyn compass

98 Two-spar wing construction
99 Two-blade constant-speed propeller
100 Spinner
101 Intake
102 Engine cowling
103 Oil filler access
104 Cowling hinge line
105 Fresh air inlet and trunking
106 Fresh air cabin ducting
107 Fuselage frames
108 External capping strip
109 Passenger entry door

110 Bench seat (eight, side-to-side)
111 Passenger windows
112 Port main undercarriage
113 Window curtains
114 Passenger entry door (port)
115 Individual lighting
116 Aileron cables
117 Passenger window
118 Antenna

119 Rear-view mirror (port only)
120 Ceiling panel (starter switches)
121 Aileron cable turnbuckles
122 Fuel gauges
123 Ceiling panel (power supply)
124 Pilot's seat
125 Control yoke
126 Co-pilot's (or passenger's) seat

127 Pilot's entry door (starboard)
128 Underfloor control cables
129 ADF sense and marker aerials
130 Control linkage
131 Engine control pedestal
132 Instrument panel shroud
133 Windshield
134 Bulkhead
135 Rudder pedals
136 Heater and blower installation
137 Radio tray
138 Nose baggage compartment door

139 Nose structure
140 Nose baggage comparment
141 Nosewheel steering (up to 20 deg each way) cable and bungee assembly

142 Forward frame
143 Glass-fibre detachable nose cone (weather scanner optional)
144 Nosewheel leg attachment
145 Upper torque link bolt
146 Nosewheel leg shock absorber
147 Steerable/self-centering nosewheel

Introduction of an autofeather system, which put the propeller into feather in the event of an engine failure at take-off, without action by the pilot, brought with it the designation BN-2A Mk III-3.

SERVICE USE

The first production Trislander flew on 6 March 1971, followed by UK certification on 14 May and US Type Approval (to FAR Pt 23) on 4 August of the same year. Aurigny Air Services in the Channel Islands took delivery of the first customer aircraft on 29 June 1971. Pilatus Britten-Norman and its predecessor companies produced 73 Trislanders for airlines around the world. Eight completed aircraft were supplied to IAC following its licence agreement with PB-N in 1982, together with components for a further 12 aircraft to be assembled in Florida. No further production is planned in the UK.

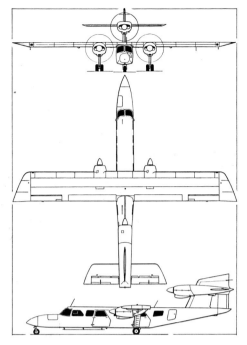

Left: The cockpit of the Trislander. Considerable ingenuity was necessary to provide a satisfactory arrangement of the engine controls and instruments in a panel having the same width as that of the twin-engined BN-2 Islander. The co-pilot has full dual controls but no flight instruments.

Above: The three-view drawing shows the basic arrangement of the BN-2A Mk III Trislander. All those built were externally similar and clearly made use of major components of the Islander. The wing was unchanged, as was the fuselage cross-section, and the long nose was originally built as an Islander option.

SPECIFICATION

Power Plant: Three Avco Lycoming O-540-E4C5 flat-six piston engines each rated at 260hp (194kW) for take-off, with Hartzell two-blade constant-speed fully-feathering propellers of 6ft 8in (2.03m) diameter. Fuel capacity 164 Imp gal (746l) in integral tanks between spars in each outer wing panel and in tanks within wing tips.
Performance: Max operating speed, 143kts (265km/h) IAS; max speed, 156kts (290km/h) at sea level; cruising speeds, 144kts (267km/h) at 75 per cent power at 6,500ft (1,980m), or 138kts (256km/h) at 67 per cent power at 9,000ft (2,470m), or 130kts (241km/h) at 59 per cent at 13,000ft (3,960m); initial rate of climb, 980ft/min (4.97m/sec); service ceiling, 13,150ft (4,010m); take-off distance to 50ft (15.2m), 1,950ft (595m); landing distance from 50ft (15.2m), 1,445ft (440m); max range at 130kts (241km/h) cruising speed, 868 naut mls (1,610km); range with max payload (no reserves), 130 naut mls (241km).
Weights: Empty equipped weight, 5,843lb (2,650kg); max payload, 3,550lb (1,610kg); max take-off weight, 10,000lb (4,540kg); max landing weight, 10,000lb (4,540kg); max zero-fuel weight, 9,700lb (4,400kg).
Dimensions: Span, 53ft 0in (16.15m); overall length, 49ft 3in (15.01m); overall height, 14ft 2in (4.32m); sweepback, nil; wing area, 337.0sq ft (31.31m²).
Accommodation: Cabin length (including rear luggage compartment), 27ft 0½in (8.24m), max width 3ft 7in (1.09m), max height, 4ft 2in (1.27m). Accommodation for up to 18 occupants (including pilot) on two individual side-by-side seats and eight bench-type seats, with no aisle, at 29-in (74cm) seat pitch; access to each seat row through individual doors, two on port and three on starboard side of fuselage. Rear baggage compartment volume, 25.0cu ft (0.71m³); optional nose luggage compartment volume, 22.0cu ft (0.62m³).

Right: The Trislander's unique configuration is well shown in this photograph, with the basic arrangement of the twin-engined Islander (see previous spread) modified by the addition of a third engine, located in a nacelle carried half way up the tail fin. The arrangement worked well and operators of the Trislander, such as Trans-Jamaican Airlines shown here, have been satisfied with the results obtained. However, the market for a piston-engined aircraft of this size dwindled after the introduction of twin-turboprop 19 seaters, and production of the Trislander was ended in the UK in 1982.

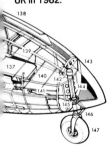

Left: Cutaway drawing of the basic Trislander, and an inset showing a possible club arrangement.

PIPER PA-31 SERIES USA

A number of related light twins produced by Piper in the PA-31 family can be traced back to the original Navajo, which first flew on 30 September 1964 as a six/eight seater with a pair of 300hp (224kW) Lycoming IO-540-MIA5 engines. Progressive variants over the next decade included a turbocharged version, the Turbo Navajo, with 310hp (231kW) TIO-540-A engines; the PA-31P Pressurized Navajo with 425hp (317kW) TGO-540-E1A engines, and the PA-31-325 Turbo Navajo CR with 325hp (243kW) TIO-540-F2BD engines and handed propellers. All these variants had applications in the air taxi and small third-level airline markets, but of more specific interest was the PA-31-350 Navajo Chieftain, which was announced in September 1972 as a lengthened version of the Navajo CR powered by 350hp (261kW) handed TIO-540-J2BD engines. A 2ft (61cm) lengthening of the fuselage allowed the Chieftain (as it is now usually known) to seat up to 10 occupants including the pilot, and all-cargo versions were also developed. Close to 2,000 Chieftains had been sold by 1986 and the success of this type in the commercial air transport market led Piper to set up an Airline Division in 1981 to support Chieftain operations and to evolve PA-31 derivatives more specifically intended for airline use, as described below.

VARIANTS

The PA-31-350, first flown on 25 September 1981, is known as the T-1020 and is a Chieftain with special interior and structural modification to suit short-haul commuter airline operation, with a high rate of

landings to flight hours. Up to 10 passengers can be accommodated in addition to the pilot, and the T-1020 has a maximum take-off weight of 7,000lb (3,175kg). In parallel with the T-1020, Piper evolved the T-1040 as an aircraft of similar capacity but offering the advantages of turboprop power. For speed of development and minimum cost, the T-1040 made use, so far as possible, of existing Piper components, by combining the fuselage of the T-1020 and Chieftain with the PT6A-11 engines of the Cheyenne I (itself a Navajo derivative, as indicated by the PA-31T-1 designation), the wings and landing gear of the Cheyenne IIXL (PA-31T-2) and the engine nacelles with baggage lockers of the larger Cheyenne IIIA (PA-42). Small improvements were made, especially to the design of the air inlets, and the first of three pre-production T-1040 airframes flew on 17 July 1981. The designation for this member of the Navajo/Cheyenne family is PA-31T-3. After deliveries had begun, Piper obtained certification of a wing-tip tank installation, giving the T-1040 an extension of some 300 naut mls (555km) in range, and another option is a cargo pod which, fitted under the fuselage, has a volume of 30cu ft ($0.85m^3$). In all-cargo configuration, the T-1040's cabin offers a volume of 246cu ft ($7m^3$) and the cargo payload is nearly 2,900lb (1,315kg). Access to the cabin is facilitated by the 'Dutch' door, the top half of which hinges up and the bottom half (incorporating steps) down. Adjacent and to the rear of this door is a second, upward-hinged hatch giving access to the rear baggage compartment. Piper has studied a stretched version of the T-1040 as the T-1050, but no decision had been taken to launch such an aircraft up to the end of 1986.

SERVICE USE

Some 500 Chieftains have been delivered specifically for commuter airline use since production of this PA-31 variant began. The T-1020 was certificated to FAR Pt 23 during 1982 and 22 were built. The T-1040 obtained FAA Type Approval, to CAR Pt 3, FAR Pt 23, FAR Pt 36 and SFAR Pt 27 as appropriate, on 25 February 1982 and first deliveries were made in May 1982. Piper built 23 T-1040s before ending production of both it and the T-1020.

Above: From its original PA-31 Navajo, Piper developed the PA-31-350 Navajo Chieftain, which had a lengthening of the fuselage to allow up to 10 people to be carried. Now usually known simply as Chieftains, numerous examples are in airline and air-taxi use.

Below: The Piper T-1040, depicted in this three-view drawing, was the final derivative of the PA-31 design. With the company designation PA-31T-3, the T-1040 is distinguished from the Chieftain and earlier PA-31 versions by its Pratt & Whitney Canada turboprop engines.

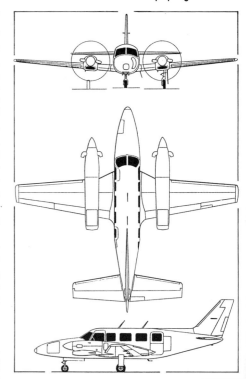

Below: Windward Island Airways International is a small operator in the Netherlands Antilles, with this Piper T-1040 in its mixed fleet in 1986.

SPECIFICATION
(T-1040)

Power Plant: Two Pratt & Whitney Canada PT6A-11 turboprops each rated at 500shp (373kW) for take-off, with Hartzell three-blade constant-speed fully-feathering propellers of 7ft 9in (2.36m) diameter. Fuel capacity, 350 Imp gal (1,135l) in wing fuel cells plus 55 Imp gal (250l) in optional wing-tip tanks.

Performance: Max operating speed, 227kts (421km/h) IAS; max cruising speed, 236kts (437km/h) at 11,000ft (3,355m); long-range cruising speed, 178kts (330km/h) at 10,000ft (3,050m); initial rate of climb, 1,610ft/min (8.2m/sec); service ceiling, 24,000ft (7,315m); take-off distance to 50ft (15.2m), 2,650ft (810m); landing distance from 50ft (15.2m), 2,100ft (640m); range with max payload, 590 naut mls (1,093km); range with max internal fuel, 670 naut mls (1,241km).

Weights: Operating weight empty, 4,624lb (2,097kg); fuel weight, 2,010lb (912kg); max payload, 2,976lb (1,350kg); max take-off weight, 9,000lb (4,082kg); max landing weight, 9,000lb (4,082kg); max zero-fuel weight, 7,600lb (3,447kg).

Dimensions: Span, 41ft 1in (12.52m); overall length, 36ft 8in (11.18m); overall height, 13ft 0in (3.96m); sweepback, nil; wing area, 229.0sq ft ($21.27m^2$).

Accommodation: Cabin length (including flight deck), 12ft 7in (3.84m), max width, 4ft 2in (1.27m), max height, 4ft 3½in (1.31m). Accommodation for up to nine passengers in high-density layouts, in addition to two pilots (or pilot and passenger) side-by-side on individual seats. Nose baggage compartment volume, 25cu ft ($0.71m^3$); nacelle baggage lockers volume 9.0cu ft ($0.25m^3$) each.

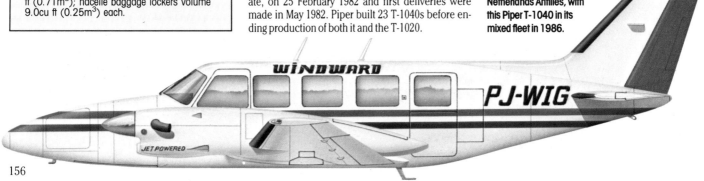

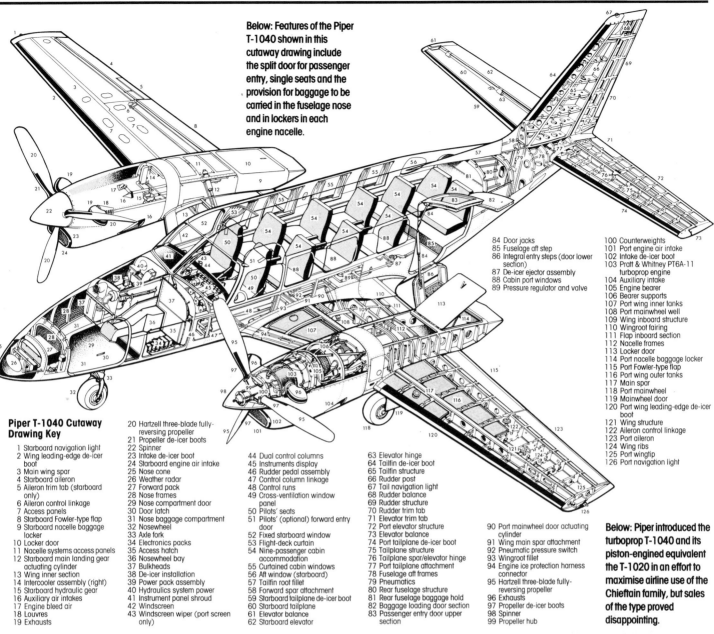

Below: Features of the Piper T-1040 shown in this cutaway drawing include the split door for passenger entry, single seats and the provision for baggage to be carried in the fuselage nose and in lockers in each engine nacelle.

Piper T-1040 Cutaway Drawing Key

1 Starboard navigation light
2 Wing leading-edge de-icer boot
3 Main wing spar
4 Starboard aileron
5 Aileron trim tab (starboard only)
6 Aileron control linkage
7 Access panels
8 Starboard Fowler-type flap
9 Starboard nacelle baggage locker
10 Locker door
11 Nacelle systems access panels
12 Starboard main landing gear actuating cylinder
13 Wing inner section
14 Intercooler assembly (right)
15 Starboard hydraulic gear
16 Auxiliary air intakes
17 Engine bleed air
18 Louvres
19 Exhausts
20 Hartzell three-blade fully-reversing propeller
21 Propeller de-icer boots
22 Spinner
23 Intake de-icer boot
24 Starboard engine air intake
25 Nose cone
26 Weather radar
27 Forward pack
28 Nose frames
29 Nose compartment door
30 Door latch
31 Nose baggage compartment
32 Nosewheel
33 Axle fork
34 Electronics packs
35 Access hatch
36 Nosewheel bay
37 Bulkheads
38 De-icer installation
39 Power pack assembly
40 Hydraulics system power
41 Instrument panel shroud
42 Windscreen
43 Windscreen wiper (port screen only)
44 Dual control columns
45 Instruments display
46 Rudder pedal assembly
47 Control column linkage
48 Control runs
49 Cross-ventilation window panel
50 Pilots' seats
51 Pilots' (optional) forward entry door
52 Fixed starboard window
53 Flight-deck curtain
54 Nine-passenger cabin accommodation
55 Curtained cabin windows
56 Aft window (starboard)
57 Tailfin root fillet
58 Forward spar attachment
59 Starboard tailplane de-icer boot
60 Starboard tailplane
61 Elevator balance
62 Starboard elevator
63 Elevator hinge
64 Tailfin de-icer boot
65 Tailfin structure
66 Rudder post
67 Tail navigation light
68 Rudder balance
69 Rudder structure
70 Rudder trim tab
71 Elevator trim tab
72 Port elevator structure
73 Elevator balance
74 Port tailplane de-icer boot
75 Tailplane structure
76 Tailplane spar/elevator hinge
77 Port tailplane attachment
78 Fuselage aft frames
79 Pneumatics
80 Rear fuselage structure
81 Rear fuselage baggage hold
82 Baggage loading door section
83 Passenger entry door upper section
84 Door jacks
85 Fuselage aft step
86 Integral entry steps (door lower section)
87 De-icer ejector assembly
88 Cabin port windows
89 Pressure regulator and valve
90 Port mainwheel door actuating cylinder
91 Wing main spar attachment
92 Pneumatic pressure switch
93 Wingroot fillet
94 Engine ice protection harness connector
95 Hartzell three-blade fully-reversing propeller
96 Exhausts
97 Propeller de-icer boots
98 Spinner
99 Propeller hub
100 Counterweights
101 Port engine air intake
102 Intake de-icer boot
103 Pratt & Whitney PT6A-11 turboprop engine
104 Auxiliary intake
105 Engine bearer
106 Bearer supports
107 Port wing inner tanks
108 Port mainwheel well
109 Wing inboard structure
110 Wingroot fairing
111 Flap inboard section
112 Nacelle frames
113 Locker door
114 Port nacelle baggage locker
115 Port Fowler-type flap
116 Port wing outer tanks
117 Main spar
118 Port mainwheel
119 Mainwheel door
120 Port wing leading-edge de-icer boot
121 Wing structure
122 Aileron control linkage
123 Port aileron
124 Wing ribs
125 Port wingtip
126 Port navigation light

Below: Piper introduced the turboprop T-1040 and its piston-engined equivalent the T-1020 in an effort to maximise airline use of the Chieftain family, but sales of the type proved disappointing.

SAAB SF-340 SWEDEN

After studying project designs for a number of possible civil aircraft, including all-cargo types, Saab-Scania of Sweden concluded an agreement with Fairchild Industries of the USA to proceed with project definition of a regional airliner. Known as the SF-340, it was to be a fully collaborative venture – the first of its kind between a European and an American company – in which each company would be responsible for the design and production of a portion of the airframe, and marketing and sales activities would be shared. All aircraft were to be assembled in Sweden, but those for the North American customers were to be finished and furnished by Fairchild in the USA. Project definition was completed during 1980 and in September of that year the two companies agreed to a full go-ahead for the SF-340, which had evolved as a twin-engined, low-wing monoplane with 34 passenger seats – hence the designation. Features of the design included a circular-section pressurized fuselage, a high aspect ratio wing with long-span single-slotted flaps, extensive use of composite materials and adhesive bonding in the structure, and a design fatigue life of 45,000 flight hours and 90,000 landings. Three aircraft were used for flight development and certification, these being first flown on 25 January, 11 May and 25 August 1983 respectively. The first full production standard aircraft flew on 5 March 1984. On 1 November 1985, Saab-Scania assumed overall control of the SF-340 programme after Fairchild indicated that it wished to relinquish its participation. By agreement, the US company remained as a sub-contractor responsible for its share of airframe production (undertaken at Fairchild's airframe manufacturing plant in Chantilly, Virginia) until 1987, when Saab also took over this work after building new production facilities at its Linkoping factory in Sweden.

VARIANTS

All SF-340s to date are of the same external configuration, although the first prototype was test flown for a time with winglets. Early production aircraft had 1,630shp CT7-5A engines, with smaller diameter propellers and a 26,000lb (11,794kg) gross weight, increased to the figures shown above in May 1985. A corporate version is available with, typically, a 12-seat interior and CT7-7E engines offering a better cruise performance at higher altitudes. A cargo version has been designed, with cargo door aft of the wing and passenger door forward, for mixed-traffic operations. Stretched derivatives, such as the 44-passenger SF-440, were studied from 1985 onwards, but had not been launched up to 1987.

SERVICE USE

Type certification obtained in Sweden on 30 May 1984 and ratified by FAA in US and by nine other European authorities (members of the JAR – Joint Airworthiness Requirements group) on 29 June 1984. Australian approval was gained on October 1984. Revenue passenger service began on 15 June 1984 in the hands of Crossair of Switzerland. Other early operators were Comair of Cinicinnati in the US, in October 1984, and Kendall Airlines of Australia in March 1985. By January 1987, some 70 SF-340s were in service with 15 airlines on three continents, and the total order book stood at 98.

SPECIFICATION

Power Plant: Two General Electric CT7-5A2 turboprops with Dowty Rotol four-bladed propellers of 11ft 0in (3.35m) diameter. Fuel capacity, 708 Imp gal (3,220l).
Performance: Max operating speed, 250kts (463km/h) EAS or Mach=0.50; max cruising speed, 274kts (508km/h) at 15,000ft (4,575m) at 25,700lb (11,657kg) weight; economical cruise, 252kts (467km/h) at 25,000ft (7,620m); service ceiling, 25,000ft (7,620m); take-off field length (FAR 25), 4,000ft (1,220m); landing field length (FAR 25), 4,000ft (1,220m); range with 35 passengers, 800 naut mls (1,500km).
Weights: Typical operating weight empty, 17,215lb (7,808kg); max fuel, 5,690lb (2,581kg); max payload, 7,785lb (3,531kg); max take-off, 27,275lb (12,371kg); max landing, 26,500lb (12,020kg); max zero fuel weight, 25,000lb (11,340kg).
Dimensions: Span, 70ft 4in (21.44m); overall length, 64ft 8in (19.72m); overall height, 22ft 6½in (6.87m); fuselage diameter, 7ft 7in (2.31m) sweepback, 3 deg at quarter chord; gross wing area, 450sq ft (41.81m²).
Accommodation: Cabin length, 34ft 8in (10.57m); max width, 7ft 1in (2.16m), max height, 6ft 0in (1.83m). Standard accommodation for 35 passengers in 2+1 arrangement at 30in (76cm) seat pitch. Baggage compartment aft of main cabin, 225cu ft (6.4m³). Flight crew of two, provision for one observer; one flight attendant.

Below: A Saab SF-340 in the colours of the Swiss airline, Crossair. The SF-340 entered service with Crossair, the launch customer for this aircraft, on 15 June 1984. It is used typically on inter-European flights from bases at Zurich, Geneva and Basle. Formed in 1975, Crossair is a relatively new European carrier with a modern fleet, its 340s being complemented by Swearingen Metro IIIs.

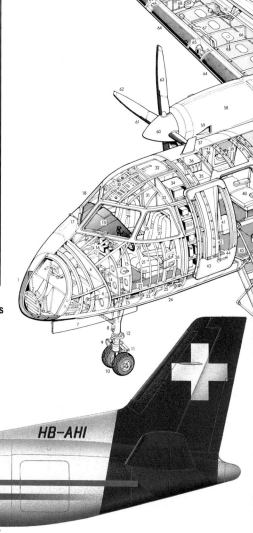

Above: An SF-340 on trial before delivery to the Norwegian carrier, Norving, which has three of these aircraft in a large mixed fleet for charter work.

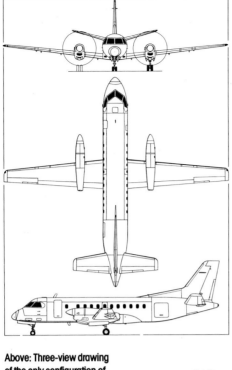

Above: Three-view drawing of the only configuration of SF-340 so far developed, although a stretched version, the SF-440, has also been studied. The low wing position is designed to reduce weight, and allow easy access to the engines for routine servicing.

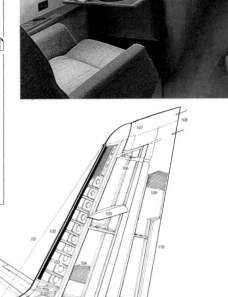

Above: This is the interior of an SF-340 as configured in its corporate/executive version. Rapid changes from one interior layout to another can be made quite easily.

Above: The SF-340 was designed specifically for short-haul low-density routes, and this cutaway emphasises the compactness and neatness of the design. Cabin accommodation is for up to 35 passengers. The wing area and planform were chosen for low operating costs over short stages.

Saab SF-340 Cutaway Drawing Key

1 Radome
2 Weather radar scanner
3 Radar transmitter/receiver
4 Front pressure bulkhead
5 Nose undercarriage wheel bay
6 Hydraulic retraction jack
7 Nosewheel doors
8 Nose undercarriage leg strut
9 Taxying lamp
10 Twin nosewheels
11 Torque scissor link
12 Steering control link
13 Nosewheel leg pivot fixing
14 Rudder pedals
15 Angle of attack transmitter
16 Instrument panel
17 Windscreen wipers
18 Windscreen panels
19 Instrument panel shroud
20 Control column handwheel
21 Pilot's seat
22 Flight deck floor level
23 Underfloor control linkages
24 External hydraulic pipe duct
25 Control mechanism access panels
26 Pitot tubes
27 Safety harness
28 Centre control pedestal
29 Co-pilot's seat
30 Overhead systems switch panel
31 Starboard side toilet compartment
32 Cockpit roof escape hatch
33 Cockpit rear bulkhead
34 Radio and electronics rack
35 Galley/closet unit
36 Wardrobe
37 VHF aerial
38 Starboard side emergency exit
39 'Pull-down' window blinds
40 Front seat row, total 34 passengers
41 Cabin attendant's folding seat
42 Airstairs stowage
43 Entry door, open position
44 Door latch
45 Entry lobby
46 Airstairs
47 Folding handrail
48 Cabin window panel
49 Sidewall seat mounting rail
50 Cabin air vent duct
51 Landing lamp
52 Floor beam construction
53 Seat mounting rails
54 Glassfibre floor panels
55 Fuselage frame and stringer construction
56 Bonded fuselage skin/stringer panel
57 ADF aerial
58 Starboard engine cowling panels
59 NACA-type cooling air intake
60 Propeller spinner
61 Propeller blade de-icing boots
62 Dowty-Rotol four-bladed variable and reversible pitch, fully feathering propeller
63 Composite propeller blades
64 Wing leading-edge de-icing boots
65 Pressure refuelling connection
66 Starboard wing outer integral fuel tank, fuel capacity 733 Imp gal (3,3311)
67 Fuel system piping
68 Overwing filler cap
69 Compass flux valve
70 Bonded wing skin/stringer panel
71 Starboard navigation lights
72 Starboard light
73 Glassfibre wing tip fairing
74 Static dischargers
75 Starboard aileron
76 Aileron geared tab
77 Aileron actuator
78 External flap hinges
79 Starboard single-slotted trailing edge flap, down position
80 Engine exhaust nozzle
81 VLF/Omega aerial (option)
82 Starboard emergency exit window panel
83 Wing spar attachment main frames
84 Wing panel centreline splice
85 Spar attachment links
86 Port emergency exit window panel
87 Cabin wall trim panelling
88 Fuselage skin panelling
89 Overhead hand-baggage lockers (option)
90 Three-abreast seating
91 Overhead conditioned air distribution duct
92 Rear four-abreast seat row
93 Passenger cabin rear bulkhead
94 Anti-collision beacon (option)
95 Fin root fillet construction
96 HF aerial coupler (option)
97 Tailplane leading-edge de-icing boot
98 Starboard tailplane
99 Static dischargers
100 Starboard elevator
101 HF aerial cable (option)
102 Fin leading-edge de-icing boot
103 Leading-edge ribs
104 Aluminium honeycomb tail unit skin panels
105 VOR aerial
106 Fin construction
107 Rudder horn balance
108 Static dischargers
109 Honeycomb rudder construction
110 Rudder tab
111 Vortex generators
112 Rudder hinge control mechanism
113 Tailcone
114 Cabin pressure valves
115 Rear pressure bulkhead
116 Elevator tab
117 Port elevator honeycomb construction
118 Elevator tip fairing
119 Tailplane construction
120 Ventral strake, port and starboard
121 Rear fuselage ventral access hatch
122 Elevator hinge control
123 Fin/tailplane attachment main frames
124 Tail control cables
125 Cockpit voice recorder
126 Air data recorder
127 Baggage compartment bulkhead
128 'Up-and-over' baggage compartment door
129 Baggage restraint net
130 Door guide rails
131 Baggage loading door
132 DME aerial (option)
133 Wing trailing edge root fillet
134 Battery
135 Air conditioning plant, port and starboard
136 Flap inboard section
137 Wing stringers
138 Port inboard integral fuel tank
139 Heat shrouded engine exhaust pipe
140 Exhaust nozzle
141 Flap hydraulic jack
142 Rear spar
143 Composite flap shroud construction
144 Flap honeycomb construction
145 Port single-slotted trailing-edge flap, down position
146 Aileron geared tab
147 Static dischargers
148 Port aileron honeycomb construction
149 Glassfibre wing tip fairing
150 Lighting power supply
151 Strobe light
152 Port navigation light
153 Wing leading edge de-icing boot
154 Wing rib construction
155 Fuel tank bay end rib
156 Overwing fuel filter cap
157 Port outer integral fuel tank
158 Front spar
159 Leading-edge nose ribs
160 Twin mainwheels
161 Main undercarriage leg strut
162 Torque scissor links
163 Mainwheel doors, closed after cycling of undercarriage leg
164 Hydraulic retraction jack
165 Main undercarriage pivot fixing
166 Engine bay fireproof bulkhead
167 Intake particle separator
168 Accessory gearbox
169 General Electric CT7-5A turboshaft engine
170 Engine nacelle construction
171 Ventral oil cooler
172 Gearbox mounting strut
173 Engine drive shaft
174 Propeller reduction gearbox
175 Propeller hub pitch change mechanism
176 Engine air intake
177 Propeller spinner
178 Port Dowty-Rotol four-bladed composite propeller

SHORTS 330 UK

Based on its experience in the design and operation of the Skyvan, Shorts began to study, in the early 1970s, the possibility of developing a larger commuter airliner, in the 30-seat category, for which there then appeared to be an emerging market. To make such an aircraft attractive to a market that was traditionally unlikely to be able to finance expensive new equipment, the company set itself the target of producing an aircraft having a first cost no greater than $1 million (about £400,000) in 1973 values. Such a restraint ruled out any possibility of starting the design of a new type from scratch. Instead, what became known initially as the SD3-30 evolved as an aircraft sharing several features with the Skyvan: it used the same outer wing panels, on a longer centre wing, had the same, basically square, cross-section for the fuselage, which was 12ft 5in (3.78m) longer, and used a similar, though enlarged, tail unit. Improving the appearance of the SD3-30 (compared with that of its progenitor) was a longer nose and a longer top fuselage fairing, extending from the flight deck to the tail. Other significant changes were the introduction of retractable landing gear and a switch from the Skyvan's Garrett engines to Pratt & Whitney Canada PT6As, judged to be more acceptable to the regional airline industry and more readily able to meet the power requirements of the enlarged aircraft, since suitably uprated PT6A-45s were already under development for the de Havilland Canada Dash 7. Helped by a UK government grant towards launching costs (to be repaid through a levy on subsequent sales) Shorts was able to announce a formal go-ahead for the SD3-30 on 23 May 1973, and construction of prototypes and pre-production aircraft was put in hand at the Queen's Island, Belfast, factory in Northern Ireland. The first and second aircraft made their initial flights there on 22 August 1974 and 8 July 1975 respectively. The first production aircraft, flown on 15 December 1975, was also used to complete the final stages of certification.

VARIANTS

The SD3-30, which was re-styled as Shorts 330 soon after entering service, was initially powered by 1,156shp (862kW) PT6A-45A engines. After delivering 26 aircraft with these engines, Shorts introduced the slightly modified PT6A-45B, and these were used in the next 40 aircraft. A switch was then made to the PT6A-45R, with slightly higher flat-rated power and a power reserve system, as recorded in the data panel, and some previously optional items of equipment became standard. The power increase

allowed the gross weight to go up by 210lb (95.3kg) from the original certification weight of 22,690lb (10,292kg). Fuel capacity in the Shorts 330 was increased in January 1985 from the original 480 Imp gal (2,182l). In this form, the aircraft is now known as the Shorts 330-200. Although the Shorts 330 is primarily a regional airliner, it is readily adaptable for all-cargo and military transport roles. Specifically for military use, the Shorts 330-UTT (Utility Tactical Transport) has a strengthened floor, inward-opening rear cabin doors for paradropping, and structural reinforcement for a max take-off weight of 24,600lb (11,158kg). For military or commercial use, this C-23A Sherpa features a full-width rear cargo ramp/door for straight-in loading, with provision for a reinforced floor and roller conveyor systems. The first Sherpa flew on 23 December 1982 and was one of 18 sold to the USAF.

SERVICE USE

The SD3-30 gained full UK certification in the transport category on 18 February 1976, and won FAA type approval to FAR Pt 25 and FAR Pt 36 on 18 June 1976. Deliveries began in the same month, and revenue service was inaugurated by Time Air in the US on 24 August 1976. Sales by early 1987 totalled 123.

Below: The interior of the Shorts 330, with three-abreast seating and enclosed overhead lockers.

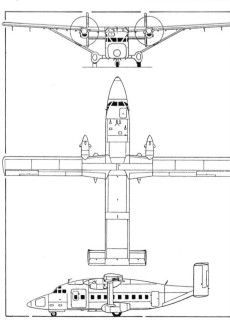

Below: Three-view drawing of the Shorts 330, showing its similarity to the smaller Skyvan.

Right: Cutaway drawing of the Shorts 330, which entered production in 1975. Construction is simple and orthodox, for ease of maintenance.

SPECIFICATION
(Shorts 330-200)

Power Plant: Two Pratt & Whitney Canada PT6A-45R turboprops each rated at 1,198shp (893kW) for take-off, with Hartzell five-blade constant-speed fully-feathering and reversing propellers. Fuel capacity, 560 Imp gal (2,546l) in wing centre section and fuselage top fairing.

Performance: Max operating speed, 195kts (361km/h) IAS; max cruising speed, 190kts (352km/h) at 10,000ft (3,050m); long-range cruising speed, 159kts (294km/h) at 10,000ft (3,050m); initial rate of climb 1,180ft/min (6.0m/sec); take-off field length (FAR Pt 25), 3,420ft (1,040m); landing distance (FAR), 3,380ft (1,030m); range with max payload, no reserves, 473 naut mls (876km); range with max fuel, no reserves, 915 naut mls (1,695km) with 4,335lb (1966kg) payload.

Weights: Operating weight empty, 14,727lb (6,680kg); fuel weight, 4,480lb (2,032kg); max passenger payload, 5,850lb (2,653kg); max cargo payload, 7,500lb (3,400kg); max take-off weight, 22,900lb (10,387kg); max landing weight, 22,600lb (10,251kg).

Dimensions: Span, 74ft 8in (22.76m); overall length, 58ft 0½in (17.69m); overall height, 16ft 3in (4.95m); sweepback, nil; wing area, 453sq ft (42.1m²).

Accommodation: Cabin length, 31ft 1in (9.47m), max width, 6ft 4in (1.93m), max height, 6ft 4in (1.93m). Standard layout provides 30 seats in a two-plus-one arrangement with offset aisle, at seat pitch of 30in (76cm). Two above-floor baggage compartments, volume 145cu ft (4.11m³). Flight crew of two.

Shorts 330 Cutaway Drawing Key

1 Glass-fibre nose cone
2 Weather radar installation
3 Nose skin panelling
4 Forward baggage compartment, 45 cu ft/400lb (1.27m³/181kg) max
5 Upward-hinged baggage door, 30.5in x 37.7in (77.5cm x 95.8cm)
6 VHF 2 aerial
7 Hydraulically steerable rearward-retracting nosewheel
8 Nosewheel fork
9 Nosewheel oleo
10 Nosewheel pivot point
11 Nosewheel box
12 Nosewheel retraction mechanism and jack
13 Undercarriage emergency actuation accumulator
14 Hydraulics bay
15 Rudder circuit linkage
16 Avionics bay (port and starboard)
17 23 Amp/hr batteries (port and starboard)
18 Seat adjustment lever
19 Seat belt
20 Heated pitot head
21 Underfloor avionics equipment
22 Elevator circuit linkage
23 Control column
24 Pilot's seat
25 Rudder pedals
26 Windscreen wipers
27 Windscreen panels (electrically heated)
28 Instrument panel coaming
29 Central control console (trim wheels)
30 Co-pilot's seat
31 Overhead panel (AC/DC power supply)
32 Fuel cocks
33 Crew escape/ditching hatch
34 Flight deck/cabin sliding door
35 Aileron circuit linkage
36 Control cable conduit (rudder and elevator trim circuits)
37 Flight deck conditioned/heating/de-misting air supply
38 Ambient-air intake
39 Combined VOR/Localiser/ILS glide-slope aerials
40 Blow-in door (ground running)

41 Turbine-blower intake
42 Heat exchanger
43 Air cycle installation
44 Engine bleed-air supply
45 Pre-cooler
46 Pre-cooler intake
47 Cabin conditioned/fresh air supply
48 Doorway-surround doubler plate
49 Cabin forward emergency exits, port 37in x 24.5in (94cm x 62cm); starboard 42in x 27in (107cm x 68.6cm)
50 Forward freight door, 65.6in x 55.6in (167cm x 141cm)
51 Freight door hinges
52 Honeycomb-sandwich floor panels
53 Corrugated inner skin
54 Cabin air distribution duct
55 Seat mounting rails
56 Rudder circuit
57 ADF sense aerials (port and starboard)
58 Rectangular fuselage section frames
59 Chemically-milled window panel
60 12-a-side cabin windows, 18.5in x 14.4in (74cm x 36.6cm)
61 Passenger accommodation: 30 seats, 3 abreast (single port/double starboard) arrangement
62 Engine bleed-air supply duct
63 Fuel tank mounting lugs
64 Forward multiple fuel tank (Cell 1)
65 Class II sealed tank dividing bulkhead
66 Fuel gravity filler
67 Forward multiple fuel tank (Cell 2)
68 Class I sealed tank dividing bulkhead
69 Forward multiple fuel tank (Cell 3)
70 Sealed containment area (tank seepage)
71 Tank/fuselage attachment
72 Wingroot fairing
73 Engine-propeller control cable runs
74 Hydraulics reservoir
75 Wing centre section
76 Chemically-milled centre section skinning
77 Dorsal anti-collision beacon
78 Centre-section front spar
79 Leading-edge access panels
80 Oil cooler
81 Engine firewall
82 Engine mounting ring
83 Exhaust ducts
84 Air intake duct (with debris deflector)
85 Propeller pitch-change mechanism
86 Hartzell constant-speed five-bladed auto-feathering propeller, 9ft (2.75m) diameter

87 Propeller de-icing boots
88 Pratt and Whitney Canada PT6A-45 turboprop engine
89 Oil filter cap
90 Outer/inner wing pin joints
91 Outer-section front spar
92 Outer wing support strut
93 Starboard landing/taxying lamp
94 Support strut pin joints
95 Strut attachment bracket
96 Fluid de-iced leading-edge (tank and pump unit mounted at rear of starboard mainwheel well)
97 Starboard navigation light
98 Glass-fibre wing-tip fairing
99 Starboard aileron
100 Aileron trim tab
101 Aileron hinge rib
102 Support strut box
103 Flap hinge ribs
104 Starboard outer flap section
105 Starboard centre flap section
106 Centre-section end rib
107 Starboard inner flap section
108 Flap actuating rod mechanism (mounted on spar)
109 Water-methanol tank and pump
110 Gravity fuel filler
111 Aft fuel tank (Cell 4)
112 Sealed containment area (tank seepage)
113 Tank/fuselage attachment
114 Elevator circuit
115 Cabin concealed ceiling lighting
116 Fuselage (detachable) top fairings
117 Overhead passenger hand-baggage lockers
118 Service door/emergency exit, 56.5in x 28.4in (143.5cm x 72cm)
119 Buffet unit storage compartment (sandwiches/biscuits etc)
120 Cabin furnishing profile
121 Coat closet
122 Toilet compartment
123 VHF 1 aerial
124 Skin outer panelling
125 Corrugated inner skin panelling
126 HF sense aerial
127 Rudder/elevator circuits
128 Emergency locator antenna
129 Rectangular section aft frame
130 Tailplane spar pin joint strip
131 Tailplane structure
132 Rudder actuation lever
133 Rudder trim tab jack
134 Leading-edge de-icing fluid lines
135 Fin skin panels
136 Rudder aerodynamics balance
137 Rudder extension fairing
138 Static dischargers
139 Rudder trim tab
140 Starboard rudder

141 Trim tab actuating rod
142 Rear navigation light (starboard lower fin only)
143 Elevator trim tab
144 Trim tab actuating rod
145 Three-section elevator
146 Elevator actuation quadrant
147 Rudder control linkage
148 Elevator spring strut
149 Trim cable pulleys
150 Port tailplane spar pin joints
151 Fluid de-iced leading-edge
152 Fin structure
153 Rudder aerodynamic balance
154 Rudder extension fairing
155 Port rudder
156 Rudder trim tab
157 Rudder actuation lever fairing
158 Fin attachment access panels
159 Fin lower section
160 De-icing system access
161 Fluid de-iced leading-edge
162 Aft fuselage structure
163 Aft baggage door, 43in x 57in (109cm x 145cm)
164 Baggage door (open)
165 Baggage restraint net
166 Stepped aft baggage compartment, 100 cu ft/600lb (2.83m³/272kg max
167 Bulkhead
168 Doorway-surround doubler plate
169 Passenger entry door, 56.5in x 28.4in (143.5cm x 72cm)
170 Cabin electrics and communication panel
171 Buffet unit heated water container/cup/stowage/trash bin
172 Cabin attendant's tip-up seat (lowered)
173 Contoured inner window surrounds
174 Cabin seating rearmost row (port seat omitted for clarity)
175 Rudder circuit linkage
176 Damper strut
177 Flap actuating rod
178 Centre-section ribs
179 Centre-section front spar

180 Firewall/bulkhead
181 Engine support structure
182 Engine mounting ring (with four dynafocal resilient mounts)
183 Exhaust duct
184 Spinner
185 Intake lip electrical de-icing
186 Oil cooler intake scoop
187 Aft gearbox integral oil tank
188 Fuselage main frames (wing/undercarriage carrying)
189 Rudder circuit
190 Stub wing front and rear spars
191 Undercarriage mounting beam
192 Undercarriage retraction jack
193 Wing support strut attachment
194 Undercarriage pivot point
195 Undercarriage levered suspension leg
196 Port main landing-gear fairing
197 Retractable mainwheel
198 Shock-absorber strut
199 Port wing support strut
200 Port landing/taxying lamp
201 Hydraulic ground service panel (fairing hinged aft section)
202 Wing outer-section front spar
203 End ribs
204 Outer/inner wing pin joints
205 Port inner flap section
206 Outrigged flap hinge arms
207 Aileron trim tab cables
208 Port centre flap section
209 Hinged trailing-edge (controls) access panels
210 Port outer flap section
211 Aileron control rods
212 Support strut box
213 Multi-angle section diffusion members
214 Pressed ribs
215 Corrugated inner skin panels
216 Aileron actuating rod
217 Cable-operated trim tab jack
218 Trim tab actuating rod
219 Aileron trim tab
220 Port aileron
221 Outer-section rear spar
222 Aileron mass-balance weights
223 Wing skin outer panelling
224 Outer-section front spar
225 Outer-section leading-edge spar
226 End rib structure/tip attachments
227 Glass-fibre port wing-tip fairing
228 Port navigation light

Above: Thai Airways, a government-owned airline responsible for domestic and regional services in Thailand, has four of these Shorts 330 Srs 200s in service in 1987, together with a pair of the related Shorts 360s (next page). Some 24 airlines were operating Shorts 330s at the end of 1986, most of these (12) being in North and South America, with nine others in the UK and Europe.

Below: A typical operator of the Shorts 330 in the UK is Guernsey Airlines, which has two in service on its network of scheduled routes radiating from Guernsey in the Channel Islands. The flat-sided 330 lends itself to flamboyant liveries.

SHORTS 360 UK

For many years, operators of commuter-style services in the USA (where a large proportion of the market for this type of aircraft exists) had been limited by the terms of the CAB Economic Regulation 298 to flying aircraft with no more than 30 passenger seats. To fly larger types required the airline to seek authority under a substantially different set of operating regulations, compliance with which frequently imposed extra costs which were necessarily passed on to the traveller and thus served to diminish the number of passengers carried. In turn this reduced viability and led, eventually, to financial collapse. The deregulation of the US airline industry in 1978 brought a relaxation of these rules and made it possible for many third-level airlines to contemplate growth of a kind previously thought impossible. One obvious impact of this sea-change in the fortunes of at least some of the commuter specialists was that the aircraft manufacturers found a new opportunity to market aircraft of more than 30-seat capacity. In the late 1970s Shorts had already been studying several ways of improving the basic Shorts 330 without increasing capacity, one such option being to use more powerful PT6A-65 engines in order to achieve higher operating weights. When the limit on capacity became less important, it became possible to combine this new engine installation (with a modified cowling and improved air intake) with a new or modified fuselage. As a first step, it was decided to restrict the 'stretch' to a modest six seats, emphasis being placed upon improvement to the rear fuselage profile to reduce drag and thus improve operating economics. Wind tunnel testing embraced several options, including a T-tail layout, but an entirely conventional low-mounted tailplane and single fin-and-rudder finally met the design objectives, allied to a somewhat lengthened rear fuselage of improved aerodynamic form. This redesign allowed one extra seat row (three passengers) at the rear of the cabin; a 36in (91.5cm) plug ahead of the wing provided for another seat row. For the most part, the remainder of the airframe was little changed from that of the Shorts 330, although Dowty landing gear was chosen to replace the earlier Menasco gear, and

Above: The Shorts 360 is a close relative of the 330, as illustrated on the previous page, the single fin being the most obvious identifying feature. This example is in the livery of Canadian airline Time Air,

which flies two on scheduled routes in the Province of Alberta. At the end of 1986, some 100 Shorts 360s were in use with 28 airlines, of which 12 were in North America and nine in Europe.

improved Hartzell propellers were matched to the new power plant, which incorporated an emergency reserve feature to provide a power boost in the event of one engine failing during the critical stages of take-off. Since the Shorts 330 designation was indicative of a 30-seat version of the basic SD-3 design, the new 36-seat project became known as the Shorts 336 in the drawing office, but this was changed to Shorts 360 for marketing purposes. The go-ahead for the Shorts 360 was given by the company's management in January 1981, and a first flight was achieved on 1 June of the same year, indicating the extent to which standard components of the Shorts 330 were appliable to the new aircraft. In the prototype, this commonality extended to the PT6A-45R engines fitted for the first six months of flight testing, the definitive PT6A-65Rs first being flown in January 1982.

VARIANTS

Between prototype first flight and production definition, some small changes were made in the control system of the Shorts 360, including deletion of one of the two trim tabs from each elevator. The first production batch of aircraft had PT6A-65R engines each rated at 1,173shp (875kW) for maximum continuous operation and at 1,327shp (990kW) with emergency reserve for take-off. During 1986, the more powerful PT6A-65AR engines were introduced in aircraft designated Shorts 360 Advanced.

SERVICE USE

The first production Shorts 360 flew on 19 August 1982 and UK certification was obtained on 3 September of that year, followed in November by FAA approval to FAR Pts 25 and 36. The first delivery was made to Suburban Airlines at Reading, Pennsylvania on 11 November 1982, and service use began on 1 December. The first Shorts 360 Advanced went to Thai Airways in early 1986. Sales totalled 120 at the end of 1986.

Shorts 360 Cutaway Dawing Key

1 Radome
2 Weather radar scanner
3 Nose skin panelling
4 Nose compartment construction
5 Door hinges
6 Forward baggage compartment
7 Baggage loading floor
8 Baggage door
9 Aft-retracting nosewheel
10 Nosewheel forks
11 Emergency hydraulic accumulator
12 Static ports
13 Nose undercarriage pivot bearing
14 Hydraulic retraction jack
15 Rudder pedals
16 Control column
17 Instrument panel
18 Windscreen wipers
19 Electrically-heated windscreen panels
20 Stand-by compass
21 Instrument panel shroud
22 Co-pilot's seat
23 Centre control console
24 Pilot's seat
25 Seat adjustment lever
26 Pitot head
27 Underfloor compartment access panels
28 Avionics equipment racks
29 Cockpit floor level
30 Cockpit bulkhead
31 Forward fuselage section frame and stringer construction
32 Side window panels
33 Overhead systems switch panels
34 Cockpit roof escape/ditching hatch
35 Rear bulkhead control duct
36 Sliding door to main cabin
37 Cockpit air supply ducting
38 Main cabin air supply ducting
39 Air conditioning system NACA-type intake
40 Pre-cooler intake
41 Heat exchanger
42 Ground running intake
43 Air conditioning plant air cycle unit
44 Cabin roof skin panelling
45 Cabin top fairing panel
46 Corrugated inner skin doubler
47 Fresh air scoop
48 Door surround skin doubler
49 Freight door

50 Forward emergency exit hatch, port and starboard
51 Freight door hinges
52 Cabin air distribution duct
53 Cockpit/centre fuselage production joint
54 Freight door construction
55 Passenger cabin floor level
56 Seat mounting rails
57 Three-abreast passenger seating, 36-seat standard layout
58 Fuselage skin panel joint strap

59 Honeycomb sandwich floor panels
60 Floor beam construction
61 Cabin window panels
62 Overhead passenger service units
63 Fresh air distribution ducts to individual punkah louvres
64 Overhead stowage bins
65 Corrugated inner skin doubler
66 Fuselage skin panelling
67 Wing spar/fuselage attachment pin joint
68 Engine bleed air ducting to air conditioning system
69 Sealed containment area (tank seepage)
70 Fuel tank mounting lug
71 Three-cell forward main fuel tank; total fuel system capacity 480 Imp gal (2,182l)
72 Fuel tank bulkheads
73 Gravity filler caps

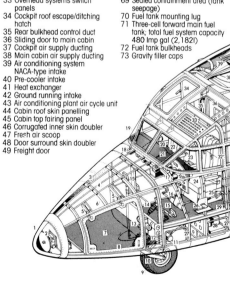

Above: Cutaway drawing of the Shorts 360 in its standard configuration.

Right: British Midland adopted this new livery for its Shorts 360s in 1986.

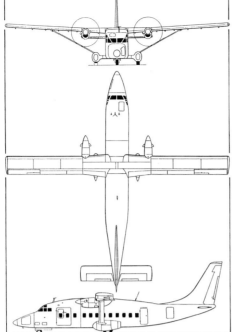

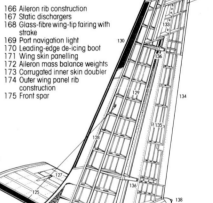

Left: Three-view drawing of the Shorts 360, which has the same wing and front fuselage as the Shorts 330, with a lengthened rear fuselage and a completely new tail unit.

Above: The cockpit of the Shorts 360 is functionally effective, and retains the traditional 'T' layout for the basic flight instruments, centred in front of each pilot's seat.

74 Hydraulic reservoirs
75 Wing centre section front spar
76 Leading-edge access panels, engine control runs
77 Engine bay fireproof bulkhead
78 Annular engine intake
79 Engine mounting ring frame
80 Exhaust stubs
81 Pratt & Whitney Canada PT6A-65R turboprop engine
82 Engine air intake
83 Propeller hub pitch-change mechanism
84 Spinner
85 Hartzell five-bladed, constant-speed, fully feathering and reversible propeller
86 Engine cowling panels
87 Starboard wing strut
88 Landing/taxiing lamp
89 Strut attachment joint
90 Starboard outboard wing panel
91 Leading-edge pneumatic de-icing boot (optional)

92 Starboard navigation light
93 Glass-fibre wing tip fairing with strake
94 Static dischargers
95 Aileron mass balance weights
96 Starboard aileron
97 Aileron hinge control
98 Aileron tab
99 Outboard Fowler-type flap segments
100 External flap hinges
101 Flap hydraulic jacks
102 Outboard/centre wing panel pin joints
103 Inboard Fowler-type flap segment
104 Flap damper strut
105 Rear spar
106 Centre wing panel rib construction
107 Anti-collision light
108 Wing skin panel centreline joint
109 Water-methanol tank
110 Gravity fuel filler cap
111 Aft single cell main fuel tank
112 Fuel tank bulkheads
113 Sealed containment area (tank seepage)
114 Cabin roof trim and concealed lighting panel
115 Tailplane control rods
116 VHF aerial

117 Rear fuselage upper fairing panels
118 Overhead stowage bins
119 Centre fuselage/tailcone joint frame
120 Starboard toilet compartment
121 Whip aerial
122 Tailcone frame and stringer construction
123 Fin root fillet
124 HF aerial cable
125 Starboard tailplane
126 Pneumatic leading-edge de-icing boot
127 Starboard elevator
128 Fin leading edge
129 Tailfin construction
130 Pneumatic leading-edge de-icing boot
131 Glass-fibre fin-tip fairing
132 Static dischargers
133 Rudder balance
134 Rudder trim tab
135 Rudder construction
136 Rudder hinges
137 Tailcone
138 Tail navigation light
139 Elevator tab
140 Port elevator construction
141 Glass-fibre tailplane tip fairing with strake
142 Tailplane rib construction

143 Three-spar torsion box tailplane construction
144 Rudder and elevator hinge controls
145 Tailplane spar/fuselage attachment joint
146 Sloping fin attachment bulkheads
147 Tailplane de-icing air valve
148 Rear baggage door
149 Baggage restraint net
150 Rear baggage compartment
151 Baggage loading floor
152 Battery compartment
153 Galley unit
154 Cabin attendant's folding seat
155 Interphone
156 Rear cabin seat row
157 Passenger entry door, emergency exit on starboard side
158 Rear cabin window panels
159 Port Fowler-type flaps
160 Rear spar
161 Flap external hinge
162 Flap hydraulic jacks
163 Flap shroud ribs, hinged access panel
164 Outer flap rib construction
165 Aileron tab

166 Aileron rib construction
167 Static dischargers
168 Glass-fibre wing-tip fairing with strake
169 Port navigation light
170 Leading-edge de-icing boot
171 Wing skin panelling
172 Aileron mass balance weights
173 Corrugated inner skin doubler
174 Outer wing panel rib construction
175 Front spar

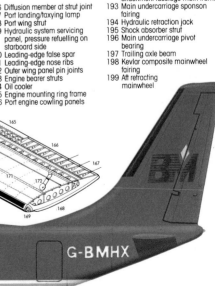

176 Diffusion member at strut joint
177 Port landing/taxiing lamp
178 Port wing strut
179 Hydraulic system servicing panel, pressure refuelling on starboard side
180 Leading-edge false spar
181 Leading-edge nose ribs
182 Outer wing panel pin joints
183 Engine bearer struts
184 Oil cooler
185 Engine mounting ring frame
186 Port engine cowling panels

187 Spinner
188 Engine air intake duct
189 Exhaust stub
190 Intake duct particle separator
191 Oil cooler air scoop
192 Wing and undercarriage attachment fuselage main frames
193 Main undercarriage sponson fairing
194 Hydraulic retraction jack
195 Shock absorber strut
196 Main undercarriage pivot bearing
197 Trailing axle beam
198 Kevlar composite mainwheel fairing
199 Aft retracting mainwheel

SHORTS SKYVAN UK

Interest in the development of a small transport aircraft aimed chiefly at the freighting market began at Short Bros and Harland in the 1950s. At that time, the Belfast-based company was much interested in the air freighter market, both civil and military, the interest eventually leading to development not only of the Skyvan, at the bottom end of the size scale, but also to the RAF's Belfast, the largest freighter built in the UK. Whilst studying its own designs in the second half of the 1950s, Shorts was also approached by F G Miles Ltd with the sugges-

tion that the two companies might collaborate in development of the latter's HDM 106 Caravan light freighter, itself a derivation of the Miles Aerovan 'pod-and-boom' light freighter combined with the Hurel Dubois high-aspect-ratio wing. Purchasing the Caravan preliminary design from Miles, Shorts continued to study aircraft of the same general configuration, leading eventually to the conclusion that twin-boom and pod-and-boom layouts were less satisfactory than a more conventional fuselage based on a payload 'box' with a 6.5ft (1.98m) square

cross-section and a length of 16ft (4.9m). A high-aspect-ratio, untapered, strut-braced high wing and fixed landing gear were also found to be desirable features for a mini-freighter, which took shape as the PD.36 project design at Belfast and acquired the drawing office number SC.7 when construction of a prototype was launched in 1959. At this point, Shorts opted to power the mini-freighter with a pair of 390hp (291kW) Continental GTSIO-520 piston engines, believing that small turboprops would not be sufficiently advanced to be incorporated in a proto-

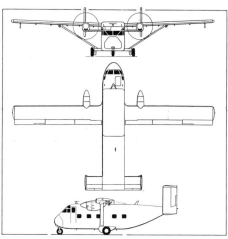

Left: Aero Services Barbados uses this Skyvan 3 to fly between the Caribbean Islands.

Above: Three-view drawing of the Skyvan Srs 3, which has been the standard version since 1967.

TUPOLEV TU-134 SOVIET UNION

The Tupolev design bureau began development of this twin-engined short/medium-range jetliner in the early 1960s, in an effort to provide Aeroflot with an aircraft in this class of better performance than the Tu-124, which had only then recently entered service. The Tu-124 was essentially a scaled-down derivative of the first Soviet jet transport, the Tu-104, which itself was adapted from the Tu-16 jet bomber and therefore lacked some of the refinements that were coming to be taken for granted by airline passengers in the west. The Tu-134 emerged in September 1964, by which time a prototype was reputed to have completed more than 100 test flights, to show that its configuration matched quite closely that chosen by BAC and Douglas for, respectively, the One-Eleven and the DC-9, aircraft both in a similar category to the Tu-134. The Soviet aircraft had more wing sweepback, however, combining this with a rugged tricycle landing gear design to allow short-field and rough-field operation, in line with Aeroflot requirements. It also had the characteristic Tupolev fairings at the wing trailing edge to house main units of the landing gear when retracted, which had been a feature of the Tu-104 and Tu-124 as well as the military Tu-16 and Tu-28. It will be noted, incidentally, that the Tupolev design bureau had followed Boeing practice in designating its jetliners in numerical series (104, 114, 124, 134 etc). The Tu-134 was assigned the NATO reporting name 'Crusty'.

VARIANTS

Six prototypes or pre-production aircraft are reported to have been used in development of the Tu-134, production of which was launched in 1964 at Kharkhov. The first production batch was followed by the appearance, in the second half of 1970, of the Tu-134A, featuring a 6ft 10½in (2.10m) fuselage 'stretch', providing for eight extra passengers (two

seat rows) in the maximum-density one-class layout. All early Tu-134s and some Tu-134As had the Tupolev glazed nose, similar to that of the original Tu-16 bomber, but later aircraft had a 'solid' nose radome containing weather radar. Soloviev D-30 Srs II engines were introduced on the Tu-134A. Further versions of the aircraft began to appear from the autumn of 1981 onwards, but it is believed that these were the result of modification programmes rather than new production, which had probably then

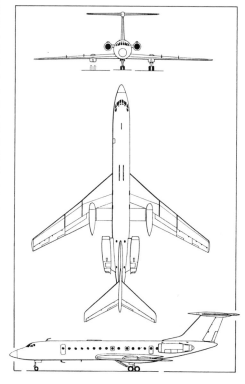

Left: The Tupolev Tu-134A is shown in this three-view drawing with the

lengthened radar-carrying nose featured by most production aircraft.

type airframe. With these engines, the SC-7 prototype flew on 17 January 1963, its construction having progressed only slowly while government launching aid was sought in order to establish a production line. Well before this approval was eventually given in 1964, it had become clear that turboprops were replacing piston engines as favoured power for commercial operation, and Shorts decided during 1962 to base future plans for the Skyvan (as the SC7 had been named) on a version with Turboméca Astazou II turboprops provid-

Above: Up to 22 seats can be provided in the Skyvan, which in its civil passenger-carrying version was sometimes known as the Skyliner. Overhead lockers and concealed lighting are featured.

SPECIFICATION
(Skyvan Series 3)

Power Plant: Two Garrett TPE 331-2-201A turboprops each rated at 715shp (533kW) for take-off, with Hartzell three-blade variable-pitch propellers of 8ft 6in (2.59m) diameter. Fuel capacity, 293 Imp gal (1,332l) in tanks in wing centre section fairing above fuselage, and provision for 97 Imp gal (441l) in tanks in fuselage sides.
Performance: Max cruising speed, 175kts (324km/h) at 10,000ft (3,050m); economical cruising speed, 150kts (278km/h) at 10,000ft (3,050m); initial rate of climb, 1,640ft/min (8.3m/sec); service ceiling, 22,500ft (6,860m); take-off distance to 50ft (15m), FAR Pt 23, 1,600ft (490m); landing distance from 50ft (15m), FAR Pt 23, 1,480ft (450m); range with max fuel at best range speed, 600 naut mls (1,115km); range with 4,000lb (1,815kg) cargo payload, 162 naut mls (300km).
Weights: Operating weight empty, passenger version, 8,100lb (3,674kg); operating weight empty, freighter, 7,600lb (3,447kg); fuel weight, standard, 2,320lb (1,052kg); fuel weight, max, 3,120lb (1,415kg); max payload, 4,600lb (2,086kg); max take-off weight, 12,500lb (5,670kg); max landing weight, 12,500lb (5,670kg).
Dimensions: Span, 64ft 11in (19.79m); overall length, no nose radar, 40ft 1in (12.21m); overall length, with nose radar, 41ft 4in (12.60m); overall height, 15ft 1in (4.60m); sweepback, nil; wing area, 378sq ft (35.12m²).
Accommodation: Cabin length, 18ft 7in (5.67m), max width, 6ft 6in (1.98m), max height, 6ft 6in (1.98m). Provision for up to 19 passengers in a two-plus-one arrangement with offset aisle. Flight crew of one or two.

---

ing 520shp (388kW) each. After completing 25 hours with the piston engines, the prototype was fitted with Astazous and, as the Skyvan IA, flew again on 2 October 1963.

VARIANTS
An initial production batch of 19 Skyvan Srs IIs were built with 730shp (545kW) Astazou XII engines, the first flight being made on 29 October 1965. The type could carry 19 passengers or 4,000lb (1,815kg) of freight and was used by several commercial operators. To produce a definitive version of the Skyvan, Shorts then switched to the Garrett TPE331-201 engine to produce the Skyvan Srs 3 which first flew on 15 December 1967. Some Srs 2s were converted to have the Garrett engines, and some aircraft were produced as Skyvan IIIAs with a 13,700lb (6,215kg) gross weight. Furnished to higher standard for airline use, the Skyliner version of the Skyvan Srs 3 could carry up to 22 passengers. Several military variants were also developed, as the Skyvan Srs 3M and Skyvan 3M-200, the latter with clearance to operate at weights up to 15,000lb (6,804kg).

SERVICE USE
Certification of the Astazou-engined Skyvan Srs 2 was obtained early in 1966, and deliveries began at that time. The Skyvan Srs 3 entered service in 1968, and in 1970 it was certificated in accordance with new UK civil airworthiness requirements for STOL operations. Some 150 Skyvans had been sold by the end of 1986, of which about 90 were for commercial operators or government agencies and the remainder for military users.

TUPOLEV TU-134

been completed. These variants included the Tu-134B with a forward-facing crew compartment including engine controls and navigation instruments on the centre panel, with a jump seat (between the two pilots' seats) for the navigator/flight engineer. The Tu-134B-1 had interior revisions, including a small reduction in toilet size, to allow an increase in basic capacity to 84 passengers, or a maximum of 90 if galley facilities were removed. The Tu-134B-3 introduced new lightweight seats permitting five-abreast seating for 96 passengers, with full toilet and galley provisions retained; improved D-30-III engines were also introduced.

SERVICE USE
Proving flights with the Tu-134 on Aeroflot routes were made before the first commercial service began in September 1967, between Moscow and Stockholm. The Tu-134A went into service in the second half of 1970. Production of all versions of the Tu-134 is estimated at more than 700, of which up to 100 were exported, for use by most of the East European airlines, by Syrian Air and by Hang Khong Vietnam. Large-scale use continued in 1987.

Below: A Tupolev Tu-134A in service with the Czech airline CSA, which had 13 of these rear engined twinjets in its fleet in 1986. The short-haul Tu-134 has been used by the airlines of all the East European nations and a few in the Middle and Far East.

TUPOLEV TU-154 SOVIET UNION

The Soviet counterpart of the Boeing 727-200 and HSA Trident, the Tu-154 was first publicized in 1966 and made its first flight on 4 October 1968. Intended to take the modernization of Aeroflot a step further following the introduction of the first generation of turbojet and turboprop transports, the Tu-154 had the same overall configuration as its two Western contemporaries, but also some significant differences to meet the operational requirements of Soviet air transport. In particular, the power-to-weight ratio is considerably higher than that of the Model 727, giving the aircraft a lively airfield performance and allowing it to operate from the relatively short and poorly-surfaced Class 2 airfields at many Soviet cities. The wing pods for landing gear stowage are also a distinctive feature of the Tupolov design. Flight development involved six prototypes and pre-production aircraft, and since entering Aeroflot service the type has undergone considerable development, as noted below. The NATO reporting name for all versions is 'Careless'.

VARIANTS

The initial production version, identified simply as Tu-154, had 20,950lb st (9,500kgp) Kuznetsov NK-8-2 engines, and a number of possible interior layouts, ranging from 128 to 167 seats. The standard all-economy layout had 160 seats, and a typical mixed-class arrangement provided 24 first-class seats in the forward cabin in place of 54 economy-class. Soviet sources indicated the availability of an all-cargo version, but this may not have appeared in definitive form until the Tu-154C was developed as a Tu-154B derivative, as noted below. The Tu-154A was the first improved version to appear, in 1973, with its uprated NK-8-2U engines (see data panel), and maximum take-off weight increased from

Above: A Tupolev Tu-154 of the Hungarian airline Malev on the approach, revealing the large-area trailing-edge flaps. These and the high power/weight ratio give the Tu-154 an outstanding field performance, for both take-off and landing.

Left: The three-man flight-deck of an early production Tupolev Tu-154.

TUPOLEV TU-204 SOVIET UNION

Left: This artist's impression of the Tupolev Tu-204 shows that it breaks new ground for design from this bureau. According to preliminary details published during 1986, the Tu-204 is likely to be the most advanced of Aeroflot's new generation of jet and turboprop airliners when it enters service in the early 'nineties.

Right: The three-view of the Tupolev Tu-204 shows that its configuration is similar to that of the Boeing 757, which it also matches in size, with up to 219 seats in a one-class layout. Other than the unsuccessful supersonic Tu-144, all previous Tupolev airliners have had wing pods into which the main gear retracts.

One of the trio of new airliners publicized in the Soviet Union in 1986 as being under development for service with Aeroflot in the 1990s, the Tu-204 has been described as the 'Soviet Boeing 757'. Dimensionally similar, the Tu-204 has slightly less sweepback than the Boeing twin, but is of the same overall configuration and similarly powered by a pair of advanced high-BPR turbofans. The

latter are of unknown provenance at the time this account was prepared, but appear to be of the same type as those specified for the four-engined Ilyushin Il-96 and are probably a product of the Soloviev bureau, perhaps as derivatives of the D-30. Like the other airliners under development in the Soviet Union, the Tu-204 makes extensive use of new materials, including composites to achieve a low

specific structure weight, which combines with the low specific fuel consumption of the new engines to produce notably good fuel efficiency. Tupolev bureau literature claims fuel consumption at 0.02kg per passenger-km (0.71lb/passenger-mile), which if confirmed would make it considerably better than the Boeing 757 – itself one of the most fuel-efficient airliners operating in the mid-1980s. The Tu-204 has

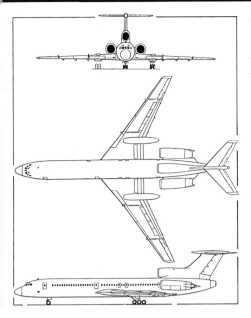

Above: This three-view drawing depicts the Tu-154M, which is the latest production version of the Tupolev tri-jet. A change of engines, from Kuznetsov to Soloviev, results in small external changes and an improvement in overall performance. The nacelles on the wings are primarily for undercarriage stowage.

198,416lb (90,000kg) to 207,235lb (94,000kg). This allowed an increase in fuel capacity, from the original 73,082lb (33,150kg), with provision for 14,550lb (6,600kg) in a centre-section tank that was not connected to the aircraft's main fuel system but the contents of which could be transferred to the main tanks at destination airports where refuelling facili-

ties were restricted or expensive. Numerous changes and improvements were made in the avionics and other systems and the cabin interior. The Tu-154B superseded the Tu-154A in 1977, and was followed by the slightly refined Tu-154B-2. This introduced a Thomson-CSF/SFIM automatic flight control and navigation system for Cat II landings and had higher operating weights, matched to a rearranged cabin layout that increased maximum seating to 180. The supplementary tank of the Tu-154A was also fully integrated into the aircraft's fuel system. As a conversion of the Tu-154B, the Tu-154C is an all-cargo carrier with a side-loading door ahead of the wing and a 1,565 naut ml (2,900km) range with 44,100lb (20,000kg) payload. The latest development is the Tu-154M (sometimes described as the Tu-164 in early references), which appeared in 1982 with Soloviev D-30KU-154-II engines derived from those of the Il-62M and each rated at 23,380lb st (10,500kg). Overall dimensions are unchanged but the tailplane is redesigned, and wing slats and spoilers modified.

SERVICE USE
Aeroflot conducted Tu-154 proving flights early in 1971 and began services in mid-year on an *ad hoc* basis, with full commercial exploitation starting on 9 February 1972 on the Moscow-Mineralnye Vady route. First international services were on the Moscow-Prague route, starting on 1 August 1972. The Tu-154A entered service in April 1974, the Tu-154B in 1977 and the Tu-154M at the beginning of 1985. Production of the TU-154 is thought to exceed 400, in all versions combined, and the type has entered service in substantial numbers with most East European airlines, Syrian Air, Alyemda, Guyana Airways, Choson Minhang, Cubana and CAAC.

SPECIFICATION
(Tu-154B)

Power Plant: Three Kuznetsov NK-8-2U turbofans, each rated at 23,150lb st (10,500kgp) for take-off, with thrust reversers on the fuselage-side engines. Fuel capacity, 9,050 Imp gal (41,140l) in integral tanks in wings, plus provision for 1,250 Imp gal (5,683l) supplementary fuel.
Performance: Max operating speed, 310kts (573km/h) IAS or Mach=0.90; max cruising speed, 486kts (898km/h) at 28,000ft (8,500m); long-range cruising speed, 405kts (749km/h) at 36,090ft (11,000m); take-off field length, 5,890 (2,100m); landing distance, 6,760ft (2,060m); range with max payload, 1,485 naut mls (2,750km); range with 120-passenger payload, 2,160 naut mls (4,000km); range with max fuel, 2,810 naut mls (5,200km) with 26,400lb (12,000kg) payload.
Weights: Basic operating weight, 111,940lb (50,775kg); max fuel weight, 87,633lb (39,750kg); max payload, 41,887lb (19,000kg); max take-off weight, 216,050lb (98,000kg); max landing weight, 176,000lb (80,000kg); max zero-fuel weight, 162,800lb (74,000kg).
Dimensions: Span, 123ft 2½in (37.55m); overall length, 157ft 1¾in (47.90m); overall height, 37ft 4¾in (11.40m); sweepback, 35 deg at quarter chord; wing area 2,169sq ft (201.45m²).
Accommodation: Cabin width, 11ft 9in (3.58m), cabin height, 6ft 7½in (2.02m). Typical one-class layout for 169 passengers in two cabins, six abreast with centre aisle at seat pitch of 29.5in (75cm). Mixed class layout has 24 seats four-abreast at 38in (96cm) pitch and 130 tourist class. Maximum high-density arrangement for 180 passengers. Three underfloor baggage/cargo holds, combined volume 1,158cu ft (43m³). Flight crew of three plus optional fourth position for navigator.

TUPOLEV TU-204

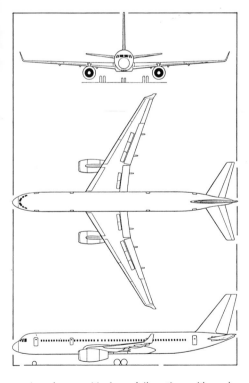

a wing of supercritical aerofoil section, with a relatively high aspect ratio, moderate sweepback (about 20-22 deg at quarter chord), and winglets. The structure is designed for a service life of 45,000 flying hours and 30,000 landings. Like the Il-96, the Tu-204 has advanced systems, which may include fly-by-wire, described in the brochure as 'electronic remote systems for control of the aircraft, and cen-

tral sticks in place of a control column'. A photograph of the cockpit mock-up shows the control sticks, each with two hand grips, centred for the use of each pilot but mounted off the instrument panel instead of the floor, apparently in an alternative to the side-stick controllers adopted in such types as the Airbus A320. The cockpit has two large 'glass' displays for each pilot, making up a four-tube EFIS, and two more display panels on the centre of the panel for systems information. Triple inertial navigation systems (INS) are fitted and the standard of equipment provides for operation in weather minima down to ICAO Cat III.

VARIANTS
No variants of the basic design have yet emerged, other than the alternative cabin layouts. The Tu-204 designation appears to be in continuation of this design bureau's series adopted for its commercial jetliners in a system paralleling Boeings '7-7' numbering. The first Tupolev jetliner (and indeed Aeroflot's first jet transport, second in revenue service in the world following the de Havilland Comet) was the Tu-104, a hastily-adapted passenger-carrying version of the Tu-16 twin-jet bomber. The Tu-20 four-turboprop bomber similarly provided the basis for the Tu-114, and the Tu-124 was a slightly smaller, more refined version of the Tu-104. Tupolev broke new ground with the Tu-134, a T-tailed twin-jet that paralleled the BAC One-Eleven and Douglas DC-9 development, and retained the same configuration for the larger Tu-154. The Tu-144 was the 'Soviet Concorde', an expensively unsuccessful attempt to develop a supersonic airliner, and the Tu-164 designation has been associated with the aircraft better known as the Tu-154M. Nothing is

known at present of Tu-174, 184 or 194 designs and these numbers may have been bypassed to give the Tu-204 a '21st century' flavour.

SERVICE USE
Introduction into Aeroflot service is expected in the early 1990s.

SPECIFICATION

Power Plant: Two high-bypass-ratio turbofans of unspecified type (probably Soloviev) each rated at 35,300lb st (16,000kgp) for take-off, with thrust reversers.
Performance: Max cruising speed, 459kts (850km/h) at 39,375ft (12,000m); economical cruising speed, 437kts (810km/h) at 36,090ft (11,000m); max cruising altitude, 40,025ft (12,200m); take-off field length, 8,200ft (2,500m); range with max fuel, 2,540 naut mls (4,700km) with 28,660lb (13,000kg) payload; range with max payload 1,300 naut mls (2,400km).
Weights: Empty equipped weight, 124,780lb (56,600kg); max payload, 48,500lb (22,000kg); max take-off weight, 207,230lb (94,000kg).
Dimensions: Span, 137ft 9½in (42.00m); overall length, 147ft 7½in (45.00m).
Accommodation: Cabin length, about 114ft 3in (34.80m), max width, about 12ft (3.65m), max height, about 8ft (2.44m). Basic aircraft layout provides 214 seats with central aisle at 32in (81cm) seat pitch; maximum one-class seating, 219. Typical three-class layouts provide 12 first-class four-abreast at 39in (99cm) pitch, 11-47 club-class six-abreast at 38in (96cm) pitch and 147-111 tourist class six-abreast at 32in (81cm) pitch. Underfloor freight holds. Flight crew of two, with provision for optional third seat.

VICKERS VISCOUNT UK

The result of project design work that began before the end of World War II under the aegis of the Brabazon Committee, the Viscount emerged in 1948 as the world's first airliner with turboprop engines, and went on to become the UK's most successful commercial aircraft production programme. As at first conceived, under the designation VC2, the Viscount was to carry 24 passengers over an 870 naut ml (1,610km) range, powered by early versions of the Rolls-Royce Dart. With government backing, Vickers launched construction of two prototypes in March 1946 and the first of these (Vickers 630) flew on 16 July 1948, with Dart RDa.1 engines and accommodation for 32 passengers. For production as the Vickers 700, the Viscount was enlarged in length and wingspan, powered by the more powerful Dart RDa.3 engines and sized to accommodate 40 passengers four-abreast. A prototype of this enlarged version flew on 19 April 1950 and provided the basis for a production order from British European Airways that allowed Vickers to establish a firm programme and launch a marketing campaign. Export orders soon followed, leading to the evolution of further variants as described below.

VARIANTS

The first production standard was defined as the Viscount 700, with Dart Mk 505 engines (replacing Dart Mk 504s in the prototype), a gross weight of 53,000lb (24,040kg) and 47 seats five-abreast. Individual 700-series type numbers applied to each customer variant, starting with 701 for the BEA aircraft and ranging up to 798 (including some unused numbers). The Type 724 for TCA (now Air Canada) introduced a new fuel system, US-style two-pilot cockpit, and 60,000lb (27,215kg) gross weight. The Type 745 for Capital Airlines introduced RDa.6 Mk 510 engines, full compliance with US regulations and a gross weight rising eventually to 64,500lb (29,256kg). In the mid-1950s Vickers stretched the Viscount's fuselage by 3ft 10in (1.17m) and moved the rear cabin bulkhead aft to obtain enough space to seat up to 71 passengers. With RDa.6 engines and 64,500lb (29,256kg) gross weight this was the Viscount 800, first flown on 27 July 1956, and with more powerful RDa.7 Mk 520 engines it was the Type 806, a BEA 'special'. The Type 806A prototype first flew on 9 August 1957. Based on the Type 806, the Viscount 810 series combined RDa.7/1 engines with structural modifications to allow the maximum take-off weight to increase to 72,500lb (32,885kg). A prototype of the Viscount 810 flew on 23 December 1957, and most of the final production batches, for several overseas operators, were of this type. All Viscounts had distinctive elliptical cabin windows but only in the 700-series were the fore and aft cabin doors also of this shape. Viscount production ended in 1964 with 444 built, of which 438 were sold to customers; the final deliveries were to CAAC, which had ordered six as the first Western equipment acquired by the Chinese airline.

SERVICE USE

The Viscount 700 obtained its UK certificate of airworthiness on 17 April 1953 and BEA put the type into service between London and Cyprus on the following day. A number of passenger-carrying proving flights had been made before this event, which was the world's first operation of a revenue scheduled airline service by turboprop airliner. In the US, FAA

approval of the Type 745 for Capital Airlines was obtained on 7 November 1955. Deliveries of the Type 802 began (to BEA) on 11 January 1957, and of the Type 806 (also to BEA) on 1 January 1958. Continental Airlines received the first of the 810-series (Type 812) in May 1958 and revenue service began on 28 May. By 1987, many Viscounts had been retired after giving long years of excellent service. Some 40 remain in regular airline use.

Below: The Vickers Viscount was designed from the outset for two-pilot operation, although an extra seat was also provided on the flight deck and was often used by a third crew member.

Vickers Viscount 810/840 Series Cutaway Drawing Key

1 Radome
2 Weather radar scanner
3 Radar tracking mechanism
4 Front pressure bulkhead
5 Radome hinge panel
6 Nose section construction
7 Pressurisation relief valve
8 Control system linkages
9 Rudder pedals
10 Pneumatic system air bottle
11 Nosewheel doors
12 Forward retracting twin nosewheels
13 Nosewheel steering jack
14 Pitot head
15 Cockpit floor level
16 Seat mounting rails
17 Conditioned air delivery duct
18 Nosewheel steering control
19 Control column handwheel
20 Instrument panel
21 Weather radar display
22 Instrument panel shroud
23 Windscreen wipers
24 Windscreen panels
25 Overhead systems switch panels
26 Co-pilot's seat
27 Direct vision opening side window panel
28 Pilot's seat
29 Cockpit rear bulkhead
30 Cockpit pressure dome
31 Folding observer's seat
32 Cockpit doorway
33 Windscreen de-icing fluid reservoir
34 Wing and engine inspection floodlight
35 Radio and electronics equipment racks
36 Underfloor autopilot controllers
37 Cockpit section frame construction
38 Folding airstairs
39 Folding handrail
40 Entry lobby
41 Forward entry doorway
42 Starboard side baggage compartment
43 HF aerial mast
44 Hydraulic equipment compartment
45 Cabin front bulkhead
46 Cockpit pressure dome aft fairing
47 Forward passenger compartment
48 Four-abreast passenger seating
49 Forward entry door, open
50 Door latch
51 Door hinge link
52 Forward 'pull-out' emergency exit window
53 Underfloor cargo hold, volume 250cu ft (7.08m^3)
54 Toilet compartments, port and starboard
55 Ventral cargo hold door, starboard side
56 Toilet compartment doors
57 Magazine rack
58 VHF aerial
59 Starboard engine nacelles
60 Engine cowling panels
61 Propeller spinner
62 Rotol four-bladed constant-speed propeller
63 Propeller blade root de-icing
64 Starboard wing central fuel cells; total fuel system capacity 1,916 Imp gal (8,710l)
65 Fuel system piping
66 Outboard fuel cells
67 Overwing fuel filler cap
68 De-icing air outlet louvres
69 Retractable landing/taxiing lamp
70 Leading-edge hot air de-icing
71 Starboard navigation light
72 Wing tip fairing
73 Static dischargers
74 Starboard aileron

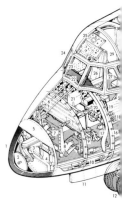

Above: Cutaway drawing of the Viscount Series 810/840, representing the final production variant of this four-engined turboprop airliner.

Below: Best-known for its operation of Boeing 747s across the North Atlantic, Virgin Atlantic Airways uses this Viscount 802 to feed its Gatwick services.

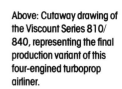

G-AOHT

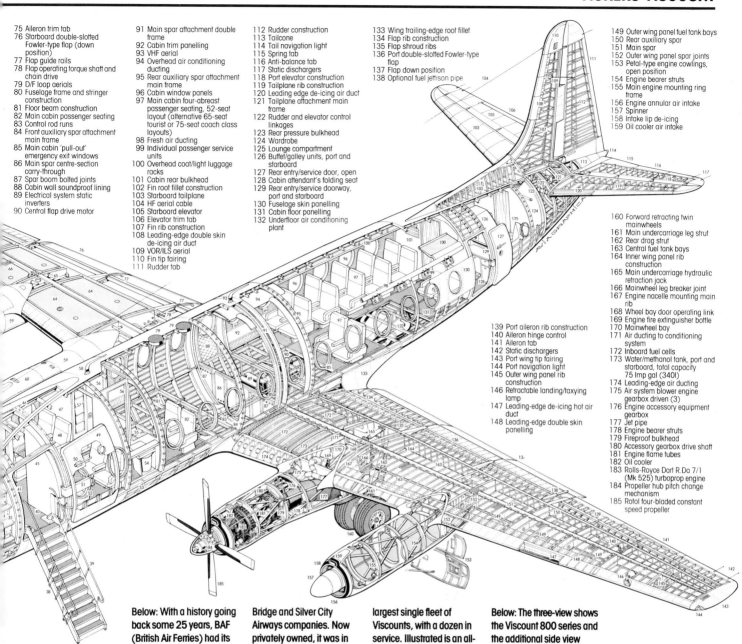

75 Aileron trim tab
76 Starboard double-slotted Fowler-type flap (down position)
77 Flap guide rails
78 Flap operating torque shaft and chain drive
79 D/F loop aerials
80 Fuselage frame and stringer construction
81 Floor beam construction
82 Main cabin passenger seating
83 Control rod runs
84 Front auxiliary spar attachment main frame
85 Main cabin 'pull-out' emergency exit windows
86 Main spar centre-section carry-through
87 Spar boom bolted joints
88 Cabin wall soundproof lining
89 Electrical system static inverters
90 Central flap drive motor

91 Main spar attachment double frame
92 Cabin trim panelling
93 VHF aerial
94 Overhead air conditioning ducting
95 Rear auxiliary spar attachment main frame
96 Cabin window panels
97 Main cabin four-abreast passenger seating, 52-seat layout (alternative 65-seat tourist or 75-seat coach class layouts)
98 Fresh air ducting
99 Individual passenger service units
100 Overhead coat/light luggage racks
101 Cabin rear bulkhead
102 Fin root fillet construction
103 Starboard tailplane
104 HF aerial cable
105 Starboard elevator
106 Elevator trim tab
107 Fin rib construction
108 Leading-edge double skin de-icing air duct
109 VOR/ILS aerial
110 Fin tip fairing
111 Rudder tab

112 Rudder construction
113 Tailcone
114 Tail navigation light
115 Spring tab
116 Anti-balance tab
117 Static dischargers
118 Port elevator construction
119 Tailplane rib construction
120 Leading edge de-icing air duct
121 Tailplane attachment main frame
122 Rudder and elevator control linkages
123 Rear pressure bulkhead
124 Wardrobe
125 Lounge compartment
126 Buffet/galley units, port and starboard
127 Rear entry/service door, open
128 Cabin attendant's folding seat
129 Rear entry/service doorway, port and starboard
130 Fuselage skin panelling
131 Cabin floor panelling
132 Underfloor air conditioning plant

133 Wing trailing-edge root fillet
134 Flap rib construction
135 Flap shroud ribs
136 Port double-slotted Fowler-type flap
137 Flap down position
138 Optional fuel jettison pipe

139 Port aileron rib construction
140 Aileron hinge control
141 Aileron tab
142 Static dischargers
143 Port wing tip fairing
144 Port navigation light
145 Outer wing panel rib construction
146 Retractable landing/taxiing lamp
147 Leading-edge de-icing hot air duct
148 Leading-edge double skin panelling

149 Outer wing panel fuel tank bays
150 Rear auxiliary spar
151 Main spar
152 Outer wing panel spar joints
153 Petal-type engine cowlings, open position
154 Engine bearer struts
155 Main engine mounting ring frame
156 Engine annular air intake
157 Spinner
158 Intake lip de-icing
159 Oil cooler air intake

160 Forward retracting twin mainwheels
161 Main undercarriage leg strut
162 Rear drag strut
163 Central fuel tank bays
164 Inner wing panel rib construction
165 Main undercarriage hydraulic retraction jack
166 Mainwheel leg breaker joint
167 Engine nacelle mounting main rib
168 Wheel bay door operating link
169 Engine fire extinguisher bottle
170 Mainwheel bay
171 Air ducting to conditioning system
172 Inboard fuel cells
173 Water/methanol tank, port and starboard, total capacity 75 Imp gal (340l)
174 Leading-edge air ducting
175 Air system blower engine gearbox driven (3)
176 Engine accessory equipment gearbox
177 Jet pipe
178 Engine bearer struts
179 Fireproof bulkhead
180 Accessory gearbox drive shaft
181 Engine flame tubes
182 Oil cooler
183 Rolls-Royce Dart R.Da 7/1 (Mk 525) turboprop engine
184 Propeller hub pitch change mechanism
185 Rotol four-bladed constant speed propeller

Below: With a history going back some 25 years, BAF (British Air Ferries) had its origins in the Channel Air Bridge and Silver City Airways companies. Now privately owned, it was in 1987 the operator of the largest single fleet of Viscounts, with a dozen in service. Illustrated is an all-cargo Freightmaster variant.

Below: The three-view shows the Viscount 800 series and the additional side view (bottom), the Viscount 700.

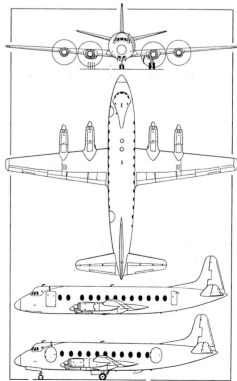

YAKOVLEV YAK-40 SOVIET UNION

Best-known for its long series of piston-engined fighters and later for jet fighters including the first Soviet VTOL types, the Yakovlev design bureau turned its attention to the small airliner class of aircraft in the early 1960s. Its interest in this category of aircraft had been shown during the 1940s with the design of several light transports, but as a replacement for the many Lisunov Li-2 (licence-built DC-3) aircraft still then in service in the Soviet Union, the Yak-40 broke new ground both for the design bureau and for Aeroflot, its principal operator. A major requirement, in this context, was that the new aircraft should be able to operate from Class 5 airfields, having no paved runways – a requirement reflecting the special needs of the Soviet Union and one which was unmatched in any contemporary jet aircraft of Western origin. With the emphasis upon good field performance, the Yakovlev design team chose a three-engined configuration for the new transport. This meant that take-off weights and runway lengths could be calculated for the 'engine out' case with the loss of only one third, rather than one half (as in a twin-engined design) of available engine power. The rear engine location also has advantages over podded engines beneath the wings in terms of possible ingestion of debris when operating on grass and gravel strips. In common with most other Soviet jet transports, the Yak-40 was designed to have a relatively high thrust-to-weight ratio, again with benefit to airfield performance (including operation at high altitude airfields), albeit with some sacrifice in operating economy. To power the aircraft as planned by Yakovlev, turbofans of about 3,000-3,500lb st (1,360 – 1,600kgp) were required, and the Ivchenko bureau undertook the development of a suitable engine

Right: Three-view of the Yakovlev Yak-40, which was the first commercial aircraft design essayed by this design bureau. The three-engined layout was similar to that used by several Western and Soviet contemporaries and helped field performance.

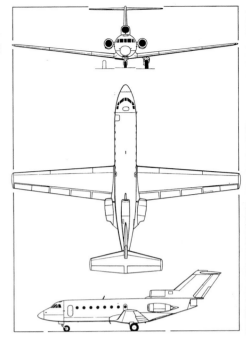

SPECIFICATION

Power Plant: Three Ivchenko AI-25 turbofans each rated at 3,300lb st (1,500kgp) for take-off, with thrust reverser on centre engine only. Fuel capacity, 860 Imp gal (3,910l) in integral tanks between wing spars.

Performance: Max cruising speed, 297kts (550km/h) at 22,965ft (7,000m); initial rate of climb, 1,575ft/min (8.0m/sec); take-off run 2,295ft (700m); landing run, 1,180ft (360m); range with max fuel, 971 naut mls (1,800km).

Weights: Empty weight, 27-seat interior, 20,725lb (9,400kg); fuel weight, 8,820lb (4,685kg); max payload, 6,000lb (2,720kg); max take-off weight, 35,275lb (16,000kg).

Dimensions: Span, 82ft 0¼in (25.00m); overall length, 66ft 9½in (20.36m); overall height, 21ft 4in (6.50m); sweepback, nil; wing area, 753.5sq ft (70.00m²).

Accommodation: Cabin length, 23ft 2½in (7.07m), max width, 7ft 0¾in (2.15m), max height, 6ft 0¾in (1.85m). Standard cabin layout has 27 seats in two-plus-one arrangement with offset aisle, at a seat pitch of 29.7in (75.5cm). Alternative high-density arrangement seats 32 in a four-abreast layout with central aisle, at the same seat pitch. Mixed-class layouts seat 18-20, with four-six passengers in a forward club lounge-type layout and 14 four-abreast seats to the rear. Executive/VIP arrangements have seven seats in the forward compartment and six seats three-abreast to the rear. No underfloor baggage. Flight crew of two, with third jump seat on flight deck.

---

specifically for this purpose, the AI-25 being a two-shaft turbofan. To minimize the requirement for ground equipment to support operation of the Yak-40 at smaller airfields, an APU was fitted as standard, primarily for engine starting, and access to the cabin was by way of a ventral airstair/door in the rear fuselage. Five prototypes were used to develop the Yak-40, whose first flight was made on 21 October 1966. The type has been assigned the NATO reporting name 'Codling'.

YAKOVLEV YAK-42 SOVIET UNION

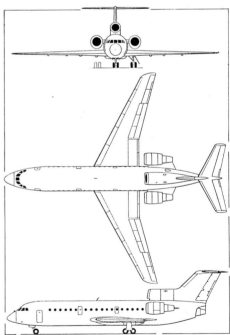

The Yak-42 was developed as a short-haul, medium-capacity jetliner for Aeroflot, to replace the Tu-134, Il-18 and An-24 primarily on the shorter domestic routes within the Soviet Union. Design began in the early 1970s, with a mock-up displayed in Moscow in mid-1973, showing that the overall configuration closely resembled that of the Yak-40, including the three-engined layout and rear-fuselage ventral stairway for access to the cabin. A key design requirement for the Yak-42 was the ability to operate reliably in the more remote regions of the USSR, in a wide range of climates, with the minimum of ground support and maintenance facilities. At the project stage, the design bureau apparently had difficulty assessing the relative merits, particularly in terms of operating economy and performance, of alternative designs with different degrees of wing sweepback. The unusual step was taken of building prototypes for comparative testing with 11 deg and 23 deg of sweepback, the first of these making its maiden flight on 7 March 1975. The 23-deg version was found to be superior and the third

Above left: First flown in 1975, the Yakovlev Yak-42 is, in configuration, an enlarged Yak-40. It has failed, to date, to match its forerunner's success, however, and after it had entered Aeroflot service in 1981, it had to be withdrawn for a programme of modifications.

Above: The three-view shows the Yak-42 in its basic production form, with the 23-deg wing sweepback and twin-wheel main undercarriage. Expected to be in service before the end of 1987, the Yak-42M has a 14ft 9in (4.50m) longer fuselage and new engines.

Left: Reflecting its early 'sixties design origin, the Yak-40's two-man flight deck lacked many of the refinements that would be expected today, as this illustration shows.

Above: The Yak-40 was built in considerable numbers for Aeroflot, but hopes that it would also prove a useful export were not realised. Czech Airlines was one of the few users.

VARIANTS

Modifications to the basic Yak-40 in the course of the production run included the introduction of a clam-shell thrust reverser on the centre engine, and deletion of an acorn fairing at the fin/tailplane leading-edge junction. Other then such changes, all production Yak-40s were externally similar, although several alternative interior layouts were available, as described in the data panel. Freight-carrying and ambulance versions also were produced. In 1970, a

Yak-40M was projected, with a lengthened fuselage, to carry 40 passengers. This may have reached prototype testing, but in any case did not proceed to production. The Yak-40V designation was used to identify an export variant, powered by AI-25T engines rated at 3,858lb st (1,750kgp) each and with the maximum take-off weight increased to 36,376lb (16,500kg). The Yak-40 achieved reasonable export success, as noted below, and in the early 1980s plans were made for an 'Americanized' version to be

developed and marketed by ICX Aviation in Washington. Known as the X-Avia, this was to have been re-engined with Garrett TFE 731-2 turbofans and was projected in three variants: the 30-seat LC-3A, the 40-seat LC-3B and the all-cargo LC-3C. The programme did not, in the end, go ahead.

SERVICE USE

The Yak-40 entered production at the Saratov factory in 1967 and deliveries to Aeroflot began in 1968, with the first passenger-carrying flight made on 30 September of that year. Production ended in 1978 with approximately 1,000 built; most entered service with Aeroflot but exports were made to Afghanistan, Bulgaria, Czechoslovakia, France, West Germany, Italy, Poland and Yugoslavia for commercial use, and elsewhere for government or military operation in a VIP role.

YAKOVLEV YAK-42

prototype was completed to the same standard while production plans were made and a first batch of 200 was put in hand at the Smolensk factory. Initial production aircraft were similar to the third prototype, but a switch was made from twin main wheels to four-wheel bogie units on the main undercarriage.

VARIANTS

The first production Yak-42s had a wing span of 112ft 2½in (34.02m) and gross weight of 117,950lb (53,500kg). The bogie main landing gear was standard, and alternative interiors were for 120 passengers in a one-class layout or 104 two-class in a local-service configuration with carry-on baggage and coat stowage compartments at the front and rear of the cabin. An enlarged loading door in the forward-fuselage port side could be fitted to allow the Yak-42 to operate in the convertible passenger/cargo role. A modification programme was undertaken in 1983 to overcome handling difficulties encountered during early service with Aeroflot, and led to a small increase in wing area (see data panel). As operating in 1985, the Yak-42 also had a higher maximum take-off weight than initially approved. The Yak-42M is a stretched derivative expected in service in 1987, powered by 16,550lb st (7,500kgp) Lotarev D-436 turbofans. Fuselage length is increased by 14ft 9in (4.50m) to 134ft 1¼in (40.88m), allowing seating to be increased to 156-168, and gross weight goes up to 145,505lb (66,000kg). Estimated performance figures for the Yak-42M include a take-off field length of 7,550ft (2,300m) at the new gross weight, and ranges of 2,160 naut mls (4,000km) with maximum fuel, 2,025 naut mls (3,750km) with a 22,050lb (10,000kg) payload and 1,350 naut mls (2,500km) with a 35,275lb (16,000kg) payload. The performance of the earlier

Yak-42 was demonstrated in 1981 when a flight was made from Moscow to Khabarovsk, a distance of 3,318 naut mls (6,145km), and a load of 44,502lb (20,186kg) was lifted to an altitude of 6,562ft (2,000m), setting class records in accordance with FAI regulations.

SERVICE USE

First passenger proving flights were made by Yak-42s in late 1980, on the Moscow-Krasnodar route, and about 20-30 aircraft were delivered to Aeroflot by the end-1981. Following an accident in 1982, the Yak-42 appears to have been withdrawn from service, and modified aircraft were put back into operation from October 1984 onwards, starting with the Saratov-Leningrad and Moscow-Pykovo routes.

Left: The long, thin tube look of a Yak-42 cabin is emphasised in this photograph, showing the six-abreast seating for 120 passengers with a single aisle, and the open overhead luggage racks.

The following pages present details, in a slightly more condensed form than in the main part of the book, of two categories of aircraft that play a part in the air transportation business. First there is a group of 'minor types' — aircraft that are in regular service carrying passengers, but which for various reasons are used only in small numbers. Some are elderly, some were not very successful, some were not primarily intended for airline use, one or two have yet to make good their promoter's expectations and enter production.

There are many other aircraft that could justify entry in this section. All over the world, small airlines and air taxi operators use light twin-engined aircraft, survivors from earlier eras and other assorted types. However, to include all of them would extend the size of this volume unacceptably.

In a second category here are the freighters — aircraft that are used only or principally to carry freight and outsize cargo items. Almost without exception these are types designed for military use, although here again can be found examples of elderly passenger transports that are ending their days as freighters.

AEROSPATIALE CORVETTE FRANCE

SPECIFICATION

Power Plant: Two Pratt & Whitney Canada JT15D-4 turbofans each rated at 2,500lb st (1,134kgp) for take-off. Fuel capacity, 365 Imp gal (1,660l) in integral wing tanks and provision for 154 Imp gal (700l) in two wing-tip tanks.
Performance: Max cruising speed, 410kts (760km/h) at 30,000ft (9,000m); economical cruising speed, 306kts (566km/h) at 39,000ft (11,900m); initial rate of climb, 2,700ft/min (13.7m/sec); service ceiling, 41,000ft (12,500m); take-off balanced field length, (FAR Pt 25), 4,560ft (1,390m); landing distance, 2,480ft (755m); max range, 840 naut mls (1555km) with 12 passengers, or 1,380 naut mls (2,555km) with tip tanks.
Weights: Empty weight, 7,738lb (3,510kg); max payload, 2,248lb (1,020kg); max take-off weight, 14,550lb (6,600kg); max landing weight, 12,550lb (5,700kg); max zero-fuel weight, 12,345lb (5,600kg).
Dimensions: Span, 42ft 2½in (12.87m); overall length, 45ft 4½in (13.83m); overall height, 13ft 10½in (4.23m), sweepback, 22 deg 32 mins at quarter chord; wing area, 236.8sq ft (22.0m²).
Accommodation: Cabin length, 18ft 9½in (5.73m), max width, 5ft 1½in (1.56m), max height, 5ft 0in (1.52m). Normal seating for up to 14 passengers in individual seats with centre aisle. Flight crew of one or two.

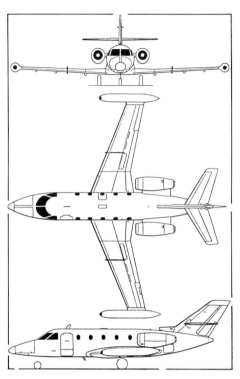

Left: Sharing the apron at Guernsey Airport in this photograph are Corvette 100s of Sterling Airways in Denmark and Sweden's Baltic Aviation.

Below: The Aérospatiale Corvette was of typical biz-jet configuration in 1970, and some of the 40 built are still used in corporate service.

The SN 600 was a project conceived jointly by the two French State-owned companies Sud and Nord shortly before their merger to form Aérospatiale, hence the 'SN' designation. It was intended as a small jet airliner suitable for use on third-level and feeder routes, as well as for executive transport use. The prototype SN 600 first flew on 16 July 1970 but was lost during flight development and small changes were made, as indicated by a change of designation to SN 601, before two more prototypes were completed, making their first flights on 20 December 1972 and 7 March 1973. The first aircraft to full production standard flew on 9 November 1973 and certification was obtained on 28 May 1974. The first two Corvette 100s, as the basic aircraft were known, were in service with Air Alpes by September 1974, and a number of others went into operation in the designed role as commuter-liners in the next two years. However, the market for the Corvette proved to be smaller than had been hoped, and production terminated after 40 had been built. The Corvette 200, projected with a 6ft 7in (2.0m) fuselage stretch to seat up to 18 passengers, was not built. A few Corvettes were still in third-level airline service in the mid-1980s.

BEECHCRAFT KING AIR USA

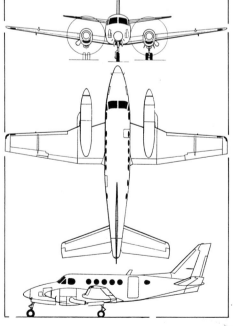

Left: The series of twin-engined transports known as King Airs include several sizes and configurations. This is a Super King Air 300.

Below: King Air 100 and smaller King Air variants have the layout shown here. A T-tail distinguishes the Super King Airs.

SPECIFICATION
(King Air C90A)

Power Plant: Two Pratt & Whitney Canada PT6A-21 turboprops each rated at 550shp (410kW) for take-off, with Hartzell three-blade constant-speed fully-feathering propellors of 7ft 9in (2.36m) diameter. Fuel capacity 320 Imp gal (1,454l) in outer wings and nacelle tanks.
Performance: Max cruising speed, 242kts (448km/h) at 12,000ft (3,660m) and 243kts (450km/h) at 21,000ft (6,400m); initial rate of climb, 2,155ft/min (10.9m/sec); service ceiling, 28,100ft (8,565m); take-off distance to 50ft (15m), 2,260ft (690m); landing distance from 50ft (15m), 2,010ft (615m); max range, 1,315 naut mls (2,437km) at 21,000ft (6,400m).
Weights: Empty weight, 5,765lb (2,615kg); max take-off weight, 9,650lb (4,377kg); max landing weight, 9,168lb (4,159kg).
Dimensions: Span, 50ft 3in (15.32m); overall length, 35ft 6in (10.82m); overall height, 14ft 3in (4.34m); sweepback, nil; wing area, 293.94sq ft (27.31m²).
Accommodation: Cabin length, 12ft 11in (3.94m), max width, 4ft 6in (1.37m), max height, 4ft 9in (1.45m). Up to eight passenger seats and crew of two. Baggage compartment volume, 53.5cu ft (1.51m³).

The King Air family was derived from the Queen Air, which itself entered production in 1958 as the largest of the Beechcraft twins. The King Air provided the basis for development of the Beechcraft 1900 Airliner, but variants of the smaller King Air are also used as third-level airliners and as air taxis by a number of operators in various parts of the world. Development of the King Air began with installation of PT6A turboprops in a Queen Air airframe, leading to construction of a true King Air prototype which first flew on 20 January 1964. Initial deliveries of the Model 90, with PT6A-6 engines, began later in 1964, this model being superseded by the A90 and B90 with slightly more powerful PT6A-20s and the C90 and C90-1 with PT6A-21s and cabin improvements. The C90A, current in 1986, introduced 'pitot' cowlings with reduced-area intakes to increase ram-air flow to the engines. The King Air 100, introduced in 1969, featured more powerful PT6A-28 engines, a lengthened cabin to provide up to 13 seats in airline commuter configuration, and reduced wing span. The A100 had a series of refinements and the B100 switched to 715shp (536kW) Garrett TPE331-6-252B engines. The E90 combined the airframe of the C90 with PT6A-28 engines of the A100 and the F90, which appeared in 1979, combined the basic Model 90 fuselage with the short span wings of the Model 100 and the T-tail of the Super King Air 200. The F90-1 features PT6A-135A engines and 'pitot' intake as on the C90A-1. More than 1,300 Model 90 King Airs have been produced for commercial use.

CESSNA TWINS USA

The Cessna company has produced a long series of twin-engined light transports over the years, primarily for business use, and these have also gone into use with local service airlines and air taxi operators in various parts of the world. The smaller of the piston-engined twins are in the 300 series, and include the original Model 310 which first flew in 1953 and was Cessna's first business twin; the pressurized Model 340; and the lightweight Model 303 Crusader. Of more specific interest to air transport operators, the Model 402 was launched in the mid-1960s and featured a convertible interior for passengers or cargo, a reinforced cabin floor and optional cargo door. More than 1,500 have been produced in Utililiner and Business liner variants. The Model 411, which had appeared in the early 1960s as Cessna's largest twin, was succeeded by the pressurized Model 421 Golden Eagle, production of which exceeded 1,900. Another piston twin with airline application was the Model 404 Titan, with up to 10 seats in the commuter role. Turboprop power was introduced with the Model 441, which first flew on 26 August 1975 and led to production of the Conquest II, with Garrett TPE331 engines and up to 10 seats, and the Conquest I with PT6A-112 engines and up to eight seats. Largest in the range in 1987 is the unpressurized Reims-Cessna F406 Caravan II, jointly developed with Cessna's European licensee as a light utility transport. First flown on 22 September 1983, the Caravan II is powered by 500shp (373kW) PT6A-112 engines and seats up to 10 in a Model 404 Titan-type fuselage, which has been locally strengthened.

SPECIFICATION
(Model 402C Utililiner)

Power Plant: Two Continental TS10-520-VB flat-six turbosupercharged air-cooled piston engines each rated at 325hp (242kW) for take-off, with McCauley three-blade constant-speed fully feathering propellers of 6ft 4½in (1.94m) diameter. Fuel capacity 178Imp gal (808l) in integral wing tanks.
Performance: Max cruising speed, 213kts (394km/h) at 20,000ft (6,095m); economical cruising speed, 142kts (263km/h) at 10,000ft (3,050m); initial rate of climb, 1,450ft/min (7.4m/sec); service ceiling, 26,900ft (8,200m); take-off distance to 50ft (15m), 2,195ft (670m); landing distance from 50ft (15m), 2,485ft (755m); range with max fuel, 1,273 naut mls (2,359km) at 10,000ft (3,050m).
Weights: Typical weight, empty, 4,126lb (1,872kg); max take-off weight, 6,850lb (3,107kg); max landing weight, 6,850lb (3,107kg); max zero-fuel weight, 6,515lb (2,955kg).
Dimensions: Span, 44ft 1½in (13.45m); overall length, 36ft 4½in (11.09m); overall height, 11ft 5½in (3.49m), sweepback nil; wing area, 225.8sq ft (20.98²).
Accommodation: Cabin length, 15ft 10in (4.83m), max width, 4ft 8in (1.42m), max height, 4ft 3in (1.30m). Up to eight occupants, in cabin in four individual and two double seats, and two pilots or pilot plus passenger. Baggage in nose compartment, at rear of cabin and in wing lockers in ends of nacelles, combined total capacity 1,500lb (680kg).

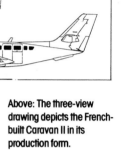

Above: The three-view drawing depicts the French-built Caravan II in its production form.

Left: Built by Reims Aviation in France, the Caravan II appeared in 1983. Wings are supplied by Cessna.

EMBRAER EMB-123 BRAZIL

Having established its position in the commuter airliner market with the EMB-110 Bandeirante and the EMB-120 Brasilia, the Brazilian Embraer company studied a number of projects in the late 1970s and early 1980s to ensure that it could maintain its foothold by introducing a new type at the appropriate time. One possibility that was given some attention was to undertake the joint development of a new commuterliner with Shorts, an agreement to this end being signed in May 1984; up to the time this volume was published, nothing had come of this agreement, however.

Meanwhile, during 1986, Embraer completed the design definition of a small pressurized twin-turboprop commuterliner conceived in the category of a replacement for the Bandeiraute, and continued negotiations with Fabrica Militar de Aviones (FMA) in Argentina with a view to the latter taking a 30-50 per cent share in detailed design and manufacture. The new design was designated EMB-123, reviving the nomenclature used some years earlier for one of the projects preceding the launch of the Brasilia. From the latter, the EMB-123 derived its fuselage, shortened by some 10ft (3.05m) for the reduced passenger capacity, and a T-tail. Completely new are its supercritical wing of very high aspect ratio (12:1) and the unusual rear-fuselage location chosen for the two turboprop engines, in pusher arrangement. Benefits of the layout claimed by Embraer are the clean wing for optimum fuel efficiency and performance, a smooth ride and quiet cabin environment. Subject to programme launch arrangements being agreed between Embraer and FMA, first deliveries were expected to be made in 1990.

SPECIFICATION

Power Plant: Two Pratt & Whitney Canada PT6A-67 derivative turboprops each rated at about 1,200shp (896kW) for take-off, with six-blade advanced-technology constant-speed and feathering propellers. Fuel capacity, 275 Imp gal (1,250l).
Performance: Max cruising speed, 340kts (630km/h) at 30,000ft (9,150m) at 95 per cent max take-off weight; initial rate of climb, 2,500ft/min (12.7m/sec); operational ceiling, 40,000ft at (12,190m); take-off field length, 3,937ft (1,200m); landing field length, 3,937ft (1,200m); range, 650 naut mls (1,200km) with 19 passengers.
Weights: Operating weight empty, 10,803lb (4,900kg); fuel weight, 2,161lb (980kg); max payload, 4,409lb (2,000kg); max take-off weight, 16,976lb (7,700kg); max landing weight, 16,645lb (7,550kg); max zero-fuel weight, 15,212lb (6,900kg).
Dimensions: Span, 54ft 0in (16.46m); overall length, 56ft 5in (17.19m); overall height, 18ft 5in (5.61m); sweepback, 8 deg at quarter chord; wing area, 236.81sq ft (22.0m²).
Accommodation: Cabin length, about 20ft 6in (6.25m), max width, 6ft 10¾in (2.10m), max height, 5ft 9in (1.76m). Basic layout provides 19 seats three-abreast with off-set aisle, at seat pitch of 31in (79cm). Baggage compartment in nose and rear fuselage, combined capacity 992lb (450kg). Flight crew of two and one cabin attendant.

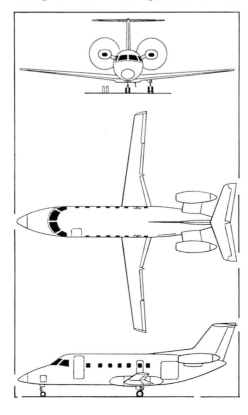

Left: A provisional three-view drawing of the EMB-123 project.

Above: Rear-mounted pusher turboprops are a feature of the EMB-123.

GRUMMAN ALBATROSS USA

SPECIFICATION
(G-111 Albatross)

Power Plant: Two Wright R-1820-982C9HE3 air-cooled radial piston engines each rated at 1,475hp (1,100kW) for take-off, with Hamilton Standard three-blade constant-speed, feathering and reversing propellers. Fuel capacity 561 Imp gal (2,550l) in tanks in inner wings. Provision for 166 Imp gal (756l) in each wingtip float.

Performance: Normal operating speed, 206kts (382km/h); economical cruising speed, 162kts (300km/h) at 5,000ft (1,525m); initial rate of climb, 1,250ft/min (6.35m/sec); max operating altitude, 8,000ft (2,440m); take-off distance to 50ft (15m), 4,400ft (1,340m) from land or 4,425ft (1,350m) from water; landing distance from 50ft (15m), 3,030ft (925m) on land, 3,170ft (965m) on water; range with 28 passengers, 273 naut mls (506km) from land or 405 naut mls (750km) from water; max ferry range, no reserves, 1,480 naut mls (2,742km).

Weights: Operating weight empty, 23,500lb (10,659kg); max payload (cargo), over 8,000lb (3,630kg); fuel load, 6,438lb (2,920kg); max take-off weight, 30,800lb (13,970kg) from land or 31,150lb (14,129kg) from water; max-landing weight, 29,160lb (13,226kg) on land or 31,150lb (14,129kg) on water.

Dimensions: Span, 96ft 8in (29.46m); overall length, 61ft 3in (18.67m); overall height on land, 25ft 10in (7.87m); sweepback, nil; wing area, 1,035sq ft (96.2m²).

Accommodation: Cabin length, 26ft 1in (7.95m); max width, 7ft 5in (2.26m), max height, 6ft 2in (1.88m). Standard interior provides 28 individual seats in cabin, with central aisle, at a pitch of 32in (81cm). Baggage compartment volume, 280cu ft (7.93m³). Flight crew of two and one cabin attendant.

The G-111 has its origins in the Grumman G-64 Albatross design of the period immediately after World War II, first flown on 24 October 1947 as the XJR2F-1 utility transport amphibian for the US Navy. Later production batches for the USAF as search and rescue amphibians were designated SA-16, and all variants later received HU-16 designations. During the late 1970s, as Albatross amphibians became available upon being retired by the USAF and USN, Grumman developed a conversion programme, in conjunction with Resorts International, for a version of the Albatross to operate in the commuter role. Identified as the G-111 (the original Grumman design number for the HU-16B variant), a prototype of this civil conversion first flew on 13 February 1979 and FAA type approval was obtained on 29 April 1980. The conversion included restoration of the airframe to zero-time standard through a full inspection and repair, removal and overhaul of the engines, modernization of the flight deck, installation of passenger seats in the cabin, with provision of suitable access doors and emergency hatches, and a lightweight, solid-state avionics system throughout. At least 12 of these G-111 conversions had been delivered to Resorts International by 1986, some of these going into service with Resorts subsidiary Chalks International and others being available for sale. A variant with Garrett TPE331-15UAR turboprops and Dowty-Rotol four-blade propellers has also been studied by Grumman and Resorts International, but had not been launched up to 1987.

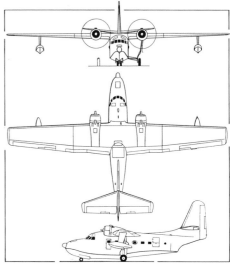

Above: The prototype G-111 conversion of the Grumman Albatross. Six of these piston-engined amphibians were in service in 1986 with Chalks International.

Right: Three-view drawing of the G-111, which is externally difficult to distinguish from the original military and maritime variants of the Grumman Albatross.

GRUMMAN GOOSE and TURBO-GOOSE USA

SPECIFICATION
(G-21A Goose, pre-World War II)

Power Plant: Two Pratt & Whitney R-985-SB Wasp Junior air-cooled radial piston engines each rated at 400hp (299kW) for take-off, with Hamilton Standard two-blade variable-pitch or constant-speed propellers. Fuel capacity, 183 Imp gal (833l).

Performance: Max speed, 175kts (323km/h) at 5,000ft (1,525m); cruising speed, 75 per cent power, 165kts (306km/h) at 9,600ft (3,925m); initial rate of climb, 1,300ft/min (6.6m/sec); service ceiling, 22,000ft (6,705m); range up to 782 naut mls (1,258km).

Weights: Empty weight, 5,450lb (2,472kg); useful load, 2,550lb (1,157kg); payload with max fuel, 778lb (353kg); max take-off weight, 8,000lb (3,629kg).

Dimensions: Span, 49ft 0in (14.94m); overall length, 38ft 4in (11.68m); overall height (on wheels), 12ft 2in (3.71m); sweepback, nil; wing area, 375sq ft (34.84m²).

Accommodation: Two pilots or pilot plus passenger in cockpit and four passengers in individual seats in cabin. Baggage compartment at rear of cabin.

SPECIFICATION
(McKinnon G-21G Turbo-Goose)

Power Plant: (A330) Two Pratt & Whitney Canada PT6A-27 turboprops each rated at 680shp (507kW) for take-off, with Hartzell three-blade constant-speed, feathering and reversing propellers. Fuel capacity, 488 Imp gal (2,218l) in wing and centre section tanks.

Performance: (A330) Max operating speed, 211kts (391km/h); cruising speed, 178kts (330km/h); service ceiling, 20,000ft (6,095m); range with max fuel, 1,390 naut mls (2,575km).

Weights: Empty equipped weight, about 6,700lb (3,040kg); max take-off weight, 12,500lb (5,670kg).

Dimensions: Span, (tip floats retracted), 50ft 10in (15.49m); overall length, 39ft 7in (12.07m); sweepback nil; wing area, 377.64sq ft (35.08m²).

Accommodation: Pilot and up to 11 passengers, in main and rear cabins. Baggage compartment capacity, 300lb (136kg).

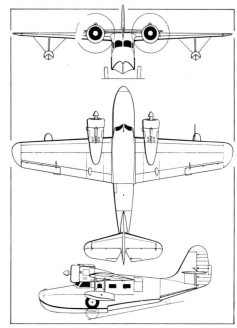

Above right: This three-view drawing shows the Grumman Goose in its original piston-engined version. Many of those that are still flying now have turboprops.

Right: Catalina Seaplanes, flying between Long Beach, California, and Catalina Island, has been a long-time user of Grumman aircraft, including two Goose amphibians in 1986.

The Goose amphibian, developed as a four/six-seat business amphibian, first flew in June 1937 and obtained US type approval on 29 September of that year in its initial G-21 form and on 5 February 1938 in improved G-21A form. Produced for USAAF and USN service during the war, numbers of Goose amphibians found applications in airline operation, especially in countries with extensive coastlines and lakes, such as Alaska, Canada, New Zealand and Scandinavia. Starting in 1958, the McKinnon company in the USA and later in Canada developed a number of Goose conversions, and

some of these were still in small-scale commercial use in 1986. The G-21C and G-21D had four 340hp (254kW) Lycoming engines in place of the original Wasp Junior, the G-21D also featuring a lengthened bow. The G-21E introduced 579eshp (432kW) Pratt & Whitney Canada PT6A-20 turboprops and the G-21G had 715eshp (534kW) PT6A-27s, optional retractable wing-tip floats and increased cabin accommodation.

GRUMMAN GULFSTREAM I and GULFSTREAM I-C USA

SPECIFICATION
(Gulfstream I)

Power Plant: Two Rolls-Royce Dart 529-8X or 529-8E (RDa.7/2) turboprops each rated at 1,990shp (1,484kW) for take-off, with Rotol four-blade constant-speed propellers of 11ft 6in (3.51m) diameter. Fuel capacity, 1,290 Imp gal (5,865l) in integral fuel tanks.
Performance: Max cruising speed, 302kts (560km/h) at 25,000ft (7,620m); economical cruising speed, 250kts (463km/h) at 25,000ft (7,620m); initial rate of climb, 1,900ft/min (9.7m/sec); service ceiling, 33,600ft (10,240m); take-off distance to 50ft (15m), 2,875ft (875m); landing distance from 50ft (15m), 2,125ft (650m); range with max fuel, 2,205 naut mls (4,088km) with 2,740lb (1,243kg) payload.
Weights: Empty equipped weight, 21,900lb (9933kg); max payload, 4,270lb (1,937kg); max take-off weight, 35,100lb (15,920kg); max landing weight, 33,600lb (15,240kg); max zero-fuel weight, 26,170lb (11,870kg).
Dimensions: Span 78ft 6in (23.92m); overall length, 63ft 9in (19.43m); overall height, 22ft 9in (6.94m); sweepback; nil; wing area, 610.3sq ft (56.7m²)
Accommodation: Cabin length, 33ft 0in (10.06m), max width 7ft 4in (2.23m), max height, 6ft 1in (1.85m). High-density seating for 24 passengers, in single seats with central aisle. Baggage compartment volume 100cu ft (2.83m³).

SPECIFICATION
(Gulfstream I-C)

Power Plant: As Gulfstream I.
Performance: Max operating speed, 308kts (571km/h); initial rate of climb 1,900ft/min (9.7m/sec); max certificated altitude, 30,000ft (9,145m); take-off field distance, 4,850ft (1,480m); landing distance 2,770ft (845m); range with max payload, 434 naut mls (804km); range with max fuel, 2,171 naut mls (4,023km).
Weights: Empty equipped weight, 23,693lb (10,747kg); fuel weight, 10,460lb (4,744kg); max payload, 7,400lb (3,356kg); max take-off weight, 36,000lb (16,329kg); max landing weight, 34,285lb (15,551kg); max zero-fuel weight, 32,250lb (14,628kg).
Dimensions: Span, 78ft 4in (23.88m); overall length, 75ft 4in (22.96m); overall height, 23ft 0in (7.01m); sweepback, nil; wing area, 610.3sq ft (56.7m²).
Accommodation: Cabin length, 43ft 4in (13.21m), max width, 7ft 4in (2.24m), max height, 6ft 1in (1.85m). Up to 37 seats in three-abreast arrangements with offset aisle. Forward and rear baggage compartments, combined volume 251cu ft (7.11m³). Flight crew of two and one cabin attendant.

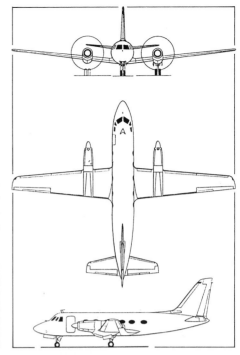

The Grumman G-159 Gulfstream I first flew on 14 August 1958 as a long-range large-capacity corporate transport with up to 19 seats. Production totalled 200, and about 20-30 of these had been acquired for airline use, with up to 24 seats, in the mid-1980s. Users included Brown Air Services and Peregrine Air Services in the UK, and Air South, Royale Airlines and Orion Air in the USA. The G-IC, first flown on 25 October 1979, was a Gulfstream I conversion with stretched fuselage. Five were made by Gulfstream American for US local service use.

Above: This three-view shows the Gulfstream I in its basic form. Five G-1C conversions by Gulfstream American have longer fuselages.

Left: The Gulfstream I, designed as a corporate transport, has found favour more recently for airline use, for example with Birmingham Executive.

GRUMMAN MALLARD and TURBO-MALLARD USA

The G-73 Mallard was developed as one of Grumman's first commercial ventures after World War II, in continuation of the company's pre-war interest in amphibious transports for the private and business owner. The Mallard first flew on 30 April 1946, powered by a pair of 600hp (448kW) Pratt & Whitney R-1340-8WH1 Wasp air-cooled radial piston engines. With a gross weight of 12,500lb (5,670kg), the Mallard cruised at 139kts (257km/h) at 8,000ft (2,440m) and had a range of 975 naut mls (1,800km). Production totalled 61, and ended in 1951. Most Mallards were purchased by private owners but a few reached airline service, and continued in this role throughout the 1960s and 1970s, primarily in Canada, Alaska and the Caribbean. In 1964, one Mallard operated by Northern Consolidated Airways in Alaska was fitted with a PT6A-9 turboprop on the starboard wing (retaining the R-1340 to port) and used for a 15-hour flight trial. After reverting to standard, this aircraft returned to NCA service but in 1969 was purchased by Frakes Aviation Inc. in Texas and modified to full Turbo-Mallard configuration as set out in the data panel. It first flew in this guise in September 1969 and after FAA type approval in October 1970 several more similar conversions were made by Frakes, for operation by Chalks International Airline on its services in the Bahamas, alongside standard Mallards already used by that company.

SPECIFICATION
(Turbo-Mallard)

Power Plant: Two Pratt & Whitney Canada PT6A-27 or PT6A-34 turboprops each flat-rated at 715shp (534kW) for take-off, with three-blade constant-speed propellers with automatic feathering system. Fuel capacity, 158 Imp gal (719l) in main wing tanks and 41.5 Imp gal (189l) each in wing tip float tanks, plus two optional 69 Imp gal (314l) tanks in wings.
Performance: Max cruising speed, 191kts (354km/h) at sea level; economical cruising speed, 187kts (348km/h) at 14,000ft (4,265m); initial rate of climb, 1,350ft/min (6.9m/sec); service ceiling, 24,500ft (7,470m); take-off distance to 50ft (15m), 3,700ft (1,130m) from land or 4,900ft (1,495m) from water; landing distance from 50ft (15m), 4,350ft (1,325m) on land or 4,500ft (1,370m) on water; range, with max payload, no reserves, 750 naut mls (1,388km); range with max fuel, no reserves, 1,400 naut mls (2,594km).
Weights: Empty equipped weight, 8,750lb (3,969kg); max take-off weight, 14,000lb (6,350kg); max landing weight 13,500lb (6,124kg).
Dimensions: Span, 66ft 8in (20.32m); overall length, 48ft 4in (14.73m); overall height (on wheels), 18ft 9in (5.72m); sweepback; nil; wing area, 444sq ft (41.25m²).
Accommodation: Up to 10 passengers and two pilots. Baggage compartments in nose and at rear of cabin, capacity 700lb (318kg).

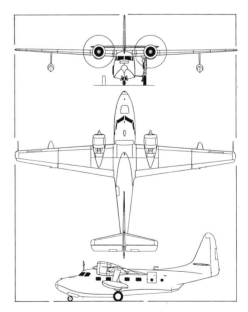

Above right: Shown in this three-view is the Grumman Mallard as originally produced. Some still in service now have been fitted with turboprops.

Right: Canadian west coast operator Air BC, now a subsidiary of Air Canada, has this Turbo Mallard in a diverse fleet of seaplanes and amphibians.

ILYUSHIN IL-14 SOVIET UNION

The Il-14 was an improved derivative of the Il-12, which was itself the first product of the Ilyushin design bureau after World War II to achieve large scale production for non-military use, although it was probably designed primarily as a replacement for the Li-2 in the role of a military tactical transport. The Il-14, which flew as a prototype in 1952, differed from the Il-12 in having a refined structure, some aerodynamic improvements, and uprated engines. Like the Il-12, the Il-14 was built for both military and 'commercial' use, the latter in the hands of Aeroflot and designated Il-14P (*Passazhirskii*) with accommodation for 18-26 passengers. In 1956, a slightly stretched version appeared, with a 3ft 4in (1.0m) section inserted in the forward fuselage, increasing accommodation to a maximum of 36. This was designated Il-14M (*Modifikatsirovanny*). Later, considerable numbers of Il-14Ps and Ms were adapted to serve Aeroflot as freighters under the designation Il-14T (*Transportny*). Up to 3,500 examples of the Il-14 are reported to have been built in the Soviet Union, and VEB Flugzeugwerke built 80 in East Germany. As the Avia 14, the type was also built in large numbers in Czechoslovakia, in several different versions. These aircraft were used in both civil and military guise by the relevant operators in East Germany and Czechoslovakia and were exported to other countries in the Soviet sphere of influence, including Romania, Bulgaria, Cuba and China. By 1987, almost all had gone, but Aeroflot was believed to have between 100 and 200 still in use for various activities and others were still being flown by CAAC in China on the equivalent of 'third-level' routes.

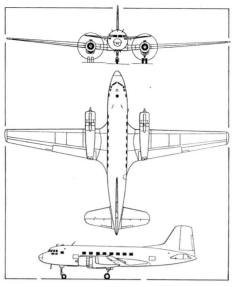

Left: Almost rivalling the famed Douglas DC-3 for longevity of service, the Ilyushin Il-14 quite closely resembles that type in its overall configuration, size and performance.

Below left: Of several thousand examples of the Il-14 built, only a hundred or two remained in use in 1986, when this one was photographed in Chinese service.

SPECIFICATION
(Il-14M)

Power Plant: Two Shvetsov ASh-821-7 air-cooled 14-cylinder two-row radial piston engines each rated at 1,930shp (1,440kW) for take-off, with four-blade feathering AV-50 propellers. Fuel capacity, 770 Imp gal (3,500l) in wing tanks.
Performance: Max level speed, 225kts (417km/h); max cruising speed, 208kts (385km/h); economical cruising speed, 168kts (311km/h) at 7,000ft (2,135m); initial rate of climb, 1,220ft/min (6.2m/sec); service ceiling, 22,000ft (6,705m); range with max payload, 558 naut mls (1,034km); range with max fuel, 1,729 naut mls (3,202km).
Weights: Operating weight empty, 27,776lb (12,600kg); max take-off weight, 39,683lb (18,000kg); max landing weight, 38,030lb (17,250kg).
Dimensions: Span, 104ft 0in (31.69m); overall length, 73ft 2in (22.30m); overall height, 25ft 11in (7.90m); sweepback, nil; wing area, 1,075sq ft (99.70m²).
Accommodation: Cabin length, 36ft 0in (10.97m), max width, 9ft 1in (2.77m), max height, 6ft 8in (2.03m). Typical layout provides up to 36 seats, four abreast with central aisle, at seat pitch of 43in (109cm). Flight crew of three or four.

SAUNDERS ST-27 CANADA

The Saunders ST-27 is a derivative of the de Havilland Heron, a four-engined light transport first flown on 10 May 1950 as a 'big brother' for the twin-engined Dove, with which it shared the fuselage cross-section. Production of the Heron totalled 148, in Srs 1 (fixed landing gear) and Srs 2 (retractable land gear) versions, and a few of these were still operating in the feederline and air taxi roles in the mid-1980s. Some airline examples were Riley Herons, with their original Gipsy Queen piston engines replaced by Lycoming flat-six engines. A more ambitious conversion scheme was that launched by Saunders Aircraft Corp in 1968 as the ST-27. This involved remanufacturing the Heron with a lengthened fuselage to increase the capacity to a maximum of 24 seats; fitting a redesigned main spar to strengthen the wing; and installing a pair of PT6A-27 turboprops. Thus modified, a prototype flew on 28 May 1969, and UK certification was obtained on 16 September 1970, with Canadian endorsement on 14 May 1971. A total of 13 Herons was remanufactured by Saunders, and these ST-27s have served with several airlines in Canada and South America. The principal operator in 1987 was City Express, based in Toronto and a successor to Air Otonabee, which previously had gathered together almost all the remaining ST-27s. The ST-28 was a modified variant of the ST-27 to comply with FAR Part 25 regulations, which first flew on 12 December 1975, but plans to manufacture ST-28s as all-new airframes did not mature.

SPECIFICATION

Power Plant: Two Pratt & Whitney Canada PT6A-34 turboprops each rated at 750shp (560kW) for take-off, with Hartzell three-blade variable-pitch constant-speed feathering and reversing propellers of 7ft 6in (2.29m) diameter. Fuel capacity, 320 Imp gal (1,455l) in wing bag tanks.
Performance: Max cruising speed, 200kts (370km/h) at 7,000ft (2,135m); economical cruising speed, 182kts (338km/h) at 7,000ft (2,135m); initial rate of climb, 1,600ft/min (8.1m/sec); service ceiling, 25,000ft (7,620m); take-off distance to 50ft (15m), 2,350ft (715m); landing distance from 50ft (15m), 1,150ft (350m); range with max payload, 100 naut mls (185km); range with max fuel, 710 naut mls (1,315km).
Weights: Operating weight empty, 7,900lb (3,583kg); max take-off weight, 13,500lb (6,124kg); max landing weight, 13,150lb (5,965kg); max zero-fuel weight, 12,850lb (5,828kg).
Dimensions: Span, 71ft 6in (21.79m); overall length, 59ft 0in (17.98m); overall height, 15ft 7in (4.75m); sweepback, nil; wing area, 499sq ft (46.36m²).
Accommodation: Cabin length, 31ft 6in (9.60m), max width, 4ft 6in (1.37m), max height, 5ft 9in (1.75m). Typical layout provides 19 or 20 individual seats at 30in (76cm) pitch, with central aisle. Forward and rear baggage compartments, combined volume 119cu ft (3.37m³). Flight crew of two and one cabin attendant.

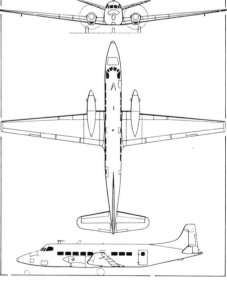

Above: This three-view drawing of the Saunders ST-27 clearly shows the aircraft's ancestry, with a recognisable de Havilland wing and fuselage from the Heron.

Left: The colourful livery of City Express is worn by most of the Saunders ST-27s still serving in 1987. Note the French rendition of the airline name in this photo.

SIAI-MARCHETTI SF.600TP CANGURO ITALY

Although it has an equal share in design and production of the ATR 42, participates in production of the McDonnell Douglas MD-80 and DC-10 and the Boeing 767, and is sharing in design of the MD-90, the Italian aircraft industry has made few efforts to produce airliners as wholly national projects. A modest attempt to amend this situation began some 10 years ago, leading to the construction of a prototype of the F600 Canguro in 1978. Powered by a pair of Lycoming TIO-540-J flat-six piston engines, and having a fixed tricycle landing gear, this prototype made its first flight on 30 December 1978, and was built by the General Avia company under the technical direction of Dr. Stelio Frati. It was followed by two more prototypes, the third being in the definitive form with turboprop engines and the optional retractable landing gear, data for which are given here. Designed to meet a broad spectrum of operational requirements, the Canguro can be produced with a sideways-hinged rear fuselage and provision is made for wing strong points to carry up to 1,763lb (800kg) of external stores. Construction of a batch of nine Canguro aircraft for demonstration purposes was reported to be underway in 1986 by SIAI-Marchetti (a member of the Agusta group of companies), which had acquired the design rights from General Avia.

SPECIFICATION

Power Plant: Two Allison 250-B17C turboprops each rated at 420shp (313kW) for take-off, with three-blade Hartzell constant-speed fully-feathering and reversing propellers of 6ft 8in (2.03m) diameter. Fuel capacity, 242 Imp gal (1,100l) in tanks in outer wings.
Performance: Max cruising speed, 165kts (306km/h) at 5,000ft (1,525m); cruising speed at 75 per cent power, 155kts (287km/h) at 10,000ft (3,050m); initial rate of climb, 1,515ft/min (7.7m/sec); service ceiling, 24,000ft (7,315m); take-off distance to 50ft (15m), 1,280ft (390m); landing distance from 50ft (15m), 985ft (300m); range with max payload (cargo), 324 naut mls (600km); range with max fuel, 853 naut mls (1,580km).
Weights: Empty equipped weight (cargo version), 3,968lb (1,800kg); operating weight empty (passenger), 4,292lb (1,947kg); max payload (cargo), 2,315lb (1,050kg); max take-off weight, 7,275lb (3,300kg).
Dimensions: Span, 49ft 2½in (15.00m); overall length, 39ft 10½in (12.15m); overall height, 15ft 1in (4.60m); sweepback, nil; wing area, 258.3sq ft (24.00m²).
Accommodation: Cabin length, 16ft 6¾in (5.05m), width, 4ft 0½in (1.23m), height, 4ft 2in (1.27m). Up to nine passengers, with three-persons rear bench-type seat and six individual seats, plus tenth passenger alongside pilot in place of second pilot. Side loading door aft of wing for cargo, with optional swing-tail arrangement for straight-in loading in dedicated cargo version. Total cabin volume 279cu ft (7.90m³). One or two pilots.

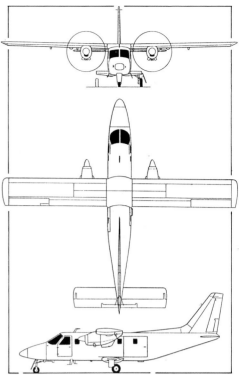

Above: This three-view drawing of the SF.600TP shows the version with a retractable undercarriage. Other options are available, such as a fixed u/c, hinged rear fuselage and fittings for military use.

Left: A prototype of the SIAI-Marchetti SF.600TP Canguro on test in 1986. After a protracted period of development, this light twin transport had entered into limited production in 1987.

TRANSALL C-160 INTERNATIONAL

The Transall C-160 was developed originally to meet the requirements of the French and German air forces, the AG Transall concern being set up to manage production as a shared activity in France and Germany, with final assembly lines in both countries. The first of three prototypes flew on 25 February 1963, these being followed by six pre-production examples and then 110 C-160Ds for the Luftwaffe, 50 C-160Fs for Armée de l'Air and nine C-160Zs for the South African Air Force. Production was completed in 1970, and in 1973 four C-160Fs were converted for operation (as C-130Ps) by Air France on the regular night mail services, primarily between Paris and Bastia, Corsica. In 1977 production of a second batch of Transalls began and the first of these improved aircraft flew on 9 April 1981. The Armée de l'Air bought 29 second-series C-160s, and six more were ordered by the Indonesian government. The latter are operated in civil guise by Pelita Air Service on the transmigration services to ferry inhabitants from Java to the less densely-populated islands of Indonesia.

SPECIFICATION

Power Plant: Two Rolls-Royce Tyne RTy.20 Mk 22 turboprops each rated at 6,100ehp (4,550kW) for take-off, with four-blade BAe Dynamics (Ratier Forest-built) constant-speed fully-feathering and reversing propellers of 18ft 0in (5.49m) diameter. Fuel capacity, 4,190 Imp gal (19,050l) in four integral wing tanks and provision for 1,980 Imp gal (9,000l) in optional centre-section tanks.
Performance: Max speed, 277kts (513km/h) at 16,000ft (4,875m); initial rate of climb, 1,300ft/min (6.6m/sec); service ceiling, 27,000ft (8,230m); take-off distance to 35ft (10m), 3,250ft (990m); landing distance from 50ft (15m), 2,850ft (870m); range, 2,750 naut mls (5,095km) with 17,640lb (8,000kg) payload and 1,000 naut miles (1,853km) with 35,275lb (16,000kg) payload.
Weights: Typical operating weight empty, 63,935lb (29,000kg); max payload, 35,275lb (16,000kg); max take-off weight, 112,435lb (51,000kg); max landing weight, 103,615lb (47,000kg); max zero-fuel weight, 99,210lb (45,000kg).
Dimensions: Span, 131ft 3in (40.0m); overall length, 106ft 3½in (32.40m); overall height, 38ft 2¾in (11.65m); sweepback, nil; wing area, 1,722sq ft (160.0m²).
Accommodation: Cabin length, 44ft 4in (13.51m), width, 10ft 3½in (3.15m), max height, 9ft 8½in (2.98m). Military versions accommodate up to 93 troops in high-density seating. Total cabin volume (including ramp area) 4,940cu ft (139.9m³) in cargo role. Flight crew of three.

Right: Although designed and produced for military use, and primarily as a freighter, the Transall is justifiably included here as an 'airliner' as six are in service in Indonesia to carry passengers on that country's ambitious transmigration scheme.

Above: The configuration of the C-160 Transall, shown in this three-view drawing, is classic for a dedicated freighter, with a high wing and a cabin floor line close to the ground for ease of loading through the rear door and ramp. Civil examples in service in 1987 in France and in Indonesia, have no external differences.

AERO SPACELINES GUPPY 201 USA (and FRANCE)

The series of Guppy outsize transports originated in an idea by the late John M.Conroy, who formed Aero Spacelines (now part of the Tracor group of companies) to modify a Boeing Stratocruiser to have a lengthened fuselage with a new upper lobe of increased diameter. Known as the Pregnant Guppy, this prototype first flew on 19 September 1962. Two further developments, intended primarily to carry stages of the Saturn rocket launchers and other space hardware between manufacturing and launch sites in the USA, were the Super Guppy, which was even larger and powered by Pratt & Whitney T34 turboprops, and the Mini Guppy, with piston engines and a swing tail. These two aircraft first flew on 31 August 1965 and 24 May 1967 respectively. A variant of the Mini Guppy with Allison 501 turboprops flew on 13 March 1970 but was lost two months later, before entering service. Finally, Aero Spacelines produced two Super Guppy 201s, which combined Allison power with the same outsize fuselage as the earlier Super Guppy prototype. First flown on 24 August 1970 and 24 August 1971, these two aircraft were acquired by Airbus Industries and, after certification on 26 August 1971, entered service in October to ferry major fuselage components and wings of the A300/A310 family from their production centres to the final assembly line in Toulouse. Two more aircraft, to similar specification, were then converted for Airbus by UTA in France, making their first flights on 11 June 1982 and 2 August 1983 respectively. All four remain in service in Europe, operated by Aeromaritime.

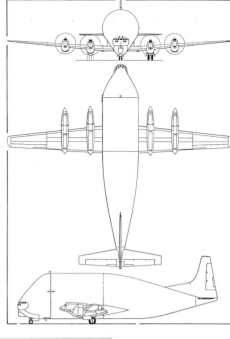

SPECIFICATION

Power Plant: Four Allison 501-D22C turboprops each rated at 4,912ehp (3,666kW) for take-off, with four-blade Hamilton Standard constant-speed propellers of 13ft 6in (4.11m) diameter. Fuel capacity, 7,580 US gal (28,700l) in wing and centre section tanks.
Performance: Max operating speed, 210kts (390km/h) IAS below 14,800ft (4,510m) or Mach = 0.413 IAS; max cruising speed, 250kts (463km/h) at 20,000ft (6,095m); economical cruising speed, 220kts (407km/h) at 20,000ft (6,095m); initial rate of climb, 1,500ft/min (7.62m/sec); certificated ceiling, 25,000ft (7,620m); take-off distance to 50ft (15m) FAA requirements, 8,400ft (2,560m); landing distance from 50ft (15m) FAA requirements, 6,750ft (2,055m); range with max payload, 440 naut mls (813km); range with max fuel, 2,540 naut mls (4,700km).
Weights: Empty equipped weight, 100,000lb (45,360kg); max payload, 54,000lb (24,494kg); max take-off weight, 170,000lb (77,100kg); max landing weight, 160,000lb (72,570kg); max zero-fuel weight, 154,000lb (69,854kg).
Dimensions: Span, 156ft 3in (47.62m); overall length, 143ft 10in (43.84m); overall height, 48ft 6in (14.78m); sweepback, nil; wing area, 1,964.6sq ft (182.52m²).
Accommodation: Cabin max length, 111ft 6in (33.99m), max width, 25ft 1in (7.65m), max height, 25ft 6in (7.77m). Usable cabin volume, 39,000cu ft (1,104m³). Sideways-hinged nose for straight-in loading. Flight crew of four.

Above: Little of the original Boeing KC-97 design but the wing remains identifiable in the Guppy.

Left: Even if their shape and bulk did not make these unmistakable, the four Guppy outsize transports used to support the Airbus programme in Europe are readily identified by their Airbus colours.

ANTONOV AN-12 SOVIET UNION

The An-12 freighter has its origins in the An-10, which appeared in 1957 as one of the first of Aeroflot's turboprop transports, entering service in 84-seat form and being developed into the 100-seat An-10A. The An-12 appeared in 1959 as a dedicated freighter and became numerically more important than the An-10, entering service both with Aeroflot and with the Soviet military forces. Its military significance was shown by the provision of a twin-gun tail turret, and this feature (less the guns) was usually retained in aircraft operated by Aeroflot on freight services and supply missions outside the Soviet Union, for which the An-12 continues to be widely used. The type has also been exported to several Soviet bloc air forces and to the airlines of some countries in the Soviet sphere of influence, including Bulgaria, China, Cuba, Iraq, Poland and Guinea. A version similar to the Soviet An-12BP production model has been manufactured in China as the Hanzhong Y-8, with Chinese-built Wojiang WJ-6 turboprops. The NATO reporting name for the An-12 variant is 'Cub'.

Left: In this three-view drawing of the An-12, the rear gun turret is faired over, but examples are often seen at civil airports with the turret still in place.

SPECIFICATION

Power Plant: Four Ivchenko AI-20K turboprops each rated at 4,000ehp (2,983kW) for take-off, with four-blade AV-68 constant-speed, feathering and reversing propellers of 14ft 9in (4.50m) diameter. Fuel capacity, 3,058 Imp gal (13,900l) in bag tanks in wings, plus provision for 923 Imp gal (4,200l) in auxiliary tanks.
Performance: Max speed, 419kts (777km/h); max cruising speed, 361kts (670km/h); economical cruising speed, 297kts (550km/h) at 24,600ft (7,500m); initial rate of climb, 1,970ft/min (10.0m/sec); service ceiling, 33,500ft (10,200m); take-off run, 2,300ft (700m); landing run, 1,640ft (500m); range with max payload, 1,940 naut mls (3,600km); range with max fuel, 3,075 naut mls (5,700km).
Weights: Empty equipped weight, 61,730lb (28,000kg); max payload, 44,090lb (20,000kg); normal take-off weight, 121,475lb (55,100kg); max take-off weight, 134,480lb (61,000kg).
Dimensions: Span, 124ft 8in (38.00m); overall length, 108ft 7.25in (33.10m); overall height, 34ft 6.5in (10.53m); sweepback, nil; wing area, 1,310sq ft (121.70m²).
Accommodation: Cabin length, 44ft 3.5in (13.50m), max width, 11ft 5.75in (3.50m), max height, 8ft 6.25in (2.60m). Rear ramp/door in rear fuselage gives access to cabin for direct loading, with reinforced floor and cargo-handling provision. Troop-carrying versions can carry 100 paratroops. Total cabin volume, 3,432.6cu ft (97.2m³). Flight crew of five.

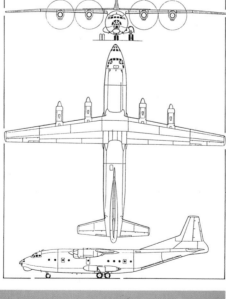

Right: The Antonov An-12 was derived from the An-10 passenger transport for use as a freighter primarily by Soviet military forces. Many operate in civil markings, but usually to carry items of freight for government or quasi-military purposes rather than genuine commercial activities.

ANTONOV AN-22 ANTEI SOVIET UNION

The An-22 was first flown on 27 February 1965, and at the time of its public debut a few years later was the world's largest transport aircraft, although it was subsequently surpassed in size by the Boeing 747 and the Lockheed C-5A Galaxy, these being exceeded, in their turn, by the Antonov An-124 described separately. The An-22 was developed by using five prototypes for flight development, and two of these were operated during 1967 experimentally by Aeroflot. The Antei (Antheus), as the An-22 is sometimes known, was designed primarily to give

the Soviet forces improved airlift capability (especially for the air transportation of tanks and outsize army vehicles). Its capacious hold was of value also for the movement of civil engineering equipment from industrial centres to more remote sites in Russia, and to ferry supplies being exported by the Soviet Union as military or general aid to other nations around the world. As a consequence, An-22s have often been seen, both within the Soviet Union and beyond its borders, operating in Aeroflot colours and civil markings. It is believed that about 80 An-22s were built, ending in 1974, and about 50 of these probably remain in service, primarily for military support duties, in 1986. The NATO reporting name for the An-22 is 'Cock'.

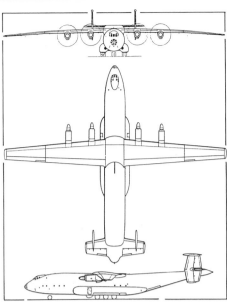

SPECIFICATION

Power Plant: Four Kuznetsov NK-12MA turboprops each rated at 15,000shp (11,186kW) for take-off, with eight-blade contra-rotating propellers of 20ft 4in (6.20m) diameter.
Performance: Max speed, 399kts (740km/h); take-off run, 4,260ft (1,300m); landing run, 2,620ft (800m); range with max payload, 2,690 naut mls (5,000km); range with max fuel, 5,900 naut mls (10,950km) with 99,200lb (45,000kg) payload.
Weights: Empty equipped weight, 251,325lb (114,000kg); max payload, 176,350lb (80,000kg); fuel weight, 94,800lb (43,000kg); max take-off weight, 551,160lb (250,000kg).
Dimensions: Span, 211ft 4in (64.40m); overall length, about 190ft 0in (57.92m); overall height, 41ft 1.5in (12.53m); sweepback, nil; wing area, 3,713sq ft (345.0m²).
Accommodation: Cabin length, 108ft 3in (33.00m), max width, 14ft 5in (4.40m), max height, 14ft 5in (4.40m). Rear loading ramp/door giving access to main cabin for cargo-carrying, with reinforced freight floor and tiedown fittings and built-in winches associated with rail-mounted gantries in cabin room. Forward passenger compartment with 28-29 seats immediately aft of flight deck. Flight crew of five or six.

Below: Like the majority of types illustrated in this section of the book, the Antonov An-22's military origins are betrayed by its configuration.

Right: The Antonov An-22 was the largest aircraft ever built with turboprop engines, and it has been operated only by Aeroflot and the Soviet military.

ANTONOV AN-124 SOVIET UNION

SPECIFICATION

Power Plant: Four Lotarev D-18T turbofans each rated at 51,650lb st (23,430kgp) for take-off, with thrust reversers. Fuel in integral wing tanks.
Performance: Max cruising speed, 467kts (865km/h); normal cruising speed, 432-459kts (800-850km/h) at 32,800-39,370ft (10,000-12,000m); take-off field length, 9,850ft (3,000m); landing run at max landing weight, 2,625ft (800m); range with max payload, 2,400 naut mls (4,500km); range with max fuel, 8,900 naut mls (16,500km).
Weights: Max payload, 330,700lb (150,000kg); max take-off weight, 892,872lb (405,000kg).
Dimensions: Span, 240ft 5.75in (73.30m), overall length, 228ft 0.25in (69.50m); overall height, 72ft 2.25in (22.00m).
Accommodation: Cargo hold length, 118ft 1.25in (36.00m), max width, 21ft 0in (6.40m), max height, 14ft 5.25in (4.40m). Upper deck cabin aft of flight deck with up to 88 seats. Access to main cargo hold through upward-hinged nose (with kneeling nosewheel leg) and/or rear loading door/ramp. Reinforced floor with cargo tie-down points and travelling cranes in roof to facilitate loading. Flight crew of six.

Above: First flown in 1982, the Antonov An-124 is an outsize military transport, included here because it is sometimes seen flying in Aeroflot livery.

Right: The three-view drawing shows a conventional design for a transport of the eighties, but some advanced technology is incorporated.

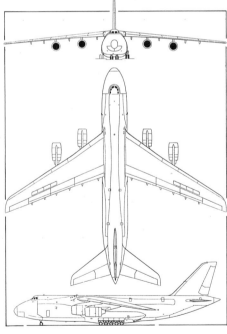

The An-124 was first reported to be under development in the late 1970s, when the designation was thought to be An-40, later changed to An-400. The definitive designation of An-124 emerged in May 1985 when an example of this very large transport made an appearance at the Paris Air Show. The first flight of the prototype had been made on 26 December 1982, and production examples were reported to be in service by early 1986. The only An-124s seen outside of the Soviet Union at the time of writing have operated in Aeroflot livery

and with civil registrations, but it is clear that so large an aircraft has as much military application as commercial. Loads carried by the An-124 range from the largest of Soviet tanks to complete SS-20 nuclear missile systems, and from earth movers to oil well equipment; like the An-22 described above, it is therefore of value in major civil engineering schemes in the Soviet Union. The An-124 is of conventional aerodynamic design but makes extensive use of composite materials in its structure, representing some 16,150sq ft (1,500m²) of surface area

and saving 3,970lb (1,800kg) of weight. The floor of the main hold is fabricated from titanium, and the flight control system is completely fly-by-wire. A 24-wheel landing gear (10 main wheels on each side of the fuselage and four nose wheels) helps to spread the weight of the An-124, which was the heaviest aircraft in the world in 1986, and allow it to operate from unprepared fields, hard-packed snow and ice-covered swampland, although not necessarily at its maximum weights. The NATO reporting name is 'Condor'.

CANADAIR CL-44 CANADA

SPECIFICATION
(Canadair CL-44 D-4)

Power Plant: Four Rolls-Royce Tyne RTy.12 Mk 515/10 turboprops each rated at 5,730shp (4,276kW) for take-off, with four-blade HSD Hydromatic constant-speed feathering and reversing propellers of 16ft 0in (4.88m) diameter. Fuel capacity, 10,150 Imp gal (46,180l) in wing and centre section tanks.
Performance: Max operating speed, 250kts (463km/h) IAS up to 25,000ft (7,620m), or Mach = 0.63; typical high-speed cruising speed, 349kts (647km/h) at 21,000ft (6,400m); long-range cruising speed, 324kts (600km/h) at 25,000ft (7,620m); take-off field length, 7,400ft (2,255m); landing field length, 6,230ft (1,900m); range with max payload, 2,850 naut mls (5,300km); range with max fuel, 4,850 naut mls (8,985km) with a 35,564lb (16,132kg) payload.
Weights: Operating weight empty, 88,952lb (40,348kg); max fuel weight, 81,448lb (36,944kg); max payload, 66,048lb (29,959kg); max cargo payload, 63,272lb (28,725kg); max take-off weight, 210,000lb (95,250kg); max landing weight, 165,000lb (74,843kg); max zero-fuel weight, 155,000lb (70,307kg).
Dimensions: Span, 142ft 3.5in (43.37m); overall length, 136ft 10in (41.70m); overall height, 38ft 8in (11.80m); sweepback, 7 deg at quarter-chord; wing area, 2,075sq ft (192.76m²).
Accommodation: Cabin length, 98ft 1in (29.90m), max floor width, 11ft 0in (3.35m), max height, 6ft 9in (2.05m). Usable cabin volume, 6,294cu ft (178.2m³); two underfloor freight holds, combined volume, 1,109cu ft (31.4m³). Rear fuselage (including tail unit) hinged to starboard for straight-in loading. Flight crew of three or four.

The CL-44 was derived in Canada from the original Bristol Britannia, initially to meet an RCAF requirement for a long-range troop and freight transport. Principal changes were a lengthening of the fuselage, increased wing span and a switch from Bristol Proteus to Rolls-Royce Tyne engines. The first of 12 CL-44D Yukons for the RCAF flew on 15 November 1959. The CL-44D-4, first flown on 16 November 1960, was optimized for commercial operation as a freighter, with a swing tail (at the time unique) and 27 were produced with first deliveries made to Flying Tiger on 31 May 1961, to Seaboard on 20 June 1961 and to Slick on 17 January 1962. Loftleidir acquired four to use as passenger transports, and for this company Canadair developed the CL-

44J with a 15ft (4.6m) fuselage stretch to increase seating from 178 to 214. Four aircraft were converted to CL-44J standard (first flight 8 November 1965) and were used by Loftleidir as Canadair 400s. A single CL-44D-4 was modified by Conroy Aircraft to 'guppy' configuration with increased-diameter upper fuselage lobe, and first flying (as the CL-44-O) on 26 November 1969. Most of the CAF Yukons were sold for commercial use when retired in 1973, but lack the swing-tail feature. About a dozen CL-44s remain in cargo use in 1987.

Below: The Canadair CL-44 was novel, when introduced in 1961, for its swing-tail arrangement to allow straight-in loading. Note the large fairings over the hinges in this picture.

Right: The origins of the Canadair CL-44 in the Bristol Britannia design are shown clearly in this three-view drawing. Fuselage length and engines were principal differences.

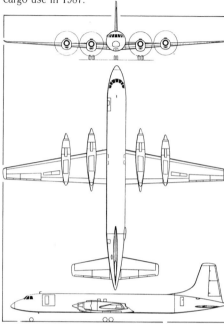

CESSNA CARAVAN I USA

Cessna launched the Model 208 as a brand-new design in 1981, aimed at providing a light general utility aircraft for passengers or cargo-carrying, and suitable for adaptation to a variety of other roles. These could include, according to Cessna, such activities as parachuting of supplies or personnel, firefighting, photographic duties, agricultural spraying, casualty evacuation, border patrol and so on. Named Caravan I, the Model 208 prototype first flew on 9 December 1982, and the

SPECIFICATION

Power Plant: One Pratt & Whitney PT6A-114 turboprop flat-rated at 600shp (447kW) to 12,500ft (3,800m), with three-blade Hartzell constant-speed, feathering and reversing propellers of 8ft 4in (2.54m) diameter. Fuel capacity, 335 US gal (1,268l) in integral wing tanks.
Performance: Max operating speed, 175kts (325km/h) IAS; max cruising speed, 184kts (341km/h) at 10,000ft (3,050m); initial rate of climb, 1,215ft/min (6.2m/sec); service ceiling, 27,600ft (8,410m); take-off distance to 50ft (15m), 1,665ft (505m); landing distance from 50ft (15m), 1,550ft (470m); range with max fuel, 1,370 naut mls (2,539km) at 20,000ft (6,095m).
Weights: Empty weight, 3,800lb (1,724kg); fuel weight, 2,224lb (1,009kg); max payload, 3,000lb (1,361kg); max take-off weight, 7,300lb (3,311kg); max landing weight, 7,300lb (3,311kg).
Dimensions: Span, 52ft 1in (15.88m); overall length, 37ft 7in (11.46m); overall height, 14ft 2in (4.32m); sweepback, nil; wing area, 279.4sq ft (25.96m²).
Accommodation: Cabin length (excluding baggage area), 15ft 0in (4.57m), max width, 5ft 2in (1.57m), max height, 4ft 3in (1.30m). Provision for up to nine seats plus pilots, two or three abreast with aisle. Total cabin volume, 341cu ft (9.66m³).

first production aircraft was rolled out in August 1984. FAA type approval was obtained on 23 October 1984, and in mid-1985 certification of a float-equipped version was completed, using Wipline floats. In December 1983, meanwhile, Cessna had obtained an order from Federal Express for 30 Caravan Is, to be used (by several independent supplemental carriers) on that operator's overnight small package delivery services. Deliveries began early in 1985, the Federal Express Model 208A featuring a windowless fuselage, an underfuselage cargo pannier, a 6in (15.2cm) upward extension of the fin and some equipment changes. Federal Express bought 10 more Model 208As (with options on another 90) and then ordered 70 of the lengthened Model 208B. First flown on 3 March 1986, the Model 208B has a 4ft (1.22m) fuselage stretch and operates at higher weights in order to take advantage of the increased cargo volume. The first Model 208B was delivered to Federal Express on 31 October 1986, (following FAA type approval on 9 October), and by the beginning of 1987 about 100 Caravan Is of all versions were in service.

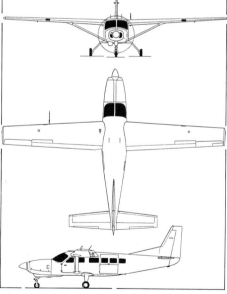

Above: Many years of experience in the design and production of single-engine light aircraft lie behind the concept of the Cessna Caravan I.

Left: A pygmy among giants, in this section of the book, the Caravan I is a specialist utility transport with a useful air freighting rôle, and is much used by Federal Express.

CURTISS C-46 USA

SPECIFICATION

Power Plant: Two Pratt & Whitney R-2800-34 air-cooled 14-cylinder two-row piston engines each rated at 2,000shp (1,496kW) for take-off, with three-blade Hamilton Standard Hydromatic constant-speed fully feathering propellers of 14ft 6in (4.42m) diameter. Fuel capacity, 1,400 US gal (5,305l) in tanks in outer wing panels.

Performance: Normal operating speed, 191kts (354km/h) IAS; normal cruising speed, 162kts (301km/h) at 7,000ft (2,135m); initial rate of climb, 1,300ft/min (6.6m/sec); service ceiling, 27,600ft (8,410m); range with max payload, 96 naut mls (117km); range with max fuel, 1,017 naut mls (1,880km) with 5,700lb (2,585kg) payload.

Weights: Empty equipped weight, 33,000lb (14,970kg); fuel weight, 8,400lb (3,810kg); max payload, 11,630lb (5,265kg); max take-off weight, 48,000lb (21,772kg); max landing weight, 46,800lb (21,228kg); max zero-fuel weight, 45,168lb (20,488kg).

Dimensions: Span, 108ft 0in (32.92m); overall length, 76ft 4in (23.27m); overall height, 21ft 8in (6.60m); wing area, 1,358sq ft (126.15m²).

Accommodation: Cabin length, 48ft 0in (14.63m), max width, 9ft 10in (2.99m), max height, 6ft 8in (2.03m). Cabin originally adapted for up to 62 seats, five-abreast at a pitch of 35in (89cm); total cabin volume, 2,300cu ft (65.13m³). Additional underfloor hold volume, 455cu ft (12.9m³). Flight crew of two.

Left: Rivalling the Douglas DC-3 in length of service, the portly Curtiss C-46 is easily recognized but is rarely seen in service nowadays.

Below: Designed as a passenger transport, the Curtiss C-46 was prevented from fulfilling its rôle by the exigencies of WWII. Those still flying serve only as freighters.

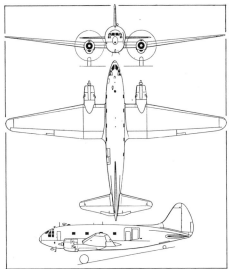

O f the types of aircraft serving the airlines in 1987, the C-46 can claim to be the second oldest, only the Douglas DC-3 having flown any earlier. Of similar configuration to the famous Douglas type, the Curtiss transport was conceived in 1937 as the CW-20. Considerably larger than the DC-3, it differed also in having a fuselage of 'double bubble' cross section, to offer the largest possible cabin volume for the smallest drag. First flown on 26 March 1940, the CW-20 appeared too late to capture any part of the pre-war airline market although, strangely enough, the prototype was impressed for military service with the USAAF and was passed to the UK, where it joined the war time fleet of BOAC. For the USAAF, Curtiss built 3,141 examples of the CW-20 in military guise, designated C-46 and named Commando. After World War II many hundreds of these aircraft were acquired by civilian operators, at first for passenger use but subsequently (and more particularly) as freighters, for which their military style cargo-loading doors made them particularly suitable. As 'aerial tramps', C-46s became much used in the US and Central and South America, and two or three dozen are still to be found flying in this role, well away from the trunk routes, in 1987.

HAWKER SIDDELEY ARGOSY UK

T he Argosy is better known in the military role through the purchase of 56 for service with the RAF, but was designed as a private venture for the commercial air freight business. As the AW650, the prototype first flew on 8 January 1959, but sales failed to come up to expectation and in the event only 17 were built for civil use. This total comprised 10 more Srs 100s (delivered to Riddle Airlines in the US and to BEA), a prototype Srs 200 (first flown 11 March 1964) with uprated engines and higher operating weights, and five similar Srs 220s for BEA, which put them into service in February 1965. After being sold by BEA (and the original US operator of the Srs 100s), Argosies continued in service with several smaller airlines, and a few of both series are still flying in 1987 in various parts of the world.

SPECIFICATION
(Argosy Srs 200)

Power Plant: Four Rolls-Royce Dart Mk 532/1 turboprops each rated at 2,230shp (1,663kW) for take-off, with four-blade Dowty Rotol constant-speed, feathering and reversing propellers of 12ft 0in (3.66m) diameter. Fuel capacity, 3,400 Imp gal (15,454l).

Performance: Normal operating speed, 235kts (435km/h) EAS; max cruising speed, 241kts (447km/h) at 10,000ft (3,050m); economical cruising speed, 226kts (419km/h) at 20,000ft (6,095m); initial rate of climb, 900ft/min (4.6m/sec); service ceiling, 21,000ft (6,400m); take-off field length, 5,150ft (1,570m); landing field length, 5,040ft (1,535m); range with max payload, 485 naut mls (780km); range with max fuel, 1,760 naut mls (2,835km) with 17,000lb (7,710kg) payload.

Weights: Operating weight empty, 48,920lb (22,186kg); fuel weight, 27,200lb (12,338kg); max payload, 31,080lb (14,095kg); max take-off weight, 93,000lb (42,185kg); max landing weight, 88,500lb (40,143kg); max zero-fuel weight, 80,000lb (36,288kg).

Dimensions: Span, 115ft 0in (35.05m); overall length, 86ft 9in (26.44m); overall height, 29ft 3in (8.91m); sweepback, nil; wing area, 1,458sq ft (135.45m²).

Accommodation: Cabin length, 47ft 0in (14.30m), width, 10ft 0in (3.05m), height, up to 8ft 9in (2.64m). Total freight volume, 3,835cu ft (108.31m³) with straight in nose and tail loading doors and floor lashing points; optional provision for up to 89 passengers. Flight crew of two.

Below: Despite the great hopes that rested upon the Argosy when it was first developed, by the Armstrong Whitworth company, wholly for the civil freighting market, it enjoyed only limited success and the major production run, in the end, was for the military.

Right: The high wing, twin-boom layout of the Argosy, shown in this three-view drawing, made it readily identifiable. The layout was adopted to allow straight-in loading through the rear clamshell doors. The nose also opened, to give a unique straight-through facility.

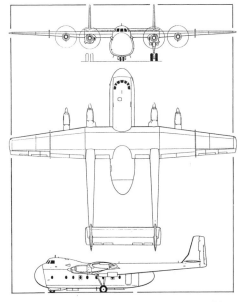

ILYUSHIN IL-76 SOVIET UNION

SPECIFICATION
(Ilyushin Il-76T)

Power Plant: Four Soloviev D-30KP turbofans each rated at 26,455lb st (12,000kgp) for take-off, with thrust reversers. Fuel capacity, about 18,000 Imp gal (81,830l) in integral wing tanks.
Performance: Max speed, 459kts (850km/h); max cruising speed, 432kts (800km/h); economical cruising speed, 405kts (750km/h); typical cruising altitude, 35,000ft (10,700m); absolute ceiling, about 50,850ft (15,500m); take-off run, 2,790ft (850m); landing run, 1,475ft (450m); range with max payload, about 2,700 naut mls (5,000km); max range, 3,617 naut mls (6,700km).
Weights: Max payload, 88,185lb (40,000kg); max take-off weight, 374,785lb (170,000kg).
Dimensions: Span, 165ft 8in (50.50m); overall length, 152ft 10.25in (46.59m); overall height, 48ft 5in (14.76m); sweepback, 25 deg at quarter chord; wing area, 3,229sq ft (300.0m²).
Accommodation: Cabin length (excluding ramp), 65ft 7.5in (20.00m), width, 11ft 1.75in (3.40m), height, 11ft 4.25in (3.46m). Pressurized cabin, with total volume of 8,310cu ft (235.3m³) has cargo handling provisions, including rear doors and ramp with built-in rollers and overhead cranes and winches. Three quick-loading modules can be carried, each with 30 passenger seats, four-abreast. Flight crew of five.

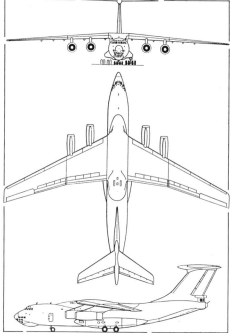

Left: The combination of a high swept-back wing and a high tail make the Il-76 readily identifiable. Civil and military versions are externally similar apart from the airline liveries.

Below: This three-view drawing shows the Il-76 in its military guise, with an armed tail turret. Some examples flown in airline markings have the turret faired over.

The design of the Il-76 began in the late 1960s to provide a heavy transport for both military and civil use, primarily as a replacement for the Antonov An-12. Key design requirements were the ability to accommodate and lift specific items of military equipment and civil engineering hardware, but also included a rough-field capability and facilities for operation in extreme climatic conditions as encountered in Siberia and elsewhere. The prototype Il-76 first flew on 25 March 1971, and examples of the military version (featuring, like the An-12, a twin-gun tail turret) were under evaluation by 1974. The original unarmed Il-76 was followed by the Il-76T, which featured increased fuel in the wing centre section and higher operating weights, and then by the Il-76TD, with improved D-30KP-1 engines and further increases in fuel capacity and weights. These versions are unarmed, whereas the Il-76M and Il-76MD have the tail turret and other features specifically for military use. Examples of both military and commercial Il-76 variants have been supplied to Iraq, Libya, Syria and Cuba, and usually operate in the colours of these countries' airlines, with civil markings. The Indian Air Force has bought 20 and uses the name Gajraj, while the NATO reporting name for the Il-76 is 'Candid'.

LOCKHEED L-100 HERCULES USA

The commercial L-100 originated as a 'civilianized' version of the C-130 Hercules military tactical transport, and was first flown in the form of a Model 382 company demonstrator on 21 April 1964. FAA type approval was obtained on 16 February 1965 and small numbers of Model 382B Hercules (some also known as L-100s) were built for commercial use from 1965 onwards. These early models had the same 97ft 9in (29.79m) overall length as the basic C-130B. The projected L-100-10, with D22A engines replacing the 4,050shp (3,022kW) 501-D22s, was followed by the L-100-20 with the same uprated engines and an 8ft 4in (2.54m) lengthening of the fuselage. The original demonstrator was converted to Model 382E (L-100-20) form and first flew on 19 April 1968, gaining type approval on 4 October that year. The L-100-30 had another 6ft 8in (2.03m) fuselage stretch and first flew on 14 August 1970, type approval being gained on 7 October. In all, just over 100 commercial Hercules have been delivered, about half being L-100-30s. Most were for all-cargo use (some by air forces), but six L-100-30s operated by Pelita Air Services in Indonesia carry up to 128 passengers on the transmigration flights, and others can be fitted with passenger-carrying modules without loss of the freight-carrying provisions.

SPECIFICATION
(Lockheed L-100-30)

Power Plant: Four Allison 501-D22A turboprops each rated at 4,680ehp (3,490kW) for take-off, with four-blade Hamilton Standard constant-speed feathering and reversing propellers of 13ft 6in (4.11m) diameter. Fuel capacity, 9,980 US gal (37,770l) in integral wing and centre section tanks, and two fixed underwing tanks.
Performance: Max cruising speed, 315kts (583km/h) at 20,000ft (6,095m) at a weight of 120,000lb (54,430kg); economical cruising speed, 300kts (556km/h) at 150,000lb (68,040kg); initial rate of climb, 1,700ft/min (8.64m/sec); take-off field length (FAR), 6,200ft (1,890m); landing field length (FAR), 4,850ft (1,480m); range with max payload, 1,363 naut mls (2,526km); range with max fuel (no payload), 4,979 naut mls (9,227km).
Weights: Operating weight empty, 77,680lb (35,235kg); fuel weight, 64,856lb (29,418kg); max payload, 51,110lb (23,183kg); max take-off weight, 155,000lb (70,308kg); max landing weight, 135,000lb (61,235kg); max zero-fuel weight, 128,790lb (58,420kg).
Dimensions: Span, 132ft 7in (40.41m); overall length, 112ft 9in (34.37m); overall height, 38ft 3in (11.66m); sweepback, nil; wing area, 1,745sq ft (162.12m²).
Accommodation: Cabin length (excluding ramp), 56ft 0in (17.07m), max width, 10ft 3in (3.12m), max height, 9ft 0in (2.74m). Cabin total volume 6,057cu ft (171.5m³) including space over rear loading ramp. Built-in cargo handling facilities including roller conveyors. Flight crew of four.

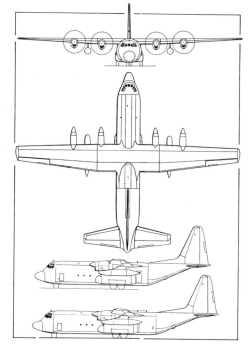

Below: A few of the commercial L-100 Hercules are passenger-carriers, such as this L-100-30 flown by Pelita.

Right: The L-100-20 version of the Hercules is shown in this three-view drawing, with an extra side view of the L-100-30.

SHORTS BELFAST UK

SPECIFICATION

Power Plant: Four Rolls-Royce Tyne RTy.12 turboprops each rated at 5,730shp (4,276kW) for take-off, with four-blade Hawker Siddeley (DH) constant-speed feathering and reversing propellers of 16ft 0in (4.88m) diameter. Fuel capacity, 10,300 Imp gal (48,822l) in integral wing tanks.

Performance: Typical cruising speed, 275kts (510km/h); take-off runway length, 8,200ft (2,500m); landing runway length, 6,800ft (2,075m); range with max payload, 850 naut mls (1,575km); range with 22,000lb (10,000kg) payload, about 3,350 naut mls (6,200km).

Weights: Typical operating weight empty, 130,000lb (58,967kg); fuel weight, 82,400lb (37,376kg); max payload, 75,000lb (34,000kg); max take-off weight, 230,000lb (104,325kg); max landing weight, 215,000lb (97,520kg); max zero-fuel weight, 205,000kg (92,986kg).

Dimensions: Span, 158ft 10in (48.41m); overall length, 136ft 5in (41.58m); overall height, 47ft 0in (14.33m); sweepback, 7.05 deg at quarter chord; wing area, 2,465sq ft (229.09m²).

Accommodation: Cabin length (including ramp), 84ft 4in (25.70m), max width, 16ft 1in (4.90m), max height, 13ft 4in (4.06m). Total cabin volume, 11,350cu ft (321.4m³), including space above rear loading ramp, with cargo handling system and built-in roller conveyors. Flight crew of three or four, and provision for up to 19 passengers on upper deck.

The Belfast was developed to meet an RAF requirement for a heavy strategic freighter, and the first of 10 ordered for military use flew on 5 January 1964. Deliveries to the RAF began on 20 January 1966 and all 10 aircraft were operated by No. 53 Squadron until retirement 10 years later, in September 1976. Five of the ex-RAF aircraft were then acquired for conversion for operation in civil guise as all-cargo transports carrying outsize loads. Conversion design, engineering and certification was handled by Marshall of Cambridge (Engineering) and involved changes to the autopilot, avionics, power plant and flight control systems to meet civil certification standards, CAA approval being obtained on 6 March 1980. Commercial operation of the Belfast began later in March 1980, the company at first being known as TAC Heavylift, subsequently simply as Heavylift after the parent TAC had gone out of business. Three Belfasts are in full-time service with Heavylift in 1987, having demonstrated their ability to carry a diversity of awkward and outsize loads to many different parts of the world. Two others remain available for conversion.

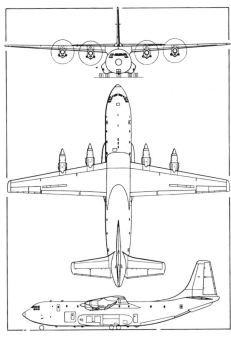

Left: Although only three examples of the Shorts Belfast are in regular service, this outsize transport has found a useful rôle to play in many parts of the world, as few other freight transports can match its capaciousness.

Above: In its day, the Shorts Belfast was among the largest military freighters in service. The design had its origins in that of the Bristol Britannia, but as this three-view drawing shows, little of the original eventually remained.

VICKERS VANGUARD UK

SPECIFICATION

Power Plant: Four Rolls-Royce Tyne RTy.11 Mk 512 turboprops each rated at 5,050shp (3,769kW) for take-off, with four-blade de Havilland constant-speed, feathering and reversing propellers of 14ft 6in (4.42m) diameter. Fuel capacity, 5,130 Imp gal (23,320l) in integral wing tanks.

Performance: Max cruising speed, 369kts (684km/h) at 20,000ft (6,095m); economical cruising speed, 365kts (676km/h) at 25,000ft (7,620m); initial rate of climb, 2,700ft/min (13.7m/sec); service ceiling, 30,000ft (9,145m); take-off distance to 35ft (11m), 6,540ft (2,000m); landing distance from 50ft (15m), 6,390ft (1,950m); range with max payload, 1,590 naut mls (2,945km); range with max fuel, 3,693 naut mls (4,990km) at 25,000ft (7,620m).

Weights: Operating weight empty, 82,500lb (37,422kg); fuel weight, 41,000lb (18,600kg); max payload, 37,000lb (16,783kg); max take-off weight, 146,500lb (66,448kg); max landing weight, 130,500lb (61,238kg); max zero-fuel weight, 122,500lb (55,564kg).

Dimensions: Span, 118ft 7in (36.15m); overall length, 122ft 10.5in (37.45m); overall height, 34ft 11in (10.64m); sweepback, nil; wing area, 1,529sq ft (142.0m²).

Accommodation: Cabin length, 90ft 0in (27.43m), width, 10ft 8in (3.26m), max height, 7ft 3in (2.21m). Typical mixed-class seating, 42 four-abreast at 39in (99cm) pitch and 55 six-abreast at 34in (86cm) pitch. Maximum seating for 139 passengers six-abreast at 34in (86cm) pitch. Underfloor freight holds volume, 1,360sq ft (38.50m²). Flight crew of two.

Design of the Vanguard was begun by Vickers (before that company became part of British Aircraft Corporation) to provide a 'big brother' for the Viscount which, as the world's first turboprop airliner, was enjoying considerable success. In the event, the rapid development of turbojet-engined airliners to serve medium-to-short stage lengths pre-empted the market for the Vanguard and sales fell far short of the high hopes that surrounded the type at the time of its first flight on 20 January 1959. Vanguards were sold only to BEA, which bought six Type 951s (first flight 22 April 1959) and 14 Type 953s with increased gross weight (first flight 1 May 1961), and to TCA, which bought 23 Type 952s (first flight 21 May 1960). By 1974, TCA (as Air Canada) had retired all its Vanguards and two years later British Airways had in service only five, all of which had been converted to Merchantman standard, this being the name for the passenger aircraft converted to all-freight configuration. The first Merchantman conversion, by Aviation Traders, flew at Southend on 10 October 1969, featuring a forward side freight door and a roller conveyor system in the floor; 12 in all were converted for BEA, which retired its last of the type in 1980. Several smaller operators have used Vanguards and Merchantmen second-hand, the majority of those still flying in 1987 being devoted to freighting.

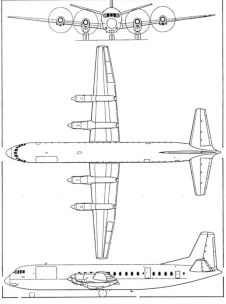

Above: The three-view drawing of the Vanguard clearly shows that it was designed to carry passengers, not freight. The forward side freight door was a later modification.

Left: Europe Air Service, one of the last operators of the Vanguard, passed its aircraft to sister French company Intercargo Service in 1987.

The airlines featured in this section represent a typical cross section of the world's major passenger carriers (which operate predominantly international services) and also the larger carriers which specialize in domestic operations. The United States is naturally well represented. The US marketplace has been transformed as a result of deregulation, a key effect of which has been a significant increase in mergers and takeovers amongst major US carriers, this in turn leading to the rapid creation of an oligopolistic market. Northwest's takeover of Republic (itself an amalgam of several operators), Delta's takeover of Western (the oldest US carrier) and the acquisition by Texas Air Corporation (owner of Continental and New York Air) of Eastern and PEOPLExpress, are clear indications of this development. The section also features the major communist-bloc airlines, including the world's largest operator, Aeroflot-Soviet Airlines, for whom only approximate statistics are available. A number of the smaller national carriers which undertake long haul operations are also included.

The airline fleet information is generally correct to the first quarter of 1987 and, wherever possible, account has been taken of confirmed aircraft orders up to that time. The statistics for aircraft yet to be delivered are contained in parentheses. Each fleet data list includes all of that airline's major passenger and freight equipment, i.e: the aircraft featured in the first section of the book. Light aircraft and helicopters, however, have been excluded.

The recession in oil prices has assisted in extending the useful economic life of many commercial airliners which are now out of production. However, the attractive operating and maintenance costs of the current and new generations of twin-engine jetliners, notably the MD-80 family, Boeing 737-300 and Airbus A320, are providing considerable impetus to the sales of these models to airlines worldwide. Increasingly stringent noise regulations also play an important role in promoting the use of these quieter aircraft and have strongly influenced the acceptance of the BAe 146 airliner at noise-sensitive airports.

AER LINGUS

Aer Lingus is the trade name under which the combined operations of Aer Lingus Teoranta and Aerlinte Eireann are known. Aer Lingus Teoranta was formed on 22 May 1936 as the national airline of the Irish Republic to operate scheduled services between Ireland and Great Britain. Aer Lingus was the first carrier outside of Great Britain to order the Viscount and was the first European operator of the Fokker F27 Friendship. The carrier initiated short haul jet services in May 1965 with BAC One-Elevens.

Aerlinte Eireann was formed on 26 February 1947 to operate transatlantic services, but due to a change in government policy the proposed services (initially to Boston and New York) were shelved. The carrier finally began operations with the inauguration of the Dublin-Shannon-New York service on 28 April 1958, using Super Constellations leased from Seaboard. Jet operations on the route began in December 1960 with the delivery of three Boeing 720-048 aircraft.

The operations of the two carriers are now fully integrated into an international and regional 29-point network of passenger and cargo services from Dublin, Shannon and Cork to London and several provincial centres throughout the UK, 14 European cities, and New York and Boston in North America. The carrier's major shareholder is the Ministry of Finance for the Irish government, with management holding a small number of qualifying shares. Aer Lingus currently employs 5,600 personnel, and carried a total of 2,267,145 passengers in the fiscal year ending in March 1986. Aer Lingus Commuter is a wholly owned subsidiary formed in 1984.

Fleet Data
3 Boeing 747-100; **(2)** 737-300; **11** 737-200; **4** BAe (BAC) One-Eleven 200; **4** Shorts 360.

Shorts 360

AEROFLOT

The Soviet state airline is the world's largest carrier. In addition to operating scheduled passenger and freight services and international charter flights, over 120 additional activities are undertaken. These include agricultural work, survey operations, fishery and ice reconnaissance, forest fire patrol and aeromedical services. Between 400,000 and 500,000 personnel are employed.

The carrier was formed in March 1923 under the name of Dobrolet, and services were operated from Moscow to Odessa, Georgia and into Central Asiatic Russia. Dobrolet merged with the Ukrainian airline Ukvozduchput in 1929 to form Dobroflot, which was subsequently reorganized as Aeroflot in 1932. However, it was not until 1960 that the last remaining separate entity, the Polar Aviation division operating services in the Arctic regions, became part of Aeroflot. During the 1930s emphasis was placed on developing the domestic route network; very few international services were operated at this time. On 15 September 1956 Aeroflot initiated jet services, on the Moscow-Irkutsk route, with the Tupolev Tu-104. From 1958 onwards substantial development of international routes was undertaken, initially

Ilyushin Il-86

to West European cities and subsequently to the underdeveloped third world countries in Asia and Africa under the organization of the Directorate of International Routes. The carrier operated its first transatlantic service on 7 January 1963.

Aeroflot currently operates to some 3,600 points within its domestic network and 122 points in 97 countries within Europe, Africa, Asia, and North and South America. International services are operated from Moscow (Sheremetiyevo) and 12 other international airports including Leningrad (Pulkovo), Kiev, Tashkent and Khabarovsk. Unduplicated route length now exceeds 621,400 miles (1,000,000km) of which 435,000 miles (700,000km) are international. Approximately 112 million passengers were carried in 1985, of which 3 million were on international services. Aeroflot carried some 3 million tonnes of cargo and mail during the same period.

Fleet Data
3,000 Antonov An-2; **150** An-12; **700** An-24/26/30; **60** Ilyushin Il-18; **170** Il-62M; **100** Il-76T/TD; **80** Il-86; **400** L-410/410 UVP; **450** Tupolev Tu-134; **500** Tu-154; **350-450** Yakovlev Yak-40; **100** Yak-42; over **2,000** helicopters including Mi-8, Mi-6, Mi-10K, Kamov Ka-24, Ka-32, and Mi-2.
(in the absence of official data the figures are provided as a guide only)

Fokker F28-1000

AEROLINEAS ARGENTINAS

Aerolineas Argentinas was founded on 14 May 1949 as a state corporation. It superseded four separate operators: Flota Aerea Mercante Argentina (FAMA), Aviacion del Litoral Fluvial Argentino (ALFA), Zonas Oeste y Norte de Aerolineas Argentinas (ZONDA), and Aeroposta Argentina. Of these, Aeroposta Argentina was the oldest, having begun operations in late 1928. ALFA had inaugurated flying-boat services in 1938 as Corporacion Sudamericana de Servicios Aereos, while ZONDA was established in February 1946 operating domestic and regional routes with DC-3 aircraft. FAMA, the largest of the four operators, was founded on 8 February 1946, and had been established as the

Argentine flag carrier. FAMA initiated services to London in September 1946 with DC-4 aircraft. The four companies ceased operations on 31 December 1949, and were merged to form the new carrier. Services from Buenos Aires to New York were initiated in March 1950 and domestic services were significantly expanded. Jet operations to Europe began in May 1959 following the acquisition of Comet 4 aircraft, and from 1962 Caravelle VI-R aircraft provided domestic and regional jet services.

Aerolineas Argentinas, presently employing 9,822 personnel, operates a network of scheduled passenger and cargo services to North, Central and South America, and to Europe.

Fleet Data
6 Boeing 747-200; **1** 747SP; **1** 707-320B; **8** 727-200; **12** 737-200; **1** Fokker F28-4000; **3** F28-1000.

McDonnell Douglas DC-10-30

AEROMEXICO

Aeromexico, Mexico's national airline, was formed on 1 September 1934 as Aeronaves de Mexico. Domestic operations were initiated with the opening of services between Mexico City and Acapulco. Between 1952 and 1962 Aeronaves took over Lineas Aereas Mexicanas SA (LAMSA), Aerovias Reforma SA, Aerolineas Mexicanas SA, and Guest Aerovias Mexico (which had been operating transatlantic services). Aeronaves was nationalized in July 1959 and a Pan American holding was acquired by the Mexican government. The first major international route, from Mexico City to New York, was opened up in December 1957 by Britannia 302 aircraft; later, DC-8 aircraft were used. In 1970, as part of a government plan, domestic operators in Mexico were rationalized into an integrated system consisting of eight smaller operators under the control of Aeronaves de Mexico. The airline changed its name to Aeromexico in February 1972.

Aeromexico, presently employing 10,350 personnel, operates a 35-point domestic network and international passenger and cargo services linking Mexico City with Panama City, Caracas, Bogota, Los Angeles, Tucson, Houston, Miami, New York, Toronto, Madrid, and Paris.

Fleet Data
3 DC-10-30; **2** DC-10-15; **5** DC-8-50; **9** MD-80; **16** DC-9-30; **8** DC-9-10.

AEROVIAS NACIONALES DE COLOMBIA (AVIANCA)

Avianca is the oldest airline in the Americas, and has the longest unbroken record of scheduled operation in the world. The carrier

was founded on 5 December 1919, under the name of Sociedad Colombo-Alemana de Transportes Aereos (SCADTA) by a group of German and Colombian businessmen. Scheduled operations began in September 1921 with services between the capital, Bogota, and the northerly port Barranquilla using Junkers F13 seaplanes. Pan American acquired an 80 per cent shareholding in the carrier in 1931 and in June 1940 SCADTA merged with Servicio

Boeing 747-259B Combi which Avianca operates on long-haul routes

Aereo Colombiano, a small domestic airline established in 1933, adopting the current name Avianca. Several domestic operators were taken over between 1941 and 1952, including in September 1951 Lineas Aereas Nacionales (LANSA), an operator serving all major points in Colombia and also Caracas.

Boeing 707-121 aircraft leased from Pan American enabled Avianca to initiate jet services to Miami and New York in October 1960 before the carrier took delivery of Boeing 720B aircraft. Pan American's remaining shareholding was purchased by Avianca in 1978.

Employing some 6,400 personnel, Avianca currently operates a large domestic network from Bogota, and international services to Madrid, Paris and Frankfurt in Europe; to Miami, New York and Los Angeles in North America; and to major points in Central and South America. Sociedad Aeronautica de Medellin Consolidad SA (SAM), a scheduled operator, and Helicopteros Nacionales de Colombia SA (Helicol) are wholly-owned subsidiaries.

Fleet Data
1 Boeing 747-200; **2** 747-100; **4** 707-320B; **(3)** 767-200; **7** 727-200; **11** 727-100.

AIR AFRIQUE

Air Afrique (Société Aérienne Africaine Multinationale) was formally constituted on March 28, 1961, with the signing of the Treaty of Yaoundé in Cameroun. The carrier was formed by Air France, the French independent airline UAT (now UTA) and 11 African states comprising Benin (then Dahomey), Cameroun, Central African Republic, Chad, Gabon, Ivory Coast, Mauritania, Niger, Republic of the Congo,

McDonnell Douglas DC-10-30

Senegal and Burkina Faso (then Upper Volta), which were formerly French colonies. The state of Togo joined the Air Afrique consortium in 1965, but Cameroun withdrew in September 1971 and Gabon in 1977, each to develop its own international carrier. Each of the member states contributes towards Air Afrique's capital with the balance held by Société pour le Développement du Transport Aérien en Afrique (Sodetraf). The carrier began services on August 19, 1961, taking over the route structure operated by Air France and UAT in French Africa and using Boeing 707 and DC-8 aircraft leased from the two carriers.

As black Africa's largest carrier, Air Afrique currently operates a route network emcompassing 22 African states and linking these with Paris, Bordeaux, Nice, Geneva, Zürich, Rome, Las Palmas, New York, and Jeddah. Some 5,200 personnel are employed by Air Afrique.

Fleet Data
3 DC-10-30; **1** DC-8-63CF; **1** DC-8F-50; **3** Airbus A300B4; **2** 727-200 (leased).

AIR ALGÉRIE

The carrier was formed as a result of the merger of the original independent Air Algérie (established in 1947) and the French operator Compagnie Air Transport in June 1953. Air Algérie officially became the country's national carrier in 1963, and was wholly government-owned by 1972.

Air Algérie (Société Nationale de Transport et de Travail Aérien), employing some 6,300 personnel, currently operates scheduled passenger and cargo services to 34 destinations in West Africa, Austria, Belgium, Bulgaria, Czechoslovakia, Egypt, Federal Republic of Germany, France, Great Britain, Greece, Italy, Jugoslavia, Libya, Romania, Soviet Union, Spain, Switzerland, and the Middle East. An extensive domestic network is also operated.

Fleet Data
2 Airbus A310-200; **11** Boeing 727-200; **16** 737-200; **3** Lockheed L-100-30; **8** Fokker F27.
(Note: A number of smaller aircraft types are operated including Grumman Ag-Cat and Beechcraft Queen Air aircraft.)

Boeing 737-2D6 Advanced

AIRCAL

AirCal was formed in 1966 to operate intra-state scheduled passenger services in California and began operations on January 16, 1967 with services between Santa Ana and San Francisco using L-188 Electras. Known until 1981 as Air California, the airline introduced jet services with leased DC-9 aircraft which were replaced from October 1968 with the first of an initial six

Boeing 737-3A4

Boeing 737s purchased by the airline.

AirCal was placed under trusteeship between 1972 and 1981 following the collapse of its owner, Westgate-California Corporation. The airline currently provides scheduled services between Orange County, Seattle/Tacoma, San Jose, San Francisco, Oakland, Portland, Sacramento, Reno, Lake Tahoe, Burbank, Los Angeles, San Diego, Ontario, Palm Springs, Chicago, Vancouver (Canada) and Anchorage (Alaska). AirCal employs approximately 3,100 personnel and was acquired by American Airlines in late 1986.

Fleet Data
8 Boeing 737-300; **23** 737-200; **2** 737-100; **6** BAe 146-200.

AIR CANADA

Air Canada was formed as Trans-Canada Airlines (TCA) by the Canadian government on 10 April 1937 to function as a wholly owned affiliate of Canadian National Railways. The carrier began scheduled operations on September 1 of that year with a passenger and airmail service between Vancouver and Seattle. Transcontinental passenger services on the Vancouver-Montreal route were inaugurated on 1 April 1939 and transatlantic services in support of the Canadian armed forces overseas began on 22 July 1943 between Montreal and Prestwick. The carrier began operating its North Atlantic services on a commercial basis on 7 May, 1947 with Canadair DC-4M North Stars.

TCA became the first operator of turboprop aircraft in the Americas with the inauguration of Viscount 724 services on 1 April 1955 between Montreal and Winnipeg. A total of 51 Viscounts eventually entered service with the carrier. DC-8-41 aircraft inaugurated jet operation for TCA on 1 April 1960 on the Montreal-Toronto-Vancouver route.

The carrier adopted its present title on 1 January 1965 and on 1 November 1966 Air Canada became the first North American airline to operate to the Soviet Union.

The flag carrier became a Crown Corporation in its own right in February 1978 and currently operates a 29-point domestic system and international services to Europe, the USA, the Caribbean, Bermuda and the Far East. A total of 62 destinations are served worldwide. 22,100 personnel are employed by Air Canada and 11,200,000 passengers were carried in 1985.

Boeing 767-233

Fleet Data
2 Boeing 747-200; **3** 747-100; **8** L-1011 TriStar 1/100; **6** L-1011 TriStar 500; **7** DC-8-73F; **14** 767-200; **36** 727-200; **35** DC-9-30.

Boeing 737-228 Advanced

AIR FRANCE

The carrier was founded on 30 August 1933, when Société Centrale pour l'Exploitation de Lignes Aériennes (formed on 17 May 1933, by the merger of four French operators) purchased the bankrupt Compagnie Générale Aérospatiale. The combination resulted in a fleet of 259 aircraft comprising 35 different types. French airlines were nationalized after World War II, Société Nationale Air France being established on 1 January 1946 but succeeded by Compagnie Nationale Air France on 16 June 1948, when the carrier was incorporated by act of parliament. Air France introduced Comet 1A services on 26 August 1953 over its Paris-Rome-Beirut route, and Viscount 708 services initially between Paris and London on 15 September 1953. The French government currently holds 99.38 per cent of the carrier's shares, with the balance in the hands of public and private interests.

Air France's current route network includes a complex structure of medium-haul routes throughout Europe and to North Africa and the Middle East, and a long-haul network which extends to North and South America, the Caribbean Islands, Africa, Madagascar and the Indian Ocean, China, Japan and other Far East destinations. Air France also operates the highly efficient Postale de Nuit internal night mail services using Fokker F27 Friendships and Transall C-160 aircraft. In all, Air France presently serves over 140 points in over 70 countries, and presently employs approximately 35,000 personnel.

The French carrier was the first airline to introduce the A300 Airbus into service (initially on the Paris-London route from May 23, 1974) and also inaugurated commercial supersonic services on 21 January 1976, with Concorde (simultaneously with British Airways).

Fleet Data
17 (+1) Boeing 747-200; **15** 747-100; **13** Airbus A300B4; **4** A300B2; **6** A310-200; **8** Concorde; **29** 727-200; **(25)** A320; **14** 737-200; **2** Transall C-160; **15** Fokker F27.

AIR-INDIA

Air-India was formed as Air-India International on 8 March 1948 by Air-India Limited (51 per cent holding) and the Indian government (49 per cent holding) to operate international services. Air-India Limited had started operations as Tata Sons Limited on 15 October 1932, providing scheduled air mail services on the Karachi-Ahmedabad-Bombay-Bellary-Madras route with de Havilland Puss Moths, the carrier changing its title to Tata Airlines in January 1938. On 29 July 1946 Tata became a public company and was re-named Air-India Limited. Vickers Viking aircraft were acquired in 1947 and during that year plans were drawn up with the Indian government for the creation of Air-India International which inaugurated service on 8 June 1948 between Bombay and London, via Cairo and Geneva, with Lockheed Constellation aircraft. Following the passage of the Air Corporations Act in March 1953, Air-India International was nationalized in August 1 of that year (Air-India Limited being absorbed into the Indian Airlines Corporation).

Jet operations were inaugurated on the Bombay-London route with Boeing 707-437 aircraft on 19 April 1960. The carrier's title was abbreviated to Air-India on 8 June 1962 by an amendment to the Air Corporations Act.

Air-India currently operates a network of scheduled passenger and cargo services from Bombay, Calcutta, Delhi, Hyderabad, Madras and Trivandrum to destinations in the Middle and Far East, Europe, Africa, Australia, the USA and Canada. Over 17,000 personnel are presently employed by the carrier. Air-India Charters (formed in September 1971) and the Hotel Corporation of India are wholly-owned subsidiaries.

Fleet Data
9 Boeing 747-200; **1** DC-8-73F (leased); **1** DC-8-63F (leased); **3** Airbus A300B4; **6** A310-300.

Airbus A310-304; note the small wing tip fences on this variant.

AIR INTER

Air Inter (Lignes Aériennes Intérieures) was established on 12 November 1954 to operate domestic services within France. Initial operations began with leased aircraft in 1958 (the first service being Paris-Strasbourg on 17 March), but this proved unsuccessful and was terminated a few months later. Full operations were resumed in June 1960 on a regular basis with leased aircraft. In 1962 Air Inter purchased its first aircraft, five Viscount 708s from Air France, and the first of the carrier's own Caravelle III aircraft entered service in March 1967. Also in 1967, protocol documents were signed with the state to authorize Air Inter's operations in the French metropolitan region, and with Air France and UTA to define the parameters of the carrier's activities in relation to the operations of the two French airlines. Air Inter attained financial autonomy during 1972 with the termination of subsidies. Air Inter became the first and only operator of the Dassault-Breguet Mercure 100 when the type entered service between Paris and Lyon on June 4, 1974. The carrier ceased charter operations in 1977 following an agreement reached with Air France, in return for which the carrier received a 20 per cent holding in Air Charter International, a formerly wholly-owned charter subsidiary of Air France established in 1966.

Air Inter operates an extensive network of scheduled passenger and cargo services radiating from Paris to some 30 destinations in France and Corsica. Based at Paris-Orly Airport, the carrier presently employs approximately 7,000 personnel.

Fleet Data
1 Airbus A300B4; **14 (+3)** A300B2; **(12)** A320; **11** Mercure 100; **12** Caravelle 12; **7** Fokker F27.

Airbus A300B2-1C

AIR LANKA

Air Lanka was established on 10 January 1979 as the national carrier of Sri Lanka, replacing Air Ceylon, which ceased operations on 31 March 1978. Scheduled passenger and cargo operations from Colombo utilizing Boeing 707 aircraft began on 1 September 1979 with management and technical assistance initially provided by Singapore Airlines under contract.

The government has a 60 per cent shareholding in the carrier with the remaining 40 per cent held by public companies in Sri Lanka.

Air Lanka currently provides services linking Sri Lanka with Bangkok, Hong Kong, Kuala Lumpur, Tokyo, Tiruchirapalli, Trivandrum, Madras, Bombay, Male, Karachi, Dubai, Bahrain, Abu Dhabi, Doha, Muscat, Dhahran, Kuwait, Copenhagen, Rome, Vienna, Zürich, Paris, Frankfurt, Amsterdam and London. The carrier employs 3,589 personnel.

Fleet Data
2 Boeing 747-200B; **2** L-1011 TriStar; **1** Boeing 737-200.

Lockheed L-1011-500 TriStar

AIR NEW ZEALAND

Air New Zealand was formed in 1939 as Tasman Empire Airways Ltd (TEAL) by the Governments of New Zealand (50 per cent), Australia (30 per cent) and the United Kingdom (20 per cent). Following delivery of two S30 Empire-class flying boats, operations commenced on 30 April, 1940, between Auckland and Sydney. The decision of the British government to withdraw from participation in the carrier in October 1953 left the New Zealand and Australian governments as sole shareholders, each with a 50 per cent holding. In July 1961 the New Zealand government took over sole ownership of TEAL in return for which Qantas was permitted to commence trans-Tasman services in competition with TEAL.

DC-8-52 aircraft entered service with TEAL on the Christchurch-Sydney route on 3 October, 1965, and the carrier adopted its current title Air New Zealand on 1 April 1965.

Fokker F27 Mk500

In 1977 the New Zealand Government decided to merge Air New Zealand with the other state owned airline New Zealand National Airways Corporation (NZNAC) and the two were amalgamated on 1 April 1978, as Air New Zealand. NZNAC had been formed as a result of an Act of Parliament in November 1945 to merge three private operators (Union Airways of New Zealand, Cook Strait Airways and Air Travel (NZ) Limited) into one national domestic airline.

Air New Zealand operates a route network encompassing 24 domestic points and international services linking Auckland and Christchurch with 18 destinations in Australasia, the Pacific, the Far East, North America and Europe. Approximately 7,000 personnel are employed by the carrier. Subsidiary companies include Safe Air (a wholly owned cargo operator) and Instant Freeline Reservations (airline, hotel and car rental reservations system).

Fleet Data
6 Boeing 747-200; **3** 767-200ER; **1** DC-8F-50; **10** 737-200; **15** Fokker F27.

AIR PORTUGAL-TAP

Air Portugal was established by the Portuguese government as a division of the Civil Aeronautics Secretariat in 1944 under the name of Transportes Aereos Portugueses SARL. Regular commercial services were inaugurated between Lisbon and Madrid on 19 September 1946, and later to Luanda (Angola), Lourenco Marques (Mozambique) and Paris, using DC-3s and subsequently DC-4 aircraft. TAP's first domestic route (Lisbon-Oporto) was opened in 1947. In 1953 the government sold its interest in the carrier, principally to a private business consortium, and TAP became a limited liability company. Super Constellations were introduced into service from July 1955 and in 1959 TAP embarked on a policy of route expansion to the African continent. Services to Rio de Janeiro via Ilha do Sal and Recife in association with Panair do Brasil (now Varig) began in 1960 using Panair DC-7C aircraft. Caravelle VI-Rs were delivered from July 1962 although jet operations had started earlier through the operation of Comet 4Bs in association with BEA. North Atlantic services were inaugurated on the Lisbon-New York route in 1969 and to Montreal in 1971. TAP once again came under state ownership when the carrier was nationalized on 15 April 1975. The carrier adopted its present name in 1979.

Air Portugal operates a network of international scheduled services to points in Europe, the Canary Islands, Africa, and North, Central and South America, as well as domestic services linking Lisbon, Oporto, Faro, Madeira and the Azores. Charter operations are also undertaken. Approximately 10,000 personnel are employed by the carrier.

Fleet Data
5 Lockheed TriStar 500; **3** Boeing 707-320B; **3** 707-320C; **4** 727-200; **4** 727-100; **7** 737-200.

Boeing 727-282 Advanced

ALIA-THE ROYAL JORDANIAN AIRLINE

Alia was founded in December 1963 as the wholly government-owned national carrier of Jordan to supersede the previous national airline, Jordanian Airways. Operations started in December 1963 with services to neighbouring Middle East countries using a leased DC-7 aircraft and subsequently two Handley Page Heralds. Jet operations began following delivery of Alia's first Caravelle 10R in July 1965 and services were inaugurated to Paris and Rome. Alia was the first Arab carrier to link the Middle East with North America inaugurating North Atlantic service in July 1977 using 747-2D3B equipment.

Alia presently operates services from Amman to 38 destinations in Europe, the Middle and Far East, North America and North Africa, and employs 4,551 personnel. Subsidiary interests of Alia include Arab Wings Company Limited (established in 1975 and operating air taxi, medical and executive jet charter services), Arab Air Services, Arab Air Cargo, and a number of hotel and travel interests.

Fleet Data
2 Boeing 747-200; **8** Lockheed TriStar 500; **(6)** Airbus A310-300; **3** 707-320C; **4** 727-200; **(6)** A320.

Lockheed L-1011-500 TriStar

ALITALIA

Alitalia (Linee Aeree Italiane) was established in its original form as Alitalia-Aviolinee Italiane Internazionali on 16 September 1946, a joint-capital company in which the Italian government subscribed 47.5 per cent of the capital, BEA subscribed 40 per cent and the remainder came from private interests. The carrier started operations between Turin, Rome and Catania on 5 May 1947, using Fiat G.12 aircraft leased from the air force. By 1955 Alitalia was one of only two carriers in Italy operating scheduled services, the other operator being LAI (Linee Aeree Italiane) which was formed by the Italian government and TWA in the same year as Alitalia. With the exception of the Rome-Turin route, operated by Alitalia, all domestic services were undertaken by LAI. Both carriers operated European, Mediterranean and transcontinental services. Alitalia changed its corporate designation to Alitalia-Linee Aeree Italiane and absorbed LAI in 1957.

The carrier inaugurated jet services in 1960 with the Caravelle VI-N starting on the Rome-London route on 23 May, and the DC-8-43 commencing operations on the Rome-New York route on 1 June. Alitalia currently operates an extensive worldwide scheduled network covering Europe, Africa, the Near, Middle and Far East, Australia, North and South America. Subsidiary interests include ATI-Aero Trasporti Italiani (a wholly owned scheduled domestic and international charter operator formed in 1963). Alitalia carried 12,800,000 passengers in 1985 and presently employs over 18,000 personnel.

Fleet Data
12 Boeing 747-200; **8** Airbus A300B4; **18 (+6)** MD-80; **20** DC-9-30.

Airbus A300B4-203

ALL NIPPON AIRWAYS

In less than three decades ANA has grown to become Japan's largest airline in terms of fleet size and passengers carried. ANA was founded in 1952 as the Japan Helicopter and Aeroplane Transport Company and began service between Tokyo and Osaka in December 1953 with de Havilland Dove aircraft. The carrier changed its name to All Nippon Airways in December 1957. The carrier merged in March 1958 with Kyokuto Airlines, a domestic airline that had started operations in March 1953 flying from Osaka to points in southern Japan. In spite of strong competition from Japan Air Lines and railway transportation, ANA experienced vigorous growth with rapid expansion in domestic travel, and in November 1963 the carrier absorbed Fujita Airlines, followed by Central Japan Airlines in 1965 and Nagasaki Airways in 1967. Jet services with a 727 aircraft leased from Boeing were introduced between Tokyo and Sapporo in May 1964. A number of routes have been transferred to Nihon Kinkyori Airways, a third-level operator formed in March 1974 by Japan Air Lines, ANA, Toa Domestic and other Japanese airlines to operate government-subsidized feeder services to isolated island communities and remote mainland destinations.

ANA currently employs 10,945 personnel and operates a scheduled passenger and cargo network covering 71 domestic and regional routes. Regional charter flights are

Boeing 767-281

operated to destinations which include Beijing, Hong Kong, Manila and Singapore, and in 1986 ANA inaugurated its first international scheduled operations with services to Los Angeles and Washington, DC.

Fleet Data
3 Boeing 747-200; **17** 747SR;
11 Lockheed TriStar 1; **25** 767-200;
(15) 767-300; **(10)** Airbus A320;
12 727-200; **14** 737-200;
19 NAMC YS-11.

Boeing 767-223

AMERICAN AIRLINES

American Airlines was formed in May 1934 as a successor to American Airways, which had been established in 1930 by the Aviation Corporation (AVCO) to unify the operations of five operators under AVCO's control. These operators in turn had succeeded many pioneer air operators with roots stretching back to 1926. American represented the conglomeration of 85 original companies. The carrier was heavily dependent upon air mail business in the early 1930s, and sponsored development of the DC-3 aircraft in order to develop passenger operations.

Since World War II American has been responsible for sponsoring the design of a number of significant commercial aircraft, including the Convair 240 and 990, Douglas DC-7 and DC-10, and Lockheed Electra. From 1945 American operated a transatlantic division, American Overseas Airlines, to serve a number of European countries, but this division was sold to Pan American in September 1950. American began nonstop transcontinental service with DC-7 aircraft between New York and Los Angeles on 29 November 1953. Jet operations with the first of many 707 aircraft began on the same route on 25 January 1959.

The carrier became the largest customer for the BAC One-Eleven aircraft which entered service on American's short-haul routes in March 1966. The world's first DC-10 service was operated by American between Los Angeles and Chicago, on 5 August 1971. In the same year American absorbed Trans Caribbean Airways and began flying to Caribbean destinations.

American, one of the world's largest carriers, currently operates a 137-point network throughout the USA, destinations in Canada, Mexico and the Caribbean, and London, Manchester, Düsseldorf, Münich, Frankfurt, and Paris. Tokyo, Zürich and Geneva will be served from 1987. In addition to its key domestic hubs at Chicago and Dallas/Fort Worth, new hubs are being developed at Nashville, San Juan and Raleigh/Durham. 41,000,000 passengers were carried in 1985 and American

presently employs approximately 50,000 personnel. AirCal was acquired in late 1986.

Fleet Data
2 Boeing 747SP; **10** DC-10-30;
46 DC-10-10; **13** 767-200;
9 (+8) 767-200ER; **125** 727-200;
39 727-100; **83 (+37)** MD-80.

AMERICA WEST AIRLINES

America West Airlines, a low-fare regional airline headquartered in Phoenix, Arizona, was incorporated in September 1981 and commenced scheduled operations on 1 August 1983 with three Boeing 737 aircraft and 280 employees. Initially serving Colorado Springs, Kansas City (since discontinued), Los Angeles, Phoenix and Wichita, America West now operates an extensive hub and spoke system centered on Phoenix Sky Harbor International Airport and serving 30 cities in 12 states and in Alberta, Canada. In order to expand its operations in Arizona, the airline acquired de Havilland Canada Dash 8 aircraft to provide feeder services to Yuma and Flagstaff from Spring 1987. Las Vegas is being developed as another important centre for operations with 'Nite Flite' services connecting the city with seven destinations. A total of 5,125,710 passengers was carried in 1985.

5 (+21) Boeing 737-300; **6 (+3)** 757;
25 (+12) 737-200; **4** 737-100; **3** Dash 8;
(25) A300-600R; **(15)** 767-300ER.

Boeing 737-3G7

ANSETT AIRLINES OF AUSTRALIA

The carrier was originally formed in February 1936 as Ansett Airways Limited by R.M. Ansett. Operations commenced between Melbourne and Hamilton using a Fokker

Boeing 767-277: this aircraft entered Ansett service on 27 June 1983.

Universal. By 1939 Ansett was operating additional routes from Melbourne to Adelaide, Broken Hill and Sydney. In late 1945 Ansett acquired three C-47s and extended its network to Hobart and Brisbane. Barrier Reef Airways, which operated seaplane routes radiating from Brisbane to Sydney, Hayman Island and Townsville, was taken over in 1952, and additional routes from Sydney were acquired from the bankrupt Trans Oceanic Airways during the following year. Convair 340 and 440 aircraft were subsequently introduced to provide low-fare services between state capitals in competition with Trans-Australia Airlines (TAA) and Australian National Airways, (ANA). Ansett is a subsidiary of Ansett Transport Industries Limited (ATI) which in 1957 succeeded in purchasing ANA to form Ansett-ANA on October 4 of that year. ANA's network stretched through Sydney and Melbourne to Tasmania and across Western Australia to Perth. As a result of subsequent acquisitions ATI now owns a number of other subsidiaries which include Ansett WA (formerly MacRobertson Miller Airlines), Ansett NT and Air New South Wales.

Ansett inaugurated Lockheed Electra turboprop services between Sydney and Melbourne on 10 March 1959, and Beoing 727-77 aircraft initiated jet services on 2 November 1964. The carrier adopted its present title in late 1968. Ansett currently operates an extensive network of scheduled services covering all the states of the Commonwealth of Australia and presently employs 8,000 personnel.

Fleet Data
5 Boeing 767-200; **13** 727-200;
12 737-300; **(8)** Airbus A320;
1 (+9) Fokker F50; **6** F27.

ATI—LINEE AEREE NAZIONALI

Linee Aeree Nazionali operates an extensive network of scheduled passenger services throughout Italy. ATI was formed in December 1963 as a subsidiary of Alitalia to operate the latter's routes previously serviced by Societa Aerea Mediterranea. The airline began operations in June 1964 and currently provides service to Turin, Milan,

Venice, Verona, Trieste, Udine, Gorizia, Genoa, Bologna, Pisa, Florence, Rome, Naples, Bari, Brindisi, Taranto, Lecce, Reggio Calabria, Messina, Catania, Palermo, Trapani, Siracusa, Marsala, Cagliari, Alghero, Sassari, and the islands of Pantellaria and Lampedusa. ATI has also operated specially equipped Fokker F27 aircraft to calibrate and check navaids. Some 1,924 personnel are employed by the airline.

Fleet Data
12 MD-80; **24** DC-9-30; **5 (+1)** ATR 42;
1 Fokker F27.

McDonnell Douglas DC-9-32: the livery deliberately mimics that of Alitalia.

Boeing 737-376

AUSTRALIAN AIRLINES

The Australian National Airlines Commission was appointed by the Commonwealth government on 12 February 1946, under the National Airlines Act to operate a network of domestic services. The Commission's operations were conducted under the name Trans-Australia Airlines (TAA), and operations began on 9 September 1946 between Melbourne and Sydney with DC-3 aircraft. By December of that year all state capitals had been linked, and principal coastal routes were operated in competition with those operated by Australian National Airways (now part of Ansett). In 1949 TAA acquired and subsequently developed the Queensland interior routes pioneered by Qantas Empire Airways Limited (now Qantas), as well as their flying doctor services. In 1960, at the request of the government, TAA acquired the Papua-New Guinea route network previously served by Qantas, and also the six DC-3s and four de Havilland Canada Otters operated by Qantas on these routes.

Jet services were inaugurated by TAA with Boeing 727-76 aircraft on 2 November 1964 simultaneously with its major competitor, Ansett-ANA. In association with Ansett, Qantas and the Australian government, TAA helped to form Air Niugini in 1973. TAA changed its title to Australian Airlines in 1986.

The airline's current network of scheduled passenger and cargo services link 32 points in Australia, including all state capitals and numerous provincial towns throughout the country. Australian presently employs nearly 8,000 personnel.

Fleet Data
4 Airbus A300B4; **(9)** A320-200;
12 Boeing 727-200; **1** 727-100C;
6 (+6) 737-300; **9** DC-9-30;
3 Fokker F27; **3** BAe Jetstream 31.

McDonnell Douglas MD-81

AUSTRIAN AIRLINES

Austrian Airlines (Österreichische Luftverkehrs AG) was founded on 30 September 1957, by a merger of Air Austria and Austrian Airways, which had been formed but had not started operations. The nation's previous operator, OLAG, had been incorporated into Deutsche Luft Hansa in 1938, and after cessation of hostilities in 1945 the Allies did not permit civil aviation activities until the State Treaty was signed in 1945. Austrian inaugurated services on 31 March 1958 between Vienna and London using chartered Viscount 779 aircraft. Jet services were introduced with Caravelle VI-Rs on 20 February 1963 to cope with the carrier's fast-growing European route system. Austrian operated its first domestic service with DC-3 on May 1 of that year.

DC-9 aircraft were progressively introduced from 19 June 1971, and on 30 October 1977 Austrian became one of the launch customers for the MD-80, which began service with the carrier in October 1980. Austrian is 99 per cent government-owned and presently operates a route network of 28,907 miles (46,519km) covering over 42 cities in 30 countries in Europe, North Africa and the Middle East. The carrier employs 3,050 personnel and carried 2,003,947 passengers in 1985 (including 465,452 passengers on charter operations).

Fleet Data
(2) Airbus A310-300; 13 (+4) MD-80; 4 DC-9-30; (2) Fokker F50.

Tupolev Tu-154B-2

BALKAN BULGARIAN AIRLINES

Bulgaria's national carrier was originally formed by the government as Bulgarshe Vazdusne Sobstenie and domestic operations began on 29 July 1947. In 1949, the carrier became a joint Bulgarian-Soviet enterprise known as TABSO (Bulgarian-Soviet Joint Stock Company for Civil Aviation, or Bulgarian Civil Air Transport as it was also known). The Soviet Union's half-interest in TABSO was bought out in 1954 and the carrier became wholly Bulgarian-owned although the title was retained until 1968.

Lisunov Li-2 aircraft were supplemented by Ilyushin Il-14s and a number of international services to European capitals were initiated. The introduction of Ilyushin Il-18 aircraft in 1962 enabled the carrier to develop services to Algiers and Tunis, and charters to Black Sea holiday resorts. Bulair was formed in 1968 as a division of the carrier to undertake passenger and cargo operations with Il-18 and An-12 aircraft leased from BALKAN Bulgarian. Bulair was integrated with the parent carrier in 1972. Jet

services were inaugurated with Tupolev Tu-134 aircraft in 1968.

BALKAN Bulgarian currently operates a network of scheduled passenger and cargo services covering 44 destinations in Europe, Africa and Asia as well as 8 domestic points. The carrier also provides aerial agricultural services and presently employs approximately 2,780 personnel.

Fleet Data
17 Tupolev Tu-154B; 3 Tu-154M; 17 Tu-134/134A/134B; 3 Antonov An-12; 7 Ilyushin Il-18; 1 An-30; 8 An-24; 12 Yakovlev Yak-40; 9 Mil Mi-8.

McDonnell Douglas DC-10-30

BANGLADESH BIMAN

Bangladesh Biman was formed on 4 January 1972 as the national airline of the People's Republic of Bangladesh. Scheduled services began on 4 February of that year on domestic routes linking Dacca, Chittagong, Sylhet and Jessore using a DC-3 aircraft. Leased Fokker F27 aircraft were subsequently used, and wet-leased Boeing 707 equipment opened up a service to London from Dacca on January 1, 1973.

A seven-point domestic network is presently operated, together with international services to Singapore, Kuala Lumpur, Bangkok, Rangoon, Kathmandu, Calcutta, Bombay, Karachi, Dubai, Abu Dhabi, Kuwait, Muscat, Doha, Dhahran, Jeddah, Tripoli, Athens, Rome, Amsterdam and London. Bangladesh employs approximately 4,500 personnel.

Fleet Data
3 DC-10-30; 5 Boeing 707-320B/C; 2 Fokker F28-4000; 3 F27-600.

BRANIFF

The Dallas-based scheduled carrier is the successor to the former Braniff International which was originally founded in 1928 by the brothers Tom and Paul Braniff. In 1929 the company became part of the Aviation Corporation which subsequently established American Airlines. The carrier was reorganized as an independent company on

3 November 1930, and its original Tulsa-Oklahoma City route operated in 1928 was extended to Wichita.

Operations from Houston to Lima via Havana began on 4 June 1948, with subsequent extensions to Rio de Janeiro, Asuncion and Buenos Aires. Braniff developed domestic services throughout the mid-western states as far west as Denver, and acquired Mid-Continent Airlines on 15 August 1952. A Dallas/Fort Worth-New York route was inaugurated in February 1956 and jet services were initiated with Boeing 707-227 aircraft on 20 December 1959. Braniff became the first operator of the BAC One-Eleven (Series 203) with service inauguration of the type on 25 April 1965. The acquisition of Pan American-Grace Airways (Panagra) on 1 February 1967 gave Braniff a number of additional South American destinations.

Braniff International ceased operations on 12 May 1982, and was restarted as Braniff with financial backing from Hyatt, Inc. Braniff recommenced operations in March 1984 on a much smaller scale. Hub and spoke services are operated from Dallas/Fort Worth and Kansas City, collectively serving Boston, Chicago, Detroit, Las Vegas, Los Angeles, Miami, Fort Lauderdale, Newark, New York, Phoenix, San Diego, San Francisco, Seattle and Washington DC. Services from San Antonio and Dallas to Mexico City and Acapulco were initiated in late 1986. Braniff employs approximately 1,600 personnel.

Fleet Data
22 Boeing 727-200.

Boeing 727-227 Advanced

BRITISH AIRWAYS

British Airways was formed on 1 September 1972 through the amalgamation of British Overseas Airways Corporation (BOAC), BOAC Associated Companies, BOAC Engine Overhauls, British European Airways Corporation (BEA), BEA Airtours, BEA Helicopters, Northeast Airlines, Cambrian Airways and International Aeradio which were brought together under the British Airways Group established by the 1971 Civil Aviation Act.

BEA had been formed on 1 August 1946, as a nationalized concern to take over the European routes operated by BOAC's British European Airways division and to absorb a number of British domestic airlines. BEA introduced the world's first turboprop service on 18 April 1953, with Viscount 701 aircraft between London and Nicosia, and began jet operations with Comet 4Bs in April 1960. BOAC was formed as a result of an act of parliament which provided for the acquisition and amalgamation of Imperial Airways (formed on 31 March 1924) and

the pre-war British Airways (established in 1935) on 1 April 1940. BOAC took over British South American Airways on 30 July 1949, and became the world's first commercial jet operator when services with the Comet 1 were inaugurated between London and Johannesburg on 2 May 1952.

British Airways operates the largest route network in the world, covering about 323,680 miles (520,900km) of unduplicated routes serving 145 destinations in 70 countries. No-reservation, guaranteed-seat 'shuttle' services, inaugurated in January 1975, link London with Glasgow, Edinburgh, Manchester and Belfast. On 21 January 1986, Concorde completed 10 years of commercial service with the carrier. Supersonic services are currently operated from London to New York, Washington DC-Dulles and Miami. Charter services are operated by British Airtours.

British Airways Helicopters (formed in 1964), British Airways Associated Companies Ltd (controlling hotel interests and the carrier's investments in Air Mauritius and GB Airways), and British Airways Engine Overhaul Ltd (undertaking engine overhaul work for the carrier and under contract for other operators) are all subsidiaries of British Airways. A total of 19,681,000 scheduled and charter passengers was carried in the 1985-86 fiscal year and 38,939 personnel are currently employed.

Fleet Data
(16) Boeing 747-400; 15 (+1) 747-200; 16 747-100; 6 Lockheed TriStar 1; 3 TriStar 50; 8 TriStar 200; 2 TriStar 500; 7 Concorde; 24 (+2) 757-200; 43 737-200; 21 One-Eleven 500; 5 One-Eleven 400; 6 BAe (HS) 748.

BRITISH CALEDONIAN AIRWAYS

BCal came into being as Caledonian/BUA in November 1970 through the acquisition of British United Airways (BUA) by Caledonian Airways. The new carrier represented the second-force airline which UK government policy favoured at that time with a view to stimulating competition. BUA had been established more than a decade earlier through the merger of Airwork Group and Hunting-Clan Air Transport in July 1960. BUA developed routes to Europe and became the launch customer for the BAC One-Eleven, inaugurating service with the type in April 1965. BUA also took over BOAC's former South American route. Caledonian Airways was formed in April 1961 as an international charter airline, commencing operations with leased DC-7C aircraft.

After the merger, and following the 1976 UK government civil aviation review, BCal took over British Airways' routes to Caracas, Bogota, Lima and Lusaka while giving up to BA its routes to East Africa and the Seychelles. BCal gained from the subsequent increase in the number of US gateway cities and experienced a substantial expansion of its long-haul network to North America and also to the Far East. On 1 April 1985, the carrier relinquished its South American network to BA in return for the latter's Saudi Arabian routes following the UK

Boeing 737-236 Advanced

McDonnell Douglas DC-10-30

government's October 1984 Airline Competition Policy document which endeavoured to balance the structure of the UK airline industry before the privatization of British Airways.

BCal operates an extensive scheduled route system linking London (Gatwick) with the USA, Europe, North, Central and West Africa, the Middle and Far East. Mainline domestic services are also operated to Glasgow, Edinburgh, Manchester and Jersey, and BCal plans to serve Kinshasa in Zaire and start a nonstop service to Tokyo.

British Caledonian Flight Training and Caledonian Far East Airways (providing airline handling and ground support services at Hong Kong-Kai Tak Airport) are wholly-owned subsidiaries of BCal. The carrier is also an equal partner with the Rank Organization in Cal Air International, an inclusive tour operator. BCal, a wholly-owned subsidiary of the British Caledonian Group, carried 2,300,000 passengers in 1985 and presently employs approximately 7,000 personnel.

Fleet Data
3 (+1) Boeing 747-200;
(9) MD-11; **11** DC-10-30;
(10) Airbus A320-200; **13** One-Eleven 500.

Airbus A310-222

CAAC

CAAC (The Civil Administration of Civil Aviation of China) was established in 1962 and superseded the Civil Aviation Administration of China (also known as CAAC) which had been formed in 1949 after the founding of the People's Republic. The operations of Skoga (People's Aviation Corporation of China), an airline formed as a joint Sino-Soviet undertaking, were taken over by CAAC following the withdrawal of Soviet participation in Skoga during 1954, leading to its dissolution in 1955. CAAC operated primarily domestic routes in the initial stages with the exception of services to the Soviet Union.

Acquisition of four Trident 1E aircraft from Pakistan International Airlines in 1970 allowed jet services to be inaugurated. The first Boeing 707-3J6B was acquired in August 1973, and, with the Il-62, enabled CAAC to develop long-haul international routes. Services to Tokyo were started in September 1974 and to Paris in October of the same year.

CAAC controls all civil aviation activities in China and operates the present domestic network which features over 180 routes covering all 29 provinces and autonomous regions except Taiwan. International services are operated to 20 countries in Asia, the Middle East, Africa, Europe and North America. CAAC operates a variety of non-airline activities in connection with the national development of industry and agriculture. Such activities include aerial survey, crop spraying and aero-medical work.

CAAC is in the process of major reorganization which will result in the separation of regulatory functions and a shift in operating autonomy to a number of regional airlines.

Fleet Data
2 (+4) Boeing 747-200; **4** 747SP;
3 Airbus A310-200; **4** 707-320B;
6 707-320C; **2 (+4)** 767-200ER;
5 Ilyushin Il-62; **5 (+25)** MD-80;
8 737-300; **15** 737-200;
3 (+12) Tupolev Tu-154M; **19** Trident 2E;
10 BAe 146-200; **3** DHC-7; **7** Shorts 360;
5 DHC-6 Twin Otter.
(Note: CAAC also operates an unspecified number of other Soviet aircraft types as well as a variety of helicopters and small aircraft.)

CANADIAN PACIFIC AIR LINES

Canadian Pacific was formed on 16 May 1942 through the purchase and amalgamation of 10 small independent operators by Canadian Pacific Railways. These had been primarily operating a network of northern air routes linking isolated communities and potentially rich mining areas with rail terminals.

In late 1948 CPAL was awarded its first international route, Vancouver to Sydney via Honolulu, Fiji and Auckland, and services started on 13 July 1949 with DC-4M North Stars.

In 1959 CPAL was finally successful in securing its first transcontinental route, from Vancouver to Montreal via Winnipeg and Toronto in competition with TCA (now Air Canada), and services commenced with Britannias on 4 May of that year. DC-8-43 aircraft entered service on long haul routes from 1961, and Boeing 737-217s entered service on domestic routes in 1968.

CPAL, known as CP Air from 1968 until January 1986, integrated services with Eastern Provincial Airways in April 1983 and acquired the operator on 31 August 1984. CPAL also acquired over 99 per cent of the stock in Nordair and plans to absorb the operations of this operator through 1987.

Headquartered in Vancouver, CPAL now serves well over 70 domestic points throughout Canada and 16 destinations in Central and South America, the Far East and Europe. 4,530,000 revenue passengers were carried in 1985 and CPAL employs approximately 10,000 personnel. It has now been acquired by Pacific Western. They will be known as Canadian Airlines Intl.

Fleet Data
12 DC-10-30; **43** Boeing 737-200;
2 L-188 Electra; **5** Fairchild FH227;
4 BAe (HS) 748; **(6)** Boeing 767-300ER.

McDonnell Douglas DC-10-30

CATHAY PACIFIC AIRWAYS

Cathay Pacific was founded on 24 September 1946, and initial operations consisted of freight and passenger services between Asia and Australia and charter

Boeing 747-367

flights to the United Kingdom using DC-3 aircraft. In 1948 the Swire Group became the major shareholder and manager of the carrier with Australian National Airways (later absorbed by Ansett Airlines of Australia) as a minority shareholder. By the end of that year Cathay Pacific operated seven DC-3 aircraft and two Catalina flying-boats on scheduled services from Hong Kong to Manila, Bangkok, Singapore and Rangoon. A DC-4 aircraft was introduced in 1949 to operate the Singapore route and open new services to Saigon, Haiphong and North Borneo. IN 1959 the carrier acquired Hong Kong Airways giving Cathay access to northern routes including Japan. Jet service was introduced in 1962 when the first of nine Convair 880-22M aircraft was delivered.

Cathay Pacific remains a private company with 70 per cent of its issued capital held by Cathay Holdings (a wholly owned subsidiary of Swire Pacific) and the

balance held by the Hong Kong and Shanghai Banking Corporation. An extensive network of scheduled passenger and cargo services is operated from Hong Kong to Abu Dhabi, Bahrain, Bangkok, Bombay, Brisbane, Dhahran, Dubai, Frankfurt, Fukuoka, Jakarta, Kaohsiung, Kota Kinabalu, Kuala Lumpur, London (Gatwick), Manila, Melbourne, Osaka, Paris, Penang, Perth, Rome, Seoul, Shanghai, Singapore, Sydney, Taipei, Tokyo and Vancouver. New services to Beijing and San Francisco were to be inaugurated during 1986. Some 6,600 personnel are employed by the carrier.

Fleet Data
(2) Boeing 747-400; **3 (+1)** 747-300;
9 (+1) 747-200; **2** Lockheed TriStar 100;
7 TriStar 1.

CESKOSLOVENSKE AEROLINIE

Ceskoslovenske Aerolinie (CSA), the national airline of Czechoslovakia, was originally formed on 29 July 1923 as Ceskoslovenske Statni Aerolinie. The carrier operated in competition with the privately-owned Ceskoslovenske Letecka Spolecnost (CLS) formed in 1927. The two carriers were absorbed into Deutsche Luft Hansa during World War II. The present carrier came into being on 1 March 1946, and began domestic and international operations with DC-3 aircraft. CSA was nationalized by the Communist government in 1949.

Jet operations began in 1957 with the delivery of Tupolev Tu-104A aircraft, which

inaugurated the first jet link between Prague and Moscow on 9 December of that year. In 1959 CSA became the first Communist carrier to operate international services outside Europe with the opening of a route to Bombay via Cairo and Bahrain. Ilyushin Il-62 operations were started with the lease of one aircraft from Aeroflot in May 1968 before the delivery of CSA's own Il-62s, and a service to New York via Amsterdam and Montreal with the type was inaugurated on 4 May 1970. In January 1976 CSA took over the third-level domestic operations of Slov-Air, which was originally formed in 1969.

In addition to its domestic system, CSA operates an extensive network of services to most European capitals and to destinations in the Near, Middle and Far East, North and West Africa, and North and Central America. Approximately 5,500 personnel are employed by CSA.

Fleet Data
6 Ilyushin Il-62M; **6** Il-62;
7 Tupolev Tu-154M; **13** Tu-134A;
2 Il-18; **5** Yakovlev Yak-40.

Tupolev Tu-134A

Boeing 767-209

CHINA AIRLINES

China Airlines Ltd (CAL) was founded by a group of retired Taiwanese air force officers on 19 December 1959, and began charter operations with two PBY Catalina amphibious aircraft. Cargo operations were subsequently initiated and various additional activities undertaken, including fishery patrol, insecticide spraying and aerial photography. Scheduled domestic services were inaugurated in October 1962 between Taipei and Taichung, and subsequently to Hualien, Tainan, Makung and Kaohsiung, for which DC-3, DC-4 and C-46 aircraft were acquired. CAL became the national carrier of Taiwan in 1965, and a year later initiated its first international service between Taipei and Saigon (now Ho Chi Minh City). Jet operations were inaugurated following delivery of CAL's first Boeing 727-109 aircraft on 3 March 1967. Following suspension of all domestic operations by Civil Air Transport (CAT) in 1968, CAL took over CAT's traffic rights to enhance its domestic system. NAMC YS-11A turboprop aircraft entered service with the carrier in 1970 on short-haul routes, and in February of that year CAL inaugurated service to San Francisco via Tokyo with a Boeing 707-309C. Direct flights to the USA were initiated in April 1977 using Boeing 747SP-09s.

CAL operates a domestic route network covering all major cities in Taiwan, including Chiayi, Hualien, Makung, Tainan, Taipei and Kaohsiung. CAL's international network serves destinations in South East Asia, the Pacific, North America, the Middle East and

Europe. CAL was the first operator of the Boeing 767 in Asia and presently employs approximately 5,900 personnel.

Fleet Data
6 Boeing 747-200; **4** 747SP; **5** Airbus A300B4; **2** 767-200; **2** 737-200.

McDonnell Douglas DC-10-30

CONTINENTAL AIRLINES

Continental's history can be traced to Varney Speed Lines (South West Division) which inaugurated passenger and air mail service on 15 July 1934 from El Paso to Pueblo with Lockheed Vegas. The carrier adopted its present title on 1 July 1937 and acquired Pioneer Airlines at the end of 1954 which gave Continental access to Pioneer's extensive network in Texas and New Mexico. On 1 May 1957 service was inaugurated between Chicago and Los Angeles via Kansas City and Denver using DC-7B aircraft, marking Continental's full transition to a mainline trunk carrier. Viscount 812 aircraft entered service between Chicago and Los Angeles on 26 May 1958, and Boeing 707-124s began jet operations for Continental on 8 June 1959.

In October 1981 Texas Air Corp, parent company of Texas International Airlines, acquired a controlling interest in Continental and the operations of the two airlines were combined on 31 October 1982 to form a single carrier under the name Continental. The carrier filed for protection under Chapter 11 in September 1983. Following approval by the US bankruptcy court of its plan for reorganization, Continental emerged from Chapter 11 in 1986 and the carrier presently services 57 domestic points, with primary hubs at Denver and Houston, and 28 international destinations in Europe, Canada, Mexico the Far East and Australasia. New York Air and PEOPLExpress are being integrated into Continental during the course of 1987.

Fleet Data
6 DC-10-30; **8** DC-10-10; **6** Airbus A300B4; **50** Boeing 727-200; **14** 727-100; **16** DC-9-30; **11** DC-9-10; **23** (+ additional) 737-300; **15** MD-80.

CYPRUS AIRWAYS

Cyprus Airways was jointly formed on 24 September 1947 by BEA (now part of British Airways, with a 40 per cent holding) and the Cyprus government (40 per cent holding), the remaining 20 per cent being held by private interests. The airline commenced operations on 6 October 1947 between Nicosia and Athens, with BEA operating the

Airbus A310-203

services until April 1948 when the airline acquired its own equipment, namely three DC-3 aircraft. BOAC acquired a 23 per cent interest in Cyprus Airways in 1950 and BEA took over all the airline's operations in February 1958. BOAC sold its shareholding to the Cyprus government in June 1959.

Jet services were inaugurated with BEA Comet 4B aircraft on 4 July 1961. The airline acquired its own jet aircraft with the delivery of the first of two Trident 2E aircraft on 19 September 1969. All operations were suspended following the Turkish invasion of Cyprus in July 1974. Cyprus Airways recommenced operations in 1975 with services between Larnaca and Athens, and Beirut and Tel Aviv, using leased equipment.

The airline currently serves 20 destinations in Europe and the Middle East, and employs over 1,100 personnel. Cyprus Airways is owned by the Cyprus government and local interests.

Fleet Data
3 Airbus A310-200; **3** Boeing 707-120B; **(4)** A320-200; **3** One-Eleven 500.

British Aerospace 146-100

DAN-AIR SERVICES (DAN-AIR LONDON)

Dan-Air was formed in 1953 as a subsidiary of Davies and Newman Ltd, the shipping brokers from whom its name was derived. Originally formed to operate charter flights, Dan-Air has also developed a network of scheduled services within Great Britain and to Europe. The carrier acquired Skyways International in April 1972, an operator formed in February 1971 to succeed Skyways Coach Air Ltd, which had pioneered coach-air services between Great Britain and France.

Dan-Air operates domestic services linking 14 points, and European services are operated from London (Gatwick), Bristol, Cardiff, Manchester, Newcastle, Teesside, Cork and Berlin. Inclusive-tour flights to resorts throughout Europe and the Mediterranean are undertaken from more than a dozen points in Great Britain, as well as from Berlin. Dan-Air also operates contract services for oil companies, ad hoc passenger and cargo charters, and night mail contracts. The carrier uplifted more passengers than any other independent operator in Great Britain during 1985, and presently employs over 3,000 personnel.

Fleet Data
1 Airbus A300B4; **6** Boeing 727-200; **4** 727-100; **1** 737-300; **6** 737-200; **11** One-Eleven 500; **5** One-Eleven 200/300; **3** BAe 146-100; **11** BAe (HS) 748.

DELTA AIR LINES

Delta was formed in 1925 as Huff Daland Dusters, the world's first crop dusting company. The carrier initially started passenger operations in 1929 between Birmingham (Alabama) and Dallas with a subsequent extension to Atlanta. Delta merged with Chicago and Southern Air Lines (founded in 1933) on 1 May 1953 and inaugurated jet services with DC-8 aircraft on 18 September 1959. In May 1960 Delta became the first airline to operate the Convair 880 and Delta premiered DC-9 service in December 1965. Northeast Airlines was acquired on 1 August 1972.

Atlanta represents the airline's main base of operations. Secondary hubs are also being developed at Dallas/Fort Worth and Cincinnati. Delta's extensive route network now covers 96 points in 35 states, DC, Puerto Rico, Bermuda, the Bahamas, Canada, Ireland, Great Britain, France and the Federal Republic of Germany. The airline carried 39,582,232 passengers in the year ending 30 June 1986, and employs

Airbus A300B4-103

38,901 personnel (including 2,364 temporary and part-time staff). Subject to the approval of the US Department of Transportation and the respective shareholders, Delta plans to acquire Western Airlines by 1987.

Fleet Data
35 L-1011 TriStar 1/100/200/500; **13** DC-8-71; **15** Boeing 767-200; **(9)** 767-300; **19 (+41)** 757-200; **102** 727-200; **33** 737-200; **36** DC-9-30; **(30)** MD-80.

Lockheed L-1011-500 TriStar: the 500 Series TriStar is a long range variant.

EASTERN AIR LINES

Eastern began life as Pitcairn Aviation, which was formed in 1927 and initiated an air mail service between Brunswick (New Jersey) and Atlanta on 1 May 1928 using PA-5 Pitcairn Mailwings. North American Aviation, Inc. purchased the carrier in July 1929 and renamed it Eastern Air Transport in January 1930. The traffic rights of New York Airways between New York and Atlantic City were acquired in 1931 and Ludington Air Lines, operating between New York, Philadelphia and Washington, DC, was taken over in 1933. The carrier assumed its present title in 1934.

On 1 June 1956, Eastern absorbed Colonial Airlines which gave the carrier routes in Canada, Bermuda, New York State and New England. Jet services with DC-8-21 aircraft began on 24 January 1960. Eastern began its now famous air shuttle operation in April 1961, and this links Washington, DC, New York and

Boston. The carrier became the world's first operator of the Boeing 727 in 1964. The absorption of Mackey Airways in January 1967 gave Eastern access to Nassau and Freeport in the Bahamas. Eastern was one of the three launch customers for the Lockheed TriStar and was the first operator of the type with services being inaugurated on 26 April 1972. The 1973 acquisition of Caribbean-Atlantic Airlines (Caribair) greatly expanded Eastern's operations between the USA and the West Indies.

Eastern services 110 cities in the USA and 34 international destinations in Mexico, Canada, the Bahamas, Bermuda, the Caribbean and South America. Some 41,736,000 passengers were carried in 1985 and the carrier presently employs approximately 40,000 personnel. In late 1986 approval was granted for Eastern to be acquired by Texas Air Corporation.

Fleet Data
24 Lockheed TriStar 1; **32** Airbus A300B4; **2** A300B2; **22 (+5)** Boeing 757-200; **95** 727-200; **32** 727-100; **21** DC-9-50; **58** DC-9-30.

EGYPTAIR

Egyptair was originally formed as Misr Airwork in May 1932 by the Misr Bank and Airwork Limited, London. The company began domestic operations in July 1933 between Cairo, Alexandria and Mersa Matruh with D.H.84 Dragons. By the end of the year Asyut, Luxor and Aswan were also served and in 1934 the carrier's first international route, to Lydda and Haifa, was opened, followed by services to Baghdad and Cyprus in 1936. After World War II, Misrair entered a period of rapidly expanding operations with the emphasis on new Middle East destinations. In 1949 it became completely Egyptian-owned, and the title was changed to Misrair SAE. On 1 January 1961 the carrier merged with Syrian Airways to form United Arab Airlines (UAA), following the union of Syria and Egypt in 1958. Syria withdrew during 1961, and the two carriers

Boeing 767-266ER

became independent once again, though the Egyptian carrier retained the UAA name.

Jet operations were started on 16 July 1960 with Comet 4C aircraft. The carrier adopted its present title on October 10, 1971, following the country's change of title to the Arab Republic of Egypt.

In addition to a six-point domestic network, Egyptair undertakes a network of scheduled international services to 30 destinations in the Middle and Far East, Europe and Africa. Over 9,000 personnel are employed by the carrier.

Fleet Data
1 (+2) Boeing 747-200; **8** Airbus A300B4; **6** 707-320C; **3** 767-200; **7** 737-200.

EL AL ISRAEL AIRLINES

EL AL was founded on 15 November 1948 as the country's national carrier. EL AL's inaugural flight took place between Geneva and Tel Aviv in September of that year, and scheduled commercial services started in July 1949 to Paris and Rome using Curtiss C-46 and DC-4 aircraft. Service to Johannesburg was started in 1950 and three Constellations were acquired in that year, initiating a Tel Aviv-London-New York route on 16 May 1951. Jet operations commenced in 1961, initially with leased Boeing 707 equipment, and subsequently with the carrier's own Boeing 707-458 aircraft which began direct New York-Tel Aviv service in June of that year.

EL AL operates a scheduled network of passenger and cargo services from Tel Aviv to Amsterdam, Athens, Boston, Brussels, Bucharest, Cairo, Chicago, Cologne, Copenhagen, Frankfurt, Geneva, Istanbul, Johannesburg, Lisbon, London, Los Angeles, Madrid, Marseilles, Miami, Montreal, München, New York, Paris, Rome, Vienna, and Zürich. Subsidiary companies of EL AL include Sun D'Or (formerly EL AL Charter Services), Teshet (partners in Laromme Hotels), and Tamam (in-flight Catering services). Some 3,605 personnel are currently employed by EL AL.

Fleet Data
7 Boeing 747-200; **1** 747-100; **4** 767-200; **5** 707-320B/C; **2** 737-200.

Boeing 747-258C

ETHIOPIAN AIRLINES

The national carrier of Ethiopia was formed on 26 December 1945 by proclamation of Emperor Hailé Selassie. Ethiopian began scheduled services on 8 April 1946, utilizing an initial fleet of five DC-3 aircraft. Trans World Airlines provided technical and management assistance under contract until 1970. The carrier developed routes to neighbouring African countries and initiated operations to Western Europe in June 1958 with services to Frankfurt. Ethiopian became the first African carrier to serve the People's Republic of China with the inauguration of scheduled services to Shanghai via Bombay on 23 February 1973.

Ethiopian Airlines operates an extensive scheduled domestic network covering over 40 destinations and an international route network from Addis Ababa to Abidjan, Abu Dhabi, Accra, Aden, Athens, Beijing,

Boeing 767-260ER

Bombay, Bujumbura, Cairo, Dar-es-Salaam, Djibouti, Douala, Dubai, Entebbe, Frankfurt, Jeddah, Khartoum, Kigali, Kilimanjaro, Kinshasa, Lagos, London, Nairobi, Paris and Rome. Ethiopian employs approximately 2,900 personnel.

Fleet Data
2 Boeing 767-200ER; **2** 707-320C; **3** 720B; **3** 727-200; **2** DHC-5A Buffalo; **9** DC-3; **6** DHC-6 Twin Otter.

FINNAIR

Finnair, the Finnish national carrier, was founded on 1 November 1923 as Aero O/Y and operations began on 24 November 1924, with a Helsinki-Reval (Tallinn) service using Junkers F13 seaplanes. 1936 saw the end of the seaplane era with the construction of airports at Helsinki and Turku. The ending of hostilities in 1944 resulted in a six-month suspension of operations, after which services recommenced from Hyvinkaa (some 30 miles, 48km, from the capital). Services were resumed from Helsinki in 1947, and the first of nine DC-3 aircraft entered service with the carrier in 1953, later initiating a Helsinki-London service on 1 September 1954. An agreement was reached between Finnair and Aeroflot in 1955 as a result of which Finnair became the first non-communist airline to be granted

traffic rights to Moscow after the war.

Jet operations with Caravelle III aircraft began on 1 April 1960 with services to Stockholm and Frankfurt. Finnair later became the first operator of the Super Caravelle when the first of eight of the type commenced operations in 1964. Transatlantic services began in January 1969 with the inauguration of a

McDonnell Douglas MD-82

Helsinki-Copenhagen-Amsterdam-New York route using DC-8-62CF aircraft.

Originally a private concern, Finnair is now a joint stock company, with the Finnish government holding 76.1 per cent of the share capital. Finnair currently operates one of the world's densest domestic networks in relation to population, serving a 21-point system. International services are operated to nearly 40 destinations from Los Angeles, Seattle, New York and Montreal in the west to Bangkok, Singapore and Tokyo in the east. Area Travel Agency, Oy Finnmatkat, Finncharter, Nordic-Hotel Oy, Kesi-Herkku Oy (catering), and Aero O/Y are wholly-owned subsidiaries. Finnair has interests in Finnaviation (providing schedule and charter services) and Karair (primarily a charter operator). Over 5,000 personnel are employed by the carrier which uplifted 3,826,603 passengers in the fiscal year ending 31 March 1986.

Fleet Data
4 DC-10-30; **2** Airbus A300B4; **5** MD-80; **12** DC-9-50; **(8)** MD-87; **(2)** MD-11; **5** DC-9-40; **1** DC-9-10; **3** Fokker F27; **(5)** ATR72; **5** ATR42-300.

Boeing 747-2U3B

GARUDA INDONESIA

Garuda was established on 31 March 1950 as the national carrier of Indonesia, with the Indonesian government and KLM as equal shareholders. Garuda succeeded the post-war Inter-Island Division of KLM, which had been operating throughout the East Indies since August 1947, and the pre-war KNILM. The carrier's initial fleet comprised 20 DC-3s and eight Catalinas. The carrier was nationalized in 1954 and began its first international service, to Singapore, in the same year. With the return of Irian Jaya (formerly Dutch New Guinea), the operations of the domestic airline De Kroonduif were absorbed by Garuda on 1 January 1963.

Jet operations were initiated following the introduction of Convair 990A aircraft in September 1963 on routes to Manila and Tokyo. Services to Rome, Prague, Frankfurt and Amsterdam through Bangkok, Bombay and Cairo were started in 1965 in association with KLM. Garuda took delivery of its first DC-8-55 in June 1966 and began services with the type to Sydney from Jakarta via Bali. DC-9-32 aircraft entered service on domestic and regional routes in 1969, followed by F28 Fellowship 1000 aircraft in 1971. In October 1978 Garuda took over Merpati Nusantara Airlines, which had been formed by the Indonesian government on 6 September 1962, and operated services in Borneo, Irian Jaya and a number of regional routes. Merpati continues to operate under its own name.

Garuda currently operates an extensive domestic network linking Jakarta with 31 destinations throughout the Indonesian

archipelago, spanning one-tenth of the globe. Scheduled international passenger and cargo services are now operated to Amsterdam, London, Frankfurt, Paris, Rome, Zürich, Athens, Abu Dhabi, Jeddah, Colombo, Penang, Manila, Bangkok, Kuala Lumpur, Singapore, Hong Kong, Tokyo, Sydney, Perth and Melbourne. Garuda employs approximately 7,000 personnel.

Fleet Data
6 Boeing 747-200; **6** DC-10-30; **9** Airbus A300B4; **19** DC-9-30; **6** Fokker F28-3000; **28** F28-4000.

McDonnell Douglas DC-10-30

GHANA AIRWAYS CORPORATION

Ghana's national carrier was formed on 4 July 1958 as the airline of the former Gold Coast to take over the Ghana operations of the former West African Airways Corporation. Ghana Airways was a BOAC associate company until February 1961, when the carrier became wholly government-owned. BOAC Boeing Stratocruisers initiated services for the carrier between Accra and London on 16 July 1958. Jet operations were inaugurated with VC10 aircraft in 1965, and DC-9-50 and Fokker F28 aircraft were subsequently introduced on Ghana Airways' regional and domestic routes.

Ghana Airways currently provides domestic services between Accra, Kumasi, Sunyani and Tamale. Regional services are operated to Abidjan, Banjul, Conakry, Cotonou, Dakar, Freetown, Lagos, Lome, and Monrovia, and long haul international services are flown to Düsseldorf, London, and Rome. Approximately 1,900 personnel are employed by the carrier.

Fleet Data
1 DC-10-30; **1** DC-9-50; **2** Fokker F28-2000/4000.

GULF AIR

Gulf Air was formed on 24 March 1950 as Gulf Aviation Company Limited by F. Bosworth, and from modest beginnings the carrier has grown rapidly to become a full international airline and the major carrier for the Gulf states of Bahrain, Qatar, Oman and the United Arab Emirates. Services connecting Bahrain, Doha, Dhahran and Sharjah began with a single Anson. In October 1951 BOAC became a major shareholder; four de Havilland Herons were purchased in the following year, at which time services to Abu Dhabi, Dubai, Kuwait, and Muscat were started. Four DC-3s were acquired to meet increasing traffic demand and also to operate charters on behalf of petroleum companies.

Jet operations started with Trident 1E aircraft chartered from Kuwait Airways before the arrival of Gulf Aviation's first One-Eleven 432 in January 1970. The carrier formally adopted its present title in 1973, and on 1 April 1974, the Gulf states of Bahrain, Oman, Qatar and the UAE became sole owners of the carrier with equal shareholdings. 'Golden Falcon' services from the Gulf to London were initiated in that year with VC10 Type 1101s purchased from British Airways. In 1985 Gulf Air ceased operations to Dubai, which set up its own official carrier, Emirates Airlines. Gulf Air currently operates a network of scheduled passenger and cargo services

Lockheed L-1011-200 TriStar: Gulf Air operates eight of the -200 variant.

linking Bahrain with Abu Dhabi, Amman, Athens, Baghdad, Beirut, Bangkok, Bombay, Cairo, Colombo, Dacca, Dhahran, Delhi, Doha, Hong Kong, Jeddah, Karachi, Khartoum, Kuwait, Larnaca, London, Muscat, Manila, Paris, Ras Al Khaimah, Salalah, Sanaa, Sharjah, Shiraz, Tehran and Tunis. Gulf Air also undertakes charter services and subsidiaries of the carrier include Gulf Helicopters Limited, and hotel and airport handling interests. Approximately 4,000 personnel are employed by the carrier.

Fleet Data
1 Boeing 747-200; **11** Lockheed TriStar 1/100/200; **8** 737-200.

Boeing 747-256B: this aircraft is named Tirso de Molina by Iberia.

IBERIA

Iberia (Lineas Aéreas de Espa6a), Spain's national carrier, was originally formed in 1927, with services starting between Madrid and Barcelona on 14 December of that year. In 1928 Iberia merged with CETA and Unión Aéreas Espa6ola to form CLASSA (Compa6ia de Linea Aéreas Subvencionadas SA) which initiated operations on 27 May 1929 from Madrid to Seville with Junkers aircraft. International service began on August 19 of that year between Madrid and Biarritz. In 1931 the carrier became Lineas Aéreas Postales Espanolas and by 1933 had opened routes to Bordeaux, Paris, Casablanca and Las Palmas. The carrier adopted its former name of Iberia in 1937. Transatlantic operations commenced with service to Buenos Aires on 22 September 1946 and jet services were introduced with DC-8-52 aircraft on the carrier's New York route in July 1961.

Iberia is controlled by the Instituto Nacional de Industria and is a member of the ATLAS Group (also comprising Air France, Alitalia, Lufthansa and Sabena) which is involved with technical co-operation.

In addition to an extensive domestic and European network Iberia operates long-haul services to North, Central and South America, Africa and the Middle and Far East. A total of 93 cities in 43 countries are served. Iberia employs 22,335 personnel and carried 13,160,775 passengers in 1985. Iberia plans to operate to Australia in 1987.

Fleet Data
6 Boeing 747-200; **8** DC-10-30; **6** Airbus A300B4; **35** 727-200; **30** DC-9-30.

Airbus A300B2-1C

INDIAN AIRLINES

Indian Airlines came into being as a State corporation on 28 May 1953, as a consequence of India's 1953 Air Corporation Act, which was aimed at rationalizing the fragmented domestic operations within the country. The assets and liabilities of eight major domestic operators were acquired by Indian Airlines, and operations by the new carrier began on 1 August 1953. The fleet comprised 99 piston-engined aircraft, including DC-3s, DC-4s and Vikings, and an equipment modernization plan was formulated. Viscount 768 aircraft joined the fleet in 1957, with service inauguration on 10 October, 1957, and the Fokker F27 Friendship 100 began operations with Indian Airlines in May 1961. The carrier entered the jet era with the introduction of Caravelle VI-Ns on routes from February 1964. These aircraft provided the mainstay of Indian Airlines' fleet until the introduction of the HS 748 (assembled under licence by Hindustan Aeronautics Limited at Kanpur) with deliveries starting in June 1967.

Indian Airlines operates as an autonomous corporation under the administrative control of the Ministry of Tourism and Civil Aviation. Operations are organized into four regions controlled from Bombay, Calcutta, Delhi and Madras, and a 73-point network is currently operated, including international services to destinations in Afghanistan, Bangladesh, the Maldive Islands, Nepal, Pakistan and Sri Lanka. Indian Airlines has developed into one of the world's largest regional carriers and currently handles over 23,000 passengers a day. In addition to scheduled and charter operations, Indian Airlines operates a night air mail system linking the country's four major cities. Over 19,000 personnel are currently employed by Indian Airlines.

Fleet Data
2 Airbus A300B4; **8** A300B2; **(19)** A320-200; **25** Boeing 737-200; **11** BAe (HS) 748; **8** Fokker F27.

INTERFLUG

Gesellschaft für Internationalen Flugverkehr GmbH (Interflug) is the national carrier of the German Democratic Republic and was formed as Deutsche Lufthansa in May 1954. Scheduled operations began on 4 February 1956 between Berlin and Warsaw using Ilyushin Il-14 aircraft. Domestic services were inaugurated on 16 June 1957 from Berlin to Barth, Dresden, Erfurt and Leipzig. On 18 September 1958 the carrier formed a subsidiary called Interflug GmbH to operate international services to the west. The subsidiary's title was determined by a ruling of the International Court of Justice at the

Hague to avoid confusion with the West German Lufthansa. The subsidiary Interflug was run jointly by its parent airline and the Deutsche Reisebüro (German State Travel Agency), and operated its first service between Copenhagen and Leipzig on 27 February 1959, in association with the Leipzig Trade Fair.

Ilyushin Il-18 turboprops entered service on the Berlin-Moscow route in 1960 and the carrier adopted the title of Interflug for all operations in September 1963. Jet operations started after delivery of Tupolev Tu-134s ordered in 1967. Ilyushin Il-62 aircraft entered service with Interflug in 1970 and inaugurated a Berlin-Havana route via Gander in 1974. The international route network was progressively expanded to include services to Baghdad, Algiers, Cairo, Damascus, Istanbul, Larnaca, Amsterdam, Helsinki, Copenhagen, Stockholm and Milan in addition to further East European destinations.

Interflug currently operates scheduled passenger and cargo services to 50 destinations in 36 countries. Charter services are also undertaken and a separate division handles agricultural and aerial survey activities. Approximately 7,000 personnel are employed.

Fleet Data
15 Ilyushin Il-62/62M; **14** Il-18; **36** Tupolev Tu-134/134A.

Tupolev Tu-134A

IRAN AIR

Iran Air (Iran National Airlines Corporation), also known as Homa (an acronym of its Persian name), was established in February 1962 through the merger of Iranian Airways and Persian Air Services to become the state-owned national carrier. Iranian Airways had been formed as a private airline in December 1944 and began operations on 31 May 1945. The first scheduled service was inaugurated in May 1946 linking Teheran and Meshed, and a domestic network was subsequently developed using DC-3 aircraft. Regional services to Baghdad, Beirut and Cairo were initiated by the end of 1946, and a route to Paris was opened in April 1947. Persian Air Services had been formed in 1954 and commenced operations the following year with a cargo service between Teheran and Geneva using Avro Yorks operated under charter by Trans Mediterranean Airways. Regional and international services were developed, and in 1960 a DC-7C was leased from Sabena, followed by a Boeing 707 leased from the same source.

Iran Air began jet operations with Boeing 727-86 aircraft on 4 July 1965, and the route network was subsequently expanded to include London, Frankfurt and Moscow. In

Airbus A300B2-203

the meantime the carrier had signed a three-year agreement with Pan American in 1964 covering the provision of management and technical assistance. Wide-bodied operations began with the introduction of Boeing 747SP-86 aircraft in March 1976, and services to New York with the type were subsequently initiated.

Scheduled passenger and cargo services are currently operated to 18 domestic points and to Abu Dhabi, Athens, Beijing, Bombay, Dhahran, Doha, Dubai, Frankfurt, Geneva, Istanbul, London, Paris, Rome, Sharjah, Tokyo, and Vienna. Charter operations are also undertaken. The change of government in 1979, and the war with Iraq, have had a significant effect on Iran Air's operations and re-equipment programme. Iran Air employs approximately 9,000 personnel.

Fleet Data
4 Boeing 747-200/200F; **1** 747-100; **4** 747SP; **4** 707-320C; **6** Airbus A300B2; **5** 727-200; **2** 727-100; **4** 737-200.

IRAQI AIRWAYS

Iraqi Airways was founded in December 1945 as a subsidiary of the government-owned Iraqi State Railways. Operations got under way on 29 January 1946, with a domestic service between Baghdad and Basra using de Havilland Rapide aircraft. By the end of that year Iraqi had started international services to Beirut, Damascus, Lydda (now Lod) and Cairo with DC-3s. Viscount 735 aircraft were acquired in 1955 and the type began operations on the Beirut service on 1 November of that year. On 1 April 1960, the carrier became financially independent of Iraqi State Railways. During Iraqi's formative years (until January 1960), BOAC provided the carrier with technical assistance and personnel.

Jet operations were initiated on London services in November 1965 following delivery of the first of three Trident 1E aircraft. A major re-equipment programme covering a fleet of Boeing 707-370C, 727-270 (Advanced) and 737-270C (Advanced) aircraft was completed during 1976 and wide-bodied services were introduced with Boeing 747-270C (SCD) aircraft in the same year. In addition to its domestic network, Iraqi Airways currently operates to a number of destinations in the Middle East, Europe, Asia and North Africa. Approximately, 5,000 personnel are employed.

Fleet Data
3 Boeing 747-200; **1** 747SP*; **20** Ilyushin Il-76*; **2** 707-320C; **6** 727-200; **5** Antonov An-12*; **3** 737-200; **2** Tupolev Tu-124*; **7** An-24. (*Operated for the Iraqi government)

Boeing 727-270 Advanced

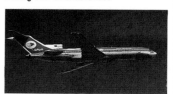

Boeing 747SR-46

JAPAN AIR LINES

JAL (Nihon Koku Kabushiki Kaisha) was established in its original form on 1 August 1951, as a private company. The previous national carrier (Greater Japan Airways) had ceased operations in 1945. JAL began services on the Tokyo-Osaka route with a leased Martin 2-0-2 on 25 October 1951. The carrier took delivery of its own aircraft, DC-4s, in October 1952, and placed an order for five DC-6A/Bs for international services. The financial requirements of such expansion resulted in dissolution of JAL in August 1953, to be replaced by a national carrier of the same name, with 50 per cent government financial participation. The carrier's first DC-6B was delivered on 15 September 1953, and began services between Tokyo and Sapporo on 2 October, the day after the new carrier had been legally established. After flight trials over the Tokyo-San Francisco route via Wake Island and Honolulu had taken place, JAL's first regular international commercial service was inaugurated over the route on 2 February 1954. International services were subsequently expanded to Hong Kong, Bangkok and Singapore. A Tokyo-Paris polar service was inaugurated with Boeing 707-328 equipment in association with Air France on 1 April 1960. Jet operations with the carrier's own equipment were started on the Tokyo-San Francisco route with DC-8-32 aircraft on 12 August 1960. Wide-bodied operations began on JAL's trans-Pacific routes from 1 July 1970, with Boeing 747-146 aircraft, and 747SR-46 (short range) aircraft began serving the Tokyo-Okinawa route in October 1973.

JAL currently operates an extensive network of scheduled passenger and cargo services covering 57 destinations in Japan, Australia, New Zealand, Asia, the Middle East, North, Central and South America, and Europe. Approximately 21,000 employees work for the carrier.

Fleet Data
5 (+4) Boeing 747-300; **32** 747-200;
6 747-100; **11** 747SR/100SR;
20 DC-10-40; **4** 767-200;
2 (+8) 767-300; **5** DC-8-61; **4** DC-8-62;
2 727-100.

JUGOSLOVENSKI AEROTRANSPORT

Jugoslovenski Aerotransport (JAT-Yugoslav Airlines) was formed by the Yugoslav government in 1946 to replace air services temporarily provided by military aircraft. Domestic operations began in 1947 with Junkers Ju 52/3m aircraft. DC-3 aircraft were subsequently introduced into service, and by the end of 1947 JAT's network radiated from Belgrade to the main cities in the country and to several East European nations including Romania, Hungary and Czechoslovakia. Operations were suspended in 1948 following Yugoslavia's break with the Soviet Union. Domestic services began to be flown again in October of that year and some international services in 1949. The emphasis switched to development of international routes to West European destinations and Convair 340

aircraft were acquired in 1953 to operate these services. JAT began jet operations following delivery of the first Caravelle VI-N and new routes to Amsterdam, Berlin and Moscow were opened with the type.

JAT currently operates a very extensive domestic system covering 16 points and scheduled passenger and cargo services are operated to 48 cities in Western and Eastern Europe, Scandinavia, North Africa, North America, and the Middle and Far East. Approximately 7,000 personnel are employed by JAT. Air Yugoslavia is a wholly-owned subsidiary formed in the late 1960s to operate charters mainly to countries such as Australia and the USA where large numbers of Yugoslav emigrants live. It charters aircraft from JAT when needed.

Fleet Data
3 DC-10-30; **4** Boeing 707-320C;
9 727-200; **7** 737-300; **11** DC-9-30.

Boeing 727-2H9 Advanced

Airbus A310-304

KENYA AIRWAYS

Kenya's national airline was formed on 22 January 1977, by the government following the demise of East African Airways Corporation (EAAC), the carrier owned jointly by Kenya, Tanzania and Uganda. Kenya Airways began operations over routes linking Nairobi with Mombasa and London on 4 February 1977, using Boeing 707-321 equipment leased from the UK independent, British Midland Airways. Operations gradually extended to cover a number of domestic and regional services previously operated by EAAC, using former EAAC Fokker F27-500 and DC-9-32 equipment. Kenya Airways acquired three ex-Northwest Orient Boeing 707-351B aircraft and expanded services to Europe.

Kenya Airways currently operates a network of scheduled passenger services which include domestic services linking Nairobi, Mombasa, Malindi and Kisumu, and international services to Athens, Rome, London, Frankfurt, Paris, Cairo, Khartoum, Dubai, Jeddah, Bombay, Addis Ababa, Mogadishu, Seychelles, Entebbe, Harare,

Dar-es-Salaam, Lusaka, Kigali, Bujumbura, Lilongwe and Zanzibar. The airline employs approximately 2,800 personnel. Kenya Flamingo Airways is the airline's charter subsidiary, leasing aircraft from the parent as required.

Fleet Data
2 Airbus A310-300; **3** Boeing 707-320B;
1 720B; **1** DC-9-30; **2** Fokker F27.

KLM-ROYAL DUTCH AIRLINES

KLM (Koninklijke Luchtvaart Maatschappij NV) was founded on 7 October 1919, and is the world's oldest airline still operating under its own name. The first and now oldest air route in the world was opened on 17 May 1920, between Amsterdam and London with a leased de Havilland D.H.16. In the subsequent years a European network was developed and various types of Fokker aircraft introduced into service. Initial services to the East Indies in 1929 led to the opening of a weekly service from Amsterdam to Batavia (now Jakarta) in October 1931. The DC-2 entered KLM service in 1935, and in 1937 the carrier became the first European operator of the DC-3 aircraft. Services in the West Indies based on Curacao were initiated in 1935 and were developed to serve Colombia, Venezuela, Barbados, Trinidad and the Guianas. These services were continued throughout World War II, and subsequently extended to Cuba and Miami. On 21 May 1946, KLM started scheduled services to New York, making the carrier the first European airline to operate flights between the two continents after the war. South America and South Africa were added to the network in 1946 and 1947 respectively, and Australia was included in KLM's route network from 1951. Viscount 803 aircraft entered service on European routes in 1957, and the Electra began serving with the carrier in 1959, primarily on Middle and Far East routes. KLM became the first non-US airline to operate the DC-8 in April 1960.

KLM currently operates an extensive route network of scheduled passenger and cargo services form Amsterdam covering Europe, North and Latin America, Africa, the Near, Middle and Far East, and Australia. The Netherlands Government holds a 54.9 per cent shareholding in KLM with the remainder of shares in private hands. The carrier currently employs approximately 19,000 personnel.

KLM owns a number of subsidiaries which include NLM City Hopper, a domestic

Boeing 747-206B SUD

and regional operator founded in 1966, KLM Helicopters established in October 1965 and undertaking general offshore support duties and charters, and KLM Aerocarto which carries out survey work.

Fleet Data
6 Boeing 747-400; **19** 747-200/300;
5 DC-10-30; **10** Airbus A310-200;
10 737-300; **18** DC-9-30; **(10)** Fokker 100;
1 DC-9-10.

Boeing 747-3B5B

KOREAN AIR

Korean Air, known until 1984 as Korean Air Lines, was formed as a government-owned carrier in June 1962 to succeed Korean National Airlines which was organized in 1945 by Captain Yong Wook Shinn, the country's first licensed pilot. Korean National was granted a permit in 1948 to establish scheduled domestic services, and operations from Seoul to Kusan, Kwanju, Pusan and Chunmunjin were started with Stinson aircraft. DC-3s were acquired in April 1950 and international services to Tokyo began in 1952, followed by services to Hong Kong in 1954.

Korean Air Lines, as it then was, introduced F27 Friendship 200 aircraft in January 1964. Services to Fukuoka and Osaka were initiated and the Hong Kong route reopened in 1966. Jet operations began following the delivery of a DC-9-32 aircraft in July 1967, and two former Eastern Air Lines Boeing 720-025s were added to the fleet in 1969. Wide-bodied operations with Boeing 747-2B5B aircraft began in May 1973, and the first DC-10-30 was delivered in February 1978. Korean became one of the early operators of the Airbus when its first A300B4-2C aircraft was delivered on 31 August, 1978.

Scheduled services are currently operated from Seoul, Pusan and Cheju to Tokyo, Nagoya, Osaka, Fukuoka, Niigata, Taipei, Manila, Hong Kong, Honolulu, New York, Los Angeles, Bangkok, Singapore, Colombo, Bahrain, Dhahran, Baghdad, Jeddah, Kuwait, Abu Dhabi, Tripoli, Zürich, Frankfurt, Amsterdam and Paris. The carrier was acquired by the Han Jin Transport Group in 1969. Approximately 10,000 personnel are employed by Korean Air.

Fleet Data
(3) Boeing 747-400; **2** 747-300;
12 747-200; **2** 747SP; **4** DC-10-30;
2 (+1) Airbus A300-600; **10** A300B4/F4;
1 707-320B; **4** 707-320C; **6** 727-200;
6 MD-80; **2** Fokker F28-4000;
1 Fokker F27; **1** Falcon 20; **1** CASA 212;
1 Cessna 500.

British Aerospace 125-700

KUWAIT AIRWAYS

The carrier was formed in late 1953 as Kuwait National Airways and began scheduled operations from Kuwait to Basra and Beirut in 1954 with DC-3 aircraft. Services to Bahrain and Cairo were introduced in 1956, and the carrier adopted the title of Kuwait Airways Corporation (KAC) in March of the following year. On 1 June 1958, BOAC took over management of the carrier under a five-year contract, and in March 1959 KAC absorbed British International Airlines, a then BOAC subsidiary providing local charter services. Operations with Viscount 754 aircraft leased from MEA were inaugurated in 1958, replacing DC-4 equipment. By 1963 the carrier had become wholly-owned by the government of Kuwait and adopted its present title.

Kuwait Airways took delivery of its first Comet 4C on 18 January 1963, and a London service with the type was inaugurated in March 1964. During the following month the carrier acquired Trans Arabia Airways, a major competitor since 1959. The latter operated a fleet of DC-6B aircraft on services throughout the Middle East and to London. Boeing 707-369Cs entered service in 1968, and wide-bodied operations began in 1978 following delivery of the carrier's first Boeing 747-269B on 28 July. Routes to New York and Manila were opened in December 1980.

Kuwait Airways now operates scheduled passenger and cargo services to 41 destinations in 38 countries in the Middle East, Europe, Africa, North America, and Asia. The carrier currently employs approximately 6,500 personnel.

Fleet Data

4 Boeing 747-200; **3** Airbus A300C-600; **5** A310-200; **3** 767-200 ER; **4** 727-200; **2** Gulfstream III; **2** BAe 125-700.

LAN-CHILE

LAN-Chile (Línea Aérea Nacional de Chile) is the second oldest airline in South America and was founded on 5 March 1929, as a branch of the Chilean air force. The carrier, originally known as Línea Aeropostal Santiago-Arica, began operations between Santiago and Arica with D.H.60G Gipsy Moths. In 1932, the carrier became independent of the air force and adopted its present title, although LAN-Chile remained a government-owned concern. Following the acquisition of Lodestars, LAN-Chile used the type in 1946 to inaugurate international operations with a service from Santiago to Buenos Aires which was later extended to

Boeing 767-216ER

Montevideo. LAN-Chile began jet operations following the delivery of the first of three Caravelle VI-R aircraft in March 1964. In April 1967, LAN-Chile initiated service to New York with a Boeing 707-330B acquired from Lufthansa, and subsequently opened a European route with the type. Passenger services to Easter Island were started on 3 April 1967, and these were later extended to Papeete (Tahiti) thereby forming the first regular air link between South America and the South Pacific. In 1974 LAN-Chile operated a Boeing 707 transpolar flight between Punta Arenas and Sydney and thus became the first airline to link South America with Australia via the South Pole.

LAN-Chile presently operates scheduled domestic services linking Santiago, Arica, Iquique, Puerto Montt, and Punta Arenas, and international services to Buenos Aires, Mendoza, Montevideo, Caracas, Rio de Janeiro, Lima, La Paz, Panama, Miami, New York, Madrid, Easter Island, Papeete, and Nandi. LAN-Chile employs approximately 1,400 personnel.

Fleet Data

2 Boeing 767-200ER; **3** 707-320B; **1** 707-320C; **3** 737-200.

Fokker F27-600

LIBYAN ARAB AIRLINES

Libyan Arab Airlines, the national carrier of the Socialist People's Libyan Arab Jamahiriya, was originally founded as Kingdom of Libya Airlines (KLA) in September 1964. KLA absorbed two existing operators, Libiavia and United Libyan Airlines, the former of which had begun services between Tripoli and Ankara in July 1958. KLA began operations with Caravelle VI-R aircraft and developed new international services while the domestic services were contracted out to Aero Trasporti Italiani (ATI) with Fokker F27 aircraft based at Tripoli. The carrier adopted its current title on 1 September 1969 following the revolution, and subsequently acquired its first Boeing 727-200 aircraft. Libyan Arab Airlines took over domestic operations, acquiring its own Fokker F27s.

In addition to a comprehensive domestic network, the carrier provides scheduled passenger and cargo services from Tripoli, Benghazi and Sebha to Algiers, Amman, Amsterdam, Athens, Belgrade, Bucharest, Casablanca, Damascus, Frankfurt, Istanbul, Jeddah, Karachi, Kuwait, Larnaca, London, Madrid, Malta, Milan, Moscow, Paris, Rome, Sfax, Sofia, Tunis, Vienna, Warsaw and Zürich. Approximately 3,600 personnel are employed.

Fleet Data

2 Airbus A310-200; **4** Boeing 707-320 B/C; **10** 727-200; **3** Fokker F28-4000; **18** F-27-400/500/600.

Tupolev Tu-154B-2 (Aeroflot lease)

LOT

LOT (Polskie Linie Lotnicze) was established as the state-owned national carrier of Poland on 1 January 1929, to take over the two existing private operators, Aerotarg and Aerolot. Aerotarg had been formed in May 1921 and operated domestic services from Warsaw. Aerolot was founded as Aerolloyd in 1922 and operated Junkers F.13 aircraft on domestic services and, in 1925, the country's first international routes to Austria and Czechoslovakia. LOT undertook a major expansion programme resulting in a network which covered 13 countries by 1939. The formidable task of re-establishing LOT after the adversities of World War II began early in 1945. Initially domestic services were restarted, and subsequently international routes to Berlin, Paris, Prague, Moscow and Stockholm were opened using Li-2 aircraft (Soviet-built DC-3s).

Jet operations with the Tupolev Tu-134 started in November 1968, and from May 1972 the Ilyushin Il-62 began serving on the London, Paris and Moscow routes. Services to New York and Montreal were subsequently inaugurated, and in September 1977 LOT initiated scheduled operations to Bangkok via Baghdad and Bombay.

LOT currently operates an 11-point domestic network and international services to 36 destinations in Europe, the Middle East, North Africa, North America and Asia. Approximately 6,000 personnel are employed by the carrier. LOT also undertakes extensive charter operations.

Fleet Data

7 Ilyushin IL-62M; **(10)** Tupolev Tu-154M; **9** Il-18; **1** Antonov An-12; **7** Tu-134A; **16** An-24.

LUFTHANSA

The carrier was formed in 1953 as Luftag to succeed its pre-war forerunner, Deutsche Luft Hansa (DLH), which had been established on 6 January 1926, through a merger of Deutscher Aero Lloyd AG and Junkers AG Luftverkehr and which ceased operations in April 1945 as a result of an Allied ban on German aviation. The origins of DLH go back to February 1919 when Deutsche Luft-Reederei, a former company, commenced scheduled services between Berlin and Weimar.

Luftag was formed on 6 January 1953. The carrier adopted its present title, Lufthansa (Deutsche Lufthansa AG), in August 1954, and scheduled operations began on 1 April 1955, with domestic services between Hamburg, Düsseldorf,

Airbus A310-203

Köln/Bonn, Frankfurt and Münich. Service to London, Paris and Madrid followed shortly afterwards. Substantial development of the domestic and European route system followed the service introduction of Convair 440 aircraft in 1957 and Viscount turboprop aircraft in 1958. Boeing 707-430 services between Frankfurt and New York from March 1960, and to San Francisco in May of that year, marked the beginning of jet operations for Lufthansa. The carrier became the first European customer for the 727 aircraft, and European services with the type commenced in 1964. Lufthansa subsequently launched the 737 airliner with an order for 21 of the type being placed in 1965.

Lufthansa currently serves 136 points covering 79 countries in Europe, Africa, the Near, Middle and Far East, Australia, North, Central and South America. Principal subsidiaries include Condor Flugdienst (a charter/inclusive-tour operator) and German Cargo Services. Major shareholdings in the carrier are held by the Federal German Government (74 percent), the State of North Rhine-Westphalia and Federal German Railways. Approximately 35,000 personnel are employed by Lufthansa.

Fleet Data

(6) Boeing 747-400; **23** 747-200; **11** DC-10-30; **7** A300-600; **5** A300B4; **10** A310-200; **(15)** A320; **(15)** A340; **28** 727-200; **10** 737-300; **40** 737-200.

Boeing 747-3H6

MALAYSIAN AIRLINE SYSTEM

MAS (Sistem Penerbangan Malaysia Berhard) was formed by the government of Malaysia in April 1971 as the national carrier to succeed Malaysia-Singapore Airlines (MSA), following the decision by the respective governments to establish separate operations. The history of the carrier dates from 1937 with the registration of Malayan Airways Limited, a company formed by the Straits Steamship Company, the Ocean Steamship Company and Imperial Airways. During its first year of operation, in 1947, domestic services between Singapore, Kuala Lumpur, Ipoh, Penang, Kuantan and Kota Baru were inaugurated. Later in the year regional services to Jakarta, Palembang and Medan began when the airline took delivery of its first DC-3 aircraft. International services to Saigon were also initiated. In 1963 the carrier was renamed Malaysian Airways Limited and two years later the carrier absorbed Borneo Airways. The title of Malaysia-Singapore Airlines was adopted following acquisition of a majority shareholding in the company by the Governments of Malaysia and Singapore in 1966.

Following the split-up of MSA, the new carrier, MAS, began operations on 1 October 1972, taking over the former MSA routes in the Malayan peninsula, Sabah and Sarawak. Based at Subang International Airport, Kuala Lumpur, MAS has now expanded its network to serve 22 international destinations in Europe, Asia and Australia and 36 domestic points, and currently employs approximately 10,500 personnel.

Fleet Data
1 Boeing 747-300; **2** 747-200; **3** DC-10-30; **4** Airbus A300B4; **12** 737-200; **11** Fokker F27; **4** DHC-6 Twin Otter.

Tupolev Tu-154B-2

MALEV (MAGYAR LÉGIKÖZLEKEDÉSI VÁLLALAT)

Malev, the Hungarian state airline, was formed in March 1946 as a joint Hungarian/Soviet undertaking under the title of Maszovlet (Magyar Szovjet Polgari Legiforgalmi Társaság). Maszovlet commenced operations on 15 October 1946, with domestic services linking Budapest, Debrecen and Nyireghaza, and utilizing Lisunov Li-2 and Polikarpov Po-2 aircraft. The airline adopted its present name on 25 November 1954, when it became wholly Hungarian-owned. Several West European destinations were added to Malev's scheduled network between 1958 and 1960, and in May 1960 the airline inaugurated turbo prop services with Ilyushin Il-18s. Jet operations commenced following the delivery of Tupolev Tu-134 aircraft in December 1968.

Malev presently undertakes domestic services and operates international services to well over 30 destinations throughout Europe and in North Africa and the Middle East. Approximately 3,600 personnel are employed by Malev.

Fleet Data
10 Tupolev Tu-154B; **10** Tu-134/134A; **4** Ilyushin Il-18.

MEXICANA

Mexicana (Compañia Mexicana de Aviacion) is the fourth oldest airline in the world and the second oldest in Latin America, having been originally founded as Compañia Mexicana de Transportes Aeros (CTMA) on 12 July 1921. Operations started from Mexico City to Tuxpan and Tampico with Lincoln Standards. The assets of CTMA were acquired in September 1924

McDonnell Douglas DC-10-15

by Compañia Mexicana de Aviacion (Mexicana) which was formed on 20 August 1924. Initial operations centred on payroll deliveries to remote oil fields (due to the vulnerability of ground routes to armed robbery). The carrier signed an air mail contract with the Mexican government for the Mexico City-Tampico route on 16 August 1926, and passenger services were subsequently introduced on the route with Fairchild 71 aircraft on 15 April 1928. Pan American purchased Mexicana in January 1929 as part of its ambitious expansion plans in Latin America though Mexicana retained its separate identity. In January 1936 Mexicana began services on its first international trunk route from Mexico City to Los Angeles with Lockheed 10 Electra aircraft.

In 1960 the carrier took delivery of its first Comet 4C jet aircraft which initiated service to Chicago on 4 July of that year. In the same year Mexicana acquired the routes of ATSA and TAMSA which gave access to the route structure in the Yucatan and additional services to Texas. Pan American sold its remaining shares in the carrier in January 1968, and Mexicana gradually expanded its international route structure to include Dallas in 1972, St Louis in 1973, Kansas City in 1974, Costa Rica in 1977, San Francisco in 1978 and Seattle in 1979. Mexicana currently operates an extensive route system which serves 27 points in Mexico, nine points in the USA and also San Jose. The airline employs approximately 12,600 personnel. The Mexican government holds 58 per cent of the shares with the remainder in the hands of board members and employees.

Fleet Data
5 DC-10-15; **40** Boeing 727-200.

Boeing 720-023B

MIDDLE EAST AIRLINES

MEA (Middle East Airlines-Air Liban) was founded as a private company in May 1945. Middle East Airlines Company SA, as it was then known, began regular commercial services on regional routes from Beirut in January 1946 with three de Havilland Rapides. DC-3 aircraft were acquired and the network was expanded to include Ankara and Istanbul in 1947 and Kuwait, Bahrain and Dhahran in 1948. Following negotiations with Pan American in 1949, MEA became a joint-stock company, Pan American acquiring a 36 per cent shareholding in the Lebanese carrier in return for which MEA received three additional DC-3s. In January 1955 the association with Pan American was terminated and in March of that year BOAC acquired a 38.74 per cent holding as a result of which MEA was able to purchase a fleet of Viscount 754 aircraft, commencing services with the type on 2 October 1955. During the next six years MEA's network was

successfully expanded to include London, Rome, Geneva, Athens, Frankfurt and Vienna in Europe, as well as additional destinations in the Middle East. Four Comet 4C aircraft were ordered in 1960 and jet operations began with Comet 4s leased from BOAC before the introduction of MEA's own Comet 4Cs on 6 January 1961. The formal association with BOAC was terminated in August of that year and the British carrier

sold its MEA stock to Lebanese shareholders.

On 7 June 1963, MEA merged with Air Liban, another major Lebanese carrier, which operated to Paris and to destinations in North and West Africa. Air France acquired a 30 per cent holding in MEA through association with Air Liban. By 1965 the two companies were fully integrated and the new carrier had adopted its current title. The major part of MEA's fleet was destroyed by an armed attack on Beirut International Airport on 28 December 1968, forcing the carrier to lease various aircraft prior to acquiring a fleet of Convair 990A and subsequently Boeing 720-023B aircraft from American Airlines. MEA absorbed Lebanese International Airways (a scheduled carrier which also served Europe and the Middle East) on 1 July 1969.

Despite the ongoing unsettled situation in the Lebanon, MEA has managed to maintain an albeit reduced network of scheduled services in the Middle East and to destinations in Europe, North and West Africa. Approximately 5,500 personnel are employed.

Fleet Data
8 Boeing 707-320C; **6** 720B.

MIDWAY AIRLINES

Midway, formed in October 1976, initially provided high-frequency low-fare scheduled services from Chicago's then little used Midway Airport. Operations started in 1979 with an initial fleet of leased DC-9-10 aircraft.

The airline now operates a network of business-class 'Metrolink' services to Boston, New York (Newark), White Plains, Philadelphia, Washington DC (National), Cleveland, Detroit, Indianapolis, Kansas City, Minneapolis/St Paul, Dallas/Fort Worth, New Orleans, Fort Myer, Fort Lauderdale, Miami, Orlando, Tampa, West Palm Beach, St Croix and St Thomas. Midway Airlines employs approximately

Boeing 737-2T4 Advanced

2,000 personnel. On 24 July 1985, the airline acquired the assets of the defunct Air Florida and formed a subsidiary called Midway Express. The operations of the subsidiary have since been integrated with those of the parent company.

Fleet Data
7 Boeing 737-200; **11** DC-9-30; **9** DC-9-10.

Boeing 737-3T0. New York Air has been integrated with Continental Airlines.

NEW YORK AIR

New York Air, a wholly owned subsidiary of Texas Air Corporation, operated a network of scheduled passenger services covering 13 states in the eastern USA. Operations began on 19 December 1980 from the carrier's initial hub at New York – La Guardia. New York Air later developed Washington – Dulles International Airport as its primary hub with Newark as the secondary hub.

New York Air served Boston, Charleston, Cleveland, Detroit, Ft Lauderdale, Greensville/Spartanburg, Hartford, Jacksonville, Knoxville, Martha's Vineyard, Nantucket, Newark, New Orleans, New York (JFK, La Guardia, MacArthur, White Plains), Orlando, Philadelphia, Raleigh/Durham, Rochester, Tampa, Washington DC (National and Dulles), and West Palm Beach. The carrier provided hourly shuttle services from Newark to Boston and Washington-National. Some 3,500,000 passengers were carried in 1985 and New York Air employed 2,000 personnel, and has now been integrated with Continental Airlines.

Fleet Data
9 (+ additional) Boeing 737-300; **6** MD-80; **19** DC-9-30.

NIGERIA AIRWAYS

Nigeria Airways began operations on 1 October 1958, as WAAC (Nigeria) Limited, taking over the domestic services of West African Airways Corporation (WAAC) in Nigeria. WAAC had operated in the former British colonies in West Africa. Services to Dakar and London were undertaken for WAAC by BOAC. The Nigerian carrier became wholly government-owned in March 1961, and Fokker F27 Friendship 200 aircraft entered service in early 1963.

A former BOAC VC 10 Type 1101 was acquired in September 1969 and Boeing 707-3F9C aircraft entered service in May

1971. The carrier adopted its present title in the same year and introduced the F28 Fellowship 2000 on domestic routes in 1973. Wide-bodied operations were initiated following delivery of Nigeria's first DC-10-30 on 14 October 1976.

Nigeria currently operates an extensive domestic network covering all 19 states in the Nigerian Federation, and international services from Lagos, Kano and Port Harcourt to Amsterdam, Frankfurt, London, Rome, Jeddah, New York, and destinations in East and West Africa. Approximately 8,000 personnel are employed by the carrier.

Fleet Data

2 DC-10-30; **3** Boeing 707-320C; **4** Airbus A310-200; **8** 737-200.

McDonnell Douglas DC-10-30

NORTHWEST AIRLINES

Northwest is the second oldest airline in the USA with a continuous identification, and was formed on 1 August 1926 as Northwest Airways. The airline began air mail service on 1 October 1926, between Minneapolis/St. Paul and Chicago, and passenger services in July of the following year. On 16 April 1933 the airline adopted the name Northwest Orient and acquired Northern Air Transport. On 1 June 1945 Northwest became the fourth US transcontinental airline when service was extended eastward from Minneapolis/St Paul to Newark and New York City via Milwaukee and Detroit. Northwest expanded its routes through Canada, Alaska and the Aleutian Islands, and on 15 July 1947 a new Great Circle route through Anchorage to Tokyo, Seoul, Shanghai, and Manila was inaugurated with DC-4 aircraft. Jet operations began on 8 July 1960 with DC-8-32 aircraft on the Far East routes.

Northwest adopted its current title when it acquired Republic Airlines on 12 August 1986, making the airline one of the largest operators in the USA. Northwest now operates an extensive route network featuring hubs at Minneapolis/St Paul, Detroit and Memphis, with service to 110 cities in 40 states and DC, Four destinations in Canada, two destinations in Mexico, and the Cayman Islands, 11 points in the Far East and eight points in Europe. Service to Bangkok is due to start in April 1987. Northwest employs 31,000 personnel and, together with the former Republic Airlines, carried nearly 32,000,000 passengers in 1985. Northwest was the launch customer for the Boeing 747-400.

Boeing 757-251

Fleet Data

(10) Boeing 747-400; **20 (+3)** 747-200; **6** 747-200F; **12** 747-100; **20** DC-10-40; **23 (+10)** 757-200; **74** 727-200; **(10)** Airbus A320; **9** 727-100; **8** MD-80; **28** DC-9-50; **64** DC-9-30; **34** DC-9-10; **13** Convair 580; **(20)** A340.

OLYMPIC AIRWAYS

Olympic was formed in January 1957 under the ownership of the Greek shipping magnate Aristotle Onassis to succeed the state-owned carrier TAE (Technical and Air Enterprises Company), which was placed into liquidation. TAE in its original form was established in 1935 to provide technical services, pilot training and air taxi charter services. In an attempt to improve the economic performance of air transportation in Greece, TAE merged with two other Greek carriers, ELL.A.S. and A.M.E., at the behest of the Greek government, to form the new TAE. The economic difficulties persisted and in 1955 the carrier was taken over by the government. Subsequent agreement was reached with Onassis as a result of which the latter acquired the assets of the carrier together with a 50-year guarantee of sole designation as national airline and a monopoly of domestic routes. Olympic began operations on 6 April 1957, with a fleet of 14 DC-3s and one DC-4 aircraft. In order to match stiff competition from other foreign operators, DC-6B aircraft were leased from UAT (now UTA) in advance of the carrier's own DC-6B fleet acquisition. The type inaugurated Olympic's first international flights on 2 June 1957, with services from Athens to Rome, Paris and London. Services to Zürich and Frankfurt were added to the network in August of the following year.

Comet jet services began on Middle East routes to Tel Aviv, Nicosia, Beirut and Cairo in May 1960. In December 1974 Onassis relinquished his rights to operate Olympic and the carrier resumed operations in January 1975 under the control of the Greek government.

Olympic Airways currently serves an intensive 31-point domestic system and an international network covering some 39 cities in Europe, Africa, Asia and North America. Olympic employs approximately 10,000 personnel.

Fleet Data

4 Boeing 747-200; **8** Airbus A300B4; **2** 707-320B; **4** 707-320C; **6** 727-200; **11** 737-200.

Shorts 330-100 (of Olympic Aviation)

British Aerospace 146-200

PACIFIC SOUTHWEST AIRLINES

Pacific Southwest Airlines was formed as a division of Friedkin Aeronautics, Inc. of San Diego to operate scheduled services in California. PSA commenced operations with a leased DC-3 in May 1949 between San Diego and Oakland. Rapid expansion of its low-fare services led to the introduction of the Boeing 727 and 737 into PSA's fleet in June 1965 and September 1968 respectively.

PSA is now the largest operator on the west coast of the USA, and operates the world's largest fleet of BAe 146 aircraft. PSA was acquired by USAir in December 1986, and now operates as a subsidiary of the latter. Scheduled services are centred on PSA's hubs in Los Angeles and San Francisco and extend to 29 destinations in seven states and to Los Cabos in Mexico. Pacific Southwest Airmotive, Pacific Northwest Airlines, Pacific Southwest Exploration, Jetair Leasing and Airline Training school are subsidiaries. Approximately 5,000 personnel are employed by PSA.

Fleet Data

31 MD-80; **4** DC-9-30; **20 (+4)** BAe 146-200.

PACIFIC WESTERN AIRLINES

The Canadian operator, presently the largest regional airline in Canada, was originally formed on 1 July 1945 as Central British Columbia Airways to provide charter services. Following the acquisition of a number of other carriers, the operator adopted its present title on 15 May 1953. In 1954, Pacific Western acquired Associated Airways (a scheduled operator and prime contractor for servicing a sector of the Distant Early Warning Line), and Queen Charlotte Airlines was acquired in July 1955.

Pacific Western inaugurated scheduled jet services on its regional routes following the delivery of its first Boeing 737 in November 1968. A Boeing 707-138B and Lockheed L-100-382 Hercules aircraft were procured in 1967 to undertake passenger and freight charters. The provincial government of Alberta acquired a 97 per cent holding in the operator in August 1974. In 1970, Pacific Western took over BC Air Lines and in May 1977 the operator acquired a 72 per cent shareholding in Transair, based in Winnipeg. Pacific Western and Transair subsequently integrated their route networks and now operate as one entity.

Pacific Western undertakes an extensive network of scheduled services throughout

British Columbia, Alberta, Saskatchewan, Manitoba, the North West Territories, and the Yukon. Pacific Western acquired Canadian Pacific Air Lines in December 1986 and the combine will be known as Canadian Airlines International.

Fleet Data

24 Boeing 737-200.

Boeing 737-275 Advanced

PAKISTAN INTERNATIONAL AIRLINES

Pakistan International Airlines (PIA) was formally established as a scheduled carrier on 11 March 1955, with the takeover of Orient Airways. PIA had, however, initiated operations with Super Constellations on 7 June 1954, between Karachi and Dacca following its formation as a department of the Pakistan Ministry of Defence in 1951. Orient Airways became a registered company in 1947 and took over the routes of the pre-partition Indian operators in East and West Pakistan. On 1 February 1955, PIA inaugurated its first international service on the Karachi-Cairo-London route. The first of an eventual fleet of five Viscount 815 aircraft entered service in January 1959.

Jet services were started on 7 March 1960, to London, with a Boeing 707-121 leased from Pan American and operations were extended to New York on 5 May 1961. PIA then acquired its own Boeing 720-040B aircraft, and the first of these began operation in February 1962. Services to Canton and Shanghai began on 29 April 1964. PIA's operations underwent substantial change following the 1971 war which resulted in East Pakistan becoming the independent state of Bangladesh, and services to and within the latter were terminated. New York services were resumed in 1972 and on 20 January 1973, PIA became the first foreign carrier to operate to Beijing.

PIA currently serves a 29-point domestic network and operates scheduled passenger and cargo services to 39 international destinations in the Middle and Far East, North and East Africa, Europe and North America. The carrier employs approximately 20,000 personnel.

Fleet Data

8 Boeing 747-200; **8** Airbus A300B4; **7** 707-320B/C; **6** 737-300; **9** Fokker F27; **2** DHC-6 Twin Otter.

Boeing 737-340

Airbus A300B4-203 (top) and A310-222

PAN AM-PAN AMERICAN WORLD AIRWAYS

Pan Am was founded on 14 March 1927, starting air mail operations between Key West (Florida) and Havana on 28 October of that year with Fokker F.VII aircraft followed by scheduled passenger services on the route on 16 January 1928. Under the leadership of Juan Trippe, Pan Am was to develop into the world's most successful and important international carrier. Substantial private backing and government support aided the carrier to develop an extensive network throughout Central and South America and the Caribbean. During the 1930s and 1940s Pan Am acquired financial interests in many Latin American operators, and pioneered services across the Pacific and Atlantic.

Pan Am acquired American Overseas Airlines (AOA) from American Airlines on 25 September 1950. AOA operated to the Federal Republic of Germany, Scandinavia, Finland and Iceland as well as scheduled services from West Berlin to points in the Federal Republic of Germany. The carrier launched both the Boeing 707 and Douglas DC-8 in October 1955, and inaugurated jet services with the Boeing 707-121 on the New York – Paris route on 26 October 1958. Pan Am also placed the launch order for the Boeing 747 on 14 April 1966, starting operations with the type to London on 22 January 1970. Pan Am acquired National Airlines on 7 January 1980, to become at that time the second largest US carrier.

In late 1985 Pan Am completed the sale of its Pacific division to United Airlines and is now concentrating on the development of its transatlantic and South American routes. The carrier now serves 26 cities throughout the USA and 63 international destinations. No-reservations, guaranteed-seat air shuttle services are now operated between Boston, New York-LaGuardia and Washington, DC in competition with Eastern. Pan Am carried 13,200,000 passengers in 1985 and presently employs 20,648 personnel.

Fleet Data
7 Boeing 747-200; **36** 747-100; **12** Airbus A300B4; **7** A310-200; **(12)** A310-300; **(16)** A320-200; **38** 727-200; **12** 737-200.

PHILIPPINE AIRLINES

Philippine Airlines (PAL) was formed on 26 February 1941 by a group of industrialists, and inaugurated flights between Manila and Baguio on 15 March of that year with a Beech 18. PAL resumed post-war operations with a Manila-Legaspi service on 14 February 1946, using newly acquired DC-3 aircraft. The carrier was designated the Philippine flag carrier to the US on 14

November 1946, and services to San Francisco with DC-4 aircraft began on 3 December. On 3 May 1947, the carrier purchased its main competitor, Far Eastern Air Transport, Inc. (FEATI). DC-6 aircraft were acquired in May 1948, and in August of that year Commercial Air Lines, Inc., (CALI) sold out to PAL making the latter the nation's only scheduled domestic airline at that time.

Jet operations were inaugurated on the Hong Kong route with Boeing 707 aircraft chartered from Pan American on 11 December 1961. BAC One-Eleven 402 aircraft entered service on PAL's domestic and regional routes in May 1966. Wide-bodied services were introduced on the Pacific route following delivery of PAL's first DC-10-30 in July 1974, and the carrier

Boeing 747-2F6B; the new livery reflects the Filipino national flag.

now also operates a fleet of Boeing 747-2F6B and Airbus A300B4-103 aircraft.

PAL currently operates an extensive 41-point domestic network and international services to 21 destinations in the Far East, Australasia, the Pacific, Europe and North America. PAL employs approximately 9,600 personnel and the government maintains a 99.7 per cent holding in the carrier.

Fleet Data
4 Boeing 747-200; **2** DC-10-30; **5** Airbus A300B4; **11** One-Eleven 500; **12** BAe (HS) 748; **4** Shorts 360.

PIEDMONT AIRLINES

Piedmont, headquartered in Winston-Salem (North Carolina), was formed on 1 January 1948, as a division of Piedmont Aviation, a general aviation sales and service operator established on 2 July 1940. Piedmont began local services on 20 February 1948, linking Wilmington (North Carolina) and Cincinnati (Ohio). Piedmont's subsequent development centered very much on these states and Kentucky, Tennessee, South Carolina, Virginia and West Virginia.

Turboprop services were initiated in November 1958 with Fairchild F-27 aircraft followed by FH-227Bs in 1966. Jet operations started with leased Boeing 727 equipment in March 1967 followed by the first of many Boeing 737 aircraft in May 1968. In January 1986 the carrier acquired Empire Airlines, a Utica-based regional carrier, as a result of which Piedmont has now become the world's largest operator of the Fokker F28. Piedmont currently serves over 100 cities in 24 states and the District of Columbia, utilising Charlotte, Dayton and Baltimore/Washington International Airport as its major hubs. Approximately 12,000 personnel work for the carrier. Henson Airlines, a regional airline, is a subsidiary of Piedmont. Piedmont itself will be acquired by USAir during 1987.

Fleet Data
34 Boeing 727-200; **19 (+17)** 737-300; **63** 737-200; **45** Fokker F28-1000/4000.

Boeing 737-301

PLUNA (PRIMERAS LINEAS URUGUAYAS DE NAVEGACION AEREA)

PLUNA, the national carrier of Uruguay, was founded in September 1935 by the Marquez Vaeza brothers and domestic operations were initiated on 15 November 1936. PLUNA ceased operations on 15 March

1943 following withdrawal of a government subsidy. The government later acquired an 83.3 per cent holding in the carrier which resumed operations on 15 September 1945 and inaugurated its first international service on 4 May 1948, to Porto Alegre in Brazil. PLUNA became totally state-owned on 12 November 1951.

D.H. Heron aircraft were ordered to supplement the fleet of DC-3s and in May 1958 the carrier took delivery of its first Viscount 769. PLUNA further expanded its network in 1967 with the takeover of routes from the defunct CAUSA-Compania Aeronautica Uruguaya SA. Jet services

Boeing 737-2A3

commenced following delivery in December 1969 of a Boeing 737-2A3. Since 1973 the transport division of the Uruguayan Air Force, TAMU, Transporte Aereo Militar Uruguayo, has been responsible for providing domestic services while PLUNA has operated the international network which currently serves Porto Alegre, San Pablo, Rio de Janeiro, Asuncion, Buenos Aires, Punta del Este and Madrid. Approximately 820 personnel are employed by the carrier.

Fleet Data
1 Boeing 707-320B; **3** 737-200.

PRESIDENTIAL

Presidential Airways was incorporated in March 1985 to provide full service, low-fare scheduled passenger services from Washington-Dulles International Airport, the carrier's hub and headquarters.

Presidential began operations on 10 October 1985 from its newly constructed midfield terminal at Washington-Dulles and flies from Dulles to Boston (Massachusetts), Hartford (Connecticut), Indianapolis (Indiana), Miami/Fort Lauderdale, West Palm Beach, Orlando, Sarasota, Daytona Beach and Melbourne (Florida), Cleveland (Ohio), Savannah and Atlanta (Georgia), Hilton Head (South Carolina), Portland (Maine), Detroit (Michigan), and Montreal (Canada).

The carrier acquired Key Airlines, a Las Vegas-based charter company, during 1985, and also Colgan Airways, a commuter operator headquartered in Manassas (Virginia). The latter was purchased through Washington Air Corp., a wholly-owned subsidiary of Presidential. Under an agreement with Continental, Presidential now operates its services as 'Continental Express'.

Fleet Data
8 Boeing 737-200; **6 (+9)** BAe 146-200.

British Aerospace 146-200 in the 'Continental Express' livery that Presidential introduced in 1987.

QANTAS AIRWAYS

Qantas was registered by two ex-flying corps Lieutenants, W. Hudson Fysh and P. J. McGinness, as The Queensland and Northern Territory Aerial Services Limited (from which 'Qantas' was derived) on 16 November 1920, with a paid-up capital of £6,037. For the first two years an Avro 504K and a B.E.2E were used to provide air taxi services and pleasure flights. The first scheduled service was inaugurated on 1 November 1922, from Charleville to Cloncurry in Queensland, via Longreach, using an Armstrong Whitworth F.K.8. A

Boeing 767-238ER

1,475-mile (2,375-km) route network in Queensland was established over the subsequent 12 years, with flying doctor services forming part of the operations. On 18 January 1934, Qantas and Imperial Airways (forerunner of BOAC) formed Qantas Empire Airways Limited to operate the Brisbane-Singapore portion of the England-Australia route. An order was placed for Constellations in October 1946, and on 3 July 1947, the Australian government purchased the remaining local shareholding in the carrier (having earlier purchased BOAC's holding) and became the sole owner of the airline, designating it Qantas Empire Airways as the operator of Australia's international air services. The carrier began its own Sydney-London Constellation services on 1 December 1947, and subsequent overseas operations were rapidly developed. During this time Qantas participated as a shareholder in Tasman Empire Airways Limited (TEAL) of New Zealand to develop air links between the two countries. The San Francisco route (opened on 15 May 1947) was extended in 1958 to New York and London, making Qantas the first operator to provide regular round the world service by linking London with the carrier's South-East Asia route to Sydney.

Jet operations were inaugurated on the North American services on 29 July 1959, following delivery of Boeing 707-138 aircraft. Lockheed Electras were also acquired in the same year and were used to start the carrier's own services to New Zealand in 1961, and on 1 August 1967, the name of the carrier was changed to Qantas Airways Limited.

Qantas currently operates a network of passenger and cargo services to Christchurch, Wellington, Auckland, Noumea, Fiji, Port Moresby, Honolulu, Los Angeles, San Francisco, Vancouver, Tokyo, Hong Kong, Manila, Bali, Jakarta, Singapore, Bangkok, Bombay, Bahrain, Athens, Belgrade, Rome, Frankfurt, Amsterdam, London, Manchester, and Harare from Perth, Darwin, Melbourne, Sydney, Brisbane, Adelaide, Port Hedland, Cairns, Townsville, Norfolk Island and Hobart. Qantas presently employs an average of 12,000 personnel.

Fleet Data
5 Boeing 747-300; **16** 747-200; **2** 747SP; **(4)** 747-400; **6** 767-200ER.

ROYAL AIR MAROC

Royal Air Maroc (Compagnie Nationale de Transports Aériens) is the national carrier of the Kingdom of Morocco, and was formed on 28 June 1953, by the merger of Air Atlas and Air Maroc, brought about largely through the efforts of the Moroccan government. Air Atlas (Compagnie Cherifienne d'Aviation) was formed in 1946 to provide local services plus international links with Algiers and key cities in southern France. Air Maroc (Société Avia Maroc Ligne Aérienne) was established in 1947 as a charter airline. Following the merger, Royal Air Maroc undertook development of both domestic and international services. Routes to Dakar, Gibraltar, Madrid and Frankfurt

Boeing 727-2B6

were opened, and Meknes, Oujda, Tetuan, Fez and Mellila-Nador were added to the domestic network.

The carrier introduced jet operations in 1960 with Caravelle III aircraft entering service on the Casablanca-Paris route on 20 May. Wide-bodied services were initiated following delivery of a Boeing 747-2B6B aircraft on 29 September 1978.

Royal Air Maroc currently operates scheduled services from Casablanca and Tangier to domestic points and to destinations in North and West Africa, the Middle East, Europe, North and South America. Charter and inclusive-tour operations are also undertaken. The Moroccan government has a 92.7 per cent holding in the carrier. Royal Air Maroc employs approximately 4,500 personnel. Royal Air Inter was formed as an associate of the carrier in 1970 to operate domestic services from Casablanca.

Fleet Data
1 Boeing 747-200; **1** 747SP; **2** 707-320C; **2** 757-200; **8** 727-200; **6** 737-200.

Airbus A310-222

SABENA-BELGIAN WORLD AIRLINES

Sabena (Société Anonyme Belge d'Exploitation de la Navigation Aerienne) was established on 23 May 1923. Principal shareholders were the Syndicat National pour l'Etude des Transports Aériens (SNETA), the Belgian government and the Belgian Congo. SNETA was Sabena's predecessor, and had been formed to develop the necessary infrastructure for the establishment of air services within Europe and to the Belgian Congo (now Zaire). Sabena's initial route development focused on air links between the Low Countries and Switzerland, and on 1 April 1924, a cargo service was inaugurated on the Rotterdam-Brussels-Strasbourg route, extended to Basle on 10 June. With the arrival of Handley Page W.8 aircraft, Sabena began passenger services on the route on 14 July 1924. In addition to building up

European operations, Sabena proceeded to develop what became an extensive network of services in the Belgian Congo, where the SNETA-formed company LARA had already pioneered air services. Delivery of DC-4 aircraft, ordered during World War II while Sabena was temporarily headquartered in Leopoldville, facilitated the inauguration of services between Brussels and New York on 4 June 1947.

In 1949 Sabena was granted a monopoly of scheduled services in the Congo, and the carrier acquired two small local independent operators, Aeromas and the original Air Congo. Following independence for the Congo, Sabena assisted in the formation in June 1961 of the new Air Congo (now Air Zaire). Sabena introduced jet operations with the Boeing 707 starting Brussels-New York services in January 1960.

Sabena currently operates an extensive scheduled network of services within Europe and to Africa, the Middle East, Far East and North America. Sabena currently employs nearly 9,000 personnel.

Fleet Data
1 Boeing 747-300; **2** 747-100; **5** DC-10-30; **3** Airbus A310-200/300; **15** 737-200.

Airbus A300-620

SAUDIA

Saudia (Saudi Arabian Airlines) was founded in 1945 by the Saudi government as the national carrier, and domestic operations started with three DC-3 aircraft on 14 March 1947. A fleet of Bristol Freighter 21 and DC-4 aircraft was introduced into service from 1949, followed by 10 Convair 340s from 1954. Three DC-6 aircraft were added in 1960 to enhance the route system within the Arab world and improve travel facilities for pilgrims. The acquisition of two Boeing 720-068B aircraft permitted jet services to be inaugurated in April 1962, progressively to cover Amman, Beirut, Cairo, Instanbul, Bombay and Karachi. In 1963 King Faisal decreed the corporate status of Saudi. 1967 marked the opening of Saudia's inaugural route to Europe, serving Geneva, Frankfurt and London, and later that year the carrier initiated services to Tripoli, Tunis and Casablanca. Acquisition of Boeing 707-368Cs enabled non-stop Jeddah-London operations to begin in 1968. Wide-bodied services were inaugurated with Lockheed TriStar 100 aircraft in 1975. A comprehensive flight training centre was opened in Jeddah in April 1979.

Saudia, the largest national airline in the Middle East, now operates a 23-point domestic network and scheduled international passenger and cargo services to a further 44 destinations in Europe, Asia, Africa, the Middle East and North America. Saudia currently employs approximately 26,000 personnel.

Fleet Data
10 Boeing 747-300; **1** 747-200; **8** 747-100; **2** 747SP; **17** TriStar 200; **11** Airbus A300-600; **5** 707-320C; **19** 737-200; **2** Fokker F28-3000.

SCANDINAVIAN AIRLINES SYSTEM

SAS is the national carrier of Denmark, Norway and Sweden, and was originally formed on 1 August 1946 as a consortium of Det Danske Luftfartselskab (DDL), Det Norske Luftfartselskap (DNL) and AB Aerotransport (ABA), the leading pre-war airlines of those three nations respectively, for intercontinental operations. Scheduled services were inaugurated on the Stockholm-Copenhagen-New York route on 17 September 1946, with DC-4 aircraft. On 18 April 1948, the three partner airlines formed the SAS European division and in July of that year Svensk Interkontinental Lufftrafik (SILA), another Swedish airline, merged with ABA. Agreement was reached on 8 February 1951, for unification of the whole SAS consortium under a centralized management, and the three participating carriers became non-operating holding companies. The consortium is owned 28.5 per cent by DDL, 28.5 per cent by DNL and 43 per cent by ABA, each of the parent airlines being a private company owned 50-50 by private shareholders and the respective government of the three countries involved.

SAS initiated service to Buenos Aires on 29 December 1946, and opened a route to Bangkok in October 1949. The carrier inaugurated the world's first scheduled polar service between Copenhagen and Los Angeles on 15 November 1954, using DC-6B aircraft. Jet operations started with a Copenhagen-Beirut Caravelle service on 26 April 1959, making SAS the first airline to put the type into scheduled operation. DC-8-32 aircraft entered service on the New York route on 1 May 1960. The carrier introduced the DC-9-21 and DC-9-41 aircraft into domestic and European service in 1968 (both models having been developed to the carrier's specifications).

SAS currently operates to over 100 destinations in Europe, Africa, the Middle and Far East, and North, Central and South America, and employs approximately 19,000 personnel.

Fleet Data
2 Boeing 747-200; **(12)** MD-11; **9** DC-10-30; **2** DC-8-63; **3** DC-8-62; **16 (+2)** MD-80; **49** DC-9-41; **2** DC-9-30; **9** DC-9-21; **8** Fokker F27.
(Note: Swedair, Busy Bee, and Fred Olsen operate certain flights for SAS)

McDonnell Douglas DC-10-30

SINGAPORE AIRLINES

Singapore Airlines (SIA) was formed on 24 January 1972, as the state-owned national carrier to succeed the jointly operated Malaysia-Singapore Airlines (MSA) following the decision in January of the preceding year by the Malaysian and Singapore governments to set up separate national airlines. SIA began operations on 1 October 1972, serving the total MSA international network with former MSA Boeing 737 and 707 aircraft. On 2 April 1973, SAI began daily services to London, and in September of that year the carrier's first two 747B aircraft were delivered. Boeing 727-212 aircraft entered SIA service on regional routes in September 1977.

Concorde services between Singapore and London via Bahrain in conjunction with British Airways were inaugurated on 10 December 1977, but suspended shortly afterwards due to the Malaysian government decision to ban supersonic operations over Malaysia. Although the service was allowed to resume in January 1979, it was finally terminated in November 1980.

Singapore Airline's route network now covers services from Singapore to Auckland, Adelaide, Brisbane, Melbourne, Perth, Sydney, Honolulu, Los Angeles, San Francisco, Osaka, Tokyo, Seoul, Taipei, Hong Kong, Bandar Seri Begawan, Manila, Jakarta, Medan, Kuala Lumpur, Kuantan, Kaohsiung, Penang, Bangkok, Colombo, Karachi, Bombay, Madras, Mauritius, Dhahran, Dubai, Abu Dhabi, Bahrain, Athens, Malta, Vienna, Amsterdam, Brussels, Copenhagen, Frankfurt, London, Paris, Rome and Zürich. Approximately 10,000 personnel are employed by SIA.

Fleet Data
(14) Boeing 747-400; 14 747-300; 9 747-200; 6 Airbus A310-200; 4 757-200.

Boeing 757-212

SOUTH AFRICAN AIRWAYS

SAA is the national airline for the Republic of South Africa and was formed on 1 February 1934, when the government (through the South African Railways Administration) took control of Union Airways which had been operating since 1929 as a private company providing air mail services from Port Elizabeth to Johannesburg, Cape Town and Durban. On 1 February 1935 SAA acquired South West African Airways which had been operating a Windhoek-Kimberley air mail service since 1932. By the outbreak of World War II SAA had established a regional network of services which encompassed all adjacent territories. Operation between Johannesburg and London, known as the 'Springbok' service, began in cooperation with BOAC on 10 November 1945. By the end of 1947 a network of domestic, regional and international services was being operated with a fleet of 41 aircraft comprising DC-3, DC-4, Viking, Lodestar and Dove aircraft.

Early in the 1950s SAA took delivery of Constellation aircraft for use on the Springbok service, and in 1953 the carrier began jet operations with Comet I aircraft

leased from BOAC. In 1956 SAA became the first airline outside the United States to operate the DC-7B, which entered service for SAA on the London route. Viscount 813 aircraft entered major domestic and regional service with the carrier in November 1958 and SAA recommenced jet operations on 1 October 1960, following delivery of Boeing 707-344 aircraft.

In addition to an 11-point domestic route system and regional operations to neighbouring African countries, SAA operates to Rio de Janeiro, New York, Perth, Sydney, Hong Kong, Ilha do Sal, Lisbon, Taipei, Madrid, Rome, Athens, Vienna, Zürich, Frankfurt, Paris, Brussels, Amsterdam, London, and Tel Aviv. Approximately 11,700 personnel are employed by SAA.

Fleet Data
2 Boeing 747-300; 7 747-200; 4 747SP; 7 Airbus A300B2/B4/C4; 15 737-200.

Boeing 747-244B

SOUTHWEST AIRLINES

Southwest was formed on 15 March 1967 as Air Southwest to provide scheduled intra-state low-fare passenger services in Texas. The current name was adopted on 29 March 1971 and services were inaugurated on 18 June of that year between Houston, Dallas and San Antonio with three Boeing 737-2H4 aircraft.

Southwest was certificated as an interstate carrier in December 1978 and now provides high-frequency, low-fare services linking 11 points in Texas with Albuquerque, Chicago, Kansas City, Las Vegas, Little Rock, Los Angeles, New Orleans, Oklahoma City, Ontario, Phoenix, St Louis, San Diego, San Francisco and Tulsa.

Muse Air was taken over on 25 June 1985 and is operated as a subsidiary under the name TranStar Airlines adopted on 17 February 1986. TranStar utilises a fleet of DC-9-50 and MD-80 aircraft. Southwest carried 11,595,602 passengers in 1985 and employs 4,567 personnel.

Fleet Data
17 (+15) Boeing 737-300; 46 737-200.

Boeing 737-3H4

McDonnell Douglas DC-10-30

SWISSAIR

Swissair was founded on 26 March 1931, through the merger of Ad Astra Aero and Balair. In April 1932 Europe's first regular services with the Lockheed Orion single engine monoplane were initiated on the Zürich-Munich-Vienna route, establishing new standards in fast air transportation. Swissair was the first European airline to employ air stewardesses, following the introduction of the 16-seat Curtiss Condor. The airline was designated as the national carrier in February 1947. Swissair's first transatlantic service, from Geneva to New York, was operated by a DC-4 on 2 May of that year, but a regular service did not begin until April 1949. Swissair began Convair 240 services in 1949, and acquired DC-6B aircraft from 1951 for long haul operations. Jet operations began on 30 May 1960, with DC-8 services to New York. Caravelles were introduced on European routes in the same year and Convair 990s entered service in 1962 to the Far East and South America. Wide-bodied services to New York began in April 1971 following delivery of two 747B aircraft. Swissair was the launch customer for the DC-9-51 and also the DC-9-81 (MD-81), the latter entering service on European routes on 5 October 1980.

Swissair currently operates a world-wide network to points in Europe, North and South America, Africa, the Middle and Far East. From 64 employees in 1931 Swissair's work force has grown to over 16,500. Approximately 78 per cent of Swissair's share capital is held by private interests, the balance being held by public institutions.

Fleet Data
4 (+1) Boeing 747-300; 11 DC-10-30/30ER; 9 Airbus A310-200/300; 18 (+3) MD-80; (6) MD-11; 2 DC-9-51; 5 DC-9-32; (8) Fokker 100.

TAROM

Tarom (Transporturile Aeriene Române) was originally formed in 1946 as Transporturi Aeriene Romana Sovietica (TARS) by the governments of Romania and the Soviet Union. TARS succeeded the pre-war state airline LARES and provided domestic and international services radiating from Bucharest. Routes to Prague, Budapest and Warsaw were opened with Li-2 aircraft, and in 1954 TARS adopted its present title when Romania took over complete control of the carrier. Ilyushin Il-14 aircraft were acquired, enabling Tarom to expand its international network, including new services to Moscow, Vienna, Zürich, Paris, Brussels and Copenhagen. Ilyushin Il-18 turboprops entered service in 1962 and further expansion took place with services to Belgrade, Sofia, Athens and Frankfurt.

Jet operations on European routes began after delivery of the first of an initial fleet of six One-Eleven 424 aircraft on 14 June 1968. Ilyushin Il-62s were acquired in 1973, primarily for holiday charter traffic, and the first of three Boeing 707-3K1C aircraft entered service in 1974. In 1975 Tarom formed Liniile Aeriene Romane (LAR), a charter subsidiary which began operating in December of that year with former Tarom

One-Eleven 424s. Tarom has been acquiring a number of One-eleven 560 aircraft built under licence in Romania.

In addition to its domestic network, Tarom currently operates scheduled international passenger and cargo services within Europe and to Tripoli, Algiers, Casablanca, Amman, Baghdad, Beirut, Cairo, Damascus, Istanbul, Kuwait, Larnaca, Tehran, Tel Aviv, Karachi, Bangkok, Singapore, Beijing and New York.

Fleet Data
4 Boeing 707-320C; 5 Ilyushin Il-62/62M; 11 Tupolev Tu-154B; 8 Il-18; 13 One-Eleven 500; 5 One-Eleven 400/475; 9 Antonov An-26; 32 An-24.

Tupolev Tu-154B-2

THAI AIRWAYS INTERNATIONAL

Thai Airways International Limited (Thai International) is the designated national flag carrier of Thailand for scheduled international services, and was formed in August 1959 by Scandinavian Airlines System (SAS) with a 30 per cent shareholding, and Thai Airways Company Limited (the government-owned domestic airline of Thailand) with a 70 per cent shareholding. Operations began in May 1960 on regional services within Asia, utilizing technical and managerial assistance provided by SAS, and three DC-6B aircraft leased from the airline. Rapid development of international routes led to the opening of 'Royal Orchid' services to Kuala Lumpur, Singapore, Jakarta, Rangoon, Calcutta, Saigon (now Ho Chi Minh City), Hong Kong, Taipei and Tokyo.

Jet services were inaugurated in 1962 with two Convair 990A aircraft on lease from SAS. Wide-bodied operations with DC-10-30 aircraft leased from SAS and UTA were initiated prior to delivery of Thai's own DC-10-30s from March 1977. On 1 April of that year, SAS's residual shareholding in the carrier was acquired by Thai Airways Company Limited.

Thai International's current route network of scheduled passenger and cargo services covers 41 destinations throughout

Airbus A300B4

South-East Asia, Australia, the Middle East, Europe, and the USA. Thai International currently employs approximately 10,500 personnel.

Fleet Data

(2) Boeing 747-300; 6 747-200; 2 DC-10-30; (2) DC-10-30ER; 4 (+4) Airbus A300-600; 12 A300B4.

TOA DOMESTIC AIRLINES (TDA)

TDA was formed in May 1971 through the merger of Japan Domestic Airlines and Toa Airways. Japan Domestic had been formed in April 1964 as a result of the merger of three domestic carriers: Tokyo-based Fuji Airlines, Osaka-based Nitto Aviation, and North Japan Airlines of Sapporo. Toa Airways had been founded on 26 November 1953, and operated services to south-west Japan.

TDA started operations on 15 May 1971, and is Japan's third major carrier, providing scheduled services on over 60 domestic and regional routes. Stockholders include Toa Airways, Japan Domestic, Japan Air Lines (9.1 per cent), Tokyu Corp., (26.2 per cent), FujiSash Industries (10.5 per cent), and Kinki Nippon Railway (8.7 per cent). TDA has a 60 per cent holding in Japan Air Commuter and presently employs approximately 3,600 personnel.

Fleet Data

9 Airbus A300B2K/C4; 13 (+2) MD-80; (4) MD-87; 14 DC-9-41; 34 NAMC YS-11/11A.

Airbus A300B2K-3C

TRANS WORLD AIRLINES

TWA can trace its history back to the formation of Western Air Express (WAE) which initiated mail services between Los Angeles and Salt Lake City in April 1926. In 1929 the carrier absorbed Standard Air Lines and in July 1930 WAE merged with Transcontinental Air Transport, Inc. (TAT) to form Transcontinental and Western Air (TWA). Prior to the merger, TAT had acquired Maddux Airlines which gave TAT access to San Francisco and San Diego. In 1934 the former WAE was bought out of TWA and subsequently became the current Western Airlines.

Constellation services were inaugurated in February 1946 between New York and Paris via Gander and Shannon, representing TWA's first international route and also the first commercial link between the USA and Paris. In 1950 the corporate name was changed to Trans World Airlines, reflecting TWA's international route expansion. On 20 March 1959, TWA operated its first jet service with the introduction of Boeing 707 aircraft. Wide-bodied services with Boeing

Lockheed L-1011-100 TriStar

747-131 aircraft were initiated in 1979, and the Lockheed TriStar, for which TWA was one of three launch customers, entered service in June 1972.

TWA currently operates a 64-point domestic network and international services to Europe and the Middle East. Approximately 27,000 personnel work for TWA. Ozark Airlines was acquired by the carrier during 1986 and is operated as a subsidiary. TWA was acquired by New York investor Carl Icahn on 26 September 1985.

Fleet Data

20 Boeing 747-100/200; 35 Lockheed TriStar 1/50/100; 10 767-200; 56 727-200; 26 727-100; 19 MD-80.

TUNIS AIR

Tunis Air (Société Tunisienne de l'Air) was founded in 1948 as a co-operative venture between the Tunisian government, Air France and various private investors who were later bought out. Operations started in 1949 with DC-3 aircraft initially serving the traditional markets between Tunisia, France and Algeria. The declaration of independence resulted in the Tunisian government taking a 51 per cent (and later, 85 per cent) controlling interest in the carrier in 1957, with Air France holding the balance. The fleet was then composed of three DC-3s and two DC-4 aircraft and the route network covered international services to Paris, Marseille, Lyon, Rome, Bonn and Algiers. The introduction of the airline's first Caravelle III in September 1961 represented a major advance for Tunis Air, and as additional Caravelles were added to the fleet, the route system was progressively expanded to

Boeing 737-2H3 Advanced

include services to Amsterdam, Brussels and Frankfurt in 1966, Zürich in 1967, and Casablanca in 1968. The carrier's first Boeing 727-2H3 entered service in 1972, during which year Luxembourg and Jeddah were added to the system. London services were inaugurated in the following year.

Tunis Air currently operates scheduled passenger and cargo services from Tunis, Djerba, Monastir, Tozeur and Sfax to 24 countries within Africa, Europe and the Middle East. The national carrier currently employs approximately 4,700 personnel.

Fleet Data

1 Airbus A300B4; 8 Boeing 727-200; 4 737-200.

TÜRK HAVA YOLLARI

THY-Turkish Airlines, Turkey's national airline, was founded on 20 May 1933, as Devlet Hava Yollari (State Airlines), and was part of the Ministry of National Defence. In 1935 the airline was transferred to the Ministry of Public Works. Operations started

Airbus A310-203

between Ankara and Istanbul with aircraft which included the de Havilland D.H. 86B Express and Rapide. On 3 June 1938, the airline became known as the General Directorate of State Airways, and the Ministry of Transportation assumed control. The airline operated only domestic services until 1947, when a route to Athens was opened. DC-3 aircraft were introduced, and the airline took delivery of the first of seven de Havilland Herons in February 1955. In May of that year the Turkish government established a corporation to handle air transportation and on 1 March 1956, the new corporation began operations under the present title of Turk Hava Yollari AO. The Turkish government had a 51 per cent holding in THY, and BOAC held 6.5 per cent of the share capital, through which THY was able to order a fleet of five Viscount 794 aircraft.

Jet services were introduced in August 1967 with a DC-9-15 leased from Douglas, and Boeing 707-321 aircraft were acquired from Pan Am in 1971. Wide-bodied services began in December 1972 with DC-10-10 aircraft.

THY currently operates from Ankara, Istanbul, Antalya, Izmir and Adana to 11 other domestic points, and international services to Austria, Belgium, Cyprus, Denmark, Egypt, France, Germany, Greece, Italy, Ireland, Iraq, Libya, the Netherlands, Pakistan, Saudi Arabia, Switzerland, the United Kingdom and the United Arab Emirates. THY is 99.9 per cent owned by the Turkish Government and employs approximately 6,200 personnel. Kibris Turk Hava Yollari (Cyprus Turkish Airlines) is a subsidiary, formed on 4 December, 1974, to provide scheduled services from Ercan, Cyprus, to Adana, Ankara, Istanbul and Izmir.

Fleet Data

2 DC-10-10; 7 Airbus A310-200; 2 Boeing 707-321C; 9 727-200; 9 DC-9-30; 3 DHC-7.

UNION DE TRANSPORTS AÉRIENS

UTA, the largest independent airline in France, was created on 1 October 1963, through the merger of Union Aéromaritime de Transport (UAT) and Compagnie de Transports Aériens Intercontinentaux (TAI). UAT had been formed in 1949 with the backing of Compagnie Maritimes des Chargeurs Reunis, a shipping company, to succeed Aeromaritime which had been founded by the same company in 1935 to operate services in French West Africa. UAT began DC-4 services in 1950 between Paris and Dakar, Pointe Noire and Saigon. Jet operations to Dakar with Comet IA aircraft were inaugurated in 1953, and were

Boeing 747-2B3B

subsequently extended to Brazzaville and Johannesburg. In 1955 UAT took over Société Aigle Azur which operated Boeing Stratoliners from Paris to Brazzaville, Madagascar, Saigon and Hanoi. Jet operations recommenced in September 1960 with the acquisition of DC-8-32 aircraft and UAT, in association with Air France, subsequently helped to form Air Afrique which took over their extensive route network in French Africa.

TAI had been formed on 1 June 1946, as a successor to Regie Air Afrique (founded in 1934), and began services to North Africa a month later with Junkers Ju 52/3m aircraft. In 1947 routes from Paris to Tananarive and Saigon were opened using DC-3 aircraft. TAI acquired DC-6Bs in 1953 and its first DC-7C at the end of 1957. On 1 January 1956, as a result of a reallocation of routes, TAI was able to extend its Saigon services to Darwin and Noumea, followed by further extension to Auckland on 4 February 1957. The Paris-Tahiti-Honolulu-Los Angeles route was opened in 1960 using DC-7Cs: this represented the world's longest route, linking with Air France in Los Angeles for the continuation through Montreal to Paris. TAI introduced DC-8 services in 1960, starting non-stop service between Los Angeles and Papeete.

UTA operates an extensive passenger and freight network linking Paris, Nice, Marseille, Lyon and Bordeaux with 24 destinations in Europe, Africa, South East Asia, the Middle East, Australasia, the Pacific and North America. Chargeurs Réunis has a 62.5 per cent holding in the airline which currently employs nearly 6,600 personnel.

Fleet Data

(2) Boeing 747-400; 2 747-300; 3 747-200; 6 DC-10-30.

UNITED AIRLINES

United traces its origin to Varney Air Lines which began air mail services between Paso, Washington and Elko, Nevada on 6 April 1926. Varney Air Lines was later merged with Pacific Air Transport and National Air Transport, both of whom were air mail carriers, into Boeing Air Transport which was part of a combine that included the Boeing Airplane Company and Pratt & Whitney, the engine manufacturer. United was organized on 1 July 1931, as the management company for the airline division. Three years later the combine broke up and the corporate divisions became separate entities. By May 1947 the route network had been expanded to include Boston, Denver, Washington DC and Hawaii. Jet operations with DC-8 aircraft were inaugurated on 18 September 1959.

United's size increased significantly on 1 June 1961, when the carrier took over Capital Airlines, founded in November 1936 as Pennsylvania Central Airlines. As a result of the merger United's route system was increased by 7,200 miles (11,600 km) and the carrier became the world's largest privately-owned airline in terms of annual passengers carried and passenger miles flown. In 1985, United concluded the purchase of Pan Am's Pacific division.

United now operates an extensive scheduled passenger and cargo route network linking a total of over 159

Boeing 767-222

destinations throughout the USA, and in Canada, the Bahamas, Japan, Hong Kong and Mexico. United currently employs nearly 50,000 personnel, and operates an all-jet fleet of over 360 aircraft.

Fleet Data

(6) Boeing 747-200; 13 747-100; 11 747SP; 7 DC-10-30; 44 DC-10-10; 6 L-1011 TriStar 500; 29 DC-8-71; 19 767-200; 104 727-200; 10 (+100) 737-300; 50 727-100; 74 737-200.

Boeing 737-2B7 Advanced; USAir operates 23 737-200s

USAIR

USAir was formed on 5 March 1937, under the name of All-American Aviation. The carrier was the first to be certificated by the former Civil Aeronautics Board following the passage of the Civil Aeronautics Acts in 1938 and began a specialized 'pick-up' air mail service to isolated communities without adequate airport facilities. With the introduction of passenger operations, the carrier changed its name to All-American Airways. The title was changed again in 1953 to Allegheny Airlines Inc. By 1959 Allegheny's system extended from Boston in the east to Cleveland and Detroit in the west. In 1963 Allegheny relocated its principal operations and maintenance base from Washington DC to Pittsburgh.

In July 1968 Allegheny merged with Indianapolis-based Lake Central Airlines. Further rapid growth was enhanced by a merger with Mohawk Airlines of Utica in April 1972. Mohawk operated in the eastern seaboard states, and also to eastern Canada. By mid-1978 the carrier had become an all-jet operator and adopted its current title in 1979.

USAir currently operates a scheduled route network covering over 100 cities in 30 states, DC and two Canadian provinces. Approximately 15,000 personnel are employed and some 21,725,000 passengers were carried in 1986. USAir has retained its responsibility to serve the smaller and intermediate-sized destinations through the Allegheny Commuter program, established in 1967. Two of the participants, Suburban Airlines and Pennsylvania Airlines, are wholly owned subsidiaries of USAir. The carrier reached agreement to acquire Pacific Southwest Airlines in December 1986, and the latter is now operated as a subsidiary.

Fleet Data

10 Boeing 727-200; 21 (+27) 737-300; 23 737-200; 70 DC-9-30; (20) Fokker 100; 20 BAe (BAC) One-Eleven 200.

VARIG

Varig (Viाção Aérea Rio Grandense), the national carrier of Brazil, was founded on 7 May 1927, with technical assistance provided by the German-backed Kondor Syndikat and proceeded to develop domestic services within the Rio Grande do Sul. Service to Montevideo began in August 1942, and Lockheed 10A Electras were acquired in 1943 inaugurating service to Rio de Janeiro via Florlanopolis, Curitiba and Sao Paulo. The acquisition of Aéro Geral in late 1951 gave Varig access to routes north of Rio de Janeiro for the first time. Buenos Aires was added to the network in the following year, and on 2 August 1955, Varig's first Super Constellation inaugurated services to New York.

Jet services were inaugurated with Caravelle IIIs on the New York route from 19 December 1959. In August 1961 Varig obtained a controlling interest in the REAL Aerovias airline consortium. REAL had been founded in February 1946 and had become the largest operator in South America through a series of mergers and takeovers, operating a very extensive domestic network as well as international services to a number of destinations REAL's route system and aircraft fleet were progressively integrated with those of Varig, and in 1965 the route network and aircraft of the bankrupt Panair do Brasil were also acquired. The Foundation of Employees (the owners of Varig, and nowadays known as the Ruben Berta Foundation) acquired control of Cruzeiro do Sul in May 1975. The two carriers maintain separate identities but have combined schedules to avoid duplication.

In addition to a 34-point network within Brazil, Varig currently serves more than 60 destinations throughout Central and South America, and in the USA, Europe, Africa and Asia. Varig currently employs nearly 17,000 personnel.

Fleet Data

2 Boeing 747-300; 3 747-200; 12 DC-10-30; 2 Airbus A300B4; 1 (+5) 767-200ER; 12 707-320C; 10 727-100; 12 L-188 Electra; 12 737-200.

Boeing 727-41

VIASA

VIASA (Venezolana Internacional de Aviacion SA) was created in January 1961 by Aerovias Venezolanas (Avensa) and Linea Aeropostal Venezolana (LAV) to take over the international routes operated by both Venezuelan carriers. Avensa had been formed in 1943, and started domestic passenger services in 1944, followed by international services in June 1955. LAV had been formed in 1933 when the government decided to nationalize the Venezuelan branch of the French Compagnie Générale Aéropostale which had been operating since 1929. Due to the financial

requirements associated with the procurement of competitive jet equipment, the Venezuelan government encouraged Avensa and LAV to form VIASA to operate international services on their behalf, with Avensa holding 45 per cent of the shares and LAV holding the balance.

VIASA began operations with Super Constellation and DC-6B aircraft acquired from its parent companies, and on 8 August 1961, the carrier began jet services to the USA with Convair 880 aircraft which had previously been on order for Avensa. Close co-operation was established with KLM, and DC-8 aircraft were leased from the Dutch airline which enabled VIASA to operate jet services from Caracas to Amsterdam via Paris and London from 6 April 1961.

VIASA currently operates scheduled passenger services from Caracas and Maracaibo across the Atlantic to Las Palmas, Lisbon, Madrid, Milan, Rome, Paris, Frankfurt, London and Amsterdam, and to New York, Miami, Mexico City, San Jose, Panama City, Bogota, Cali, Quito, Lima, Rio de Janeiro, Buenos Aires, Curacao, Santo Domingo, San Juan, Port of Spain and Barbados in North, Central and South America and the Caribbean. The carrier is wholly government-owned and currently employs approximately 2,000 personnel.

Fleet Data

5 DC-10-30; 1 DC-8-63.

McDonnell Douglas DC-10-30

Boeing 737-247

WESTERN AIRLINES

Western Airlines (WAL) was incorporated on 13 July 1925, as Western Air Express (WAE) and is the oldest US carrier. Operations began with air mail services between Los Angeles and Salt Lake City via Las Vegas on 17 April 1926, using Douglas M-2 aircraft. Passenger services on the route began on 23 May of that year, and this represented the first scheduled passenger service in the USA. By early 1930 WAE had taken over Colorado Airways, Pacific Marine Airways, West Coast Air Transport and Standard Air Lines. On 16 July of that year, under pressure from the Postmaster General, WAE merged with Transcontinental Air Transport to form TWA in order to gain the mail contract for the Los Angeles-Kansas City section of the transcontinental route which had previously been flown by both airlines. In 1934 WAE was bought out from TWA and operated for a while as General Air Lines. On 17 April 1941, the carrier officially changed its title to Western Airlines. By this time Boeing 247-D and DC-3 aircraft had been acquired, and National Parks Airways been absorbed. Services on the carrier's old Los Angeles-San Francisco route were

restarted in 1944 and extended to Portland and Seattle in 1947.

The first of 12 Lockheed Electra turboprops flew on the Los Angeles-Seattle route in August 1959, and jet services were inaugurated on 1 June 1960, with Boeing 707-139 aircraft leased from the manufacturer prior to delivery of the carrier's first Boeing 720-047Bs in April 1961. On 1 July 1967, Seattle-based Pacific Northern Airlines (PNA) was merged into Western. Founded in 1932 as Woodley Airways, PNA operated services linking southern Alaska with Washington state and Oregon.

Western, headquartered in Los Angeles, agreed to merge with Delta Airlines on 9 September 1986. Initially Western is operating as a subsidiary but will subsequently be fully integrated with Delta. Western operates scheduled passenger and cargo services to 67 cities in the USA (including Honolulu and Anchorage), and to several points in Canada and Mexico. The carrier employs approximately 10,000 personnel.

Fleet Data

9 DC-10-10; 38 Boeing 727-200; 13 737-300; 28 (+14) 737-200.

ZAMBIA AIRWAYS CORPORATION

Zambia Airways, the national carrier of Zambia, was originally formed in April 1964 as a subsidiary of Central African Airways Corporation (CAAC). Operations on domestic and regional routes using DC-3 and Beaver aircraft commenced on 1 July of that year. Following the dissolution of CAAC, Zambia Airways became an independent wholly government-owned carrier on 1 September 1967. Initial technical and managerial assistance was provided by Alitalia. Zambia subsequently contracted

with Aer Lingus in 1974 and Ethiopian Airlines in March 1982 for technical and managerial support. BAC One-Eleven 207AJ aircraft entered service in January 1968, and on 1 November of that year a new service linking Lusaka and London via Nairobi and Rome was initiated with a DC-8 leased from Alitalia.

Zambia currently provides domestic services and also operates international services to Nairobi, Dar-es-Salaam, Harare, Johannesburg, Mauritius, London, Rome, Larnaca, and Bombay. Nearly 1,700 personnel are employed by the carrier.

Fleet Data

1 DC-10-30; 2 Boeing 707-320C; 1 737-200; 2 BAe (HS) 748.

McDonnell Douglas DC-10-30

Note: Page numbers set in **bold** type refer to the principal entries on specific aircraft or airlines; page numbers set in *italics* refer to subjects that are mentioned in captions to illustrations.